Summa metaphysicae ad mentem Sancti Thomae

Studies in Philosophy and the History of Philosophy

General Editor: John C. McCarthy

Volume 68

Summa metaphysicae ad mentem Sancti Thomae
Essays in Honor of John F. Wippel

Edited by Therese Scarpelli Cory and Gregory T. Doolan

The Catholic University of America Press
Washington, D.C.

Copyright © 2024
The Catholic University of America Press
All rights reserved
The paper used in this publication meets the minimum
requirements of American National Standards for Information
Science—Permanence of Paper for Printed Library Materials,
ANSI Z39.48-1992.
∞

Cataloging-in-Publication Data is available from the Library of
Congress

ISBN: 978-0-8132-3727-5
eISBN: 978-0-8132-3728-2

Printed in Canada

John F. Wippel,
1933–2023

Contents

List of Abbreviations of Works by Thomas Aquinas   ix

Introduction (*Therese Scarpelli Cory and Gregory T. Doolan*)   xi

PART 1: METAPHYSICS AS A SCIENCE

1. *Gregory T. Doolan* (*The Catholic University of America*), Discovering the Perspective from Which Being Is Considered as Being: Aquinas, Wippel, and the Separative Analysis of Substance   3

2. *Philip Neri Reese, OP* (*Pontifical University of St. Thomas Aquinas / The Angelicum*), Omne ens est creatum: A *propter quid* Metaphysical Demonstration   42

PART 2: THE PROBLEM OF THE ONE AND THE MANY IN THE ORDER OF BEING

3. *Mark D. Gossiaux* (*Loyola University New Orleans*), Thomas Aquinas and the Origin of the Controversy concerning the Real Distinction between Essence and Existence   67

4. *David Twetten* (*Marquette University*), A Defense of Essence-Realism as the Key to Aquinas's Arguments for the Essence-*Esse* Real Distinction   96

5. *Therese Scarpelli Cory* (*University of Notre Dame*), Likeness and Agency in Aquinas: A Study   130

PART 3: THE ESSENTIAL STRUCTURE OF FINITE BEING

6. *Stephen Brock* (*Pontifical University of Santa Croce / University of Chicago*), Created Form as Act and Potency in the Metaphysics of Thomas Aquinas   177

7. Gloria Frost (*University of St. Thomas, Minnesota*), Aquinas on How Accidental Forms Vary in Themselves 207

PART 4: FIRST CAUSAL PRINCIPLES: FROM FINITE BEING TO UNCREATED BEING

8. Francis Feingold (*Kenrick-Glennon Seminary*), Can Angels Know Being without Judgment 227

9. Gaven Kerr (*St. Patrick's Pontifical University, Maynooth*), Aquinas's Metaphysical Way to God 276

10. Brian Carl (*University of St. Thomas, Texas*), The Kataphatic and Apophatic Propriety of '*Qui Est*' 297

11. Michael Rubin (*Christendom College*), Aquinas on 'Beauty' as a Divine Name 317

12. Jason Mitchell (*Independent Scholar*), Aquinas on Divine Application 348

Appendix: *Vita Sapientis*: A Biographical Interview with John F. Wippel (*Nick Kahm and Miriam Pritschet*) 373

Select Bibliography 381

Contributor Biographies 401

Index of Terms 405

Index of Names 410

List of Abbreviations of Works by Thomas Aquinas

Comp. theol.	*Compendium theologiae*
De aet. mun.	*De aeternitate mundi*
De car.	*Quaestio disputata de caritate* [= *De virtutibus, q. 2*]
De ente	*De ente et essentia*
De malo	*Quaestiones disputatae de malo*
De pot.	*Quaestiones disputatae de potentia*
De prin. nat.	*De principiis naturae*
De sub. sep.	*De substantiis separatis*
De ver.	*Quaestiones disputatae de veritate*
De virt. card.	*Quaestio disputata de virtutibus cardinalibus*
De virt. in com.	*Quaestio disputata de virtutibus in communi*
In De an.	*Sententia libri De anima*
In De caus.	*Super librum De causis expositio*
In De div. nom.	*In librum Beati Dionysii De divinis nominibus expositio*
In De gen.	*In librum De generatione et corruptione Aristotelis expositio*
In De hebd.	*Super Boetii De ebdomadibus*
In De sensu	*Sentencia libri De sensu et sensato*
In De Trin.	*Super Boetii De Trinitate*
In Ethic.	*Sententia libri Ethicorum*
In Meta.	*In duodecim libros Metaphysicorum Aristotelis expositio*
In Peri herm.	*Expositio libri Peryermenias*

List of Abbreviation

In Phys.	*In VIII libros Physicorum*
In Politic.	*Sententia libri Politicorum*
In Post. an.	*Expositio libri Posteriorum*
In Sent.	*Scriptum super libros sententiarum magistri Petri Lombardi*
Q. de an.	*Quaestiones disputatae de anima*
Quod.	*Quaestiones de quolibet*
SCG	*Summa contra Gentiles*
ST	*Summa theologiae*

Therese Scarpelli Cory and Gregory T. Doolan

Introduction

With the encyclical *Aeterni Patris* issued in 1879, Pope Leo XIII called for a restoration of Christian philosophy *ad mentem Sancti Thomae*: "according to the mind of St. Thomas." There, Leo instructs that "teachers should strive to instill the teaching of Thomas Aquinas ... into the minds of their students and clearly to set forth his solidity and excellence over others."[1] Few teachers have done this with the dedication and thoroughness of John F. Wippel.[2] In teaching Aquinas's thought, Wippel did more than take the aforementioned phrase to mean doing so "in the spirit of St. Thomas." Such an approach, laudable in itself, is rightly termed Thomism.

Wippel's own approach, however, was instead to treat the preposition *ad* in this phrase more literally as a "getting up next to"—if you will, adjacent to—Aquinas's very mind, so that with him, his students can peer

---

1. Pope Leo XIII, *Aeterni Patris*, Encyclical Letter, August 4, 1879, no. 31 (available at www.vatican.va): "Ceterum, doctrinam Thomae Aquinatis studeant magistri, a Vobis intelligenter lecti, in discipulorum animos insinuare; eiusque prae ceteris soliditatem atque excellentiam in perspicuo ponant. Eamdem Academiae a Vobis institutae aut instituendae illustrent ac tueantur, et ad grassantium errorum refutationem adhibeant.—Ne autem supposita pro vera, neu corrupta pro sincera bibatur, providete ut sapientia Thomae ex ipsis eius fontibus hauriatur, aut saltem ex iis rivis, quos ab ipso fonte deductos, adhuc integros et illimes decurrere certa et concors doctorum hominum sententia est: sed ab iis, qui exinde Auxisse dicuntur, re autem alienis et non salubribus aquis creverunt, adolescentium animos arcendos curate."

2. Those of us who are fortunate enough to have been his students know well that our professor, in his humility, preferred to be addressed as "Fr. Wippel" despite his having been granted the title "Monsignor." Moreover, in professional circles, Fr. Wippel published simply by the name John F. Wippel. With that in mind, in the introduction to this volume, we will refer to him as such.

inside to see the master's thought arising at its source and watch it develop throughout his career. It is an approach to Aquinas well evidenced in both the title and pages of Wippel's magnum opus, *The Metaphysical Thought of Thomas Aquinas*. Honoring the historical Thomas, Wippel shows how this metaphysical thought—although spread throughout Aquinas's writings on various topics—is nevertheless unified as part of an implicitly systematic metaphysics. Wippel thus explains his approach to presenting Aquinas as follows: "While acknowledging that he did not write a *Summa metaphysicae*, I have now presented the kind of metaphysical book he might have written had he chosen to do so, in accord with the philosophical order and methodology as he himself defines this."[3] Thus, to describe Wippel's teaching simply as Thomism is woefully inadequate, for what he teaches us is instead Thomas himself. And in doing so, Wippel perfectly fulfills the exhortation of *Aeterni Patris* for the teacher of philosophy to "take care that the wisdom of Thomas be drawn from his own fonts."[4]

In this faithful manner, for almost six decades, Wippel taught the philosophical thought of Thomas Aquinas to generations of students, shaping their minds *ad mentem Sancti Thomae*. It was fitting, therefore, that a volume honoring Wippel was published in 2012: *The Science of Being as Being*. That Festschrift contains contributions from a number of students and colleagues influenced by Wippel over the years. Since the time of its publication, however, Wippel continued his teaching, shaping the minds of another generation, both in the classroom and through his writings. Hence, it is entirely appropriate that he *again* be honored, namely, by that next generation. In that spirit, we present to you this new Festschrift, *Summa metaphysicae ad mentem Sancti Thomae: Essays in Honor of John F. Wippel*. It had been our hope to present this volume to him in a ceremony in his honor, but unfortunately Wippel passed away only a few months prior to its publication. We are, however, reassured by the thought that he knew of its impending publication and expressed appreciation for all of the efforts of the contributors.

This volume offers the reader contributions on a number of metaphysical themes, with each essay living up to Wippel's own scholarly

---

3. John F. Wippel, *The Metaphysical Thought of Thomas Aquinas: From Finite Being to Uncreated Being* (Washington, DC: The Catholic University of America Press, 2000), 594.
4. Pope Leo XIII, *Aeterni Patris*, no. 31.

standards for original research. The contributions, moreover, are presented according to the systematic metaphysical divisions found in his work, *The Metaphysical Thought of Thomas Aquinas*. After examining the nature of the science of metaphysics, Wippel considers issues arising from its subject matter, being *qua* being (organized around the Problem of the One and the Many), followed by issues pertaining specifically to finite being (organized around the essentially composite character of all finite being), and finally the difficulties attendant on reasoning from finite being to its principle, uncreated being. In his introduction to that monograph, Wippel explains that he follows the philosophical order that Aquinas himself might have taken, "had he chosen to write a *Summa metaphysicae*." Characteristically, Wippel does not invent this order out of whole cloth, but extracts it, with meticulous documentation, from Aquinas's own practice. Our *Summa metaphysicae ad mentem Sancti Thomae* follows the same trajectory. Thus, the first part of this Festschrift addresses themes pertaining to the nature and discovery of the science of metaphysics. The second examines themes concerned with the Problem of the One and the Many in the order of being. The third considers themes related to the essential structure of finite being. And, finally, the fourth part addresses topics regarding the first causal principles, moving, as Wippel does in his own investigations, from the consideration of finite beings to the Uncreated Being.

The first part of the volume ("Metaphysics as a Science") opens with two studies by Gregory T. Doolan and Philip Neri Reese regarding the science of metaphysics as the ultimate philosophical project.

Doolan's chapter, "Discovering the Perspective from Which Being Is Considered as Being: Aquinas, Wippel, and the Separative Analysis of Substance," tackles a controversy that defined one of Wippel's most important contributions to our understanding of Aquinas, namely, how we come to know the subject of metaphysics, *ens commune*, or being-in-general. Whereas proponents of the River Forest School have argued that being-in-general can be grasped only after proving the existence of an immaterial substance, Wippel has argued that being-in-general can be grasped even by someone who is aware only of the existence of material beings, by a separation (*separatio*) or judgment that separates materiality from the concept of being. Thus, one need recognize only that the concept of being that founds metaphysics is neutrally immaterial. In response to a criticism of Wippel's interpretation, Doolan shows that for Wippel, this separating judgment asserts only that materiality is conceptually separable from being, not that there are or can be immaterial substances. Doolan then goes on to argue, importantly, that this separating judgment does not have to bear the full responsibility for establishing the notion of being-in-general. Properly speaking, the notion of being-in-general is discovered when being is recognized as common to substance and accident, across the categories. From there, the separating judgment is the final step of judging that materiality is not essential to the notion of being-in-general; and it is with this final refinement that metaphysics can be identified as a science distinct from physics.

If metaphysics, the science of *ens commune*, is a science (*scientia*) in the proper sense, then it ought to be able to produce demonstrations that conform to the paradigm of *epistēmē* that Aristotle lays out in the *Posterior Analytics*. Reese's chapter, "*Omne ens est creatum*: A *propter quid* Metaphysical Demonstration?" takes up one aspect of this complicated question. Aquinas claims that metaphysics is a science. But if so, then—as Reese points out—metaphysics must be able to formulate *propter quid* demonstrations, that is, valid syllogisms that draw explanatory conclusions from *per se* known and immediate premises. But are any metaphysical demonstrations found in Aquinas's writings? Reese locates one in *Summa theologiae* I, q. 44, a. 1, ad 1. There, he contends, Aquinas offers a *propter quid* demonstration that is meant to explain the conclusion "every being is created," where "every being" means "every instance of *ens commune*." This particular demonstration, he argues, cannot be formulated by any science other than metaphysics. Thus Aquinas's metaphysics is properly a science capable of demonstrations, and can be shown to be as systematic as the rest of his philosophical thought.

The next part ("The Problem of the One and the Many in the Order of Being") dives into the content of metaphysics, examining issues that are "as broad in extension as the subject [of metaphysics], itself," that is, being *qua* being. The preeminent distinction concerning being *qua* being is that between essence and existence, which Aquinas famously insists are not merely conceptually, but really distinct principles. It is this distinction that is discussed by the first two contributions offered by Mark Gossiaux and David Twetten.

Gossiaux's study, "Thomas Aquinas and the Origin of the Controversy concerning the Real Distinction between Essence and Existence," examines the extent of the influence of Aquinas and Giles of Rome, respectively, on their successors in the debate about the real distinction between essence and existence in the 1270s, shortly after Aquinas's death. Few scholars today would accept Chossat's claim from 1910 that Giles of Rome was the originator of the real distinction. Nonetheless, there remains a substantial lack of clarity about the degree to which the historical controversy about the real distinction was shaped by Giles or by Aquinas himself. To map out the origins of the controversy, Gossiaux takes the reader on a tour of the treatments in Giles of Rome, Siger of Brabant, and Henry of Ghent. As he argues, Giles (in his early *Ordinatio*) roughly reproduces Aquinas's account of the real distinction. Subsequently, however, in his *Theoremata de corpore Christi*—perhaps due to the criticisms of Siger of Brabant—Giles becomes concerned that Aquinas's position is insufficiently developed, and eventually attempts to remedy the inadequacy himself with a stronger formulation of the distinction in *Theoremata de ente et essentia*. As Gossiaux shows, the concerns that Giles raises about Aquinas's version of the doctrine are similar to those of Siger. These concerns suggest a circulating state of discontent with Aquinas's position, a discontent that boils over in Henry of Ghent's well-known attack on the real distinction in his *Quodlibet* I, q. 9. As Gossiaux shows, even though Giles is already active in the controversy, Henry is actually responding principally to Thomas Aquinas's formulation. Nonetheless, as the controversy progresses, it is Giles's development of the real distinction that will become the canonical view.

But how philosophically plausible is this doctrine of the real distinction between essence and existence? Twetten offers a new approach to the topic in his study, "A Defense of Essence-Realism as the Key to Aquinas's Arguments for the Essence-*Esse* Real Distinction." Twetten argues that Aquinas's Genus Argument, which is famously rejected by most scholars who consider this topic, needs to be reread in light of Aquinas's teachings on the real distinction between nature and supposit. Considering human nature as an example, Twetten considers Aquinas's position that an individual such as Diotima cannot be really identical with her humanity; otherwise, to be human would be to be Diotima. From this distinction, Twetten concludes that Aquinas is committed to a much stronger realism about essences than standard readings recognize. With this stronger realism in place, Twetten contends, it becomes possible to give a robust new force to Aquinas's Genus Argument, to demonstrate that essence and *esse* are really distinct principles in a created being.

As Wippel has shown, for Aquinas, it is the essence principle within the essence-*esse* composition of beings that accounts for diversification and, hence, multiplication of *esse*. At the same time, being is not a genus; the many kinds of beings, each with its own essence, are not reducible to a single natural kind. What types of unities occur, then, within this world of diverse beings?

The answer is found in Aquinas's theory of likeness (*similitudo*). In "Likeness and Agency in Aquinas: A Study," Cory argues that, although Aquinas usually defines likeness quite narrowly as a relation grounded on unity of quality, in reality he understands likeness more sweepingly as a relation grounded on any mode of unity, short of numerical unity. Thus, there are as many modes of likeness as there are of unity, falling conveniently under a four-part taxonomy that Cory here reconstructs. She draws out implications for Aquinas's axiom, "Every agent makes something like itself," arguing that for Aquinas, there can be acting only where there can be likeness. The possibility of unities beyond that of common natures allows the world of creatures to be drawn into a single schema of action, even though no single shared nature exists throughout the whole.

Aquinas's distinction between essence and existence leads to the view that every creature falls short of perfect simplicity, being composed at least of act and potency, if not also of form and matter. Thus, the volume's third part ("The Essential Structure of Finite Being") focuses on these composite structures of creaturely being, with a study by Stephen Brock focusing on act and potency, and one by Gloria Frost on substance and accident.

Brock's chapter, "Created Form as Act and Potency in the Metaphysics of Thomas Aquinas," tackles the problem of how Aquinas applies his fundamental act-potency distinction to form. Puzzlingly, Aquinas describes form both as act (*actus*) and as potency for being (*esse*), but act is opposed to potency. How can form be both? On one prominent Thomistic interpretation, the solution is to posit two orders: form is act in the one order (the essential order), and potency in another order (the

Introduction   xvii

existential or transcendental order). But if forms are potency in the existential order, several problems emerge. For instance: how can the divine essence be, as Aquinas insists, the form whereby God exists? Instead of the two-order solution, Brock argues, we should understand form's being act and potency in light of Aquinas's claim that form is the immediate principle of the actuality that is *esse*. It is act in the sense of a principle of *actuality*, but it is potency in the sense of being a *principle* of actuality (rather than identical with that actuality).

Another major act-potency composition in Aquinas's metaphysics is that of substance and accident. Turning to accidental form, Frost's chapter, "Aquinas on How Accidental Forms Vary in Themselves," examines Aquinas's controversial, but surprisingly understudied, view on the increase and decrease in accidental qualities. In Aquinas's view, as my soup cools, its quality of heat does not in itself diminish; rather, he claims somewhat cryptically that the soup participates less and less in the quality of heat. As Frost shows, interestingly, what underlies this cryptic claim is an absolute commitment to the unity and indivisibility of form, which leads Aquinas to insist that all the variation is only the side of the subject—that is, deriving from how the subject receives and is actualized by the form. As she also shows, however, the view is more nuanced than is usually recognized: Aquinas allows for some interesting exceptions. For instance, certain forms that constitute an order or proportion among parts toward some end—for example, health—are measured relative to that end, and thus can vary in themselves according to their success in promoting the relevant end. Something parallel is true of forms like scientific knowledge, which can encompass larger or smaller numbers of cases and hence can vary internally in that respect.

The fourth and final part of the volume ("First Causal Principles: From Finite Being to Uncreated Being") follows the trajectory from creatures to the Creator, approaching the divine as investigated in metaphysics, that is, separate substances, and most of all God, as cause(s) of being *qua* being. This part includes five wide-ranging studies.

Between finite bodies and the Creator there are finite separate substances: angels, which are too seldom considered in the context of Thomistic metaphysics. In his study on the angelic judgment of existence (*esse*), "Can Angels Know Being without Judgment?," Francis Feingold uncovers a surprisingly neglected problem that angels pose for

Aquinas's metaphysical commitments. As Feingold observes, Aquinas's essence-existence distinction in beings is also reflected in human cognition, because we cognize essences through simple apprehension and existence through a judgment that composes and divides. Indeed, many Thomistic commentators have taken for granted that it is precisely because of the real distinction that our cognition of essence and existence is similarly distinguished. And yet, Aquinas holds that angels cognize existence even though, unlike us, they do not compose and divide. How, then, can they cognize existence without composing and dividing? Through detailed textual analysis, Feingold shows that, in fact, Aquinas holds that the need to cognize existence through composition and division is an artifact of how human intellectual cognition occurs. Cognition of existence is internal to a causal relationship, and cognitive composition (which involves turning back to phantasms and thus to the original causal action of the object on the human being) is needed in order to recover that original causal contact. Angels, however, cognize in a different mode, which captures existence by reflecting God's causality of creatures. Aquinas thus allows that angels have judgment, and judge a thing's existence, but not that they compose and divide. Feingold's account sheds light not only on a poorly-understood aspect of Aquinas's angelology, but also on what it takes to cognize existence (including for God), and why the embodied intellect can grasp existence only through turning to phantasms and sense.

Aquinas holds that creaturely being provides the starting point from which we can reason to the existence of God. His many arguments for God's existence are famous. Gaven Kerr's study, "Aquinas's Metaphysical Way to God," argues that behind them all, there is a common metaphysical strategy, according to which Aquinas begins from a derivative or participated actuality and reasons to something that has that actuality *per se*. This strategy is found *par excellence* in Aquinas's argument in the fourth chapter of the *De ente et essentia*, from a creaturely distinction between essence and *esse*, to God as pure *esse* itself. But whereas some Thomists such as Joseph Owens and John F. X. Knasas hold that the *De ente* argument unifies all of Aquinas's argumentation for the existence of God, Kerr maintains that such a reduction is not possible. Rather, he argues, what in fact unifies Aquinas's various forms of argument is the schema of reasoning from that which is *per aliud* to that which is *per se*.

Creaturely being also provides the only available starting point for saying anything philosophically about God—a topic explored by Carl and Rubin. Carl, in "The Kataphatic and Apophatic Propriety of '*Qui Est*,'" offers a new angle on the longstanding questions of whether '*qui est*,' or 'He Who Is,' is the most proper name of God, and whether this name communicates anything positive about God or remains in the realm of pure apophaticism. Carl helpfully unpacks what it means for one divine name to be "more proper" than another. Then, building on developments in Aquinas's doctrine on divine naming that have been highlighted by Wippel, he explores how the early treatment in *In Sent*. I, d. 8, q. 1. a. 1, and the mature treatment in *Summa theologiae* I, q. 13, a. 11, help to shed light on the significance of '*qui est*' as a name drawn from being (*esse*) itself. He identifies three arguments in Aquinas to explain the propriety of '*qui est*' as a divine name. Two are apophatic: '*qui est*' is drawn from being (*esse*), which just is the divine essence; and '*qui est*' consignifies present existence and hence appropriately indicates divine eternity. But a third argument harbors kataphatic elements: namely, that being (*esse*) is most universal and least determinate; therefore, there is the least to negate from the name '*qui est*.' By drawing on some clarifications from Aquinas's earlier *In Sent*. text, Carl is able to show that what makes '*qui est*' the *most* proper name is therefore its kataphatic character as the name from which the least has to be negated.

Rubin's study, "Aquinas on 'Beauty' as a Divine Name," tackles the longstanding dispute over whether 'beautiful' is a distinct transcendental for Aquinas, alongside 'one,' 'true,' and 'good,' or whether it is reducible to the combination of 'true' and 'good.' Where other interpreters have sought to resolve the dispute by examining the *ratio* of beauty, Rubin points out that another cache of evidence has remained unexplored, that is, Aquinas's reasoning about "Beauty" as one of the divine names. Since divine names are distinct only by their *rationes*, if "Beauty" turns out to be a distinct divine name in its own right, we will have powerful evidence that Aquinas thinks it has a unique *ratio* and therefore is a transcendental distinct from the others. Rubin goes on to show that Aquinas does indeed consider "Beauty" to be a distinct divine name, reviewing first a series of texts in which Aquinas attributes beauty to the divine essence, and second the texts in which Aquinas argues for appropriating the name "Beauty" to the Second Person of the Trinity. From these texts,

Rubin argues, several important findings emerge in favor of considering "beautiful" as a distinct transcendental attribute of being: namely, Aquinas *does* regularly treat "Beauty" as a distinct divine name; he has a distinctive way of arguing to God's Beauty from creaturely beauty; and in so arguing, Aquinas uses a notion of creaturely beauty that is not restricted to one genus of beings, but encompasses both spiritual and bodily beauty—that is, a properly transcendental notion of beauty.

The volume concludes—as does Wippel's *Metaphysical Thought*—by turning back from God to creatures, with a chapter by Jason Mitchell, "Aquinas on Divine Application." In response to the Bañez-Molina debate on how God moves creatures, Mitchell argues that Aquinas himself offers a third alternative that has to date not been sufficiently explored: namely, that God moves creatures by applying creaturely powers to their operations. Aquinas's theory of divine application, Mitchell argues, cannot be understood except by taking seriously the "existential" reading of Aquinas, according to which the act of being (*actus essendi*) is primary in each creature and is further limited by essence and accidents. Given that a thing's powers flow from its act of being, which itself is dependent in an ongoing way on the Creator, a thing can exercise its powers in operation only if God further applies those powers to their operations.

Our contributors do not always agree on every point of interpretation, of course. But the picture that emerges from this volume of Aquinas's metaphysics is, we hope, nonetheless unified by the detectable guiding influence of its "first principle," the teacher, mentor, and exemplar, whom his students know simply as "Fr. Wippel," and to whose memory we dedicate this volume with immense gratitude and respect. In that spirit, the volume includes an appendix narrating Wippel's trajectory from his childhood on an Ohio farm, to his time as a seminarian and student, and eventually to his ordination and career to become, for more than the past half century, one of the most eminent scholars of Aquinas. This narrative is drawn from an interview with Wippel in 2020 conducted by Nick Kahm and written by Miriam Pritschet. We hope that this biography and the anecdotes that Wippel tells will more fully bring to life the character of this remarkable scholar.

Acknowledgments: We would like to thank Andreas Waldstein for his work preparing the manuscript, Jane Spencer for compiling the index, as well as John Martino of The Catholic University of America Press for his support.

Part 1 ∞ Metaphysics as a Science

Gregory T. Doolan

1   Discovering the Perspective from Which Being Is Considered as Being

Aquinas, Wippel, and the Separative Analysis of Substance

Among scholars of medieval philosophy, John F. Wippel is well known for his invaluable contributions to the study of the metaphysical thought of Thomas Aquinas. Although he wrote on numerous topics in this area, Wippel is perhaps best known for his treatment of certain signature themes, such as the problem of Christian philosophy, the role of participation in Aquinas's metaphysical thought, and the argument in the fourth chapter of the *De ente et essentia* for the real distinction between essence and *esse*. In this chapter, I will examine another signature theme addressed by Wippel, namely, the discovery of the subject of metaphysics by means of the intellectual act that Aquinas terms *separatio*. My aim in doing so is twofold: first, to confirm this approach as Aquinas's own and, second, to situate it as a step in what I take to be a broader methodology employed by Aquinas for discovering *ens commune* as the subject of metaphysics.

On three different occasions over the course of his career, Wippel provided dedicated presentations of this theme: in the fourth chapter of his 1984 volume *Metaphysical Themes in Thomas Aquinas*,[1] the second chapter of his 2000 magnum opus, *The Metaphysical Thought of Thomas*

---

1. *Metaphysical Themes in Thomas Aquinas* (Washington, DC: The Catholic University of America Press, 1984), 69–104. This chapter was previously published as the article, "Metaphysics and *Separatio* According to Thomas Aquinas," *The Review of Metaphysics* 31 (1978): 431–70.

Aquinas,[2] and most recently in his 2021 volume *Metaphysical Themes in Thomas Aquinas III*.[3] A review of these three treatments reveals that, over the years, Wippel remained committed to the same fundamental position on this topic that he had maintained earlier in his career: for Aquinas, the discovery of the subject matter of metaphysics as BEING-IN-GENERAL (*ens commune*) follows upon an act of *separatio* whereby one comes to judge that SUBSTANCE and, hence, BEING need not be material.[4] In recognizing that the *ratio* of BEING is, in Wippel's terms, "neutrally immaterial," we discern that there is need for a science beyond that of physics. And, he contends, we can discover this distinctive subject matter of metaphysics prior to and independent of any knowledge of what he terms "positively immaterial" beings that, by their nature, never exist in matter.

Although Wippel's presentation of this reading of Aquinas remained fundamentally identical over the years, his subsequent treatments offer the reader helpful clarifications in response to the objections of other scholars. Perhaps the most well-known of these objections is advanced by the likes of Ralph McInerny and Benedict Ashley.[5] Their position, which I will call the Laval/River Forest Interpretation, maintains that various textual observations by Aquinas indicate that he held that the subject of

---

2. *The Metaphysical Thought of Thomas Aquinas: From Finite Being to Uncreated Being* (Washington, DC: The Catholic University of America Press, 2000), 23–62.

3. *Metaphysical Themes in Thomas Aquinas III* (Washington, DC: The Catholic University of America Press, 2021), 42–72. This chapter was previously published as "Aquinas on *separatio* and Our Discovery of Being as Being," in *The Discovery of Being & Thomas Aquinas*, ed. Christopher M. Cullen, SJ, and Franklin T. Harkins (Washington, DC: The Catholic University of America Press, 2019), 11–42. As with the other essays in that volume, Wippel's was originally presented at the 31st Annual Conference of the Center for Medieval Studies at Fordham University in 2011, entitled "The Metaphysics of Aquinas and Its Modern Interpreters: Theological and Philosophical Perspectives."

4. In this chapter, I will employ the following conventions when translating the Latin term *ens*: when speaking of the universal *ens commune*, I will employs small caps: e.g., BEING, BEING-IN-GENERAL; when speaking about an individual existing thing, I will employ lowercase Roman type: e.g., a being, beings; when speaking about the term *as* a term, I will employ single quotation marks: e.g., 'being.' I will translate the Latin term *esse* that signifies for Aquinas *actus essendi* as follows: to be, existing, the act of existing, or existence. I will similarly employ small caps when speaking of SUBSTANCE as a nature and single quotation marks when referring to the name, 'substance.'

5. For a presentation of their views, see Ralph McInerny, *Praeambula Fidei: Thomism and the God of the Philosophers* (Washington, DC: The Catholic University of America Press, 2006), 188–218; Benedict Ashley, *The Way toward Wisdom: An Interdisciplinary and Intercultural Introduction to Metaphysics* (Notre Dame, IN: University of Notre Dame Press, 2006), 132–69.

metaphysics is established only after the existence of at least one positively immaterial entity has been proven in natural science (physics). Going beyond this textual point, they also maintain that Wippel's approach is philosophically problematic: to conclude to the neutrally immaterial character of BEING is unwarranted unless one has first proven the existence of some positively immaterial entity (e.g., a prime mover in physics). Only then, we are told, can one legitimately perform the relevant act of *separatio* to conclude that BEING need not be material and, thereby, discover the distinctive subject matter of metaphysics.

In what follows, I will focus principally on the philosophical concerns raised by the Laval/River Forest Interpretation, but in the course of doing so, will have occasion to reply briefly to its textual objections as well. As I will show, McInerny and Ashley misread both Wippel and Aquinas on this topic of *separatio*. Contrary to their concerns, the approach pointed to us by Wippel is not one of proving the *possibility* of the existence of positively immaterial beings prior to proving their actuality. Instead, the key issue is a *perspectival* one, namely, of providing a methodology by which even the material beings of our experience can be considered from a nonmaterial perspective *as* beings prior to, and independent of, any awareness or consideration of positively immaterial entities.

To this end, this chapter will have five parts. (1) First, I will offer a summary of Wippel's general stance on the role of *separatio* for Aquinas, noting the similar critique of him offered by both McInerny and Ashley. (2) In the second part, I will show how Wippel's general stance is informed by a particular application of *separatio* presented in the commentary on Boethius's *De Trinitate*. There, Aquinas provides a separative analysis to show that materiality is not part of the *ratio* of SUBSTANCE and, consequently, not part of the *ratio* of BEING (*ens*). In other words, this analysis reveals the neutrally immaterial character of both SUBSTANCE and BEING, providing a different perspective from which to study them than as bodies. (3) After having considered Wippel's reading of this text, I will next turn to a supporting text from *De spiritualibus creaturis*, in which Aquinas offers a parallel analysis of the *ratio* of SUBSTANCE. As I will show, this additional text not only supports Wippel's reading of Aquinas, but also provides a vantage point from which to respond to both McInerny and Ashley. (4) In the fourth part of my chapter, I will respond to a concern of McInerny's that Wippel's approach to the analysis of SUBSTANCE and BEING is merely dialectical and, thus, insufficient for establishing the subject of metaphysics. (5) Finally, I will go beyond Wippel's reading to show how the separative act that he discusses is in fact part of a broader approach employed by Aquinas to establish both the unity of the subject of metaphysics (*ens commune*) and its diversity from the subjects of other speculative sciences.

WIPPEL ON THE ROLE OF *SEPARATIO* IN METAPHYSICS

In Part I of his 1984 volume *Metaphysical Themes in Thomas Aquinas*, Wippel considers (in the fourth chapter) the nature and subject of metaphysics, focusing much of his attention on Aquinas's early commentary on Boethius's *De Trinitate* (1257–59).[6] He begins by turning to q. 5, a. 1, which considers whether the speculative sciences are suitably divided into natural, mathematical, and divine science (metaphysics). In this article, Aquinas not only acknowledges the suitability of this division, but also provides a rationale for it. We are told that these three sciences are distinguished by the objects that they study and the degree to which those objects are separated from—or connected with—matter and motion.

Aquinas explains that one class of speculative objects depends upon matter for their extra-mental reality (*secundum esse*), since they can exist only in matter. Moreover, such objects are dependent upon matter also for their being understood (*secundum intellectum*). For example, a human exists with flesh and bones, and a proper understanding of *what a*

---

6. *In De Trin*. For all dating of Aquinas's works, I will follow Jean-Pierre Torrell's *Initiation à saint Thomas d'Aquin: Sa personne et son œuvre, Nouvelle édition profondément remaniée*, vol. 1 (Paris: Les Éditions du Cerf, 2015). Although the fourth chapter of Wippel's volume can stand on its own, ideally it should be read in light of the two chapters that precede it to have a full sense of Wippel's positions. In the second chapter, he compares Aquinas and Avicenna on the relationship between first philosophy and the other theoretical sciences. There, among other points, Wippel clearly acknowledges that for Aquinas the study of metaphysics comes after the study of both mathematics and the natural sciences, following the pedagogical order of learning (*Metaphysical Themes*, 41–44). In chapter 3, he examines the sense in which metaphysics for Aquinas is "first philosophy." There, Wippel reiterates the position noted in the prior chapter: metaphysics is not called "first philosophy" because it is first in the order of discovery, nor because it is first in the pedagogical order of learning, but rather because it gives principles to the other sciences. Thus, he notes, it is first in the order of synthesis. But in the order of analysis, it is last and after physics; hence it is a meta- or trans-physics. Wippel also shows that in another respect, metaphysics is analytically first for Aquinas because it studies the first causes; hence, it is called "first philosophy" for that reason as well (*Metaphysical Themes*, 55–67, esp. 67).

human is includes an acknowledgement of this condition, as evidenced by the fact that the definition of HUMAN includes mention of sensible matter. The sorts of speculative objects in this first class are studied in natural science (physics).[7] The second class of speculative objects, like this first, also depends upon sensible matter for their extra-mental reality, because in reality they never exist apart from it; but unlike the first class, the second does not depend upon sensible matter to be understood. These are mathematical objects, such as lines and numbers, in whose definitions sensible matter is not included.[8]

Finally, the third class of objects do not depend upon sensible matter either for their being understood or for their very existence (*esse*). And Aquinas identifies two types of such objects. Some are separate from matter in reality (*secundum esse*) such that they *never* exist in matter, for example God and the angels. The other sort of speculative object in this third class are such that they do not depend upon matter for their reality even though they are sometimes found in matter. In other words, objects of this sort *can* exist under material conditions, but need not exist that way. Aquinas gives as examples SUBSTANCE, QUALITY, BEING (*ens*), POTENCY, ACT, ONE and MANY, and "so forth" (*huiusmodi*), indicating that this list is not intended to be exhaustive.[9] He tells us that both types of objects in this third class of *speculabilia* are studied in the science that is alternatively named divine science (or theology), metaphysics, and first philosophy.[10]

Wippel provides a helpful nomenclature to classify these two sorts of objects that are separate from matter and motion in both thought and reality. The first sort he terms "positively immaterial" objects and the second "negatively" or "neutrally immaterial."[11] The labels are to a degree straightforward, but it is helpful that in his later treatments of this topic, Wippel tells us the rationale for his choice of these terms. In his 2000 volume, *The Metaphysical Thought of Thomas Aquinas*, he explains that

> objects of the first type are not and cannot be realized in matter because they positively exclude materiality. Hence one may, as I have suggested in another

---

7. *In De Trin.*, q. 5, a. 1, co. (Leon. 50.137:93–149); *Metaphysical Themes*, 71.
8. *In De Trin.*, q. 5, a. 1, co. (Leon. 50.138:149–54); *Metaphysical Themes*, 72.
9. As I have done before, I am using small caps for terms that are intended to reference notions or natures. See note 4 above.
10. *In De Trin.*, q. 5, a. 1, co. (Leon. 50.138:154–67); *Metaphysical Themes*, 72.
11. See, e.g., *Metaphysical Themes*, 72–73, 78, 82–83.

context, describe them as *positively immaterial*. Objects of the second type do not have to be realized in matter in order to exist, even though they may be.... Hence we may describe things of this type as *negatively immaterial*, meaning thereby that they do not have to be present in matter in order to exist. We may also describe them as *neutrally immaterial*, meaning by this that they may or may not be present in matter.[12]

If we return to Wippel's earlier *Metaphysical Themes* volume, we find him considering these two sorts of immaterial objects and asking whether it is possible to begin a study of BEING as BEING without prior knowledge of the positively immaterial: "In other words, will knowledge of the second type of 'immaterial,' the 'neutrally immaterial,' if one may so phrase it, be sufficient to begin metaphysics? Will knowledge of this kind of immaterial even be possible without presupposing the reality of the immaterial in the first or stronger and positive sense?"[13] Wippel's answer in response to both of these questions is "yes."

In support of his position, Wippel turns our attention to q. 5, a. 3, of the *De Trinitate* commentary, in which Aquinas examines whether the objects studied in mathematics exist in matter, yet without consideration of matter and motion.[14] Aquinas answers this question by looking at the operations of the intellect to discern how the intellect comes to have abstract knowledge. Following Aristotle, he identifies its operations as twofold: (1) the first entails the "understanding of indivisibles" (*intelligentia indivisibilium*) by which the intellect knows *what* something is (*quid est*); (2) the second operation entails "composing and dividing," by which the intellect forms either an affirmative or negative enunciation. These two operations are perhaps better known to us as simple apprehension and judgment. And Aquinas tells us that they correspond to two aspects of things in reality (*in rebus*).

As Aquinas explains, the first operation concerns the nature of a thing, whether as something whole or as something incomplete in the manner of a part or an accident. By contrast, the second operation concerns the *esse* of a thing, which in a composite thing results from the

---

12. *Metaphysical Thought*, 8 (emphasis added). Wippel's reference to "another context" is to his treatment of this topic in his *Metaphysical Themes* book. For simplicity's sake, moving forward, I will dispense with language of the 'negatively immaterial' when speaking of the second sense of immateriality noted here and instead use only the term 'neutrally immaterial.'
13. *Metaphysical Themes*, 72–73.
14. *In De Trin.*, q. 5, a. 3 (Leon. 50.144–51).

union (*congregatio*) of principles, but in a simple substance accompanies the simple nature itself.[15] "Needless to say," Wippel observes, "this text, together with its parallels, strongly supports those who insist that for Thomas one must have recourse to judgment, not merely to simple apprehension, if one is to grasp being as existing or as real, or if one is to grasp existence as such." And, indeed, Wippel makes clear that this is his own view.[16]

What follows next in Aquinas's text, as well as in Wippel's analysis of it, is a detailed examination of the role played by each of these intellectual operations in forming different sorts of abstract knowledge. I will, however, focus here principally on the second operation since that is the one that most concerns us. Regarding this operation, Aquinas is clear that not every sort of judgment is abstractive, but only a negative judgment inasmuch as it signifies the separation of things.[17] Moreover, since the truth of the intellect results from its conformity to reality, he adds that a negative judgment truly abstracts (*uere abstraere*) only if what it separates is truly separate in reality. To illustrate this point, Aquinas asks us to consider a man who, in reality, is white: if we were to assert of him that "the man *is not* white," our judgment would be false, precisely because the two items are not separate in reality. By contrast, it *would* be true to assert that "the man *is not* a donkey," because these two are really separate.[18]

Aquinas then draws a terminological distinction between the abstractive act of *separatio* and the sort of abstractive act entailed in the intellect's first operation (whereby we know *what* something is). Only the former, he tells us, is properly called 'separation' (*separatio*); the latter act should instead be called 'abstraction' (*abstractio*). Wippel helpfully clarifies for us the shift at this point in Aquinas's terminology: "Abstraction

---

15. *In De Trin.*, q. 5, a. 3, co. (Leon. 50.147:89–105).
16. *Metaphysical Themes*, 74–75.
17. On this point, see Aquinas's later commentary on Aristotle's *Peri Hermeneias* (1270–71): "negatio uero dicitur diuisio in quantum significat rerum separationem." *In Peri herm.* I.3 (Leon. 1*/1.15:77–78).
18. *In De Trin.*, q. 5, a. 3, co. (Leon. 50.147:105–18). Aquinas then proceeds to explain that, in contrast to the second operation of the intellect, the first operation can, in certain cases, abstract things that are not separate in reality. As Wippel explains, "In brief, such is possible when and only when the intelligibility of that which is abstracted does not depend on the other thing with which it is united in reality" (*Metaphysical Themes*, 75). For Aquinas's detailed explanation of this point and his examples, see *In De Trin.*, q. 5, a. 3, co. (Leon. 50.147:119–58).

has now taken on a narrower meaning, being restricted to the intellect's first operation. *Separatio* refers to the intellect's second operation, or judgment, and since it is a distinguishing or dividing operation, is often described by commentators on Thomas as a 'negative judgment.'"[19] Having highlighted that it is this sort of operation that is properly called *separatio*, Aquinas then observes that *separatio* properly belongs to divine science, or metaphysics.[20]

In considering this text, Wippel highlights the importance of judgment in general for Aquinas's metaphysics, noting that "there is strong reason to suggest that an existential judgment or a judgment of existence has some role to play in one's discovery of being as existing according to Thomas." Still, he cautions that if one were to stop there, one would have arrived at a notion of BEING (*ens*) only as material and changing, which is not the subject of metaphysics; rather, this sort of concept is what Wippel terms the "primitive notion of being."[21]

How then does one get beyond this restricted notion of BEING, which is reached through an affirmative judgment? According to Wippel, one does so by means of the sort of negative judgment that Aquinas terms *separatio*. Whereas the process of abstraction performed in the first operation of the intellect is sufficient to attain the subject matters of the other theoretical sciences, it is insufficient to attain the subject of metaphysics because abstraction strictly taken cannot arrive at the neutrally

---

19. *Metaphysical Themes*, 76; *In De Trin.*, q. 5, a. 3, co. (Leon. 50.148:159–71).

20. Of course, negative judgments can occur in any science. Presumably, in saying that *separatio* properly belongs to metaphysics, Aquinas means as an abstractive technique or methodology. In contrast to this sort of abstractive negative judgment, the first operation of the intellect abstracts in one of two ways: either by abstracting form from sensible matter or by abstracting a universal from a particular. The former sort of abstraction, he explains, is proper to mathematics, whereas the latter is proper to physics but also, he adds, to all of the sciences in general. *In De Trin.*, q. 5, a. 3, co. (Leon. 50.149:275–86).

21. *Metaphysical Themes*, 77–78. Regarding Wippel's distinction between a "primitive" or "prephilosophical" concept of BEING and a "philosophical" or "metaphysical" one, I am sympathetic with Rudi te Velde's criticism that it is not borne out by the texts *if* by these terms Wippel is speaking of different concepts in the knower. If, however, he simply means by these terms that the so-called metaphysical concept of BEING entails a refinement of one's concept (comparable to discovering that whales are in fact mammals and not fish), then I see no problem with this language. As I will argue below, even a prephilosophical grasp of BEING in this latter sense is flexible enough to extend across the categories, prior to a grasp of the neutrally immaterial character of BEING-IN-GENERAL. For te Velde's critique of Wippel on these points, see "The Knowledge of Being: Thomistic Metaphysics in the Contemporary Debate," in *The Discovery of Being & Thomas Aquinas* (ed. Cullen and Harkins), 46–50.

The Perspective for Considering Being as Being

immaterial notion of BEING-IN-GENERAL (*ens commune*).²² By contrast, the operation of *separatio* can do just that.

In his *Metaphysical Themes* volume, Wippel nicely sums up this position, so it is worth quoting him at length here. What follows, however, is a dense paragraph, so for the reader's benefit I will parse out the sentences, adding italics for points of emphasis and clarification:

> 1. To express Thomas's understanding of *separatio* in other terms, it is the process through which the mind explicitly acknowledges and asserts that *that by reason of which something is recognized as being* need not be identified with *that by which it is recognized as material being*, or *changing being*, or *being of a given kind*.
>
> 2. One may describe it as a negative judgment in that it denies that *that by reason of which something is described as being* is to be identified with *that by reason of which it is being of a given kind*, for instance, material and changing being, or quantified being, or, for that matter, spiritual being.
>
> 3. One may describe it as *separatio* because by reason of this judgment one distinguishes or separates *that intelligibility in virtue of which something is described as being* from all lesser and more restrictive intelligibilities that indicate its kind of being.
>
> 4. As a result of *separatio*, therefore, one asserts that in order for something to be or to be real, it need not be material or changing or quantified.
>
> 5. Thus one asserts the negative immateriality, the neutral character, of being.²³

We find Wippel presenting in this paragraph a number of helpful distinctions regarding his reading of Aquinas on *separatio*. Still, the relations between these distinctions might leave the reader uncertain about Wippel's principal point: Does it concern simply our *consideration* of BEING, or is it a point about reality itself and what could possibly exist? In sentence 1, we find him presenting *separatio* as a "mental process"

---

22. Regarding why it is problematic to hold that this metaphysical notion of BEING is arrived at by means of abstraction strictly taken, see Wippel, *Metaphysical Themes*, 78–81. One particular problem noted by Wippel is that "If one abstracts from individual differences, from sensible matter, and from quantity in arriving at one's notion of being, how can one apply such an abstracted notion to these same individual differences, to sensible matter, and to quantity? Perhaps by adding something to the notion of being that does not fall under the same. But that could only be nonbeing" (*Metaphysical Themes*, 80). The problematic abstractive approach that he describes calls to mind Hegel's conclusion that BEING is the emptiest of all concepts—a position with which Aquinas would clearly disagree.

23. *Metaphysical Themes*, 79. With the exception of the term *separatio*, all emphasis has been added.

directed toward that by which the mind "recognizes" beings as beings. Then, in sentence 2, he clarifies that this mental process entails a negative judgment concerning how beings, as beings, should (and should not) be "described."

Thus far, Wippel's language suggests that the relevant separative judgment entails a conceptual analysis of the notion of BEING. This reading is further indicated in sentence 3, where he clarifies why this mental process is called *separatio,* namely, because by it the mind separates lesser and restrictive "intelligibilities" from the "intelligibility in virtue of which something is described as being." What are these restrictive intelligibilities? Presumably they are the intelligibilities indicated in the prior two sentences: the notions of BEING as material, changing, quantified, or even as spiritual (i.e., positively immaterial). All of these, he tells us, indicate a *kind* of being rather than BEING as such.

In sentence 4, however, Wippel appears to shift from a conceptual consideration of intelligibilities about BEING to a claim about reality itself: he tells us that the aforementioned consideration of the "recognition" and "description" of the "intelligibility" by which beings are beings justifies us in asserting that "for something to be or to be real, it need not be material." Finally, in sentence 5, Wippel concludes that to affirm the conclusions reached by the aforementioned mental process known as *separatio* is to assert the negative, or neutrally, immaterial character of BEING.

This paragraph raises two major questions regarding Wippel's position. First, we might ask why he thinks that we are justified in moving from a conceptual consideration of intelligibilities to an assertion about reality. Second, we might ask whether Wippel is attempting to prove the neutrally immaterial character of BEING by first establishing the *possibility* of the existence of positively immaterial substances. We find these sorts of questions raised by McInerny, in his work *Praeambula Fidei.* There, he observes that "Wippel apparently takes *separatio* to be a mental act whereby we just recognize that being is sometimes immaterial, that substance is sometimes immaterial, and so on."[24]

As McInerny presents Wippel's account of *separatio,* it amounts to no more than hand-waving. On its own, McInerny contends, this mental act

---

24. McInerny, *Praeambula Fidei,* 195.

The Perspective for Considering Being as Being

is insufficient to discern the neutrally immaterial character of BEING. To justify such a separative judgment, he maintains, one must already know that *at least one* positively immaterial being or substance exists, as otherwise "one has no basis for saying that some substances exist apart from matter and motion."[25] This criticism prompts McInerny to ask rhetorically, "Does Wippel think that simply ignoring the features of sensible being puts one into contact with immaterial being? Or does he think the conceptual possibility—the dialectical or logical possibility—suffices to establish the subject of the science we are seeking?"[26]

We find a similar critique raised by Benedict Ashley in his work, *The Way toward Wisdom*.[27] Going beyond McInerny's rhetorical questions, Ashley more pointedly criticizes Wippel's view that one can establish the neutrally immaterial character of BEING by judging that it need not be material, changing, or quantified: "One may indeed *make* this judgment, but," Ashley asks, "what *validates* it?" Looking at Wippel's later *Metaphysical Thought of Thomas Aquinas*, Ashley observes that Wippel "casts no further light on this inescapable question."[28]

Are McInerny's and Ashley's criticism of Wippel on this point accurate, though? Is it indeed the case that Wippel merely asserts that BEING need not be material, offering no validation for the sort of judgment of separation that he presents? To answer these questions, we need to look more closely at Wippel's three presentations of this topic. Doing so will show a development over time—not in terms of the substance of his position—but in terms of a point of clarification, namely regarding Aquinas's analysis of the *ratio* of SUBSTANCE. And all of these considerations will put us in a better position ultimately to see the role of *separatio* for

---

25. Ibid.
26. Ibid.
27. Expressing concerns with Wippel's language of BEING as "neutrally immaterial," Ashley notes, "More correctly, Wippel also says that metaphysical Being is 'unrestricted' to the material. But how can we judge this to be the case if the only being that we know is material being? While it is true that *ens* potentially, or if you like, virtually, contains whatever is or can be known, our direct knowledge of it based on the senses tells us only about the material and sensible things directly experienced by us." See Ashley, *Way toward Wisdom*, 157.
28. Ibid., 158. Ashley grants with Wippel that "the object of metaphysics (Metascience) is known only by a judgment of separation, but for that judgment to be valid, somehow it must first be known that immaterial substances really exist" (Ashley, *Way toward Wisdom*, 158). For both McInerny and Ashley, then, it belongs to natural science to provide such knowledge, for example by means of an argument such as Aristotle's in *Physics* VIII for the existence of a prime mover that is pure act.

Aquinas as an integral part of what I take to be a broader approach employed by him to establish the subject matter of metaphysics.

WIPPEL, *SEPARATIO*, AND THE ANALYSIS OF SUBSTANCE

In their critiques of Wippel, both McInerny and Ashley focus their attention on the 2000 volume, *The Metaphysical Thought of Thomas Aquinas*. For that reason, we should turn to that text to see what Wippel in fact has to say on this topic. And because Ashley cites chapter 2 of this volume as making supposedly unvalidated claims about the role of *separatio*, it is worth looking at an extended quotation from that chapter.

There, as before, Wippel provides a close summary and analysis of q. 5, a. 3, from the *De Trinitate* commentary, after which he draws the following conclusions about *separatio* for Aquinas:

> [1] First of all, separation is a judging operation, whereby the intellect distinguishes one thing from another by noting that the one is not found in the other. In other words, it is a negative judgment. [2] Secondly, Thomas also writes within this same article that when we are dealing with things which *can* exist in separation from one another, separation obtains rather than abstraction. [3] Thirdly, he remarks that substance, which he also refers to as the intelligible matter for quantity, can exist without quantity. Therefore to consider substance as such apart from quantity pertains to separation rather than to abstraction.
>
> This third point is especially important because in q. 5, a. 1 of this same Commentary, Thomas has included substance along with being *(ens)* as illustrations of that which is found in matter in certain instances but not in others, that is, of that which is negatively or neutrally immaterial. If it is through separation that one may consider substance as such rather than as quantified (or as material, we may add), so too it is through separation that one may consider being as such or as being rather than as quantified or material. In sum, it is through separation that one discovers being as being, the subject of metaphysics. This follows both from the fact that Thomas cites substance and being as illustrations of that which is negatively or neutrally immaterial, to use our terminology, and because for Thomas, as for Aristotle, substance is the primary referent of being.[29]

---

29. *Metaphysical Thought*, 47.

With these observations, then, we find Wippel again affirming the role of *separatio* in the judgment that BEING need not be considered as material. We also find that he in fact does more than merely affirm this role: Wippel provides precisely what Ashley claims is missing, namely, *validation* of this judgment. And this validation is provided no less than by Aquinas himself in q. 5, a. 3, of the *De Trinitate* commentary. It is to this text that Wippel points us, where Aquinas shows how, through a negative judgment, one can arrive at the conclusion that SUBSTANCE need not be quantified and, hence, need not be material. With that in mind, I will now turn to examine that passage, which I will refer to as the "*Separatio*-Analysis Text": the passage in which Aquinas explicitly provides a separative analysis of SUBSTANCE.[30]

This passage appears toward the end of q. 5, a. 3, of the *De Trinitate* commentary—an article that is, in fact, dedicated to addressing how mathematical objects can rightly be considered without matter even though their existence is *in* matter. After again drawing distinctions between the intellect's different operations, Aquinas begins to address the question at hand concerning mathematical objects, noting that a form can legitimately be abstracted from a given kind of matter if the *ratio* of its essence does not depend on that sort of matter.[31] By contrast, if the *ratio* of the essence of some form in fact depends upon the relevant kind of matter, then that form cannot be abstracted from such matter. Having enunciated this general principle, Aquinas next explains that all accidents are related to a substance as to their subject in the manner of form to matter. Hence, the *ratio* of any accident depends upon the *ratio*

---

30. As in prior sections of this chapter, in this section I will be placing in small caps terms such as SUBSTANCE, QUANTITY, and QUALITY to indicate that they reference notions or natures. On my use of this convention, see notes 4 and 9 above.

31. Perhaps Aquinas's most thorough treatment of the term *ratio* occurs in *In Sent.* I, d. 2, q. 1, a. 3, co. (Mandonnet/Moos 1.66–71). There, he clarifies that that the term *ratio* signifies what the intellect apprehends from the signification of some name. For items that have a definition, this is the definition of the thing. To be precise, he notes, *ratio* does not signify the very concept of the intellect but rather the intention (*intentio*) that is signified by the concept. Thus, the term *ratio* is a second intentional term, like the term 'genus' or 'definition' and signifies something in the mind. Nevertheless, Aquinas clarifies that in a way the term can also signify something that is in an extra-mental thing when the intellect conceives the likeness of a thing existing outside of the mind. Thus, Aquinas explains, the *ratio* of HUMAN can be said to be in an actually existing human as well as in the mind's concept of HUMAN as the intentional similitude of the extra-mental thing. And, we might add, as with the *ratio* of HUMAN, so too with the *ratio* of SUBSTANCE.

of SUBSTANCE and, for this reason, it is impossible for any accidental form to be separated from a substance. Aquinas then observes that accidents "befall" a (sensible) substance (*superueniunt substantie*) in a certain order, with quantities first, followed by (sensible) qualities, and then passions and motions.[32]

Those of us fortunate enough to have had Wippel as a teacher may remember from his "Metaphysical Themes" course the rare helpful diagram that he provided on the chalkboard, showing Aquinas's presentation of this order.

Figure 1: Interrelations Between Accidents and Substance

The diagram depicts in a visual way the relation of dependence that these accidents have—not only to SUBSTANCE—but also *to each other*, with the intelligibility of the posterior presupposing that of the prior. Thus, a proper understanding of posterior accidents presupposes an understanding of the prior, but the inverse is not the case. For example, whereas sensible qualities cannot be understood without a consideration of QUANTITY, by contrast, QUANTITY itself *can* be understood without consideration of sensible qualities.[33] And Aquinas concludes that, since we call matter "sensible" because of its sensible qualities, the *ratio* of

---

32. *In De Trin.*, q. 5, a. 3, co. (Leon. 50.148:180–91).

33. Toward the end of his *responsio* in this article, Aquinas illustrates this dependence of the intelligibility of posterior sensible accidents upon the prior with the examples of SURFACE, COLOR, and MOTION presupposing the intelligibility of QUANTITY. See *In De Trin.*, q. 5, a. 3, co. (Leon. 50.149:266–70).

QUANTITY does not depend upon sensible matter to be understood even though quantities cannot exist apart from matter. Thus, the sort of quantitative objects studied in mathematics, such as figures, are justifiably abstracted from sensible matter.[34]

Aquinas is careful to note, however, that even though the *ratio* of QUANTITY does not entail a dependence upon sensible matter for its intelligibility, it still depends upon what he terms "intelligible matter," namely, SUBSTANCE itself. To clarify this terminology, he adds that SUBSTANCE considered as it is in itself, without any accidents, is not comprehensible by any sense power, but by the intellect alone.[35] In this way, Aquinas indicates that even QUANTITY as abstracted from sensible matter must still be understood to be the quantity *of* something, namely, of a substance. Thus, the *ratio* of QUANTITY presupposes and depends upon the *ratio* of SUBSTANCE. But the same is not the case the other way around. Aquinas makes this position clear toward the end of his *responsio* in the *Separatio*-Analysis Text: "Now SUBSTANCE, which is the intelligible matter of QUANTITY, can exist *(potest esse)* without QUANTITY. Hence, the consideration of SUBSTANCE without QUANTITY belongs to the kind [of operation that is] *separatio* rather than to that of abstraction."[36]

What is it about the *ratio* of SUBSTANCE that allows us to move beyond a quidditative act of abstraction to make this negative existential judgment about it? Aquinas does not go into more detail in these lines, but we will see clarification from other texts shortly. Suffice it to say, in citing the *Separatio*-Analysis Text, Wippel provides precisely what Ashley claims he does not: *validation* for his reading of how Aquinas establishes the neutrally immaterial character of SUBSTANCE. Having done so, he then simply makes explicit what is left implicit by Aquinas: because

---

34. *In De Trin.*, q. 5, a. 3, co. (Leon. 50.148:180–202). Hence, Aquinas refers to this operation as "abstraction of form from sensible matter" in contrast to "abstraction of a universal from a particular." The latter sort of abstraction, he explains, belongs to physics and is common to all of the sciences, whereas the former belongs to mathematics. *In De Trin.*, q. 5, a. 3 (Leon. 50.149:279–85).

35. *In De Trin.*, q. 5, a. 3, co. (Leon. 50.148:194–200).

36. *In De Trin.*, q. 5, a. 3 (Leon. 50.149:270–74): "Substantia autem, que est materia intelligibilis quantitates, potest esse sine quantitate; unde considerare substantiam sine quantitate magis pertinet ad genus separationis quam abstractionis." Note Aquinas's language and methodology here: he is discussing the *consideration (considerare)* of the *ratio* of SUBSTANCE, not the *possibility* of the existence of immaterial substance. As will be discussed below, both McInerny and Ashley misread Wippel as focusing on the latter point rather than the former.

we can conclude in this way that SUBSTANCE is a neutrally immaterial object of consideration—and because SUBSTANCE is the primary instance of BEING—we are further validated in judging that BEING itself need not be considered as material.[37]

It is worth noting here that Wippel's conclusion about BEING is precisely that: a conclusion. He is not telling us that Aquinas's separative analysis *presupposes* knowledge that substances, and hence certain beings, can exist without matter; rather, as Wippel indicates, this is a conclusion that *follows from* the separative analysis described above. This is a point we will return to below. Suffice it to say that both McInerny and Ashley, looking at Wippel's *Metaphysical Thought* (2000), miss this point. It is a point that Wippel brings out even more clearly in his third and final treatment of this topic, "Aquinas on *separatio* and Our Discovery of Being as Being" (2019).[38] Still, the attentive reader can see in all of Wippel's presentations the clear textual support that he offers for his reading of Aquinas on the discovery of the subject of metaphysics.[39] In sum, although Wippel does not put it precisely in these terms, Aquinas validates the separative judgment of BEING as neutrally immaterial by means of an analysis of the *ratio* of SUBSTANCE.

This reading of the text is brought out in the subsequent article from Aquinas's commentary on the *De Trinitate*. There, in q. 5, a. 4, he considers whether the divine science, or metaphysics, concerns things that are separate from matter and motion.[40] In one objection, it is noted that the subject of metaphysics is BEING *(ens)* and principally the sort of being that is SUBSTANCE. Now, the objector argues, if either of these abstracted from matter, then we would not find any beings that would have matter (which is clearly not the case).[41] In reply, Aquinas explains what he means in saying that BEING and SUBSTANCE are separate from matter and motion. They are not separate in the way that the *ratio* of DONKEY excludes REASON; if they were, then their *rationes* would indeed be without the characteristics of matter in such a way that those

---

37. Wippel, *Metaphysical Thought*, 47.
38. "Aquinas on *separatio*," 31–32.
39. For Wippel's summary from his earlier *Metaphysical Thought* regarding the role of *separatio* in judging that SUBSTANCE need not be material, see the passage quoted above (page 14). For his still earlier summary treatment of the topic, see *Metaphysical Themes*, 78–79.
40. *In De Trin.*, q. 5, a. 4 (Leon. 50.151–56).
41. *In De Trin.*, q. 5. a. 4, obj. 5 (Leon. 50.152:34–41).

characteristics would be entirely excluded. Instead, he clarifies, the *rationes* of BEING and SUBSTANCE are separate from matter and motion in the way that ANIMAL abstracts from REASON, even though some animals are rational.[42]

At this point, we might well ask: What is it precisely about SUBSTANCE that allows us to judge that it can be without QUANTITY, thereby excluding matter and motion from its *ratio*? Furthermore, we might wonder whether Aquinas's analysis in this text implicitly presumes the existence of positively immaterial substances to validate his *separative* judgment. To answer these questions, it is helpful to turn to another analysis of SUBSTANCE offered by Aquinas, an analysis that is not addressed by Wippel himself, but which I would argue both supports his reading of the *Separatio*-Analysis Text and even strengthens his case.

THE *RATIO* OF SUBSTANCE AND THE NONDEPENDENCE PRINCIPLE

In his later *De spiritualibus creaturis* (1267–68), Aquinas considers in the fifth article the question of whether there are any created spiritual substances that are not united to a body.[43] After offering a brief historical summary of views on this topic, he provides three arguments to prove that there do indeed exist created spiritual, or separate, substances. It is the first of these arguments that concerns us, in which Aquinas begins with the observation that if we consider the perfection of the universe, "it is clear (*apparet*) that there exist certain substances that are entirely without bodies."[44]

As he explains, we see that the perfection of the universe is such that it should not lack any nature that is possible to exist. His intention, of course, is to show that the perfection of the universe requires the existence of created spiritual substances that are entirely incorporeal, which he begins to do by enunciating the following principle:

> It is clear that if there are two of anything (*aliqua duo sunt*), of which one does *not* depend upon the other according to its *ratio*, it is possible for the [one] to

---

42. *In De Trin.*, q. 5, a. 4, ad 5 (Leon. 305–13).
43. *De spir. creat.* 5 (Leon. 24/2.55–64).
44. *De spir. creat.* 5, co. (Leon. 24/2.61:195–97): "Primo igitur apparet esse aliquas substantias omnino a corpore absolutas ex perfectione uniuersi."

be found without the other. For example, ANIMAL—according to its *ratio*—does not depend upon RATIONAL. Hence, it is possible for there to be found nonrational animals.[45]

Here we find Aquinas developing his reasoning in the earlier text, considered just above, from the *De Trinitate* commentary: the possibility for the existence of nonrational animals such as donkeys is that REASON does not belong to the *ratio* of ANIMAL. Still, in that earlier text, he had noted simply that ANIMAL abstracts from REASON, whereas in this text Aquinas goes beyond abstraction to make an existential judgment about what *could* be. We might wonder, then, about the legitimacy of his application of what I will term the "*Ratio*-Nondependence Principle" enunciated in this text: if there are two of anything, of which one does not depend upon the other according to its *ratio*, it is possible for the one to be found—that is, to exist in reality—without the other. We may recall at this point what Aquinas had told us in his *De Trinitate* commentary, namely, that abstraction is the first operation of the intellect, by means of which we grasp *what* something is, not *that* it is. It is instead by means of an act of judgment, the intellect's second operation, that we understand something to exist.[46] Is Aquinas now making the error of moving from the mind to the world, judging that because we can, in this way, *understand* ANIMAL as nonrational that therefore such animals do in fact exist? No. Rather, he is indicating that this analysis of the *ratio* simply reveals the possibility that, in principle, there *could* exist nonrational animals.[47]

---

45. *De spir. creat.* 5, co. (Leon. 24/2.61:200–206): "Manifestum est autem quod, si aliqua duo sunt, quorum unum ex altero non dependeat secundum suam rationem, possibile est illud sine alio inueniri: sicut animal secundum suam rationem non dependet a rationali; unde possibile est inueniri animalia non rationalia." Emphasis added in translation.

46. See above, pages 8–9.

47. Aquinas's use of the *Ratio*-Nondependence Principle (hereafter RNP) here might lend to the accusation that he is opening the door to a rationalistic approach to metaphysics that is the hallmark of a conceptualist ontology, but I do not see that to be the case. Although Aquinas does not tell us here what justifies employing the RNP to draw conclusions about reality, presumably it is due to the connection he sees between the *rationes* of real things and their corresponding *modi essendi*. For Aquinas, things "have their proper mode of existence in accordance with their proper *ratio / habent proprium modum essendi secundum propriam rationem*." Thus, to grasp what belongs or does *not* belong to the *ratio* of a given type of being is to grasp how such a type of being can or cannot exist. With that said, I do not take Aquinas's position here to mean that we can infer aspects of reality from simply any *ratio* that we can conceive; rather, I see him indicating that the application of the RNP as a metaphysical tool pertains only to those *rationes* that have what he describes elsewhere as an "immediate

The Perspective for Considering Being as Being

Having enunciated and illustrated for us this *Ratio*-Nondependence Principle, Aquinas then applies it to an analysis of SUBSTANCE in this text from the *De spiritualibus creaturis* that I will call the "*Ratio*-Nondependence Text":

> Now, it belongs to the *ratio* of SUBSTANCE that it subsist *per se*, which in no way (*nullo modo*) depends upon the *ratio* of BODY. For the *ratio* of BODY in a certain way references (*aliquo modo respiciat*) certain accidents, namely dimensions, by which it is not caused to subsist. It remains, therefore, that after God, who is not contained in any genus, there are found in the genus of SUBSTANCE some substances entirely without bodies.[48]

As in his earlier *Separatio*-Analysis Text, Aquinas here employs the method of *separatio* in analyzing the *ratio* of SUBSTANCE, even if he does not identify that intellectual operation by name. As he indicates, in our consideration of the *ratio* of SUBSTANCE, we can discern not only what belongs to that *ratio* but also what does *not* belong to it. What fundamentally belongs to substances as such is the mode of existence called 'subsistence,' that is, *per se* existence.[49] But SUBSISTENCE, he explains,

---

foundation" in reality: in other words, *rationes* that pertain to known quidditative content. This is why, in his example above, Aquinas sees the RNP as applicable to an analysis of ANIMAL; for we can come to know such quidditative content through encountering animals such as humans, which have a genuine essence. But the principle would *not* be applicable to an analysis of a fictional creature such as the Chimera, whose *ratio* Aquinas tells us has no foundation in reality—or, again, to the goatstag, which Aquinas tells us has no quiddity or essence, because its *ratio* is simply composed of several names. Thus, even though we can know what the names 'Chimera' or 'goatstag' signify, it is impossible for us to know the *whatnesses* of such "things" because, in fact, there are no such things: their *rationes*, Aquinas tells us, have neither an immediate nor even a remote foundation (unlike an intention such as GENUS or a privation such as BLINDNESS, which at least has a remote foundation). In sum, I do not see Aquinas here as indicating that the RNP can be employed as a metaphysical tool for analyzing simply any *ratio*, or concept, as such, but only for *rationes* known to have an immediate foundation in reality. On the connection between a being's proper *modus essendi* and its proper *ratio*, see SCG IV, c. 14 (Marietti 275). On Aquinas's treatment of the notion of *ratio*, see above note 31. For his treatment of the *ratio* of the goatstag, see *In Post. an.* II.6 (Leon. 1*/2.194:12–26). For a consideration of Aquinas's treatment of fictional beasts like the Chimera, see Gyula Klima, "The Semantic Principles Underlying Saint Thomas Aquinas's Metaphysics of Being," *Medieval Philosophy and Theology* 5 (1996): 125–27. For more discussion of Aquinas's use of logical methodology in metaphysics, see the fourth section of this chapter, below.

48. *De spir. creat.* 5, co. (Leon. 24/2.61:206–14): "Est autem de ratione substantie quod per se subsistat, quod nullo modo dependet a corporis ratione, cum ratio corporis quedam accidentia, scilicet dimensiones, aliquo modo respiciat, a quibus non causatur subsistere. Relinquitur igitur quod post Deum, qui non continetur in aliquo genere, inueniantur in genere substantie alique substantie a corporibus absolute."

49. Considering the etymology of the term 'substance' (*substantia*), Aquinas tells us that

does not in any way depend upon the *ratio* of BODY. Bodies, considered as such, have certain accidents, namely dimensions, which the *ratio* of BODY references (*respiciat*). What does Aquinas mean by this? Certainly not that the accidents of dimensions are themselves part of that *ratio*: if they were, then a genus in the category of SUBSTANCE would depend upon accidents in its definition and essence, which is impossible.

Rather, as Aquinas makes clear in an earlier article of the same *De spiritualibus creaturis*, dimensions are the proper accidents of a body and thus follow necessarily from the *ratio* of that genus.[50] Elsewhere, he

---

this name is imposed from the fact that a substance *substands* accidents. Nevertheless, considering the signification of the term 'substance,' he frequently indicates that that *for which* it is imposed (what the name signifies) is SUBSISTING THING (*res subsistens*). Thus, on those occasions when he explicitly discusses the *ratio* of SUBSTANCE, Aquinas does not mention its substanding but, instead, focuses on its mode of existence: SUBSISTENCE. At other times, however, he is careful to indicate that the subsistence of a substance is not identical with its essence, because the essence of a substance is really distinct from its *esse*. For this reason, Aquinas does not think that the formulation *ens per se* is suitable as a definition, or *ratio*, of SUBSTANCE, as will be discussed in more detail below. Rather, over the course of his career, he offers versions of what, in one text, he terms the "quasi definition" of SUBSTANCE: "a thing having a quiddity for which *esse* is acquired, or had, as *not* in another" (*res habens quidditatem, cui acquiritur esse, vel debetur, ut non in alio*). This formulation acknowledges the real distinction between essence and *esse* in created substances while at the same time still highlighting SUBSISTENCE as their mode of being. For Aquinas on the etymology of the term 'substance,' see *In Sent.* I, d. 23, q. 1, a. 1, co. (Mandonnet 554–57); *ST* I, q. 29, a. 3, ad 3 (Leon. 4.332). For his treatment of SUBSISTENCE as fundamental to the *ratio* of SUBSTANCE, see *In Sent.* II, d. 3, q. 1, a. 1, ad 1 (Mandonnet 2.88); *In Sent.* III, d. 6, q. 1, a. 1, qc. 1, co. (Moos 3.225.23); *De spir. creat.* 5, co. (Leon. 24/2.61:206–14). For occasions when Aquinas employs the formulation *ens per se* to speak of SUBSTANCE, see *De ver.*, q. 1, a. 1, co. (Leon. 22/1.5:100–123); *ST* I, q. 52, a. 1, co. (Leon. 5.20); *De pot.*, q. 5, a. 10, co. (Marietti 2.155–56); *In Meta.* IV.1 (Marietti 159:539). For what Aquinas terms the "quasi definition of SUBSTANCE," see *In Sent.* IV, d. 12, q. 1, a. 1, qc. 1, ad 2 (Moos 4.499). For similar formulations of this quasi definition, see *SCG* I, c. 25 (Marietti 36.236:B6–12); *De pot.*, q. 7, a. 3, ad 4 (Marietti 2.194); *ST* I, q. 3, a. 5, ad 1 (Leon. 4.44); *In Phys.* 77.1, ad 2 (Leon. 12.194). For discussions of Aquinas's account of SUBSTANCE, see Gregory T. Doolan, "Aquinas on *Substance* as a Metaphysical Genus," in *The Science of Being as Being: Metaphysical Investigations*, ed. Gregory T. Doolan (Washington, DC: The Catholic University of America Press, 2012), 99–128; Wippel, *Metaphysical Thought*, 198–208 and 228–37; Étienne Gilson, "Quasi Definitio Substantiae," in *St. Thomas Aquinas 1274–1974: Commemorative Studies*, ed. Armand Maurer (Toronto: Pontifical Institute for Mediaeval Studies, 1974), 1:111–29.

50. *De spir. creat.* 3, ad 18 (Leon. 24/2.48:619–27). Thus, elsewhere, he explains that "the *ratio* of BODY consists in this: that it is of such a nature so that in it there can be designated three dimensions" (*ratio corporis in hoc consistat quod sit talis naturae, ut in eo possint designari tres dimensiones*). *In Sent.* I, d. 25, q. 1, a. 2, ad 2 (Mandonnet 1.602–3). Considering the term 'body' as said of an animal, Aquinas draws a distinction between two ways in which 'body' may be said in accordance with this basic *ratio*. In one way, it signifies matter as an integral part of an animal that is completed by form. In another way, 'body' signifies a thing having the sort of nature perfected by any form from which there can be designated in it three dimensions; in this

explains that the name 'body' is "imposed" (i.e., taken) *from* the exterior properties of the sort of substance that has three dimensions; nevertheless, what the term is imposed *to signify* is not those dimensions but, rather, a certain genus of SUBSTANCE. The fact that we understand the *ratio* of BODY in light of these properties is due to the nature of our intellect, which comes to know the quiddities of sensible things from their exterior accidents.[51] Aquinas explains, in this way, how the exterior accidents of dimensions are requisite for our understanding of the *ratio* of BODY even though they are not as such part of that *ratio*. By contrast, the consideration of dimensions is in no way requisite for our understanding of SUBSTANCE as such because in no way are they either *part of* or *referenced in* its *ratio*. This is what Aquinas intends to bring out in the *Ratio*-Nondependence Text from the *De spiritualibus creaturis*.

We find, then, that in both this text and the *Separatio*-Analysis Text from the *De Trinitate* commentary, Aquinas's line of reasoning exhibits a robust optimism—not only that we can understand the *ratio* of SUBSTANCE—but that, independent of any consideration of positively immaterial substances, we can understand it as not dependent upon the *ratio* of BODY. Thus, I take Aquinas to be indicating that from our experience of bodily substances, we can come to understand what it is for a body to subsist in distinction from what it is for that same body to be the sort of thing to which the accidents of dimensions belong, recognizing that the *ratio* of SUBSTANCE "in no way depends upon the *ratio* of BODY." In short, through this analysis of the *ratio* of SUBSTANCE, Aquinas shows by an act of *separatio* that the *ratio* and genus of SUBSTANCE is—in Wippel's terms—neutrally immaterial and, following from this analysis, he concludes that a substance as such need not be material.

---

second way, it is taken as a genus and signifies the whole animal. We are concerned here with the latter sense of 'body', taken as a genus contained under the supreme genus of SUBSTANCE. See *In Meta.* VII.12 (Marietti 373.1547); *De ente*, c. 2 (Leon. 43.371–72:105–50). In these last cited texts, Aquinas not only draws the same distinction regarding the signification of the term 'body', but also identifies a third. As he explains, the three designated dimensions can themselves be called 'body'. Taken in this way, 'body' names a genus in the category of QUANTITY. It is according to this third sense of the term 'body' that the mathematician is said to study bodies. See, e.g., *In De Trin.*, q. 5, a. 3, ad 2 (Leon. 50.150:302–17). On Aquinas's treatment of dimensions and these various senses of the term 'body', see Joseph Bobik, *Aquinas on Being and Essence: A Translation and Interpretation* (Notre Dame, IN: University of Notre Dame Press, 1965), 86–100.

51. *ST* I, q. 18, a. 2, co. (Leon. 4.226).

If we consider the *Ratio*-Nondependence Text in particular, it is worth highlighting the stark contrast between Aquinas's analysis of the *ratio* of SUBSTANCE and the claim of both McInerny and Ashley. According to them, one must first prove the existence of a positively immaterial being to discover the neutrally immaterial character of SUBSTANCE. Here, Aquinas's approach is precisely the inverse: he proves both the possibility and the actuality of the existence of the positively immaterial *after* having established the neutrally immaterial character of SUBSTANCE.[52]

Whether or not we take Aquinas's ultimate conclusion in this argument to be demonstrative (namely, that created immaterial substances do in fact exist), the key takeaway for our own consideration concerns the intermediate step in which he offers an analysis of SUBSTANCE in light of the *Ratio*-Nondependence Principle.[53] As with the *Separatio*-Analysis Text that Wippel focuses on, so with this *Ratio*-Nondependence Text: Aquinas provides a clear methodology to validate the claim that SUBSTANCE (and hence BEING) need not be material or considered as such.

The line of reasoning in these two texts also provides a response to McInerny's concern that Wippel is "simply ignoring the features of sensible being," and then (supposedly) asserting without argument that this "puts one into contact with immaterial being."[54] Instead, what we have seen is that Wippel's approach (indeed, Aquinas's) entails precisely an

---

52. To be clear, however, Aquinas does not present the application of the RNP in this analysis as sufficient to prove that spiritual substances in fact exist but merely that it is possible for there to be such beings within the genus of SUBSTANCE. Why, then, does Aquinas's argument ultimately conclude to the *actual* existence of created immaterial beings? Because, at the outset of the argument, he also enunciates the principle that the perfection of the universe is such that it is not lacking any kind of nature that could possibly exist. Granting that God exists, and having established the possibility of created incorporeal substances, Aquinas then concludes that the perfection of the universe requires the *actual* existence of these beings. See *De spir. creat.* 5, co. (Leon. 24/2.61:195–99).

53. Most scholarship that addresses Aquinas's arguments for the existence of angels treats those arguments as merely dialectical, or probable, arguments rather than as demonstrative, with few scholars addressing Aquinas's own views of the strength of these arguments. As I have argued elsewhere, however, Aquinas himself appears to consider at least some of his arguments to be demonstrative, including this argument from *De spir. creat.* 5. For this reading, see my "Aquinas on the Demonstrability of Angels," in *A Companion to Angels in Medieval Philosophy*, ed. Tobias Hoffmann (Leiden: Brill, 2012), 13–44. For support of my interpretation, see Stephen L. Brock, *The Philosophy of Saint Thomas Aquinas* (Eugene, OR: Cascade Books, 2015), 119. For a summary of differing interpretative views of these arguments, see my "Demonstrability of Angels," 13–14, esp. nn2–3.

54. See above, page 13.

acknowledgment of the features of sensible beings *as* sensible, coupled with a recognition that those features are not requisite for our understanding of them as subsistent beings. The relevant act of *separatio* in Aquinas that Wippel highlights is simply a *via negativa* clarifying what SUBSTANCE is by showing what it is not.

Still, it might be objected that the separative analysis of SUBSTANCE described above is not a distinctly metaphysical analysis but, rather, a dialectical one that is insufficient for establishing the subject of metaphysics, which concerns real BEING. Indeed, as we have seen, McInerny himself raises this very concern, noting that Wippel (supposedly) seems to think it sufficient to identify the *conceptual* possibility of the positively immaterial in order to establish the subject of metaphysics. If this is indeed the case, McInerny observes, Wippel would merely be showing the "dialectical or logical possibility" of the immaterial, which McInerny indicates would be insufficient for establishing the subject of this science.[55] With this concern in mind, I will now turn to the fourth part of my chapter to examine Aquinas's methodology in more detail as well as to clarify further what I take to be Wippel's position.

AQUINAS'S USE OF LOGICAL METHODOLOGY IN METAPHYSICS

Before we address an implicit response to McInerny's concern that we can find in Wippel, it is worth acknowledging that Aquinas's argumentation in both the *Separatio*-Analysis Text and the *Ratio*-Nondependence Text might well seem to be dialectical in their procedure. We have seen that in these two texts, Aquinas's line of reasoning entails an analysis of the *ratio* and genus of SUBSTANCE. Now, both a *ratio* and a genus are logical intentions formed by the intellect; and, as Aquinas explains elsewhere, it belongs to dialectics to proceed in its argumentation through a consideration of intentions of reason.[56] Therefore, at first glance, these arguments could well be seen to be dialectical rather than demonstrative.

Nevertheless, we should keep in mind that for Aquinas, not all

---

55. See above, page 13.
56. See above, note 31. For Aquinas's reference to GENUS as a logical intention, see e.g., *De ente*, prol. (Leon. 43.369:9–10); for his treatment of *ratio* as an intention, see, e.g., *In Sent.* I, d. 2, q. 1, a. 3, co. (Mandonnet 1.66–67). On the consideration of intentions in dialectics, see *In Meta.* IV.4 (Marietti 160.574); *In Post. an.* I.20 (Leon. 1*/2.75:111–74).

arguments that reason from intentions are *ipso facto* dialectical.[57] As he explains, although none of the special (i.e., particular) sciences can reason demonstratively from such intentions, metaphysics is justified in doing so because of the affinity that it shares with logic. Commenting on Aristotle's *Metaphysics*, Aquinas explains that both metaphysics and logic are universal sciences that consider all things; thus, they can be said to have, in a way, the same subject matter: BEING. But whereas metaphysics is concerned with REAL BEING (*ens naturae*) as its subject matter, logic is concerned only with BEING OF REASON (*ens rationis*).[58] Thus, logic considers intentions such as GENUS, SPECIES, and so forth, that reason discerns or "devises" (*adinvenit*) through its consideration of real things. Aquinas explains that because such intentions are equal in extension with real beings (*entibus naturae aequiparantur*), the subject of logic extends to everything of which REAL BEING is predicated, even though logic does not itself study real beings as such.[59]

Whereas logic is not properly concerned with real beings, metaphysics is properly concerned with them *as well as* with the logical intentions that are beings of reason. As Aquinas explains, this is because metaphysics studies the *per se* accidents of BEING (*per se entis accidentia*), among which are common logical intentions such as GENUS and SPECIES "because these too are accidents of BEING inasmuch as it is BEING."[60] In

---

57. Nor do all dialectical arguments reason from common intentions. The distinguishing characteristic of a dialectical argument is that it is marked by probability rather than by the certitude of a demonstration. Reasoning from common intentions is one way in which some arguments may be probable, but so too is reasoning based upon opinions held, for example, by the wise or the many. Thus, an otherwise demonstrative argument would be dialectical if the premises are not comprehended by the one reasoning but held only by opinion. See, e.g., *ST* I, q. 12, a. 7, co. (Leon. 4.127).

58. On *ens rationis* as the subject of logic, see Robert W. Schmidt, SJ, *The Domain of Logic According to Saint Thomas Aquinas* (The Hague: Martinus Nijhoff, 1966), 49–174.

59. *In Meta.* IV.4, nn. 573–74 (Marietti 160). In his earlier commentary on Boethius's *De Trinitate*, Aquinas notes of logic and metaphysics that "both sciences are universal and, in a way, have the same subject matter" (*utraque scientia communis est et circa idem subiectum quodammodo*). See *In De Trin.*, q. 6, a. 1, co. (Leon. 50.159:133–36). Regarding Aquinas's justification of the use of a logical methodology in metaphysics, see James B. Reichmann, "Logic and the Method of Metaphysics," *The Thomist* 29 (1965): 341–95; Rudi te Velde, "Metaphysics, Dialectics and the *Modus Logicus* According to Thomas Aquinas," *Recherches de Théologie et Philosophie médiévales* 63 (1996): 15–35; Wippel, *Metaphysical Thought*, 209–11.

60. *In Meta.* IV.4, n. 587 (Marietti 162): "Et non solum est considerativa istorum, de quibus ostensum est singillatim propriis rationibus, quae cadunt in consideratione huius scientiae; sed etiam considerat de priori et posteriori, genere et specie, toto et parte, et aliis huiusmodi, pari ratione, quia haec etiam sunt accidentia entis inquantum est ens." In Aquinas's saying that logical intentions such as GENUS and SPECIES are *per se* accidents of BEING, I take him to mean

other texts, he explains that these logical intentions are the result of an operation of reason acting upon cognition of reality. Thus, even though they are "devised" by reason with no immediate foundation in reality, they nevertheless have an ultimate foundation there.[61] In this way, Aquinas indicates that the metaphysician can, with care, reason in what I take to be a *quia* manner, back from intentions as *effects* of REAL BEING to draw conclusions about real beings as their *cause*.[62]

Aquinas explains that if the particular sciences were to employ this method, treating it as demonstrative, they would fall into error (*peccatum*) precisely because such sciences are not universal. For the particular sciences to reason demonstratively, they must instead proceed according to their own proper principles. But, again, metaphysics is a universal science; as such, he tells us, it is justified in appropriating and employing this sort of logical methodology in its distinctly scientific investigations.[63] In sum, for the metaphysician to reason about SUBSTANCE from

---

that BEING (i.e. BEING-IN-GENERAL, or CREATED BEING) as such is intelligible, and if it *is* known (namely, by human knowers) it cannot but be known except through logical intentions such as the aforementioned. In a parallel way, the notion of NUMBER itself is neither odd nor even, but *if* there is a given number, it must be one or the other. Hence, Aquinas sees ODD and EVEN as *per se* accidents of number (*In Meta.*, n. 571).

61. Aquinas explains that a genus, for example, has its immediate foundation in the intellect with reference to several species understood by the mind, and yet it still has a remote foundation in extra-mental things; in a similar way, the term *ratio* signifies an intention of the mind, but a *ratio* is nevertheless said to be *in* a thing inasmuch as there is something outside of the mind that corresponds to the conception that signifies the thing. On both points, see *In Sent.* I, d. 2, q. 1, a. 3, co. (Mandonnet 1.66–67).

62. Thus, he is quite comfortable, for example, defending the unicity of substantial form by employing the logical technique of the method of predication (*via praedicationis*) in *ST* I, q. 76, a. 3, co. (Leon. 5.221). Similarly, he approvingly sees Aristotle as employing this logical method in *Metaphysics* VII.3.1029a8–27 to prove the distinction of prime matter from form by showing the metaphysical need for an ultimate substratum of all predication and, hence, of all form; see *In Meta.* VII.2, n. 1287 (Marietti 323). And to prove the real distinction between essence and *esse* in finite beings, one line of reasoning that he offers on a number of occasions is the so-called Genus Argument, which reasons from a being's inclusion in a genus to the real distinction of these metaphysical principles within that being (e.g., *SCG* I, c. 25 [Marietti 2.35–36:230]). Regarding the *quia* line of reasoning in metaphysics from logical intentions, see my "Aquinas's Methodology for Deriving the Categories: Convergences with Albert's *Sufficientia Praedicamentorum*," *Documenti e studi sulla tradizione filosofica medievale* 30 (2019): 654–89. For a detailed presentation of Aquinas's use of the method of predication to defend the unicity of substantial form, see Reichmann, "Method of Metaphysics," 381–83. On Aquinas's use of the same method to prove the reality of prime matter, see Wippel, *Metaphysical Thought*, 303, and Reichmann, "Method of Metaphysics," 376–81.

63. For Aquinas's discussion of this logical methodology and its place in the sciences, see his treatment of different rational methods in *In De Trin.*, q. 6, a. 1, co. (Leon. 50.159–60:119–99). For a detailed analysis of this text, see Reichmann, "Method of Metaphysics," 341–95.

its *ratio*—from what belongs both *to* it and *in* it—is not to engage in dialectics but, rather, is to engage in genuinely metaphysical reasoning.[64] With the foregoing in mind, we find that McInerny's concern that the sort of separative analysis of BEING advanced by Wippel is merely dialectical turns out to be both unwarranted and, in a way, irrelevant. It is unwarranted when it comes to reading Aquinas himself and irrelevant when it comes to reading Wippel on Aquinas.

Regarding Aquinas himself, I say that the concern is unwarranted because in both of his analyses of SUBSTANCE examined above, he reasons from a consideration of corporeal substances and their material features to a distinctly metaphysical (i.e., nondialectical) consideration of them *as* substances, with the recognition that the *ratio* of SUBSTANCE is neutrally immaterial. Moreover, we have seen Aquinas explicitly argue in the *Ratio*-Nondependence Text from *De spiritualibus creaturis* that, having identified the neutrally immaterial character of SUBSTANCE, we may then infer the real possibility of the existence of positively immaterial beings prior to having proven their *actual* existence.[65] In short, in these analyses, the question of the existence of such beings—whether in terms of either actuality or possibility—is subsequent to establishing the *ratio* of SUBSTANCE as neutrally immaterial.

64. Hence, Aquinas tells us at the outset of his opusculum *De ente et essentia* that his goal is to clarify "quid nomine essentie et entis significetur, et quomodo in diuersis inueniatur, et quomodo se habeat ad intentiones logicas, scilicet genus, speciem et differentiam" (*De ente*, prol. [Leon. 43.369:7–10]). Given Aquinas's observation here and his approach in this work of investigating metaphysical themes in comparison with logical intentions, the editor of the Leonine edition observes that "il est difficile de classer ce petit *compendium* où logique et métaphysique vont de pair" (*De ente*, Préface [Leon. 43.320B]). Armand Maurer grants this general point, but adds that "perhaps it is more exact to say simply that it is a metaphysical work using a dialectical method." Although I am sympathetic with Maurer's efforts to show in this way how the *De ente* is a metaphysical treatise, I disagree with his conclusion that this method is therefore dialectical. For Maurer's interpretation, see his "Dialectic in the *De ente et essentia* of St. Thomas Aquinas," in *Roma, magistra mundi. Itineraria culturae medievalis: Mélanges offerts au Père L.E. Boyle à l'occasion de son 75e anniversaire*, ed. J. Hamiss, Textes et études du moyen âge 10 (Louvain-la-Neuve: Fédération des Instituts d'Etudes Médiévales, 1998), 573–83, esp. 583.

65. This conclusion stands in stark contrast to the following claim by McInerny: "But of course unless one knows there is at least one immaterial being or one immaterial substance, one has no basis for saying that some substances exist apart from matter and motion" (*Praeambula Fidei*, 195). Although it is true to say that one has no *immediate* basis for saying that there exist some substances apart from matter and motion, Aquinas clearly holds that one does have an immediate basis for demonstrating the *possibility* of the existence of such substances and, moreover, he presents such a demonstration as an intermediate step to proving their *actual* existence.

The Perspective for Considering Being as Being

Regarding McInerny's reading of Wippel on the discovery of the subject matter of metaphysics, I have also noted that his concern turns out to be irrelevant. Wippel himself is not, as McInerny reads him, trying to prove "the conceptual possibility—the dialectical or logical possibility" of positively immaterial entities at all! Instead, Wippel makes clear, his intent is to show, through a separative analysis of SUBSTANCE and BEING, that we can come to discover that "we may investigate one and the same physical and changing thing from different *perspectives*. We may study it insofar as it is material and mobile, or insofar as it is living, or insofar as it is quantified. But we may also study it insofar as it enjoys reality at all, i.e., insofar as it is a being."[66]

I take this perspectival point about the consideration of BEING to be at the heart of the approach that Wippel sees in Aquinas. With that in mind, it is worth quoting at length what Wippel himself expresses in his third and final treatment of this topic:

> To summarize my thinking on this, just as it is possible for us to investigate a material and changing being from different *perspectives*—for instance, as mobile, as quantified, as living or dead—so is it possible for us to investigate such a being simply insofar as it is real or insofar as it enjoys being. This inquiry does not require that we investigate it as material or as quantified even though such a being may exist only in such a way. Once we have formulated a pre-philosophical notion of being as "that which is," we can always ask ourselves how widely we can apply it: Must we restrict it to the particular kinds of beings we have experienced, or can we extend this notion so that it may be applied to anything of which we can say "it is"? To accept the latter alternative is to acknowledge that if we should encounter or demonstrate the reality of some positively immaterial being, we could then recognize it as enjoying being and hence as "that which is." To acknowledge this does not require us to assume in advance that such a being exists, *or even to defend its possibility in the absolute sense*, that is, intrinsically (as lacking contradiction) and extrinsically in that causes might exist that could bring such an entity into existence. All we need to do is not to exclude any such entity from being recognized *as* a being *if* we should encounter or demonstrate its existence.[67]

It is in this last of Wippel's three major treatments on the topic of *separatio* that we find him most explicitly clarifying his position. The separative analysis he presents is not intended in *any way* to show the possibility

---

66. Wippel, *Metaphysical Thought*, 61; emphasis added. For this language of perspectives, see also his "Aquinas on *separatio*," 41–42.
67. "Aquinas on *separatio*," 72; emphasis added.

of the existence of positively immaterial entities. Nor is it intended to show that BEING is broader in scope and more universal than BODY, as McInerny and Ashley presume that he is trying to do. Rather, Wippel is arguing that for Aquinas, the act of *separatio* allows us to consider even the material beings of our experience from a perspective not captured in the science of physics. In a way, as I take it, Wippel does himself a disservice in speaking of BEING as "neutrally immaterial," because this language of immateriality could easily mislead a reader. Wippel's real point is not that BEING is *im*-material, but rather that, in its *ratio*, BEING is *a*-material, or *non*-material. Thus, to consider even a bodily substance as a being is to consider it from a different perspective than from that of its nature as a body. In short, what Wippel is showing is that, for Aquinas, our discovery of this perspectival consideration of BEING is what enables us to discern the need for a science distinct from that of physics.

Still, even if both McInerny and Ashley were to grant Wippel's perspectival point, I think we may safely presume that they would respond by saying that it is impossible to attain such a perspective about material beings without having first proven the existence of positively immaterial ones. Until that is done, they both indicate, we are not justified in shifting our perspective on material being as material and moving beyond the subject of physics, which is MOBILE BEING (*ens mobile*). With this concern in mind, I will now turn to the fifth and final part of this chapter, in which I will offer both support for Wippel's perspectival approach to the study of BEING as well as my own reading of how *separatio* factors into the discovery of BEING-IN-GENERAL (*ens commune*) as the distinctive subject of metaphysics.

THE UNITY AND DIVERSITY OF THE SUBJECT OF METAPHYSICS

The question of how we discern the distinctiveness of a science's subject matter is, of course, not unique to the consideration of metaphysics. Aquinas addresses this general question on more than one occasion; he also at times addresses the more specific question of how to distinguish between seemingly identical scientific subject matters. On this point, we can see that Aquinas makes the very sort of perspectival point made by Wippel regarding the study of sensible substances. Addressing the studies of geometry and the philosophy of nature, Aquinas tells us that both sciences consider the same subjects (*subiecta*), namely, points, lines, surfaces, and bodies. As a result, he notes, we might be tempted at first to think that these two sciences are in fact one and the same.[68] The reason they are not, however, is that the philosopher of nature considers these subjects insofar as they are the termini of natural bodies whereas the mathematician does not. Drawing out the broader implication, Aquinas notes in commenting on Aristotle's *Physics* that "it is not inappropriate (*inconveniens*) that the same [object] falls under the consideration of diverse sciences according to diverse considerations."[69]

Of course, mere diversity of perspectival consideration is not, as such, sufficient to account for the diversity of sciences. Commenting on Aristotle's *Posterior Analytics*, Aquinas explains the further conditions required for such a diversity: whatever is the same according to nature must not only be considered in diverse *ways* but, more importantly, according to diverse *principles*. It is for this reason, we are told, that the consideration of BODY in mathematics differs from the consideration of that same nature in physics.[70] In reality, a mathematical body is not separate from a natural one; nevertheless, a mathematical body is known by principles of QUANTITY, whereas a natural body is known by principles of motion. For that reason, geometry and natural philosophy are different sciences even though, in a way, they study the same thing. "It is clear, therefore," Aquinas concludes, "that for the diversification of the sciences, [what] suffices is a diversity of principles that accompany the diversity of knowable genera."[71] It is those genera, in turn, that account for the *unity* of each science; for the unity of a science, he explains, follows from the terminus of the relevant knowledge concerning some, one genus.[72]

---

68. *In Phys.* II.3.2 (Leon. 2.61).

69. *In Phys.* II.3.4 (Leon. 2.62): "Non est autem inconveniens quod idem cadat sub consideratione diuersarum scientiarum secundum diuersas considerationes."

70. As I have in the prior sections of this chapter, I am here employing small caps for terms such as BEING, QUANTITY, and BODY when such terms are intended to reference notions or natures.

71. *In Post. an.* I.41 (Leon. 1*/2.155:270–75): "Patet ergo quod ad diuersificandum sciencias sufficit diuersitas principiorum, quam concomitatur diuersitas generis scibilis, ad hoc autem quod sit una sciencia simpliciter utrumque requiritur, et unitas subiecti et unitas principiorum."

72. *In Post. an.* I.41 (Leon. 1*/2.153:131–53): "Cuius ratio est quia processus sciencie cuiusque est quasi quidam motus rationis; cuiuslibet autem motus unitas ex termino principaliter consideratur, ut patet in V Phisicorum, et ideo tenet quod unitas sciencie consideretur ex fine siue

In sum, following Aristotle's *Posterior Analytics*, Aquinas identifies two criteria for establishing or "discovering" the subject of a science: (1) the first is what we could call the "Unity Criterion," which holds that whatever a given science studies must pertain to a single genus as its subject matter, thereby making it *one* science; (2) the second standard is what we could call the "Diversity Criterion," which holds that the unified subject genus studied by a given science is distinguished from the subject of another science if the principles pertaining to it are diverse from those pertaining to the subject of that other science.[73] Following this Diversity Criterion, Aquinas shows that what might at first appear to be the same subject genus of two sciences can be revealed to be diverse through a recognition of the diversity of their relevant principles. Thus, one and the same body can be considered in two respects: as under a genus contained in the category of SUBSTANCE and also according to the genus contained in the category of QUANTITY. For this reason, a body as such can be studied in two different sciences: in the philosophy of nature insofar as it is the subject of motion and in geometry insofar as it is measured.[74] Each of these sciences has its unity from its respective genus of study, with philosophy of nature studying MOBILE BEING (*ens mobile*) and geometry studying MAGNITUDE (i.e., continuous quantity).[75]

In a similar way, I would argue, we find Aquinas applying both the

---

ex termino sciencie; est autem cuiuslibet sciencie finis seu terminus genus circa quod est sciencia, quia in speculatiuis scienciis nichil aliud queritur quam cognitio generis subiecti; sicut in geometria intenditur quasi finis cognitio magnitudinis, que est subiectum geometrie."

73. We should note the difference here between the principle for the division of the sciences for Aristotle and Aquinas in terms of their *objects* and their *subject matter*. We have seen that the former division is presented in terms of the degree of separation that objects have from matter and motion (*Metaphysics* VI.1; *In De Trin.*, q. 5, a. 1 [Leon. 50.136–42]). This is a division of the speculative sciences *as speculative* and not in terms of their subjects, properly speaking. The concern there for both authors is that—unlike the practical sciences, which are diversified based upon their diverse ends—the speculative sciences share the same end, which is knowledge of the truth for its own sake. Hence, the speculative sciences as such are distinguished from each other by the type of *objects* they study. By contrast, the division of the sciences presented by Aristotle in his *Posterior Analytics* (and by Aquinas in his commentary on that work) is presented in terms of their distinctive *subject matters*. For a helpful summary overview of the medieval distinction between a subject and object in scientific investigation, see Jan A. Aertsen, *Medieval Philosophy and the Transcendentals: The Case of Thomas Aquinas*, Studien Und Texte Zur Geistesgeschichte Des Mittelalters 52 (New York: E. J. Brill, 1996), 118.

74. *In De cael.* I.2, n. 2 (Leon. 3.4).

75. For Aquinas on *ens mobile* as the subject of physics, see, e.g., *In Phys.* I.1 (Leon. 2.4:3); on MAGNITUDE as the subject of geometry, see, e.g., *In Post. an.* I.41 (Leon. 1*/2.153:141–43). On this point about geometry, see the Latin in note 72 above.

Unity and Diversity Criteria to establish, or "discover," the subject of metaphysics, revealing the distinctness of its subject matter from that of the philosophy of nature. A bodily substance can be considered not only inasmuch as it is a mobile being but also inasmuch as it simply *is*. Indeed, to say of a body that "it is" is not the same as to say that "it is mobile." The latter predication is more limited than the former. As we have seen, following the Unity Criterion, Aquinas identifies the genus of study in physics as MOBILE BEING—a genus that does not include accidents as its members, as is evidenced by the fact that neither the terms 'mobile being' nor 'body' are predicable of accidents.[76] By contrast, the terms 'is' and 'being' *can* be predicated of accidents as well as of substances precisely inasmuch as both of them *are*.

I take such a recognition to be nothing less than an application of the Unity Criterion for establishing the subject of metaphysics. And, in fact, we find Aquinas indicating as much in his commentary on the opening chapter of *Metaphysics* IV. There, in *lectio* 1, Aquinas notes that it is in this chapter of the *Metaphysics* that Aristotle begins to proceed demonstratively in considering this science, following his dialectical considerations in Book III. Outlining Aristotle's presentation in IV.1, Aquinas tells us that "first, he establishes (*stabilit*) the subject of this science."[77] How? By doing three things: (1) proposing that there is a science whose subject is BEING; (2) showing that it is not any of the particular sciences but is, instead, a universal science; and (3) showing that this is the science of first principles and causes. In other words, what we find is Aquinas indicating to us that what is about to follow in the text entails (1′) the identification of the subject of this science as *ens commune* and then an application of (2′) the Unity and (3′) Diversity Criteria to confirm what has been established.

---

76. That Aquinas considers *ens mobile* to be convertible with BODY is clear from the opening *lectio* of his commentary on the *Physics*, when discussing the subject of that science. He sees the convertibility of these notions as a fact that is demonstrated in the course of the study of physics: "Non dico autem *corpus mobile*, quia omne mobile esse corpus probatur in isto libro [i.e., in the *Physics*]; nulla autem scientia probat suum subiectum: et ideo statim in principio libri *de Caelo*, qui sequitur ad istum, incipitur a notificatione corporis" (*In Phys.* I.1, n. 1 [Leon. 2.4]).

77. *In Meta.* IV.1 (Marietti 150.529): "Primo *subiectum stabilit huius scientiae*." On this language of *stabilit* in this context and the Avicennian influence, see Aertsen, *The Transcendentals*, 136–37. Aertsen notes that "by introducing the notion of 'subject,' which is absent in Aristotle's text, he [Aquinas] places this theme more expressly within the framework of the theory of science than Aristotle does" (ibid., 136).

Let us recall again that according to the Unity Criterion, what makes any science *one* science is its subject of study, which is some, one genus. Of course, BEING is not properly a genus. Still, Aquinas reminds us in commenting on this passage from *Metaphysics* IV.1, there are also sciences whose subjects follow from a unity of predication that is analogical.[78] "But 'being' (*ens*) is predicated in this way of all beings. Therefore," he concludes, "all beings belong to the consideration of a single science that considers BEING inasmuch as it is BEING, namely both substances and accidents."[79] Carefully noting to the reader that Aristotle here offers a demonstrative argument to prove the unity of BEING as the subject of metaphysics, Aquinas dedicates most of the remainder of the *lectio* to parsing out this demonstration.[80] For our purposes, it is sufficient to note the conclusion to this argument, which, again, is that "all beings belong to the consideration of a single science that considers BEING inasmuch as it is BEING, namely both substances and accidents." In short, following the resolutive method (*via resolutionis*) that Aquinas sees as most proper to metaphysics, he shows how all notions resolve to the first and must fundamental notion of BEING.[81]

78. For this reason, Aquinas will at times call BEING (*ens*) a genus, by which I take him to mean that it is *like* a genus as a unified subject of study. See, e.g., *In Meta.*, proem. (Marietti 2): "Unde oportet quod ad eamdem scientiam pertineat considerare substantias separatas, et ens commune, quod est genus, cuius sunt praedictae substantiae communes et universales causae." On this points, see Doolan, "*Substance* as Metaphysical Genus," 117–18.

79. *In Meta.* IV.1 (Marietti 151.534): "Circa primum, utitur tali ratione. Quaecumque communiter unius recipiunt praedicationem, licet non univoce, sed analogice de his praedicetur, pertinent ad unius scientiae considerationem: sed ens hoc modo praedicatur de omnibus entibus: ergo omnia entia pertinent ad considerationem unius scientiae, quae considerat ens inquantum est ens, scilicet tam substantias quam accidentia."

80. Aquinas first identifies the minor premise of the argument as the position that 'being' (*ens*), or 'what is' (*quod est*), can be said in many analogical ways: primarily of substances and secondarily of accidents with reference back to substances as the point of focal unity, namely as a referent that is one as a subject. He then proceeds to present further declining senses of 'being' inasmuch as the term is said also of motions as well as of privations and negations (*In Meta.* IV.1 [Marietti 151.535–43]). Aquinas next identifies the major premise of the demonstration as follows: "Hic *ponit maiorem* primae rationis; dicens, quod est unius scientiae speculari non solum illa quae dicuntur «secundum unum», idest secundum unam rationem omnino, sed etiam eorum quae dicuntur per respectum ad unam naturam secundum habitudines diversas. Et huius ratio est propter unitatem eius ad quod ista dicuntur; sicut patet quod de omnibus sanativis considerat una scientia, scilicet medicinalis, et similiter de aliis quae eodem modo dicuntur" (*In Meta.* IV.1 [Marietti 151.544]).

81. For Aquinas on the role of the *via resolutionis* in metaphysics, see *In De Trin.*, q. 6, a. 2 (Leon. 50.162–63). For his discussion of BEING (*ens*) as the first concept of the intellect to which all other concepts resolve, see *De ver.*, q. 1, a. 1, co. (Leon. 22/1.4–5:95–128). For Wippel's

The Perspective for Considering Being as Being   35

As Aquinas presents the situation, then, the universality and hence the unity of metaphysics as a science can be recognized in this resolutive way through a discernment that BEING is both inclusive of everything and is predicated of everything analogically. It is worth emphasizing here the sort of universality to which he directs our attention: it is not, as Ashley and McInerny claim, the universality of BEING as inclusive of both the material and immaterial.[82] Instead, following Aristotle, Aquinas points simply to the predicability of BEING across the categories, such that it includes accidents as well as substances. Of course, it will turn out that BEING is also universal precisely in the manner that Ashley and McInerny indicate. But as Aquinas himself presents the situation, that sort of universality is established only once metaphysics is underway. Hence, when Aristotle later, in Book XI, raises the question of whether there are any substances separable from sensible ones, Aquinas tells us that "it belongs to *this* science [i.e., metaphysics] to investigate *whether or not* there exists anything separate from sensible substances."[83] In short, the answer to this question is not required to establish the

---

treatment of *resolutio* in Aquinas, see *Metaphysical Thought*, 42–44. See also Jan A. Aertsen, "Method and Metaphysics: The *via resolutionis* in Thomas Aquinas," *The New Scholasticism* 63 (1989): 405–18. For Aertsen's view of the role of this *via* in discerning the subject of metaphysics as *ens commune*, see his *The Transcendentals*, esp. 130 and 134–36. For a comparison of Aertsen's view on this topic with that of Cornelio Fabro, see Jason A. Mitchell, "Knowledge of *ens* as *primum cognitum* and the Discovery of *ens qua ens* according to Cornelio Fabro and Jan A. Aertsen," in *The Discovery of Being & Thomas Aquinas* (ed. Cullen and Harkins), 106–24.

82. Ashley, *Way toward Wisdom*, 53: "There can be no valid metaphysics formally distinct from natural science unless its subject, Being as Being (*esse*), as it analogically includes both material and immaterial being, has first been validated in a manner proper to the foundations integral to natural science by a demonstration of the existence of immaterial being as the cause of material beings." If Ashley is correct, one might well wonder why neither Aristotle in *Metaphysics* IV nor Aquinas in commenting on that text makes mention of immaterial being as the cause of material beings when they identify the subject of this science. Taking note of this fact, and responding to the River Forest school, Lawrence Dewan notes that Aquinas "everywhere treats the metaphysicals as a domain unto themselves, even though they are objects first encountered by us in sensible reality. So considered, they are already analogical. Thus, when Aristotle presents the doctrine of 'being' as something 'said in many ways,' or as Thomas calls it, the 'analogical predication' of 'being,' there is no appeal to immaterial being in the explanation.... That is, for him it is not only the concepts of physics which are encountered in sensible things." See Lawrence Dewan, OP, "St. Thomas, Physics, and the Principle of Metaphysics," in *Form and Being: Studies in Thomistic Metaphysics*, Studies in Philosophy and the History of Philosophy 45 (Washington, DC: The Catholic University of America Press, 2006), 49.

83. *In Meta*. XI.2 (Marietti 514.2175): "Et est *utrum sit aliqua substantia separabilis* praeter sensibiles substantias, quae sunt hic et nunc. Et haec quaestio necessaria est hic ad quaerendum; quia si nihil est praeter sensibilia, tunc sola sensibilia sunt entia. Et, cum sapientia sit scientia entium, sequitur quod sapientia sit circa sola sensibilia, cum tamen in hac scientia

subject of metaphysics; instead, as Aquinas indicated when commenting earlier on *Metaphysics* IV.1, the acknowledgment of the universality of BEING according to the doctrine of predicamental analogy provides a sufficient application of the Unity Criterion for identifying the subject "genus" of this science.

But what about the Diversity Criterion, according to which the subject of a science is shown to be distinct from the subjects of other sciences? In a way, the diversity of the subject of metaphysics is established precisely in the recognition of its very universality: particular sciences, Aquinas explains, consider only some part of BEING. "But the common science [i.e., metaphysics] considers universal BEING *as* BEING; therefore, it is not the same as any of the particular sciences."[84] Still, Aqui-

---

videamur quaerere quamdam aliam naturam separatam. Et sic ad propositum huius scientiae pertinet quaerere, si est aliquid separatum a sensibilibus, vel non" (emphasis added in translation). For Aristotle's observation, see *Metaphysics* XI.2.1060a7–12; for the translation, see *Metaphysics*, ed. Jonathan Barnes, trans. W. D. Ross, in *The Complete Works of Aristotle*, vol. 1 (Princeton, NJ: Princeton University Press, 1984), 1675. One might wonder, then, what we should make of Aristotle's noteworthy observation in *Metaphysics* VI.1 that "if there were no substance other than those which are formed by nature, natural science will be the first science; but if there is an immovable substance, the science of this must be prior and must be first philosophy, and universal in this way, because it is first." (*Metaphysics*, 1026a27–30 [1620])? Both McInerny and Ashley cite these lines as evidence that Aquinas thinks that one must first prove the existence of separate substance to recognize that the science of BEING is distinct from physics. What they neglect, however, is how Aquinas responds to the repeat of these words in *Metaphysics* XI.7.1064b6–12 (1681). Just prior to that, Aristotle notes that "Therefore about that which can exist apart and is unmovable there is a science different from both of these, if there *is* a substance of this nature (I mean separable and immovable), as we shall try to prove there is" (*Metaphysics* XI.7.1064a32–36 [1681]). Aquinas explains that "[Aristotle] says this because he has *not yet* proven that there exists any such substance. Rather, he *intends* to show this" (*Et hoc dicit, quia nondum est probatum aliquam talem substantiam esse. Sed hoc ostendere intendit*); emphasis added. See *In Meta.* XI.7 (Marietti 536.2262). In other words, Aquinas is indicating that by Book XI, Aristotle still has not proven the existence of separate substances. His observation about physics as a hypothesized first science were there no separate substances should thus be read in light of this other observation indicating that the metaphysical investigations conducted so far do not presume their existence, as their existence has yet to be proven. A number of different responses have been offered by scholars regarding Aquinas's treatment of the text from *Metaphysics* VI.1. See, e.g., Wippel, *Metaphysical Thought*, 58–59; Steven A. Long, *Analogia Entis: On the Analogy of Being, Metaphysics, and the Act of Faith* (Notre Dame, IN: University of Notre Dame Press, 2011), 20–21; Dewan, "Physics and Principle of Metaphysics," 51 and 51n11.

84. *In Meta.* IV.1 (Marietti 151.532): "Hic ostendit, *quod ista scientia non sit aliqua particularium scientiarum*, tali ratione. Nulla scientia particularis considerat ens universale inquantum huiusmodi, sed solum aliquam partem entis divisam ab aliis; circa quam speculatur per se accidens, sicut scientiae mathematicae aliquod ens speculantur, scilicet ens quantum. Scientia autem communis considerat universale ens secundum quod ens: ergo non est eadem alicui

nas's explanation here is not presented in terms of the Diversity Criterion itself, which holds that the diversity of scientific subjects is accounted for by the diversity of their principles. Instead, we find that criterion addressed at the end of this *lectio* commenting on *Metaphysics* IV.1.

In the remaining lines of the *lectio*, Aquinas notes that after Aristotle has shown the analogical unity of the subject of metaphysics, he goes on to state that this science is principally concerned with substances because they are the primary instances of BEING. "Therefore," Aquinas tells us, "the philosopher who considers all beings, should first and principally consider the principles and causes of substances."[85] Although other sciences study substances, Aquinas acknowledges, they do so only insofar as they study *such* substances: LION or OX. Metaphysics alone studies substances inasmuch as they are substances or beings.[86] With that in mind, if we follow the Diversity Criterion, we see that the study of the principles of substances *as* substances is what principally diversifies the subject of metaphysics from the subjects of other sciences. At this point, of course, the objection of McInerny and Ashley may well be raised again: if we do not yet know that separate substances exist, would we not simply be seeking the principles of bodies in seeking the principles of substances?

Aquinas himself raises this question when commenting on *Metaphysics* XI.1, noting that if this science *is* concerned with sensible substances, it might not seem to differ from natural science. But immediately after raising this concern, he tells us that "the truth regarding this question is that this science [metaphysics] treats of sensible substances

---

scientiarum particularium." Commenting on Book XI, Aquinas makes clear that physics is a particular science, contrasting the "particularis scientia de natura" with the universal science of BEING QUA BEING, again focusing on the relevant universality as one that concerns every genus of BEING rather than as a universality that embraces the material and positively immaterial. See *In Meta.* XI.7 (Marietti 535.2248 and 2252).

85. "Ergo philosophus qui considerat omnia entia, primo et principaliter debet habere in sua consideratione principia et causas substantiarum." *In Meta.* IV.1 (Marietti 153.546); emphasis added in translation. Commenting on *Metaphysics* XII, Aquinas clarifies that this is not to say that the most common principles of all the categories are in the genus SUBSTANCE or, indeed, in any of the other genera. Rather, he explains, the principles of all of them are the same proportionally and universally. Moreover, the first principles in the category of SUBSTANCE are causally the principles of the other categories inasmuch as accidents are caused by substances. See *In Meta.* XII.4 (Marietti 578–81, esp. nn. 2460, 2464, 2475, 2483).

86. "Nam omnes substantiae, inquantum sunt entia vel substantiae, pertinent ad considerationem huius scientiae: inquantum autem sunt talis vel talis substantia, ut leo vel bos, pertinent ad scientias speciales" (*In Meta.* IV.1 [Marietti 153.546]).

inasmuch as they are substances—*not* inasmuch as they are sensible and mobile. For this properly belongs to natural science."[87] Nor does it seem that he thinks we need to know the existence of separate substances to make this distinction regarding perspective of consideration, if we consider that, not long after this observation, he tells us that even by Book XI of the *Metaphysics*, Aristotle "has not yet proven that there exists any such substance."[88] In short, Aquinas thinks that Aristotle (and us readers along with him) have been engaging in metaphysical investigations the whole time, without evidence of separate substances offered thus far. Sensible substances can be considered either inasmuch as they are sensible or inasmuch as they are substances. The former investigation, as we have seen, entails a consideration of their principles as mobile beings, but the latter considers their principles as substances as such and, hence, as beings.

What, then, are these distinctive principles of SUBSTANCE as such? The answer to this question is not required to begin the science of metaphysics; rather, there simply must be at the outset a knowledge *that* there must be distinctive principles to account for a different sort of effect than that of motion.[89] As we have seen, the sort of principles that are sought here are principles of a substance's subsistence.[90] With that in mind, it is

---

87. *In Meta.* XI.1 (Marietti 510.2158–59): "Est autem veritas huius quaestionis, quod ista scientia determinat de substantiis sensibilibus, inquantum sunt substantiae, non inquantum sunt sensibiles et mobiles. Hoc enim proprie pertinet ad naturalem. Sed propria consideratio huius scientiae est de substantiis, quae non sunt ideae, nec mathematica separata, sed primi motores, ut infra patebit" (emphasis added in translation). Note that in this last sentence, for Aquinas to say that the proper consideration of this science is of the first movers is not to claim that we must know of their existence *prior* to beginning this science or to establish its subject matter.

88. Moreover, it is in the *lectio* that immediately follows where he tells us that it in fact belongs to metaphysics "to investigate whether or not there exists anything separate from sensible substances." For the Latin of both texts, see note 83 above.

89. As Wippel argues, developing Aquinas's own comparison between the scientific approach of physics and that of metaphysics in the proemium of his commentary on the *Metaphysics*, just as physics does not presuppose the principles and causes of its subject, neither does metaphysics; rather, such knowledge is the end of goal of a science (*Metaphysical Thought*, 54; *In Meta.*, proem. [Marietti 1–2]). Of course, the ultimate extrinsic principle of a substance as such for Aquinas will turn out to be God, whose own existence does not need to be presupposed to begin to do metaphysics. The same basic assessment is true regarding intrinsic principles: identifying the precise intrinsic principles of the subject of a science is discovered in the process of examining that subject.

90. It might be objected that the intrinsic principles of sensible substances taken *as* substances are the same as those of such substances taken as mobile, namely, form and matter. Here, again, we can offer the perspectival point that the consideration of form and matter as

here that we return to the theme of *separatio* and its role in the discovery of the subject matter of metaphysics. For, as we have seen, Aquinas holds that by means of a separative analysis of the *ratio* of SUBSTANCE, we are able to discern that its *ratio* "in no way depends upon the *ratio* of BODY."[91] It is this negative judgment of *separatio*, then, that reveals the need to identify and investigate the distinctive principles of sensible substances taken *as* substances. *Separatio* thus reveals the limits of physics, which is incapable of investigating either SUBSTANCE or BEING from this nonmaterial perspective. And in this way, the act of *separatio* also reveals the need for a science beyond that of physics, one with its own distinctive perspective on BEING, namely, metaphysics.

CONCLUDING THOUGHTS

In the epilogue to his magisterial work, *The Metaphysical Thought of Thomas Aquinas*, Wippel reminds us that in considering Aquinas's metaphysics, we must acknowledge from the outset that he never wrote a *Summa metaphysicae*. Thus, when presenting his metaphysics as a system of thought, we must, in Wippel's words, "reconstruct essential elements," yet reconstruct them in a manner "guided by his own remarks."[92] Following the spirit of this observation, we should acknowledge that on the topic of the subject matter of metaphysics, Aquinas himself at no point explicitly states to us, "*This* is how that subject is discovered." It is precisely for this reason that there remains ongoing debate among scholars regarding this fundamental topic, with each side guided by various remarks of

---

principles of motion in sensible substances is different from that of form and matter as principles of them *as* substances. Going beyond this perspectival consideration, I would add that the further analysis of sensible substances as regards the real distinction in them between essence and supposit does not concern an analysis of principles of motion but is a distinctly metaphysical analysis. This is all the more so, of course, for the consideration of *esse* as a really distinct principle from essence in a sensible substance, which Aquinas shows by means of at least some arguments that do not presuppose the existence of God or other positively immaterial entities. For considerations of Aquinas on the essence/nature-supposit distinction, see Wippel, *Metaphysical Thought*, 238–53, and the contributions to this volume by Stephen Brock and David Twetten. For a catalog and analysis of those argument in Aquinas for the real distinction between essence and *esse* that do not presuppose the existence of God, see Wippel, *Metaphysical Thought*, 132–76.

91. See note 48 above.
92. *Metaphysical Thought*, 594.

Aquinas.[93] With that said, I hope to have shown that the clearest and strongest statement by Aquinas on this topic occurs in his commentary on the *Metaphysics*, where he tells how the subject of this science is "established" (*stabilit*). What he presents there is an approach that supports Wippel's general position that the systematic study of a science of BEING-IN-GENERAL (*ens commune*) does not presuppose knowledge of the existence of the positively immaterial.[94]

With that said, what I also hope to have shown is that although the act of *separatio* to which Wippel points is a necessary condition to discover the subject of metaphysics, it is not a sufficient one. Instead, the separative analysis of SUBSTANCE provides an instrumental step in the process of this discovery. Prior to any philosophical consideration, there is the prephilosophical recognition of BEING as WHAT IS (*quod est*). Then, the first philosophical step toward the discovery of *ens commune* comes with the recognition that BEING is not limited to what is in the category of SUBSTANCE but that it extends to all that is in the categories of accidents as well. In other words, there is a recognition that all of the categories resolve to the more fundamental concept of BEING. Following this *via resolutionis*, the intellect is presented with a unified subject of study. It is only at this point that we are provided with the frame of reference to ask the pertinent question, namely, is this science of BEING distinct from physics?

At this point, an additional step is needed: to confirm what has already been indicated by the *via resolutionis*, that is, the distinctiveness of *ens commune* as a subject of study. It is here, I would argue, that we see the key instrumental role of *separatio* in the analysis of the *ratio* of SUBSTANCE. It is through a separative judgment that we come to recognize the neutrally immaterial character of SUBSTANCE and, hence, of BEING-IN-GENERAL. In this way, the act of *separatio* confirms our initial resolutive assumption that there is a subject of study beyond that

---

93. See, e.g., the recent paper by Glen Coughlin, "The Role of Natural Philosophy in the Beginning of Metaphysics," *The Thomist* 84, no. 3 (2020): 395–434.

94. As noted above, and as Wippel observes, this is not to deny that an insight into the neutrally immaterial character of BEING-IN-GENERAL might follow according to the according of discovery from a prior awareness of the positively immaterial, whether it be through a faith in God, adoption of cultural beliefs, discovery of the Prime Mover in physics, etc. Again, the point at stake is that such knowledge is neither a necessary condition to begin the science of metaphysics nor part of the scientific order of investigation that leads to an awareness of *ens commune*.

of physics. For by means of this separative analysis of SUBSTANCE, we come to affirm that the material substances first presented to the intellect can be considered from a distinctive perspective, namely, the perspective of BEING as BEING.[95]

[95]. I would like to express my thanks to Therese Cory, Barry Jones, and Jeffrey Wilson for reading earlier drafts of this chapter and for offering valuable feedback to improve it.

Philip-Neri Reese, OP

2 ∽ *Omne ens est creatum*
A *propter quid* Metaphysical Demonstration?

The history of philosophy has been punctuated by moments and movements of intense systematic aspiration. In modernity, one need only think of figures like Hegel or Spinoza to find clear examples of bold system-builders. In antiquity, Neo-Platonists like Plotinus and Proclus come to mind. But for every Hegel, there is also a Kierkegaard, a thinker who vehemently eschews the project of system-building; and for every Plotinus there is an Epictetus, a thinker who is simply not interested in such a project. This mix of aspiration, antipathy, and apathy toward systematization was no less present in the medieval period than it was in modernity and antiquity. There may, for example, be much of philosophical interest in the thought of figures like Peter Damian and Bernard of Clairvaux, but they were by no means systematizers. The Albertists of fifteenth-century Cologne, however, undoubtedly were.[1]

On the spectrum that runs from unsystematic (whether antipathetic or apathetic) to highly systematic thinkers, it would be foolish to place Thomas Aquinas anywhere other than on its highly systematic end. Nevertheless, scholars and followers of Aquinas have disagreed with respect to precisely *how* systematic he is. Is it possible, for example, to extract his philosophical thought—and in particular his metaphysical

---

1. See, for example, Maarten J. F. M. Hoenen, "Thomismus, Skotismus und Albertismus: Das Entstehen und die Bedeutung von philosophischen Schulen im späten Mittelalter," *Bochumer Philosophisches Jahrbuch für Antike und Mittelalter* 2 (1997): 81–103, and Mario Meliadò, "Axiomatic Thought: Boethius' *De hebdomadibus* and the *Liber de causis* in Late-Medieval Albertism," *Bulletin de philosophie médiévale* 55 (2013): 71–131.

thought—from his theological writings?² If so, what is the best way to present that thought, once extracted? The Neo-Thomistic manuals of the early-to-mid-twentieth century present Aquinas's metaphysics as a rigorous system of theses, proofs, corollaries, and scholia.³ More recent works on the same topic—foremost among which is Fr. Wippel's magisterial *The Metaphysical Thought of Thomas Aquinas*—do not.⁴ And it is unlikely that Aquinas himself, had he written a *Summa philosophiae* or a *Summa metaphysicae*, would have adopted such a *more geometrico*.⁵

But even if there are good reasons not to present the whole of Aquinas's metaphysical thought as an axiomatized system, it is still legitimate to wonder how demonstrative Aquinas's metaphysics is. Are there first principles proper to metaphysics from which the metaphysician can demonstrate *propter quid* conclusions? Are there metaphysical facts the truth of which can not only be established but also *explained*? Few, if any,

---

2. The later Gilson provides an example of someone who held the answer to this question to be "no." See, e.g., Etienne Gilson, *Elements of Christian Philosophy* (Garden City, NY: Doubleday, 1960), 282n6. For more on the debate over Christian philosophy—within which this question played an important role—see Gregory B. Sadler (ed. and trans.), *Reason Fulfilled by Revelation: The 1930s Christian Philosophy Debates in France* (Washington, DC: The Catholic University of America Press, 2011).

3. See, e.g., Joseph Gredt, OSB, *Elementa Philosophiae Aristotelico Thomisticae*, vol. 2 (Freiburg: Herder, 1937). See also Avery R. Dulles, SJ, James M. Demske, SJ, and Robert J. O'Connell, SJ, *Introductory Metaphysics: A Course Combining Matter Treated in Ontology, Cosmology, and Natural Theology* (New York: Sheed and Ward, 1955). The latter text, while not as rigorous in its presentation as Gredt's, nevertheless ends each of its sections with a syllogism the premises of which summarize the content of that section.

4. See John F. Wippel, *The Metaphysical Thought of Thomas Aquinas: From Finite Being to Uncreated Being* (Washington, DC: The Catholic University of America Press, 2000), but see also Leo J. Elders, SVD, *The Metaphysics of Being of St. Thomas Aquinas in a Historical Perspective* (Leiden: Brill, 1993), W. Norris Clarke, SJ, *The One and the Many: A Contemporary Thomistic Metaphysics* (Notre Dame, IN: University of Notre Dame Press, 2001); Lawrence Dewan, OP, *Form and Being: Studies in Thomistic Metaphysics* (Washington, DC: The Catholic University of America Press, 2006); and Benedict Ashley, OP, *The Way toward Wisdom* (South Bend, IN: University of Notre Dame Press, 2006). For a suggestive consideration of different *rationes* of presentation, see William Baumgaertner, "Metaphysics and the Second Analytics" *New Scholasticism* 29 (1955): 423–26.

5. The method was not unknown in Aquinas's day. The *De hebdomadibus* of Boethius and the *Liber de causis*, each of which Aquinas commented upon, were both written in this manner. Moreover, Aquinas's student, Giles of Rome, adopted the method for his *Theoremata de esse et essentia*, which was significantly influenced by Aquinas's *De ente et essentia*. But Thomas's short opusculum was not written in the same way, and a number of his methodological comments—especially those in SCG II, c. 4—give us reason to think that he would not have adopted the method for a longer work, either. On this, I am in substantive agreement with Wippel, *Metaphysical Thought*, xvii–xxvii.

recent studies have approached Aquinas's metaphysics from this perspective.[6] This is surprising for at least two reasons. First, even though Aquinas considered the *via resolutionis* to be of special importance in metaphysics, he never denied that metaphysics also proceeds according to the *via compositionis*—that is, demonstratively.[7] Second, if there are no *propter quid* demonstrations in Aquinas's metaphysics, then his metaphysics cannot count as *scientia* in the truest sense, for Aquinas thinks that the paradigmatic instances of *scientia* are those produced by *propter quid* demonstrations.[8] As Aquinas clearly thinks that metaphysics *is*

6. The debate between Joseph Owens and Joseph Bobik on the proper methodology of Thomistic metaphysics is relevant, though largely second-order. See Joseph Owens, *St. Thomas and the Future of Metaphysics* (Milwaukee, Wis.: Marquette University Press, 1957); Joseph Bobik, "Some Remarks on Father Owens' 'St. Thomas and the Future of Metaphysics,'" *The New Scholasticism* 33 (1959): 68–85; Joseph Owens, "St. Thomas and Elucidation," *The New Scholasticism* 35 (1961): 59–63; Joseph Bobik, "Some Remarks on Fr. Owens' 'St. Thomas and Elucidation,'" *The New Scholasticism* 37 (1963): 59–63; Joseph Owens, "Existential Act, Divine Being, and the Subject of Metaphysics," *The New Scholasticism* 37 (1963): 359–63; Joseph Bobik, "Some Disputable Points Apropos of St. Thomas and Metaphysics," *The New Scholasticism* 37 (1963): 411–30; and, finally, Joseph Owens, "The 'Analytics' and Thomistic Metaphysical Procedure," *Mediaeval Studies* 20 (1964): 83–108. See also Lawrence Dewan, OP, "St. Thomas, Metaphysical Procedure, and the Formal Cause," in his *Form and Being: Studies in Thomistic Metaphysics* (Washington, DC: The Catholic University of America Press, 2006), 167–74, and R. E. Houser, "The Real Distinction and the Principles of Metaphysics," in *Laudemus viros gloriosos: Essays in Honor of Armand Maurer, CSB*, ed. R. E. Houser (Notre Dame, IN: University of Notre Dame Press, 2007), 75–108.

7. See Aquinas, *In De Trin.*, q. 6, a. 1 (Leon. 50.162:362–82). See also L.-M. Régis, OP, "Analyse et synthèse dans l'oeuvre de saint Thomas," *Studia Medievalia* (Bruges, 1948): 303–30; Edmund Dolan, "Resolution and Composition in Speculative and Practical Discourse," *Laval Théologique et Philosophique* 6 (1950): 9–62; L. Oeing-Hanhoff, "Die Methoden der Metaphysik im Mittelalter," in *Die Metaphysik im Mittelalter, Ihr Ursprung und ihre Bedeutung*, ed. Paul Wilpert and Willehad P. Eckert (Berlin: De Gruyter, 1963), 71–91; L. Oeing-Hanhoff, "Analyse/Synthese," *Historisches Wörterbuch der Philosophie* I (1971): 232–48; John F. Wippel, "The Title *First Philosophy* According to Thomas Aquinas and His Different Justifications for the Same," *Review of Metaphysics* 27 (1974): 585–600; Jan A. Aertsen, "Method and Metaphysics: The *via resolutionis* in Thomas Aquinas," *New Scholasticism* 63 (1989): 405–18; Eileen Sweeney, "Three Notions of *Resolutio* and the Structure of Reasoning in Aquinas," *The Thomist* 58 (1994): 197–243; Jan Aertsen, "What Is First and Most Fundamental? The Beginnings of Transcendental Philosophy," in *Was ist Philosophie im Mittelalter?*, ed. J. A. Aertsen and A. Speer (Berlin: De Gruyter, 1998), 177–92; and, more recently, Michael Chase, "Quod est primum in compositione, est ultimum in resolutione. Notes on analysis and synthesis in Late Antiquity," *Anuario Filosófico* 48 (2015): 103–39.

8. For an adequate appreciation of Aquinas's account of *scientia*, it is important to recognize that (1) both demonstration *propter quid* and demonstration *quia* genuinely yield *scientia*, and (2) the *scientia* which results from *propter quid* demonstration is a better, or truer, *scientia* than that which results from demonstration *quia*. With respect to (1), see Aquinas, *In Post. an.* I.23 (Leon. 1*/2.84a–b:14–23). With respect to (2), see Aquinas, *In Post. an.* I.41 (Leon. 1*/2.151a–b:15–30).

a *scientia* in the truest sense, it behooves the Thomistic metaphysician to be able to produce *propter quid* metaphysical demonstrations. Unfortunately, that is not an easy task. To accomplish it, one would have to (a) understand Aquinas's account of the requirements for *propter quid* demonstration in general, (b) identify a plausible candidate demonstration drawn from Thomas's metaphysics, and (c) show how the demonstration identified in (b) meets the requirements outlined in (a). The aim of this chapter is to do precisely that. As we shall see, *ST* I, q. 44, a. 1, ad 1, offers a plausible example of a *propter quid* metaphysical demonstration explaining why *omne ens est creatum*.

AQUINAS ON *PROPTER QUID* DEMONSTRATIONS

A *propter quid* demonstration is a process of reasoning that leads necessarily to the truth by means of immediate principles that express the proper causes of that truth.[9] It is a demonstration that explains *why* something is the way it is, not merely *that* it is the way it is.[10] In Aquinas's day, the question of how such demonstrations ought to be constructed was a matter of some debate. According to both Albert the Great, before him, and Giles of Rome, after him, the middle term of a *propter quid* demonstration—at least paradigmatically—should be the definition of the property that is to be demonstrated.[11] But Aquinas disagreed. In

---

9. See *In Post. an.* I.23, where Aquinas identifies (a) mediacy and (b) causality as the fault lines that divide *demonstratio quia* from *demonstratio propter quid*. See also *ST* I, q. 2, a. 2, co.; *In De Trin.* q. 6, a. 4, ad 2 (Leon. 50.171a–b:159–75). For contrasting forms of reasoning and their corresponding epistemic states, see *In Post. an.*, proem. (Leon. 1*/2.4b–7a:46–123).

10. In other words, while *quia* demonstrations answer the third of Aristotle's four scientific questions ("what is it like?"), *propter quid* demonstrations answer both the third and also the fourth ("why is it like that?"). See *In Post. an.* II.1 (Leon. 1*/2.174b–175a:68–96).

11. See Albertus Magnus, *Liber Posteriorum Analyticorum* II, t. 2, c. 10, ed. A. Borgnet (Paris: Vivès, 1890), 189a–b. For Giles's view, see Jan Pinborg's edition of Giles's *Quaestio quid sit medium in demonstratione* in Jan Pinborg, "Diskussionen um die Wissenschaftstheorie an der Artistenfakultät," *Miscellanea medievalia* 10 (1976): 254–68. See also John Longeway, "Aegidius Romanus and Albertus Magnus vs. Thomas Aquinas on the Highest Sort of Demonstration (*demonstratio potissima*)," *Documenti e studi sulla tradizione filosofica medieval* 13 (2002): 373–434, as well as the lengthy introduction in John Longeway, *Demonstration and Scientific Knowledge in William of Ockham: A Translation of "Summa Logicae" III-II: "De Syllogismo Demonstrativo," and selections from the Prologue to the "Ordinatio"* (Notre Dame, IN: University of Notre Dame Press, 2007). The caveat "paradigmatically" is important. All parties involved in the debate agree that chains of *propter quid* demonstration are possible, and that demonstrative syllogisms appearing later in a chain will count as *propter quid* just in case they can be reduced back to *propter quid* syllogisms appearing earlier in the chain. The question, then, is not what

a striking passage from the beginning of his commentary on the second book of Aristotle's *Posterior Analytics*, Thomas takes aim at Albert's view. He says:

> Aristotle here *seems* to say that the definition of the property is the middle term of the demonstration. But it must be considered that the definition [of the property] cannot be brought to completion without the definition of the subject; for it is obvious that the principles containing the definition of the subject are the principles of the property. Therefore, a demonstration is not resolved back to a first cause unless the definition of the subject is taken as the middle term of the demonstration. In this way, then, it is necessary (1) to conclude the property of the subject through the definition of the property, and then, further, (2) to conclude the definition of the property through the definition of the subject. Whence, it was said in the beginning of [the *Posterior Analytics*] that it is necessary to know ahead of time not only what the property is, but also what the subject is—which would not be the case unless the demonstrator [were to employ] the definition of the subject in demonstrating.[12]

To clarify Aquinas's point, we can let P stand for the property to be demonstrated, DP stand for the definition of that property, S stand for the subject of the property, and DS stand for the definition of that subject. Using this shorthand, we can construct a schema capturing Albert's exemplar demonstration:

Albert's Exemplar Demonstration

1. Every DP is P
2. Every S has DP
3. Every S has P

---

the middle term of every *propter quid* demonstration must be (as that can change), but rather what the middle term of the initial *propter quid* demonstration should be. This is the *demonstratio potissima*.

12. "*Videtur* hic Aristoteles dicere quod diffinitio passionis sit medium in demonstratione. Set considerandum est quod diffinitio <passionis> perfici non potest sine diffinitione subiecti: manifestum est enim quod principia que continet diffinitio subiecti sunt principia passionis. Non ergo demonstratio resoluet in primam causam, nisi accipiatur ut medium demonstrationis diffinitio subiecti. Sic igitur oportet passionem concludere de subiecto per diffinitionem passionis, et ulterius diffinitionem passionis concludere de subiecto per diffinitionem subiecti. Vnde et in principio libri dictum est quod oportet precognoscere quid est non solum de passione, set etiam de subiecto, quod non oporteret nisi demonstrator diffinitione subiecti <uteretur> in demonstrando." Aquinas, *In Post. an.* II.1 (Leon. 1*/2.177a:250–66); emphasis added.

The problem, Aquinas thinks, is the minor premise. To capture the ideal structure of *propter quid* demonstrations, both premises ought to be *per se nota*, and thus not susceptible to further *propter quid* proof. But the minor premise in the Albertinian schema is not *per se nota*. Why not? Because it can be proven by appeal to the definition of the subject. It is this further proof that Aquinas sees as capturing the ultimate stage in every chain of *propter quid* reasoning, and so it is this further proof that he proposes as the exemplar of *propter quid* demonstration.

Aquinas's Exemplar Demonstration

1. Every *DS* has *DP*
2. Every *S* is *DS*
3. Every *S* has *DP*

Unlike its Albertinian counterpart, both premises in this schema will be *per se nota*—at least to the wise.[13] The minor premise, because it involves predicating the definition of the *definitum*, will be *per se nota* in the first mode of perseity, namely, according to formal causality.[14] The major premise, because it involves predicating the property of its proper subject, will be *per se nota* in the second mode of perseity, namely, according to material causality.[15] This is why Aquinas says in the passage quoted above that "the definition [of the property] cannot be brought to completion without the definition of the subject," for a complete definition must invoke the real, proper causes of the thing defined, and that includes its proper subject. Furthermore, Aquinas seems to think that the major premise can also be *per se nota* in the fourth mode of perseity, namely, according to extrinsic (that is, efficient or final) causality, though he does not say so explicitly.[16]

---

13. For Aquinas's appropriation of the Boethian distinction between principles that are *per se nota* to all and principles that are *per se nota* to the wise, see *In De heb.*, c. 1 (Leon. 50.269a-b:118–85).

14. See Aquinas, *In Post. an.* I.10 (Leon. 1*/2.39a:25–30). While Aristotle discusses four modes of perseity, Aquinas clarifies in lecture 10 that only Aristotle's first, second, and fourth modes of the *per se* are ways of *speaking or predicating*. He interprets Aristotle's third mode of perseity as a way of *being*.

15. See Aquinas, *In Post. an.* I.10 (Leon. 1*/2.39b:51–67).

16. Aquinas states that the conclusions of *propter quid* demonstrations are predicated in both the second and the fourth modes of perseity, but he is silent regarding the major premise. Two points support the view that it, too, can be predicated in the fourth mode. First, there is Aquinas's claim in the *In Post. an.* II.1 text, quoted above, that the principles of the subject are

TABLE 1: COMPARISON OF BOTH DEMONSTRATIONS

Demonstration 1	Demonstration 2
(1) Everything that has the capacity to laugh is risible.	(1) Every rational animal has the capacity to laugh.
(2) Every human has the capacity to laugh.	(2) Every human is a rational animal.
(3) Every human is risible.	(3) Every human has the capacity to laugh.

We can illustrate these points—along with the difference between the competing accounts—with a concrete comparison (see the table above).[17]

Because "having the capacity to laugh" is the definition of risibility and "rational animal" is the definition of human, it should be clear that the first demonstration (D1) follows Albert's schema, while the second (D2) follows Thomas's. The major premise in D1 is *per se nota* in the first mode, as it predicates "having the capacity to laugh" of risibility. But the minor premise in D1 is not *per se nota* at all—D2 is proof (literally) of that. Unlike D1, D2's major premise is *per se nota* in the second mode as it predicates the property's definition ("having the capacity to laugh") of its proper subject (rational animal). Also unlike D1, D2's minor premise is *per se nota*—this time in the first mode—as it predicates "rational animal" of human. Moreover, the middle term of D2 (like the middle term of D1) is a real, causal definition, for "rational animal" formally expresses the essence of a human being.[18] D1, then, will yield *propter quid*

---

the principles of the property, which would seem to be as true of external principles as it is of internal principles. Second, whatever is contained in the conclusion must be contained in one of the premises; but the fourth mode of perseity is contained in the conclusion; so it must be contained in one of the premises—and as it is not contained in the minor premise, it must be contained in the major premise. Still, Aquinas does introduce the dual character of demonstrative conclusions only after distinguishing them from principles known by way of *intellectus*, so there may be some reason to think they are unique in this respect. See Aquinas, *In Post. an.* I.10 (Leon. 1*/2.40b–41b:138–46).

17. Aquinas himself gives examples drawn from mathematics and music. See Aquinas, *In Post. an.* II.1 (Leon. 1*/2.177a:267–76, 277–90).

18. One might worry that Aquinas's distinction between form and essence in composite substances falsifies this claim. For the essence of a composite substance, which is expressed by its definition, includes sensible matter abstracted from individual matter, while the form of a composite substance does not—for the form of a composite substance is precisely the principle that must enter into composition with matter in order to constitute the natural substance. See, e.g., Aquinas, *De ente*, c. 2 (Leon. 43.370b:10–25). This is true, but it is also not the whole story. For Aquinas also thinks that there is a genuine sense in which essence stands as form *vis-à-vis*

knowledge if it is joined to D2, while D2 is *propter quid* in its own right.[19] As such, Aquinas seems to have the better of the debate.[20]

It should now be clear what Aquinas would expect from a *propter quid* metaphysical demonstration, namely, (1) its minor premise ought to predicate the definition of the subject matter of metaphysics of that subject matter; (2) its major premise ought to predicate the definition of a metaphysical property of the definition of metaphysics' subject matter; and (3) the middle term of the demonstration—that is, the definition of the subject matter of metaphysics—ought to be a real, causal definition, not just a nominal one. I would like to suggest that precisely such a proof can be found in *ST* I, q. 44, a. 1, ad 1, to which we now turn.

THE ARGUMENT OF Q. 44, A. 1, AD 1

This article of the *Summa* asks whether every being must be created by God. As our candidate for a *propter quid* metaphysical demonstration appears in the reply to the first objection, we begin by quoting that objection:

> It seems unnecessary for every being to be created by God, because nothing precludes a thing from being found without a [feature] that does not belong to its *ratio* (e.g., a human can be found without whiteness). But the relation of a caused thing to its cause does not seem to belong to the *ratio* of beings, since some beings can be understood without that [feature]. Therefore, they can *be* without that [feature]. Therefore, nothing precludes some beings from not being created by God.[21]

---

individual matter. In fact, he explicitly distinguishes between two senses of "form": one, the *forma totius*, signifies the essence, while the other, the *forma partis*, signifies the formal principle of the essence. See Aquinas, *De ente*, c. 2 (Leon. 43.373b:274–91). I am grateful to Gregory Doolan for drawing my attention to the relevance of this distinction to the point at issue here. For more on these distinctions in Aquinas, see Wippel, *Metaphysical Thought*, 205–6, and Joshua Hochschild, "Form, Essence, Soul: Distinguishing Principles of Thomistic Metaphysics," in *Distinctions of Being: Philosophical Approaches to Reality*, ed. Nikolaj Zunic (Washington, DC: American Maritain Association, 2013), 21–35.

19. This is because the minor premise of D1 must be either (1) accepted as probable, (2) known through a prior *quia* demonstration, or (3) known through D2 (or an equivalent *propter quid* demonstration given through a causal definition in another order of causality). If (1), D2 will not demonstrate at all. If (2), it will only demonstrate *quia*. Thus, if D1 is to be *propter quid*, it must be by way of D2 (or its equivalent).

20. Much more can be—and was—said on both sides of this debate. See note 11 above.

21. "Videtur quod non sit necessarium omne ens esse creatum a Deo. Nihil enim prohibet inveniri rem sine eo quod non est de ratione rei, sicut hominem sine albedine. Sed habitudo

The core of the objection is that the nonessential features of a thing are existentially separable from that thing. As createdness is a nonessential feature of beings, it is existentially separable from them. But how do we know that createdness is a nonessential feature of beings? We know this, the objector thinks, because if it *were* an essential feature of beings it would be included in the *ratio* of *a being*—which it is not.[22] We can call this the "*Ratio Entis* Objection."

The *Ratio Entis* Objection

1. Every feature that does not belong to the *ratio entis* is a feature that some *ens* can be without

2. The relation of a caused thing to its cause is a feature that does not belong to the *ratio entis*

3. The relation of a caused thing to its cause is a feature that some *ens* can be without[23]

It is important to note that the objector is not claiming that createdness is a feature existentially separable from *every* being. The claim is simply that createdness is existentially separable from *some* being. The example of whiteness is apt to mislead in this regard. Not only does it not belong to the *ratio* of *a human*, but it is also existentially separable from *all* humans. Compare this with rationality. Rationality does not belong to the *ratio* of *an animal*, but it is nevertheless not existentially separable from *all* animals (e.g., it is not existentially separable from humans). The objector's point, then, seems to be this: if feature *x* does not pertain to the *ratio* of kind *y*, then it is possible for some instance of *y* to exist without

---

causati ad causam non videtur esse de ratione entium: quia sine hac possunt aliqua entia intelligi. Ergo sine hac possunt esse. Ergo nihil prohibet esse aliqua entia non creata a Deo." *ST* I, q. 44, a. 1, obj. 1 (Leon. 4.455a).

22. We should note, however, that for Aquinas there is a distinction between the *quid nominis* (the signification or meaning of a term) and the *quid rei* (the essence of a thing). While terms really do signify things, what a given term means is not always expressive of the essence of the thing it signifies. Thus, we can take the term "a god" to mean "a premier efficient cause" without committing to the stronger claim that "a premier efficient cause" expresses the *essence* of the thing we call "a god." While the *quid nominis* yields a *nominal* definition of the thing (i.e., it "defines" that thing by way of the meaning of the term that refers to it), the *quid rei* yields a *real* definition of the thing (i.e., it *defines* the thing by expressing the essential features of that thing).

23. It is surprising that the subject term in the objector's argument is not "being created," but rather "the relation of a caused thing to its cause." This ambiguity will be addressed in greater detail in §4.

feature *x*. In the present context, this means that while createdness may well be proper to the more specific *ratio* of *some* beings, it is not proper to the *ratio entis* itself. As such, it is possible for there to be a being that is not created by God.

The proof of premise 2 in the Ratio Entis Objection comes in the form of an enthymeme. We know that the relation of a caused thing to its cause is not a part of the *ratio entis* because "some beings can be understood without that [feature]." The suppressed premise must be that if a being can be understood without some feature, then that feature must not be included in the *ratio* of *a being*. If this is right, then the proof of premise 2 runs as follows:

(2a) Every feature that is not required for *ens* to be understood is a feature that does not belong to the *ratio entis*

(2b) The relation of a caused thing to its cause is a feature that is not required for *ens* to be understood

(2) The relation of a caused thing to its cause is a feature that does not belong to the *ratio entis*

The point is that the *ratio* or intelligible structure of a thing is that which is captured and expressed by the definition of the thing in question. As such, to understand something just *is* to grasp the features that constitute that thing's *ratio*. Thus, if createdness is not required for us to understand something as a being, then createdness is not a part of the *ratio entis*. And if createdness is not a part of the *ratio entis*, then at least some being can *be* without being created.

Thus far, the objection. Now, Aquinas's response:

> It must be said that even though the relation [of a caused thing] to a cause does not enter into the definition of a being that is caused, it nevertheless follows upon the [features] that *do* belong to its *ratio*. This is because it follows from the fact that something is a being by participation that it should be caused by another. Whence, a being of this sort cannot *be* unless it *be caused* (just as neither [can there be] a human being, unless it be able to laugh). But since being caused does not belong to the *ratio* of a being, simply-speaking, a being is found that is not caused.[24]

24. "Ad primum ergo dicendum quod, licet habitudo ad causam non intret definitionem entis quod est causatum, tamen sequitur ad ea quae sunt de eius ratione: quia ex hoc quod aliquid per participationem est ens, sequitur quod sit causatum ab alio. Unde huiusmodi ens non potest esse, quin sit causatum; sicut nec homo, quin sit risibile. Sed quia esse causatum non est

Aquinas's reply trades on a distinction between two different *rationes* of *ens*. The first is the *ratio* "a being, simply-speaking" (*ens simpliciter*), while the second is the *ratio* "a being by participation" (*ens per participationem*). He concedes to the objector that being caused is included in neither *ratio*, but insists that it does follow upon "being by participation"—which is included in the definition of every caused being.

Thus, Thomas seems to grant the *Ratio Entis* Objection's minor premise (and the proof thereof), but not its major premise. This is because Aquinas thinks that not all the features that necessarily belong to a thing are included in that thing's *ratio*. The example of risibility makes this clear. Even though the capacity for laughter is not included in the definition of a human being, that capacity necessarily belongs to human beings because it follows upon features that *are* included in that *ratio* (that is, rationality and animality). As such, the capacity to laugh assumes a middle position between (1) features that are included in the *ratio* of a thing and (2) features that are entirely coincidental thereto. Items in the first category are predicated in the first mode of perseity. Items in the second category are not predicated *per se* at all. But items in the middle category are *per se accidentia*—properties that belong necessarily to their subjects without constituting their essences. And as we saw in §1, such properties are predicated in a *propter quid* demonstration according to the second mode of perseity.

Aquinas clearly thinks that all of this applies to the case of being. While it is true that no being can be without a feature belonging to the *ratio entis*, it is not true that any feature that does *not* so belong is a feature some being can be without. Like humanity, being can have *per se* accidents, that is, properties that follow upon—rather than enter into—its *ratio*. The question, then, is whether createdness is such a property. And this is where the distinction between *rationes* of being makes a difference. If the *ratio* we have in mind is *ens simpliciter*, then Aquinas's answer is "no." But if the *ratio* we have in mind is *ens per participationem*, then his answer is "yes." We just need to understand why.

The literal conclusion of Aquinas's argument is: "Whence, a being of this sort [*huiusmodi ens*] cannot *be* unless it *be caused*." For simplicity's sake, we can convert this conclusion from (a) a negation to an

---

de ratione entis simpliciter, propter hoc invenitur aliquod ens non causatum." *ST* I, q. 44, a. 1, ad 1 (Leon. 4.455b).

affirmation, (b) a conditional affirmation to a categorical affirmation, and (c) a modal categorical affirmation to a nonmodal categorical affirmation. The resulting conclusion is: "Every being of this sort is caused."

Both the subject term and the predicate term are problematic. The subject term is problematic because it is unclear what "of this sort" refers to. The predicate term is problematic for two reasons: first, because it is not an exact match with the one that appeared earlier in Aquinas's reply, namely, "is caused *by another*"; and second, because neither "is caused" nor "is caused by another" seems equivalent to "is created," which is the predicate at issue in the article.

Regarding the predicate, it seems safe (and charitable) to assume that the "is caused" in Aquinas's conclusion is shorthand for the "is caused by another" that appeared earlier in his argument. The question of how this relates to "is created" is a harder problem and will be taken up in the final section of this chapter. Regarding the subject, there are two grammatical possibilities for the antecedent of *huiusmodi*, namely, "being by participation" and "being that is caused." To adjudicate between these possibilities, it will be helpful to reconstruct the whole argument as literally as possible.

As we have already seen, Aquinas presents *ens per participationem* as the *ratio* contained in the definition of every being that is caused, and it is upon this *ratio* that "being caused by another" follows. Thus, "being caused by another" ought to be the major extreme, "being by participation" ought to be the middle term, and "being that is caused" ought to be the minor extreme. This yields the following syllogism:

1. Every being by participation is caused by another
2. Every being that is caused is a being by participation
3. Every being of this sort is caused [by another]

What, then, does "of this sort" refer to? The less plausible reading interprets "of this sort" as referring to "being by participation." On that reading, the conclusion would reduplicate the major premise, rendering the syllogism invalid. The more plausible reading takes "of this sort" to refer to "being that is caused," making the conclusion "every being that is caused is caused by another."[25] Given the fact that the first article of

---

25. This provides additional support for reading the "is caused" in the conclusion as shorthand for "is caused by another." If the conclusion were simply "every being that is caused is

q. 44 is specifically concerned with efficient causality, and that Aquinas thinks that efficient causes are *extrinsic* cause, one might worry that this conclusion is analytically true, and so stands in no need of proof. But there is good reason to think that Aquinas only intends "being that is caused" to function extensionally, here—that is, to pick out the right domain of quantification—rather than to function intensionally, as the *ratio* that is doing the work in the argument is *ens per participationem*, not *ens causatum*. If this is right, then "being that is caused" is simply picking out every being that is not *uncaused*. In other words, it is extensionally picking out *ens commune*, the subject matter of metaphysics.[26] As such, a less-literal but still-faithful reconstruction of Aquinas's argument in q. 44, a. 1, ad 1, runs as follows:

1. Every being by participation is caused by another
2. Every [instance of] *ens commune* is a being by participation
3. Every [instance of] *ens commune* is caused by another[27]

To see whether this argument might plausibly count as a *propter quid* metaphysical demonstration, we will have to consider each premise in turn, checking to see whether it meets the requirements laid out in the first section of this chapter. We will begin with the minor premise.

EVALUATING THE MINOR PREMISE

If the proof reconstructed above is to be a *propter quid* demonstration, then its minor premise must satisfy two conditions: first, it must be *per se nota* in the first mode of perseity, such that the predicate term is the definition of the subject term; second, the definition in question must be a real definition, and not merely a nominal one. Does the proposition "every [instance of] *ens commune* is a being by participation" meet these requirements?

As noted above, Aquinas thinks that *ens commune* is the subject

---

caused" it would be manifestly redundant.

26. See Aquinas, *SCG* II, c. 54; *ST* I-II, q. 66, a. 5, ad 4; *In Meta.*, proem. See also Wippel, *Metaphysical Thought*, 11–22 and 53–56.

27. I have added "instance of" in brackets for the sake of style, but it is important to recognize that such an addition is not required. Like "animal" or "human," *ens commune* functions as a kind-term from a logical point of view. Thus, while it may be awkward to do so in English, it is just as permissible is say "every *ens commune* is a being by participation" as it is to say "every animal is sensate" or "every human is risible."

matter of metaphysics, and is thus equivalent to *ens inquantum ens*. But this does not mean that he thinks that the subject matter of metaphysics includes everything that might count as "a being" in any sense of the term. Rather, he is clear that there are numerous senses of "a being" that fall *outside* of the subject matter of metaphysics, that is, outside of the sense of "a being" that corresponds to *ens commune* or *ens inquantum ens*. The first of these is "a being *per accidens*."[28] The musical builder, the mathematical grammarian, and the priest professor can all be called "beings," but they are not beings *per se* because they neither posit one thing within the ten categories,[29] nor are they the proper termini of causal processes.[30] The latter point is especially relevant. As we have already seen, Aquinas grants that being caused does not follow upon the *ratio* of *ens simpliciter*, and so it is possible to find a being that is not caused. If he intends *ens simpliciter* to include being *per accidens*, then this concession makes sense—for beings *per accidens* do not have proper causes.[31]

Once we have narrowed our focus to the sense of "a being" that corresponds to being *per se*, we come upon a further sense of "a being" that must also be excluded from the subject matter of metaphysics. This is the sense that corresponds to propositional truth.[32] As it is true to say that "blindness *is* an affliction of the eye" and "nonbeing *is* nonbeing" there must be some sense in which blindness and nonbeing can be said to be—and so some sense in which they count as "a being." Nevertheless, these privative and negative terms do not posit anything in reality, and so they do not posit anything that could fall under *ens commune* or *ens inquantum ens*.

With these two senses of "a being" set aside, Aquinas characterizes

28. For a detailed study of the importance of this exclusion for Aquinas's metaphysical methodology, see Lawrence Dewan, "Being *per se*, Being *per accidens*, and St. Thomas's Metaphysics," *Science et Esprit* 30 (1978): 169–84.

29. This is because they posit *multiple* items within the (potentially multiple) categories of being. See *In Sent.* II, d. 9, q. 1, a. 1, obj. 3, "*si dicatur*..." (and reply); *SCG* III, c. 74 (Leon. 14.218b:6–17); *In Meta.* V.9, VI.3, XI.8.

30. See Aquinas, *ST* II-II, q. 95, a. 5, co.; *In Meta.* V.9, VI.3, XI.8.

31. This is not to say that Aquinas's concession will *only* make sense if *ens per accidens* is included within *ens simpliciter*, for Aquinas may also have God in mind as an example of an uncaused *ens*. Still, it is striking that in the corpus of the article, the only context in which Aquinas applies the term *ens* to God is in the quotation from Aristotle. When speaking in his own voice, he only refers to God as (*ipsum*) *esse*.

32. See Aquinas, *De ente*, c. 1 (Leon. 43.370a–b:1–13); *In Sent.* II, d. 34, q. 1, a. 1, co., and d. 37, q. 1, a. 2, ad 3; *SCG* III, c. 9 (Leon. 14.22b:14–21); *De pot.*, q. 7, a. 2, ad 1; *ST* I, q. 48, a. 2, ad 2; *De malo*, q. 1, a. 1, ad 19; *In Meta.* V.9, VI.4, VII.1, IX.1, X.3.

the sense that remains—the sense of "a being" that constitutes the subject matter of metaphysics and corresponds to *ens commune* and *ens in-quantum ens*—as that which signifies the essence,[33] nature,[34] or entity[35] that is outside the soul,[36] divided into the ten categories[37] and divided by act and potency.[38] The question, then, is whether *ens per participationem* might be the real definition of "a being" in precisely this sense.

Aquinas's commentary on Boethius's *De hebdomadibus* gives us good reason to think that it is. Boethius begins his short treatise by laying out certain *terminos, regulas,* and *conceptiones,* which Aquinas interprets as *per se nota* propositions, distinguishing between those that are *per se nota* to all and those that are *per se nota* to the wise.[39] He clarifies that Boethius's *conceptiones* are *per se nota* to the wise and then divides them into (a) those that pertain to *a being,* (b) those that pertain to *a one,* and (c) those that pertain to *a good.*[40] With respect to the *per se nota* propositions that pertain to *a being,* Aquinas further distinguishes between (a1) those that arise from a comparison between *esse* and the subject of *esse* and (a2) those that arise from a comparison between *esse simpliciter* and *esse aliquid.*[41] Aquinas characterizes one proposition belonging to the first group as a way of clarifying an earlier proposition ("*esse* and that-which-is are diverse") in terms of participation. The clarificatory proposition reads "what-is can participate in something, but *esse* itself in no way participates in anything."[42]

It is in explaining this proposition that Aquinas distinguishes three

---

33. Aquinas, *De ente,* c. 1 (Leon. 43.370a-b:1-18); *In Sent.* II, d. 37, q. 1, a. 2, ad 3; *SCG* III, c. 9 (Leon. 14.22b:14-21); *De pot.*, q. 7, a. 2, ad 1.
34. Aquinas, *De malo,* q. 1, a. 1, ad 19; *In Meta.* X.3.
35. Aquinas, *ST* I, q. 48, a. 2, ad 2.
36. Aquinas, *De ente,* c. 1 (Leon. 43.370a-b:1-18); *In Sent.* II, d. 34, q. 1, a. 1, co., and d. 37, q. 1, a. 2, ad 3; *In Meta.* VII.1.
37. Aquinas, *De ente,* c. 1 (Leon. 43.370a-b:1-18); *In Sent.* II, d. 34, q. 1, a. 1, co.; *SCG* III, c. 9 (Leon. 14.22b:14-21); *ST* I, q. 48, a. 2, ad 2; *De malo,* q. 1, a. 1, ad 19; *In Meta.* V.9, VI.4, VII.1, X.1, X.3.
38. Aquinas, *SCG* II, c. 54; *De pot.*, q. 3, a. 1, ad 12; *In Meta.* VII.1, IX.1, X.3.
39. See Aquinas, *In De heb.*, c. 1 (Leon. 50.269a-b:118-85).
40. See Aquinas, *In De heb.*, c. 2 (Leon. 50.270a:2-18). Aquinas may use the distinction between principles that are *per se nota* to all and those that are *per se nota* to the wise to track the Aristotelian distinction between the common principles that apply to every science and the proper principles that pertain to a single science, but I cannot argue for that here.
41. See Aquinas, *In De heb.*, c. 2 (Leon. 50.270a-b:19-30).
42. "Quod est participare aliquo potest, set ipsum esse nullo modo aliquo participat." *In De heb.*, c. 2 (Leon. 50.270a:4-5).

modes of participation, namely, (1) logical participation, exemplified by an individual participating in a species or a species participating in a genus, (2) formal participation, exemplified by matter participating in substantial form or a subject participating in accidental form, and (3) causal participation, exemplified by an effect participating in its efficient cause.[43] In light of this distinction, Aquinas qualifies Boethius's axiom. He grants that "what-is can participate in something" in all three ways, but he restricts the claim that "*esse* itself in no way participates in anything" to the logical and formal modes—implying, though not explicitly stating, that *esse* can participate in something in the efficient mode.[44] What is important for us is the fact that Aquinas presents participation as belonging to the *ratio entis*. At least to the wise, that is, to those who understand the difference between the intensions "a being" (*ens*) and "to be" (*esse*), the diversity of the two will be self-evident.

This becomes even clearer when we turn to Thomas's comments on one of the *conceptiones* pertaining to *a one* ("in every composite thing, *esse* is other than what-is"). He says:

> Next, when [Boethius] says "Everything composite ...," he sets down axioms regarding the composite and the simple—which pertain to the *ratio* of the one; and it must be considered that the discussion above regarding the diversity between *esse* and that-which-is [proceeded] according to their *intensions*. Here, he shows how it applies to the *things*. And he shows this, first, in composite things, and second, in simple things (where he says "Everything simple ..."). First, therefore, it must be considered that just as *esse* and what-is differ according to their intensions, so do they differ *really* in composite things. This is clear from the foregoing. For it was said above that *esse* neither participates

---

43. See Aquinas, *In De heb.*, c. 2 (Leon. 50.271a–b:69–85). See also Rudi A. te Velde, *Participation and Substantiality in Thomas Aquinas* (New York: Brill, 1995), 11–15 and 76–82; Wippel, *Metaphysical Thought*, 96–110; and Stephen Brock, "Harmonizing Plato and Aristotle on *esse*: Thomas Aquinas and the *De hebdomadibus*," *Nova et Vetera* (English Edition) 5 (2007): 478–88.

44. See Aquinas, *In De heb.*, c. 2 (Leon. 50.271b:85–113). The modal qualification in the axiom is important. The word *ens*, in virtue of its concrete mode of signification, is open to the possibility of these three modes of participation. But Aquinas is not making the stronger claim—at least here—that every *ens* actually participates according to all three modes. The possibility that Aquinas in fact holds the stronger view was explored in a set of articles published in a recent issue of *The Thomist*. See Jason A. Mitchell, "Aquinas on *esse commune* and the First Mode of Participation," *The Thomist* 82 (2018): 543–72; Daniel D. De Haan, "Aquinas on *actus essendi* and the Second Mode of Participation," *The Thomist* 82 (2018): 573–609; and Gregory T. Doolan, "Aquinas on *esse subsistens* and the Third Mode of Participation," *The Thomist* 82 (2018): 611–42.

something, such that its *ratio* should be constituted from a multiplicity, nor does it have something extrinsic mixed with it such that there would be an accidental composition in it. Thus, *esse* itself is not a composite. The composite thing, therefore, is not its *esse*. Thus, he says that in every composite thing, to be a being is something other than the composite thing itself, which is by participating *esse*.[45]

It is important to recognize that the "composite things" at issue in this quotation are not just *hylomorphic* composites. Aquinas counts created separate substances, too, as "composite" in this context.[46] The proposition, then, concerns nothing less than *ens commune*. And when we look at his explanation of that proposition, we find him asserting not just that participation pertains to the *intension* of "a being," but that it pertains to the reality of what it is to be a being: to be a being is to be something that really participates in *esse*.[47] If this is correct, then the proposition "all *ens commune* is being by participation" will, in fact, be *per se nota*—at least to the wise—in the first mode, for the predicate term expresses what the subject term really is. To be an essence, nature, or entity outside the soul, divided by the categories and divided by potency and act is to be something that participates *esse*.

---

45. "Deinde cum dicit: *Omni composito* etc., ponit conceptiones de composito et simplici, que pertinent ad rationem unius, et est considerandum quod ea que supra dicta sunt de diuersitate ipsius esse et eius quod est, est secundum ipsas intentiones. Hic ostendit quomodo applicetur ad res; et primo ostendit hoc in compositis, secundo in simplicibus, ibi: *Omne simplex* etc. Est ergo primo considerandum quod sicut esse et quod est differunt secundum intentiones, ita in compositis differunt realiter. Quod quidem manifestum est ex premissis. Dictum est enim supra quod ipsum esse neque participat aliquid ut eius ratio constituatur ex multis, neque habet aliquid extrinsecum admixtum ut sit in eo compositio accidentalis; et ideo ipsum esse non est compositum; res ergo composita non est suum esse; et ideo dicit quod in omni composito aliud est esse ens et aliud ipsum compositum quod est participando ipsum esse." Aquinas, *In De heb.*, c. 2 (Leon. 50.272b–73a:196–215). There is some controversy regarding whether the final instance of *ens* in this passage should be removed or retained. See Wippel, *Metaphysical Thought*, 162n80. I have chosen to retain it, but to underline the preceding instance of *esse* so as to convey the same meaning as if the *ens* had been removed. I have also underlined the *est* in the last sentence in order to highlight the parallelism.

46. See Aquinas, *In De heb.*, c. 2 (Leon. 50.273a:221–36).

47. Further support for this conclusion can be found in Aquinas, *In De caus.* 4 (Saffrey 47.8–18), where Aquinas argues that because "a being" is something that finitely participates in *esse*, while the first cause is infinite *esse* itself, it follows that the first cause is beyond "a being."

EVALUATING THE MAJOR PREMISE

If "a being by participation" expresses the real *ratio*[48] of *ens commune*, then the minor premise of our candidate *propter quid* demonstration meets the requirements we would expect it to meet. Can the same thing be said of the major premise? That depends on two things. First, it must be *per se nota* in the second mode—according to which the subject term is contained in the definition of the predicate term. Second, the predicate term must express the definition of the property that is ultimately being proved to belong to the subject. So, is the proposition "every being by participation is caused by another" *per se nota* in the second mode? And, if so, is "caused by another" the real definition of the property at issue in q. 44, a. 1, ad 1?

We can begin with the first question. In order to determine whether or not the major premise of Aquinas's proof is *per se nota* in the second mode, we will have to consider more carefully the sort of participation involved in the argument's middle term—that is, the sort of participation involved when we say that (1) "a being by participation" expresses the real *ratio* of *ens commune* and (2) every "being by participation" is caused by another. As we saw in the previous section, Aquinas acknowledges three different kinds of participation, which we referred to as logical, formal, and causal. These, then, are our candidates.

If we understand "participation" to mean logical participation, will the proposition "every being by participation is caused by another" be *per se nota* in the second mode of perseity? No. Consider the following disjunctive argument: Either it is possible for *ens* to participate in *esse* according to the first kind of participation, or it is not. If it is not, then it follows that the proposition thus understood cannot be *per se nota*, as it would be false.[49] But if it *is* possible for *ens* to participate in *esse* according to the first kind of participation, this would be because the participation of the concrete (*ens*) in the abstract (*esse*) would count as an instance of

---

48. I say "real *ratio*" rather than "real definition" because a real definition is properly given in terms of proximate genus and specific difference. As being is (a) not a genus, and (b) has no specific differences that contract it "from outside," as it were, it does not admit of a proper definition. Nevertheless, there remains a difference between the *ratio nominis* "*entis*" and the *ratio rei entis*.

49. For examples of contemporary interpreters who think that *ens* cannot participate *esse* according to the first mode, see Wippel, *Metaphysical Thought*, 128, and Gavin Kerr, *Aquinas's Way to God: The Proof in "De Ente et Essentia"* (Oxford: Oxford University Press, 2015), 61–62.

the first kind of participation. Unfortunately, that is hard to square with the text, for it would require understanding the first kind of participation as having to do not with the participation of the less-common in the more-common, but rather with there being a merely rational distinction between participant and participated.[50] But suppose, for the sake of argument, that this *were* the case. It would, then, still be false that "every being by participation is caused by another," for negative terms like "a nonbeing" and "the non-hot" would be "beings-by-participation" thus understood, and yet they are not caused by another in any proper sense.[51] Moreover, and for the same reason, this reading of "a being by participation" would prevent it from expressing the real *ratio* of *ens commune*, as the above section argues it does, because its extension would be too wide.

What about the second kind of participation? In this case, the first prong of our disjunctive argument is more successful than the second. If it is not possible for *ens* to participate in *esse* according to the second kind of participation, then understanding the proposition "every being by participation is caused by another" in this way will render it false.[52] If it *is* possible for *ens* to participate in *esse* according to the second kind of participation, this will presumably be because the formal participation of each being in its *actus essendi* (and the real composition resulting therefrom), counts as an instance of the second kind of participation.[53] Unlike our first attempt, this interpretation of "a being by participation" seems to apply exclusively and exhaustively to *ens commune*, for that which enters into real composition with *actus essendi* is an essence, nature, or entity outside the soul, divided into the categories, and divided by act

---

50. See Aquinas, *In De heb.*, c. 2 (Leon. 50.271b:97–102). It is important to point out that this is *not* the view of Jason Mitchell, who has recently argued that every finite being participates in *esse commune* according to the first kind of participation. See Mitchell, "Aquinas on *esse commune* and the First Mode of Participation," 556. This *does*, however, seem to be the view of Daniel De Haan, whose taxonomy of the three kinds of participation emphasizes the non-ontological character of the first kind. See De Haan, "Aquinas on *actus essendi* and the Second Mode of Participation," 607.

51. See, e.g., Aquinas, *De malo*, q. 1, a. 3, co. (Leon. 23.14b–15a:139–74), where Aquinas offers three arguments in support of the claim that privations like the bad (*malum*) cannot have *per se* causes.

52. Here, again, Wippel and Kerr offer good examples of contemporary interpreters who would take the first prong. See note 49 above.

53. For proponents of this view, see Elders, *The Metaphysics of Being of Thomas Aquinas*, 228; Tomas Tyn, OP, *Metafisica della sostanza: Partecipazione e "analogia entis"* (Verona: Fede & Cultura, 2009), 239; De Haan, "Aquinas on *actus essendi* and the Second Mode of Participation."

and potency. Moreover, this sort of participation in *esse*, because it is not self-explanatory, is plausibly connected in an immediate—though not analytic—way with being caused by another. As such, it could provide a reading of the major premise that is *per se nota* in the second mode.

Finally, what about the third kind of participation? In this case, our disjunctive argument is unnecessary, as there is widespread scholarly agreement that *ens* participates in *esse* according to the third kind of participation—that is, as an effect participates in its cause.[54] This is because God is *ipsum esse subsistens* and God is the efficient cause of *ens commune*. Thus, *ens commune* stands to *ipsum esse* as effect stands to cause.[55] Whence, the former participates in the latter according to the third kind of participation. But does this interpretation yield a *per se nota* proposition in the second mode of perseity? Unfortunately, it does not. Recall that the proposition in question is "every being by participation is caused by another." If "a being by participation" means "a being effected through efficient causality" then the analyzed proposition will be "every being that is effected through efficient causality is caused by another." While that proposition is both true and *per se nota*, it is not *per se nota* in the *second* mode of perseity, but rather in the *first*. Furthermore, this interpretation of the major premise would seem to falsify Aquinas's claim in *ST* I, q. 44, a. 1, ad 1, that "the relation [of a caused thing] to a cause does not enter into the definition of a being that is caused." Thus, if Aquinas's argument is to be a *propter quid* demonstration, it seems that we have to interpret its middle term as involving the second kind of participation.[56]

Now that we have answered the question of whether the major premise might plausibly be read as *per se nota* in the second mode, we can turn to the question of whether "caused by another" might plausibly be read as the definition of the property at issue in this text. One of the most puzzling features of this passage is the fact that, even though the article as a whole is concerned with whether all things are created by God,

---

54. The disagreement is not about whether *ens* participates in *esse* according to the third kind of participation, but rather about whether *ens* participates in *esse* in that way *only*.

55. For more on the nuances involved in the participation of *ens* in (the likeness of) *ipsum esse subsistens*, see Doolan, "Aquinas on *esse subsistens* and the Third Mode of Participation."

56. This does not, of course, prove that *ens* participates in *esse* according to the second kind of participation. It only proves that *if* the argument is *propter quid*, *then* *ens* participates in *esse* according to the second kind of participation. One man's *modus ponens*, however, can always be another man's *modus tollens*.

Aquinas's argument proves only that all things are caused by another. This is puzzling for two reasons. First, because "is caused" seems like a weaker predicate than "is created," and second, because "by another" seems like a weaker qualification than "by God." Is Aquinas making his task easier than it should be?

I think not. The first objection begins and ends by speaking of "creation," even though its actual argument is framed in terms of the relation of a caused thing to its cause. I see two possible explanations. The first is that the objection is arguing *a maiore ad minus*—that is, showing that some beings are not created by showing that some beings are not caused, the former being an instance of the latter. The second possibility is that the objection—and Aquinas, as well—somehow intends "caused" to be interchangeable with "created." Three points militate against the first option: (1) it makes the objection implausibly truncated, (2) it makes Aquinas's response criminally inadequate, and (3) it ignores the fact that in the other objections, in the body of Aquinas's response, and in Aquinas's other replies, "caused by God," "created by God," and "from God" all seem to be used interchangeably. As such, the best reading of the text is one that understands "caused" as coextensive with "created."

But is such a reading possible? I think it is. Aquinas consistently contrasts creation with change. While both are instances of efficient causality, creation is the efficient causing of the *whole being* of a thing, while changing is the efficient causing that presupposes matter (whether prime or otherwise).[57] Thus, if "caused by another" is intended to be short for "efficiently caused in its whole being by another" then the predicate term in Aquinas's argument (like the subject-term in the *Ratio Entis* Objection) is, in fact, the definition of the property that is ultimately at issue in q. 44, a. 1—namely, createdness.[58] This would yield the following demonstrations:

As we saw in the first section of this chapter, Aquinas thinks that D1 will be a *propter quid* demonstration only when it is reduced back to D2, as its minor premise is not *per se nota*. Each premise in D2, however, is *per se nota* in its own right. If this is correct—and if D2 is an accurate

---

57. See, for example, Aquinas, *In Sent.* II, d. 1, q. 1, aa. 2–3, and d. 11, q. 1, a. 2; *In Sent.* IV, d. 11, q. 1, a. 2, qc. 3; *De ver.*, q. 5, a. 8, ad 2; *SCG* II, c. 17; *De pot.*, q. 3; *Comp. theol.* I.99; *De 108 artic.*, 14; *ST* I, q. 45, a. 1, and q. 65, a. 1; *De sub. sep.* 10.

58. While this does not address the worry about the difference between "by another" and "by God," addressing that worry is not required for identifying a *propter quid* proof.

TABLE 2: *PROPTER QUID* DEMONSTRATIONS IN THOMAS

Demonstration 1 (D1)	Demonstration 2 (D2)
(1) Everything efficiently caused in its whole being by another is created.	(1) Every being by participation is efficiently caused in its whole being by another.
(1) Every [instance of] *ens commune* is efficiently caused in its whole being by another.	(2) Every [instance of] *ens commune* is a being by participation.
(2) Every [instance of] *ens commune* is created.	(3) Every [instance of] *ens commune* is efficiently caused in its whole being by another.

reconstruction of Aquinas's argument in q. 44, a. 1, ad 1—then we have arrived at a *propter quid* metaphysical demonstration for the fact that every being is created. That, I take it, would be a welcome contribution to Thomistic metaphysics. But if I am mistaken—about either the status of Aquinas's argument as a *propter quid* demonstration or the accurate reconstruction of that argument—then the welcome contribution to Thomistic metaphysics will lie in the correction of my mistake(s). At the very least, I hope that this study will encourage others to approach St. Thomas's metaphysics from a demonstrative point of view, and thus help us grow in appreciation for the deeply systematic character of his thought.

Part 2 ∽ The Problem of the One and the
Many in the Order of Being

Mark D. Gossiaux

3 ∞ Thomas Aquinas and the Origin of the Controversy concerning the Real Distinction between Essence and Existence

In a lengthy article published more than a hundred years ago in the *Dictionnaire de théologie catholique*, M. Chossat made the provocative remark that the first Scholastic thinker to have defended the real distinction between essence and existence was not Thomas Aquinas, but Giles of Rome.[1] Chossat's claim drew a lively response from students of Thomas, who moved quickly to show that Aquinas did indeed defend the real distinction.[2] Today most scholars would agree that the real distinction between essence and existence is one of the cornerstones of Thomas's metaphysics, as it serves to ground the ontological distinction between God (as pure act) and creatures (which are compounds of act and potency), and it provides a solution to the Problem of the One and the Many in

---

1. M. Chossat, "Dieu. Sa nature selon les scolastiques," in *Dictionnaire de théologie catholique*, vol. 4 (Paris: Letouzey et Ané, 1910), col. 1180: "Le premier scolastique dont un historien, dans l'état actuel de nos connaissances, puisse dire sans controverse qu'il ait admis cette distinction est Gilles de Rome, quelques années après la mort de saint Thomas."

2. For some of the early reactions to Chossat's article, see A. Gardeil, "'Destruction des destructions' du R. P. Chossat," *Revue thomiste* 18 (1910): 361–91; P. Mandonnet, "Les premières disputes sur la distinction réelle entre l'essence et l'existence," *Revue thomiste* 18 (1910): 741–65; M. Grabmann, "Doctrina S. Thomae de distinctione reali inter essentiam et esse ex documentis ineditis saeculi XIII illustratur," in *Acta hebdomadae Thomisticae Romae celebratae 19–25 Novembris 1923 in laudem S. Thomae Aquinatis* (Rome: Apud sedem Academiae S. Thomae Aquinatis, 1924), 131–90. For more on the scholarly reaction to Chossat's article, see P. Porro, "Ancora sulle polemiche tra Egidio Romano e Enrico di Gand: due questioni sul tempo angelico," *Medioevo* 14 (1988): 107–48 (esp. 109–14); S. Mercier, *Gilles de Rome. Théorèmes sur l'être et l'essence* (Paris: Les Belles Lettres, 2011), 76–84.

the order of being. There are many different kinds of being, because existence (*esse*, or act of being) is limited and thereby multiplied by its reception in the essence of a creature.[3]

However, Chossat's claim about Giles of Rome is not without some foundation. The historical controversies concerning the relationship between essence and existence occur *after* Thomas's death. It is common to trace the origin of these controversies to 1276, the year of Henry of Ghent's first quodlibetal debate. There Henry considered and rejected the view that the existence of a creature is really distinct from its essence. The consensus among scholars today is that the target of Henry's criticisms was Giles of Rome, not Thomas Aquinas. At that time Giles was still a bachelor in the theology faculty at Paris, and he had not yet composed a systematic treatment of essence and existence. A few years later Giles did expound the theory at length in two works, the *Theoremata de esse et essentia* (1278–84) and the *Quaestiones de esse et essentia* (1285–87). With these works Giles emerged as the chief spokesman for the real distinction. When scholars rejected the real distinction—and a great many did—it will be the version of Giles of Rome that they attack.[4]

---

3. The literature on Thomas's metaphysics of essence and existence is vast. For an authoritative treatment with an extensive bibliography, see John F. Wippel, *The Metaphysical Thought of Thomas Aquinas: From Finite Being to Uncreated Being* (Washington, DC: The Catholic University of America Press, 2000). Also quite helpful is C. Fabro, *La nozione metafisica di partecipazione secondo S. Tommaso d'Aquino*, 3rd ed. (Turin: SEI, 1963); and J. Owens, "The Accidental and Essential Character of Being in the Doctrine of St. Thomas Aquinas," *Mediaeval Studies* 20 (1958): 1–40.

4. On the thirteenth-century controversy concerning essence and existence, see E. Hocedez, "Gilles de Rome et Henri de Gand sur la distinction réelle (1276–1287)," *Gregorianum* 8 (1927): 358–84; "Le premier quodlibet d'Henri de Gand (1276)," *Gregorianum* 9 (1928): 92–117; J. Paulus, "Les disputes d'Henri de Gand et de Gilles de Rome sur la distinction de l'essence et de l'existence," *Archives d'histoire doctrinale et littéraire du moyen âge* 13 (1940–42): 323–58; R. Imbach, "Averroistische Stellungnahmen zur Diskussion über das Verhältnis von Esse und Essentia," in *Studi sul XIV secolo in memoria di Anneliese Maier*, ed. A. Maierù and A. P. Bagliani (Rome: Storia e letteratura, 1981), 299–319; John F. Wippel, "Essence and Existence," in *The Cambridge History of Later Medieval Philosophy*, ed. N. Kretzmann, A. Kenny, and J. Pinborg (New York: Cambridge University Press, 1982), 385–410; C. Luna, "Nouveaux textes d'Henri de Gand, de Gilles de Rome et de Godefroid de Fontaines: les questions du ms. Bologne, Collegio di Spagna 133. Contribution à l'étude des questions disputées," *Archives d'histoire doctrinale et littéraire du moyen âge* 65 (1998): 151–272; P. Porro, *Tommaso d'Aquino. L'ente e l'essenza* (Milan: Bompiani, 2002), 183–202; C. König-Pralong, *Avènement de l'aristotélisme en terre chrétienne* (Paris: Vrin, 2005), 35–127, and *Être, essence et contingence. Henri de Gand, Gilles de Rome, Godefroid de Fontaines* (Paris: Les Belles Lettres, 2006). For the Latin text of Giles's *Theoremata*, see *Aegidii Romani Theoremata de esse et essentia*, ed. E. Hocedez (Louvain: Museum Lessianum, 1930).

The Real Distinction between Essence and Existence

In this chapter I wish to examine the influence that Thomas Aquinas may have had on the origins of the historical controversy concerning the relationship between essence and existence. Three thinkers played a leading role in the early debate on the real distinction: Giles of Rome, Siger of Brabant, and Henry of Ghent. Accordingly, this chapter is divided into three main parts: the first considers the influence of Thomas on the early teaching of Giles, the second looks at Siger's criticisms of Thomas's understanding of essence and *esse*, and the third examines whether Thomas can be regarded as a target of Henry's attack on the real distinction in his first quodlibetal debate.

THOMAS AND THE EARLY TEACHING OF GILES OF ROME

Giles's first treatment of essence and existence can be found in his commentary on Peter Lombard's *Sentences*. Giles read the *Sentences* probably in 1270–72. A *reportatio* of his lectures was discovered and edited some years ago by C. Luna.[5] Giles's revision of his lectures on Book I (*Ordinatio* I) dates from 1271–73; the revision of Book II (*Ordinatio* II) was not completed prior to 1309.[6] It is generally agreed that Giles began his academic career as a student of Thomas Aquinas during the latter's second Parisian regency. Giles's relation to Aquinas, however, was a relatively complex one. Although he appears to share many of Aquinas's philosophical positions, Giles is often quite critical of Thomas. Sometimes it is the position defended by Thomas that he attacks; at other times Giles agrees with the conclusion that Aquinas defends, but he finds Thomas's arguments to support it to be objectionable. One sees this attitude prominently displayed in his treatment of essence and existence in *Ordinatio* I.[7]

---

5. *Aegidii Romani Opera Omnia III.2. Reportatio lecturae super libros I–IV Sententiarum: Reportatio Monacensis. Excerpta Godefridi de Fontibus*, ed. C. Luna (Florence: SISMEL, 2003).

6. For Giles's life and career, see F. Del Punta, S. Donati, and C. Luna, "Egidio Romano," in *Dizionario biografico degli Italiani* (Rome: Istituto della Enciclopedia Italiana, 1993), 42:319–41. For the chonology of Giles's writings, see R. Wielockx, *Aegidi Romani Opera Omnia III.1. Apologia* (Florence: Leo S. Olschki, 1985), 229–40; S. Donati, "Studi per una cronologia delle opere di Egidio Romano," *Documenti e studi sulla tradizione filosofica medievale* 1 (1990): 1–111; 2 (1991): 1–74.

7. Giles was summoned to appear before Bishop Tempier and his advisors in March 1277 to retract fifty-one articles (drawn from *Ordinatio* I) which were deemed erroneous by members of the Faculty of Theology at Paris. Rather than retract these articles, Giles offered a defense of them (*Apologia*), which resulted in his exile from the University until his rehabilitation

TABLE 3: GILES AND THOMAS ON THE MEANINGS OF *ESSE*

Giles, Ord. I, d. 33, pr. 1, q. 2, ad 1:	Thomas, In Sent. I, d. 33, q. 1, a. 1:
Ad primum dicendum quod consuevit distingui triplex esse. Primo prout sumitur pro esse quidditativo, secundum quod dicimus quod diffinitio est sermo indicans quid est esse.	Sed sciendum, quod esse dicitur tripliciter. Uno modo dicitur esse ipsa quidditas vel natura rei, sicut dicitur quod definitio est oratio significans quid est esse; definitio enim quidditatem rei significat.
Secundo accipitur pro actu essentiae secundum quem modum dicimus quod esse est actus entis.	Alio modo dicitur esse ipse actus essentiae; sicut vivere, quod est esse viventibus, est animae actus; non actus secundus, qui est operatio, sed actus primus.
Tertio prout dicit veritatem compositionis.	Tertio modo dicitur esse quod significat veritatem compositionis in propositionibus, secundum quod 'est' dicitur copula: et secundum hoc est in intellectu componente et dividente quantum ad sui complementum; sed fundatur in esse rei, quod est actus essentiae.

One of the distinctive characteristics of Giles's mature teaching on essence and existence is his description of *esse* as a "thing" (*res*), and the real distinction as one obtaining between two things (*inter rem et rem*). This language, scholars have pointed out, is quite foreign to Thomas Aquinas.[8] It should be noted, however, that this *res*-language is not to be found in *Ordinatio* I. Consider the following interesting text (see the table above). Both Giles and Thomas describe the same three meanings for *esse*. In the first sense, *esse* signifies the quiddity or whatness of a thing; in this sense a definition tells us what a thing is (*quod quid erat esse*). In a second sense, *esse* signifies the act of an essence, which Thomas understands not as second act (i.e., operation), but as first act, and which Giles indicates as the act of being (*actus entis*). In this sense, *esse* signifies the existence of a thing. Finally, in the third sense of *esse* distinguished by Giles and Thomas, it signifies the truth of composition. In this sense *esse* functions as the logical copula. One should note that there is no hint of

---

in 1285. As Wielockx has shown, thirty of these fifty-one articles were also taught by Thomas Aquinas. See *Aegidi Romani Opera Omnia III.1. Apologia*, 179–224. On Giles's ambivalent attitude toward Thomas, see E. Hocedez, "Gilles de Rome et Saint Thomas," in *Mélanges Mandonnet. Études d'histoire littéraire et doctrinale du Moyen-Âge* (Paris: Vrin, 1930), 1:385–409.

8. For discussion, see Hocedez, *Aegidii Romani Theorematia de esse et essentia*, (43)–(67).

The Real Distinction between Essence and Existence 71

res-language in Giles's text; instead, his thinking is aligned with that of Thomas.

The influence of Thomas can also be seen in Giles's treatment of essence and existence. The eighth distinction in Peter Lombard's *Sentences* is concerned with the truth, immutability, and simplicity of the divine essence. It is also where one usually finds discussions of essence and existence. The first question that Giles asks is whether being (*esse*) is proper to God alone. Giles begins his reply by offering what appears to be a division of being. Being (*esse*), he tells us, can be viewed in two ways. First, as particularized and determined to a genus or species (for example, we might speak of *this* being or *that* being). Secondly, being may be considered absolutely (*esse simpliciter*). As such it is free from limitation and materiality, and it is not determined to some particular genus. Only the latter may be assigned to God, as he is not a particular kind of being, but rather being itself (*ipsum esse*) or pure being (*esse purum*).[9]

Having distinguished God as *esse simpliciter* from particular or determinate instantiations of being, Giles is also careful to distinguish him from *esse commune*, that is, from the being that is common to all things. He notes three differences between *esse simpliciter* and *esse commune*. First, while any creature exists by means of *esse commune*, God does not, as he is the cause of *esse commune*. Second, while all creatures participate *esse commune*, God does not; instead, *esse commune* participates divine *esse*. Thirdly, *esse commune* does not include divine *esse*, though it does in some way comprehend created *esse*; by contrast, divine *esse* contains and comprehends *esse commune*. According to Giles, then, God does not fall under *esse commune*, though *esse commune* may be said to be included under divine *esse*, insofar as it is caused by and participates in divine *esse*.[10]

---

9. *Ord.* I, d. 8, p. 1, pr. 1, q. 1: "Propter primum notandum quod esse dupliciter potest accipi. Uno modo particulatum et contractum ad aliquod genus vel speciem, ut hoc esse vel illud. Alio modo simpliciter. Cum quaeritur utrum Deo competat esse, si loquimur de esse contracto, non solum tale esse non est Dei proprium, immo habet aliquo modo repugnantiam ad esse divinum ... Viso quod esse contractum, ut hoc vel illud, Deo non competit, restat videre quomodo esse simpliciter ei competat. Propter quod notandum quod esse simpliciter dicitur illud quod est a contractione et materialitate abstractum, non determinatum ad aliquod genus entis... sed est esse simpliciter et abstractum ab omnia contractione, quia est esse purum secundum actualem existentiam et rei veritatem" (fol. 46vOPQ).

10. "Differt autem illud esse simpliciter ab esse communi sive universaliter sumpto in tribus. Primo: quia licet per illud esse, scilicet commune, quodlibet creatum sit, quia quicquid est per esse, esse habet; ipsum tamen esse sic acceptum comparatum ad divinum esse, Deus non

In the final part of his reply, Giles explains how *esse* is proper to God alone. He notes that the word "proper" (*proprium*) can have two meanings: it may refer to the quiddity of a thing or it may indicate a proper accident. As there can be no accidents in God, the latter meaning cannot apply to him. However, if one construes *proprium* to refer to the quiddity of a thing, then *esse simpliciter* is proper to God alone, because only in God is *esse* identical with quiddity. By contrast, every creature has an *esse* distinct from its quiddity.[11]

In this question Giles has drawn a sharp contrast between the way *esse* is found in God and the way it is found in creatures. In God, *esse* is not limited or contracted; it is uncaused, and it is identical with his essence. In creatures, *esse* is limited and contracted, it is participated and caused, and it is distinct from essence. Although no mention has been made yet of the kind of distinction involved, or of whether *esse* and essence enter into composition in creatures, it is significant that Giles affirms a link between what is participated, what is limited, and what is caused.

Later in this same distinction, Giles asks whether in God there is a composition of *esse* and essence. He begins his discussion by criticizing the argument given by Aquinas in *De pot.*, q. 7, a. 2, to prove such an identity. As Giles explains that argument, when several causes individually are able to bring about a given effect, it is necessary that there be another cause, which is the proper cause of that effect, in virtue of which the other causes bring about that effect. For example, if pepper and ginger both produce heat, it is necessary that this action of heating should be reduced to the proper cause of heat, namely, fire. Now all causes agree in giving *esse*, but they are diversified according to the different kinds of

---

est illo, sed e converso. Nec habet rationem causae, sed causati: nam et ipsius esse communis Deus est causa. Secundo differt: quia ipso esse sic communiter sumpto omnia creata participant, sed si tale esse ad Deum referatur, Deus non participat eo, sed illud tale esse divino esse participat, quia cum creatura sit, oportet ipsam esse participatione summae entitatis. Tertia est ex eo quod tale esse non comprehendit divinum esse, licit aliquo modo omne esse creatum comprehendat; ipsum tamen divinum esse etiam tale esse continet et comprehendit" (fol. 46vQ–47rA).

11. "Cum ergo quaeritur, utrum esse sit proprium Dei: si accipiatur proprium pro propria passione, quia tale proprium manat de genere accidentium, non est Deo proprium, ubi nihil per accidens. Sed si proprium intelligitur pro ipsa quidditate: accipiendo esse non pro esse contracto sed abstracto, non abstracto secundum intellectum sed pro esse puro secundum rei veritatem, tunc esse soli Deo est proprium, quia in solo Deo esse est sua quidditas. Omnis alia creatura habet esse distans a quidditate" (fol. 47rB).

esse that they cause. Thus some give to their effect to be a human (*esse homo*), others to be lion (*esse leo*), and so on. Therefore, there must be a cause whose proper effect is *esse*, and this in turn will be the first cause, because the first effect must be brought about by the first cause. This is confirmed by *De causis*, pr. 4 ("The first of created things is *esse*, and there is nothing created before it"). Therefore, since *esse* is the first effect, it belongs to God (as the first cause) to cause *esse*, and since it is proper to God to give *esse*, it follows that God is *ipsum esse*.[12]

Against this reasoning Giles brings two criticisms. The first concerns the form of the argument. If an effect belonging to several causes is reduced to one as to a proper cause, it is evident that this effect belongs to its proper cause primarily and *per se*; however, from this it does not follow that this effect does not enter into composition with the cause. Thus, if *esse* is reduced to God as to a proper cause, it is evident that *esse* primarily and *per se* belongs to God; however, it does not follow that *esse* does not enter into composition with the divine essence. According to Giles, therefore, more work is needed to draw the conclusion that Thomas wishes to draw.

Giles's criticism, however, does not appear to be particularly strong. When one turns to the text of the *De potentia*, one finds that Giles has omitted a key step in Thomas's argument. Having shown that *esse* is the proper effect of God, Thomas then reasons that the proper effect of any cause proceeds from it according to the likeness of its nature (*secundum similitudinem suae naturae*). This calls to mind a key principle of Thomas's understanding of causality, namely, that every agent brings about something similar to itself (*omne agens agit simile sibi*).[13] A proper

---

12. *Ord.* I, d. 8, p. 2, pr. 1, q. 2: "Quidam sic probant esse Dei non facere compositionem in Deo: quia quando aliquis effectus convenit pluribus causis, oportet illud appropriari uni causae, sicut nos videmus quod piper et cinciber conveniunt in hoc effectu, quia utrumque calefacit. Necesse est ipsum calefacere reduci in causam unam ut in ignem, ita quod proprium erit igni calefacere. Cum igitur videamus omnes causas communicare in dare esse; diversificari autem secundum diversa esse, quia quaedam dant suis causatis esse hominem, quaedam esse leonem, et sic de aliis. Igitur oportet aliquam causam esse cuius sit proprium causare esse, et ista causa est causa prima, quia oportet primum causatum esse a causa prima et e converso. Huic sententiae videtur concordare Auctor *De Causis*, quia in quarta propositione illius libri ait quod prima rerum creatarum est esse, et non est ante ipsum creatum aliud. Quia igitur esse est primum causatum, Dei est dare esse tamquam primae causae, et quia proprium est Deo dare esse, erit ipsum esse" (fol. 52vMN).

13. For discussion of this, see John F. Wippel, "Thomas Aquinas on our Knowledge of God and the Axiom that Every Agent Produces Something Like Itself," *Proceedings of the American*

effect is produced by its cause in accordance with its own proper nature or form. If *esse* is the proper effect of God, then it follows that *esse* is the substance or nature of God. It is with this in mind that Thomas appeals to the *De causis*. *Esse* is the first of all created effects precisely because God is his very *esse*, and *esse* is his proper effect.[14]

Giles's second criticism concerns Thomas's use of the fourth proposition of the *De causis*: *Prima rerum creatarum est esse*. According to Giles, if one considers the Platonic source of the text, one realizes that it implies, not that God is being (*ipsum esse*), but that he is superior to being (*super esse*):

> For the *Book of Causes*, where that proposition is written, was extracted from a book of Proclus, who was a disciple of Plato. But Plato maintained that the order of divinities is in accordance with the order of separated [entities], such that all [secondary] divinities depended upon a first god as participating in him. Now this was the order of abstract entities: for being (*ens*) was not said of all things, since prime matter and those things which are wholly in potency are not beings. But one (*unum*) and good (*bonum*) were said of all things, such that the essence of unity and the essence of goodness were the first god. And because after good and one, there is not something [caused] by God [that is as] common as being, *esse* was first not simply, but in the genus of created things. Therefore, when he said, "the first of created things is *esse*," he added, "and there is not anything created before it." For this reason, it is said in the comment that, "after the first cause there is no created thing more extensive or prior than it." Following this path God is not *esse*, nor is *esse* proper to him, but he is above *esse* (*super esse*). However, because our intention is to speak about the *esse* that is in God and is God himself, this authority (*auctoritas*) is irrelevant.[15]

Catholic Philosophical Association 74 (2000): 81–101, reprinted in his *Metaphysical Themes in Thomas Aquinas II* (Washington, DC: The Catholic University of America Press, 2007), 152–71.

14. *De pot.*, q. 7, a. 2 (Marietti 191): "Ad cuius evidentiam considerandum est quod, cum aliquae causae effectus diversos producentes communicant in uno effectu, praeter diversos effectus, oportet quod illud commune producant ex virtute alicuius superioris causae cuius illud est proprius effectus. Et hoc ideo quia, cum proprius effectus producatur ab aliqua causa secundum suam propriam naturam vel formam, diversae causae habentes diversas naturas et formas oportet quod habeant proprios effectus diversos ... Proprius autem effectus cuiuslibet causae procedit ab ipsa secundum similitudinem suae naturae. Oportet ergo quod hoc quod est esse, sit substantia vel natura Dei. Et propter hoc dicitur in lib. *de Causis* [prop. 9] quod intelligentia non dat esse nisi in quantum est divina, et quod primus effectus est esse, et non est ante ipsum creatum aliquid."

15. *Ord.* I, d. 8, p. 2, pr. 1, q. 2: "Nam liber de causis ubi illa propositio scribitur extractus fuit ex libro Procli, qui fuit discipulus Platonis. Plato autem posuit ordinem deorum secundum ordinem abstractorum, ita quod omnes dii dependebant a primo deo tamquam participantes

It is difficult not to be perplexed by Giles's remarks. He appears to be faulting Thomas for not knowing the Platonic origins of the *De causis*. However, it is commonly agreed today that Aquinas was the first Latin thinker to recognize (1272) that the *De causis* was not a work of Aristotle, but rather a compilation based on Proclus's *Elements of Theology*, which was translated by William of Moerbeke in 1268.[16] As Thomas's *De potentia* predates the Moerbeke translation of Proclus, Giles's remark seems somewhat uncharitable. Whether Giles learned of the true origins of the *De causis* from Aquinas, or whether he discovered it on his own, or whether it was a subject of idle talk at Paris in the months leading up to Aquinas's own commentary on the *De causis*, is unclear. In any event, Giles's criticism of Thomas's use of the fourth proposition of the *De causis* appears to miss the mark. For Thomas cites this proposition not to establish the identity of essence and *esse* in God (as Giles suggests), but rather as external confirmation of the claim that the proper effect of God is to cause *esse*. The latter is the proper effect of God, precisely because God is his *esse*.

Having rejected Thomas's argument, Giles proceeds to give his own argument to establish the identity of essence and *esse* in God, which he grounds on the notion of participation. Appealing to the principle that those things that act in virtue of another are not identical with their power, Giles notes that fire is not its own heat, as it acts in virtue of the heavenly bodies. However, if fire were the first cause, and heat that in virtue of which all things caused by fire participate fire, then it would

---

ipso. Ordo autem abstractorum hic erat. Nam ens non dicebatur de omnibus, quia materia prima et ea quae sunt penitus in potentia non sunt entia. Sed unum et bonum dicebantur de omnibus, ita quod essentia unitatis et bonitatis erat deus primus, et quia post bonum et unum non est aliquid a deo commune sicut ens, ipsum esse erat primum non simpliciter sed in genere creatorum. Et ideo cum dixisset prima res creatarum est esse, subdit et non est ante ipsum creatum aliud. Ideo in commento dicitur quod post causam primam non est latius neque prius creatum ipso. Ista viam sectando Deus non est esse, nec est proprium ei esse, sed est super esse. Sed quia intentio nostra est loqui de esse quod est in Deo et est ipse Deus, auctoritas non est ad propositum" (fol. 52vO). Unless otherwise noted, all translations are my own.

16. See Thomas, *In De caus.*, proem. (Saffrey 3): "Inveniuntur igitur quaedam de primis principiis conscripta, per diversas propositiones distincta, quasi per modum sigillatim considerantium aliquas veritates. Et in graeco quidem invenitur sic traditus liber Procli Platonici, continens ccxi propositiones, qui intitulatur *Elementatio theologica*; in arabico vero invenitur hic liber qui apud Latinos *De causis* dicitur, quem constat de arabico esse translatum et in graeco penitus non haberi: unde videtur ab aliquo philosophorum arabum ex praedicto libro Procli excerptus, praesertim quia omnia quae in hoc libro continentur, multo plenius et diffusius continentur in illo."

follow that fire would be its own heat (i.e., it would be hot by its own essence). Similarly, because all things have *esse* through the *esse* of the first cause, one may infer that God is his own *esse*, because he is the first cause, and through his *esse* all creatures exist. Thus, because God's *esse* is not caused by another, nor does he participate his *esse*, it follows that God is his *esse*.[17]

Later in this same distinction, Giles turns to consider creatures and asks whether every creature is composite. He presents two arguments to show that in all created substances there is a composition of *quod est* (that which is) and *esse*. The first argument follows the way of causality. Giles reasons that if something is created, it has *esse* from another. But everything that has *esse* from another is in potency to *esse*, and therefore is distinct from its *esse*. For if it were identical with its *esse*, it would be pure act, lacking any potentiality; hence it would not require something essentially different from itself to produce it in being. Therefore, to maintain that a creature is its own *esse* is to hold that a creature is not a creature, which is absurd.[18]

One finds an argument similar to this in Thomas's *SCG* II, c. 52. There Thomas reasons that the substance of a thing belongs to it *per se* and not by reason of another (*per aliud*). But *esse* belongs to any created thing by means of another; otherwise, it would not be caused. Therefore, the *esse* of no created substance is identical with its essence.[19] In another

---

17. *Ord.* d. 8, p. 2, pr. 1, q. 2: "Ideo notandum quod ut habitum est: ea quae agunt in virtute alterius non sunt sua virtus; unde ignis non est suus calor, quia agit in virtute supercaelestis corporis. Sed si ignis esset primum agens et calor esset illud cuius virtute omnia causata ab igne participarent igne, ignis esset suus calor. Cum igitur omnia habeant esse per esse primi, iuxta illud Commentatorem in II° *Metaphysicae*, unum est igitur per se ens et per se verum, et omnia alia sunt entia et vera per esse et veritatem eius. Deus igitur erit ipsum esse, cum sit primum agens et per eius esse omnia habeant esse" (fol. 52vP). For the reference to Averroes, see *In II Meta.*, com. 4, in *Aristotelis opera cum Averrois commentariis* (Venice, 1562-74), vol. 8, fol. 30rC.

18. *Ord.* I, d. 8, p. 2, pr. 2, q. 1: "Respondeo dicendum quod in omni creato quod habet per se esse oportet nos concedere esse compositionem ex quod est et esse. Et est ratio: quia si creatum est, ab alio habet esse. Omne quod ab alio habet esse est in potentia ad esse, et non est ipsum esse, quia si ipsum esse esset, tunc esset actus purus sine aliqua potentialitate. Non igitur indigeret aliquo essentialiter differente ab eo qui ipsum ad esse produceret. Ponere igitur creatum sic esse, est ponere creatum non esse creatum" (fol. 54rA).

19. *SCG* II, c. 52 (Leon. 13.145): "Amplius. Substantia uniuscuiusque est ei per se et non per aliud: unde esse lucidum actu non est de substantia aeris, quia est ei per aliud. Sed cuilibet rei creatae suum esse est ei per aliud: alias non esset causatum. Nullius igitur substantiae creatae suum esse est sua substantia."

The Real Distinction between Essence and Existence 77

text, Thomas remarks that it belongs to the nature (*ratio*) of any caused thing that it possesses some composition, because, at the very least, its *esse* is other than its quiddity.[20]

Giles's second argument follows the way of predication. When an abstract term is predicated of a subject, there is nothing in the subject that is other than the predicate. For example, if humanity (*humanitas*) were predicated of Socrates, there would be nothing in Socrates that would not pertain to humanity, and vice versa. In this case, Socrates and humanity would be identical. Giles then applies this reasoning to the case of *esse*, which is also predicated in the abstract. If there were a created being that were its *esse*, then there would be nothing in that being that were not *esse*. Such a being would thus be identical with *esse*, and, Giles notes, it would have *esse* in the maximal degree (*maxime*).[21] Drawing upon Aristotle, Giles observes that what is in the highest degree such (*maxime tale*) in every genus is first (*primo tale*) and the cause of all others in that genus. Therefore, if there is a creature that has *esse* in the highest degree, it will cause all other things to be and its own *esse* will be uncaused. But if this were so, then the creature would become the creator, which of course is absurd. Giles concludes that only God is *esse* alone; in all others, one finds a composition of what participates *esse* and *esse*, or of *quod est* and *esse*.[22]

In these texts from the eighth distinction, Giles has argued that God alone is his quiddity; in all other things essence and existence are distinct. Whereas God is absolutely simple, all creatures possess some form of metaphysical composition. In creatures, being is limited, participated,

---

20. *ST* I, q. 3, a. 7, ad 1 (Leon. 4.47): "Est autem hoc de ratione causati, quod sit aliquo modo compositum: quia ad minus esse eius est aliud quam quod quid est, ut infra patebit."

21. "Item sicut superius dicebatur: quando aliquid in abstracto de aliquo praedicatur, nihil est in eo quod sit aliud a tali praedicato: ut si natura hominis de homine praedicaretur in abstracto, nihil esset in homine quod non pertineret ad humanitatem, et e converso. Et quia si nihil esset in homine aliud a natura sua, homo esset sua humanitas. Si igitur esset aliquod ens creatum in quo non esset nisi esse, tunc illud ens creatum esset suum esse, et maxime haberet esse" (fol. 54rAB). Like Aquinas, Giles holds that when *esse* is said of a subject, it is predicated in the abstract. For this in Thomas, see *In De heb.*, 2 (Leon. 50.270–71).

22. *Ord.* I, d. 8, p. 2, pr. 2, q. 1, fol. 54rB: "Sed quod est maxime tale in omni genere est primo tale et causa omnium aliorum, ut potest patere per Philosophum, II° *Metaphysicae*. Creatum igitur quod sic ponitur maxime habebit esse et omnia alia producet ad esse. Et nihil erit causa ipsius esse, ac per hoc creatum non erit, sed creator omnium. Non est igitur aliquid citra Primum in quo sit tantum esse et in quo non sit aliquid quod participat esse." For the reference to Aristotle, see *Metaphysics* II.1.993b24–27.

and caused, and because their being is caused, creatures are in potency with regard to it. The limitation of being is explained by its reception in a distinct receiving principle. In order to account, therefore, for the limited and participated character of created being, essence and *esse* must enter into composition with each other. Thus, in all creatures there must be a real composition of essence and *esse*. On all of these points, Giles's thinking is in harmony with Thomas Aquinas's.

However, one can discern the beginnings of an evolution in Giles's thinking on essence and existence when one turns to his *Theoremata de corpore Christi* (1274). In Theorem 29, Giles makes some brief, but extremely important, remarks about essence and existence, which are occasioned by his analysis of the relation between matter and extension. As he indicates in this text, matter is extended not by its essence, but by participation, by virtue of the inherence in it of quantity. Giles describes the extension of matter as a quantitative mode that matter receives when it is subject to quantity. This quantitative mode is accidental to the nature of matter and is really distinct from it. Quantity, by contrast, is extended essentially, by its very nature. Extension is not added to the nature of quantity, nor does quantity participate in extension. Thus, one cannot understand quantity without understanding it to be extended.[23]

However, just as quantity is identical with its extension, so is the divine essence identical with its *esse*. According to Giles, *esse* is not something superadded to the divine nature: God has *esse* of himself (*a seipsa*); he does not acquire it from another. Thus God has *esse* not by participation but essentially. One does not understand the divine nature without understanding it to exist. However, because other beings possess *esse* from the divine essence, *esse* denotes something added to their nature. Hence *esse* does not belong to the nature of a created being, but is

---

23. *Theoremata de Corpore Christi*, pr. 29 (Rome, 1554; reprinted in Frankfurt am Main: Minerva, 1968), 18rA–18vA: "Quicquid enim est extensum, vel est quantitas, vel hoc habet ex quantitate et ut induit quendam quantitativum modum ... Videmus enim quod sola quantitas est sua extensio, quia extensio in quantitate non est aliquid superadditum quantitati. Non enim quantitas est extensa per aliud, sed seipsa est quid extensum. Propter quod quia non competit ei extensio participatione, sed essentialiter est ipsa extensio, ideo non potest intelligi quantitas, si non intelligeretur extensa. Pertinet enim ad ipsam quidditatem quantitatis extensio. Unde si diffiniretur quantitas diffinitione non per additamentum, extensio pertineret ad quidditatem ipsius. Caetera autem praeter quantitatem sunt extensa per participationem, et extensio dicit quiddam additum naturae eorum, quae si non diffinirentur per additamenta, extensio non ingrederetur diffinitionem eorum, et possent intelligi non intellecta extensione."

The Real Distinction between Essence and Existence

accidental to it and is received in the nature, and thereby is really distinct from it.[24]

Having reached this point, Giles's discussion of essence and existence comes to an abrupt end. He notes that questions such as whether *esse* denotes an essence added to the nature of the creature; how essence and *esse* are really distinct; whether essence and *esse* can be called two things (*duae res*); and how *esse* flows from essence and is its act, are outside of his present concern. He closes with the following remark: "Nevertheless, because students for the most part become weary concerning the *esse* of creatures, and many, when they speak of *esse* and essence, support themselves in words only, when the opportunity arises (Lord granting), we intend to treat [this topic] more extensively."[25]

There are, I think, a number of things in this quotation that are worthy of note. First, Giles promises at a later time to devote more attention to the relationship between essence and existence. He kept this promise by writing the *Theoremata de esse et essentia* (ca. 1278–84) during his period of exile from Paris. Second, Giles tells us that there is a need for a more thorough investigation of the relationship between essence and existence. Students become worn out debating this problem, perhaps because they make little progress in understanding it. Many (*multi*), when they discuss this topic, do so superficially; they content themselves with mere words and fail to get at the heart of the central issues. Third, it seems reasonable to construe Giles's remarks as a criticism of his previous treatment of essence and existence in his *Sentences* commentary. More importantly, however, Giles's remarks can be taken as a criticism of Thomas Aquinas. In Giles's view, an adequate presentation of the real distinction has not yet been given. Although he does not refer to Thomas by name, it is natural to think that Giles would indeed include Thomas

---

24. "Nam sola essentia divina est suum esse, quia esse in essentia dei non dicit aliquid superadditum naturae eius. Est autem natura divina a seipsa et non acquirit esse per aliud. Propter quod quia non habet esse per participationem, sed essentialiter est suum esse, ideo non potest intelligi natura divina non intellecto ipsius esse ... Caetera autem entia, quia habent esse per divinam essentiam, esse dicit aliquid additum naturae eorum, propter quod esse non pertinet ad naturam alicuius entis creati ... Ex his autem clare patet, quod esse accidit cuilibet creaturae, et dicit aliquid receptum in natura cuiuslibet creati, et dicit aliquid additum in natura cuiuslibet entis creati, et facit realem differentiam in rebus creatis" (fol. 18v).

25. "Tamen quia ut plurimum circa esse creaturarum fatigantur adiscentes, et multi, cum loquuntur de esse et essentia, in solis verbis sustentantur, cum locus occurrerit, domino concedente, intendimus hoc diffusius pertractare" (fol. 18v).

among the *multi* who speak only superficially of essence and *esse*. As we shall see, this view of Thomas was shared by Siger of Brabant.

SIGER OF BRABANT'S CRITICISM OF THOMAS AQUINAS

Siger of Brabant examines the relationship between essence and existence in his *Quaestiones in Metaphysicam* (ca. 1273).[26] In one of the questions from the introduction to this text, Siger asks whether being (*ens*) or existence (*esse*) belongs to the essence of caused things, that is, whether existence is something added to their essence.[27] This question is evidently motivated by the conflict between two different understandings of being: the one, derived from Avicenna, maintains a distinction between a thing (*res*) and its being (*ens*); the other, represented by Aristotle and Averroes, holds that being adds nothing to the nature of a thing. Before turning to Siger's discussion, it is helpful to review briefly the background of this problem.

Avicenna establishes a distinction between thing (*res*) and being (*ens*) in *Metaphysics* I.5. There Avicenna observes that thing, being, and the necessary (*necesse*) are primary concepts, which are "immediately impressed on the soul by a first impression." These concepts are primary in the sense that they are not derived from other, better-known, concepts.[28] In this text, Avicenna focuses much of his attention on the relationship between *res* and *ens*. He argues that they are distinct notions (*duae intentiones*): being (*ens*) is connected to existence in reality or in the mind;

---

26. This work survives as a *reportatio* in four versions (Munich, Vienna, Cambridge, Paris), which is available today in two volumes: *Siger de Brabant, Quaestiones in Metaphysicam. Édition revue de la reportation de Munich. Texte inédit de la reportation de Vienne*, ed. W. Dunphy (Louvain-La-Neuve: Éditions de L'Institut supérieur de philosophie, 1981); *Siger de Brabant, Quaestiones in Metaphysicam. Texte inédit de la reportation de Cambridge. Édition revue de la reportation de Paris*, ed. A. Maurer (Louvain-La-Neuve: Éditions de L'Institut supérieur de philosophie, 1983). For the chronology of Siger's works, see F. Van Steenberghen, *Maître Siger de Brabant* (Louvain: Publications Universitaires, 1977), 217–21.

27. The question is preserved in only three of the four *reportationes*. For the text, see Siger, *Quaestiones in Metaphysicam*, Introductio, q. 7, Munich version (ed. Dunphy), 41–49; Cambridge version (ed. Maurer), 30–37; Introductio, q. 2, Paris version (ed. Mauer), 397–99.

28. Avicenna, *Liber de Philosophia prima sive Scientia divina*, ed. S. Van Riet (Leiden: E. J. Brill, 1977), Book I, c. 5 (1:31.2–1:32.5): "Dicemus igitur quod res et ens et necesse talia sunt quod statim imprimuntur in anima prima impressione, quae non acquiritur ex aliis notioribus se, sicut credulitas quae habet prima principia, ex quibus ipsa provenit per se, et est alia ab eis, sed propter ea."

The Real Distinction between Essence and Existence 81

thing (*res*), by contrast, is that which has a nature (*certitudo*) or essence.[29] Moreover, *ens* and *res* necessarily accompany one another, and neither can be separated from the other.[30]

Thomas Aquinas knows this chapter from Avicenna very well. In his derivation of the transcendentals in *De veritate*, q. 1, a. 1, he famously draws upon it: "But that which the intellect first conceives as most known (*quasi notissimum*), and into which it resolves all of its concepts, is being (*ens*), as Avicenna says in the beginning of his *Metaphysics*."[31] Because being is the primary concept, Thomas's task in this question is to explain how other concepts can make an addition to it. Avicenna, however, maintains that there is a plurality of primary concepts. It is natural to wonder whether there is an order in these concepts: is thing (*res*) prior to being (*ens*), or is being (*ens*) prior to thing (*res*)?[32] Thanks in part to Averroes, medieval Latin thinkers often interpret Avicenna as having defended a priority of thing. Thus, the question arises, how and what does *ens* add to *res*?

Averroes's criticism of Avicenna is occasioned by Aristotle's comments in *Metaphysics* IV.2 about the relation between being and unity:

> If, now, being and unity are the same and are one thing in the sense that they are implied in one another as principle and cause are, not in the sense that they are explained by the same formula (though it makes no difference even if

---

29. Avicenna, *Liber de Philosophia prima sive Scientia divina* (1:34.50–1:35.61): "Dico ergo quod intentio entis et intentio rei imaginantur in animabus duae intentiones; ens vero et aliquid sunt nomina multivoca unius intentionis nec dubitabis quin intentio istorum non sit iam impressa in anima legentis hunc librum. Sed res et quicquid aequipollet ei, significat etiam aliquid aliud in omnibus linguis; unaquaeque enim res habet certitudinem qua est id quod est, sicut triangulus habet certitudinem qua est triangulus, et albedo habet certitudinem qua est albedo. Et hoc est quod fortasse appellamus esse proprium, nec intendimus per illud nisi intentionem esse affirmativi, quia verbum *ens* significat etiam multas intentiones, ex quibus est certitudo qua est unaquaeque res, et est sicut esse proprium rei."

30. Avicenna, *Liber de Philosophia prima sive Scientia divina* (1:36.78–83): "Si autem non fuerit hoc propositum et haec coniunctio utriusque, non scietur quid sit res cuius quaerimus intentionem, nec separabitur a comitantia intelligendi ens cum illa ullo modo, quoniam intellectus de ente semper comitabitur illam, quia illa habet esse vel in singularibus vel in aestimatione vel intellectu. Si autem non esset ita, tunc non esset res."

31. Thomas, *De ver.*, q. 1, a. 1 (Leon. 22.1, 5:100–104): "Illud autem quod primo intellectus concipit quasi notissimum et in quod conceptiones omnes resolvit est ens, ut Avicenna dicit in principio suae Metaphysicae."

32. For some discussion of this problem by Arabic scholars, see R. Wisnovsky, "Notes on Avicenna's Concept of Thingness (Šay'iyya)," *Arabic Sciences and Philosophy* 10 (2000): 181–221; T.-A. Druart, "*Shay'* or *Res* as Concomitant of 'Being' in Avicenna," *Documenti e studi sulla tradizione filosofica medievale* 12 (2001): 125–42.

we interpret them similarly—in fact this would strengthen our case); for one man and a man are the same thing and existent man and a man are the same thing, and the doubling of the words in "one man" and "one existent man" does not give any new meaning (it is clear that they are not separated either in coming to be or in ceasing to be); and similarly with "one," so that it is obvious that the addition in these cases means the same thing, and unity is nothing apart from being.[33]

In this passage Aristotle asserts that being (*ens*) and one (*unum*) are convertible terms that are predicated of anything that exists. Of any extra-mental object, one can say that it is a being, and that it is one. Although *ens* and *unum* are extensionally equivalent, they are in fact distinct notions (i.e., they do not share the same definition), and neither adds anything real to that of which it is said.

In his commentary on this passage, Averroes seizes the opportunity to rebuke Avicenna:

> But Avicenna erred (*peccavit*) greatly in this, because he thought that "one" (*unum*) and "being" (*ens*) signify dispositions added to the essence of a thing. And it is astounding how this man was led astray by such an error. He listened to the teachers of our Law (*loquentes in nostra lege*), since he mixed his own divine science with their preaching.[34]

Averroes interprets Avicenna to mean that one (*unum*) and being (*ens*) are accidental dispositions added to the essence of a thing. He thinks that Avicenna was led to this error under the influence of Islamic theologians, who teach that all beings are created by God. Since all things receive their being from God, their being must be accidental to them. In Averroes's judgment, such a view is metaphysically problematic, for two reasons. First, if a thing were one through some accidental reality added to its nature, then nothing would be one *per se* and through its substance. Thus the beings of our experience would no longer possess substantial unity. Second, if a thing were one by means of an intention added to its essence, an infinite regress would result, as that intention in turn would be one by means of an intention added to it, and so on. This

---

33. Aristotle, *Metaphysics* IV.2.1003b23–31, in *The Complete Works of Aristotle*, ed. J. Barnes, 2 vols. (Princeton, NJ: Princeton University Press, 1984), 2:1585.

34. Averroes, *In IV Meta.*, com. 3, fol. 67rB: "Avicenna autem peccavit multum in hoc quod existimavit quod unum et ens significant dispositiones additas essentiae rei. Et mirum est de isto homine, quomodo erravit tali errore. Et iste audivit loquentes in nostra lege, cum quorum sermonibus admiscuit suam scientiam Divinam."

infinite regress argument will be a powerful weapon in the hands of Latin thinkers who wish to attack the real distinction.[35]

When one turns back to Siger's *Metaphysics* commentary, one notices immediately the strong influence of Averroes. Siger begins his reply by rejecting two alternative positions. The first view is that of Avicenna, which holds that a thing (*res*) exists by means of a disposition added to its essence. Accordingly, thing (*res*) and being (*ens*) are distinct intentions, and existence (*esse*) is something added to an essence. The second view is that of Thomas Aquinas, which Siger regards as an attempt to chart a middle course between the positions of Aristotle and Avicenna. Citing a famous passage from Thomas's *Metaphysics* commentary, Siger reports that his view was that *esse* is added to the essence of a thing, though it is not an accident, nor does it belong to the essence; rather, it is something constituted by the principles of the essence.[36]

Although Siger agrees with Thomas that *esse* is constituted by the principles of the essence, he finds Thomas's explanation for this to be unintelligible, if not logically absurd. According to Siger, if *esse* belongs to a thing, it is either a part of the thing's essence (e.g., matter or form), or it is the composite essence itself, or it is an accident. However, Thomas denies that *esse* is added to a thing as an accident. If *esse* were part of the essence, or if it were the whole essence, it would not make sense to speak of it as *added* to the essence. In Siger's view, it is self-contradictory to maintain (as Thomas does) that *esse* is added to a thing and also constituted by the principles of that thing. Since what is constituted by the principles of the essence is the thing itself, it follows that the *esse* of a thing simply

---

35. Averroes, *In IV Meta.*, com. 3, fol. 67vG. Note in particular: "Si res esset unum per aliquam rem additam suae naturae, sicut credit Avicenna, tunc nihil esset unum per se, et per suam substantiam, sed per rem additam suae substantiae. Et illa res, quae est una, si dicitur quod est una per intentionem additam suae essentiae, quaeretur etiam de illa re, per quam fit una, et per quid fit una: si igitur fit una per intentionem additam illi, revertitur quaestio, et procedetur in infinitum." For some applications of this infinity argument among later Latin thinkers, see Henry of Ghent, *Henrici de Gandavo opera omnia*, vol. 5: *Quodlibet I*, ed. R. Macken (Leuven: Leuven University Press, 1979), 51.14–24; and Godfrey of Fontaines, *Les quatre premiers Quodlibets de Godefroid de Fontaines*, ed. M. De Wulf and A. Pelzer (Louvain: Institute Supérieur de Philosophie de l'Université de Louvain, 1904), 163–64.

36. Siger, *Quaestiones in Metaphysicam*, Cambridge version, 32: "Alia est hic opinio, et fuit Thomae de Aquino. Quia enim Aristoteles et Avicenna videbantur in hoc contradicentes, ideo mediantes dicunt sic, quod in entibus causatis esse est additum essentiae, non tamen tamquam accidens, sed tamquam ens aliquid per essentiae principia constitutum." Here Siger quotes from Thomas, *In Meta.* IV.2; see *In duodecim libros Metaphysicorum Aristotelis expositio*, ed. M.-R. Cathala and R. Spiazzi (Rome: Marietti, 1950), n. 558.

is the thing itself. But if so, *esse* would not be something added to the essence. As a good Aristotelian, Siger holds that the totality of the real contains only essences, their constituent principles, and accidents. Since Thomas's notion of *esse* fits under none of these headings, Siger accuses him of inventing "a fourth nature" in reality (*quarta natura in entibus*).[37]

Siger's own view is that *esse* belongs to the essence of a thing; it is not something added to an essence. Against Avicenna, Siger holds that *res* and *ens* do not signify diverse intentions. Instead, *res* and *ens* are extensionally equivalent; they are merely two different ways of signifying one and the same object. *Ens* signifies the substance of a thing in the manner of an act (*per modum actus*), because the notion of being (*ens*) is derived from the act of being (*actus essendi*); *res* signifies the substance of anything in the manner of a potency.[38] For Siger, the distinction between essence and *esse* is merely linguistic. Avicenna's great mistake, in his judgment, was his failure to distinguish between names that signify diverse intentions and names that signify the same essence but in different ways. Thus, in recognizing that *res* and *ens* have diverse significations, Avicenna thought that this implied a diversity of essences. In other words, Avicenna mistakenly thought that a distinction in signification entails a distinction in the order of reality.

It is evident that Siger's understanding of *esse* is quite different from that of Thomas. The latter understands *esse* as the act of being (*actus*

---

37. *Quaestiones in Metaphysicam*, Cambridge version, 32–33: "Sed quidquid sit de conclusione, modus ponendi non est conveniens, quia omne pertinens ad rem aut est res ipsa, aut pars essentiae rei, aut accidens essentiae. Ponere igitur quod esse in entibus causatis sit additum tale, ut dictum est, erit ponere quartam naturam in entibus. Item, si esse in entibus causatis est aliquid constitutum per essentiae principia, et quod constitutum est per essentiae principia est res ipsa, sequitur quod esse rei sit res ipsa. Non igitur est aliquid additum." The Munich version reads: "Etsi conclusio vera sit, modum tamen ponendi non intelligo, quia esse quod pertinet ad rem, aut est pars essentiae rei, ut materia vel forma, aut res ipsa composita ex his, aut accidens. Sed si accidens, tunc erit additum essentiae rei: quod est contra dictam opinionem proximam. Sed dicere quod esse sit aliquid additum essentiae rei, ita quod non sit res ipsa, neque pars essentiae, ut materia et forma, et dicere quod non sit accidens, est ponere quartam naturam in rebus" (45). The Paris version reads: "Dicere quod esse non est essentia rei, sed aliquid constitutum per essentiae principia, est idem affirmare et negare, cum constitutum per essentiae principia nihil aliud sit quam ipsa res ex illis constituta. Ponere etiam quod esse sit aliquid additum essentiae et non essentia rei, cum universaliter omne pertinens ad rem, aut est pars essentiae, ut materia et forma, aut essentia, aut accidens essentiae, hoc est ponere quartam naturam in entibus" (398).

38. *Quaestiones in Metaphysicam*, Cambridge version, 33–34: "Ens enim significat substantiam uniuscuiusque per modum actus, quia ratio entis ab actu essendi sumitur. Res autem significat substantiam uniuscuiusque per modum potentiae magis."

essendi). It is that by which any being is or exists. A being (*ens*) is that which has *esse* (*habens esse*).[39] By contrast, Siger regards *ens* and *esse* as equivalent: both terms signify the essence of a thing insofar as it is in act.[40] It is not surprising, therefore, that Siger would be puzzled by Thomas's claim that *esse* is added to the essence of a thing, and yet it is constituted by the principles of the essence.

Siger's perplexity about the nature of Thomas's teaching was probably quite common at that time. Siger's text sheds some light on Giles's comments in the *De corpore Christi*. The questions that Giles had identified as needing further discussion, namely, whether *esse* is an essence added to the nature of a thing; how essence and *esse* are really distinct; whether essence and *esse* are two things; and how *esse* follows from essence and is its act are precisely the concerns of Siger. While Giles retained his belief in a real distinction, Siger granted only a conceptual distinction between essence and *esse*.

THE IMPLICATION OF THOMAS AQUINAS IN HENRY OF GHENT'S DISCUSSION IN *QUODLIBET* I, Q. 9

In *Quodlibet* I, q. 9, Henry was asked whether the essence of a creature is its *esse*. In formulating his answer he examines and rejects any real distinction between essence and existence. It is often said today that Henry's target in this text was Giles of Rome.[41] As is well known, the two carried on a lively and often acerbic debate on this issue during Giles's Parisian regency (1285–92). However, at the time of Henry's first *Quodlibet* (1276), Giles had not yet published a systematic treatment of essence and existence. It has been hypothesized that Giles was perhaps an oral participant in Henry's disputation, and so the arguments in favor of the real distinction that Henry criticized could have been offered by Giles himself. Although this conjecture has a great deal of plausibility, there remains the question of the role played by Thomas Aquinas. Obviously Thomas could not have participated in Henry's disputation, as he had died two years earlier. However, one might wonder whether Thomas was

---

39. Thomas, *In Meta.* XII.1, n. 2419: "Nam ens dicitur quasi esse habens."
40. Siger, *Quaestiones in Metaphysicam*, Cambridge version, 35: "Quia igitur esse vel ens significat essentiam rei secundum quod in actu, res autem secundum quod in potentia."
41. This claim was first advanced by E. Hocedez, "Le premier Quodlibet d'Henri de Gand (1276)," *Gregorianum* 9 (1928): 92–117.

also targeted by Henry in this question. When Henry rejected the theory of real distinction, did he have Thomas in mind? In order to resolve this question, it is necessary to look closely at Henry's text.

The opening objections in *Quodlibet* I, q. 9, attempt to establish that the essence of a creature is not its *esse*. The first argument reasons that, because a creature is something subsistent (*quid subsistens*), if it were identical with its *esse*, then it would be *esse subsistens*. But the latter is the same as pure *esse* (*esse purum*), which is God. Thus, if a creature were its *esse*, it would be God.[42] This argument claims that a distinction between essence and *esse* is needed to distinguish the creature from God. The language used in the objection is common to both Giles and Thomas. In his *Sentences* commentary, Giles distinguished between God as pure *esse* and creatures as participated *esse*. Giles also described divine *esse* as something subsistent (*quid subsistens*), as uncaused, and as pure act indistinct from the divine *esse*. Thomas also uses the terms *esse subsistens* and *esse purum* to refer to God.[43] Both thinkers view the composition of essence and existence to be one of act and potency, and both appeal to this composition to distinguish creatures from God, who is absolutely simple pure act.

The second objection in favor of the real distinction reasons that if a creature is not really other (*aliud re*) than its *esse*, then, since *esse* as such is not limited, any creature in its nature would be infinite.[44] In the *Sentences*, Giles had maintained that the *esse* of a creature is limited because it is received in a nature that is distinct from it.[45] In his mature writings, Giles develops this as an argument for the real distinction. Because it is

---

42. Henry, *Quod.* I, q. 9, 47:10–13: "Primo quia, cum creatura ipsa sit quid subsistens, si ipsa esset suum esse, ipsa esset esse subsistens. Esse subsistens est esse purum, quod non est nisi Deus. Creatura ergo esset Deus. Hoc autem falsum est. Ergo etc."

43. Descriptions of God as *esse subsistens* are scattered throughout Thomas's works. For one text where he describes God as *esse subsistens* and *esse purum*, see *De ver.*, q. 21, a. 5 (Leon. 22.3, 606:137–43): "Ipsa autem natura vel essentia divina est eius esse; natura autem vel essentia cuiuslibet rei creatae non est suum esse sed est esse participans ab alio. Et sic in Deo est esse purum, quia ipse Deus est suum esse subsistens; in creatura autem est esse receptum vel participatum."

44. Henry, *Quod.* I, q. 9, 47:14–17: "Secundo quia, si creatura non est aliud re a suo esse, cum ipsum esse, in quantum huiusmodi, non est limitatum, et ita infinitum, esset quaelibet creatura in natura sua infinita, quod falsum est. Ergo et primum similiter."

45. Giles, *Ord.* I, d. 19, p. 2, pr. 2, q. 3: "Nam illud dicitur terminatum quod est in alio receptum, quia quicquid recipitur in aliquo recipitur secundum capacitatem rei recipientis, et non secundum modum suum. Ideo omne tale terminatum est propter quod omnis creatura habet esse limitatum, quia habet esse in natura receptum" (fol. 112vPQ).

The Real Distinction between Essence and Existence 87

contrary to the nature of a creature that it be simply infinite, one may infer that in all creatures *esse* is received in an essence and is thereby limited by it.[46] Although Thomas does not appear to have formulated this as an argument for the real distinction, the gist of the argument is consistent with his metaphysical principles. Thomas holds, for example, that act is limited only by its reception in a potency, and that act which is not received is unlimited.[47] Furthermore, he describes *esse* as "the act of all acts and the perfection of all perfections."[48] It follows, then, that if there were a being whose essence and *esse* were identical, the *esse* of that being would be infinite, since its *esse* would not be limited by a distinct receiving principle. Moreover, in *De ente*, c. 4, Thomas had argued that there can be only one instance of a being whose essence is identical with its *esse*. Hence, in all other beings essence and *esse* enter into real composition.[49] Consequently, Thomas would surely have agreed with the claim that without the real distinction the creature would be infinite in its being.

The third objection in Henry's text is based upon the contingent character of created being. The argument proceeds as follows. If a creature were not really distinct from its *esse*, then, because *esse* cannot be separated from itself, *esse* would not be separated from a created thing. But in that case the creature would be wholly incorruptible.[50] One finds traces of this argument in Giles's *Sentences* commentary. There he reasoned that if something is created, then it has *esse* from another; from this it follows that it is in potency to *esse*, and therefore it is distinct from its *esse*.[51] Moreover, since all creatures receive their *esse* from God, all

---

46. Giles, *Theoremata de esse et essentia*, Th. V, 25:11–18: "Et quia hoc repugnat cuilibet creaturae quod sit simpliciter infinita, eo quod creatura quaelibet est certis limitibus circumscripta, impossibile est naturam intellegentiarum non esse differentem ab esse. Et quia quaecumque compositio habet esse in substantiis separatis, habet esse in corporalibus rebus, oportet haec corporalia et per consequens omnia creata habere naturam differentem ab esse."

47. For discussion of these two important metaphysical principles, see J. D. Robert, "Le principe: 'Actus non limitatur nisi per potentiam subjectivam realiter distinctam,'" *Revue philosophique de Louvain* 47 (1949): 44–70; W. N. Clarke, "The Limitation of Act by Potency in St. Thomas: Aristotelianism or Neoplatonism?," *New Scholasticism* 26 (1952): 167–94; John F. Wippel, "Thomas Aquinas and the Axiom that Unreceived Act is Unlimited," *Review of Metaphysics* 51 (1998): 533–64, reprinted in *Metaphysical Themes in Thomas Aquinas II*, 123–51.

48. Thomas, *De pot.*, q. 7, a. 2, ad 9 (Marietti 192): "Unde patet quod hoc quod dico *esse* est actualitas omnium actuum, et propter hoc est perfectio omnium perfectionum."

49. Thomas, *De ente*, c. 4 (Leon. 43.376:103–377:123).

50. Henry, *Quod.* I, q. 9, 47:18–20: "Tertio, quia, si creatura non est aliud re a suo esse, cum ipsum esse non potest a se ipso separari, esse non posset separari a re creata, et sic es<se>t omnino incorruptibile. Quod falsum est."

51. *Ord.* I, d. 8, p. 2, pr. 2, q. 1, fol. 54rA.

are capable of losing their *esse*, and in this way are able to be reduced to nonbeing.[52] In Giles's mature writings, however, the need to preserve the contingent nature of created being plays a leading role in his efforts to establish the real distinction. Giles never tires of repeating that the doctrine of creation cannot be maintained without the real distinction. Moreover, in his *Quaestiones de esse et essentia*, q. 12, he argues at length that a creature could not be annihilated by God if essence and *esse* did not really differ in it.[53]

It has been pointed out by others that contingency is of little significance in Thomas's argumentation for the real distinction. While Thomas often introduces the distinction between essence and *esse* to distinguish simple substances (such as angels) from God, he also asserts that such substances are necessary, though their necessity is caused by God.[54] One wonders, then, whether Thomas himself would have accepted the reasoning behind the third objection in Henry's text. Does the real distinction entail that creatures are able not to be? Strictly speaking, of course, Thomas allows that only material beings are corruptible, since corruption involves a separation of matter and form.[55] Thus, where there is no matter, there is no corruption. Thomas regards intellectual substances, such as angels and human souls, as incorruptible.[56] Nevertheless, this does not mean that such substances could not be annihilated by God.

Thomas takes up this very issue in *De pot.*, q. 5, a. 3, where he asks

52. *Ord.* I, d. 37, p. 1, pr. 1, q. 3: "Nam quaelibet creatura a sua substantia recedere potest, quia quod a versione incipit, versioni subiectum est: eo ipso quod ex nihilo omnia facta sunt in nihilum omnia redigibilia existunt. Quodlibet igitur quia potest non esse quod est, a sui substantia recedere potest. Deus autem qui omnino immutabilis est a sui substantia non potest discedere, nec potest non esse quod est" (fol. 192rB).

53. For Giles's arguments, see *Quaestiones de esse et essentia*, q. 12 (Venice, 1503; reprinted in Frankfurt am Main, 1968), fol. 31rB–32rA.

54. For this interpretation, see P. Porro, *Tommaso. L'ente e l'essenza*, 199–200. Note in particular: "Se dunque l'interpretazione dell'essenza in termini di potenza rispetto all'atto di essere servisse a legittimare la contingenza, ci si troverebbe di fronte ad una situazione quanto meno singolare: da una parte, la distinzione tra essere e essenza viene quasi sempre introdotta, nelle opere di Tommaso, per giustificare la diversità delle forme semplici da Dio; dall'altra, Tommaso stesso non mostra nessuna esitazione nell'asserire che tali forme sono poi necessarie al pari di Dio (anche se la loro necessità deriva pur sempre da Dio). Ma—per l'appunto—non è la contingenza ciò che sta a cuore qui a Tommaso" (200).

55. *SCG* II, c. 55 (Leon. 13.147): "Omnis enim corruptio est per separationem formae a materia: simplex quidem corruptio per separationem formae substantialis; corruptio autem secundum quid per separationem formae accidentalis."

56. For Thomas's arguments to establish the incorruptibility of the human soul, see *Quod.* X.3.2; *SCG* II, cc. 79–81; *ST* I, q. 75, a. 6; *Q. de an.* 14.

whether God could reduce a creature to nothing. He begins his reply with a distinction. In things that are produced by God, something is said to be possible in two ways. In one way, by the sole power of the agent; for example, one can say that before the universe was made, it was possible for it to exist at a future moment, not by means of any potency possessed by a creature (because no creatures existed), but only by the power of God, who could bring the universe into being. But in a second way, something is possible by means of potency in the things that are made; for example, it is possible for a body composed of matter and form to be corrupted.[57] The distinction that Thomas has drawn is between something that is possible by virtue of an active power (i.e., something is possible because there exists a cause that can bring it about), and something that is possible by virtue of a passive power that it possesses (e.g., it is possible for wood to burn, because the nature of wood is such that it is combustible). But there is another sense of possibility that Thomas has not yet mentioned, namely, something is possible because its realization does not imply a logical contradiction. As we shall see, this sense becomes vitally important later in Thomas's discussion.

In the next part of Thomas's text, he applies the distinction that he has drawn to the problem at hand. The creature's possibility to be reduced to nothing, he notes, can be viewed in two ways: either from the standpoint of the creature or from that of God. Considering this possibility first from the side of creatures, Thomas draws a contrast between the teaching of Avicenna and that of Averroes. According to Avicenna, all creatures have within themselves a possibility for both being and nonbeing. This is so because the *esse* of any created thing is outside of its nature. Consequently, when the nature of a creature is considered *per se*, it is merely something that is possible to be; it has the necessity of being only from its cause, whose nature is its own being. This cause is a *per se* necessary being, which Avicenna identifies as God. However, Thomas notes, Averroes maintained that some beings (namely, the heavenly bodies) do not have a possibility for nonbeing.[58] In Thomas's judgment,

---

57. *De pot.*, q. 5, a. 3 (Marietti 135): "Dicendum, quod in rebus a Deo factis dicitur aliquid esse possibile dupliciter. Uno modo per potentiam agentis tantum; sicut antequam mundus fieret, possibile fuit mundum fore, non per potentiam creaturae, quae nulla erat, sed solum per potentiam Dei, qui mundum in esse producere poterat. Alio modo per potentiam quae est in rebus factis; sicut possibile est corpus compositum corrumpi."

58. Thomas is alluding to Averroes's argument that what is possible of itself cannot acquire sempiternal existence from another. For this in Averroes, see *In XII Meta.* com. 41, 324vH-L.

the position of Averroes is more reasonable (*rationabilior*) than that of Avicenna. For the possibility of being and nonbeing belongs to a thing because of its matter, which is pure potency. Thus, when matter exists under one form, it is in potency to another. Therefore, a creature has a possibility for nonbeing, not because its essence and existence are distinct, but because it possesses matter.[59]

Thomas continues by distinguishing two ways in which a possibility for nonbeing may be lacking to the nature of a creature. In one way, this is because it is an immaterial substance. A subsistent form, such as an angel, cannot not be, nor can being (*esse*) be separated from it.[60] In a second way, the matter of a created being may lack a potentiality for another form. This is the case with the heavenly bodies; the matter of such bodies is so actualized by its form that it has no potentiality to receive another form.[61]

From this one may gather that Thomas believes that there are some creatures (e.g., angels, heavenly bodies) that are necessary beings, in the sense that they do not have within themselves the possibility for nonbeing.[62] Such beings are incorruptible, and the *esse* that they possess cannot be separated from them. If Thomas's discussion were to end here, one

---

59. *De pot.*, q. 5, a. 3 (Marietti 135): "Et haec quidem positio [scilicet opinio Commentatoris] videtur rationabilior. Potentia enim ad esse et non esse non convenit alicui nisi ratione materiae, quae est pura potentia. Materia etiam, cum non possit esse sine forma, non potest esse in potentia ad non esse, nisi quatenus existens sub una forma, est in potentia ad aliam formam."

60. Ibid.: "Dupliciter ergo potest contingere quod in natura alicuius rei non sit possibilitas ad non esse. Uno modo per hoc quod res illa sit forma tantum subsistens in esse suo, sicut substantiae incorporeae, quae sunt penitus immateriales. Si enim forma ex hoc quod inest materiae, est principium essendi in rebus materialibus, nec res materialis potest non esse nisi per separationem formae; ubi ipsa forma in esse suo subsistit nullo modo poterit non esse; sicut nec esse potest a se ipso separari." See too Thomas's remarks in *De spir. creat.* 1 (Leon. 24.14:395–400): "Remoto igitur fundamento materie, si remaneat aliqua forma determinate nature per se subsistens—non in materia—adhuc comparabitur ad suum esse ut potentia ad actum: non dico autem ut potentia separabilis ab actu, set quam semper suus actus comitetur."

61. For a very fine discussion of this in Thomas, see Thomas Litt, *Les corps célestes dans l'univers de saint Thomas d'Aquin* (Louvain: Publications universitaires, 1963), 58–86.

62. See also Thomas's interesting remarks at *SCG* II, c. 30 (Leon. 13.338): "Licet autem omnia ex Dei voluntate dependeant sicut ex prima causa, quae in operando necessitatem non habet nisi ex sui propositi suppositione, non tamen propter hoc absoluta necessitas a rebus excluditur, ut sit necessarium nos fateri omnia contingentia esse:—quod posset alicui videri, ex hoc quod a causa sua non de necessitate absoluta fluxerunt: cum soleat in rebus esse contingens effectus qui ex causa sua non de necessitate procedit. Sunt enim quaedam in rebus creatis quae simpliciter et absolute necesse est esse."

might conclude that he would not accept the reasoning behind Henry's third objection.

However, Thomas continues his analysis. If the possibility for nonbeing is viewed from the standpoint of God's power, he notes, then all creatures can be reduced to nothing. In other words, even those creatures that are formally necessary (i.e., that have no internal principle of nonbeing) are still capable of being annihilated by God. In his effort to establish this claim, Thomas argues that there are only two reasons why God could not reduce a creature to nonbeing. The first reason is that it is in itself impossible, since it would imply a logical contradiction. However, Thomas sees no logical contradiction in the nonexistence of creatures, because creatures are not identical with their existence. In other words, existence is not included within the nature of a creature, in the way that, for example, rational animal is included within the definition of man. Thus, while the proposition "Man is not a rational animal" entails a logical contradiction, no such contradiction is implied by the nonexistence of creatures. Consequently, that God could annihilate a creature is not in itself impossible.[63] A second reason why God might be unable to reduce a creature to nonbeing is that it is necessary for him to will the being of creatures. Thomas rejects this reason because God is not constrained by the necessity of his nature to will creatures, nor is his willing creatures to exist a necessary condition for his beatitude, which is something that God necessarily wills. Thomas concludes that it is not impossible for God to reduce creatures to nonbeing.

In this highly interesting text, Thomas has affirmed not only that some creatures are incorruptible, but also that God can reduce all creatures to nothing. What is particularly striking is that the distinction between essence and existence plays some role in establishing both of these claims. It plays a negative role in establishing the incorruptibility of creatures, in the sense that Thomas thinks that one cannot appeal to the distinction between essence and existence to conclude to the corruptibility of all

---

63. Thomas, *De pot.*, q. 5, a. 3 (Mandonnet 136): "Si autem recurramus ad potentiam Dei facientis, sic considerandum est, quod dupliciter dicitur aliquid Deo esse impossibile: uno modo quod est secundum se impossibile, quod quia non natum est alicui potentiae subiici; sicut sunt illa quae contradictionem implicant ... Creaturas autem simpliciter non esse, non est in se impossibile quasi contradictionem implicans, alias ab aeterno fuissent. Et hoc ideo est, quia non sunt suum esse, ut sic cum dicitur, Creatura non est omnino, oppositum praedicati includatur in definitione, ut si dicatur, Homo non est animal rationale: huiusmodi enim contradictionem implicant, et sunt secundum se impossibilia."

creatures. However, it plays a positive role in establishing the claim that God could reduce all creatures to nonbeing. Since existence is not included within the essence of a creature, there is no logical contradiction implied by the nonexistence of creatures. Since Aquinas holds that God can bring about whatever is not logically impossible, he is justified in concluding that God can reduce all creatures to nonbeing.

It is evident that for Thomas the incorruptibility of some creatures has nothing to do with God's ability to annihilate them. A creature is incorruptible because it has within itself no principle or source of its corruption. However, it is not contrary to the notion of a necessary or incorruptible being that its existence depend upon God as upon a cause. An immaterial being such as an angel does not acquire its being by generation, but by creation; so too, it cannot lose its being by corruption, but it can be annihilated by God.

From the foregoing I would conclude that Thomas would have accepted the spirit of the argument of Henry's third objection, though not its letter. Thomas does not think that all creatures are corruptible, nor does he allow for the separability of essence and *esse* in separate substances. However, he affirms that God could reduce all creatures to nonbeing. A necessary condition for this possibility is the real distinction between essence and *esse*. If any creature were identical with its *esse*, then the nonbeing of that creature would entail a logical contradiction, and God would be unable to annihilate it.

In the corpus of *Quodlibet* I, q. 9, Henry presents a series of arguments against the real distinction, and then develops his own view. The essence and existence of a creature are intentionally distinct, which he explains is less than a real distinction but more than a conceptual one. For our purposes, however, what is more interesting are Henry's remarks in the beginning of his reply, where he links the essence/existence question to the nature of participation.

According to Henry, the theory of the real distinction is grounded on a certain way of conceiving how the creature participates being (*esse*) from God. This view, which Henry describes as a false imagination (*phantastica imaginatio*), regards the essence of the creature as a substrate, and *esse* as something that is received in it as a kind of form. Thus the creature is said to exist in the manner in which a body is said to be white having received in itself the form of whiteness. It is in this way, Henry tells us, that those who defend the real distinction understand the participation of creatures in being:

> Whence they say that creatures are related to God as air to the shining sun, so that just as the sun is shining by its own nature—and furthermore, we maintain, by its essence, as it is not other than light itself—so God has *esse* through his nature and essence, because he himself is nothing other than *esse*. And just as air of itself is dark, and from its own nature it does not partake of light unless it is illuminated by the sun—thereby participating light from the sun—so too the creature of itself and from its own essence does not have being, but is in the darkness of nonbeing, unless it is illuminated by God and to it is given the *esse* which it participates.[64]

What is striking about this passage is that the analogy that Henry cites, namely, that the creature is related to God as air to the light of the sun, comes directly from Thomas Aquinas.[65] It is found in *ST* I, q. 104, a. 1, where Thomas directs himself to the question regarding whether creatures need to be conserved in being by God. Henry knows this text quite well, and he cited it in an earlier question in this same *Quodlibet*, in his discussion of the eternity of the world. There Henry attacked Thomas's claim that creation and conservation are not distinct actions.[66]

Since Henry has connected this way of understanding the participation of creatures in being with the real distinction, his quotation of Thomas's text provides very strong evidence that he regards Thomas as a defender of the theory that he will reject in this text. When we take into account also the initial series of objections that are meant to argue for the real distinction, we have very good reasons to regard Thomas as

---

64. Henry, *Quod.* I, 9, 48:45–49:52: "Unde dicunt quod creaturae se habent ad Deum sicut aer ad solem illuminantem, ut sicut solem qui est lucens per suam naturam, etiam ponamus per suam essentiam, ut non sit aliud quam ipsa lux, sic Deus habet esse per suam naturam et essentiam, quia non est aliud nisi esse. Et sicut aer de se est obscurus, et de sua natura non est omnino particeps lucis nisi a sole illuminetur, participans per hoc lumen a sole, sic creatura de se et sua essentia non habet aliam rationem esse, sed est in tenebris non entitatis, nisi a Deo illustretur et detur ei esse suum quo participet."

65. For more on Thomas's use of this analogy, see A. T. LaZella, "As Light Belongs to Air: Thomas Aquinas and Meister Eckhart on the Existential Rootlessness of Creatures," *American Catholic Philosophical Quarterly* 87 (2013): 567–91.

66. Henry, *Quod.* I, 7–8, 37:55–38:57: "Unde patet quod valde insipienter dicunt aliqui quod eadem actione Deus res creat et conservat, sicut sol eadem actione causat et conservat lumen in medio." See Thomas, *ST* I, q. 104, a. 1, ad 4: "Ad quartem dicendum quod conservatio rerum a Deo non est per aliquam novam actionem; sed per continuationem actionis qua dat esse, quae quidem actio est sine motu et tempore. Sicut etiam conservatio luminis in aere est per continuatum influxum a sole" (464).

a target of attack in Henry's question. The evidence that we have considered does not indicate that Thomas was the sole target of Henry's attack, or that Giles was not also visualized by Henry as a defender of the real distinction. Our conclusion is rather that Henry did intend to include Thomas as a defender of a theory that he deemed to be wrong-headed, namely, the real distinction between essence and existence.

CONCLUSION

In various ways Thomas Aquinas exerted a great influence on the origin of the historical controversies concerning the relationship between essence and existence. In his early writings, Giles of Rome defended a theory of the real distinction that is in harmony with the principles of Thomas's metaphysical thought. Like Thomas, Giles conceived of *esse* as the act of being, and he drew a sharp distinction between God, who is being essentially (*esse purum; esse subsistens*), and creatures, in whom being is participated, limited, and composed. There is no trace in his *Sentences* commentary of Giles's later conception of *esse* as a *res*.

Giles's thinking begins to show some signs of evolution in his *Theoremata de Corpore Christi*. In this writing he shows some dissatisfaction with current discussions of the real distinction (and by extension, with his own treatment of it in the *Sentences*). Giles's unease may have been caused by the critique of Thomas's view of essence and *esse* by Siger of Brabant. What is perplexing to Siger is Thomas's claim that *esse* is added to the essence of a thing and constituted by the principles of the essence. What is needed is a more detailed explanation of the doctrine of *esse* as existential act. This is something that Giles will strive to do in his mature works, beginning with the *Theoremata de esse et essentia*.

The public controversy over essence and existence breaks out with Henry of Ghent's first quodlibetal debate in 1276. While it is likely that Giles was an oral participant in the debate, there is strong evidence that Henry viewed Thomas Aquinas as a proponent of the real distinction that he targeted for attack. The theory of participation that underwrites the real distinction is that of Thomas, and the initial objections that Henry cites in favor of the real distinction are inspired, either directly or indirectly, by Thomas. Thus, one should regard Thomas as a target (with Giles) of Henry's quodlibetal question.

In sum, Thomas Aquinas played a leading role in the development of the historical controversy concerning the relationship between essence and existence. One may describe his influence as positive, inasmuch as he inspired the early teaching of Giles of Rome, and also negative, inasmuch as it was the criticism of Thomas by Siger of Brabant and Henry of Ghent that pushed Giles to develop his mature teaching on essence and existence, wherein the real distinction is understood as a distinction between two things (*inter rem et rem*).

David Twetten

4   A Defense of Essence-Realism as the Key to Aquinas's Arguments for the Essence-*Esse* Real Distinction

THE "GREATEST FOUNDATION OF AQUINAS'S TEACHING" (CAJETAN)

As everyone knows, Thomas Aquinas developed a metaphysics that is the fruit of some 1,500 years of philosophical reflection on first causes, a reflection whose sources include the late antique pagan Greek Neo-Platonists, Proclus and Ammonius Hermeiou, but whose proximate source is the Arabic philosopher, Avicenna.[1] Under the influence of Avicenna, Aquinas places at the center of his philosophical "system" a doctrine of *esse*, or act of being,[2] and he purports to prove philosophically that all things but one are produced out of nothing (*ex nihilo*) by a first

---

1. Especially significant are the suggestions of Cornelio Fabro, *Partecipazione e causalità secondo s. Tommaso d'Aquino* (1960, 1963), in *Opere complete*, vol. 19 (Rome: Editrice del Verbo Incarnato, 2010), as brought out in the well-researched study of Jason Mitchell, *Being and Participation: The Method and Structure of Metaphysical Reflection according to Cornelio Fabro* (Rome: Ateneo Pontificio Regina Apostolorum, 2012), 49–155. For one side of this history, see Twetten, "Aristotelian Cosmology and Causality in Classical Arabic Philosophy and its Greek Background," in *Ideas in Motion in Baghdad and Beyond: Philosophical and Theological Exchanges between Christians and Muslims in the Third/Ninth and Fourth/Tenth Centuries*, ed. Damien Janos (Leiden: Brill, 2015), 312–433, at 319–79.

2. As recently as 1977 in the critical edition of the Latin Avicenna, Aquinas's doctrine of *esse* as the ultimate act of essence in potency was thought to be Aquinas's innovation upon Avicenna; Gerard Verbeke, "Introduction," 79*, in Avicenna, *Liber de philosophia prima sive Scientia divina*, I–IV, ed. Simone Van Riet (Louvain: Peeters, 1977). It is now possible to establish the source in Avicenna, as I show in "The Source of Aquinas's 'Being as Act' (*esse ut actus*) in Arabic Philosophy" (unpublished).

cause, God, even if our universe had an eternal past, that is (as we might say), even if there were no Big Bang (*sans* the inflationary universe theory). The great Étienne Gilson puts the matter as follows: "As soon as the sensible world is regarded as the result of a creative act, which not only gives it existence but conserves it in existence through all successive moments of its duration, it becomes so utterly dependent as to be struck through with contingency down to the very roots of its being."[3]

At the heart of Aquinas's argument lies what has been called, under Cajetan's inspiration, "the foundational truth of Christian philosophy,"[4] namely, the fact of a real or extra-mental distinction between *esse* and essence in all things but one.[5] On this distinction, as on a foundation,

---

3. Étienne Gilson, *The Spirit of Mediaeval Philosophy*, trans. Alfred Howard Campbell Downes (New York: C. Scribner's Sons, 1936), 43; for the original, see Étienne Gilson, *L'esprit de la philosophie médiévale* (Gifford lectures, Université d'Aberdeen), 2nd rev. ed. (Paris: Vrin, 1969), 72–73. Gilson's use of "contingency" as coextensive with created reality here must be clarified, as the term must be able to embrace those creatures that, for Thomas, once created, cannot possibly of themselves cease to exist, namely, the heavenly bodies, immaterial substances, and the human soul; see Lawrence Dewan, "Thomas Aquinas, Creation, and Two Historians," *Laval théologique et philosophique* 50, no. 2 (1994): 363–87, at 373.

4. Norbertus del Prado, "La vérité fondamentale de la philosophie chrétienne selon saint Thomas," *Revue thomiste* 18, nos. 2–3 (1910): 209–27 and 340–60, at 342. In other places, del Prado considers this truth as one with the claim that in God, essence and *esse* are not really distinct. In Norbertus del Prado, *De veritate fundamentali philosophiae Christianae* (Fribourg: Société Saint Paul, 1911), xxxvii, 58, 161, he cites Cajetan, *In libros posteriorum analyticorum Aristotelicos* 2.6: "hoc in loco expresse Aristoteles dicit quod esse non est ipsa essentia rei, quod est maximum fundamentum doctrinae Sancti Thomae"; in Tommaso de Vio (Cajetanus), *In Praedicabilia Porphyrii, Praedicamenta, et libros Posteriorum analyticorum Aristotelis castigatissima commentaria* (Lyons: Symphorien Beraud, 1578), 579.35–36. But del Prado borrows the precise phrase from and cites (xxxviii–xxxix and 196) Cardinal González, who writes: "Hanc thesim [In rebus creatis essentia realiter distinguitur ab existentia] Angelicus Doctor habet tanquam veritatem fundamentalem philosophiae christianae, eam sexcentis plus minus locis vehementer propugnat"; Ceferino González y Díaz Tuñón, *Philosophia elementaria ad usum academicae ac praesertim ecclesiasticae iuventutis*, vol. 2: *Ontologia, cosmologia et theodicea* (Madrid: Policarpo López, 1868), 30; emphasis added. For Fabro, the essence-*esse* distinction is the central truth of metaphysics, whereas the notion of participation is the fundamental truth that commands this capital thesis; Fabro, "Sviluppo, significato e valore della 'IV via,'" *Doctor Communis* 7 (1954): 71–109, at 91.

5. Aquinas does use the expression *distinctio realis* (versus *distinctio intelligibilis* or *distinctio rationis*) over fifty times, nearly always in discussing divine attributes and persons, but twice in denying that an entity's genus and species require a real distinction among forms within it; Aquinas, *De spir. creat.* 3, ad 3 and ad 15 (Leon. 24.2, 45:450–63, 47:604–8). In the context of the essence-*esse* distinction, as is often observed, he speaks of what *differt re* or *differunt realiter* and of a *diversitas realis* or *compositio realis*; see Joseph Owens, "The Accidental and Essential Character of Being in the Doctrine of St. Thomas Aquinas," *Mediaeval Studies* 20 (1958): 1–40, at 35–36n46, and his *Aquinas on Being and Thing* (Niagara Falls, NY: Niagara University Press, 1981), 1–5. "Real" signifies "not produced by the human mind alone," or "extra-mental," not, of

depends the rest of Aquinas's philosophy of creation. Nevertheless, sharp disagreements have arisen, even among sympathizers with Aquinas, as to how and even whether Thomas "proves" this distinction as in reality, outside the mind.[6] Gilson and Cornelio Fabro, the two Thomists who remain the most influential today, came to doubt, it appears, that it can be "demonstrated." The case of Gilson is most obvious, as he writes: "No one has ever been able to demonstrate the conclusion that, in a caused substance, existence is a distinct element, other than essence, and its act."[7] Fabro writes, somewhat obscurely, but to a similar effect:

> Metaphysical reflection or 'reduction' discovers the distinction ... between essence and *esse*, as [between] potency and act. This is the supreme distinction (and composition) for the 'founding' of the 'real' under its determination as 'being [*ens*] through participation.' This determination certainly does not claim to have an immediate and direct reference to experience, as does that of substance and accident, of essence and *existence*. But this [fact] does not mean that the determination of 'being [*ens*] through participation' *is the result of demonstration*: it is 'shown' at the 'founding' of being [*ens*], or through the process of 'reduction' of being [*ens*] to *esse*, in the first phase of the ascending metaphysical reflection, which is that of the manifestation of the 'to be' [*esse*] of a being [*ens*]. The Thomistic distinction, then, of essence and *esse*, on which the definitive *determination* of '*ens* through participation' *is founded*, flows from [this] very 'resolution.'[8]

---

course, that what is distinct can exist on its own in reality. Form versus matter or accidents versus substance would be widely accepted as extra-mentally distinct than essence versus *esse*. To one who insists that "real distinction" signifies what is distinct as one *res* to another, separable *res*, what is "extra-mentally distinct" is like Scotus's formal distinction, which has been significantly clarified in Stephen Dumont, "Duns Scotus's Parisian Question on the Formal Distinction," *Vivarium* 43, no. 1 (2005): 7–62.

6. See, e.g., Francis Cunningham, *Essence and Existence in Thomism: A Mental vs. the "Real Distinction?"* (Lanham, MD: University Press of America, 1988).

7. Étienne Gilson, *Elements of Christian Philosophy* (Garden City, NY: Doubleday, 1960), 128; see 130–31. A similar conclusion is drawn in Étienne Gilson, *Introduction à la philosophie chrétienne*, 2nd ed. (Paris: Vrin, 2007; page numbers for the 1960 first edition are bracketed), 67 [55]: "Sans doute, bien des raisons suggèrent la composition d'essence et d'être dans les étants, mais aucune ne la démontre à la rigueur." Gilson here acknowledges that that the real distinction is demonstrable *under certain conditions*, as in the "three types of arguments" found in *De ente*, c. 4 (103–4 [98]); but each presupposes the Thomistic notion of being, which, once granted, leaves nothing left to be demonstrated (107–8 [102–3]). In effect, many Christian philosophers are displeased that "the fundamental truth of Christian philosophy" should be treated as an arbitrary assertion, and so they have undertaken to "demonstrate" it (103 [97–98]).

8. "La riflessione o riduzione metafisica scopre la distinzione o 'Diremtion' fra l'essenza e l'*esse*, come potenza ed atto. Questa è la distinzione (e composizione) suprema per la fondazione del reale nella sua determinazione di 'ente per partecipazione'; questa determinazione

I shall begin, in the first section below, with an objection to the project of proving the "real distinction" (as henceforth labeled) based on one of Aquinas's proofs, the "Genus Argument." The second section offers a response to the objection that appeals to Aquinas's often overlooked "essence-supposit" real distinction. In the third section, I reread the "Genus Argument" in light of the proof of the "essence-supposit" real distinction. The appeal to this simple line of reasoning, if it is correct, apparently makes most of Aquinas's proofs for the "real distinction" cogent (contrary to the position I maintained in my "Really Distinguishing,"

---

certamente non pretende di avere un riferimento immediato e diretto alla esperienza come quella di sostanza e accidenti, di essenza e di esistenza. Questo però non significa che la determinazione di ente per partecipazione sia frutto di dimostrazione: essa 'si mostra' al fondo dell'ente ovvero mediante il processo di 'riduzione' dell'ente all'*esse*, nella prima fase della riflessione metafisica ascendente ch'è quella della manifestazione dell'essere dell'ente. La distinzione quindi tomistica di essenza ed esse, sulla quale si fonda la determinazione definitiva di ente per partecipazione, scaturisce dalla 'risoluzione' stessa dell'essere dell'ente che San Tommaso ha espresso mediante il principio della 'perfectio separata.'" Fabro, *Partecipazione e causalità*, 232–33; in addition to references to this, the definitive edition, I shall place in brackets [...] the pagination of the French version (except where, as in the present case, there is no parallel): Cornelio Fabro, *Participation et causalité selon s. Thomas d'Aquin* (Louvain: Publications universitaires de Louvain, 1961). Out of context, it is difficult to convey in English the meaning of this quotation, so I have added paraphrases in brackets, italics, and *double* quotation marks to help the reader. For further explanation of Fabro's position, see the appendix below. Fabro is quite clear here that the apprehension of creatures' participated being is, in the systematic order, posterior to the apprehension of the "real distinction." At the very least, this passage undermines Fabro's previously preferred "Participation Argument," which *begins* from "*ens* through participation": an argument repeated in 1941, 1948, and 1954 (but within God-to-creatures reasoning, or, better, through the "principle of separated perfection"). See Cornelio Fabro, *La nozione metafisica di partecipazione secondo San Tommaso* (1939, 1950, 1963), in *Opere complete*, vol. 3 (Rome: Editrice del Verbo Incarnato, 2005), 243–44 [249 in first edition]; Mitchell, *Being and Participation*, 386–88, 391–92, 404. Also, as Fabro rejects the "Avicennian logical reasoning" as standing on its own, it cannot be considered a successful *quia* demonstration of a *real* distinction; see, in addition to note 17 below, Alain Contat, "Le figure della differenza ontologica nel tomismo del Novecento (seconda parte)," *Alpha Omega* 11 (2008): 213–50, at 236–38. Finally, Fabro's separation of *existentia* from *actus essendi* (the immediate context of the quotation above) could correspond to Aquinas's language and presentation of the analogous senses of being if Aquinas used *existere* exclusively of propositional being. Nevertheless, Fabro is correct to criticize formulae that confuse propositional being with extra-mental being by speaking of *esse* as a "positing" or *positio* of a possible being outside of its cause; see Cornelio Fabro, "Per la semantica originaria dell'*esse*' tomistico," *Euntes Docete* 9 (1956): 437–66, at 456, on John of St. Thomas, *Cursus theologicus*, ed. Solesmes (Paris: Desclée, 1931) I, d. 4, a. 3, n. 1 (448a): "Nomine ergo exsistentiae intelligitur communiter apud omnes illud, quo aliquid denominatur positum extra causas, et extra nihil in facto esse." See also the account of Fabro's development by the excellent scholar Christian Ferraro, *L'atto di essere nel "tomismo intensivo" di Cornelio Fabro* (Rome: Edizioni Tomismo intensivo, 2017), who also similarly highlights the quoted text (92–93; see 88–89 and 99).

written before 2005).[9] Many readers of Aquinas (my past self included), by focusing on *esse* or the act of being, have overlooked his realist notion of essence—the foundation on which, I argue, rests the famous "real distinction" and the arguments on its behalf.[10] If twentieth-century readings of Thomas are correctly held to be "existentialist," I submit, ours would do well to supplement them with some "essentialism" (properly defined), or, better, with "essence realism."[11]

---

9. David Twetten, "Really Distinguishing Essence from *Esse*," in *Wisdom's Apprentice: Thomistic Essays in Honor of Lawrence Dewan, O.P.*, ed. Peter Kwasniewski (Washington, DC: The Catholic University of America Press, 2007), 40–84. My new position is perhaps suggested by words of Aimé Forest, *La structure métaphysique du concret selon Saint Thomas d'Aquin* (Paris: Vrin, 1931; 2nd ed., 1956); I cite the second edition, which conforms to the first. Forest ascribes to Aquinas the "essence-supposit" distinction as extra-mental (149), and holds that Averroes's denial of it, and his denial that essences are extra-mental, is bound up with his denying the "essence-*esse*" real distinction (159). At the same time, Forest anticipates Fabro by criticizing Aquinas's early argument for the "essence-*esse*" real distinction, e.g., in *De ente*, c. 4 (Leon. 43.148–49), and by presenting as the "essential argument" what amounts to an argument from participation (Leon. 43.163).

10. The "essence-supposit" real or extra-mental distinction has been recognized in Aquinas, especially recently, in excellent studies: John F. Wippel, *The Metaphysical Thought of Thomas Aquinas* (Washington, DC: The Catholic University of America Press, 2000), 238–53; Gabriele Galluzzo, "Aquinas on Common Nature and Universals," *Recherches de théologie et philosophie médiévales* 70 (2004): 131–71; Galluzzo, "Two Senses of 'Common': Avicenna's Doctrine of Essence and Aquinas's View on Individuation," in *The Arabic, Hebrew and Latin Reception of Avicenna's Metaphysics*, ed. Amos Bertolacci and Dag Hasse (Berlin: De Gruyter, 2011), 309–37, at 315; Jason West, "Aquinas on the Real Distinction between a Supposit and its Nature," in *Wisdom's Apprentice*, 85–106. Nevertheless, the grounds in Aquinas are too obvious to have been missed in previous studies, such as Johannes Urráburu, *Institutiones philosophicae quas Romae in Pontificia Universitate Gregoriana*, vol. 2: *Ontologia* (Vallisoleti: Cuesta, 1891), 851–54 and 870–75; Jacques Winandy, "Le Quodlibet ii, art. 4 de saint Thomas et la notion de suppôt," *Ephemerides theologicae Lovanienses* 2 (1934): 5–29; Cornelio Fabro, *La nozione*, 346n9 [356]; Cornelio Fabro, "Neotomismo e Neosuarezismo: una battaglia di principi," *Divus Thomas* (Piac.) 44 (1941): 167–215 and 420–98, at 426–31 and 496; Edward Rousseau, *The Distinction between Essence and Supposit in the Angel according to St. Thomas Aquinas* (PhD diss., Fordham University, 1954), 64–105; Peter Geach, "Form and Existence," *Proceedings of the Aristotelian Society* 55 (1954–55): 251–72, at 251; Gilson, *Elements of Christian Philosophy*, 116–17, following Boethius; Lawrence Dewan, *The Doctrine of Being of John Capreolus: A Contribution to the History of the Notion of "esse"* (PhD diss., University of Toronto, 1967), 17–123. In del Prado, *De veritate fundamentali*, 13–14 and 141–42, the "essence-supposit" real distinction is understood to follow from the "essence-*esse*" real distinction, although not in the case of separated substances (20, 139, 377; but see 142, 257, 550): "essence-*esse*" is the first composition without which no other composition is possible (21, 49, 69, 166, 170, 255). For similar accounts of the relation among these "real distinctions," see Marie-Dominique Roland-Gosselin, "La distinction réelle entre l'essence et l'être," in *Le « De ente et essentia » de saint Thomas d'Aquin. Texte établi d'après les manuscrits parisiens. Introduction, notes et études historiques par M.-D. Roland-Gosselin* (Paris: Vrin, 1948; first edition in 1926), 135–205, at 192–93; Gallus Manser, *Das Wesen des Thomismus*, 3rd ed. (Fribourg: Paulusverlag, 1949; first edition in 1930), 554; Fabro, "Neotomismo e Neosuarezismo," 430n22.

11. See above for the definition of Avicennian essentialism. I take up senses of "essentialism"

Aquinas's Arguments for the Essence-*Esse* Real Distinction

Of course, there is a catch to my line of argument. Aquinas's essence realism rests on a premise that you and I in our philosophical mode will find easy to doubt: "Two different substances that are the same in kind must have something in them that makes them the same." The fourth section of this chapter suggests that the history of analytic philosophy gives us good dialectical grounds for rejecting this doubt. Given that the last major stage in the standard histories of twentieth-century analytic philosophy is Kripke's essentialist reaction to Quine's attack on Aristotelian essences (a stage strongly endorsed and developed by Fine's Aristotelian realism), there are grounds for thinking that essence realism and *esse* as really distinct from essence should gain in plausibility in the twenty-first century.[12] Furthermore, contemporary philosophy helps to draw attention to an implicit premise in the arguments for the "real distinction," a premise, in fact, on which much of classical philosophy depends. Finally, the fifth section proposes a new proof of God's existence based on Aquinas's essence realism, which allows us to see the universe of being (even if our universe is embedded in a multiverse or antecedently explained under inflationary or string cosmology), as immediately caused by God. I hope that the reader will agree that this reflection on the so-called fundamental truth of Aquinas's philosophy celebrates the author of the best book on Aquinas's metaphysics, Fr. John F. Wippel.

SOME TERMINOLOGY

- Essence: the common feature of things signified by their definition (see *De ente*, c. 2).[13]

---

in a forthcoming paper, "Locke and Aquinas as Alternatives to Neo-Aristotelian Universal Realism."

12. Geach's 1954 acceptance of the essence-*esse* real distinction may turn out to be "prophetic": see Geach, "Form and Existence," 269, where he marshals an updated form of the "Genus Argument." Jeffrey Brower, the author of the best contemporary paper on Aquinas's account of essence, affirms the essence-supposit real distinction in his "Aquinas on the Problem of Universals," *Philosophy and Phenomenological Research* 92 (2016): 715–35, at 724, while rejecting the essence-*esse* real distinction; see also his *Aquinas's Ontology of the Material World: Change, Hylomorphism, and Material Objects* (Oxford: Oxford University Press, 2014), 17.

13. All of the most general terms are used in many senses. An angelic essence would be an intelligible content that in itself is other than the accidents and acts that belong to the angelic subject; the divine essence is shared by three subsistent relations, for Thomas.

- *Esse* or "to be" (act of being): the feature that makes some individual be, that is, actually be in reality versus in mind alone.[14]
- Real distinction: a property belonging to (two distinct substances, or) two features within one substance that are not only conceptually but also extra-mentally distinct (whether or not they can exist on their own).
- Essence realism: there is something extra-mental in an individual that is the same in kind with, or "common" to, what is in other individuals (potential or actual), namely, the essence [versus "essence nominalism": nothing in two individuals is the same in kind; essences are in the mind or in language alone].
- Avicennian moderate realism or Avicennian essentialism: essence in itself (neither universal or particular) is the source of sameness in kind across individual things and between things and essence in the intellect; it is to essence in things that individuating conditions are added, and to essence in the intellect that universality is added.[15]

THE PROBLEM IN PROVING THE REAL DISTINCTION AND THE GENUS ARGUMENT

Let us begin, then, with what is commonly acknowledged to be one of the worst of Aquinas's arguments for the real distinction, the Genus Argument, which Aquinas ascribes to Avicenna (see *In Sent.* I, d. 8, q. 4, a. 2, co.). I systematize the argument's premises in an expanded form below the following quotation, but the essential steps can be identified even within the text:

ST I, q. 3, a. 5, co. (the Genus Argument):

> [**Premise (1)**] All things that are in one genus agree (*communicant*) in the quiddity or essence of the genus, which is predicated of them quidditatively

---

14. Throughout this chapter, I use "essence" (or, interchangeably, "nature") and "*esse* as act," by way of convenience, as they belong to the genus of substance. But we should also recognize an analogous sense of *esse* and *essentia* that belongs to accidents.

15. Joseph Owens, "Aristotle on Categories," *The Review of Metaphysics* 14 (1960): 73–90, at 81n24, captures the point very well in defending Avicenna's description of essence in itself as "neither universal nor particular": "that way of understanding the nature of a sensible thing as *just in itself* was a commonplace among mediaeval readers of Aristotle, in the wake of Avicenna. It is not at all a question of attributing to the common nature an existence outside the particular and outside the universal, but rather of maintaining that it is the same common nature that has existence either as individual in reality or as universal in the intellect" (emphasis added). Aquinas in *De ente*, c. 3, speaks of the essence in individuals, not as individual, but as *individuated*.

(*in eo quod quid est*). But [**Premise (2)**] they differ with respect to being (*esse*). For [**Premise (3)**] the being (*esse*) of (a) a human and of a horse, and (b) of this human and that human, are not the same [as they would be, were there no "essence-*esse* real distinction"]. And so, [**Premise (4)**] for whatever things belong to a genus, being and what it is, namely, essence, must differ. But in God, [being and what is] do not differ, as was shown. Hence, it is evident that God is not in a genus as a species.

ST I, q. 3, a. 5, co. (Leon. 1:44):

[(1)] Omnia quae sunt in genere uno, communicant in quidditate vel essentia generis, quod praedicatur de eis in *eo quod quid est*. [(2)] Differunt autem secundum esse: [(3)] non enim idem est esse hominis et equi, nec huius hominis et illius hominis. Et sic [(4)] oportet quod quaecumque sunt in genere, differant in eis esse et *quod quid est*, idest essentia. In Deo autem non differt, ut ostensum est. Unde manifestum est quod Deus non est in genere sicut species.

(1´) Every member of a genus or class shares to that extent the same essence as every other.

(2´) Yet, every *member* of a genus or class differs in *esse*.

(3´) Otherwise, each member would be the same; that is, for one "to be" would be for the other "to be."

(4´) Therefore, the essence of everything in a genus must be really distinct from its *esse*.

Cornelio Fabro came to reject the Genus Argument as early Avicennian[16] logical reasoning[17] (although four of the seven versions of the

---

16. Fabro, relying in part on Roland-Gosselin, Goichon, Saliba, and Forest, speaks of Aquinas's early doctrine on the essence-*esse* real distinction as depending almost exclusively on Avicenna: Fabro, *La nozione*, 116b, 214c, 217c [113 and 220]; Cornelio Fabro, "Circa la divisione dell'essere in atto e potenza," *Divus Thomas* (Piac.) 42 (1939): 529–62, at 533n5, and his "Neotomismo e Neosuarezismo," 173n3. Fabro expressly ascribes to Avicenna both the "Genus Argument" (Fabro's *La nozione*, 218b [221], and *Partecipazione e causalità*, 621 [305]) and the "*Intellectus essentiae* Argument," which is said to be (perhaps under the influence of Pretzl's misreading of al-Fārābī; see Fabro, *La nozione*, 116n66) "Avicenna's Most Characteristic Argument for the Real Distinction," in Fabro, "Neotomismo e Neosuarezismo," 175; see also his *Partecipazione e causalità*, 612n20 [292n111]. The second stage of the argument of *De ente*, c. 4, is also ascribed to Avicenna, namely, to *Metaphysica* 8.5; Cornelio Fabro, "Un itinéraire de saint Thomas," *Revue de Philosophie* 39 (1939): 285–310, at 297n5. In contrast, I believe that Aquinas is the first to give *ex professo* arguments for the essence-*esse* real distinction, though I show elsewhere how they are, nonetheless, inspired by his reading of Avicennian texts.

17. Fabro, *La nozione*, 218i,b [221] speaks of what we now call the "*Intellectus essentiae* Argument" as a "logical argument," and the "Genus Argument" as a "logico-metaphysical argument." These arguments are contrasted with "metaphysical" arguments, especially those using

argument are not from early works, including the important passage quoted in *ST* I, q. 3, showing that God is not in a genus). The problem with the Genus Argument, all agree, is that it proves at best only that there must be *some* really distinct principle to distinguish two things that "actually are" and that belong to the same class. But why is *esse* ("to be") an ontologically special component necessary to make them distinct? Why does individuating matter not suffice? Accordingly, Fr. Wippel objects that the proof begs the question, by assuming in the second premise that *esse* "already signifies an act principle which is really distinct from the essence principle of each particular substance."[18] As Fr. Owens puts it with regard to another proof: "Nothing has been introduced to show that existing adds a positive content of its own over and above the quidditative content of the thing."[19] Gilson has generalized the same objection for all possible proofs. They all assume Aquinas's special doctrine of *esse*: *esse* as act that makes a contribution other than essence. He writes: "All the arguments one can use to establish the distinction between being and essence in Thomas Aquinas's doctrine presuppose the prior recognition of

---

participation, which latter are introduced by Aquinas after 1260 starting with *SCG*; *La nozione*, 218–21; see 243–44 [221–25, 249]. For Fabro, the "logical argument" should not be taken to stand on its own independent of the metaphysical arguments, such as we find in the second and third stages of *De ente*, c. 4, itself; *La nozione*, 219 [222–23]. Given the presence of "considerations of reason and notional aspects" rather than real elements, Aquinas makes no explicit affirmation of a real distinction as long as he stays on the "logico-metaphysical" plane (as in the "Genus Argument," it appears); in fact, a logical "account of *esse*" (*razione de essere*) can be given even in the case of God; *La nozione*, 213 [216]. Similarly, participation in Plato, Boethius, and Porphyry remains at this plane, which is at base logical; *La nozione*, 70b, 107c, 184–85, 187 [62–63, 103, 187]. See the appendix for the subsequent history of Fabro's defense of the real distinction. In Fabro's mature works, the Avicennian argumentation (formal thought arising from the logical sphere) is regarded merely as a preparatory but surpassed stage in Aquinas's gradual development, one that focuses, following Aristotle's question "whether *x* exists," on the *fact* of an essence's existing, on the realization of a *possible* essence, its *existentia*, rather than on the intensive act of being or *actus essendi* such as is ever more deeply meditated upon in Aquinas's mature thought; see Fabro, *Partecipazione e causalità*, 58–60, 62–63, 176n10, 177, 177n14, 181, 198, 198n63, 202–3, 234–37 [74–76, 79–80, 214n72, 216, 216n78, 221–22, 260–61, 261n34, 266–67], and "Il fondamento metafisico," 49–50. Avicenna's "extrinsicism" is manifested, in part, by the distinction originated by Fabro's Avicenna between *esse essentiae* and *esse existentiae*; Fabro, *Partecipazione e causalità*, 198–99; see 566, 584, 649 [261n34, 283, 314–15; see 579, 585, 636]. The mature thought on the "real distinction" of Fabro's Aquinas involves "being freed from all Avicennian influence" (Fabro, *Partecipazione e causalità*, 171 [209]).

18. Wippel, *Metaphysical Thought*, 161.

19. Joseph Owens, "Aquinas' Distinction at *De ente et essentia* 4.119–123," *Mediaeval Studies* 48 (1986): 264–87, at 282.

the notion of the 'act of being' (*esse*)."[20] Thus, if "Thomist *esse*" is rejected, as by an Aristotelian of the strict observance, all the proofs fail.

On the other hand, here is a recipe for making the Genus Argument succeed—indeed, for potentially making all nine of Aquinas's proofs succeed. If we could show that:

(1.1′) To possess an essence [in Premise (1′)] is to have a component within the whole substance that is really distinct from the whole, and that

(2.1′) *Esse* [in Premise (2′)], whatever it is, belongs to the whole thing in the genus or class, not to its essence, then we would know that *essence* corresponding to class membership in Premise (1′) is ontologically other than *esse*. But this is precisely what Aquinas purports elsewhere to prove. Without further ado, let me turn directly to this argument.

AQUINAS'S PROOF OF THE ESSENCE-SUPPOSIT REAL DISTINCTION

Although there are parallels, the best statement of the proof is found in Aquinas's discussion in *Summa theologiae* III as to whether the incarnation involves union with a divine Person (or supposit) rather than with the divine nature. Again, I identify the essential premises in the text below, which I itemize in an expanded form as follows:

(1′) [Essence realism:] Two different substances that are the same in kind must have something in them that makes them the same, by which we name them and know them. In short, the very nature of the species is included in the supposit or individual substance.

(2′) There is something in most extra-mental things (e.g., individuating principles such as prime matter under quantity, necessary and contingent attributes, etc.) that does not belong to the essence of a thing as such.

(3′) Otherwise, each individual subsisting in a nature would be entirely the same as its nature; thus

(3.1′) all individuals of the same nature would be the same individual.

(4′) Therefore, essence and supposit, the individual substance as a

---

20. Gilson, *Elements of Christian Philosophy*, 130.

TABLE 4: AQUINAS'S PROOF OF THE ESSENCE-SUPPOSIT
REAL DISTINCTION

Aquinas, ST III, q. 2, a. 2, co.:	Aquinas, ST III, q. 2, a. 2, co. (Leon. 11:25):
"Person" signifies something other [in reality] than nature.[1] For "nature" signifies the essence of the species that the definition signifies. And, if, in fact, nothing else could be found adjoined to what pertains to the notion of the species, *there would be no necessity to distinguish nature from a "supposit of the nature"*—which is the individual subsisting in that nature. For [**Premise (3)**] each individual subsisting in a nature would be entirely the same as its nature. However, [**Premise (2)**] in certain subsisting things there does happen to be found something that does not pertain to the notion of [their] species, namely, [their] accidents and individuating principles, just as is especially apparent in these things that are composed of matter and form. And, for this reason, [**Premise (4)] in such things, nature and supposit differ even in reality, not as if they are entirely separate**,[2] but because [**Premise (1): essence realism**] **the very nature of the species is included in the supposit**, and certain other items are superadded that are apart from the intelligibility of the species ...[3] What is said of the supposit should be understood of the person in a rational or intellectual creature. For a person is nothing other than an individual substance of a rational nature, according to Boethius.	Dicendum quod persona aliud significat quam natura. Natura enim significat essentiam speciei, quam significat definitio. Et si quidem his quae ad rationem speciei pertinent nihil aliud adiunctum inveniri posset, nulla necessitas esset distinguendi naturam a supposito naturae, quod est individuum subsistens in natura illa, quia [(3)] unumquodque individuum subsistens in natura aliqua esset omnino idem cum sua natura. [(2)] Contingit autem in quibusdam rebus subsistentibus inveniri aliquid quod non pertinet ad rationem speciei, scilicet accidentia et principia individuantia, sicut maxime apparet in his quae sunt ex materia et forma composita. Et ideo [(4)] in talibus etiam secundum rem differt natura et suppositum, non quasi omnino aliqua separata, sed quia [(1)] in supposito includitur ipsa natura speciei, et superadduntur quaedam alia quae sunt praeter rationem speciei ... Et quod est dictum de supposito, intelligendum est de persona in creatura rationali vel intellectuali, quia nihil aliud est persona quam rationalis naturae individua substantia, secundum Boetium.

1. I add the bracketed phrase to make clear the conclusion defended by Aquinas. Several lines below, Aquinas introduces language for an extramental or "real" versus a mere conceptual distinction: *secundum rem differt* or *aliud secundum rem* versus *solum secundum rationem intelligendi*.

2. "Not as if they are entirely separate" can be expanded by Aquinas's teaching elsewhere, e.g., Aquinas, *De pot.*, q. 9, a. 1, co. (Marietti 226a): "The essence in material substances is not the same with them in reality, nor is it absolutely diverse, since it stands as a formal part" (Essentia vero in substantiis quidem materialibus non est idem cum eis secundum rem, neque penitus diversum, cum se habeat ut pars formalis).

3. Aquinas adds: "Hence the supposit is signified as a whole, having a nature as a formal part that is perfective of it [the whole]. Therefore, in things composed of matter and form, the nature is not predicated of the supposit; for we do not say that this human is his or her humanity" (Unde suppositum significatur ut totum, habens naturam sicut partem formalem et perfectivam sui. Et propter hoc in compositis ex materia et forma natura non praedicatur de supposito, non enim dicimus quod hic homo sit sua humanitas).

whole [e.g., Socrates's humanity and Socrates], are really distinct insofar as the former excludes what individuates.[21]

The reasoning is clear enough *if* one accepts Premise (1′) and essence realism, which I shall examine in my final section below. The reasoning is based on the so-called *phenomenon of sameness and difference* in things. I bring out the reasoning by focusing especially on the individuating differences of a thing. Here is the point: Socrates and his humanity are extra-mentally distinct, because human-ness is in him [Premise 1′], and human-ness excludes what makes him an individual [Premise 2′]; otherwise either essence would not be common [contrary to Premise 1′], or Socrates and Diotima would be the same human [Premise 3.1′].

RETURN TO THE GENUS ARGUMENT AS PROOF OF THE ESSENCE-*ESSE* REAL DISTINCTION

Given this proof, namely, of the essence-supposit real distinction, we may go back to the problematic proof of the essence-*esse* real distinction examined above, the Genus Argument:

1. Obama and Trump both actually are: "actually to be," whatever it is, belongs to each as a whole, as a supposit or individual substance.

2. Obama and Trump have within them a feature that is really distinct from themselves by which they are in one of the ten categories, that

---

21. The first term in the essence-supposit extra-mental distinction should be expressed abstractly, with e.g., *humanity*, which prescinds from all that is outside the essence (esp. all that is individual), rather concretely, e.g., with *human*. Essence with precision signifies a "formal part" (*forma totius* rather than *forma partis*, e.g., the soul—a distinction found in Albert with roots in Avicenna). Contrary to what may appear, the term "essence absolutely considered" signifies concretely, without precision, e.g., *human*. It is sometimes inferred that, given a predication theory in which there is a certain identity between what the predicate and the subject signify (*ST* I, q. 13, a. 12, co., and q. 85, a. 5, co.), "human" said of Socrates involves no extra-mental distinctions. This claim would entail the denial of an essence-supposit extra-mental distinction. Instead, *human* is said essentially of Biden in virtue of a formal part that is formally the same as the essence of Obama; that is, in virtue of a feature that is extra-mentally distinct from Biden as a whole. See Gyula Klima, *Ars Artium: Essays in Logical Semantics, Medieval and Modern* (Budapest: Institute of Philosophy of the Hungarian Academy of Sciences, 1988), 88 and 88n3, where the Geachian language of "individualized form" is also used; Joseph Owens, "Quiddity and Real Distinction in St Thomas Aquinas," *Mediaeval Studies* 27 (1965): 1–22, at 9–10; Owens, "Aquinas's Distinction at *De ente et essentia* 4.119–123," *Mediaeval Studies* 48 (1986): 264–87, at 267; and Wippel, *Metaphysical Thought*, 161.

is, in a genus: their humanity (see the proof of the essence-supposit real distinction, above).

3. "Actually to be" is not part of the essence of any individual: *human* does not exist or have an act of being by definition; and Obama and Trump are not the same actually existing human.

4. Therefore, essence and "actually to be" are really distinct from each other in Obama and Trump.

In other words, once we know that individuals have a really distinct essence within themselves, it is an easy matter to show that what accounts for their act of being, whatever else it is, is not part of that essence. Still, something in them must account for their *esse*, if their essence does not, nor do their other properties, such as being the leader of a nation, being wise, and whatever makes them individual: individuating matter (or the individuating principle) and individuated form. "Actually to be," whatever it is, belongs in common to each individual, so it is not as such what individuates.[22] So, something else must be the semantic anchor for the verb in our statement: "Trump *actually is*." I conclude: the striking fact that individual substances have a really distinct essence that makes them what they are—an essence that quite obviously does not contain the act of being, that does not of itself actually be—requires that something else serve as their act of being.

An objection arises: "actually is" or "actually exists" is a strange predicate or property. It needs no "semantic anchor," and in quantificational logic, it is reducible to a quantificational function. The objection allows us to make explicit the "predicate truth-maker" principle implicit in classical semantics (whether Platonic, Aristotelian, or Stoic):

5. The positive predicates of all true affirmations about something present in extra-mental reality must be made true by something inherent in some way in a thing or must be reducible to some such inherent component(s).[23]

---

22. It will be said that each thing's act of being is incommunicably its own. Each thing's matter is incommunicable, but that fact does not rule out "common matter"; so also we may speak of *esse commune* (in each sense of the term). Unlike matter as a principle of individuation under dimensive quantity, *esse* does not individuate but is individuated, as is essence (although only the latter is an intelligible content, the object of definition).

23. For valuable discussion of what constitutes a Thomistic truth-maker principle, see Timothy Pawl's *A Thomistic Account of Truthmakers for Modal Truths* (PhD diss., St. Louis University, 2008), and "A Thomistic Truthmaker Principle," *Acta Philosophica* 25 (2016): 45–64.

Aquinas's Arguments for the Essence-*Esse* Real Distinction

The claim of essence realism, as opposed to the essence nominalism here defined, is that something in reality makes Obama and Trump the same as humans: the essence *humanity* is in each. Similarly, something different makes them actually exist while they exist: their act of being (*esse*). The true statement, after an explosion in their vicinity, "Obama and Trump exist!" is not saved by their wisdom, their leadership role, their humanity, etc. Something in reality must save this true predicate, whether immediately or ultimately. Admittedly, "actually to exist" is an unusual predicate and property, with its own characteristics. To say that this predicate is reducible to the individual quantifier is false.[24] To say that this predicate is unsayable or excluded from speech by the constraints of our logic is arbitrary, as well as inconsistent with the purposes of logic.[25]

If the proof of the essence-*esse* real distinction is as easily explained as now appears, why has it caused such consternation among Aquinas scholars? The fact is that most are nominalists about essence; we associate essence realism with Scotus, not Aquinas, or, if we affirm it, we do not appeal to Aquinas's proof of essence realism as a foundation for the essence-*esse* real distinction. My conjecture, which I will not attempt to prove, is that in the enthusiasm for existentialism,[26] which helped Gilson and Fabro correctly rediscover *esse* in a twentieth-century context, they also adopted an anti-essentialism that turns out to make the "fundamental claims" of Aquinas's philosophy difficult to defend.[27] An

---

24. See especially Michael Wreen's "Existence as a Property," *Acta Analytica* 32 (2017): 297–312, and "Existence as a Perfection," *History of Philosophy & Logical Analysis* 20 (2017): 161–72.

25. See Gyula Klima, "Being," in *Encyclopedia of Medieval Philosophy: Philosophy Between 500 and 1500*, ed. Henrik Lagerlund (Dordrecht: Springer, 2011), 150–59, at 150. I have developed the semantic principle in Premise (5) in David Twetten, "How Save Aquinas' '*Intellectus essentiae*' Argument for the Real Distinction between Essence and *esse*?," *Annals of Philosophy* 67 (2019): 129–43, at 138–39.

26. A full historical picture must include the anti-idealist reaction of Bergson against the abstract idea of being, a reaction that inspired the work of Gilson's student Aimé Forest and others; see Helen John, *The Thomist Spectrum* (New York: Fordham University Press, 1966), 55–57 and 63–64.

27. The existentialist appears to regard concepts, like essences, as limited, abstract, and inert, in comparison to concrete, dynamic existence, such as is known in judgment. This stance gains life as a reaction to a prior dialectic, which is brought out in a penetrating way in John, *The Thomist Spectrum*, 82–83. Many Thomists prior to Fabro, she observes, accepted the (Neo-)Suárezian identification of *being* with "real" or "realized" essence. In the resulting dialectic, either "essence" seems too real to need a further existence, or, if abstracted from existence, it is too unreal to ground a real distinction (61 and 78–79). She continues (82): "Even when Maritain in *Sept leçons sur l'être* of 1934 apparently becomes the first to refer to thomism as an 'existential' philosophy, he insists: 'where existence is contingent, simply posited as a fact, as is the

anti-essentialist will sometimes deny, for example, that God has an essence.[28] Similarly, an anti-essentialist takes Thomas to hold that essence in itself is just nothing.[29] Joseph Owens, for example, writes:

> St. Thomas is regarding the essence just in itself as without any being whatever, and consequently without any intelligibility ...[30] Absolutely in itself it just cannot be grasped by the intellect, for there is *nothing* there to grasp! Only as already having real being in the outside world, or as having cognitional being through the act of being known, can the essence function as a direct object of intellectual consideration. In itself, absolutely considered, the essence, contrary to the views of other types of metaphysics, has no being and no intelligibility at all ... Actually, the essence is a *nothing*; yet potentially it is something. In this way, and in this way only, an essence differs from nothing.[31]

---

case with all created being, it [philosophy] must, because of this defect in its object, be directly orientated only to possible existence. Which does not mean that it is restricted to a realm of pure essences. Its goal is still existence. It considers the essences as capable of actualisation, of being posited outside the mind.'" She is quoting Jacques Maritain, *A Preface to Metaphysics: Seven Lectures on Being* (New York: Sheed and Ward, 1945), 21–22. At the root of the problem seems to be an insufficient grasp of the semantics behind Aquinas's analogous senses of "being," so that conceptualization of essences comes to be set against judgment of the act of being. Maritain writes (19–20): "The Platonists show a general tendency to confine the object of the human intellect to essences, whereas the profound tendency of St. Thomas's philosophy leads the intellect and therefore philosophy and metaphysics, not only to essences but to existence itself ... It is in the second operation of the mind, in the judgement, by composition and division, that the speculative intellect grasps being, not only from the standpoint of essence but from that of existence itself, actual or possible." For clarifications, see especially Rosa Vargas, *Thomas Aquinas on the Apprehension of Being: The Role of Judgment in Light of 13th C. Semantics* (PhD diss., Marquette University, 2013).

28. See Gilson, *Elements of Christian Philosophy*, 121, 127, 133–36; Fabro, *Partecipazione e causalità*, 221 [252], where the conclusion would also follow from statements on 25 (35), 66 (83), and 203 [267] to the effect that essence is limited, and that *esse* can be without essence. For a correction, see Cornelio Fabro, "La determinazione dell'atto nella metafisica tomistica," in his *Esegesi tomistica* (Rome: Libreria Editrice della Pontificia Università Lateranese, 1969), 329–50, at 331n4 and 335. Although form is said to be finite at the transcendental level (at 350), "transcendental" probably refers to *esse*/essence discourse regarding creatures. Given that Fabro strongly accepts "essence realism," "existentialism" should not be seen as the inspiration of his early or foundational work; see notes 10 and 26–27 above, as well as at note 39 below.

29. References could be multiplied; see Frederick Wilhelmsen, "A Note: The Absolute Consideration of Nature in *Quaestiones Quodlibetales*, VIII," *The New Scholasticism* 57 (1983): 352–61, at 353–54.

30. See the position ascribed to Fabro, that in itself essence has no similitude to and does not participate in the divine, but only insofar as it is actualized by *esse*; Alain Contat, "*Esse, essentia, ordo*. Verso una metafisica della partecipazione operativa," *Espíritu* 61 (2012): 9–71, at 18–19.

31. Joseph Owens, *Saint Thomas and the Future of Metaphysics*, Aquinas Lecture 22 (Milwaukee, Wis.: Marquette University Press, 1957), 43–45; emphasis added. There is some rhetoric in this lecture. But it is odd to hold that concrete predicates are unknown. Thomas appeals to such predicates with good reason in *De ente*, c. 3, to explicate essence absolutely considered,

Elsewhere Owens sums up the point: "The only being of the essence is existence."[32] As a result, Paul Spade, the eminent logician and Toronto-trained Ockham scholar, in presenting Joseph Owens's view, uses it to ascribe to Aquinas essence-nominalism:

---

according to the pre-modist semantic tag that predicates are taken only formally, whereas subjects are taken together with what they "suppose for" (e.g., Aquinas, *ST* I, q. 13, a. 12, co.). It would follow that no definition predicated of its general *definiendum* is known. Perhaps Owens has in mind his striking claim elsewhere: the fact that essence absolutely considered is neither one nor many (neither universal nor particular) stems from the fact that it is not a being and so not subject to the principle of noncontradiction: no being can both be F and not-F, but the essence can be either, he says. See Joseph Owens, "Thomistic Common Nature and Platonic Idea," *Mediaeval Studies* 21 (1959): 211–23, at 220: "The common nature for St. Thomas contains within its own self no being whatsoever . . . In this way it escapes the application of the first principle of being, the principle of noncontradiction." It is no wonder that essence becomes unintelligible: anything true of it would also be false. Nevertheless, Thomas says that essence is neither one nor not-one, not that essence is or can be both one and not one in the same respect. *De ente*, c. 3, does not exclude from essence in itself what belongs to its *ratio* or *intellectus*, such as, in the case of "human," rational, animal, a being, a thing, or one in kind (the latter three are "transcendent" properties of all things); but it expressly excludes unity in the sense of "community" (a one-in-many sameness-relation) that belongs to the notion of "universal" as such (Leon. 43.374–75:73–82, 85–87, 113–19); as well as numeral unity, such as belongs to an individual substance in reality or to a universal concept existing in an individual human intellect (374–75:32–45, 52–53, 56–67, 105–12). Thomas does not deny of an essence such as *human* the transcendental property of being "undivided in itself" or formally one. If we think of unity as an analogous term, we need not think of these two senses of unity as simply "greater" and "less" one. By contrast, Owens holds that "in an absolute sense there can be a unity of essence only where there is one existential act," and concludes: "The essence just in itself is merely a consideration, not a being"; Joseph Owens, "Unity and Essence in St. Thomas Aquinas," *Mediaeval Studies* 23 (1961): 240–59, at 245 and 247.

32. Joseph Owens, *An Elementary Christian Metaphysics* (Milwaukee, Wis.: Bruce, 1963), 134n8. Owens explains (133n5): "The utter novelty of St. Thomas' doctrine that essence is wholly devoid of being and is made to be by an existential act other than itself, has been expressed by a modern writer as follows: 'Aquinas invented a new kind of nonexistent and a third use or meaning of "being." The new nonexistents are called natures.'" Owens cites, as the source, Gustav Bergmann, *Meaning and Existence* (Madison: University of Wisconsin Press, 1960), 192. In addition to the argument from the principle of noncontradiction (see previous note), Owens apparently offers a second argument for essence as nonbeing from the fact that, in thirteenth-century early modist semantics, subject and predicate in affirmations about the world are one in the supposit: Socrates is risible because "risible" signifies a formality that Socrates already has (again, see Aquinas, *ST* I, q. 13, a. 12, co.). If the predicate had its own being (i.e., existence), argues Owens, then no identity would be possible; Joseph Owens, "Common Nature: A Point of Comparison between Thomistic and Scotistic Metaphysics," *Mediaeval Studies* 19 (1957): 1–14, at 6 and 13. Nevertheless, I suggest, predicational identity is saved by the formal consideration of the predicate, and does not require a unique Thomistic doctrine of *esse*. Elsewhere Owens makes the predicate existential by reason of the copula, and he admits the absence of perfect identity between subject and predicate (except in the case of God); Owens, *Saint Thomas and the Future of Metaphysics*, 53–54.

The only kind of being a thing has is its act of existing, its *esse*[33] ... Humanity, then, does not exist ... The common nature ... does not exist ... since it excludes *esse* ... There is nothing answering to the nature so taken.... Nothing at all! So it looks as if Aquinas is heading straight for nominalism. *There is nothing out there that is really common.*[34]

Now, of course, it is correct that essence in itself does not exist. Accordingly, Aquinas's *On the Eternity of the World* says that were a thing left to itself, without divine efficient causality, it would be nothing; so,

---

33. Spade presents Owens's famous paper, which states, "the nature absolutely considered abstracts from all being whatsoever," and concludes: "For St. Thomas, a finite essence just in itself has no being or entity whatsoever." Owens, "Common Nature," 5 and 13. If one wants to avoid the consequence that essence is merely negative, one could appeal here to the doctrine that *ens* and even *esse* are said in many senses. When (as in most contexts) the predication of *ens* emphasizes the *id quod* in its descriptive formula *id quod est*, it is a transcendental term and an essential predicate of any positive subject; whereas when, as sometimes occurs, it emphasizes *est*, it is an accidental predicate said truly only of those things that actually are. See in addition to texts cited in note 60 below: Aquinas, *In Peri herm.* I.5 (Leon. 1*/1.31:363–76); *Quod.* 2.2.1, co. (Leon. 25/1.215:55–72); *De ente*, c. 1 (Leon. 43.369:18–26); Ralph McInerny, "Being and Predication," in *Being and Predication: Thomistic Interpretations* (Washington, DC: The Catholic University of America Press, 1986), 173–228. Similarly, *esse* sometimes signifies not the act of being but the essence, or what it is to be a thing, *quid est esse*; see Aquinas, *In Sent.* I, d. 33, q. 1, a. 1, ad 1 (Mandonnet 766). Thus, essence taken "with precision" can be said to signify the *esse* or *quod quid erat esse* of a thing; and essence taken "without prescinding" as "essence absolutely considered" is a being (*ens*) as an essential predicate. *Human* is necessarily an *ens*, in this sense (not in the sense of an "existent"), as well as an essence and a "thing." Owens's phrasing arises from the fact that he frequently uses "being" almost as a univocal term for "existent."

34. Paul Spade, *A Survey of Mediaeval Philosophy (Course in a Box)* 2.0 (1985), chap. 57, 7–13; available at http://www.pvspade.com/Logic/docs/The%20Course%20in%20the%20Box%20Version%202_0.pdf. Spade's reading of Owens is incorrect: for Owens, essences do have existence in individual existing things, as even Spade's Aquinas affirms (12). Spade's intent, however, is to charge Owens and Aquinas with inconsistencies. Owens, in fact, disagrees with the radical "existentialist" claims of Gerald Phelan, Norris Clarke, and William Carlo, namely, in Clarke's words, that essence, rather than being something "heavy" or "solid," "must be understood ... as a negating principle which contains nothing positive of its own at all (though always attached to a positive [that is, its act of being]) but performs the sole function of limiting from within the act of *esse*." Norris Clarke, "Preface," viii, in William Carlo, *The Ultimate Reducibility of Essence to Existence in Existential Metaphysics* (The Hague: Martinus Nijhoff, 1966). Owens argues with great insight: "to speak of the limiting function of essence as though it were apparently negative in character ... would amount to conceiving the being [*esse*] of creatures as a 'what,' a quiddity, and making it the 'what is.' Rather, ... what properly constitutes the limitation of being in every case is the positive content of these essences. In being positively what it is, a stone or a tree or any other finite thing limits that very being.... There can hardly be any question, then, of conceiving the being of creatures as a nature which is made to stop at the definite limits already set up by the finite essence. Rather, the only nature there is the finite quiddity, which is always other than its being, and with which it forms but one reality. Because it is a tree or a stone or some other positive finite nature, its being is the being of that restricted nature and of nothing else." Owens, *Saint Thomas and the Future of Metaphysics*, 69–71n23.

only because of the first cause does *esse* belong to the universe "after" it was "first" nothing—first not in time, but in the order of nature.[35] Still, it is not correct to infer that for Aquinas there is nothing "out there" that is really common, that there is nothing "answering to" essence in itself, and that Aquinas, unlike Scotus, is an essence nominalist. As I have shown, Aquinas argues that essences are real components of individuals, *in which* and *through which* such individuals have *esse*, according to the formula of the *De ente*.[36] He appears to be playing with the etymology of *esse-ntia*: perhaps, in English, essence is their "to be-ship."[37] Essence in creatures, accordingly, determines, limits, or participates their *esse* such that it be the *esse* of a given essence "F." For Thomas, essence is the formal cause of *esse*, Dewan has reminded us.[38]

In sum, as we have attended to Aquinas's distinctive account of *esse* as act of being perhaps we have forgotten essence, thereby losing sight of the semantic and ontological grounds that make Aquinas's account reasonable and required. Fabro himself, in an important concluding moment, has intuited the point. One cannot speak of a real distinction, he writes, if one of the terms is missing the character of reality.[39] In fact, in the same work he observes that the ten categories must share the essence-*esse* real distinction and therefore be diversified only by their different modes of being. For this reason, both Avicenna and Aquinas offer the Genus Argument in proof of the real distinction. Far from being guilty of exaggerated realism, the argument is most valid once seen against its principles.[40]

---

35. Aquinas, *De aet. mun.* (Leon. 43.88:189–208). See also *De pot.*, q. 2, a. 1, obj. 11 and 25.
36. Aquinas, *De ente*, c. 1 (Leon. 43.370:50–52).
37. See also Aquinas, *In Sent.* I, d. 23, q. 1, a. 1, co., quoted below in note 57.
38. Lawrence Dewan, "St. Thomas, Metaphysical Procedure, and the Formal Cause," *The New Scholasticism* 63 (1989): 173–82, at 174, 177, 180n22. Dewan usually speaks of *form* as the principle or cause of *esse*; but see Dewan, "St. Thomas, Metaphysics, and Formal Causality," *Laval théologique et philosophique* 36 (1980): 285–316, at 295–96 and 310–14. If Dewan is correct, we must qualify the description of *esse* as having "absolute priority over essence" by adding "within its own order"; Owens, *Saint Thomas and the Future of Metaphysics*, 37 and 45. Aquinas famously says that "nothing is more intimate to a thing than its *esse*," *not* that nothing is more intimate to a thing's *esse* than its essence; see *ST* I, q. 8, a. 1, co.
39. Fabro addresses the Neo-Suárezian retranslation of the essence-*esse* distinction as essence possible versus essence realized: "Ma perchè San Tommaso non concepisce la distinzione in questione come una distinzione fra la essenza 'in statu possibilitatis' e la essenza realizzata? Per la ragione anzitutto che in tal caso non si può parlare di distinzione reale, mancando ad uno dei termini il carattere di realtà." Fabro, "Neotomismo e Neosuarezismo," 498.
40. "Ricondotto ai suoi principi, l'argomento è validissimo"; Fabro, "Neotomismo e

A DIALECTICAL ARGUMENT FOR PREMISE (1′) ON ESSENCE REALISM

So far I have presented Aquinas's proof of the essence-supposit real distinction, and I have used it to defend his proofs of the famous essence-*esse* real distinction. But my entire argument hinges on one's acceptance of this Premise (1′) for essence realism: "Two different substances that are the same in kind must have something in them that makes them the same—by which we name them and know them."

There is no proof of this premise—and very little direct, positive discussion—in all of classical philosophy. In a sense, the premise is simply an expression of the "semantic triangle" common to mainstream classical thought prior to Ockham. The three vertices of the "triangle" are: (1) language, (2) concepts in minds, and (3) world. As Aristotle puts it in *De interpretatione* 1: words are signs or symbols of what is in the intellect (especially universals), which is impressed in us as a likeness of reality. Plato has the same triangle, but his one-over-the-many argument, recorded in Aristotle's *De ideis*,[41] places the sameness not in this world, but in a separate world. So how do we know that the ultimate grounds of sameness, namely, essence, is in things in *this* world, not in a separate world, and not merely in language, as for Ockham's nominalism?

Albert the Great calls a premise very like Premise (1′) a *"per se* known." So, let us agree that accounting for sameness and difference in things through an intrinsic principle is close to a primary axiom. How does one defend *per se* known principles? By assuming the contradictory,

---

Neosuarezismo," 473. How would early Fabro develop this insight? If the "Genus Argument" depends on the essence-*esse* real distinction, it is circular. Or, does he perhaps refer to the claim (above, note 17) that, as in *De ente*, c. 4, the "logical argument" depends on the "metaphysical argument"? The answer is, yes, if *ricondotto* refers, as it appears, to his immediately previous "theoretical analysis," that is, to one of the best presentations in his writings of the "God-to-creatures" "Participation Argument" for the "real distinction" (471). For alternate reading, see the forthcoming work of Nathaniel Taylor, *The Argument for the Real Distinction between Being and Essence from the Categories: Avicenna, Aquinas and the Greek Background*, which is inspired by seeing the genera of the "Genus Argument" as the metaphysical categories rather than as mere logical classes. In short, the "Genus Argument" is a metaphysical, not a logical, argument. It should rather be named the "Categories Argument," just as the "*Intellectus Essentiae* Argument" might be renamed the "Essence-Realism Argument." See Twetten, "How Save Aquinas' *'Intellectus essentiae'* Argument."

41. See Gail Fine, *On Ideas: Aristotle's Criticism of Plato's Theory of Forms* (Oxford: Oxford University Press, 1993), chap. 8.

and testing for absurdity. Aquinas does not worry about the premise, but we must, given Ockham's success in making the ontological simplicity of nominalism appealing (especially against the background of our already highly complex scientific world). So, let us take nominalism as the claim denying Premise (1′) and maintaining that everything in reality is through and through individual, and that commonness is only the result of the mind's way of "taking" individuals, or a mere property of language.

Ockham's principal target is Scotus, and his nominalism can sound deceptively close to Aristotle and Aquinas insofar as both hold (with Scotus) that universals are only in the mind, and that only individuals exist. Yet, as I have argued, Aquinas follows Avicenna's realism about essences: there is a really distinct "region of intelligibility" within individuals that is common to Socrates and Diotima. Individuals are not bare particulars or blobs, lacking any "conceptual content" or "property-determined structure" within them.

So, what is the problem with nominalism? My line of attack is to think of much of the subsequent history of philosophy as testing the denial of Premise (1′). Ockham is no skeptic, but as Gyula Klima observes, his new semantics alters the "semantic triangle" by thinning the "*world→mind*" "line" that is at the triangle's base, by stripping epistemology of all formal causality.[42] What happens if efficient causality alone connects mind to world? Individuals become mere stimulants for the mind's operation in taking sets of individuals together as similar. We may have good "externalist" grounds for thinking that the mind can do this successfully, as long as our mental powers are working well. But the *nominalist* triangle is systematically vulnerable to demon skepticism, as Klima has brought out and Buridan had already seen in roughly 1350.[43] An omnipotent God could place the ideas in our minds without the "prompts." What prevents

---

42. Gyula Klima, "Ontological Alternatives vs. Alternative Semantics in Medieval Philosophy," *S: European Journal for Semiotic Studies* 3, no. 4 (1991): 587–618, at 602, 605–6, 608; Gyula Klima, "Tradition and Innovation in Medieval Theories of Mental Representation," *Proceedings of the Society for Medieval Logic and Metaphysics* 4 (2004): 4–11, at 6–10.

43. Gyula Klima, "The Demonic Temptations of Medieval Nominalism: Mental Representation and 'Demon Skepticism,'" *Proceedings of the Society for Medieval Logic and Metaphysics* 4 (2004): 37–44; Klima, "The Anti-Skepticism of John Buridan and Thomas Aquinas: Putting Skeptics in Their Place vs. Stopping Them in Their Tracks," in *Rethinking the History of Skepticism*, ed. Henrik Lagerlund (Leiden: Brill, 2010), 145–70; Klima, "Thought-Transplants, Demons, and Modalities," in *The Language of Thought in Late Medieval Philosophy: Essays in Honor of Claude Panaccio*, ed. Jenny Pelletier and Magali Roques (Dordrecht: Springer, 2017), 369–81.

an evil genius from doing the same? The question becomes an important one for the great anti-skeptic Descartes, after he adopts Galileo's "real" revolution, the claim that all perceptible qualities are only in the mind.[44] How can we be sure that invisible, inaudible, intangible, imperceivable quantitatively extended bodies are stimulating our mind, and that they are not merely the products of our mind?

My interest is not to rehearse the major "moves" of modern philosophy but to remind us that that tradition does not get started without the nominalist rejection of real essences. If "knowing" by definition signifies an extra-mental form or essence's coming to be in the cognitive power, then the specialized form of skepticism that is "demonic" is not tenable.[45] By contrast, the common starting point of contemporary philosophy is the rejection of Cartesian rationalism—without a return to the classical "semantic triangle." A typical single-author introductory text to contemporary analytic philosophy of language begins by making trouble for Locke, as if for him the classical triangle has mainly become a "language→mind semantic line": words are signs of each one's private ideas so that each can communicate one's thoughts to other minds.[46] Remember that it is anti-psychologism that motivates key starting points in Frege's semantics. Just as he rejects Mill's empiricism as irrelevant to arithmetic, so he objectifies Concepts (with a capital C), Senses (with a capital S), and Thoughts (with a capital T), making them publicly available in a "third realm" reminiscent of Plato. So, in the *Foundations of Arithmetic* (1884), Frege writes (or shouts):

> Arithmetic has nothing at all to do with sensations. Just as little has it to do with mental images, compounded from the traces of earlier sense impressions. . . . A proposition just as little ceases to be true when I am no longer

---

44. Galileo, *Il Saggiatore*, ed. Ottavio Besomi and Mario Helbing (Rome: Antenore, 2005), 284–85.

45. See Klima's "The Demonic Temptations of Medieval Nominalism," 44; "Intentional Transfer in Averroes, Indifference of Nature in Avicenna, and the Representationalism of Aquinas," *Proceedings of the Society for Medieval Logic and Metaphysics* 5 (2005): 33–37, at 35–36; "The Anti-Skepticism of John Buridan," 162–68; and "Is Ockham off the Hook?," available at http://www.fordham.edu/gsas/phil/klima/index.htm.

46. Michael Morris, *An Introduction to the Philosophy of Language* (Cambridge: Cambridge University, 2006), chap. 1. Especially valuable on Locke are the observations of Claude Panaccio, "Ockham and Locke on Mental Language," in *The Medieval Heritage in Early Modern Metaphysics and Modal Theory, 1400–1700*, ed. Russell Friedman and Lauge Nielsen (Dordrecht: Springer, 2003), 37–51.

thinking of it as the Sun is extinguished when I close my eyes. Otherwise we would end up finding it necessary to take account of the phosphorous content of our brain in proving Pythagoras' theorem.[47]

We cannot mistake the tenor of *Der Gedanke* (1918):

> Is a thought an idea? If other people can assent to the thought I express in the Pythagorean theorem just as I do, then it does not belong to the content of my consciousness, I am not its owner . . . [otherwise] we should not really say 'the Pythagorean theorem,' but 'my Pythagorean theorem,' 'his Pythagorean theorem,' and these would be different. . . . Could the sense of my Pythagorean theorem be true and the sense of his false? I said that the word 'red' was applicable only in the sphere of my consciousness if it was not meant to state a property of things but to characterize some of my own sense impressions. Therefore the words 'true' and 'false,' as I understand them, might also be applicable only in the realm of my consciousness, if they were not meant to apply to something of which I was not the owner.[48]

It is worth recalling that the founders of analytic philosophy, Frege, Moore, and early Russell, were realists about color (at least Frege) and realists about universals. Their foundational move was to replace the "language→mind semantic line" with a "language→world semantic line," "hooking up" language directly to reality, as we say. The reality corresponding to Frege's Thoughts is in Russell the Platonic realm of facts.[49] Facts, or the anti-empiricists' "propositions" are "part of the furniture of the universe."

Contemporary philosophers often do not attend to the "linguistic turn" and to the semantic commitments that regularly accompany the learning of elementary quantificational logic. The original vision of Frege fits first with a sort of Platonic realism. Frege's concept-script replaces both subject and predicate of Aristotelian logic with mini-propositions or, better, functions. The student of predicate logic is taught to isolate the conceptual content, indicated by upper-case symbols F & G, which refer to, or "hook up to," on Frege's account, an objective third realm. Conceptual contents are divided from apparently content-less individuals, (bare?) particulars in this world, to which lower-case symbols a, b,

---

47. Frege, *Foundations of Arithmetic* (1884), *The Frege Reader*, trans. Beaney, 87–88.
48. Frege, "The Thought" (1918), trans. Geach, in *The Frege Reader* (1997), 336.
49. Bertrand Russell, *Philosophy of Logical Atomism* (1918), chap. 1, in *Logic and Knowledge*, ed. R. C. Marsh (London: Allen & Unwin, 1956).

or c refer.⁵⁰ The proposition is like a mathematical function in which a and b are processed by concept-functions, truth-value-functions, and quantifier-functions. The logic has the rigor of math and serves well the purpose of mathematical proof. The jury is still out as to how well it serves metaphysics. Again, the most natural fit is with a modified Platonism, combined with a nominalist realism about this world. In Russell's logical atomism, the nominalist foundation consists of individual sense data, whereas Wittgenstein's Tractarianism reduces out universals altogether, replacing them with individual windowless monads in concatenations forming states of affairs.

Such thin metaphysical speculations were simply red flags, inviting elimination by the logical empiricists in the name of simplicity and science. If Quine's "On Two Dogmas" criticizes Carnap's project, it also marks the beginning of a much more radical nominalism that seeks to eliminate all meanings or intensions as but a "creature of the dark." The mark of classic texts is that they always reward rereading. So, let us examine again this famous passage from "On Two Dogmas":

> The Aristotelian notion of essence was the forerunner, no doubt, of the modern notion of intension or meaning. For Aristotle it was essential in men to be rational, accidental to be two-legged. But there is an important difference between this attitude and the doctrine of meaning. From the latter point of view it may indeed be conceded (if only for the sake of argument) that rationality is involved in the meaning of the word 'man' while two-leggedness is not; but two-leggedness may at the same time be viewed as involved in the meaning of 'biped' while rationality is not. Thus from the point of view of the doctrine of meaning it makes no sense to say of the actual individual, who is at once a man and a biped, that his rationality is essential and his two-leggedness accidental or vice versa. Things had essences, for Aristotle, but only linguistic forms have meanings. Meaning is what essence becomes when it is divorced from the object of reference and wedded to the word.⁵¹

Quine goes on to say that once meaning is so divorced, "it is a short step to recognizing as the business of the theory of meaning simply the synonymy of linguistic forms [behavioristically determined] and the

---

50. For discussion see Gregory McCulloch, *The Game of the Name: Introducing Logic, Language and Mind* (Oxford: Clarendon Press, 1989), 4–22; Arthur Sullivan, "Introduction," 37–65, in *Logicism and the Philosophy of Language: Selections from Frege and Russell*, ed. Arthur Sullivan (Toronto: Broadview Press, 2003).

51. Quine, "On Two Dogmas" (1951), sect. 1.

analyticity of statements; meanings themselves, as obscure intermediary entities, may well be abandoned." Notice that for Quine, "meanings ain't in the head," as for Putnam and conceptualist moderns like Locke (see Lockean universal "essences"). Rather, since Frege, they have been detached from individual objects, where Aristotle had placed them, and are attached rather to linguistic forms as functions related in a nonessential way to individuals. Human beings, featured in the language of "ordinary physical objects," are just as mythical, for Quine, as the Greek gods; meaning belongs properly to entire theories, each of which is "underdetermined" by the empirical data. Quine subsequently launches an attack on these meanings, reducing "intensions" to "extensions," and meaning to behavior. According to Quine's own account of the position arrived at in *Word and Object* (1960), "there is nothing in linguistic meaning, then, beyond what is to be gleaned from overt behavior in overt circumstances."[52] And, Quine accepts the consequences of understanding language in radically behavioristic terms: we all stand before each other, and even before our temporally prior selves, as the field translator who writes "rabbit" in his translation manual when the native cries "Gavagai." But we cannot be sure that the *stimulus meaning* would not be better translated as "undetached rabbit parts," or the "fusion" of all individual rabbits, "that single discontinuous portion of the spatiotemporal world that consists of rabbits"; or "the Holy Spirit which lives in rabbits"; or the anti-rabbit "rabbit hollow": the entire world except where the rabbit is. Every interpretation is underdetermined by the evidence at hand. "Sameness of meaning is sameness of use," judged behavioristically.[53]

Just as Frege's Platonism was a red flag for Carnap's logical empiricism, so Quine's nominalism was an invitation to Kripke to develop a "possible worlds essentialism" in the 1970s. The intuition behind Putnam's "Twin Earth" thought experiment indicates whether you are an empiricist or a metaphysician at heart. Imagine another world exactly like our world, with the same history, except that water, a clear, potable liquid, is made up not of H2O but of a highly complex formula unknown to us, which we may summarize as "XYZ." The question is: in 1789, well

52. Willard Van Orman Quine, "Indeterminacy of Translation Again," *Journal of Philosophy* 84 (1987): 5–10, at 5.
53. Willard Van Orman Quine, "Use and its Place in Meaning," *Erkenntnis* 13 (1978): 1–8, at 2.

before the discovery of the atomic table and of H2O, when someone on Twin Earth *refers* to "water," is she referring to the same thing as we on Earth when we use the same word? There is sameness of one's psychological state in relation to "water" across Earth and Twin Earth, but does "water" have the same *meaning* in both places? Michael Morris, author of the outstanding *An Introduction to the Philosophy of Language* textbook (2006), cannot make sense of Putnam's example, as Morris's intuition is that both would still be water (regardless of their various contents). By contrast, Putnam himself originally proclaimed that "meanings ain't just in the head," agreeing with Kripke that if this table had been made out of ice (without anyone's being able to discern a difference), it nonetheless would not be the same table as this, despite its "spatio-temporal" overlap. It's essential to a given table to be made of wood, just as for the pages of this chapter, in the hard copy version to be made of cellulose, that is, $C_6H_{10}O_5$. Putnam may have come to realize that he was defending an Aristotelian view. He subsequently self-identified as a Neo-Kantian.

Fregean semantics continues to control the range of our contemporary metaphysical choices, and Kripke himself has not taken great interest in developing the metaphysical side of his essentialism, even if he remains committed to it. Nevertheless, our options have greatly expanded since Quine's "On Two Dogmas." Let us review for a moment the surprising history of contemporary metaphysics. In the 1950s A. J. Ayer, having given up on logical positivism, affirmed a "bundle theory" of objects: ordinary things are nothing but bundles of real, individual properties, including colors. Equally shocking is the adoption and defense of a realist view of universals since the 1950s by Vienna Circle member Gustav Bergmann. The first theory of choice for metaphysical realists à la Bergmann is a "substrate theory," in which universals are layer-caked over bare particulars that "individuate" them. "Substrate theory" avoids the well-known problem with "bundles," conceived of as mere sets: what individuates each bundle is simply the co-presence of all its properties, so that *any* change in one property yields a brand new individual; the items in any set belong to the set necessarily and eternally. If so, a criminal would appear to have a legitimate argument before the court: "I am not the same individual I was, but a new and different set." The judge's response is weak: "you are so similar to that other person that you are guilty." In "substrate theory," by contrast, the substrate, rather than the (set of) properties, individuates. Thus, the two former logical positivists, Ayer and Bergmann, in the end abandoned every sort of austere nominalist "blob theory," of which David Lewis's "possible worlds nominalism" is perhaps the best example: ordinary objects are in themselves mere unintelligible blobs, lacking any structure; no two blobs are the same (including across possible worlds), even though they are grouped together in our language. The fact that blobs are individuated also from moment to moment in time has helped to encourage "space-time 4-dimensionalism": Olympic speed-skater Eric Heiden is really two different aggregates or "space-time worms," summer, "cycling Eric" and winter, "skating Eric." Arguably, only one of the two individual Erics really won the Olympic medal.

What motivates Bergmann, David Armstrong, and other anti-blob realists is the problem that they see with all nominalisms. It seems that there is a possible world in which only two creatures exist: two motionless red, steel spheres exactly alike. On this hypothesis, their shape seems to be, not "exactly" similar, constituted by two—as nominalists sometimes say, "perfectly similar," but individual, "shape tropes"—as for "trope nominalism." Instead, the realist insists, the spheres can be hypothesized to be the *same* shape; whereas two things "exactly" or "perfectly similar" must involve difference, or else they are, not similar, but "the same." On the other hand, bare particular substrates purportedly allow two identical bundles (as in the steel spheres) to be individuated distinctly from each other. What is puzzling, then, is the relation between the essence-less/property-less substrate and the universals bundled into them; is it an essential or an accidental relation? If, for one bare particular *a*, another contentless bare particular *b* were "substituted in" so as to be the substrate of the same universals, would the result be the same ordinary object? If not, why not?

So far in this section I have been letting the history of philosophy play its role as the philosopher's laboratory, providing a sort of *reductio* argument against the rejection of essences as grounds of sameness in things. Let me summarize. The accidental relation between the mind and world of the idealist moderns, a relation made possible by Ockham, is overcome if one accepts Frege's realism: there results a direct relation (a "language→world semantic line") between an ideal, scientific, symbolic "language" and a Platonic realm of Concepts and Thoughts with a capital C and T.[54] True Thoughts are, in the paradigm case, descriptions of individuals in this world, individuals that instantiate Concepts. This position itself has difficulties, and the rejection of the Platonic element leads to other difficulties. I have also suggested that Kripke's essentialism gives grounds for affirming again essences in extra-mental individual things. The sameness and individuation in things keeps reemerging and blocking the various attractive simplifications of nominalism from declaring a definitive victory.

The founders of the U.S. say: "We hold these truths to be self-evident... that all blobs drawn together under the set of things labeled 'human' are equal." But which declaration would have freed the African slaves? "That all contentless substrata that exemplify the publicly available conceptual content 'human' are equal"? or "That all human beings, as having the same human essence, are equal"? I suggest that Aquinas's Avicennian account of essence, which makes essence a formal part really distinct from the whole, is at least not more bizarre than the theories that must be taken seriously in the recent "rebirth of metaphysics" of the twenty-first century. What is more unreasonable? That we have no knowledge regarding whether an extra-mental world exists (early Hume), or what it is (Kant)? Or that such knowledge requires affirming a separate additional world that grounds it (Frege, Russell)? Or that the affirmation of all conventional things in this world makes them as mythical as the Greek gods (Quine)? Or that there are in individual things with non-universal "conceptual contents" that ground our knowledge and our language? Essence realism is surely no less plausible than the alternatives, given that some theory must ground our knowledge and our language.

A PROOF OF GOD'S EXISTENCE THAT "ONLY A METAPHYSICIAN COULD LOVE"

In the last section of this chapter I return to the beginning and to the grand project of connecting the world to the first cause through the doctrine of being. The real distinction between essence and *esse* has been

---

54. Frege, of course, thinks there is a mind. But the mind seems to drop out once symbols are assigned: even computer language hooks up to the world. We sometimes overlook the mental training that lies behind the assigning of symbols in predicate logic.

said to be the fundamental truth of Christian philosophy, which, once in hand, enables us to finish the project. It certainly appears that Aquinas gives an argument such as the following in *De ente*, c. 4: if Obama actually is, he cannot have caused himself to be actually, so he must be caused by something else that, if its *esse* is really distinct from its essence, must itself receive its *esse* from another, and so on, ad infinitum. If this causal regress is impossible, there must be a first cause whose essence is *esse* itself.

I have been teaching this argument for years without giving a very persuasive solution to a worry that, I submit, is among the reasons that Aquinas never rehearses this argument in works subsequent to the *De ente*. As Dewan has decisively shown,[55] creatures are contingent, not because they need a creator to keep *creating* them at each moment, or because they are constantly lapsing into nonexistence, and thus need a conserver. I add: they are contingent in the sense that their essence, considered in itself, lacks *esse*. Once they actually are, granting primary causes, they can cease to be, for Aquinas, only if they contain matter that can lose form (unlike the matter of the heavenly bodies). *Esse* is, for Thomas, a quasi-necessary consequent of an existing thing's essence, which, though other than it, a thing is at no risk of losing, given primary causes.[56] *Esse* is the very act of the essence by which the individual

---

55. Dewan, *St. Thomas and Form as Something Divine in Things*, Aquinas Lecture 71 (Milwaukee, WI: Marquette University Press, 2007). See also Fabro, "Il fondamento metafisico," 69.

56. The most important text is perhaps Aquinas, *Q. de an.* 14, co. (Leon. 24/1.125–26:165–85), on the everlasting perdurance of the human soul: *esse per se consequitur formam*. For recognition of the doctrine, see, for example, Owens, *Saint Thomas and the Future of Metaphysics*, 44–45, who accordingly speaks of *esse* as essential rather than "accidental," and interprets the causal order as one of formal rather than efficient causality. See also Étienne Gilson, *Being and Some Philosophers*, 2nd ed. (Toronto: Pontifical Institute of Mediaeval Studies, 1952), 171–72 and 174. Owens, of course, also emphasizes the accidentality of *esse*, and that *esse* belongs to the efficient as opposed to the formal order of causality. I would follow Dewan's lead in seeing *esse* as an effect of form and essence in the order of formal causality *under the efficient causality* of primary causes; see Lawrence Dewan, "The Individual as a Mode of Being according to Thomas Aquinas," *The Thomist* 63 (1999): 403–24, at 406–8, and "Discussion on Anthony Kenny's Aquinas on Being," *Nova et Vetera* 3, no. 2 (2005): 335–400, at 341–42. Thus, Dewan emphasizes that *esse* should not be called a principle or co-principle within things, but an effect of form: under efficient causality, I add. God is the first efficient cause of the *esse* of things through form. See Lawrence Dewan, "Étienne Gilson and the *Actus Essendi*," *Études Maritainiennes/Maritain Studies* 15 (1999): 70–96, at 94–96. Dewan, moreover, uses *De pot.*, q. 5, a. 4, ad 3, to argue that *esse* is even more united to, more intimate to a substance's essence than is a necessary property, for *esse* belongs to the genus of substance as its very act. See Dewan, "St. Thomas, Metaphysical Procedure," 176n14 and 182. See also Aquinas, *In Meta.* IV.2, n. 558 (Marietti

substance *is*, we may say.⁵⁷ It follows *per se* upon substantial form, just as also do a thing's natural motions or actions. The character of *esse* as a quasi-necessary consequent, as opposed to an accident, is essential to Aquinas's argument for the immortality of the soul, for example. So, to argue from Obama's "actually being" to an *immediate* creator or conserver at each moment of his "actually being" is somewhat problematic. Obama at each moment is neither being created *ex nihilo* nor being preserved from lapsing into nonbeing. On the other hand, if the argument traces Obama to his parents, who are unnecessary for his current "actually being," the reasoning of the *De ente* faces a different sort of objection: Aquinas expressly denies that it is possible to disprove an infinite series in the temporal past, a so-called horizontal and *per accidens* ordered series, for example, of past billiard balls. Proofs for God's existence in Aquinas reject, instead, an infinite "vertical" series of *per se causes* on which change or "actually being," etc., right now depend in order to be. But it is hard to see how one could use the "real distinction" to mount such a proof.

I propose an alternative approach, which at least an "Aquinas enthusiast" will appreciate. The subject matter of metaphysics, says Thomas, is being *qua* being, *ens commune* or *ens universale*: being in general.⁵⁸ He also remarks that *ens commune* is created.⁵⁹ In fact, I observe, comparatively

---

155): "Esse enim rei quamvis sit aliud ab eius essentia, non tamen est intelligendum quod sit aliquod superadditum ad modum accidentis, sed quasi constituitur per principia essentiae."

57. See Aquinas, *In Sent*. I, d. 23, q. 1, a. 1, co. (Mandonnet 555.12–18): "Unde dico, quod « essentia » dicitur cujus actus est esse, « subsistentia » cujus actus est subsistere, « substantia » cujus actu est substare . . . Esse enim est actus alicujus . . . ut quo est, scilicet quo denominatur esse, sicut calefacere est actus caloris." Also, *In Sent*. I, d. 4, q. 1, a. 1, ad 2 (Mandonnet 132): "non potest essentia communicari alteri supposito, nisi secundum aliud esse, quod est actus essentiae in qua est."

58. For *ens universale*, see Aquinas, *ST* I, q. 78, a. 1, co. (Leon. 5.251a): "Sunt duo genera potentiarum, scilicet sensitivum . . . et intellectivum, respectu obiecti communissimi, quod est ens universale." Aquinas, *De ver.*, q. 21, a. 1, co. (Leon. 22/3.592:90–92, 593:124–28): "Non autem potest esse quod super ens universale aliquid addat aliquid primo modo [id est, quod addat aliquam rem quae sit extra essentiam illius rei cui dicitur addi]; . . . nulla enim res naturae est quae sit extra essentiam entis universalis."

59. *ST* I-II, q. 66, a. 5, ad 4 (Leon. 6.436b): "ens commune est proprius effectus causae altissimae, scilicet Dei." Aquinas, *In Meta.*, proem. (Marietti 2): "Unde oportet quod ad eamdem scientiam pertineat considerare substantias separatas, et ens commune, quod est genus, cuius sunt praedictae substantiae communes et universales causae." Therefore, for Aquinas, God is not part of *ens commune*, the subject of metaphysics, but enters into the discipline as a cause of the subject.

few beings are created *ex nihilo* individually, apart from the whole. These include: all immaterial beings, such as angels and human souls, the everlasting heavenly spheres (according to Aquinas's cosmology), and prime matter. So, how is it that being in general is created *ex nihilo*? I argue as follows:

1. Being in general (*ens universale*) signifies *primarily* the "essence of extra-mental things in general" under the notion (*ratio*) of its *act of being* (by contrast with "thing" or *res*, which, as a transcendental term, names "being in general" under the notion of essence). Thus, Aquinas writes: "[A being (*ens*)] in one sense signifies the essence of a thing that exists outside the soul."[60]

2. Given the proof of the essence-supposit real distinction (see the second section above), essence in general (*essentia universalis*; as in *In De div. nom.* 5.1, n. 610), as belonging to the subject of metaphysics, is really distinct from the *esse* of things in general (*esse universale*; see *ST* I, q. 105, a. 5, co.: "God himself is properly the cause of 'universal *esse*' in all things, which among all is the most interior to [those] things").[61]

3. Therefore, the being in general (*ens universale*), unless it causes itself, must receive its *esse* from something "beyond" or "other than" *ens universale*. However:

4. Nothing that is is beyond "being in general" except that whose very essence *is* being (*esse*), from which alone "being in general" can receive the act of being (proving this fact, says Thomas following Avicenna, is the "end" or goal of metaphysics).

5. Therefore, such a cause must actually be if "being in general" actually is.

This argument, not stated in Aquinas, is quite close to the reasoning of the Fourth Way, which uses, instead, Aristotle's principle that the first in

---

60. *In Sent.* II, d. 37, q. 1, a. 2, ad 3 (Mandonnet 947); "Uno modo [ens] significat essentiam rei extra animam existentis"; see *De ver.*, q. 1, a. 1, co. (Leon. 22/1.5: 137–39): "A being" (*ens*) is taken from the act of being (*actus essendi*), whereas the name "thing" expresses the quiddity or essence of "a being" (*ens sumitur ab actu essendi, sed nomen rei exprimit quidditatem vel essentiam entis*). See also note 34 above.

61. *In De div. nom.* 5.1, n. 610 (Marietti 232); *ST* I, q. 105, a. 5, co. (Leon. 4.476); "Ipse Deus est proprie causa ipsius esse universalis in rebus omnibus, quod inter omnia est magis intimum rebus."

any genus is the cause of all else in the genus.[62] The virtue of my argument is that it establishes a *per se* vertical series without availing itself (implicitly) of the eternal heavens as universal generative causes, as do many of Aquinas's best arguments. At the same time, as Thomas himself prefers, this argument does not rely on a temporal beginning of the universe.

It is true that this is the sort of argument that "only a metaphysician can love." Nevertheless, the cogency of its reasoning for a first cause of "being in general" (*ens universale*) lends further support to the proposal of this chapter, that the *foundation* of the "foundational principle of Aquinas's metaphysics" is the proof of the essence-supposit distinction and the dialectical argument for essence realism, that is, for sameness-grounding essences as "out there" in things and as really distinct from things as individual substances. Two items are the same in kind because they possess within them the same conceptual content, which is extra-mentally distinct from those things as a whole, and therefore from their very act of being (*esse*). This *prior* real distinction between essence and individual substance, I argue, allows us to link all such things immediately, without invoking an infinite regress, to the first cause of the *esse* of all *as a whole*.[63]

---

62. Several other arguments, less well known, provide even closer parallels: Aquinas, *Lectura super Ioannem*, prol., n. 5 (Marietti 2), and *De pot.*, q. 3, a. 5, co. (Marietti 49) (three arguments). See Jules Baisnée, "St. Thomas Aquinas's Proofs of the Existence of God Presented in Their Chronological Order," in *Philosophical Studies in Honor of the Very Reverend Ignatius Smith, O.P.*, ed. John K. Ryan (Westminster, MD: Newman Press, 1952), 29–64, at 64. Compare also the reasoning in *SCG* II, c. 15, nn. 1–6 (Marietti 123–24, nn. 922–26), and *ST* I, q. 44, a. 1, co., and q. 65, a. 1, co.

63. I am grateful to the Quinn family and Rev. R. Gabriel Pivarnik for hosting this talk as the Aquinas Lecture at Providence University in 2012. The paper was subsequently delivered in Italy and Spain, and it is the culmination of a line of thinking previously tested before audiences in New Orleans (2009) and New York (2011). I am grateful to Greg Doolan for important suggestions and gracious collegiality, to Mike Wreen and Nathaniel Taylor for comments on an early draft, to Paul Quesnel for research assistance, and to the indefatigable and trustworthy aid of John Lund and team. A rich historical awareness of the role of Avicennian metaphysics of the categories, a completion of Alexander of Aphrodisias's account of (common) nature, would make the ascription of essence nominalism to Aquinas, and therefore the perspective against which this chapter was composed, inconceivable.

APPENDIX: FABRO'S MATURE THOUGHT ON THE REAL DISTINCTION

Cornelio Fabro modified his defense of the real distinction in stages subsequent to *La nozione* of 1939. In 1941, Fabro presents Aquinas's texts as offering two fundamental arguments for the essence-*esse* real distinction, each "taken from the tradition": the logical argument, which can be fleshed out as either the "Genus" or the "*Intellectus essentiae*" Argument; and the metaphysical argument from separate perfection, which is best elaborated through participation.[64] In 1954 Fabro highlights the centrality of three moments of the "dialectic of participation" for Aquinas's metaphysics of created things, within which dialectic the argument through participation becomes for the mature Aquinas the exclusive way to demonstrate the "real distinction."[65] In *Partecipazione e causalità* (1960) Fabro denies that the real distinction is known through demonstration, and he usually speaks of an argument or demonstration only in reference to Aquinas's early Avicennian reasoning (which for Fabro is also found in the initial arguments of *SCG* II, c. 52).[66] Subsequent accounts rarely make mention of an "argument" or "demonstration" for the "real distinction."[67]

Perhaps the shift in Fabro's thinking results from something like the following dialectic. Subsequent to the presentations in 1941 through 1954 that use God-to-creatures reasoning,[68] Fabro sometimes sees that he does not need—and does not want—to base the "real distinction" on the essence-*esse* identity in God.[69] But it is not clear how the "Participation

---

64. Fabro, Neotomismo e Neosuarezismo, 471 and 497.

65. Fabro, "Sviluppo, significato e valore," 89–92.

66. Fabro, *Partecipazione e causalità*, 176, 612n20, 621 [French ed.: 216, 292n111, 305]; for a possible exception, see 55n94 [70n98].

67. The exceptions include (besides a chapter borrowed from the opening half of the "Conclusione" in *La nozione*): Fabro, Introduzione a S. Tommaso: La metafisica tomista e il pensiero moderno (Milan: Ares, 1983), 274 and 279; "Il fondamento metafisico della 'IV via,'" Doctor Communis 18 (1965): 49–70, at 68–69; "Existence," in *The New Catholic Encyclopedia* (Washington, DC: The Catholic University of America Press, 1966), 5:721–24, at 724; and "L'esse' tomistico e la ripresa della metafisica," Angelicum 3 (1967): 281–314, at 307 (where it is unclear what demonstration is intended).

68. See notes 8 and 16–17 above.

69. In fact, circular reasoning would have to be ascribed to Aquinas, *ST* I, q. 3, a. 4, co., as Contat, "Le figure," 237–38, astutely observes. See also Mario Pangallo, "L'itinerario metafisico di Cornelio Fabro," Euntes Docete 50 (1997): 7–31, at 19, and Ferraro, *L'atto di essere*, 89–93.

Argument" of *La nozione* (identified in note 8 above) can accomplish this result. After 1956, Fabro apparently treats the essence-*esse* real distinction as "*per se* known to the wise," the result, not merely of an intuition or experience, nor merely of judgment, but of a metaphysical reflection on an intensive, Parmenidean apprehension of *esse*—which was obscured by both Plato and Aristotle—which is open to the infinite, in contrast with essence as abstracted from creatures and therefore finite.[70] Consequently, the "Participation Argument" would be used to prove, not the "real distinction," but the fact that all participated beings are caused by an unparticipated First.[71]

The problem with Fabro's approach is that in order that it succeed, he must remove essence from the transcendental terms that are conceptually distinct from and found within primordial intensive *esse*.[72] Such *esse* is obviously really distinct from *finite* essence. But if essence is *not* a transcendental incorporated within intensive *esse* (which *esse* has

70. In addition to Fabro, *Partecipazione e causalità*, 229 and 238, and the quotation in note 8 above, see 63 [80]: "il metodo della metafisica tomistica non è nè intuitivo, nè dimostrativo, ma 'risolutivo'... Questa forma di 'passare' non è dimostrazione nè intuizione, ma potrebbe esser detta 'fondazione.'" For the dialectic, see Cornelio Fabro, "Notes pour la fondation métaphysique de l'être," *Revue Thomiste* 111 (2011), Hors-série: 113–39, at 114 (reprint of *Revue Thomiste* 2 [1966]: 214–37): "mais qu'est alors cet acte d'être, qui est un au-delà de l'essence et de l'existence, et cependant n'est pas Dieu? Il doit être, cet *esse*, l'acte de tout acte; mais comment le découvrons- nous? Par expérience ou par démonstration? Par expérience, nous connaissons le fait de l'existence (la nôtre et celle d'autrui); par démonstration, nous obtenons, par exemple, l'exigence de l'existence de Dieu; par réflexion ou abstraction, nous accédons aux essences des choses. D'après saint Thomas, l'esse comme *actus omnium actuum* est saisi, semble-t-il, non proprement par abstraction, ce qui vaut pour les essences, mais par 'réduction' ou résolution, ce qui est un passage d'acte à acte. D'où la centralité en thomisme de la distinction réelle d'essence et *esse* ... Il n'est pourtant pas facile de montrer le processus de cette 'résolution'; et saint Thomas semble n'aller guère au-delà d'un renvoi aux sources (Ex. 3, 14; Boèce, Denys, *De Causis* ...) ou de l'exigence théologique de concevoir Dieu comme Acte pur." From this "resolution" can immediately result the recognition of the participation of finite, potential essence in primordial, intensive *esse* as act of being; see Alain Contat, "Fabro et l'être intensif: Présentation historico-doctrinale," in Cornelio Fabro, *Participation et causalité* (Paris: Parole et Silence, 2015), xv–lxxx, at xxxiii and xxxvi.

71. See Alain Contat, "L'étant, l'*esse* et la participation selon Cornelio Fabro," *Revue Thomiste* 111 (2011): 357–402, at 383–86 and 394, where these two stages in the "resolution through participation" are, in effect, ably distinguished and laid out. See also the twofold mediated knowledge at Fabro, *Partecipazione e causalità*, 231.

72. Accordingly, Fabro writes in *Partecipazione e causalità*, 66 [83]: "Nella concezione tomistica dell'essere il processo all'infinito del pensiero formale viene superato e dominato dalla qualità metafisica originale dell'esse come 'atto' ... atto di tutti gli atti, l'*esse* è l'unico atto che s'impone nella sua realtà, senza un proprio contenuto e perciò è senza limite perchè l'esse non è e non ha un'essenza ma è l'essenza che ha l'*esse*."

transcendence over essence[73]), then either God has no essence (as some texts of Fabro say), or there is a real distinction between God's essence and God's *esse*: Godhood is a participation in primordial *esse*. No one will say the latter (unless Godhood is a "divine energy" that manifests an unspeakable, prior singularity). On the other hand, if essence is merely conceptually distinct within intensive *esse*, then why is it not merely conceptually distinct from creaturely *esse* as well? Fabro's fluctuations on whether essence and form can be infinite and therefore in God are telling.[74]

---

73. See Cornelio Fabro, "Intorno al fondamento della metafisica tomistica," *Aquinas* 3 (1960): 83–135, at 128.

74. See ibid. Aquinas, *ST* I, q. 3, a. 3, co., and a. 7, co., ascribe form and essence to God.

Therese Scarpelli Cory

5 ❧ Likeness and Agency in Aquinas
A Study

Omne agens agit sibi simile: "Every agent makes something like itself." This axiom, rooted in Aristotle and acquiring its distinctive Scholastic formulation in the Latin translation of Averroes's *Long Commentary on De anima*,[1] is widely used throughout Aquinas's corpus.[2] At an impressionistic distance, the axiom seems intuitively appealing. After all, cats beget cats. Fire generates more fire. Up close, however, apparent exceptions begin to multiply: fire hardens clay; fertilizer helps corn grow; Velázquez's paintbrush produces a masterpiece; a new book brings a gleam into the bibliophile's eye; carpenter ants drill holes in a tree; friction generates a spark. How is the architect's idea of a kitchen "like" the kitchen, or vice versa? At the furthest extreme, how are creatures "like" God?

---

1. Gauthier traces the underlying idea to Aristotle's *De gen. et corr.* I.324a10–11, *De gen. animal.* II.735a20, and *Metaphysics* VII.6.1032a25, b11, and VII.8.1034a22, but the axiom itself to Averroes's *Commentarium magnum in De anima* 2, comm. 118, ed. F. Crawford (Cambridge, MA: Mediaeval Academy of America, 1953), 314.13. See Gauthier's note to 198.35 in the Leonine edition of Aquinas's *In De an.* 2.30. On Aquinas's use of this axiom, see Wippel, "Aquinas on Our Knowledge of God and the Axiom that Every Agent Produces Something Like Itself," in *Metaphysical Themes in Thomas Aquinas II* (Washington, DC: The Catholic University of America Press, 2007), 161–65; Pierson, "Aquinas on the Principle *Omne agens agit sibi simile*" (PhD diss., The Catholic University of America, 2015), 24–46; and Battista Mondin, *The Principle of Analogy in Protestant and Catholic Theology*, 2nd rev. ed. (The Hague: Martinus Nijhoff, 1968), 86–93, where the account of how the axiom is grounded is somewhat dubious. For a broader narrative about agency and likeness, see Rosemann, *Omne Agens Agit Sibi Simile: A "Repetition" of Scholastic Metaphysics* (Leuven: Leuven University Press, 1996).

2. Pierson, "Aquinas on the Principle *Omne agens*," 233–95, comprehensively documents 220 occurrences of this axiom and variants in Aquinas's corpus and groups the contexts into three categories: natural theology, philosophy of nature, and philosophy of knowledge.

Careful readers of Aquinas already know that the *Omne agens* axiom is more restricted than at first appears: the *agens* in question must be acting *per se*, that is, through a power arising from its own nature and essentially ordered toward the effect in question.³ This restriction nullifies many apparent counterexamples, such as the first three above (fire, fertilizer, and the paintbrush).⁴

Nevertheless, this clarification does not wholly lift the strain on the axiom. One might worry, indeed, that there is no serious connection between likeness and agency, and that Aquinas is just forcibly calling some relationships likenesses in order to prop up the *Omne agens* axiom.⁵ Indeed, his readers often feel compelled to explain away Aquinas's appeals to likeness.⁶ So creaturely likeness is sometimes taken to mean that creatures provide information about God,⁷ and the mind's having "likenesses" of things is often taken as just a way of saying that concepts are about things.⁸

---

3. See *In De gen.* I.13, n. 4. Mondin, *The Principle of Analogy*, 89–93, summarizes the conditions for counting as an *agens*: The agent must (1) cause *per se*, that is, by a power arising from its own nature ordered toward that effect; (2) be the principal cause, not the instrumental cause. Mondin cites *In Sent.* IV, d. 1, q. 1, a. 4, qc. 1, ad 3; *De malo*, q. 1, a. 3, ad 2, ad 14, and ad 15; *De malo*, q. 4, a. 3, co.; *ST* III, q. 62, a. 1, co.; *In Meta.* V.3, n. 789. Mondin adds a third point which is really just a clarification, not a condition: namely, a cause is not responsible for assimilating the effect to itself "to the degree the effect is the result of the action of other causes," where he cites *De pot.*, q. 7, a. 5, ad 8; *In De caus.* 12; *ST* I, q. 49, a. 1, and q. 105, a. 1, ad 1. Yet mistakes on this point are responsible for a good deal of confusion about the *Omne agens* axiom; see, e.g., Roger M. White, *Talking About God: the Concept of Analogy and the Problem of Religious Language* (Burlington, Vt.: Ashgate, 2010), 95. For Aquinas's account of efficient causation more broadly, see Gloria Frost, *Aquinas on Efficient Causation and Causal Powers* (Cambridge: Cambridge University Press, 2022), and F.-X. Meehan, "Efficient Causality in Aristotle and St. Thomas" (PhD diss., The Catholic University of America, 1940), 157–405.

4. That is, hardening bricks is not an effect to which fire is oriented by its form, but rather the result of how brick-matter responds to being heated. Fertilizer's promoting of plant growth is *per accidens* causation. The paintbrush's production of a portrait is instrumental causation.

5. For a somewhat skeptical treatment, see White, *Talking About God*, 73–103, esp. 93–95.

6. See Brian Davies, *The Thought of Thomas Aquinas* (Oxford: Clarendon Press, 1992), associating analogy with Wittgensteinian family resemblances (74–75), or explaining it in terms of resembling or copying (83), all of which is just to redescribe loosely, rather than give an account.

7. E.g., Kretzmann veers toward collapsing likeness into manifestation-to-someone, resulting in a strained interpretation of Aquinas's *SCG* II, c. 46, on why the universe's perfect likeness to God requires intellectual knowers. See Norman Kretzmann, *Metaphysics of Creation: Aquinas's Natural Theology in "Summa contra gentiles" II* (Oxford: Oxford University Press, 2001), 166n46 and 238–39.

8. E.g., P. King, *Rethinking Representation in the Middle Ages*, in *Representation and Objects of Thought in Medieval Philosophy*, ed. H. Lagerlund (Aldershot: Ashgate, 2005), 84–85; Fabrizio

But Aquinas was not bound to apply the *Omne agens* axiom as widely as he did. In fact, many of his contemporaries applied it more narrowly to univocal causation alone, where an agent makes a patient belong to the same kind (e.g., fire generating fire).[9] So the weight that the axiom bears in Aquinas is no accident: he puts that weight there deliberately. But is his notion of likeness robust enough to carry the extra load? A great deal rides on the answer. Likeness is central to Aquinas's theories of creation, nature, action, cognition, metaphysics, virtue, redemption, grace, and most importantly, the knowledge of God.[10] Indeed, likeness is arguably a structuring concept within Aquinas's systematic thought, enabling him to unify his metaphysics around *ens commune*, even though beings are arranged into irreducibly diverse "orders"—his so-called analogy of being.[11] If Aquinas's notion of likeness cannot stand up to scrutiny, his famously unified systematic project fragments into a set of smaller, incommensurable, localized projects.

Amerini, *Tommaso d'Aquino e l'intenzionalitá* (Pisa: Edizioni ETS, 2013), 97; Jeffrey E. Brower and Susan Brower-Toland, "Aquinas on Mental Representation," *The Philosophical Review* 117, no. 2 (2008): 199–200 and 225. Brian Leftow, "Aquinas on Attributes," *Medieval Philosophy and Theology* 11, no. 1 (2003): 17, says that Aquinas's talk of cognitive likeness is a "façon de parler."

9. Albert, *Sentences* IV, d. 43, q. 5: "Causa efficiens aequivoca dicitur quando causa cum effectu non est ejusdem speciei, sicut dicitur, quod sol generat hominem … Causa vero efficiens univoca habitualis dicitur, quae efficit simile sibi in specie, sicut homo generat hominem"; Bonaventure, *Sentences* II, d. 30, q. 3, a. 1, *conclusio*: "Non est generatio naturalis nisi ea, in qua natura est vere agens et vere producens sibi simile. Si igitur multiplicatio hominis ex homine esset per virtutem supra naturam, et non per virtutem ipsius naturae, generatio hominis ex homine non esset naturalis; et si hoc, non esset generatio vera." See also Bonaventure, *Commentarius in Ecclesiasten*, c. 3, qq. ad 3. In contrast, the *Summa fratris Alexandri*, p. 1, inq. 1, tr. 1, s. 1, q. 1, tit. 1, memb. 4, c. 2, n. 18, appears to extend the axiom beyond cases of shared kind into cases of "proportional disposition." I am grateful to Andreas Waldstein for pointing out these texts.

10. For Wippel's important work on the latter, see "Aquinas on Our Knowledge of God and the Axiom That Every Agent Produces Something Like Itself," *Metaphysical Themes II*, 157–71; "Thomas Aquinas on What Philosophers Can Know about God," *American Catholic Philosophical Quarterly* 66 (1992): 279–97; "Quidditative Knowledge of God," in *Metaphysical Themes*, 215–41; *Metaphysical Thought*, 501–75.

11. Wippel, *Metaphysical Thought*, 79–93; Bernard Montagnes, *The Doctrine of the Analogy of Being according to Thomas Aquinas*, trans. E. Macierowski (Milwaukee, WI: Marquette University Press, 2004), 11–14. See also Mondin, *The Principle of Analogy*; Thomas Joseph White, "How Barth Got Aquinas Wrong: A Reply to Archie J. Spencer on Causality and Christocentrism," *Nova et Vetera* (English Edition) 7 (2009): 241–70. For the historical background of analogous predication in Aquinas, see E. J. Ashworth, "Signification and Modes of Signifying in Thirteenth-Century Logic: A Preface to Aquinas on Analogy," *Medieval Philosophy and Theology* (1991): 39–67; and Ashworth, "Analogy and Equivocation in Thirteenth-Century Logic: Aquinas in Context," *Mediaeval Studies* 54 (1992): 94–135.

But what *is* Aquinas's notion of likeness? Scholars have found occasion to discuss likeness in Aquinas only in connection with associated problems—for example, cognition, analogical predication, knowledge of God, univocal causation—where the full notion of likeness itself is not completely in focus. The present study tackles Aquinas's notion of likeness in its own right. In this way, I hope to show, by way of paying tribute to Wippel's own important work on this and other axioms in Aquinas, that a systematic, unified vision of likeness informs Aquinas's *Omne agens* axiom.[12]

My first section below reconstructs Aquinas's notion of likeness as a relation grounded in any unity short of numerical unity—a concept much broader than his own much narrower official definition might suggest. This breadth might seem to make him liable to the well-known objection that likeness is just sameness-in-some-respect. But I show that Aquinas's understanding of "unity" allows him, intriguingly, to evade that objection. The second section sketches a taxonomy that can handle all Aquinas's variegated examples of likeness. I show that he admits four basic modes of likeness, grounded in different modes of unity, each of which plays its own indispensable role in his metaphysics. This metaphysically robust theory of likeness, I will show in the conclusion, is strong enough to tackle the traditional worries about Aquinas's *Omne agens* axiom. Indeed, likeness turns out to be a core metaphysical notion: Aquinas relies on it to justify the possibility of agency within a cosmos that is structured into "grades of being," and thus more fundamentally, the possibility of diversifying being into such grades at all.

AQUINAS'S VIEW OF LIKENESS: A RELATION GROUNDED IN UNITY-WITH-DIVERSITY

Aquinas has many different ways of characterizing likeness throughout his writings. Rather than try to make a case for prioritizing some over others, I want to take a bit of an unusual, but I hope more effective,

---

12. In *Metaphysical Themes II*, Wippel writes that Aquinas's axioms "deserve greater attention from Thomistic scholars" (3). Besides "Aquinas on our Knowledge of God and the Axiom that Every Agent Produces Something Like Itself," Wippel has written on "Aquinas and the Axiom 'What is Received is Received according to the Mode of the Receiver'"; and "Aquinas and the Axiom that Unreceived Act is Unlimited" (all reprinted in *Metaphysical Themes II*). I will not here discuss what it means for a proposition to be an axiom.

strategy. I will start by showing why Aquinas's official (restrictive) definition of likeness cannot be taken at face value as his final word on likeness. Nonetheless, I will argue, there is a reason why he keeps repeating it: this insufficient definition does tell us three important things about what he actually *does* think likeness is. By the expedient of working through those three things, we will uncover the dimensions of his real view of likeness.

An overly restrictive definition

In contexts where Aquinas seems to be defining likeness officially, he defines it quite restrictively. Following Aristotle and Boethius,[13] he asserts that likeness is a relation grounded in unity of quality, alongside sameness (a relation grounded in unity of substance), and equality (a relation grounded in unity of quantity): "Unity in substance makes for identity (*idem*); unity in quantity makes for equality (*aequale*); unity in quality makes for likeness (*simile*)."[14] On this restrictive definition, roughly, two things are alike when they share[15] a quality.

At first, this definition seems to correspond pretty well to common usage. When we judge, for instance, that this child is astonishingly like her mother, or that this statue is a good likeness of Napoleon, the characteristics we have in mind are ones that Aquinas would identify as qualities: for example, facial shape, hair color, personality traits, etc. Our judgments of likeness do not depend so much on having the same size (the child is smaller than the mother, and the statue may be smaller or

---

13. In discussing the various senses of "relative" in *Metaphysics* V.15.1021a10–15, Aristotle writes that likeness is one of the relations grounded on unity. Boethius likewise defines likeness in terms of qualities, but emphasizes that likeness (as opposed to identity) requires numerically different subjects: "Likeness [obtains when there is] the same quality belonging to different things" (as cited by Aquinas in *In Sent.* I, d. 34, q. 3, a. 1, obj. 2; the source is Boethius, *In Porph.*, lib. III, col. 99, t. II, cap. "De specie"). On these relations, see Svoboda, "Aquinas on Real Relation," *Acta Universitatis Carolinae Theologica* 6 (2016): 147–72.

14. *In Meta.* V.17, n. 1022 (Marietti, 268), on *Metaphysics* V.15, where he describes these as "relativa, quae accipiuntur secundum unitatem, et non per comparationem numeri ad unum vel ad numerum ... Haec enim dicuntur secundum unitatem. Nam eadem sunt, quorum substantia est una. Similia, quorum qualitas est una. Aequalia, quorum quantitas est una." He uses this definition across his career. For early examples, see, e.g., *In Sent.* I, d. 2, q. 1, a. 1, ad 5 expos.; d. 19, q. 1, a. 1; and d. 34, q. 31, obj. 2. For mid-to-late examples, see *SCG* IV, c. 14, and *De pot.*, q. 8, a. 3, ad 15.

15. In English, one would usually colloquially say that "they have the same quality." However, I want to avoid such language until we can clear up the technical significance (see pages 144–50 below).

larger than Napoleon), or even belonging to the same kind (the statue is a stone artifact, whereas Napoleon was a human being).

But the definition barely touches upon the examples of likeness that Aquinas himself cites all over his work, as the following list illustrates:

1. Creatures are like God.[16]
2. A human son is like a human father in being human.[17]
3. Two instances of exactly the same intensity of white are like each other.[18]
4. A stone statue and the human being it honors are alike in shape.[19]
5. Heat in our terrestrial world is like something in the sun (which in Aquinas's cosmology is not hot, as heat is restricted to the terrestrial realm).[20]
6. The form in the cognizer is like the form in the thing cognized.[21]
7. A "fiery" mixed body—for example, a red-hot poker—is like the pure element of fire.[22]
8. The relationship of water to stains is like the relationship of grace to sins.[23]

---

16. See *ST* I, q. 4, a. 3, among countless other texts.

17. *ST* I, q. 41, a. 5 (Leon. 4.430): "Omne autem producens aliquid per suam actionem, producit sibi simile quantum ad formam qua agit, sicut homo genitus est similis generanti in natura humana, cuius virtute pater potest generare hominem. Illud ergo est potentia generativa in aliquo generante, in quo genitum similatur generanti." See also *ST* I, q. 4, a. 3. For two fires, see *In Sent.* III, d. 3, q. 4, a. 2, ad 4.

18. *In Sent.* I, d. 19, q. 1, a. 1, ad 3 (Mandonnet 462): "Quaecumque aequalia sunt in colore, sunt etiam similia." See *In Sent.* I, d. 48, q. 1, a. 1, for "duo albi."

19. *In Sent.* I, d. 28, q. 2, a. 1, ad 3 (Mandonnet 679): "Lapis dicitur esse imago hominis inquantum habet similem figuram."

20. *SCG* I, c. 29 (Marietti 42): "Unde forma effectus in causa excedente invenitur quidem aliqualiter, sed secundum alium modum et aliam rationem, ratione cuius causa aequivoca dicitur. Sol enim in corporibus inferioribus calorem causat agendo secundum quod actu est; unde oportet quod calor a sole generatus aliqualem similitudinem obtineat ad virtutem activam solis, per quam calor in istis inferioribus causatur, ratione cuius sol calidus dicitur, quamvis non una ratione."

21. *In Sent.* IV, d. 49, q. 2, a. 1 (Parma 483): "Ad hoc autem quod visus cognoscat albedinem, oportet quod recipiatur in eo similitudo albedinis secundum rationem suae speciei, quamvis non secundum eumdem modum essendi: quia habet alterius modi esse forma in sensu, et in re extra animam."

22. *In Sent.* I, d. 48, q. 1, a. 1 (Mandonnet 1080): "Vel ex eo quod unum quod participative habet formam, imitatur illud quod essentialiter habet. Sicut si corpus album diceretur simile albedini separatae, vel corpus mixtum igneitate ipsi igni."

23. *In Sent.* IV, d. 1, q. 1, a. 1, qc. 5, ad 3 (Moos 16): "Corporalia et spiritualia non attenditur similitudo per participationem ejusdem qualitatis, sed per proportionalitatem, quae est similitudo proportionatorum; ut sicut se habet aqua ad delendas maculas corporales, ita gratia ad

Most of these examples have nothing to do with qualities. God does not have qualities at all, let alone any in common with creatures. "Human" is a substance-kind, not a quality-kind. And so forth.

So already it proves difficult to pin down what Aquinas thinks likeness is. Although he defines likeness restrictively as "a relation grounded in unity of quality," he does not adhere to that definition with any consistency. So why does he keep citing it? Surely the authority of Aristotle and Boethius provides some motivation. But what I want to show in what follows is that Aquinas's motivation is also philosophical. His real notion of likeness, as we will see, is intriguingly broad and flexible: likeness is a relation founded *on any unity within a wide range of unities*. The key to understanding likeness, then, is to understand how broad and flexible the underlying notion of "unity" is. The reason that Aquinas allows himself to repeat Aristotle's much more restrictive definition, I would argue, is that "unity in quality" can helpfully illustrate *the "play" within the wide range of unities that can ground likeness*.

So in order to take the full measure of Aquinas's concept of likeness, let us take a look at three important things that "unity of quality" can tell us about the much wider range of unities that can *actually* ground likeness.

Extending likeness from quality into substance

The first way that "unity in quality" can help to illuminate Aquinas's real notion of likeness lies in the special way that qualities signal a thing's nature. For Aquinas, accidents in general often serve as windows onto their essences.[24] Operations play a special role in this regard,[25] but he gives the quality of shape the most important role of all:

> Among all qualities, shape most of all follows and shows forth the species of things. This is evident most of all among plants and animals, whose diversity of species can be judged with no judgment more certain than by the diversity of their shapes. And the reason is that just as quantity is closest to substance

---

abluendum spirituales; et secundum hunc modum similitudinis transferuntur etiam corporalia ad spiritualia."

24. *In Sent.* II, d. 3, q. 1, a. 6 (Mandonnet 104): "Quia differentiae essentiales, quae ignotae et innominatae sunt, secundum philosophum designantur differentiis accidentalibus, quae ex essentialibus causantur, sicut causa designatur per suum effectum; sicut calidum et frigidum assignantur differentiae ignis et aquae."

25. See *Quod.* 8.2.2; *ST* I, q. 13, a. 8.

among all other accidents, so too shape, which is the quality with respect to quantity, is closest to the form of the substance.... And that is why an image, which is the expressed representation of a thing, is most powerfully found through shape, more than through color or anything else.[26]

In short, the quality of shape is, for Aquinas, the most immediate expression of a substantial kind.[27] And thus in our knowledge, unity in quality can stand for unity in substance.

Aquinas makes this point in *In Meta.* X.4—an important text to which we will return several times below—when he confronts a puzzle in Aristotle's distinction among three kinds of sameness and four kinds of likeness (*Metaphysics* X.3.1054a20–1055a1). There, Aristotle states that the third kind of sameness occurs where the "*ratio* of primary substance is one,"[28] which Aquinas takes to mean "sameness in species or genus of substance without numerical sameness."[29] For example, Bucephalus and Marengo are not numerically the same horse, but they are the same in species, both being horses. But curiously, Aristotle then goes on to describe the first kind of likeness in just the same way—that is, two things have the first kind of likeness if they are "the same in species."[30] As Aquinas thus notices, it looks as though Aristotle has identified the first kind of *likeness* with the third kind of *sameness*.[31]

---

26. *In Phys.* VII.5.5 (Leon. 2.339): "Ad evidentiam autem harum rationum considerandum est, quod inter omnes qualitates, figurae maxime consequuntur et demonstrant speciem rerum. Quod maxime in plantis et animalibus patet, in quibus nullo certiori iudicio diversitas specierum diiudicari potest, quam diversitate figurarum. Et hoc ideo, quia sicut quantitas propinquissime se habet ad substantiam inter alia accidentia, ita figura, quae est qualitas circa quantitatem, propinquissime se habet ad formam substantiae. Unde sicut posuerunt aliqui dimensiones esse substantiam rerum, ita posuerunt aliqui figuras esse substantiales formas. Et ex hoc contingit quod imago, quae est expressa rei repraesentatio, secundum figuram potissime attendatur, magis quam secundum colorem vel aliquid aliud." See also *In Sent.* I, d. 28, q. 2, a. 1.
27. *ST* I, q. 35, a. 1; III, q. 74, a. 3, ad 2.
28. Aristotle, *Metaphysics* X.3.1054b1–2. The Latin translation of the lemma, as printed in the Marietti edition of Aquinas's *In Meta.* X.4 (Marietti 474), has: "Amplius autem si ratio primae substantiae una fuerit, ut aequales lineae rectae eadem et aequalia, et isagonia, et tetragonia, et etiam plura. Sed in his aequalitas unitas."
29. *In Meta.* X.4, n. 2005: "Tertio modo dicitur idem quando 'ratio primae substantiae,' idest suppositi est una, licet suppositum non sit unum. Et hoc est idem specie vel genere, sed non numero."
30. Aristotle, *Metaphysics* X.3.1054b5. The Latin translation of the lemma has: "Similia vero, si non eadem simpliciter entia, nec secundum substantiam indifferentia subiectam, sed si secundum speciem eadem sint" (Marietti 1983). The original Greek has "same in form (*eidos*)" (Loeb 287.18–19).
31. Aquinas, *In Meta.* X.4, n. 2006 (Marietti 477): "Ostendit quot modis dicitur simile; et ponit quatuor modos; quorum primus respondet tertio modo eius, quod dicitur idem."

But in *Metaphysics* V.15, Aristotle had distinguished sameness and likeness as relations pertaining to unity in different categories, that is, substance versus quality.[32] So a puzzle emerges: why does he now say that Bucephalus's and Marengo's "both being horses" are not only a kind of sameness, but also a kind of likeness?

To solve the puzzle, Aquinas offers a series of remarks, the first of which are devoted to the point I just raised, that is, the special relationship of substances and qualities. Aquinas explains that when two substances are of the same kind, they will also be alike. For instance, if Bucephalus and Marengo are both horses, they should both have a horse-shape too: "Because quality and quantity are grounded in substance, therefore where there is unity of substance, unity of quantity and quality follow. Nevertheless, unity is not named from the quantity or quality, but from what is more primary, namely, substance. And therefore, where there is unity of substance, it is not called likeness or equality, but only sameness (*identitas*)."[33] The point is that because certain qualities follow from and express a thing's substantial kind, some relations of likeness can be expected to follow from and express relations of sameness in substantial kind.

Here one might suppose that our task is complete: Aquinas has not only solved his interpretive problem, but also showed us why he happily keeps using Aristotle's own improperly restrictive definition of likeness. By identifying sameness in substantial kind as a kind of likeness, Aristotle merely means that some likeness-relations can *stand for* some sameness-relations. And then similarly, Aquinas allows himself to employ Aristotle's unsuitably restrictive definition of likeness on the assumption that "unity of quality" can stand for "unity of substance" as needed (making the restrictive definition becomes equivalent to the more expansive definition of likeness via unity of form generally).

But this is not the whole story. Of course, in *In Meta.* X.4 Aquinas

---

32. Aristotle, *Metaphysics* V.15.1021a10–15.

33. *In Meta.* X.4, nn. 2006–07 (Marietti 477): "Quia enim idem est unum in substantia, simile vero unum in qualitate, oportet illud, secundum quod dicitur simile, se habere ad id, secundum quod dicitur idem, sicut se habet qualitas ad substantiam. Et quia usus est aequalitate quasi unitate in substantia, utitur figura et proportione quasi qualitate. Attendendum etiam est, quod cum qualitas et quantitas fundentur in substantia: ubi est unitas substantiae, sequitur quod sit unitas quantitatis et qualitatis, non tamen unitas nominatur a quantitate et qualitate, sed a principaliori, scilicet substantia. Et ideo ubi est unitas substantiae, non dicitur similitudo vel aequalitas, sed identitas tantum."

does want to underscore that various unity-grounded relations can stand for each other. Indeed, throughout this comment he repeatedly draws attention to Aristotle's use of mathematical examples, which are relevant only if Aristotle is allowing unity of quantity to stand for unity of substance or quality.[34] Nevertheless, Aquinas is pursuing a much more radical solution: namely, he will subsume sameness of substantial kind under an enormously expanded concept of likeness that can be grounded in *almost any unity whatsoever*.

Likeness as founded in unity (where the subjects are numerically diverse)

This brings us to a second way in which "unity of quality" helps to illuminate Aquinas's real views on likeness: namely, *defining likeness through unity of quality excludes the one kind of unity that cannot ground likeness, that is, numerical unity*. Quality, of course, is an accident, and accidents are individuated by their subjects. There are two horse-shapes only because there are two horses. Therefore, if likeness-relations are grounded in unity of quality, then they require numerically different subjects. "Likeness is only of things that differ, as Boethius says."[35] Bucephalus is the same as himself, but he is not like himself. One must bring Marengo into the stable in order to be able to say anything about "likeness." Numerical unity, in short, is outside the limits of likeness.

Now what I want to suggest is that for Aquinas, numerical unity is the *only* kind of unity that cannot ground likeness. *Every other unity* is able to ground some sort of likeness. Interestingly, in the continuation of In Meta. X.4, Aquinas gently pushes toward this vastly expanded range of unities, as he goes on trying to explain why Aristotle had said that the first mode of likeness is just sameness in substantial kind:

---

34. For instance, Aquinas points out that Aristotle uses the equality of two same-sized tetragons to stand in for "unity of substance" (thus the two same-sized tetragons are said to be the "same in species"; *In Meta.* X.4, n. 2005), whereas a difference in quantity is given as an example of likeness (thus a larger and smaller tetragon are said to be "alike"; *In Meta.* X.4, n. 2008).

35. *In Sent.* I, d. 48, q. 1, a. 1 (Mandonnet 1080): "Similitudo non sit nisi differentium, secundum Boetium." These could be different substances, but also presumably spatially separate parts of the same substance (such that the white of Bucephalus's tail can be like the white of Bucephalus's fetlock).

[A] Therefore for likeness and equality, there is required a diversity of substance. And for that reason he said that some things are said to be alike even if they are not the same *simpliciter* in their substantial species, as long as they are different in the subject-substance which is called the supposit, but as the same in some way in their species. For instance, the larger tetragon is said to be like the smaller tetragon, namely when the angles of one are equal to the angles of the other, and the equal sides containing the angles are proportional.

[B] It can also be considered here that when the unity is according to the perfect *ratio* of the species, there is said to be sameness (*identitas*); but when the unity is not according to the whole *ratio* of the species, there is said to be likeness—as if one were to say that things that are one in genus are alike, but things that are one in species are the same, as the examples given suggest. For he said that equal straight lines and equal tetragons have sameness with respect to each other; but unequal tetragons and unequal straight lines have likeness.[36]

Interestingly, the substance versus quality distinction no longer even registers in distinguishing sameness and likeness. Instead, Aquinas is focused on the *degrees of unity and difference that two things must have* in order to be considered "same" or "alike." The result is a massive expansion of the scope of likeness, well beyond the boundaries of quality, allowing it to be grounded in almost any unity.

In order to see how, let us first ward off a potential misreading of the text that would make Aquinas's remarks here rather less interesting. On a quick skim, one might think that in both [A] and [B], Aquinas repeats roughly the same point, that is, that unity of substantial species grounds sameness (e.g., two horses, two chipmunks), while more generic unities (two mammals, two living things) will ground mere likeness. Now

---

36. *In Meta.* X.4, n. 2008 (Marietti 477): "Ad similitudinem ergo vel aequalitatem requiritur diversitas substantiae. Et propter hoc dicit quod similia dicuntur aliqua, licet non sint simpliciter eadem secundum speciem substantiae, et si non sint etiam indifferentia secundum substantiam subiectam quae dicitur suppositum, sed sunt eadem secundum speciem aliquo modo, sicut maius tetragonum dicitur esse simile minori tetragono, quando scilicet anguli unius sunt aequales angulis alterius, et latera aequales angulos continentia sunt proportionalia. Sic igitur patet quod haec similitudo attenditur secundum unitatem figurae et proportionis. Et similiter multae rectae lineae inaequales non sunt eaedem simpliciter, licet sint similes. Potest autem et hic considerari quod quando est unitas secundum rationem perfectam speciei, dicitur identitas; quando autem est unitas non secundum totam rationem speciei, dicitur similitudo. Ut si quis dicat quod ea quae sunt unum genere, sunt similia; ea vero quae sunt unum specie, sunt eadem; ut videntur innuere exempla posita. Nam lineas rectas aequales et tetragona aequalia dixit habere identitatem adinvicem; tetragona autem inaequalia et rectas lineas inaequales habere similitudinem."

that would already be an important step, expanding likeness beyond the realm of qualitative unities into the realm of substantial unities, though without managing to embrace the full range of the examples of likeness that Aquinas offers elsewhere.

But a closer look at the passage reveals something more subtle and interesting. What I want to suggest is that Aquinas is offering [A] and [B] as two different ways of explaining why Aristotle re-labels the third mode of sameness as "likeness,"[37] and that in doing so, Aquinas actually provides the necessary materials for pinning down his own notion of likeness.

If we examine [A] more closely, we notice that it stipulates a minimum diversity required for likeness: namely, likeness requires two numerically different subjects.[38] The required unity, however, is formulated quite open-endedly. Aquinas merely says that things that are alike should be "the same in species in some way," "even if they are not (*licet non sint*) the same in species *simpliciter*." What does this mean?

First, the subjunctive formulation (*licet non sint*) does not exclude likeness for two things that *are* the same in species *simpliciter*—for example, two horses or two red things (no distinction is made between quality or substance here). Aquinas does not say that two things that are specifically the same *simpliciter* are *not* alike—just that they *need not be* specifically the same *simpliciter* in order to be alike. So it appears that likeness encompasses sameness in species. In fact, as in the list of examples in the previous section, elsewhere Aquinas frequently cites two things of the same species (two white things, two men, two fires) as examples of likeness.

Second, conversely, whereas one might assume that "being the same in species in some way" requires having some common genus, that is not what Aquinas says here. Instead, he goes on to note that in Aristotle's tetragon examples, the unities that ground likeness are unity of shape

---

37. The phrase "it can also be considered that," at the start of [B], is typical for marking a new thought, not a continuation of the previous thought. Aquinas does not use any contrasting language to indicate that the new thought is in opposition to the old one, and perhaps he thinks the two interpretations just come down to different ways of specifying the term 'same.'

38. Aquinas says the same elsewhere; see, e.g., *In Sent.* I, d. 7, q. 2, a. 2, ad qc. 1 and ad 2 (Mandonnet 185): "Ubicumque est similitudo, oportet quod ibi sit aliqua distinctio: quia, secundum Boetium, similitudo est rerum differentium eadem qualitas, alias non esset similitudo, sed identitas." See also *In Sent.* I, d. 2, q. 1, a. 5 expos., and d. 19, q. 1, a. 1, ad 2; *De ver.*, q. 2, a. 2, ad 3; and *De pot.*, q. 8, a. 3, ad 15.

and unity of *proportion*. But two things can be proportionate to each other without having any common genus; as we will see later, for Aquinas, proportion can obtain across different degrees of perfection as well.

So [A] seems to open up an astonishingly large scope for likeness. As long as two things have *some* unity and are at minimum numerically diverse, they can be alike. Does [B] contradict this thought? No. Whereas [A] was occupied with the minimum diversity required for likeness, [B] offers a different approach, specifying the minimum unity required for sameness: namely, unity in the "perfect *ratio* of the species," for example, the sameness of two horses. Where unity falls short of this standard, the two things are merely alike, as in the case of two things that belong to one genus, but not one species (e.g., a horse and a crocodile).[39] But the genus example is just that—an example. Again, Aquinas's negative characterization opens the door to a much more sweeping construal of likeness as grounded on *any* unity that *in any way* falls short of perfect sameness in kind.

Where does all this leave us? In terms of resolving the puzzle in Aristotle's text, Aquinas has offered two more explanations of what Aristotle might have been thinking when he identified the first mode of likeness with sameness in substantial species or genus. Both involve subsuming sameness partially under likeness—with the exception of numerical sameness according to [A], or with the exception of sameness of species according to [B].

Now if we combine Aquinas's depiction of likeness in [A] and his depiction of sameness in [B], we get a consistent, complete picture of Aquinas's own position. On this basic picture, there is exactly one sameness that likeness excludes: that is, numerical sameness. There are some kinds of sameness that fall under likeness, that is, as when two things belong to the same natural genus or species (apparently without any restriction by category). And there are some kinds of likeness that are not sameness, that is, likenesses grounded in more tenuous unities beyond the unity of natural kind. We will explore this entire taxonomy in §3.

In short, on Aquinas's understanding, likeness is a relation grounded in unity-with-(at minimum)-numerical-diversity. On this view, paired

---

39. Thus Aquinas suggests in [B] above that Aristotle's smaller and larger tetragons can be understood to be alike, not the same, because they are generically both tetragons, but not specifically the same kind of tetragon.

with a sufficiently variegated notion of unities, it becomes possible to accommodate his entire range of examples listed earlier, as we will see below.

Likeness and degrees of unity

"Unity in quality" usefully illuminates the flexible notion of "unity" undergirding Aquinas's real notion of likeness also in a third way: the category of quality admits of a special kind of difference that is crucial for understanding likeness in Aquinas, that is, differences in degree of perfection. For Aquinas, qualities are susceptible to intension and remission: that is, they can exist in a subject in differing degrees of perfection. A tablecloth can be more or less white; and the water can be more or less hot.[40] Thus returning again to *In Meta.* X.4, we find Aquinas explaining that Aristotle's second kind of likeness occurs when the same quality (here described as "a form to which it belongs to be more and less") is repeated in two things: for example, two instances of 97-degree heat in two mugs of water. But the third kind of likeness consists in each thing's having that quality in different degrees of perfection: for example, 42-degree heat in one mug and 97-degree heat in another.[41]

Now, famously, Aquinas (following Aristotle) holds that there is no intension and remission of form within the category of substance. Bucephalus can be faster or more courageous in battle than Marengo, but he cannot be "more a horse" than Marengo. One horse is just as much a horse as any other (first actuality), even if the two vary in their successful performance of horse-activities (second actuality).

Nevertheless, Aquinas *does* allow, in Dionysian fashion, for degrees of perfection within the category of substance. He ranks the so-called orders of being vertically according to their ontological perfection: inanimate beings, then living things (divided further into plants, animals,

---

40. On the intension and remission of forms, see Gloria Frost's contribution to this volume, "Aquinas on How Accidental Forms Vary in Themselves," which includes a summary of the relevant literature.
41. *In Meta.* X.4, nn. 2010–12 (Marietti 477): "Secundus modus est si aliqua conveniunt in una forma quae nata sit suscipere magis et minus, et tamen participent illam formam sine magis et minus: sicut albedo recipit intensionem et remissionem; unde si aliqua sunt alba aequaliter sine magis et minus, dicuntur similia. Tertius modus est quando aliqua conveniunt in una forma aut passione, etiam secundum magis et minus; sicut magis album et minus album dicuntur similia, quia est una species, idest qualitas ipsorum." There is a fourth kind, uninteresting for our purposes.

humans), then celestial bodies, then pure immaterial intellects (angels), etc.[42]

As we will see later, these grades of perfection are not always unified by common generic nature. But it is crucial to Aquinas's unified metaphysical project that likeness can cross all grades. Because qualities can occur with different degrees of intensity, "unity of quality" usefully models *a unity that can occur at different degrees of ontological perfection*.[43] (This is consistent with the claim we saw in the previous section, that two things can be alike without both preserving the "perfect *ratio* of a species," as well as with his broad characterization of likeness noted above: "Those that communicate in one form can be said to be alike, even if they participate that form unequally."[44]) Indeed, Aquinas's most exotic cases of likeness precisely arise when the *relata* are members of different orders of being.

Likeness revealed: A relation grounded in unity with numerical diversity

Aquinas's actual view of likeness, then, is much broader than his apparently official definitions would suggest. The restrictive definition of likeness through qualities alone does not precisely reflect his own real notion of likeness, though it nicely illustrates important features of that notion. In reality, for Aquinas, *any* unity, short of numerical unity, is sufficient to ground some kind of likeness.

But one might immediately object to this more sweeping construal of likeness. Instead of insisting that likeness "follows upon" unity, and even that "unity causes likeness,"[45] should not Aquinas have said that

---

42. See, e.g., *ST* I, q. 47, a. 2; *SCG* II, c. 44. Similarly, the species of angels are differentiated only by the degree of perfection with which each angel possesses the angelic nature; see *De spir. creat.* 8.

43. Notice how the relation of "less white" to "more white" is used as an example of the diverse modes of participation that can undergird likeness in cases of two things that do not belong to the same kind; *ST* I-II, q. 52, a. 3 (Leon. 6.336): "Similitudo autem et dissimilitudo non solum attenditur secundum qualitatem eandem vel diversam; sed etiam secundum eundem vel diversum participationis modum. Est enim dissimile non solum nigrum albo, sed etiam minus album magis albo, nam etiam motus fit a minus albo in magis album, tanquam ex opposito in oppositum, ut dicitur in V Physic."

44. *ST* I, q. 42, a. 1, ad 2, cited in note 59 below; observe that the example is again of the quality of heat.

45. *In Meta.* V.17, n. 1006 (Marietti 266), categorizing *similitudo* among "relationes quae consequuntur unitatem absolute." See also *In Sent.* I, d. 48, q. 1, a. 1 (Mandonnet 1080): "Conformitas est convenientia in forma una, et sic idem est quod similitudo quam causat unitas

likeness *is* unity-in-some-respect or sameness-in-some-respect?[46] Either way, he seems liable to Quine's objection that likeness is philosophically uninteresting, because it is just reducible to sharing some property.[47] (Indeed, Kretzmann defines likeness in Aquinas as "sameness in respect of sharing at least one form.")[48] The underlying question here is whether Aquinas ought to have reduced likeness to some kind of unity, and further reduced that kind of unity to sameness. To understand why he does neither, we must first clarify what Aquinas assumes by calling likeness a relation, and then show why unity as such is nonrelative.

First, for Aquinas, a relation is not something between *A* and *B*. Rather, it is an orientation to something (*ad aliud*): for example, *A*'s orientation to *B*, which is usually reciprocated by *B*'s orientation to *A*.[49] A relation requires a "foundation," which is some "absolute" feature of the bearer, that is, a feature not tied to the existence of any other subject (*ab-solutum*). *A* has that feature regardless of whether or not *B* exists, but as soon as *B* exists, that feature in *A* instantly grounds a relation to *B*.[50] For instance, Thing¹ is 30 centimeters tall regardless of whether

---

qualitatis," and *SCG* IV, c. 14, cited below in note 50. Aquinas makes similar remarks about equality in *In Sent.* I, d. 31, q. 1, a. 1 (Mandonnet 719): "Aequalitas est relatio quaedam fundata supra unitatem quantitatis ... Unde de aequalitate dupliciter convenit loqui: aut quantum ad unitatem quantitatis, quae est causa ipsius; aut quantum ad relationem consequentem. Si quantum ad unitatem quantitatis, supra quam fundatur talis relatio, sic ratio ejus consistit in privatione, sicut et ratio unitatis, ut supra dictum est, dist. 24, quaest. 1, art. 3: et ideo dicit philosophus, quod aequale opponitur privative magno et parvo, sicut unum multo; et idem in littera innuitur." See also *Quod.* 9.2.3, obj. 4.

46. Indeed, with respect to the parallel relation of equality Aquinas explicitly insists (with important Trinitarian implications) that "aequalitas non est unitas, sed relatio unitatem consequens." *In Sent.* I, d. 31, q. 3, a. 1, ad 3 (Mandonnet 720); see also q. 1, a. 1, ad 3.

47. The point is to show that because likeness is reducible to property-sharing, property-sharing itself cannot be reduced to likeness, on pain of circularity. Willard Quine, "Natural Kinds," in *Ontological Relativity and Other Essays* (New York: Columbia University Press, 1969), 117–18.

48. Norman Kretzmann, *The Metaphysics of Theism: Aquinas's Natural Theology in "Summa Contra Gentiles" I* (Oxford: Clarendon, 1997), 145.

49. When *A*'s real relation to *B* is not reciprocated by another real relation in *B* itself, then the mind conceptualizes *B* nonetheless as related to *A*—a "rational relation" (*secundum rationem*). For example, a thought is really related to the tree, but the tree is not conversely really related to the thought. See *ST* I, q. 13, a. 7.

50. *SCG* IV, c. 14 (Marietti 275): "Quia enim omnia accidentia sunt formae quaedam substantiae superadditae, et a principiis substantiae causatae; oportet quod eorum esse sit superadditum supra esse substantiae, et ab ipso dependens; et tanto uniuscuiusque eorum esse est prius vel posterius, quanto forma accidentalis, secundum propriam rationem, fuerit propinquior substantiae vel magis perfecta. Propter quod et relatio realiter substantiae adveniens et postremum et imperfectissimum esse habet: postremum quidem, quia non solum praeexigit

anything else exists. But as soon as there is a Thing² that is 30 centimeters tall, immediately Thing¹ begins to be equal-in-height to Thing², a relation flowing from Thing¹'s height.⁵¹ (Simultaneously Thing² acquires, from its own height, its own relation of equality-in-height to Thing¹).

So Aquinas's notion of likeness as a relation founded on unity amounts to the following: likeness is *A*'s orientation to some numerical "other" (*aliud*) *B*, grounded on some kind of unity that is an absolute feature of *A*. Because a relation is not reducible to its foundation, likeness is not reducible to unity.⁵²

Second, furthermore, "unity" here cannot be just another name for sameness, regardless of whether we take sameness in Aquinas's technical sense, or even in a looser sense.

(a) In the technical sense, sameness in Aquinas is a relation. But what we are looking for here is the *foundation* of a relation, and a foundation has to be something absolute. This point is perhaps a bit difficult for the modern reader. One naturally talks of unity as though it were itself relative, as a unity *among* multiple things, in the sense of "sharing" or "having something in common." For instance, we say that "Frank Lloyd Wright's architecture becomes one with its natural environment," or "Socrates is one with other humans in his humanity." Here in Aquinas, however, "unity" has to be understood in its transcendental sense as undividedness. "One is nothing other than undivided being."⁵³ For

---

esse substantiae, sed etiam esse aliorum accidentium, ex quibus causatur relatio, sicut unum in quantitate causat aequalitatem, et unum in qualitate similitudinem; imperfectissimum autem, quia propria relationis ratio consistit in eo quod est ad alterum, unde esse eius proprium, quod substantiae superaddit, non solum dependet ab esse substantiae, sed etiam ab esse alicuius exterioris." For Aquinas's theory of relations, see Mark Henninger, *Relations: Medieval Theories 1250–1325* (Oxford: Clarendon, 1989), and David Svoboda, "Aquinas on Real Relation."

51. See *In Phys.* V.8, and discussion in Svoboda, "Aquinas on Real Relation," 163–65; and *De pot.*, q. 7, a. 9, ad 7.

52. Of course Aquinas speaks in various texts with varying degrees of precision, and sometimes he seems to say that it is all the same to him whether likeness is equated with unity or caused by unity. See *ST* I, q. 93, a. 9 (Leon. 5.412): "Similitudo quaedam unitas est, unum enim in qualitate similitudinem causat, ut dicitur in V Metaphys." See also *In Ioann.* 15.4, as well as *In Sent.* I, d. 38, q. 1, a. 1, obj. 2 (Mandonnet 897): "Praeterea, cum similitudo sit quaedam unitas in forma, oportet quod in omni assimilatione vel unum similium sit causa alterius, vel utrumque ab una causa deducatur; quia unitas in effectu designat unitatem causae" (the response does not reject the principle but only its application to God's knowledge of evils).

53. *De ver.*, q. 1, a. 1 (Leon. 22/1.5:141–42): "Nihil aliud enim est unum quam ens indivisum"; see also *In Meta.* X.1, n. 1932 (Marietti 463): "Et omnia haec dicuntur unum per rationem unam, scilicet per hoc quod est esse indivisibile. Nam proprie unum est ens indivisibile." On

Aquinas, unity in this sense is nonrelative. It does not imply the existence of anything else.[54]

For clarity, it may help here to speak of the foundation of likeness as "a one [*unum*]." Whatever grounds likeness does so insofar as it is "a one" or *unum*. And to identify an *unum* is to mark off what has integrity in itself without being further divided (even if it *could* be further divided): scarlet, 30 centimeters, three-dimensional, chipmunk, carbon-based, musician, etc. Of course, likeness requires numerically diverse subjects. So an *unum* grounds likeness only on condition that this *unum* is multiplied, that is, occurring in more than one instance.[55] But the likeness-relation's foundation in *A* is not the multiplicity of the *unum*, or the *unum*-as-held-in-common-with-*B*, but just the *unum* whose existence in *A* is "absolute."

Thus even when Aquinas says that two things are "one" in some respect (e.g., Socrates and Plato are one in their humanity), he is not introducing a notion of unity as a kind of sharing or bond. Rather, to say that two things are one is just to say that when all their distinguishing features are stripped away, what is left is some *unum*.

In short: the *unum* founding *A*'s likeness-relation to *B* is a nonrelative "one" that is "undivided in itself." And that *unum* gives rise to a likeness-relation whereby *A* becomes like (oriented to) something, only on the condition that there exists some numerically distinct "other" in which that *unum* is also found. To illustrate: if God creates the universe containing just one lonely star Vega, that star already exemplifies the *unum* "to be star" (and also other *una*; to be celestial, to be body, to be bright, etc.). But if God creates a second star, Betelgeuse, which also exemplifies the *unum* "to be star," Vega's star-being instantly gives rise to a likeness-relation, in Vega, to Betelgeuse's star-being. Thus unity is not

---

Aquinas on unity, see, e.g., David Svoboda, "The *Ratio* of Unity: Positive or Negative? The Case of Thomas Aquinas," *American Catholic Philosophical Quarterly* 86 (2012): 47–70.

54. Aquinas is careful to specify that this undivided one is prior to any notion of division of one from another and hence to any notion of multiplication. See *De ver.*, q. 1, a. 1 (Leon. 22/1.5:142–50): "Si autem modus entis accipiatur secundo modo, scilicet secundum ordinem unius ad alterum, hoc potest esse dupliciter. Uno modo secundum divisionem unius ab altero; et hoc exprimit hoc nomen aliquid: dicitur enim aliquid quasi aliud quid; unde sicut ens dicitur unum, in quantum est indivisum in se, ita dicitur aliquid, in quantum est ab aliis divisum."

55. Scholars have attempted to explain in a variety of ways how the "multiplication" of an *unum* is supposed to work in Aquinas. Sometimes the problem is framed as a problem of universals, or of individuating / instantiating essences. For a classic treatment, though one that is not without interpretive difficulties, see Joseph Owens, "Common Nature: A Point of Comparison between Thomistic and Scotistic Metaphysics," *Mediaeval Studies* 19 (1957): 1–14.

sameness in Aquinas's technical sense; rather, it is something absolute (nonrelative) that can serve as a foundation to *ground* a sameness-relation to something else.

(b) But this unity that grounds likeness also should not be understood as sameness in a looser sense, such that likeness could be reduced to some familiar notion of property-sharing or sameness-in-some-respect. The reason is that, for Aquinas, *there can be likeness even where there is no sameness at all.*

Let me explain: When we speak of two things as being "the same" in some respect, we generally mean some kind of point-by-point correspondence—some feature that straightforwardly repeats even though everything else differs. Incidentally, while his terminology is not always consistent,[56] it is safe to say that likewise in Aquinas, "same" (*idem*) usually suggests membership in a shared natural kind. Two plants are the same because they are members of one species of daisy; and quality control at a Jeep manufacturer aims to ensure that the parts are all the same shape. Sameness occurs when a form is multiplied across individuals. The reason is that forms give being within some kind.[57] So if *form* is the foundation of a likeness-relation, then two alike things will always wind up as members of the same natural kind. If *A* and *B* are alike in both having the form of redness, they will both be red things.

But for Aquinas, as we will see in the second section of this chapter (below), there are kinds of unity that can obtain even where there is no "one" that straightforwardly repeats in *A* and *B*. Namely, as we will see, Aquinas wants to allow for likeness-relations that can occur even when the *relata* have *no properties univocally in common*, that is, when they are not members of a common natural kind, and there is no natural "one" that recurs in both. (Recall from *In Meta.* X.4 that Aquinas portrays sameness as one of the kinds of likeness, rather than the other way around.)[58]

In short, for Aquinas, likeness can obtain even across diverse modes of being and orders of perfection. And the reason he can hold such a view is that he thinks there are unities other than unity of form, and those unities can repeat even in the absence of any shared form and hence

---

56. See, e.g., *De prin. nat.* 6, where Aquinas speaks of analogical sameness.
57. See Brock's chapter in this volume, "Created Form as Act and Potency in the Metaphysics of Thomas Aquinas."
58. *In Meta.* X.4, n. 2008, in note 36 above.

Likeness and Agency in Aquinas 149

shared kind. That line of thought explains why Aquinas sometimes describes likeness-relations as "convergence" or "agreement" (*convenientia*, literally a coming-together) or "conformity" (*conformitas*) or "communication" (*communicatio*) or "participation" (*participatio*) in form.[59] The deliberate looseness of such formulations allows situations in which *A* does not exactly duplicate *B*'s form, but only approaches *B*'s form to some degree.

And thus we can see why it is preferable to say that Aquinas's likeness-relations are grounded on *unity*, rather than on, for example, form or being. Aquinas does say sometimes that likeness consists in *sharing one form*, giving examples of qualities and substances. "From the fact that two things are alike—having, as it were, one form—they are in a certain way one in that form, as two humans are one in the species of humanity, and two white things are one in the species of whiteness."[60] But clearly these examples of form-sharing simply do not exhaust all the kinds of

---

59. If these are not the same relations as likeness, then they are neighboring relations or subcategories of likeness. *In Sent*. III, d. 3, q. 4, a. 2, ad 4 (Moos 135): "Similitudo et convenientia, magis attenditur secundum formam quam materiam; ut si ignis generet ex aere ignem, ignis generatus magis convenit cum igne generante, cum quo convenit secundum formam, quam cum aere ex quo materialiter generatus est"; *De ver.*, q. 23, a. 7, ad 11 (Leon. 22/3.672:343–59): "Similitudo et conformitas, quamvis sint relationes aequiparantiae, non tamen semper utrumque extremorum denominatur in respectu ad alterum; sed tunc tantum quando forma secundum quam attenditur similitudo vel conformitas, eadem ratione in utroque extremorum existit, sicut albedo in duobus hominibus, eo quod uterque convenienter potest dici alterius formam habere; quod significatur cum aliquid simile alteri dicitur. Sed quando forma est in uno principaliter, in altero vero quasi secundario, non recipitur similitudinis reciprocatio; sicut dicimus statuam Herculis similem Herculi, sed non e converso; non enim potest dici quod Hercules habeat formam statuae, sed solum quod statua habeat Herculis formam"; *ST* I, q. 4, a. 3 (Leon. 4.53): "Similitudo attendatur secundum convenientiam vel communicationem in forma"; *ST* I, q. 42, a. 1, ad 2 (Leon. 4.436): "Quaecumque enim communicant in una forma, possunt dici similia, etiamsi inaequaliter illam formam participant, sicut si dicatur aer esse similis igni in calore, sed non possunt dici aequalia, si unum altero perfectius formam illam participet." See also *ST* I, q. 93, a. 9 (Leon. 4.412): "Similitudo quaedam unitas est, unum enim in qualitate similitudinem causat, ut dicitur in V Metaphys." From the rest of the text it is clear that unity in quality is not essential to likeness, but an example of likeness. For participation, see *In Sent*. I, d. 34, q. 3, a. 1, ad 2 (Mandonnet 798): "Similitudo est duplex: quaedam enim est per participationem ejusdem formae; et talis similitudo non est corporalium ad divina, ut objectio probat. Est etiam quaedam similitudo proportionalitatis ..." (we will return to the contrast later).

60. *ST* I-II, q. 27, a. 3 (Leon. 6.194): "Ex hoc enim quod aliqui duo sunt similes, quasi habentes unam formam, sunt quodammodo unum in forma illa, sicut duo homines sunt unum in specie humanitatis, et duo albi in albedine." See also *ST* I, q. 5, a. 4, ad 1 (Leon. 4.61): "Similitudo autem respicit formam" and *SCG* I, c. 29 (Marietti 42): "Simile enim alicui dicitur quod eius possidet qualitatem vel formam."

likeness that Aquinas wants to accommodate, as a quick look back at the list above illustrates (see page [[135]]).

Thus, to summarize: Aquinas's concept of likeness is not the "street" notion of similarity that Quine reduces to property-sharing. For Aquinas, likeness is a thing's orientation toward another, founded on a "unity" in its being: that is, some aspect of its being that has integrity in its own right (i.e., is undivided) and that can be instantiated in multiple subjects, though not necessarily by way of exact replication. All this precision enables Aquinas (a) to ground likeness-relations in a properly absolute foundation; (b) to accommodate *relata* with no common properties, occupying different modes of being and orders of perfection.

AQUINAS'S MANIFOLD WAYS OF "AGREEING IN FORM"

Agency and likeness: The taxonomy

Now let us turn to the question of taxonomy: what types of likeness does Aquinas admit? Aquinas asserts that "because likeness is had according to agreement or communication in form, likeness is manifold, according to the many modes of communicating in form."[61] But he never offers a single taxonomy of this "manifold" that would accommodate all the examples he himself scatters through his writings. Rather, he provides only partial lists.

An overarching taxonomy cannot be reconstructed merely by gluing together these partial lists, as they do not map nicely onto each other. For one thing, Aquinas uses terms like "same form," "same *ratio*," or "same mode of being" in differentiating various modes of unity, but does not apply the labels consistently. More importantly, the contexts can introduce misleading distortions: Aquinas typically discusses likeness in connection with cause-and-effect relationships (distinguishing univocal versus nonunivocal causes; ways of "participating" in something[62]) or ways of predicating (distinguishing univocal, equivocal, analogical predication; or that grounded in proportion versus proportionality).

It is easy to assume that these familiar causal distinctions also divide

---

61. *ST* I, q. 4, a. 3 (Leon. 4.53): "Respondeo dicendum quod, cum similitudo attendatur secundum convenientiam vel communicationem in forma, multiplex est similitudo, secundum multos modos communicandi in forma."

62. *In Sent.* I, d. 48, q. 1, a.1.

up the types of likeness.[63] But in reality, I would argue, the "joints" that carve up likeness follow the varying modes of unity upon which likeness-relations can be grounded. There are four relevant modes of unity, organized by how far they fall short of the unity of natural kind. The first two fall to some degree within a natural kind (hence "kind-bound unities"). The third only involves proportions among natural kinds (hence "kind-proportional unities"), and the fourth wholly abstracts from any natural kind (hence "unbound unities").[64]

A taxonomy of likeness
Kind-bound unities:
1. Kind-likeness (= sameness in kind): "ones" that are natural kinds (whether species or genera), had in common.
2. *Ratio*-likeness: "ones" that are *rationes* (a subessential unity, *something of* a natural kind), had in common.

Kind-proportional unities:
3. Mere power-likeness (could also be called "eminent likeness"): "ones" that are naturally proportioned, not had in common.

Unbound unities
4. Likeness of proportions: "ones" that are proportions, had in common.

---

63. E.g., one might try dividing likenesses in terms of "univocal causation" (where an agent succeeds in recruiting the patient to its kind), and equivocal or nonunivocal causation (where it does not). But as we will see, nonunivocal causation results in very different arrangements with different modes of unity. Using univocal / nonunivocal causation as the main "cut" in the taxonomy makes it difficult to distinguish mind-world likeness from other kinds. See *In Sent.* IV, d. 44, q. 3, a. 1, qc. 3, ad 2, which connects mind-world likeness to equivocal causation. Rudi te Velde, *Participation and Substantiality in Thomas Aquinas*, 98–102, provides a more detailed division into univocal causality, generic causality, and causality that "does not fall under a genus." This is enough for him to locate God's causality, but still not enough to differentiate the various modes of unities that result from nonunivocal causation, and the corresponding types of likeness. For more on univocal causation, see note 71 below.

64. *De prin. nat.* 6 also distinguishes four modes of unity (numerical unity, unity of species, unity of genus, and analogical unity). But this set of distinctions is not so useful to us. Numerical unity is irrelevant; unity of species and genus both fall under unity of natural kind (1), and analogical unity is insufficient to distinguish (2), (3), and (4). See also *In Meta.* X.1, n. 1932 (Marietti 463), where the four modes of unity pertain to a continuum, a whole, a singular, and a universal.

Let us sketch the big picture before diving into the details. This taxonomy of likeness has to be understood in light of Aquinas's view of agency (in the proper sense[65]) as likeness-generation.[66] For Aquinas, *per se* action proceeds from what is actual in the agent, aiming to make the patient actual—and therefore acting is assimilating.[67] "Because every agent acts insofar as it is in actuality, that which the agent causes must be in some way in the agent, and that is why every agent makes something like itself."[68] "It belongs to the nature of action that the agent makes something like itself, for each thing acts insofar as it is actual."[69]

On this theory, *per se* acting is essentially *the expression of the agent's nature*, and aims at unifying the patient with the agent. In the paradigm case of such unifying, the agent successfully recruits patients to its own natural kind, communicating the "one" of its kind either wholly (in the same species) or partly (only in the same genus). Hence the paradigm case of likeness is sameness in kind (1).

But a less successful agent may still be able to communicate *something of* its own natural kind, because the basic "one" of a natural kind itself can be subatomically fractured into the unities of *ratio* and mode of being. So even if agent and patient do not share a natural kind, they may be one in *ratio* and hence alike to that extent (2).

Sometimes, however, the agent even fails to make the patient have any "one" in common with itself. Still, even there a likeness arises from "ones" that are not had in common by both *relata*, but that are naturally proportionate to each other (3). This arrangement enables

---

65. Recall notes 3–4 above.

66. On causation and analogy / likeness, see Fabro, *Participation et causalité selon S. Thomas d'Aquin* (Louvain: Publications Universitaires de Louvain, 1961), 509–37; Bernhard-Thomas Blankenhorn, "The Good as Self-Diffusive in Thomas Aquinas," *Angelicum* 79, no. 4 (2002): 803–37, at 808–15; Can Laurens Löwe, *Thomas Aquinas on the Metaphysics of the Human Act* (Cambridge: Cambridge University Press, 2021); Mondin, *The Principle of Analogy*, 86–87.

67. See *In De an.* II. 10 (Leon. 45/1.109:121–24): "Dicit ergo quod omnia que sunt in potencia paciuntur et mouentur ab actiuo et existente in actu, quod scilicet dum facit esse in actu ea que paciuntur assimilat ea sibi." On the role of the axiom that "Every agent acts insofar as it is actual" in Aquinas's understanding of acting as assimilating, see Pierson, "Aquinas on the Principle *Omne agens agit sibi simile*," 196–97, where he cites, among others, the texts I have reproduced in the next two notes.

68. *De ver.*, q. 2, a. 3 (Leon. 22/1.51:236–40): "Sciendum est igitur quod cum omne agens agat in quantum est in actu, oportet quod illud quod per agentem efficitur aliquo modo sit in agente, et inde est quod omne agens agit sibi simile."

69. *SCG* I, c. 29 (Marietti 42): "De natura enim actionis est ut agens sibi simile agat cum unumquodque agat secundum quod actu est."

likeness-relations even where the *relata* have no nature in common, and is inextricably linked with the possibility of acting across orders of being.

This agent-centered account of the origins of various modes of likeness has an interesting corollary. Because Aquinas traces effects at each level to smaller and smaller numbers of agents at higher levels (ultimately resolving into one First Cause for all), it is not surprising that various patterns—that is, unities that are internal proportions—recur across different natures and orders of being that are not themselves directly causally related (4). Let us now examine each type of likeness in detail.

Kind-likeness

"Kind-likeness" is the likeness founded on the unity of a natural kind, whether substantial or qualitative.[70] For instance, Koala A and Koala B are alike in kind inasmuch as they each exemplify one kind of substance or quality: they are both koalas, or both shaped or colored a certain way.

Kind-likeness is the paradigm case of likeness from which all other kinds of likeness diverge. As we saw, Aquinas identifies it with sameness in kind.[71] It cannot be stressed enough that Aquinas is far from the English usage of "same" to denote exact correspondence, and "like" to denote less-than-exact correspondence. *Kind-likeness just is sameness in*

---

70. I have not found any examples in Aquinas of likeness grounded in sameness of other categorial kinds such as "quantity" (for which the corresponding relation is typically called equality), "place," or "habit."

71. Indeed, Aquinas initially had trouble explaining how an effect can be "like" a cause *without* sharing its natural kind—except in the case of creaturely likeness to the Creator. In *In Sent.* I, d. 8, q. 1, a. 2 (Mandonnet 198), he distinguishes univocal causes (that recruits patients to their kind) from equivocal causes, in which "effectus non convenit cum causa nec nomine nec ratione: sicut sol facit calorem qui non est calidus." It appears that such effects have no likeness to their equivocal causes, because he then introduces "analogical" causation to explain the likeness of creatures to God. However, by *In Sent.* II, d. 1, q. 2, a. 2 (Mandonnet 48), Aquinas now allows equivocal causation to produce "a certain likeness" despite the absence of a unity of natural kind, citing the same example of the sun and terrestrial heat: "Unde effectus non consequitur speciem agentis, sed aliquam similitudinem ejus quantum potest, sicut est in omnibus agentibus aequivoce, ut sol calefacere dicitur." Interestingly, some of Aquinas's immediate predecessors and contemporaries likewise hold that there is no likeness without sameness in kind *except* in the Creator-creature case. See note 9 above for the references to Albert the Great, Bonaventure, and the *Summa Fratris Alexandri* (the latter of which offers a workaround allowing creatures to have a likeness to God in virtue of the "proportional disposition" of effects to their agents, when those agents are operating by will). It is worth noting that given the view I present in this chapter, it follows that there is no genuinely equivocal causation in Aquinas except in cases of accidental causation, as every *per se* agent produces something like itself in some sense. I am grateful to an anonymous referee for this observation.

kind, a relation grounded in the unity of a natural species or genus. (In fact, kind-likeness occurs also where one quality occurs in different intensities: for example, *A* is whiter or hotter than *B*.)[72]

What is so important about the unity of natural kinds? If substances are the basic units of Aquinas's ontology, natural kinds are the *basic kind-units*—discrete, indivisible substantial, and accidental ways of being. Each natural kind has its own type of matter, common to all members of that kind (e.g., organic versus inorganic matter, or lion-matter versus fish-matter), which gives rise to a set of distinctive properties (e.g., corruptibility, divisibility, metabolic activity, reproductive capacity). Correspondingly, natural kinds bear their own distinctive principles of motion and rest, or activity and passivity.[73]

Thus Aquinas distinguishes between natural kinds, or genera, united by a common matter, and logical or metaphysical genera such as 'body' or 'substance,' which are unified by something that is not a single natural kind.[74] For instance, as Wippel has pointed out, Aquinas's category of substance is not a natural genus with a common matter, which would then be subdivided by adding further differences. Rather, substances naturally occur in three irreducibly fundamental "orders" or genera, representing distinct grades of creaturely perfection: the order of intellects, the order of celestial bodies, and the order of terrestrial bodies.[75] (It is precisely the prospect of action across those orders that demands the more sophisticated modes of unity grounding exotic modes of likeness, as we will see in considering the remaining types of likeness.)

---

72. See *In Meta.* X.4, cited in note 41 above.

73. I would speculatively suggest that kinds of accidental wholes, such as "musician" or "beast of burden," can be reduced to the natural kinds composing those wholes; e.g., because musicality is an exercise of rationality, musicians are essentially human, and similarly, beasts of burden are essentially beasts.

74. See *In Sent.* I, d. 19, q. 5, a. 2, ad 1. On logical and metaphysical genera, see Doolan, "Aquinas on Substance as a Metaphysical Genus," showing that a logical genus is unified by any 'one' picked out by the mind (see *In Meta.* X.12), and a metaphysical genus is not a genus properly speaking but rather an analogical community, in the sense that, e.g., substance and accident are both beings (see *De Spir. Creat.* 1, ad 10); and Dewan, *Form and Being: Studies in Thomistic Metaphysics* (Washington, DC: The Catholic University of America Press, 2006), 81–95.

75. Wippel interestingly suggests that there may in fact be irreducibility, triggering analogical predication, at every level of Aquinas's Porphyrian tree, that is, so that "living being" is predicated analogically of plants and animals, and "animal" is predicated analogically of insects and mammal, and even that *esse* is predicated of individuals analogically (*Metaphysical Thought*, 90–92). I am inclined to agree, though documenting that interpretation would require a study in its own right, and may complicate Aquinas's account of likeness.

Just having a form of some natural kind is sufficient to ground a kind-likeness to anything else with a form of the same kind.[76] Therefore kind-likeness is always in some way rooted in what Aquinas calls univocal agents, that is, those that successfully recruit patients to their own kind—as when a parent koala generates a baby koala.[77] If two things are alike in kind (e.g., two koala siblings) without one being the univocal cause of the other, then there is a common univocal agent somewhere in the background.[78]

Ratio-*likeness*

Within the "one" that is a natural kind, one can distinguish two sub-essential "ones" that I call "*ratio*" and "mode of being."[79] These can sometimes come apart, leaving a unity of *ratio* that grounds a second type of likeness, which I call "*ratio*-likeness" (2). This type encompasses the following examples of Aquinas's mind-world pairs, such as this physical horse and an intellect thinking about horseness, or a carpenter's mental plan and the table she produces; and pairs in which one member has something "essentially" and the other has it "participatively," such as

---

76. *SCG* I, c. 72 (Marietti 86): "Cuicumque inest aliqua forma, habet per illam formam habitudinem ad ea quae sunt in rerum natura: sicut lignum album per suam albedinem est aliquibus simile et quibusdam dissimile."

77. See *In Sent.* IV, d. 43, q. 1, a. 2, ad qc. 1 (Parma 278): "Causa autem univoca agens producit effectum in similitudine suae formae; unde non solum est causa efficiens, sed exemplaris, istius effectus," and Mondin, *The Principle of Analogy*, 91–93. Usually Aquinas's examples involve substantial kinds, but he occasionally mentions qualities; see *In Sent.* IV, d. 44, q. 3, a. 1, ad qc. 3 ad 2.

78. *In Sent.* II, d. 3, q. 3, a. 1, ad 2; *SCG* II, c. 15.

79. Unfortunately, *ratio* and *modus* are highly fluid terms. (1) Sometimes "same *ratio*" describes unity of natural kind; see *ST* I, q. 4, a. 3, equating sameness of species with "[similitudo] secundum eandem rationem speciei," as well as *ST* I-II, q. 60, a. 2, and *De pot.*, q. 7, a. 5. (2) Sometimes "same *modus*" describes unity of natural kind; see *In Sent.* IV, d. 44, q. 3, a. 1, ad qc. 3 ad 2, and *In Meta.* VII.8: "according to the same mode of being and in similar matter." And (3) *modus* and *ratio* even sometimes occur interchangeably; e.g., in *De pot.*, q. 7, a. 1, ad 8: "not according to the same *ratio*, but in a more sublime mode" (see also *In Meta.* VII.8). As we will see, however, Aquinas also distinguishes *modus* and *ratio* as two different factors in unity of natural kind, which is how I will use the terms here. On *modus* generally, see John Tomarchio, "Aquinas's Division of Being into Modes of Existing," *The Review of Metaphysics* 54, no. 3 (2001): 585–613. For an overview of the senses of *ratio* in Aquinas, see the massive entry in Roy Deferrari, *A Lexicon of St. Thomas Aquinas Based on the "Summa Theologica" and Selected Passages of His Other Works* (Washington, DC: The Catholic University of America Press, 1948), s.v. "ratio," 937b–942b, which, however, only glancingly makes contact with the sense of *ratio* here presented.

fire and a fiery poker, or the sun and the illuminated air.[80] On what unity is *ratio*-likeness grounded? Let us try to reconstruct the answer by examining more closely the mind-world examples.

In explaining how a cognitive power becomes like its object in cognizing them, Aquinas explains:

> In order for sight to cognize whiteness, there must be received in it a likeness of whiteness according to the *ratio* of its species, although not according to the same mode of being (for the form in sense has to be of one mode in sense, and of another mode in the thing outside the soul). For if the form of yellowness came to be in the eye, one would not be said to see whiteness. And in the same way, in order for the intellect to intelligize some quiddity, there must come to be in it a likeness of the same *ratio* in species, even if perchance both may not be of the same mode of being. For the form existing in intellect or sense is the principle of cognition, not according to the mode of being that it has in both, but according to the *ratio* that it shares with the exterior thing.[81]

And regarding the likeness of, for example, a table to the conception whereby the artisan brings it about, Aquinas writes: "In those that act by art, the forms of effects preexist according to the same *ratio*, but not in the same mode of being. For in the effects [of art] they have material being, but in the mind of the artisan they have intelligible being."[82] Thus: mind-world likeness-relations are grounded on a unity of *ratio*, where the modes of being are different.[83] So what is unity of *ratio*?

Unfortunately, the terminology of *ratio* (which I here leave deliberately untranslated) is famously obscure in Aquinas. But at least it is immediately clear what *ratio* does *not* mean in this context. One of the

---

80. Aquinas also calls the whiter the "same in *ratio* but different in mode" relative to the less white. But this is just difference of intensity.

81. *In Sent.* IV, d. 49, q. 2, a. 1 (Parma 483): "Ad hoc autem quod visus cognoscat albedinem, oportet quod recipiatur in eo similitudo albedinis secundum rationem suae speciei, quamvis non secundum eumdem modum essendi: quia habet alterius modi esse forma in sensu, et in re extra animam. Si enim fuerit in oculo forma citrini, non dicetur videre albedinem; et similiter ad hoc quod intellectus intelligat aliquam quidditatem, oportet quod in eo fiat similitudo ejusdem rationis secundum speciem, quamvis forte non sit idem modus essendi utrobique. Non enim forma existens in intellectu vel sensu, est principium cognitionis secundum modum essendi quem habet utrobique, sed secundum rationem in qua communicat cum re exteriori."

82. *De pot.*, q. 7, a. 1, ad 8 (Marietti 190): "In agentibus autem per artem, formae effectuum praeexistunt secundum eamdem rationem, non autem eodem modo essendi, nam in effectibus habent esse materiale, in mente vero artificis habent esse intelligibile."

83. Aquinas carries the "same *ratio*, not same mode of being" distinction through right into the divine mind; see *De pot.*, q. 7, a. 7, ad 6 (Marietti 204). I am grateful to Greg Doolan for pointing this out.

Likeness and Agency in Aquinas   157

main uses of *ratio* for Aquinas is to refer to a mental conception or notion.[84] But the *ratio* we are looking for is clearly not a definition or concept. Horse-thought and horse do not have the same definition—because they have no common natural kind. Nor is "having the *ratio* of X" here a circumlocution for knowing X's definition, or thinking about X. Sight does not cognize definitions, but according to the text excerpted above, seeing white has the *ratio* of the species "whiteness." And the table has the *ratio* of the carpenter's thought, but is not itself thinking about that thought.

Instead, therefore, the *ratio* we are looking for must be able to be in both mental and nonmental realities.[85] But clearly a *ratio* here is not a natural kind,[86] for a table that the carpenter constructs does not have a common natural kind with the carpenter's thought.[87] Similarly, a *ratio* here is not an essence. Anything whose essence is "human" is a human being. So if what my thought and Socrates share is the essence "human," then they would both have to be human beings. But thoughts are not human beings; they are immaterial accidents.

Rather, I propose that *ratio* in the present context refers to the *underlying determinate pattern* or *specification* of a natural kind. If there is a "one" that is the natural kind "cat," the *ratio* of that unity is, so to say, its "cattishness." In other words, within the "one" that is a natural kind, it is possible to distinguish both the *ratio* and the mode of being for that kind. For instance, being a cat implies being specified by a cat-*ratio* (its being is determinately *cattish* rather than anything else), and existing according to a cat-mode-of-being.[88] But a kind's *ratio* is separable from its mode of being. For instance, cat-*ratio* can specify—that is, determine or

---

84. This is the first sense of *ratio* described in *In Sent.* I, d. 2, q. 1, a. 3 (Mandonnet 66), that is, as a "second intention," naming a way that the mind conceptualizes things, rather than directly naming things themselves (like "genus," "species," or "definition").

85. This is the second sense of *ratio* described in *In Sent.* I, d. 2, q. 1, a. 3 (Mandonnet 67), such that *rationes* can be said to be "in things." See the usage in *In Sent.* IV, d. 49, q. 2, a. 5, ad 1 (Parma 494–95): "In una enim re est multas rationes intelligibiles considerare, sicut diversas ejus proprietates et habitudines ad res alias; et possibile est quod eadem re scita communiter a duobus, unus alio plures rationes percipiat, et has rationes unus ab alio accipiat."

86. Caution is warranted in sifting the terminology, because "same *ratio*" is often precisely how Aquinas refers to unity in natural kind; see *De pot.*, q. 7, a. 1, ad 8.

87. Aquinas puts mind-world causal relationships under equivocal causation in *In Sent.* IV, d. 44, q. 3, a. 1, qc. 3, ad 2.

88. On the existential significance of the "mode of being," see Tomarchio, "Aquinas's Division of Being," 603.

render "cattish"—an entirely different kind of being, such as a thought, or a chunk of wood.

The *ratio* here is a *subessential pattern* that can be realized in different things, each belonging to its own natural kind with its own mode of being.[89] It is like the story of Hamlet, which can exist in the very different media of a performance, a book, or Shakespeare's imagination. A *ratio* in this sense, I would argue, is the "nature absolutely considered" that Aquinas adopts from Avicenna, which has no being in its own right, but which is able to be realized in various modes of being.[90] This subessential "one" grounds what I am calling *ratio*-likeness. And just as unity in *ratio* is thinner than unity in natural kind, so too *ratio*-likeness is thinner than kind-likeness.

In laying out the whole taxonomy above, I have bundled *ratio*-likeness together with kind-likeness as types of likeness that are grounded on "kind-bound unities." In what sense is the unity of *ratio* bound to a natural kind, though, as agent and patient do not share a natural kind? The reason is that the artisan making a table, or a sense-object acting on sense powers, do leave *something of* their natural kinds in their effect. The specific *ratio* that makes the artisan's productive thought be a *table*-thought is transferred to this wooden body, constraining it to be a *table*-body. The *ratio* that constrains this accident to be *the color white* also constrains this act of seeing to a *white*-seeing. Thus when Aquinas describes things that have a "likeness of form," he gives examples both of kind-likeness (the generated fire and the generating fire) and of *ratio*-likeness (a statue of Mercury relative to Mercury).[91] To be "one in *ratio*" with an agent is to having *something* of its form or more precisely, of its natural kind. A *ratio* is thus the minimal "one" that a patient can have in common with its agent before wholly losing track of the agent's natural kind.

---

89. I am concerned here with *rationes* that are bound to (are originally found in) a natural kind. Perhaps there is an extended sense in which we could speak of even fictional *rationes* as replicable across different modes of being (e.g., Hamlet or the Chimaera in thought, story, visual depiction, or performance), even though they have no foundation in any natural kind. See *In Sent.* I, d. 2, q. 1, a. 3 (Mandonnet 67): "Aliquando vero id quod significatur per nomen, non habet fundamentum in re, neque proximum neque remotum, sicut conceptio Chimerae: quia neque est similitudo alicujus rei extra animam, neque consequitur ex modo intelligendi rem aliquam naturae: et ideo ista conceptio est falsa."

90. See *De ente*, c. 3. However, the "nature absolutely considered," is said to have two modes (intellectual and material), whereas *ratio* in our current sense applies across a variety of modes of being.

91. See note 92 below.

Our examples of *ratio*-likeness have been mind-world pairs, but there are also arguably nonmental examples in Aquinas. One is a statue's likeness to its model: the statue shares a *ratio* but not "the same sort of being" as "the human form in flesh and bones."[92] (Here, though, there is still a mental intermediary: the human *ratio* is communicated to some artisan's mind, who then produces the statue.)

More speculatively, another example of *ratio*-likeness may occur where a patient that acquires *x* accidentally or participatively,[93] from an agent that has *x* essentially. For instance, a red-hot poker is like fire insofar as it "participates the fieriness from that which is fire by its essence [that is, fire]."[94] (Interestingly, Aquinas states that were there such a thing as the Platonic Form of Whiteness, individual white things would be related to it in the same way.)[95]

Here Aquinas does not use "one *ratio*" language.[96] Rather, he says that what fire is essentially, the poker is by participation. Still, the relationship appears to follow the pattern seen above. Fire and the red-hot poker do arguably have one *ratio*: Aquinas ascribes "fieriness" [*igneitas*] and even "the nature of fire" to both.[97] But the two surely differ in mode of being: the agent has something *substantially*, being fire, that the patient has *accidentally*, being fiery. Arguably, then, the fire and the fiery

---

92. *De ver.*, q. 10, a. 4, ad 4 (Leon. 22/2.308:171–75): "Non enim oportet quod eiusmodi esse habeat similitudo et id cuius est similitudo, sed solum quod in ratione conveniant; sicut forma hominis in statua aurea, quale esse habet forma hominis in carne et ossibus"; *ST* I, q. 45, a. 7 (Leon. 4.475): "Aliquis autem effectus repraesentat causam quantum ad similitudinem formae eius, sicut ignis generatus ignem generantem, et statua Mercurii Mercurium, et haec est repraesentatio imaginis."

93. Not that participation language always indicates derivative kind-likeness. Sometimes *participative* just means "derivatively," e.g., in *In Sent.* II, d. 24, q. 2, a. 4, ad 2 (Mandonnet 614): "ad liberum arbitrium pertinet judicium quasi participative." And of course, Aquinas applies participation language to God and creatures, where unity of *ratio* is not preserved.

94. *Comp. theol.* I.68 (Leon. 42.103:18–22): "Omne quod habet aliquid per participationem, reducitur in id quod habet illud per essentiam, sicut in principium et causam; sicut ferrum ignitum participat igneitatem ab eo quod est ignis per essentiam suam"; *In Meta.* VII.3, n. 23. The same apparently also applies to the "fieriness" of a mixed body containing a large proportion of the element of fire; see *In Sent.* I, d. 48, q. 1, a. 1; *In De caus.* 12.

95. *Quod.* 3.8.

96. Probably because the fiery poker usually serves as an analogy of creaturely participation in divine being, where there is no common *ratio*.

97. *De pot.*, q. 6, a. 6 (Marietti 174): "Si ignis natura particulariter, et quodammodo participative, invenitur in ferro, oportet prius inveniri igneam naturam in eo quod est per essentiam ignis."

quality in the poker are one in *ratio* and differ in mode of being, and thus constitute an example of *ratio*-likeness.

Mere power-likeness (3)

So far the likeness-grounding unities we have been examining fall in some way within the framework of a natural kind, even if only its *ratio*. From here on down, the lesser modes of unity do not meet even that bar. Nevertheless, the next mode of unity to consider will still at least involve natural proportions among kinds: hence I call it "kind-proportional unity." This unity grounds what I call "mere power-likeness," applicable to agent-patient pairs even if they share no common matter. (It could equally well be called "eminent likeness," using a term that became important to early modern debates about causation, but as we will see, the label "power-likeness" helps to make the rationale for this kind of likeness clearer.)

"Mere power-likeness" explains the possibility of actions that cross orders of being. The most interesting such case, for post-Cartesian readers, might be the case of angels moving bodies. But we will look at Aquinas's favorite example—the sun's causing heat—which is actually more informative, if trickier to unpack due to its premodern scientific framework.[98]

Now the likeness here might seem obvious: a hot sun makes other things hot, like itself. However, the sun of Aquinas's cosmology cannot be hot. Recall that he views celestial bodies (such as the sun, moon, planets, and stars) and terrestrial bodies (such as grass, dirt, oxen, and humans) as belonging to two irreducibly fundamental genera of being. The reason is that sharing a natural kind requires sharing some kind of matter. But celestial bodies are made of an incorruptible stuff that Aquinas calls the "fifth essence," while terrestrial bodies are made of corruptible mixtures of the four elements.

Thus, crucially, there is no generic common nature of 'body' to which the sun and my car could be commonly reduced. Of course, both the sun and my car are extended in three dimensions. But dimensionality is just a proper accident flowing from each fundamental nature, rather

---

98. Recall that this case counts as likeness only from Aquinas's *In Sent.* II onward (see note 71 above). The sun is also involved as a universal cause in the generation of terrestrial substances; see *ST* I-II, q. 60, a. 1.

Likeness and Agency in Aquinas 161

than a nature in its own right that both have in common. In other words: while post-Cartesian readers might naturally think of 'body' as *res extensa*, for Aquinas 'body' is not some natural kind that is had in common by the sun and terrestrial substances. Rather, when construed as embracing both, it is a logical genus created by abstracting three-dimensionality from the real natures that give rise to it.

Thus there can be no unity of natural kind in the sun-heat case; the sun and terrestrial substances have irreducibly diverse natures. Nor do they have heat in common, as heat is a quality proper to a terrestrial element and a source of change for terrestrial bodies. The imperishable sun cannot be hot.

But then what unity grounds sun-heat likeness?[99] *De pot.*, q. 7, a. 1, ad 8, provides a clue by contrasting it with mind-world cases (that is, derivative kind-likeness). In the sun-heat case, "the effect is not perfectly assimilated to the agent, namely, not measuring up to the agent's power. And then the form of the effect is in the agent, not according to the same *ratio*, but in a more sublime mode, as appears in equivocal agents, as when the sun generates fire." But in the mind-world case, "the forms of effects preexist [in the artisan] according to the same *ratio* but not in the same mode of being."[100] So whereas mind-world pairs are one in *ratio* with different modes of being, the sun and terrestrial heat are neither one in mode of being, nor even one in *ratio*.

The comparison looks initially unhelpful: the sun and its effect have no "ones" in common! And yet there is Aquinas insisting that the "form of the effect is in the agent," and indeed "in a more sublime mode." His remarks echo other texts in which he says that sun and the heated

---

99. After an extended discussion, Kretzmann, *Metaphysics of Theism*, 150–57, only succeeds in repeating Aquinas's own formulations so as to assert that the effect is in the cause "somehow."

100. *De pot.*, q. 7, a. 1, ad 8 (Marietti 190): "Forma effectus invenitur aliter in agente naturali, et aliter in agente per artem. In agente namque per naturam, invenitur forma effectus secundum quod agens in sua natura assimilat sibi effectum, eo quod omne agens agit sibi simile. Quod quidem contingit dupliciter: [1] quando enim effectus perfecte assimilatur agenti, utpote adaequans agentis virtutem, tunc forma effectus est in agente secundum eamdem rationem, ut patet in agentibus univocis, ut cum ignis generat ignem; [2] quando vero effectus non perfecte assimilatur agenti, utpote non adaequans agentis virtutem, tunc forma effectus est in agente non secundum eamdem rationem, sed sublimiori modo; ut patet in agentibus aequivocis, ut cum sol generat ignem. In agentibus autem per artem, formae effectuum praeexistunt secundum eamdem rationem, non autem eodem modo essendi, nam in effectibus habent esse materiale, in mente vero artificis habent esse intelligibile."

terrestrial body are alike by "communicating in the same form," if only "in some way" or "in another mode" or "in another *ratio*"[101]—or that heat "preexists," "exists more eminently," "exists in power," or "exists causally" in the sun.[102]

So *something* must ground sun-heat likeness, and that must be *some* unity, but in what sense? Now recall that earlier, it was necessary to distinguish between unity in the sense of undividedness (the nature of fire is a "one" in the fire), and unity in the sense of commonality (two fires are one in nature). In the cases considered so far, those two senses of unity have been inseparable: the "one" that grounds A's likeness to B occurs in both A and B, *and therefore* A and B are "one in that respect," that is, having something in common.

In the sun-heat case, I propose that those two senses of unity come apart. The "ones" that ground likeness *are not had in common* by both relata, but are rather *essentially proportioned to each other*. Thus in *De veritate*, q. 2, a. 11, ad 2, Aquinas distinguishes the likeness that arises from proportion from the likeness grounded in unity of natural kind:

> One [mode of likeness] is found in diverse genera, and this one is had according to proportion or proportionality, as when one is related to the other as other-and-other... The other mode [of likeness] is found in those which belong to the same genus, as when the same inheres in diverse things.[103]

In fact, however, Aquinas also clarifies elsewhere that proportion itself does constitute a sort of declining unity, in the sense that it is a measure derivative on the fundamental measure that is the number "one."

> Proportionality is not only found in the number of unities, which is number *simpliciter* ... but it is universally found in everything in which number is found. And this is the case because proportionality is nothing other than

---

101. See *In Sent.* II, d. 15, q. 1, a. 2, ad 4 (Mandonnet 373): "In eadem forma communicant; sed contingit quod illam formam non uniformiter participant quaedam; quia quod est in uno deficienter, in altero est eminentius ... et talis similitudo sufficit ad actionem agentis non univoce." See also *De ver.*, q. 11, a. 3, ad 4 (*alio modo*); *SCG* I, c. 29 (*aliqualiter, alio modo, alia ratione*); *In Phys.* II.11 (*alia est ratio*).

102. *De pot.*, q. 7, a. 5, ad 8 (*eminentior*); *ST* I, q. 6, a. 2 (*excellentior*); *ST* I, q. 4, a. 2 (*praeexistit eminentiori modi, virtute*); *In Meta.* VII.8 (*in virtute*); *In De caus.* 12 (*causaliter*).

103. *De ver.*, q. 2, a. 11, ad 2 (Leon. 22/1.80:214–22): "Philosophus, in I Topic., ponit duplicem modum similitudinis. Unum qui invenitur in diversis generibus; et hic attenditur secundum proportionem vel proportionalitatem, ut quando alterum se habet ad alterum sicut aliud ad aliud, ut ipse ibidem dicit. Alium modum in his quae sunt eiusdem generis, ut quando idem diversis inest."

Likeness and Agency in Aquinas 163

the equality of proportion, namely when this has an equal proportion to this, and that to that. But proportion is nothing other than an orientation of one quantity to another. And quantity has the nature of a measure, which is found primarily in the number of unities, and derives thence to the whole genus of quantity, as is clear from *Metaphysics* X. And therefore number is indeed first found in the number of unities and from there derives to every other genus of quantity that is measured according to the *ratio* of number.[104]

Proportion, therefore, is a kind of unity, in the extended sense of being a measure dependent on unity. So even if two things have no nature or *ratio* in common, their proportion constitutes a certain declining unity or commonality. Thus Aquinas links proportion with "analogical commonality" (*communitas analogiae*) and "agreement" (*convenientia*).[105]

The relevant proportion for our purpose is "orientation (*habitudinis*) ... of effect to cause,"[106] that is, the proportion of heat to the sun's active power:

> Because every agent makes something like itself, the agent's effect must be in the agent in some way. Indeed, in some agents, [the effect] is there as the same according to species, and these are called univocal agents, as heat is in the heating fire. And in other agents, [the effect] is there as the same according to

---

104. *In Ethic.* V.5 (Leon. 47/2.280:17–34): "Proportionalitas non solum invenitur in numero unitatum qui est numerus simpliciter et hic vocatur numerus monadicus, sed universaliter invenitur proportionalitas in quibuscumque invenitur numerus. Et hoc ideo quia proportionalitas nihil est aliud quam aequalitas proportionis, cum scilicet aequalem proportionem habet hoc ad hoc et illud ad illud; proportio autem nihil est aliud quam habitudo unius quantitatis ad aliam; quantitas autem habet rationem mensurae, quae primo quidem invenitur in unitate numerali et ex inde derivatur ad omne genus quantitatis, ut patet in X Metaphysicae; et ideo numerus primo quidem invenitur in numero unitatum et ex inde derivatur ad omne aliud quantitatis genus quod secundum rationem numeri mensuratur." See also *In De div. nom.* 4.8, describing proportion again in terms of quantity ("habitudo unius quantitatis ad aliam"). Such remarks additionally confirm my suggestion on pages 143–44 that one reason Aquinas finds the overly restrictive traditional Aristotelian definition of likeness is that qualities are liable to different degrees (= quantities) of intensity, and that proportions among quantities can thus aptly stand for the proportions among different grades of being.

105. *De ver.*, q. 2, a. 11 (Leon. 22/1.79:139–46): "Convenientia autem secundum proportionem potest esse dupliciter: et secundum haec duo attenditur analogiae communitas. Est enim quaedam convenientia inter ipsa quorum est ad invicem proportio, eo quod habent determinatam distantiam vel aliam habitudinem ad invicem, sicut binarius cum unitate, eo quod est eius duplum." On the history of *analogia* as *proportio* and *proportionalitas*, see Ashworth, "Analogy and Equivocation," esp. 97–100.

106. Proportion here is meant not in the sense of the commensurateness of two things on the same ontological level (see *In Sent.* III, d. 23, q. 1, a. 2; *SCG* III, c. 54), but in the sense of "quamcumque habitudinem unius ad alterum, ut materiae ad formam, vel causae ad effectum" (*SCG* III, c. 54 [Marietti 74]).

proportion or analogy, as when the sun heats. For in the sun there is something that makes it engage in heating, in the same way as the heat that makes fire hot. And accordingly, heat is attributed to the sun equivocally. Thence it is clear that what is in the effect as a form giving being is also in the agent as an active power. And thus the agent is situated with respect to containing the form of the effect in whatever way it is situated to that active power.[107]

The agent's "containing the form of the effect as an active power" (or, as he puts it elsewhere, "having the effect's form eminently"), I contend, is just the unity of proportion—specifically an agent-effect proportion.

In this way, we can make sense of Aquinas's saying that the "form of heat" is in the sun, even though the sun is not hot, and even though there is no nature in common for celestial and terrestrial things. Heat is in the sun *as its active power for heating*. The proportion of heat and the active power is a kind of unity—but not a unity of natures or *rationes*. This unity allows Aquinas to include within a genus the universal cause of all beings of a certain natural kind, and all the beings it causes. Obviously if this genus were a natural genus, the universal cause would, *per impossibile*, be the cause of itself. What unifies such a genus is therefore not directly membership in a natural kind, but rather, more loosely, a natural proportion to that natural kind.[108]

The kind of likeness that arises in such contexts is what I call "mere power-likeness" (or "eminent likeness"). The heat in the effect is like the active power in the sun. Power-likeness also explains why an electric eel numbs the hand, or why a doctor warms a patient through friction. The eel and the doctor are neither numb nor warm themselves, but they have the power-versions of numbness and warmth (*in virtute*)—such that the corresponding effects are genuine expressions of the agent's form.[109]

Mere power-likeness is, like any likeness, a relation grounded on unity. But evidently, such a claim must be carefully specified. On the one

---

107. *In Sent.* IV, d. 1, q. 1, a. 4, ad qc. 4 (Moos 37): "Quia omne agens agit sibi simile, ideo effectus agentis oportet quod aliquo modo sit in agente. In quibusdam enim est idem secundum speciem; et ista dicuntur agentia univoca, sicut calor est in igne calefaciente. In quibusdam vero est idem secundum proportionem sive analogiam, sicut cum sol calefacit. Est enim in sole aliquid quod ita facit eum calefacientem sicut calor facit ignem calidum; et secundum hoc calor dicitur esse in sole aequivoce, ut dicitur in libro de substantia orbis. Ex quo patet quod illud quod est in effectu ut forma dans esse, est in agente, inquantum hujusmodi, ut virtus activa; et ideo sicut se habet agens ad virtutem activam, ita se habet ad continendam formam effectus."

108. Hence the sun's power to heat belongs "in some way" to the genus of heat (*SCG* I, c. 31, note 116). See Kretzmann, *Metaphysics of Theism*, 150–58.

109. *In Meta.* VII.8.

hand, as we saw, relations must have an "absolute" foundation in each *relatum*. For the sun, this founding "one" is its active heating power. For the terrestrial body, this founding "one" is the quality of heat. Thus each *relatum* has its own relation grounded on the relevant "one"—just as in the kind-likeness and derivative kind-likeness we saw previously.

On the other hand, in those other types of likeness, the founding "one" is had in common by both *relata*, so that the unity on which the relations are founded was equally a "unity of two things in some respect." In the sun-heat case, however, commonality is replaced by a proportion. Here, then, the two are "one in some respect," not in the sense that they are *absolutely* one, but *proportionate*, which in Aquinas's count is a sort of declining unity, a measure of discrete units. (Incidentally Aquinas follows Aristotle in comparing discrete natures to discrete numbers.)[110]

This view has an interesting upshot: by making room for mere power-likeness, Aquinas is essentially allowing that point-by-point correspondence, or being the same in some respect, is not necessary for likeness. Two things can have *nothing in common*, such that they are not one in any respect—and yet be alike, insofar as each has something (a "one") that is essentially proportioned to something ("a one") in the other.

Now here one might object: with this account, it seems that Aquinas is twisting himself into knots to save the *Omne agens* axiom, which is threatened by actions across orders of being. Aquinas forcibly redescribes agent-patient relationships in general as unities, so that by definition they will always ground likenesses whether the agent and patient have anything in common or not.

Responding to this objection can help to clear up an important puzzle. The key to a response is as follows: Aquinas is not redescribing the agent-effect relationship as a proportion. Nor is he reducing "being in proportion" to an agent-effect relationship that is itself basic or irreducible. Rather, he is *explaining the agent-effect relationship itself in virtue of a certain proportion*. The proportioning of one being to another—which amounts to their having a certain kind of unity—is prior to, and explains, agency.

Let me explain. In Aquinas's metaphysics, the pairing of this agent with that effect is not a brute, inexplicable fact. Nor is this pairing imposed from outside the natures involved (as in occasionalist theories). Rather,

110. *SCG* IV, c. 41; *ST* I, q. 5, a. 5.

Aquinas wants to explain the very possibility of agency in terms of the agent's having in its nature some unity with the form to be effected. More specifically, effects are essentially the expression of the agent's form. Or to put it more strongly: when an agent acts at a lower level of being, the effect *exactly expresses what the agent's own form would be like at that lower level.*

Now we can understand why, despite denying that the sun and heat are "one in being" or even "one in ratio," Aquinas nonetheless says that the form of one is in the other. Of course the agent's form and the effect's form are not one in natural kind, or even in the *ratio* of a kind. Nonetheless, they are one in the sense that the latter is the proper expression, at a lower level, of what the former is at a higher level. That is what Aquinas means by saying that the effect's form is contained in the agent "eminently" or "as an active power."[111] As he puts it in commenting on the *Liber de causis*, the heat is in the sun "causally" (*causaliter*), while the sun is in heat "by participation" (*participative*).[112] Or as the *Summa contra Gentiles* explains:

> Effects [of equivocal causes] are in their causes virtually [or: in power, *virtute*], like heat in the sun. But unless a power of this sort belonged to the genus of heat, the sun acting by it would not generate something like itself. From this power, therefore, the sun is said to be hot, not only because it causes heat, but because the power whereby it does this is something conformed to heat (*conforme calori*).[113]

---

111. Note that *forma* in Aquinas does not always mean the formal principle of being (*forma partis*) nor even the essence that grants a thing membership in a certain kind (*forma totius*). For instance, he often says that "forms" exist in two modes of being (*ST* I, q. 14, a. 6, ad 1; *Q. de an.* 18), where he actually means the *ratio* of the nature. Here, then, the sense in which the patient's *forma* is in the agent is even more attenuated, indicating a unity of proportion without any commonality.

112. *In De caus.* 12 (Saffrey 79–80): "Tripliciter aliquid de aliquo dicitur: uno modo causaliter, sicut calor de sole, alio modo essentialiter sive naturaliter, sicut calor de igne, tertio modo secundum quamdam posthabitionem, id est consecutionem sive participationem, quando scilicet aliquid non plene habetur sed posteriori modo et particulariter, sicut calor invenitur in corporibus elementatis non in ea plenitudine secundum quam est in igne. Sic igitur illud quod est essentialiter in primo, est participative in secundo et tertio; quod autem est essentialiter in secundo, est in primo quidem causaliter et in ultimo participative; quod vero est in tertio essentialiter, est causaliter in primo et in secundo. Et per hunc modum omnia sunt in omnibus." See *In De div. nom.* 4.5, n. 340 (Marietti 113): "Superiora sunt in inferioribus, secundum participationem; inferiora vero sunt in superioribus, per excellentiam quamdam et sic omnia sunt in omnibus."

113. *SCG* I, c. 31 (Marietti 43): "Qui quidem effectus in suis causis sunt virtute, ut calor in sole. Virtus autem huiusmodi nisi aliqualiter esset de genere caloris, sol per eam agens non sibi simile generaret. Ex hac igitur virtute sol calidus dicitur, non solum quia calorem facit, sed quia virtus per quam hoc facit, est aliquid conforme calori."

Thus despite having no kind or *ratio* in common, agent and patient still have a "communication in form."[114]

There is an important lesson here for grasping Aquinas's understanding of agency: namely, *the only reason that there is any agency at all is that form fundamentally has the power of self-expression.* Agency is possible only where unity is possible, which is to say: where an expression of the agent is possible. Indeed, to be an effect just is nothing other than to be the expression of the agent's form.

Moreover, if it is possible to act across orders of being—where agent and effect can have no nature in common—then it must be possible for form's self-expression to be realized at a radically lower level of being. Indeed, this possibility must be one of the most basic structuring principles of reality, because the very first action—God's creating—produces an effect at a lower order: namely, creatures.[115] So for Aquinas, what explains creaturely agent-effect pairings is just what explains why there can be anything other than God in the first place: namely, action is the self-expression of form, and this self-expression can be realized at ontological levels far below that of the agent in itself, without the need for any common nature.

To return to the objection, then: for Aquinas, "having heat eminently" is not reducible to "having the power to cause heat," but is rather what fundamentally *explains* having the power to cause heat. Causal pairings are more fundamentally explained by the self-expressive possibilities of form. "The likeness makes nonunivocal causation possible," as Aquinas says in the *Sentences* commentary.[116] Agency is self-expression; and

---

114. See note 59 above.

115. This point can be put in terms of causal participation; see Gregory T. Doolan, "Aquinas on *Esse Subsistens* and the Third Mode of Participation," *The Thomist* 82 (2018): 611–42; te Velde, *Participation and Substantiality*, 92: "An effect may be said to participate in its cause, especially when it is not equal to the power of that cause (*non adaequat virtutem causae*).... The effect falls short of its cause, receives only partly what the cause has fully and undiminished" (citing Aquinas's example of the air's participation in the light of the sun in *In De hebd.* 2, n. 24, and *ST* I, q. 104, a. 1).

116. *In Sent.* II, d. 15, q. 1, a. 2, ad 4 (Mandonnet 373): "Similia sunt quae in eadem forma communicant; sed contingit quod illam formam non uniformiter participant quaedam; quia quod est in uno deficienter, in altero est eminentius: et hoc oportet inveniri, secundum Dionysium, in omnibus causis essentialibus: et ideo ipse dicit quod sol uniformiter praeaccepit in se omnia ea quae divisim per actionem in aliis causantur: et secundum hoc dico, quod calor et frigus et hujusmodi inveniuntur in corporibus caelestibus nobiliori modo quam in elementis; non quod istis qualitatibus afficiantur et denominentur, sed sunt in eis sicut in virtute activa; et talis similitudo sufficit ad actionem agentis non univoce"; *In Sent.* III, d. 1, q. 1, a. 1, ad 3

therefore an agent has a proportion to (unity with) any X that constitutes an expression of its own form. "Being X preeminently" consists in having such a proportion. And being preeminently X is supposed to explain why this being has a causal power to bring about X—*not the other way around*.

Likeness of proportionality (4)

Now that we know that a proportion can be a kind of unity, we can make sense of our fourth kind of likeness: namely, likeness of proportionality.[117] The "one" that founds these likeness-relations is neither a natural "one," nor the *ratio* of some natural kind. Rather, it is a "one" which is a proportion among items. Likeness of proportionality arises when the proportion ordering one set of items (A-B) is also found in another set (C-D). In that case, A and C each stand in the same proportion *x* to something else (A:B and C:D). So A and C are one in their proportion to B and D, respectively, and that unity grounds a "likeness of proportionality." Aquinas's standard example is mathematical: six is to three, as four is to two. Within each number pair, the proportion of higher number to lower number is "double." And therefore *six is like four* in the extremely thin sense that both stand in a doubling relationship to other numbers with which they are paired: six is the double of three, and four is the double of two.[118]

(Moos 10): "Movens et motum debent esse proportionabilia, et agens et patiens, ut scilicet sicut agens potest imprimere aliquem effectum, ita patiens possit recipere eumdem"; *De ver.*, q. 2, a. 3 (Leon. 22/1.51:237-40): "Cum omne agens agat in quantum est in actu oportet quod illud quod per agentem efficitur aliquo modo sit in agente, et inde est quod omne agens agit sibi simile"; *In De div. nom.* 2.2 (Marietti 46): "Per effectus progredientes ab ipso [Deo] manifestatur, et quodammodo ipsa deitas in effectus procedit, dump sui similitudinem rebus tradit, secundum earum proportionem, ita tamen, quod sua excellentia et singularitas sibi remanet, incommunicata rebus et occulta nobis."

117. "Likeness of proportionality" is the metaphysical underpinning for a type of analogical predication that scholars call "analogy of proportionality," using language that derives from *De ver.*, q. 2, a. 11 (see below). This type of analogical predication has triggered a longstanding debate about its role in Aquinas's theory of divine naming, and whether it was eventually superseded by the so-called analogy of many-to-one. See, on the one side, e.g., Wippel, *Metaphysical Thought*, 543-72; and on the other side, e.g., Joshua Hochschild, "Proportionality vs. Divine Naming: Did Aquinas Change His Mind about Analogy?," *The Thomist* 77 (2013): 531-58. I set aside this debate about divine naming; my sole concern here is to parse this fourth kind of likeness metaphysically, and not to draw any implications for Aquinas's views on divine naming.

118. *De ver.*, q. 2, a. 11 (Leon. 22/1.79:146-65): "Convenientia etiam quandoque attenditur non duorum ad invicem inter quae sit proportio sed magis duarum ad invicem proportionum, sicut senarius convenit cum quaternario ex hoc quod sicut senarius est duplum ternarii, ita

This likeness is founded in unities wholly unbound from natural kinds: namely, the unity of two sets whose members have the same relationship to each other. So just as in kind-likeness and *ratio*-likeness, likeness of proportionality is founded on a "one" that is had in common by the *relata*. However, this unity is the thinnest mode of unity in the whole taxonomy. A proportion is a declining kind of unity and need not have anything to do with a natural kind.[119] For instance, "defect" is a proportion found in the sinful incorporeal will and a mustard-spotted white linen shirt, relative to their very different perfections. Likeness of proportionality, in short, is grounded on schematic patterns that recur indifferently to the natures in which they occur.[120]

Thus likeness of proportionality is the thinnest of Aquinas's mode of likeness. Nevertheless, it plays an important role in Aquinas's thought. His examples are abundant and delightful. Grace is like water, in that each removes a defect (sin on the one hand, dirt on the other).[121] Flowering is like laughing, in that each perfectively ornaments some nature (a field, a human being).[122] Roots are like a mouth, in that each is the nutritional intake for some being (plants, animals). God is like fire, in that each consumes its contraries (cold, wickedness).[123] Aquinas even appeals to likeness of proportionality to explain why, because love arises from likeness, one can nonetheless love a friend for having a strength that one lacks. A good singer can love a good scribe, because they both have what is proper to their profession (a well-trained voice, elegant penmanship).[124] Indeed, likeness of proportionality thus provides Aquinas with a principled account of metaphor, because where there are proportional

---

quaternarius binarii"; Aquinas labels this a "convenientia proportionalitatis," and connects it with a certain type of analogical predication, "sicut nomen visus dicitur de visu corporali et intellectu, eo quod sicut visus est in oculo, ita intellectus in mente."

119. Of course some proportions follow from natures, as natural orientations, like the proportion of active power to effect (as the expression of the agent's form). But the point is that likeness of proportionality can be founded on *any* proportion, as a *habitudo* or ordering, without requiring the proportion to be a natural orientation. See, e.g., In De div. nom. 4.8 (Marietti 129), distinguishing proportions that are "convenientes secundum naturam et conditionem rerum" from those that are not.

120. As Hochschild puts it, "Four-term proportionality is a way of describing a relation of likeness that need not involve a common quality or form shared by the relata" ("Proportionality vs. Divine Naming," 546–47).

121. See note 23 above.
122. ST I, q. 13, a. 6.
123. In Sent. I, d. 45, q. 1, a. 4
124. ST I-II, q. 27, a. 3, ad 2.

pairs, the names of one can be cross-applied to another (e.g., "laughing fields").[125]

Likeness of proportionality also does serious work for Aquinas's metaphysics. He uses likeness of proportionality to develop metaphysical notions that apply across the categories. For instance, "whatness" (*quid*) is properly substantial. Nonetheless, unity of proportion makes it possible to answer the question of "what it is" concerning an accident: "color" stands to "whiteness" as "animal" stands to "human."[126] Again, likeness of proportionality helps him explain why it is legitimate for Aristotle to analyze the structure of natural substances (e.g., a tree composed of tree-form and prime matter) by means of the structure of artifacts (i.e., a statue composed of shape and bronze). Artifacts are accidental wholes, and substantial and accidental wholeness are irreducibly diverse modes of wholeness. But they can be compared via a form-matter proportion that is "one" once we abstract from those modes.[127]

In fact, Aquinas's examples are so many, and so diverse, that one might be inclined not to take this classification very seriously. Likeness of proportionality might look like an enormous basket into which Aquinas tosses not only technical metaphysical notions, but also colorful metaphors, pedagogical illustrations, and instructive comparisons (*simile est ... non simile est*). It is tempting to pick some cases as philosophically "serious" and dismiss others as mere rhetorical flourishes.

I would suggest, however, that there is something quite sophisticated going on here. These ascriptions of likeness are possible only in virtue of some one proportion that is *really there* in the "deep structure" of created reality, underneath all the other usual sorts of expected commonalities (unity of kind, unity of ratio, agent-effect proportion, etc.). The fact that one proportion is intellectually detectable only by abstracting from a thing's real nature does not mean that the unity is not real. If someone can be praised for having "a heart of gold," that is because the metaphor *uncovers* some real unity, according to which there is *already* one proportion in virtue-to-character and gold-to-value.[128]

---

125. *ST* I, q. 13, a. 6.
126. *In Meta.* VII.4, n. 4.
127. *In Meta.* VII.2, n. 8.
128. Similarly, Ralph McInerny, *Aquinas on Analogy* (Washington, DC: The Catholic University of America Press, 2012), chap. 6, takes Aquinas's talk of metaphor seriously, though he is more concerned with predication than likeness. However, he gives an account in terms of

Aquinas's notion of likeness of proportionality is therefore somewhat like the contemporary scientific notion of "modeling by analogy," where one reality is understood by means of another due to a correspondence of pattern found in each.[129] Intriguingly, however, Aquinas's metaphysics offers *a principled account of why such modeling is possible*. That is to say, Aquinas can explain *why* the same proportions—patterns—are repeated across creaturely beings of different natural kinds and even of different "orders of being." The reason is that agents at higher orders of being (those that induce "power-likeness") act as universal causes on entire genera of substances to bring about a variety of effects that express the agent's power in different ways. The sun, for instance, does not just heat the terrestrial world, but is also the universal cause of every substance in the genus "terrestrial body," even though generating those substances usually also requires an intermediate cause in the same species: a sheep is generated by the parent sheep as particular cause and the sun as universal cause. Indeed as I mentioned earlier, Aquinas insists that unity of kind in many individuals (e.g., single genus or species) requires one efficient cause that brings about all members of that kind without itself being a member of that kind. And the entire causal order reduces to one single cause at the top: God as universal cause of all created being (with angels in between, using the heavenly bodies as instruments).

Thus we can see why the same proportions are found across diverse natures: namely, because whole regions of created realities are unified by depending on some universal cause, and indeed all of created being is unified by depending on God; and because agents make something like themselves. Because diverse effects can be the expression of some universal agent (and indeed all created effects are the expression of divine power), we should expect that they will be internally structured according to the same proportions. It is no accident that for both fields and humans there is something that perfectively decorates each, or that the notion of "defect removal" properly encompasses both grace and laundry

---

likeness: "The thing named metaphorically has a property or effect similar to an effect or property of that which the term properly signifies" (133). I, however, am concerned with specifying the kind of likeness in question.

129. See, e.g., Mary B. Hesse, *Models and Analogies in Science* (Notre Dame, IN: University of Notre Dame Press, 1966); and more recently Daniela M. Bailer-Jones, "Models, Metaphors, and Analogies," in *The Blackwell Guide to the Philosophy of Science* (Oxford: Blackwell, 2002), 108–27.

treatment spray. The "one" of a proportion is a real unity that can be found within and across various orders and kinds of being. The unities—and therefore the accompanying likeness-relations—are *there already* to be discovered.

CONCLUSION: EVERY AGENT PRODUCES SOMETHING LIKE ITSELF

In summary, I hope to have justified the following broad theses concerning Aquinas's concept of likeness:

1. Aquinas's notion of likeness goes beyond the strict boundaries of the Aristotelian definition of likeness as "a relation grounded in unity of quality."

2. Nonetheless, there are some special characteristics of quality that make "unity of quality" an apt stand-in for Aquinas's highly flexible and diverse notion of what *does* ground likeness.

3. Aquinas's actual reconstructed view is that likeness is a relation grounded on *any* unity short of numerical unity.

4. Four modes of likeness can be identified in his writings, grounded on four modes of unity: unity of natural kind, unity of *ratio*, kind-proportional unities, and unity of proportion.

Let us now return to the *Omne agens* axiom to draw out some implications.

In the introduction, I noted that the *Omne agens* axiom has drawn skepticism on the grounds that it is either obviously false (because some patients do not turn out like their agents), or that it is only artificially made to be true by relabeling any old causal relationship as "likeness." As I mentioned there already, this skepticism is only partly dissolved by a well-known clarification:

5. The *Omne agens* axiom applies only to agents acting *per se*.

But the key to dissolving the remaining skepticism lies in two further claims about the theory of agency undergirding the axiom, which I hope to have justified in this chapter:

6. Aquinas understands *per se* action as nothing other than the expression of form.

7. Some agents are capable of expressing what they have at another level of being with which they share no common nature.

From there, we can gain two important insights into why Aquinas takes the *Omne agens* axiom as sweepingly true, and why it is important for his metaphysics.

First, we can now see that it is getting things exactly backward to construe the *Omne agens* axiom as ascribing some arbitrary characteristic to causation, which Aquinas must then tie himself in knots to protect. In reality, this axiom *specifies the nature of agency in terms of self-expression*. Agents necessarily draw their patients into a certain unity with themselves, because by acting they are doing nothing other than expressing their own form. Therefore the possibility of agency is *explained by* the possibility for likeness—and therefore, more fundamentally, by the possibility for unity where there is numerical diversity.

In Aquinas's metaphysics, then, the notion of likeness is more fundamental than the notion of agency itself. And therefore Aquinas has a principled way of explaining why any given agent is paired with any given effect. The pairing is not unprincipled and inexplicable, nor is it imposed extrinsically. Rather, because *per se* agency is self-expression, an agent is naturally paired with whatever is capable of becoming in some way one with (and therefore like) the agent itself.

The second insight is that the unity that grounds likeness does not need to be the unity of some natural "one" held in common by agent and patient. One of the obstacles to understanding the *Omne agens* axiom is the tendency to believe that if two things are alike, they must have some discrete feature in common (same shape, color, size, substantial species, etc.). This belief is what underwrites the common assumption, even among readers of Aquinas, that likeness is really just "sameness in some respect." And if we do not see any common features in agent and patient, we assume that there must be no likeness.

In reality, as we saw, Aquinas admits many modes of unity: for example, unity in *ratio* (where the *ratio* at least is had in common), the unity that is the proportion of a power and its expression (where there is no "one" in common at all), and the unity of proportions themselves (where the unity is purely schematic, abstracting completely from the natures in which those proportions are found). Crucially, then, likeness is not a partial sameness. Far less is it a kind of resemblance. Instead, we could think of likeness in Aquinas's sense as a relational affinity of one thing for another, arising from some degree of unity (and indeed, Aquinas connects love with likeness). On this construal, two *relata* that have no single common feature or even any single common *ratio* of a feature can nonetheless have a degree of unity and, to that extent, a degree of likeness. And because the possibility for unity is the possibility for agency, we can see how Aquinas makes action possible across orders of being that are embraced by no common genus.

Aquinas's notion of likeness, in short, is central to his notion of being as structured into orders that are not generically reducible to some undifferentiated univocal "substance," while still preserving the possibility for causality across orders.[130] Being is one and many only because being implicitly entails the possibility of likeness.

---

130. Thus *contra* McInerny, *Aquinas on Analogy,* 161–63, it is not true that there is nothing in Aquinas corresponding to what is usually called the "analogy of being." Rather, orders of being are irreducibly diverse, but nonetheless alike, in such a way as to make possible a cascade of causal relationships.

Part 3 ～ The Essential Structure of Finite Being

Stephen L. Brock

6 ∞ Created Form as Act and Potency in the Metaphysics of Thomas Aquinas

INTRODUCTION: THE QUESTION

Much of the work of philosophy consists in making good distinctions (and fixing bad ones). In the thought of St. Thomas Aquinas, few distinctions are more fundamental, or have wider ranges of application, than the distinction between potency (*potentia*) and act (*actus*).[1] Why it is so important is not difficult to say. It is a division of that nature which for Thomas is the most fundamental and wide-ranging of all: what he calls *ens*. In these pages I call it 'entity.'[2] He regards entity, insofar as it is entity, as the subject of the highest philosophical science—metaphysics—and one cannot go far into his metaphysics without encountering the distinction between potency and act.[3] Msgr. Wippel has done important work on the notion of the reception of act by potency and on the metaphysical principle that a receptive potency limits the act that it receives.[4]

In this chapter I propose to raise and to resolve a difficulty regarding

---

1. All translations into English in this chapter are mine. Unless otherwise indicated, citations of works of Thomas Aquinas refer to the Leonine edition.

2. It is more often rendered *being*. But I reserve that term for Thomas's *esse*, about which I will have much to say.

3. For example, it already shows up as something that "follows upon" entity, in the *proemium* (brief as it is) of *In Meta.* (Marietti 1). The *Metaphysics* commentary is one of Thomas's last works. The distinction between potency and act also appears at the very beginning of one of his earliest works, *De prin. nat.* 1 (Leon. 43.39:1–4).

4. John F. Wippel, "Thomas Aquinas and the Axiom that Unreceived Act Is Unlimited," in Wippel, *Metaphysical Themes in Thomas Aquinas II* (Washington, DC: The Catholic University of America, 2007), 123–51.

Thomas's metaphysics of potency and act. The difficulty concerns their application to another metaphysical distinction of his, the well-known distinction between *essentia* and *esse*, essence and being, in all created entities. The core of the difficulty is how Thomas characterizes creaturely form. On the one hand, he often presents form as a kind of act. On the other, he sometimes describes created form as a kind of potency. It is a receptive potency for the act that is being itself, *esse*, or (as he occasionally calls it) *actus essendi*. So the question is evident. If, as Aristotle teaches, potency and act somehow divide some field, namely entity, how can one thing be both? Does created form really stand on both sides of the division?

To my knowledge, this question has not been given extended or thematic treatment in the literature on Thomas's metaphysics. However, as I shall indicate in due course, several prominent interpreters, including Msgr. Wippel, have touched upon it in significant ways. The chapter proceeds as follows. The first section sets Thomas's conception of form as act in its Aristotelian context. By this I mean two things: Aristotle's distinction between potency and act, and his account of form as cause of being. In the second section, after spelling out the aforesaid difficulty a little more, I observe that Aristotle himself seems to associate at least one kind of form—that is, soul—with certain potencies, and I look at Thomas's metaphysical analysis of this association. What I find is that, if anything, this analysis only makes it harder to understand how form can be potency for anything. In the third section, I sketch the sort of resolution of the difficulty that I think many Thomists today would give, and I raise a problem about it. The fourth and fifth sections present my own resolution; in the fourth section, I determine the sense in which created form is act, while in the fifth section, I pin down the nature of its potency for being, and then I argue that, so understood, it does not after all stand on both sides of the division of entity according to act and potency. I end the chapter with a consideration of how this reading dovetails with Thomas's extension of the notion of form to the deity.

THE *METAPHYSICS* COMMENTARY AND FORM AS ACT

Book V of Aristotle's *Metaphysics* is a little dictionary of thirty terms. Most of the terms have several meanings, which Aristotle works to distinguish and set in order. St. Thomas, in his commentary, judges that

Created Form as Act and Potency 179

all the terms figure in the science of metaphysics. Some, he says, signify causes of this science's subject, which is entity (*ens*). Others signify either the subject itself, or parts of it. Still others signify attributes of it. The twelfth term is *potentia*, potency.[5] Thomas says that Aristotle here begins to distinguish terms signifying parts of entity, and that he first treats the division of entity into *potentia et actus*, potency and act.[6]

This last assertion is a little surprising, given that *act* is not among the terms examined in Book V.[7] It is not given thematic treatment in the *Metaphysics* until Book IX. Thomas, however, thinks he can explain this. Taking the *Metaphysics* as a unified work, he says that Aristotle does not examine *act* in Book V because "he could not explain its meaning sufficiently unless the nature of forms were first made clear, as he will do in Books VIII and IX."[8] Now, Thomas does not say how the nature of forms helps explain *act*. I think, however, that we can at least glimpse something of the importance of form for the understanding of act, if we consider some remarks from Thomas's commentary on Book IX, together with others from his *Physics* and *De anima* commentaries.

Metaphysics IX begins the discussion of *act* (*energeia*) by saying, somewhat obscurely, that it applies to "*entelecheia* and other things, chiefly from motion."[9] Thomas glosses *entelecheia* as "perfection, that is, form," and he says that the "other things" are operations of any sort. As for motion, he says it is that to which the term *act* was first applied. This is not because motion has the nature of act most perfectly or to the highest degree, but simply because it is apparent to the senses.[10] Later in Book IX, we learn that some operations are not motions, but are rather what Aristotle calls perfect operations; for example, sensing.[11] These lines of Book IX do not figure in Thomas's *Metaphysics* commentary.[12] But in his

---

5. Aristotle, *Metaphysics* V.12, starting at 1019a15.
6. Aquinas, *In Meta.* V.14, n. 954. Throughout this chapter, I use the term *act* to render Thomas's *actus*.
7. It does, however, make an important brief appearance there; see below, at note 133.
8. "Nomen autem actus praetermittit, quia eius significationem sufficienter explicare non poterat, nisi prius natura formarum esset manifesta, quod faciet in octavo et nono": Aquinas, *In Meta.* V.14, n. 954 (Marietti 305). I wonder a little whether originally the last four words were not *in septimo et octavo*. We await the critical edition.
9. "ἐλήλυθε δ᾽ ἡ ἐνέργεια τοὔνομα, ἡ πρὸς τὴν ἐντελέχειαν συντιθεμένη, καὶ ἐπὶ τὰ ἄλλα ἐκ τῶν κινήσεων μάλιστα," in Aristotle, *Metaphysics*, vol. II, ed. W. D. Ross (Oxford: Oxford University Press, 1924), IX.3.1047a30–31.
10. Aquinas, *In Meta.* IX.3, n. 1805.
11. Aristotle, *Metaphysics* IX.6.1048b18–36.
12. They are missing from both of the Latin translations of the *Metaphysics* to which

De anima commentary, he explains that sensing is a perfect operation inasmuch as its subject is already in act through the form (the *species*) of the object that defines the operation. By contrast, the subject of motion—that is, the sort of bodily motion that is treated in Aristotle's *Physics*—is merely in potency to the form that terminates or completes the motion, and such motion is defined as the act of what is in potency.[13] To this we can add a point from Thomas's interpretation, in his *Physics* commentary, of this definition of motion. An act that is a motion is a partial possession of the form that functions as the motion's endpoint. For example, in a process of heating, the endpoint is some degree of heat, and the act that is the heating itself is a lesser, gradually increasing share of heat.[14] Both perfect operation and motion, then, seem somehow to derive their natures as acts from the act that is form.

The extension of the term *act* beyond motion to perfect operation and to form also impacts the term *potency*. Most properly, Aristotle says, *potency* means some principle of motion; either active potency, for moving something, or passive potency, for being moved by something.[15] But he says that this meaning is not what mainly interests him, and that *potency* extends beyond motion.[16] Principles of other types of act are also potencies. Matter is potency for form; sight, for seeing. Thomas adds that potency and act are also in intellectual things.[17] In the *Summa theologiae* he says generally that "potency signifies nothing other than a principle of some act."[18]

For Thomas, then, form is certainly a type of act. If anything, he seems to insist on this point even more strongly than Aristotle does. Nor is the point confined to Thomas's Aristotelian commentaries. The full list of places in his works where form is called act would be very long. He is also clear that it is not just sometimes or by association that the name of

---

Thomas had access. See *Aristoteles Latinus XXV 2, Metaphysica, Lib. I–X, XII–XIV, Translatio Anonyma sive 'Media,'* ed. Gudrun Vuillemin-Diem (Leiden: Brill, 1976), 175; *Aristoteles Latinus XXV 3.2, Metaphysica, Lib. I–XIV, Recensio et Translatio Guillelmi de Moerbeke*, ed. Gudrun Vuillemin-Diem (Leiden: Brill, 1995), 186.

13. *In De an.* III.6 (Leon. 45/1.230:17–36).
14. *In Phys.* III.2, n. 285.
15. Aristotle, *Metaphysics* IX.1.1046a9–15.
16. Ibid., 1045b35–1046a2 and 1048a25–30.
17. Aquinas, *In Meta.* IX.1, n. 1770. On the extension of *potency*, see also *In Meta.* IX.5, n. 1824.
18. *ST* I, q. 41, a. 4 (Leon. 4.428): "Potentia nihil aliud significet quam principium alicuius actus."

act applies to form. "Form insofar as it is form is act."[19] Form "by its essence is act."[20]

What does Thomas mean by this? I think the simplest answer is that form, just as form, is that by which, immediately, a thing is somehow *in act*. Being in act follows at once on any form, because it is a form. We can build on this answer by considering that, for Thomas, being in act is itself what is properly meant by entity, *ens*, itself.[21] Properly speaking, things that are not in act, but only in potency, *are not*. In countless places, Thomas presents form as that by which a thing is in act and has being. "Form, according to what it is, is act, and by it, things exist in act."[22] Once he even says "that which is act is form."[23] There he is explaining why matter cannot be without form. It would be "an entity in act without act, which implies a contradiction."[24] The places are innumerable, and span Thomas's entire career, where he says that "form gives being to matter."[25]

At least part of what it means to call form act, then, is that a form is that through which a thing somehow is. Form is, as Aristotle says, the "primary cause of being," *prima causa essendi*.[26] Now, this expression, "primary cause of being," is one that Thomas mostly reserves for God.

---

19. *ST* I, q. 75, a. 5 (Leon. 5.202): "Forma inquantum forma est actus."

20. *ST* I, q. 76, a. 7 (Leon. 5.231): "Forma autem per seipsam facit rem esse in actu, cum per essentiam suam sit actus." See also *ST* I, q. 77, a. 1, discussed in the second section below. Following are just a few examples of Thomas's calling form act in earlier works: "quia forma facit esse in actu, ideo forma dicitur esse actus" (*De prin. nat.* 1 [Leon. 43.39:42–43]); "omnis forma actus dicitur, etiam ipsae formae separatae" (*In Sent.* I, d. 42, q. 1, a. 1, ad 1 [Mandonnet 1.983]); "sicut forma est actus, ita materia est potentia" (*In Sent.* II, d. 12, q. 1, a. 1, s.c. 1 [Mandonnet 2.301]); "forma comparatur ad materiam ut actus ad potentiam" (*De ver.*, q. 8, a. 9 [Leon. 22/2.249:105–6]); "quidquid enim in rerum natura invenitur, actu existit, quod quidem non habet materia nisi per formam, quae est actus eius; unde non habet sine forma in rerum natura inveniri" (*De pot.*, q. 4, a. 1 [Marietti 105]); "omnis forma est actus" (*De spir. creat.* 3 [Leon. 44/2.39:237]). But it is in one of his very last works that, in my opinion, he puts it mostly strongly, saying "esse formam alicuius est esse actus eiusdem" (*De sub. sep.* 7 [Leon. 40/D.53:115–16]).

21. *ST* I, q. 5, a. 1, ad 1 (Leon. 4.56): "Cum ens dicat aliquid proprie esse in actu."

22. *SCG* II, c. 30 (Leon. 13.339:a2–3): "Forma autem, secundum id quod est, actus est, et per eam res actu existunt."

23. *ST* I, q. 66, a. 1 (Leon. 5.154): "Ipsum autem quod est actus, est forma."

24. Ibid.: "Dicere igitur materiam praecedere sine forma, est dicere ens actu sine actu, quod implicat contradictionem."

25. On the origin of the formula *forma dat esse materiae*, see Lawrence Dewan, OP, *Form and Being: Studies in Thomistic Metaphysics* (Washington, DC: The Catholic University of America Press, 2006), 171n18.

26. Aristotle, *Metaphysics* VII.17.1041b28: "αἴτιον πρῶτον τοῦ εἶναι."

Nevertheless he accepts Aristotle's description without comment.[27] I think he can do so because he is taking it to mean that this *kind* of cause, the intrinsic formal cause, is cause of a thing's being more truly and properly than any other kind is.[28] To be sure, the other kinds of cause that a thing may have—end, agent, matter—are also somehow causes of its being.[29] But they may be exercising their causality even before the thing exists, while it is still only in potency, on the way toward being; that is, they may be causing the process of its generation. Sometimes the process is cut short, so that the thing never actually exists. That is because its form is never reached. The thing cannot be without its form. But the formal cause, as such, *only* causes what is an entity in act.[30] Indeed, upon receiving its form, a thing's being in act follows *necessarily*.[31] The thing cannot cease to be except by losing its form. Nor is form a cause of only certain types or modes of being. It is cause of any being whatsoever, *causa cuiuslibet essendi*.[32] Perhaps we can say that the formal cause is primary in the sense that it is the *immediate* cause of a thing's being.

FORMS WHOSE ESSENCE INCLUDES ACT AND POTENCY

For anyone familiar with Thomas's metaphysics, this insistence on form as act surely invites the question that I posed at the beginning. Nothing in his metaphysics is more famous than the distinction between essence and being in every creature.[33] He says they relate as potency to act. Now the essence of many creatures is not form alone. In bodily creatures, part of the essence is (common) matter, which is potency and not act. But form is part of their essence too.[34] And in spiritual creatures, essence is

---

27. See Aquinas, *In Meta.* VII.17, n. 1678.
28. This is in no way to deny that creaturely form is God's effect; see below, at note 85.
29. *In Post. an.* II.7 (Leon. 1*/2.198:31–48).
30. See *ST* I, q. 5, a. 2, ad 2, and Aristotle, *Metaphysics* XII.3.1070a21–24.
31. See, e.g., *ST* I, q. 50, a. 5, and q. 75, a. 6; see also note 116 below.
32. Aquinas, *In Meta.* VIII.2, n. 1696 (Marietti 492). On the formal cause as cause of being and in relation to other causes, I would call special attention to the work of Lawrence Dewan, OP, particularly his *Form and Being* and *St. Thomas and Form as Something Divine in Things* (Milwaukee, Wis.: Marquette University Press, 2007).
33. For a thorough presentation of the many texts in which the distinction appears, and of Thomas's arguments for it, see John F. Wippel, *The Metaphysical Thought of Thomas Aquinas* (Washington, DC: The Catholic University of America Press, 2000), 132–76.
34. This is what Thomas occasionally calls *forma partis*, having in view the fact that the

nothing but form. An angel is *ipsa forma subsistens*—a form itself, subsisting.[35] Is this not paradoxical? How can it be that form is act, that a created essence is potency, and that a created essence either includes a form or is even nothing but a form? To be in potency and to be in act are opposed. Entity, *ens*, is divided according to act and potency. Created form seems to straddle the division. How can this be?

The question can be set in sharper relief by recalling that Aristotle himself seems to associate at least some forms, souls, with potencies of some sort. In *Metaphysics* IX, for instance, sight and knowledge are presented as potencies for seeing and for speculating.[36] In *De anima* III, intellectual soul is called a form, indeed a "form of forms" (εἶδος εἰδῶν),[37] and its nature is said to be in potency to the intelligibles.[38] Also, in *De anima* II, soul in general is defined as first act of a body having life in potency, and Aristotle is careful to add that what has life in potency is the body *with* soul.[39] This sounds rather as though the potency for life is soul itself.

We should notice, however, that these potencies are all for operation, not for being. Even in the general definition of soul, the word *life* signifies vital operation. Or at least that is how Thomas takes it.[40] It is not life in the sense of the very being of a living thing. Of course Thomas knows that Aristotle does also speak of life in this sense. He does so just a little later in *De anima* II, when he argues that soul, as cause of life, is cause of being, and that therefore it is "substance" (οὐσία)—that is, what the Scholastics will call substantial form.[41] But here, in defining soul, Aristotle ascribes no potency for being, or for life so taken, to soul; nor does Thomas in his commentary. The only thing indicated there as substantial potency, or as potency for life understood as the being of the living thing, is the animated body or matter.

---

whole essence of a bodily substance, even though really composed of form and (common) matter, can be taken abstractly and thereby treated as a form as well, called *forma totius*; see, e.g., *Quod.* 2.2.2. Throughout this chapter I am speaking only about forms that are *not* really composites of form and matter, forms that either inhere in or exist separately from matter.

35. *ST* I, q. 50, a. 5.
36. Aristotle, *Metaphysics* IX.6.1048b2, IX.8.1050a10–14, 1050b36–1051a3.
37. Aristotle, *De anima* III.8.432a1–3.
38. Aristotle, *De anima* III.4.429a27–29.
39. Aristotle, *De anima* II.1.412b25–26.
40. See Aquinas, *In De an.* II.2 (Leon. 45/1.75–76:105–38); *ST* I, q. 76, a. 4, ad 1, and q. 77, a. 1; *In Ethic.* IX.7 (Leon. 47/2.525:89–95).
41. Aristotle, *De anima* II.4.415b12–14; Aquinas, *In De an.* II.7 (Leon. 45/1.97–98:172–87).

Even more interesting is Thomas's own highly metaphysical account, in the *Summa theologiae*, of the human soul's potency for vital operations. There he insists on distinguishing between soul's one essence and the many immediate principles of its operations. His reason is that soul "according to its essence is act" (*secundum suam essentiam est actus*), whereas what actually has soul does not always have the vital operations; that is, the operations may be only in potency. "For nothing is in potency by reason of an act, insofar as it is act."[42] For this reason, the immediate operative principles must be potencies, *potentiae*, that are distinct from and added to soul's essence as accidents. Thomas also remarks that, insofar as it is act, soul is not ordered to further act, but is the ultimate terminus of generation. If it is called *first* act, indicating order toward further act, this is not according to its essence alone, or just insofar as it is a form, but only "insofar as it underlies its potency."[43]

In this same article, Thomas also says that what actually has soul, although not always operating, always is alive. The reason is precisely that soul by its essence is act. Here, clearly, life is to be understood as the being of the living thing; yet he is not identifying soul with life. He is seeing soul as a principle of life—as the *immediate* principle, by its essence and not through added potencies. Strikingly, however, in the sixth reply of this very article, Thomas insists that soul has something of potentiality "mixed in" (*admixtum*). This does not mean joined on as an accident. It means belonging to soul's very essence. This essential potentiality is needed in order to explain how soul can underlie accidents at all. A "pure" act cannot be a subject of accidents. This explanation is not *ad hoc*; a few pages earlier, he states that, although containing no matter, soul participates its being and so relates to it as potency to act.[44] He clearly meant that it does so by its own essence. But what is striking is that he is using this point precisely to defend the argument that soul's operative potencies must be *outside* its essence *because* it is essentially act.

---

42. *ST* I, q. 77, a. 1 (Leon. 5.237): "Nihil enim est in potentia secundum actum, inquantum est actus."

43. Ibid.: "Ipsa anima, secundum quod subest suae potentiae, dicitur actus primus, ordinatus ad actum secundum." Along this line, in the *De anima* commentary, which is contemporary with the *Prima pars*, Thomas says that Aristotle calls soul first act in order to distinguish it not only from operation but also from the forms of the elements, which "always have their action, unless they are impeded" (*semper habent suam actionem nisi impediantur*); *In De an.* II.1 (Leon. 45/1.71:319).

44. *ST* I, q. 75, a. 5, ad 4. For a similar account of angels, see *ST* I, q. 54, a. 3, ad 2, and q. 50, a. 2, ad 2 and ad 3.

In short, that in virtue of which this form, soul, is act *is* that in virtue of which it is potency for its being; namely, its own incomposite self, its simple essence. This only heightens our difficulty. The same thing is both potency and act, and even what makes it be both is the same. How is this?

A COMMON RESOLUTION, AND A PROBLEM

To this question, my impression is that many readers of Thomas today would respond along lines that can be traced to two great twentieth-century Thomists, Étienne Gilson and Cornelio Fabro.[45] Of course these two thinkers did not agree on everything, and Thomism now has many strands. But I do think the answers offered by many—I shall cite some prominent examples as I proceed—would take a common shape, which is roughly as follows.

The reason why one created form, according to its simple essence, can be both potency and act is that it belongs to two different orders of being. One is the essential or formal order, also sometimes termed predicamental or categorial. In this order, form is indeed act, and even the cause of being, taken in a certain sense; namely, as categorial being. This is primarily being in the category, or genus, of substance; secondarily, it is being in some genus of accident. A form causes such being by completing the indeterminate potency of its matter and constituting a fully determinate species within the genus. This is form as Aristotelian act and cause of being.

Thomas's metaphysics of creation, however, introduces a new order of being. Gilson calls it *existential*; Fabro, *transcendental*. At its core is being in the sense of *actus essendi*. In this order, form itself is a potency, also of a new type. This potency is not indeterminate, as matter is, awaiting specification. It does, however, resemble the potency of matter, because it limits its act. Matter limits the form in it to one individual of the species that the form constitutes. Form limits its *actus essendi* to the species itself. Moreover, the way in which a thing's form "causes" its *actus essendi* is, at best, like the way in which its matter "causes" its form. Its matter is what enables it to have its form, and its form is what enables it to have its *actus essendi*.

---

45. A helpful discussion regarding Gilson, Fabro, and others on essence and being is Alain Contat, "Le figure della differenza ontologica nel tomismo del Novecento," *Alpha Omega* 11, no. 1 (2008): 77–129, and no. 2 (2008): 213–50.

Thus Gilson says that "by constituting substances, the forms give rise to the receiving subjects of existence, and, to that extent, they are causes of existence itself. In short, forms are 'formal' causes of existence, to the whole extent to which they contribute to the establishment of substances which are capable of existing."[46] He also says that "actual existence ... is the efficient cause by which essence in its turn is the formal cause which makes an actual existence to be 'such an existence.'"[47]

On Fabro's reading, the thesis "form gives being" holds only in the predicamental order.[48] "Every essence, although an act in the formal order, is created as potency to be actualized by the participated *esse* which it receives, so that its actuality is 'mediated' through the *esse*."[49] And more explicitly,

> form is said to bestow *esse*, inasmuch as it is only the real essence, determined by form as by its formal act, that is the true subject of the *actus essendi* ... Clearly, then, form is the true cause of *esse* but only within its order, inasmuch as it is the predicamental mediator between created finite being and the *esse per essentiam*, which is the First Cause.[50]

The potency of finite essence with respect to being is, for Fabro, the expression of the "positivity of the Thomistic nothingness in relation to the perfect actuality of God."[51]

---

46. Étienne Gilson, *Being and Some Philosophers* (Toronto: PIMS, 1952), 169; on formal versus existential actuality, see 170.

47. Gilson, *Being and Some Philosophers*, 172. Joseph Owens takes up and develops Gilson's position. See Joseph Owens, "The Accidental and Essential Character of Being in the Doctrine of St. Thomas Aquinas," in his *St. Thomas Aquinas on the Existence of God: Collected Papers of Joseph Owens, C.Ss.R.*, ed. John R. Catan (Albany: State University of New York Press, 1980), 52–96, esp. 76 and 93–96, where he argues that a creature's essence or form causes its *esse* in virtue of that very *esse*. See also Owens, *An Elementary Christian Metaphysics* (Milwaukee, WI: Bruce, 1963), esp. 75–76, 101n6, 105, 147. For a similar view, see Gaven Kerr, OP, *Aquinas's Way to God: The Proof in "De Ente et Essentia"* (Oxford: Oxford University Press, 2015), 58–62.

48. See Cornelio Fabro, *Participation et causalité selon S. Thomas d'Aquin* (Louvain: Publications universitaires de Louvain, 1961), 348.

49. Cornelio Fabro, "The Intensive Hermeneutics of Thomistic Philosophy. The Notion of Participation," *The Review of Metaphysics* 27, no. 3 (March 1974): 449–91, at 474.

50. Fabro, "The Intensive Hermeneutics," 475. Benedict M. Ashley, OP, *The Way toward Wisdom: An Interdisciplinary and Intercultural Introduction to Metaphysics* (Notre Dame, IN: University of Notre Dame Press, 2006), 339, calls form actuality and cause of existence; but then (341–43) he agrees with Fabro that the chief role of form and essence in relation to being is limiting, with all positivity coming from being itself. Pasquale Porro, *Thomas Aquinas: A Historical and Philosophical Profile*, trans. Joseph G. Trabbic and Roger W. Nutt (Washington, DC: The Catholic University of America Press, 2015), 158–59 and 213, presents form as act of matter, constituting a corporeal entity's essence, and as potency for being.

51. See Cornelio Fabro, "The Problem of Being and the Destiny of Man," *International*

Finally, on this "two-orders" view, just as the nature of form does not absolutely require matter—there are spiritual, subsistent forms—so too the nature of *actus essendi* does not absolutely require form. *Actus essendi* is first found in a pure, infinite way, subsisting. This is the true cause of all finite reality, the creator.

> God is by definition the Infinite and the Incomprehensible, because He is *Esse ipsum*; He therefore escapes every grasp of a finite presence, such as is created knowledge. Consciousness as speculative reason attains to form, and God does not have form but is *esse ipsum*. It [speculative reason] grasps the idea, but God is only real; He is the *Ens realissimum* that has no possibility in itself.[52]

Pasquale Porro is even more emphatic about God's not having a form. "The true novelty of Thomas's metaphysical thought," he declares, "is in its positing a radical caesura between what is being *and* form, viz., being determined by an essence (all of creation), and what is subsistent being alone, indeterminate and unobjectifiable."[53] He explains:

Philosophical Quarterly 1 (1961): 407–36, at 431. Going farther than Gilson, Fabro, and even Owens toward denying any positive role for form is W. Norris Clarke, SJ. Clarke first announced his "thin essence" view in "Limitation of Act by Potency: Aristotelianism or Neoplatonism," *The New Scholasticism* 26, no. 2 (1952): 167–94. Clarke criticizes Fabro and Owens for making essence a distinct positive subject; see "The Role of Essence within St. Thomas' Essence-Existence Doctrine: Positive or Negative Principle? A Dispute within Thomism," in *Tommaso d'Aquino nel suo settimo centenario: Atti del Congresso Internazionale*, vol. 6: *L'Essere* (Naples: Edizioni Domenicane Italiane, 1977), 109–15. See also Clarke's "What Cannot Be Said in St. Thomas' Essence-Existence Doctrine," *The New Scholasticism* 48, no. 1 (1974): 19–39, esp. 36–37, and his book, *The One and the Many: A Contemporary Thomistic Metaphysics* (Notre Dame, IN: University of Notre Dame Press, 2001), esp. 82–83, 153, 159, 318; see also 142 and 157, where he presents form as act, but only in relation to matter, as terminus of change.

52. "Dio è l'Infinito e l'Incomprensibile per definizione, poiché è l'Esse ipsum: sfugge perciò ad ogni presa di una presenza finita com'è il conoscere creato. La coscienza come ragione speculativa attinge la forma, e Dio non ha forma ma è l'esse ipsum. Essa comprende l'idea, ma Dio è soltanto reale; è l'*Ens realissimum* che non ha in sé possibilità." Cornelio Fabro, *La preghiera nel pensiero moderno* (Rome: Edizioni di storia e letteratura, 1983), 43. On God as having no form, less categorical than Fabro, but tending in that direction, is Étienne Gilson, *The Elements of Christian Philosophy* (New York: Doubleday, 1960), 113–48; on this see Lawrence Dewan, OP, "Etienne Gilson and the *Actus Essendi*," *Maritain Studies* 15 (1999): 1–27. Clarke shows a similar tendency; see Clarke, "The Role of Essence," 112–13, and *The One and the Many*, 234 and 237. To be sure, not all interpreters who are sympathetic with Fabro hold this view. Msgr. Wippel, for example, seems quite untroubled by Thomas's ascribing form to God; see Wippel, *The Metaphysical Thought*, 508, 511, 513, 535n124.

53. Porro, *Thomas Aquinas*, 23. My reasons for disagreeing with this reading of Thomas will come out in what follows, but it should also be observed that such a teaching would hardly be a "novelty" on Thomas's part, as its Neo-Platonic pedigree is well documented. See, for instance, the commentary on Plato's *Parmenides* attributed to Porphyry in Pierre Hadot, *Porphyre et Victorinus*, 2 vols. (Paris: Études Augustiniennes, 1968), esp. 1:132, 1:489–90, 2:107; David Bradshaw, "Neoplatonic Origins of the Act of Being," *The Review of Metaphysics* 53, no. 2

To say that in God his essence is resolved into his being is to maintain a negative position; it means recognizing that divine being—insofar as it is unlimited, that is, not determined by a quidditative content—is unrepresentable and unthinkable by us ... Thomas's God is not beyond being in the manner of Proclus's One, and, nevertheless, like the latter, he is above every form, every formal determination ... For Thomas, being is no longer a form but indicates what is other than form, other than essence. Pure being, then, will be what transcends every form, unlimited being.[54]

As I said, I think the "two-orders" reading of Thomas on form has become rather common.[55] Still, not all interpreters seem to have taken it on board. I am thinking, for example, of the late Lawrence Dewan, OP, and of the eminent Dutch expert on Aquinas's metaphysics, Rudi te Velde.[56] And I do think that such a reading faces serious problems. Here I will mention just one that is especially pertinent to my present topic.

Now it is clear that Thomas does not confine the doctrine of form as act to the domain of corporeal beings. Form is act even when it is not the act of any matter. "Every form is called act, even separate forms themselves."[57] Such act divides all the more from what is merely in potency. It is separate, subsistent act. There are many such immaterial acts. Every angel is one.[58] Each is a subsistent essence and form.[59] What an angel

---

(December 1999): 383–401; and Eric Perl, *Thinking Being: Introduction to Metaphysics in the Classical Tradition* (Leiden: Brill, 2014), esp. 151–65 (showing how close to Plotinus a reading like Porro's puts Thomas).

54. Porro, *Thomas Aquinas*, 202. See also 213, 344, 350–51.

55. See above, notes 45–54. Msgr. Wippel distinguishes two "levels," on one of which form is act, of matter, and on the other of which it is potency, for *esse*; see Wippel, *Metaphysical Thought*, 333. In a later writing, citing Fabro approvingly, Wippel says form is act "in the order of essence" or as "formal act," serving as a specifying and determining principle. This is how "it can be said to 'cause' the *esse* it receives": it makes the *esse* "be the act of existing of this kind of thing." But in the "order of existence," the form is nothing but a potential principle that receives and limits *esse*, as matter does form. See Wippel, "Thomas Aquinas and Creatures as Causes of *Esse*," in *Metaphysical Themes II*, 172–93, at 176–78. Wippel offers an extended study of Fabro on essence and *esse* in his "Cornelio Fabro on the Distinction and Composition of Essence and *Esse* in the Metaphysics of Thomas Aquinas," *The Review of Metaphysics* 68, no. 3 (March 2015): 573–92. In this article the status of form as act is not addressed.

56. For Dewan, see the works cited above in note 32. For te Velde, see his *Participation and Substantiality in Thomas Aquinas* (New York: E. J. Brill, 1995), esp. 212–33. I offer a synopsis of te Velde's book, and some reflections on it, in a review published in *Acta Philosophica*, VIII.1 (1999): 178–84.

57. *In Sent.* I, d. 42, q. 1, a. 1, ad 1 (Mandonnet 1.983): "Omnis forma actus dicitur, etiam ipsae formae separatae."

58. Aquinas, *De spir. creat.* 1, ad 22.

59. See Aquinas, *In Meta.* IX.11, n. 1912.

is not, however, is *pure* act.⁶⁰ The angelic form is an act "mixed" (*admixtum*) with potency.⁶¹ It is potency with respect to its being. And the potency of the angel's form limits its being to the species of a genus. So perhaps the "two-orders" reading of Thomas can acknowledge that even immaterial, subsistent forms are acts. They would still be so only in the categorial or formal order, as constituting complete essences and species. In the existential or transcendental order, they would only be potency.

Far more difficult for this reading, however, are the places where Thomas ascribes form to God himself.⁶² The truth is that Thomas insists, sometimes quite strongly, on there being a divine form. He calls it *deitas*.⁶³ God is "through his essence form" and "maximally a simple form."⁶⁴ Again, he is a "pure form" and a "form subsisting per se."⁶⁵ In one place Thomas even calls God *determinate*, in the sense of being just himself, distinct from all else.⁶⁶ Of course it is not that God is limited.⁶⁷ Nevertheless he is "specified" by his form, even "individuated" by it.⁶⁸ In short, God has (to say the least) his own identity, and to consider this just is to consider in him a function of form.⁶⁹ Particularly striking is a text that all but assigns a formal *cause* to God:

> Since the preposition *through* denotes a cause, that is said to stand or subsist through itself which does not have any other cause of being than itself. But there is a twofold cause of being, namely the form through which something is in act, and the agent that makes it be in act. If therefore that is called *standing through itself* which does not depend on a superior agent, to stand thus through itself belongs only to God ...⁷⁰

---

60. Aquinas, *De spir. creat.* 1, ad 17; *ST* I, q. 50, a. 2, ad 3, and q. 54, a. 3, ad 2.
61. *ST* I, q. 54, a. 1.
62. See the quotation from Fabro above at note 52.
63. Ascribing form to God may seem to derogate from his transcendence, but I argue the contrary; see Stephen L. Brock, "On Whether Aquinas's *Ipsum Esse* is 'Platonism,'" *The Review of Metaphysics* 60 (December 2006): 269–303, esp. 300–303.
64. *ST* I, q. 3, a. 2, and q. 13, a. 12, obj. 2.
65. *De car.*, q. un., a. 1, obj. 18 and ad 18 (Marietti, 754 and 757).
66. *Quod.* 7.1.1, ad 1. This article affirms our mind's capacity to see God's essence immediately, or in other words, the possibility for us of the Beatific Vision. Compare this passage with the Fabro and Porro quotations above at notes 52–54. I discuss the passage in "Formal Infinity, Perfection, and Determinacy in the Metaphysics of St. Thomas Aquinas," *Forum: Supplement to Acta Philosophica* 2 (2016): 103–23, at 115–17.
67. See *ST* I, q. 7, a. 1, and q. 4, a. 2.
68. Specification: *ST* I, q. 14, a. 5, ad 3. Individuation: *ST* I, q. 3, a. 2, ad 3, and a. 3; q. 11, a. 3; and q. 13, a. 9.
69. Identity is substantial unity: Aristotle, *Metaphysics* V.15.1021a11.
70. *In De caus.* 26 (Saffrey 128:2–7): "Cum praepositio per denotet causam, illud dicitur

We can hardly say there is nothing through which God is in act. He is in act through himself.

For Thomas, it seems to me, the idea of a reality that is being without form is no less absurd than that of matter existing without form. Form without matter is intelligible. Being without form is not. "Every being and good is considered through some form."[71] Granted, Thomas sometimes calls God *esse tantum*, being alone.[72] But he does not mean that God is formless being. He means that God is not composed of his being and anything else. That which is God's being and that which is God's form are the same.

Of course God's form has no receptive potency. But this only suggests that such potency is not essential to form as form. Nor, however, is it simply repugnant to form; created forms have it. This is our difficulty. In the next two sections I shall present my own resolution of it. Then, to conclude, I shall return to the question of the ascription of form to God.

RESOLUTION (1): HOW CREATED FORM IS ACT

The reader may already have surmised how I think Thomas's conception of form as act stands with respect to his conception of being as *actus essendi*. But I wish to spell it out as fully as possible, because it is essential for resolving our difficulty.

First, let me return to a point made in the first section, above: form, or the formal cause, is in a sense the "primary cause of being." I suggested that this means that it is the immediate principle of a thing's being.[73] Now, in another sense, what Thomas regards as the "primary cause of being" is not created form, but God. In fact, God is primary in various

---

per se stare sive subsistere quod non habet aliam causam essendi nisi seipsum. Est autem duplex causa essendi, scilicet forma per quam aliquid actu est et agens quod facit actu esse. Si ergo dicatur stans per seipsum quod non dependet a superiori agente, sic stare per seipsum convenit soli Deo." Another passage in which Thomas almost ascribes a formal cause to God is *ST* I, q. 39, a. 2, ad 5.

71. *ST* I-II, q. 85, a. 2.

72. See, e.g., *De ente*, c. 4 (Leon. 43.377:145–46); *De pot.*, q. 6, a. 6, ad 5; *De sub. sep.* 8; *In De caus.* 9.

73. Very pertinent: "id quod est separatum omnino a materia, quod est suum quod quid erat esse ... statim est unum, sicut et statim est ens; non enim est in eo materia expectans formam, a qua habeat unitatem et esse ... Sed illa quae non habent materiam simpliciter, per seipsa sunt aliquid unum, sicut aliquid existens." Aquinas, *In Meta.* VIII.5, nn. 1764 and 1767 (Marietti 510), on Aristotle, *Metaphysics* VIII.6.1045a36–b8, b24; see *ST* I, q. 61, a. 1, obj. 2 and ad 2.

senses. For one thing, his causality with respect to being is the most universal. For even though any created entity whatsoever has a formal cause, no single created form (or any single created cause) is the cause of *all* being; and God causes not only the being (*esse*) itself of things but also whatever pertains in any way to their being, including all of the things' other causes, even their matter.[74] For another thing, God is the *proper* cause of being, as being. That is, he and he alone is a cause that is fully proportioned to the whole nature of being.[75] Nothing else causes being except in virtue of God.[76] Being is more the effect of God than of any other cause.[77] It transcends the power of its other causes. Thomas is quite clear that while the intrinsic, essential principles of an entity, namely its matter and form, are causes of its being—and this is especially true of its form[78]—nevertheless they are not sufficient by themselves to cause the entity's being.[79] "Being follows per se on the form of a creature," he tells us, "yet on the supposition of God's influence."[80]

Now if this is so, can form really be the *immediate* cause of being? Can it somehow mediate God's own causality, coming "between" Him and the being of a thing? Does not Thomas famously say that God "works intimately" in all, and this precisely as cause of the being of all?[81] I raise this objection with a view to pinning down the causal role of form with respect to being. It seems to me that the answer is that there is indeed nothing that *works* more intimately in things than God. There is no more intimate *agent* coming between God and the being of things. But it is crucial to bear in mind that a thing's form is not an agent or efficient cause of its being.[82] Any active role played by the forms of things presupposes their being—their being *in act*. Their causality with respect to

---

74. *ST* I, q. 44, a. 2.
75. *ST* I-II, q. 66, a. 5, ad 4 (Leon. 6.436): "Ens commune est proprius effectus causae altissimae, scilicet Dei." See also *ST* I, q. 45, a. 5, ad 1.
76. On creatures as causes of being, see Wippel, "Thomas Aquinas and Creatures as Causes of *Esse*."
77. *In De caus*. 1.
78. See *De ente*, c. 4 (Leon. 43.371:54–57).
79. *ST* I, q. 3, a. 4.
80. *ST* I, q. 104, a. 1 (Leon. 5.464): "Esse per se consequitur formam creaturae, supposito tamen influxu Dei."
81. *ST* I, q. 105, a. 5 (Leon. 5.476): "Ipse Deus est proprie causa ipsius esse universalis in rebus omnibus, quod inter omnia est magis intimum rebus." See also *ST* I, q. 8, a. 1.
82. This is stressed in Wippel, "Thomas Aquinas and Creatures as Causes of *Esse*," 175–76. See *De ente*, c. 4 (Leon. 43.377:131–35).

their being itself takes another shape. I hope it will come more into focus as we proceed. But they and their causality with respect to their being *presuppose* an efficient cause. As we just saw, they presuppose God's influence.[83]

With this in mind, I think it is not so difficult to accept the idea that a thing's form does come "between" God and the being of a thing. God gives a thing its being *by way of* giving its form. "God created natural being without an efficient means, but not without a formal means. For He gave to each a form by which it would be."[84] Indeed, if God is the first, universal agent of the being of things, it can only be because he is also the first cause of their forms. "Just as being is first among effects, so also it corresponds to the first cause, as proper effect. But being is through form and not through matter. Therefore, the first causality of forms is to be attributed most of all to the first cause."[85] Thomas is clear: "if some agent is not cause of a form as such, it will not be per se a cause of the being that follows upon such form."[86]

Here let me remark on a common objection to the very idea of form as cause of being. The objection is that nothing is a cause unless it exists—unless it already has or shares in being. How can form be a cause of the very being that it shares in? Without its being, it would not be a cause at all! I grant that nothing is a cause unless it somehow has being. But the real question, I believe, is whether it is a cause *by virtue* of its being. This depends on what sort of causality it enjoys. An agent or efficient cause causes insofar as it is in act, which is to say, in virtue of the being or the actuality that it has. And so indeed it is not a cause of its own being. By contrast, a thing's matter, which shares in the thing's being, is nevertheless a cause of the thing's being; the thing cannot be without it!

---

83. *ST* I-II, q. 2, a. 5, obj. 3 (Leon. 6.21): "Causalitas causae efficientis consideratur secundum influentiam."

84. *De car.*, q. 1, ad 13 (Marietti 756): "Deus esse naturale creavit sine medio efficiente, non tamen sine medio formali. Nam unicuique dedit formam per quam esset." See *De ver.*, q. 27, a. 1, ad 3.

85. *SCG* II, c. 43 (Leon. 13.367:b27–31): "Sicut esse est primum in effectibus, ita respondet primae causae ut proprius effectus. Esse autem est per formam, et non per materiam. Prima igitur causalitas formarum maxime est primae causae attribuenda."

86. *ST* I, q. 104, a. 1 (Leon. 5.464): "Si aliquod agens non est causa formae inquantum huiusmodi, non erit per se causa esse quod consequitur ad talem formam." There is need for care in how we think of the causing of the nonsubsistent forms of corporeal things; see *ST* I, q. 65, a. 4 (Leon. 5.152): "Formae corporales causantur, non quasi influxae ab aliqua immateriali forma, sed quasi materia reducta de potentia in actum ab aliquo agente composito."

This is possible because it is not in virtue of the thing's being that the matter causes the thing's being. The matter's causality is not a function of the actuality that it has, but of its potency, which is its very nature. Now a thing's form is even more bound to the thing's being than its matter is, because its form can never share in any *other* being and is not a cause at all unless it shares in *this* being. Nevertheless it is not by *virtue* of this being that the form causes this being. Again, the causality of a thing's form with respect to the thing's being is not efficient causality. The objection, then, merely serves to remind us that neither a creature's material cause (if it has one), nor its formal cause, nor both together, are *sufficient* by themselves to cause the creature's being. This is precisely *because* they do not cause it in virtue of any prior being of their own. An extrinsic agent, causing the creature's being in virtue of its own prior being, is needed.[87] But its causing the creature's being involves its causing those intrinsic kinds of cause as well.

So now I come to the question: in what sense can all created form, whether inhering in matter or separate, be called an act? Here I take a cue from a work probably composed by the far too neglected English Thomist, Thomas of Sutton (d. ca. 1315). It says: "There are not two acts in soul, namely its essence, which is its potentiality, and its being, but its being is its actuality, by reason of which the very essence of soul is the act of the body. For every form shares in the act that is essentially primary; but this comes about analogically."[88] In the chief and unqualified sense, act is being. "Primary among all acts is being."[89] *Actus essendi* is indeed the act of all acts. But form too is act, and created form is other than being. They are not, however, two species of a genus, as though act were said of them univocally. Nor are they called act merely in virtue of having similar relations to different things, as though it were only a

---

87. Gilson and Owens make an essence's own existence the efficient cause by which the essence is formal cause of that existence (see above, note 47). This does make the essence cause its being by virtue of its being. But is it intelligible?

88. "Non enim in anima sunt duo actus, scilicet sua essentia quae est sua potentialitas, et esse suum, sed esse suum est sua actualitas, ratione cuius ipsa essentia animae est actus corporis: omnis enim forma participat actum qui est primus per essentiam; sed hoc analogice fit." [Thomas of Sutton?], *De principio individuationis*, in Aquinas, *Opuscula philosophica*, ed. R. Spiazzi, OP (Turin: Marietti, 1954), 150n424. Compare Porro, *Thomas Aquinas*, 345: "Each creature is such because it has a form (an actuality) to which a further actuality is added (existence)."

89. *ST* I, q. 76, a. 6 (Leon. 5.229): "Primum autem inter omnes actus est esse."

proportionality. Rather, act is said of them *per prius et posterius*, according to a simple analogy or proportion. What is act in the primary sense is being.[90] Form is act by its proportion—its relation or order—to its being.

This order is not simply form's sharing in being. That would not justify the name of act. Both matter and the composite of matter and form share in being (through the form), yet neither matter nor the composite is called act.[91] Not even form's being some sort of principle of being, by itself, would justify the name of act. For even a thing's matter is some sort of principle of its being. But upon its form, its being follows immediately. Form's order to being is both *per se* and immediate. Indeed, "the primary effect of form is being, for everything has being according to its form."[92] Being is an inseparable, necessary effect of form (though the necessity is itself caused—on which more later).[93] And so form shares not only in being itself but also in being's name of act. Thus, "being belongs per se to form, which is act."[94] And "every thing is an entity (*ens*) in act through a form, either according to substantial being or according to accidental being; *whence* every form is an act."[95] Thomas calls *both* form

---

90. In *De ver.*, q. 5, a. 8, obj. 10 (Leon. 22/1.157:88–92), an early work, Aquinas seems to present form itself as primary and being as secondary: "Duplex est creaturae actus: scilicet primus et secundus. Primus autem est forma, et esse quod forma dat; quorum forma dicitur primo primus, et esse secundo primus: secundus autem actus est operatio." I do not think he is saying that form has the nature of act by priority. How then is it prior? Another work attributed to Thomas of Sutton says that form is prior to being, not in the order of acts or formal principles, but according to *inherence*. See *De quatuor oppositis*, in Aquinas, *Opuscula philosophica*, cap. 1, 208, nn. 586–87. In any case, notice that the *De ver.* text puts form and being together as *one* act. I am arguing that this is why form is called act.

91. Especially strong, in this sense, is *ST* I, q. 75, a. 5 (Leon. 5.202), on why matter cannot be part of soul: "form, insofar as it is form, is act; and that which is merely in potency cannot be a part of act, since potency is repugnant to act, as divided against act" (forma, inquantum forma, est actus; id autem quod est in potentia tantum, non potest esse pars actus, cum potentia repugnet actui, utpote contra actum divisa). See also *ST* I, q. 75, a. 1 for the claim that soul is act and therefore cannot be a body. The thought, I take it, is that being *in* potency is repugnant to being *in* act (in the same respect). See above at note 42, and below at note 134.

92. *ST* I, q. 42, a. 1, ad 1 (Leon. 4.436): "Primus autem effectus formae est esse, nam omnis res habet esse secundum suam formam." Notice that he is talking about the perfection of the Persons of the Trinity.

93. See below at note 116.

94. *ST* I, q. 75, a. 6.

95. *De spir. creat.* 3 (Leon. 44/2.38–39:234–37): "Est autem unumquodque ens actu per formam, siue secundum esse substantiale, siue secundum esse accidentale: unde omnis forma est actus." Similarly, see *De prin. nat.* 1 (Leon. 43.39:42–43): "quia forma facit esse in actu, ideo forma dicitur esse actus," and *Quod.* 1.4.1, s.c. (Marietti 6): "quaelibet forma, cum sit actus, facit esse in actu."

and being *first act*, even in the same work.[96] He also calls both of them the terminus of generation.[97] In all of this, being can only be understood as *actus essendi*.

Created form is not its being, but it cannot lack its being. It is in act *per se*, necessarily and immediately.[98] It is never *in* potency to its being, that is, ordered toward but not joined to its being. "With the foundation of matter removed, if there remains any form of a determinate nature subsisting per se and not in matter, it will still be compared to its being as potency to act; but I do not say as a potency that is separable from its act, but that its act always accompanies."[99] Let me stress that I am talking about a form in its own reality, not about how it may be in the potency or power of an agent causing it. What is in the agent is not the caused form in its own reality but another form that is equal or superior to it. By contrast, the matter that is potency for a given form can be found in its own reality without that form, having some other form instead.

Let me also stress that I am not talking only about the relation between subsistent forms (angels, human souls) and being. What is special about those is that they not only are that "by which" something is or has being, but also have being in themselves and properly "are." But even nonsubsistent forms are causes of being for their composites, bringing being with them, necessarily. This is why the only way for a composite to cease to be is to lose its form.[100]

A form is not joined to its being through the mediation of any distinct principle within it. A creature's form not only determines its mode of being, but also determines it *to* its being, utterly excluding its nonbeing

---

96. This happens in a striking way in *De ver.*; see above, note 90. It also happens, even if not as strikingly, in the *Sentences* commentary: see *In Sent.* I, d. 7, q. 1, a. 1, ad 2, and d. 33, q. 1, a. 1, ad 1. On form, see *In Sent.* II, d. 35, q. 1, a. 1, and IV, d. 17, q. 1, a. 4, qc. 2, s.c. 2, and d. 49, q. 3, a. 2. In *In Sent.* II, d. 27, q. 1, a. 1, ad 3, as an example of first act, Thomas gives *esse*, understood as *actus formae*.

97. On *esse*, see *In Phys.* VI.13, n. 880(2); *In Meta.* II.3, n. 311, and V.19, n. 1046. On form, see *De prin. nat.* 3; *In Sent.* II, d. 32, q. 1, a. 2, ad 3; *ST* I, q. 76, a. 1, ad 1; and *In Meta.* XII.3, n. 2446. Especially interesting is *In Sent.* II, d. 34, q. 1, a. 2, ad 5 (Mandonnet 2.878): the terminus of generation is form, *because* [generation] is a change toward being (terminus enim generationis est forma, quia est mutatio ad esse)."

98. *ST* I, q. 76, a. 7.

99. *De spir. creat.* 1 (Leon. 24/2.14:395–400): "Remoto igitur fundamento materie, si remaneat aliqua forma determinate nature per se subsistens, non in materia, adhuc comparabitur ad suum esse ut potentia ad actum: non dico autem ut potentiam separabilem ab actu, sed quam semper suus actus comitetur."

100. *ST* I, q. 75, a. 6.

and any other being. And *therefore* the form is an act. Notice that, instead of *act*, Thomas often calls being the *actualitas*—as it were the very "actness"—of that act which is a form.[101] An act without its actness is nonsense. And so is an actness without an act. The actness is essentially *of* the act. This is just what every created being is: the complement and the actuality of some form.[102] "Being belongs on its own account to form, for each thing is an entity in act insofar as it has a form."[103]

Now this, I submit, just is Thomas's metaphysics of creation. To repeat, "God created natural being without an efficient means, but not without a formal means. For He gave to each a form by which it would be."[104] A thing's form causes the thing's being, and in a way it is the primary cause, because the being follows on it immediately. But the form is not an agent or an efficient cause of the thing's being, and if the being is caused at all, there must be an agent cause of it.[105] The form's causality presupposes the agent's. Being follows upon form only on the supposition of divine influence. I think we can say this: the agent actively determines the thing to its being, and the thing's form just *is* the determination to its being that the agent gives the thing (thereby fully *constituting* the thing). In creation, the only agent is God. In physical generation, there are also created, secondary agents (which however only cause the thing to *begin* to be). But quite generally, an agent causes a thing's being just insofar as it causes the thing's form.[106] And because being as a

---

101. See, e.g., *ST* I, q. 3. a. 4, and q. 4, a. 1, ad 3, which echo a passage often cited as a description of *actus essendi* in *De pot.*, q. 7, a. 2, ad 9. See also *ST* I, q. 5, a. 1; q. 54, a. 1; *ST* I-II, q. 85, a. 4; *In Sent.* I, d. 33, q. 1, a. 1, ad 1; and *De pot.*, q. 5, a. 4, ad 3.

102. See *Quod.* 12.5.1. On this account, form and being are so close to each other, so akin, that the real difficulty may lie in seeing how they might be distinct, especially from an Aristotelian perspective, in which form is unquestionably act. I address this in "How Many Acts of Being Can a Substance Have? An Aristotelian Approach to Aquinas's Real Distinction," *International Philosophical Quarterly* 54, no. 3 (September 2014): 317–31. For an Aristotelian, it can also be difficult to see how the being is distinct from the essence, even when the essence includes matter. For Thomas says that the *actus essendi* is "constituted by the principles of the essence," which of course is also true of the essence itself; *In Meta.* IV.2, n. 558 (Marietti 187). As Owens points out, the very Aristotelian thinker Siger of Brabant found this passage baffling. See Owens, "The Accidental and Essential," 75. I address this question in "On Whether Aquinas's *Ipsum Esse* is 'Platonism,'" 277–80.

103. *ST* I, q. 50, a. 5 (Leon. 5.12): "Esse autem secundum se competit formae, unumquodque enim est ens actu secundum quod habet formam."

104. See above, note 84.

105. See *ST* I, q. 3, a. 4.

106. See Wippel, "Thomas Aquinas and Creatures as Causes of *Esse*," 192.

whole is God's proper effect, and being is through form (and not through matter), therefore God is *maximally* cause of forms.[107]

In short, "form is act" and "form gives being" do not refer only to the fact that form gives a determinate species—Fabro's "formal being." Thomas's form is itself something essentially "existential" and "transcendental." It is so in its relation to matter as well. What it gives to matter is *"esse et speciem,"* being *and* species.[108] The substantial form of a thing both places it in some species of the genus of substance *and* gives it *esse simpliciter*, being without qualification. This is nothing other than the thing's substantial being. This being is what *first* divides a thing from what is merely in potency—what "is not," absolutely speaking.[109] It is that according to which the thing simply *exists*. "It is therefore impossible to understand matter to be hot or so much prior to being in act. And it has being in act through a substantial form, which makes be without qualification."[110]

And even matter is existential. Speaking of being as that in creatures by which they are like God, Thomas says that "the very thing that matter is" is "potency for being, which is through form."[111] In fact it would be a mistake to see form as giving only a determinate species to matter. In itself, matter does not even have a *genus*, properly speaking. It is not even a body, or a substance, except potentially. It is an *entity* merely in potency (*ens in potentia tantum*). "It is essentially one and the same form through which a man is an entity in act, and through which he is a body, and through which he is alive, and through which he is an animal, and through which he is a man."[112] Form gives matter not only the nature of a species but also that of a genus, even an ultimate genus, an immediate

---

107. See above, at note 85.
108. *Q. de an.* 10, co., ad 2, ad 16, and ad 17 (Leon. 24/1.90:157–68, 92: 287–88, and 94:397, 403).
109. *ST* I, q. 5, a. 1, ad 1 (Leon. 4.56): "Secundum hoc simpliciter aliquid dicitur ens, secundum quod primo discernitur ab eo quod est in potentia tantum. Hoc autem est esse substantiale rei uniuscuiusque; unde per suum esse substantiale dicitur unumquodque ens simpliciter."
110. *ST* I, q. 76, a. 6 (Leon. 5.229): "Impossibile est ergo intelligere materiam prius esse calidam vel quantam, quam esse in actu. Esse autem in actu habet per formam substantialem, quae facit esse simpliciter." See *Q. de an.* 9 (Leon. 24/1.79–80:139–50).
111. *Comp. theol.* 74 (Leon. 42.105:26–27): "Cum autem materia hoc ipsum quod est sit potentia ad esse quod est per formam."
112. *ST* I, q. 76, a. 6, ad 1 (Leon. 5.229): "Una enim et eadem forma est per essentiam, per quam homo est ens actu, et per quam est corpus, et per quam est vivum, et per quam est animal, et per quam est homo."

categorial division of being. Its doing so coincides with its giving the nature of entity in the proper sense; that is, something in act, something with being.

This of course sets our difficulty squarely before us. For such form is also potency for being. We must see how form's potency for being compares with matter's potency for form-and-being.

RESOLUTION (2): A POTENCY THAT IS *PER SE* IN ACT, AND HOW POTENCY AND ACT DIVIDE *ENS*

The basic idea seems clear. Created form is potency for being in the sense that it is a principle of receiving being. It is that by which the creature receives and appropriates to itself an influx of being from God. To this extent, the potency of form does resemble that of matter.

Form's potency is also like matter's in that it limits or contracts what it receives. A created form contracts being to a finite nature and mode. The being that is received through it does not contain all the perfection of being as a whole. This is why a multitude of creatures is more perfect than any one of them. The being of each adds something.[113] And a single creature, beyond its substantial being, can receive more perfection. Its full perfection requires additional actuality, in qualified modes, received through accidental forms. Its substantial form does not immediately determine it to all such additional actuality, but only puts it in potency thereto.[114]

At the same time, however, there are considerable differences between the potency of form for being and the potency of matter for form-and-being. Matter is potency for, and a cause of, generable things. It receives or undergoes the act of generation, which is a substantial change. It passes from one substantial form to another and, thereby, from the substantial being of one to that of the other. In short, matter's potency for form is indeterminate. Its nature is open to many different forms. By contrast, a thing's substantial form is not in potency to any substantial being other than that of this thing. (And because the form is part of the thing's essence, neither is the thing itself.) A thing's form

---

113. See, e.g., *ST* I, q. 7, a. 2; q. 11, a. 4; q. 14, a. 12, ad 3; q. 50, a. 2, ad 4; q. 55, a. 4; and *De spir. creat.* 1.

114. See, e.g., *De spir. creat.* 1 ad 1, quoted below at note 142.

does not follow on its matter *per se* or necessarily; they are separable. But its form and its being are utterly inseparable. In a word, although created form is in some sense a receptive potency, its potentiality is not contingent or binary. It is quite determinate. It is not potency for opposites. It cannot go from lacking to having its being, or vice versa. It is potency *only* for the being that it has, not for nonbeing or for any other being.

Being follows on form necessarily.[115] This is why separate created substances are what Thomas calls absolutely necessary entities.[116] The whole doctrine of incorruptible creatures rests on the understanding of form as act and cause of being.

> Form, according to what it is, is act, and through it things exist in act. Whence, in certain things, necessity to be arises from it. This happens either because those things are forms not in matter, and there is no potency to nonbeing in them, but through their form they are always in the strength of being (*in virtute essendi*), as is the case in separate substances; or because their forms, by their perfection, measure up to the whole potency of the matter, such that there remains no potency for another form, nor, consequently, for nonbeing, as is the case in the celestial bodies.[117]

In a certain respect, then, form's potency for being is like a type of potency treated in *Metaphysics* IX; namely, natural *active* potency. Such potency is determined to one kind of effect. It is in no way for the opposite

---

115. Owens grants this necessity and then takes it away again; see Owens, "The Accidental and Essential," 77. Kerr, *Aquinas's Way to God*, 33, says that "if form is so construed as to be not only a structuring principle of a thing but also a principle of the existence of a thing, then all forms would self-exist, since if form and existence are identical, then that form (of whatever kind) must exist." But to say that form is a principle of the existence of a thing is hardly to say that form and existence are identical. Nor does it entail that the form "self-exists" or that its being a principle of existence has no cause; see the next note.

116. Certainly this necessity is caused. Being follows on form only on the supposition of God's freely given influence, yet the necessity is absolute, not merely "suppositional," for it pertains to the very nature of what has it. On absolute necessity in creatures, see especially *SCG* II, c. 30, entitled "Qualiter in rebus creatis esse potest necessitas absoluta." See also *ST* I, q. 2, a. 3, *tertia via*; q. 50, a. 5, co. and ad 3; q. 75, a. 6; *In De cael.* I.6, n. 62(5); and *In Phys.* VIII.21, n. 1153(13).

117. *SCG* II, c. 30 (Leon. 13.339:a2–12): "Forma autem, secundum id quod est, actus est: et per eam res actu existunt. Unde ex ipsa provenit necessitas ad esse in quibusdam. Quod contingit vel quia res illae sunt formae non in materia: et sic non inest ei potentia ad non esse, sed per suam formam semper sunt in virtute essendi; sicut est in substantiis separatis. Vel quia formae earum sua perfectione adaequant totam potentiam materiae, ut sic non remaneat potentia ad aliam formam, nec per consequens ad non esse: sicut est in corporibus caelestibus." See also Aquinas, *In Phys.* VIII.21, n. 1153(13).

kind.[118] Fire can only heat, not cool. Likewise, a form can only bring being according to its own kind, as soul can only bring life. The similarity, however, is only very qualified. One way in which it falls short is that an individual active potency can be the source of many instances of its kind of effect, as a single fire can effect many heatings. But a single form can be the formal cause of only a single instance of being. This is why numerically distinct instances of the same kind, instances distinct in being, must have distinct forms.[119] Another way in which the comparison with active potency limps is that fire can be blocked from heating, by not being applied to anything heatable. By contrast, a form cannot be blocked from receiving its being. It is the immediate principle of its being. The being that a form is potency for cannot be lacking to it or fail to belong to it. This, I believe, means that even though it is potency for its being, it cannot be said to be *in* potency to its being. I shall return to this point shortly.

Form's potency for being also differs from natural active potency in a much more radical way. As we have seen, formal causality with respect to being is not agent or efficient causality. The form of a thing is absolutely *not* an active potency for the thing's being. "The potency of a creature for being," Thomas says, "is only receptive. But the active potency is God's, from whom is the influx of being."[120]

Should we say then that form is a *passive* potency for being?[121] Certainly a passive potency is a receptive potency. But I think that Thomas deliberately avoids calling form a passive potency for being. This is because a passive potency is a capacity for a *passio*, and a *passio* is some sort of change.[122] A passive potency, as such, enables something to change

---

118. Aristotle, *Metaphysics* IX.2.1046b4–24 and IX.5.1048a3–8.

119. *ST* I, q. 76, a. 2 (Leon. 5.216): "Impossibile est enim plurium numero diversorum esse unam formam, sicut impossibile est quod eorum sit unum esse, nam forma est essendi principium."

120. *ST* I, q. 104, a. 4, ad 2 (Leon. 5.469): "Potentia creaturae ad essendum est receptiva tantum; sed potentia activa est ipsius Dei, a quo est influxus essendi." No operation of a creature is the same as its being (*ST* I, q. 54, a. 3), and the way in which a thing's form is a principle of its being is not as a principle of action; thus, "forma naturalis, inquantum est forma manens in eo cui dat esse, non nominat principium actionis" (*ST* I, q. 14, a. 8 [Leon. 4.179]).

121. Oliva Blanchette, *Philosophy of Being: A Reconstructive Essay in Metaphysics* (Washington, DC: The Catholic University of America Press, 2003), 345, calls substance a "passive potency, one that only receives its act and does not in any way produce it, as an active potency does."

122. Thus *ST* I, q. 97, a. 2 (Leon. 5.432): "dicitur passio communiter secundum quamcumque mutationem."

somehow—either from having something to lacking it, or from lacking something to having it. According to a passive potency, "something is said to be able to be *and* not be."[123] But a form only enables something to be. It does not enable a thing to change with respect to being—to pass from being to nonbeing, or even from nonbeing to being. That is the sort of potency that matter has. The reception of being through a form is not, in itself, a change, a coming into being. Form is not a cause of coming into being, but only of being.[124] It is the very terminus of the coming into being of what has it. And, of course, so is the being of what has it—because it brings the being with it. As soon as the thing has its form, it already has its being too. The soul of a horse does not enable the horse to come into being. If a portion of matter has a horse-soul, then a horse has already come into being. The potency is receptive, but rather than calling it potency by which a thing *can* receive being, perhaps we should call it potency by which a thing *is receiving* its being, so long as it is.[125]

No doubt it also limits the thing's being. But this is hardly its primary or proper function *qua* potency for being. For obviously not every principle that limits an act is a potency for that act. Is it enough to say that form's function is to make a thing "capable" of its being?[126] That is true, but weak. Form *gives being*, period. Through it, a thing actually is.[127] Even form can be called *quo est*, "that by which something is"—not of course in the sense that it *is* the very act of being, but in the sense that it is the "principle of being," *principium essendi*.[128] Being follows upon form, immediately.

In Thomas's cosmology, this point is worth stressing, because for him the matter of a celestial body has its form necessarily. It is not potency

---

123. *In Meta.* IX.9, n. 1868 (Marietti 542): "Loquitur [Aristoteles] hic de potentia passiva, secundum quam aliquid dicitur possibile esse et non esse."

124. *In Phys.* II.10, n. 15 (Leon. 2.86): "Cum causa sit ad quam sequitur esse alterius, esse eius quod habet causam, potest considerari dupliciter: uno modo absolute, et sic causa essendi est forma per quam aliquid est in actu; alio modo secundum quod de potentia ente fit actu ens."

125. As Dewan puts it, form and being are "given together" (*Form and Being*, 169).

126. As Gilson says; see above, note 47.

127. And goes on being. A thing's form "tenet rem in esse postquam fuerit" (*ST* I, q. 59, a. 2 [Leon. 5.93]). Everything has a certain *virtus essendi*, strength to endure in being, which is its form: see *In De cael.* I.6, n. 62(5); *SCG* II, c. 30 (Leon. 13.339:a7–8); *In Phys.* VIII.21, n. 1153(13). Similarly, see again *ST* I, q. 42, a. 1, ad 1: as being is the first effect of form, things with more perfect natures are of greater duration.

128. *SCG* II, c. 54 (Leon. 13.392:a28–29).

for any form, or for any substantial being, other than for what it actually has. This is why the body is ungenerable and incorruptible. Yet the celestial body's matter and its form still differ with respect to its being. Its being does not follow immediately on its matter, but reaches the matter through the form. Its matter, of itself, does yield a certain indeterminacy; namely, as to the unity or division of its parts. That there is matter at all in the celestial bodies is shown only by their still being somehow in potency, viz., by their mobility with respect to place; and this depends on their having dimensive quantity, which, as such, is infinitely divisible and so is always in itself somehow in potency.[129] But substantial form, in itself, is simple. It has no quantity *per se*, and it only gives unity.[130] Bodies have quantity by reason of their matter.

So a body is not whole and undivided by virtue of its matter alone. Form in matter determines matter to unity. I would suggest that this is the precise role of the formal cause with respect to being: to constitute the essential unity that being requires.[131] Such unity completes a thing's potential for its being, and its being immediately "flows in."

In characterizing created form as potency for being, Thomas is evidently taking advantage of the fact that Aristotle had already judged potency to have many senses. The sense in which the term applies to created form with respect to being seems about as far as possible from that most proper sense, the sense of an active principle of motion. But I doubt whether Thomas thinks that the sense in which form is potency for being is to be found in Aristotle. If he cites any source, it is the *Liber de causis*.[132]

One last consideration should serve to fully resolve our difficulty. As we saw, Aristotle examines the meanings of *potency* in *Metaphysics* V, but not those of *act*. However, the term *act* does make a brief appearance there. This comes before the chapter on *potency*, in the chapter on senses

---

129. See *In Meta.* XII.2, n. 2436, and *ST* I, q. 3, a. 1.
130. See *ST* I, q. 76, aa. 3 and 8.
131. Unity is even closer to a thing's essence than its being is. See *ST* I, q. 6, a. 3, co., ad 1 and ad 3.
132. See, e.g., *De ente*, c. 4 (Leon. 43.376:36–40); *In Sent.* II, d. 3, q. 1, a. 2; *ST* I, q. 50, a. 2, ad 4. The *Liber de causis* says that an intelligence (an immaterial creature) has *yliatim* because it has form and being. Thomas mistakenly interprets *yliatim* as *aliquid materiale vel ad modum materiae se habens*, and then he says that the intelligence is a form subsisting in participated being and relating to its being as potency to act and as matter to form: *In De caus.* 9 (Saffrey 64:6–14). See Richard Taylor, "St. Thomas and the *Liber de causis* on the Hylomorphic Composition of Separate Substances," *Mediaeval Studies* 41 (1979): 506–13.

of *being*. Here *act* appears, along with some examples, precisely in the discussion of the distinction between *being in potency* and *being in act*.[133] This distinction, Aristotle says, cuts across all the categories. (In Thomas's language, this means that it is transcendental.) And the two senses do seem to be mutually exclusive. Being in potency means being *not* in act but only ordered toward being in act. One of Aristotle's examples is of what "is" corn even though it is not yet ripe.

Now clearly this distinction, between *in potency* and *in act* as senses in which *being* is predicated, is not quite the same as the distinction between these two predicates in themselves, *potency* and *act*. And I see no reason why these two predicates must always be mutually exclusive, especially if they themselves both have various senses. As we saw, in his discussion of the powers of the soul, Thomas said that nothing is *in* potency by reason of an act, as act.[134] But this does not mean that what is an act cannot also be a potency. It can be, if it is a potency that cannot be merely *in* potency but is *per se* and immediately in act.[135] A created form is a potency to be, but it cannot be *in* potency. Either it is in act, or it is not at all, even in potency. It is distinct from its being, but it can in no way be considered as lacking its being. Can there be a dead soul, a soul-cadaver? The notion is simply incoherent.

Thomas does say that what is not pure act, an act "mixed" with potentiality, cannot be its own *actualitas*, its "actness," because this is repugnant to *potentialitas*, "potentialness."[136] Created form is act, but it is not its *actualitas*. Its *actualitas* is its being, which is distinct from it. Its *potentialitas*, I take it, is its essence—which is the form itself.[137] But it has

---

133. Aristotle, *Metaphysics* V.7.1017b1–9.
134. *ST* I, q. 77, a. 1.
135. Besides the potency of form for its being and the potency of celestial matter for its form, another potency that is always in act and never merely in potency to what it is potency for is that of angelic intellect; see *ST* I, q. 54, a. 4; q. 56, a. 1; q. 58, a. 1. However, just as celestial matter is in act, not immediately, but through its form, so angelic intellect is first in act, not through itself, but through its primary object, the angel's essence; see *ST* I, q. 54, a. 2, obj. 2 and ad 2, and q. 56, a. 1.
136. *ST* I, q. 54, a. 1 (Leon. 5.39): "Impossibile est autem quod aliquid quod non est purus actus, sed aliquid habet de potentia admixtum, sit sua actualitas, quia actualitas potentialitati repugnat."
137. Or perhaps more precisely, the essence of the form is the form taken abstractly. Even in the case of an immaterial creature, that which is signified concretely (the supposit) is the same in intrinsic *ratio* or in constitution as that which is signified abstractly (its essence or nature), but they do differ *per accidens*: see *Quod.* 2.2.2.

its *actualitas*, its being, *per se*, immediately, and with absolute necessity. That is what it means to call form act.

As we saw, the common notion of potency, for Thomas, is "principle of act." The common notion of "act" is hardly definable, but we can say that it is what an entity has insofar as it is *not* merely "in potency."[138] To be *in* potency, then, is to have a principle of act but to lack the corresponding act. To be *in* act is to have the act. Obviously this does not entail lacking its principle; quite the contrary. So there is no incoherence in the notion of something that is both a potency and an act. Created form is potency inasmuch as it is a receptive principle of an act, namely being, and is other than this act. It is act inasmuch as it is joined to this act necessarily, *per se*, and immediately, and so can itself be said to be that by which an entity is in act. Created form, then, does not at all straddle the division between being *in* potency and being *in* act. In itself, created form is entirely on the side of being in act. This is how I resolve the difficulty.

CONCLUSION: ASCRIBING FORM TO THE DEITY

One may wonder: if created form is always a mixture of actuality and potentiality, and if all of our direct experience is of created things, so that our notion of form is taken from created form, how can the notion be applied properly to God? Of course the same question could be raised about being (*esse*) itself, as no creaturely being subsists, and all of it is finite. It is certainly important to keep in mind that, for Thomas, no term can be univocal as applied commonly to God and creatures. However, a term said properly of creatures can also be said properly—that is, not just metaphorically—of God. This is possible insofar as the notion that the term signifies, when taken absolutely, does not entail anything pertaining to imperfection or limitation.[139] Even though all created form is imperfect and limited, it does not follow that our very notion of form, taken absolutely, entails these features. After all, every created entity is caused, but being caused is not entailed by the notion of entity (*ens*) taken absolutely; if it were, there could be no uncaused entity.[140] Is mere receptive potency, and therewith, imperfection and limitation, in the very notion

---

138. See Aristotle, *Metaphysics* IX.6.1048a31.
139. See *ST* I, q. 13, a. 3, ad 1, and q. 9, a. 3.
140. See *ST* I, q. 44, a. 1, ad 1.

Created Form as Act and Potency 205

of form, as form? Or does the notion of form, as form, only include act? Is it simply "that by which something is in act" and "by which it is an entity (ens)"?[141]

Thomas, I believe, thinks that it is. In a discussion of the distinction between the human soul and its powers that is practically contemporaneous with that of the *Summa theologiae*, he says that the notion of form, *ratio formae*, is opposed to the notion of subject, *ratio subiecti*. Here is why:

> Every form, as such, is act, whereas every subject is compared to what it is subject of as potency to act. If therefore there is any form that is only act, such as the divine essence, it can in no way be a subject ... But if there is some form that is in some respect in act and in some respect in potency, it will be a subject only in this respect in which it is in potency. Spiritual substances, however, though subsistent forms, are nevertheless in potency, insofar as they have finite and limited being. And ... in the intellect and will of a created substance there always remains potency to something that is outside it. Whence if one rightly considers, spiritual substances are not found to be subjects except of the accidents that pertain to intellect and will.[142]

Notice that Thomas is *not* saying that these substances are subjects of their substantial being, nor is he saying that they are in potency to their substantial being.[143] This is so even though a few lines earlier, in the corpus of the same article, he had said that they compare to their being as potency to act. For he went on at once to say that it is a potency whose act always accompanies it.[144] But because that act—its substantial being—is finite and limited, therefore they are *in* potency to, and subjects of, the

---

141. The latter phrase is from the fundamental presentation of the causal roles of form in *ST* I, q. 5, a. 4.

142. *De spir. creat.* 1, ad 1 (Leon. 24/2.14:410–29): "Omnis forma in quantum huiusmodi est actus; omne autem subiectum comparatur ad id cuius est subiectum, ut potentia ad actum. Si qua ergo forma est que sit actus tantum, ut diuina essentia, illa nullo modo potest esse subiectum .... Si autem aliqua forma sit que secundum aliquid sit in actu et secundum aliquid in potentia; secundum hoc tantum erit subiectum, secundum quod est in potentia. Substantie autem spirituales, licet sint forme subsistentes, sunt tamen in potentia, in quantum habent esse finitum et limitatum. Et ... remanet semper in intellectu et voluntate substantie create potentia ad aliquid quod est extra se. Unde si quis recte consideret, substantie spirituales non inveniuntur esse subiecte nisi accidentium que pertinent ad intellectum et voluntatem." On *forma* and *subiectum*, see also *ST* I, q. 29, a. 2, ad 5.

143. In *De prin. nat.* 1 (Leon. 43.39:20–32), Thomas says that, properly speaking, a subject is something in potency to accidental being, whereas what is in potency to substantial being is properly called matter; and that a substantial form is not properly said to be in a subject, because a subject is what per se has "complete being" (*esse completum*).

144. See above, at note 99.

further actuality of the accidents pertaining to intellect and will. Their potency for substantial being is very different from their being *in* potency to the being of some accident.

The "two-orders" view does not make this distinction sufficiently. It limits the role of substantial form to that of completing a substance's species. It misses what is primarily meant by saying that form is act, namely, that it is the immediate cause of a thing's being. As a result, this view makes a substance's relation to its being indistinguishable from a subject's relation to what it underlies. It makes substantial being look too much like an accident.

But most importantly, in this passage there is no doubt that the divine essence is a form in the proper sense. The term *form* is common to God and creatures, not univocally, but by analogy. But if so—and as the passage suggests—then although the term *form* was first fashioned to refer to creaturely forms, the nature of form belongs primarily to God.[145] And it is of Him that the term is said most properly.[146] God is "pure act and simple and the primary form."[147] Created form is not just act but also potency. Nevertheless, to call it form is only to say that by it, an entity is in act. "Form is something divine in things, insofar as it is a certain participation of the primary act."[148] The primary act is a form that is identical with its being. Other forms are distinct from, but immediately joined to, their being. And so they too are acts. In the one metaphysical order—the order of entity insofar as it is entity—all form, insofar as it is form, is act.

---

145. See *ST* I, q. 13, a. 6.
146. See *ST* I, q. 13, a. 3.
147. *In Sent.* I, d. 22, q. 1, a. 1, ad 2 (Mandonnet 1.532).
148. *In De cael.* III.2, n. 552 (Leon. 3.233:2). The thought is gathered from Aristotle, *Physics* I.9.192a16–17; see *In Phys.* I.15, n. 135(7). Similarly, see *SCG* II, c. 43 (Leon. 13.367:b35–37): "omnia similantur Deo qui est actus purus, inquantum habent formas, per quas fiunt in actu." See also *SCG* III, c. 97 (Leon. 14.299:a30–b2).

Gloria Frost

---

7 ∞ Aquinas on How Accidental Forms Vary in Themselves

Consider a lawn chair that is left outside in the sun until its color eventually fades. Now consider a pot of water on the stove that becomes hotter and hotter until it boils.[1] While these two cases may initially seem like they have nothing in common, they are both cases in which a quality in a subject, its *green color* or its *heat*, increases or decreases its intensity. Variation in the intensity of qualities is not limited to sensible qualities. Qualities of intellect and character can likewise become stronger or weaker over time. Consider the courageous soldier whose disposition to act courageously becomes even more intense through repeated actions on the battlefield; or a student whose ability to solve geometry problems grows weaker through lack of practice. Such cases involve both continuity and change: the subject continues to have the same type or species of quality, but its degree of intensity varies. For instance, the water remains hot, but becomes more intensely so; the student remains able to reason about geometry, but with less facility.

One pressing question about cases of qualitative increase and decrease concerns what it is that undergoes change. Is it the subject or the subject's quality that changes? For instance, when the soldier becomes more courageous, is it only the soldier who changes, or does the quality of courage, that is, the form by which he is courageous, vary in itself? Put more generally, do qualitative forms themselves vary throughout the intensification

---

1. When possible, I quote Aquinas's texts the Leonine edition. For texts not included in the Leonine edition or superseded by other editions, see the bibliography. All English translations are my own.

process, or do forms remain fixed and constant while their subjects vary in relation to them? A related question also arises: are all instances of the same species of qualitative form exactly the same or do they vary in such a way that one is more or less perfect than another? For example, can one form of courage be a more perfect courage than another form of courage? These questions were widely discussed in the Middle Ages because of their connection with an important theological teaching. Medieval Christians believed that the point of life on earth was to grow in charity, that is, the virtue that enables love of God, and that human beings would be united to God in the afterlife in accord with the degree of their charity. Understanding these theological beliefs required thinkers to develop a metaphysical account of qualitative increase and decrease.[2]

The goal of this chapter is to investigate Thomas Aquinas's views on whether and how qualities can increase and decrease *in themselves*. Aquinas's views are especially intriguing because they raise questions about both the development in his thought over time as well as its internal consistency. On the one hand, Aquinas argues throughout his works that any addition to or subtraction from a form itself would entail a change in the species of a subject's quality. According to him, qualities cannot increase and decrease in virtue of the form gaining or losing something, as this would result in a different type of quality, rather than a more intense quality of the same kind. Throughout his works, he argues that a subject's quality increases in its intensity in virtue of the subject participating more perfectly in the same invariable form. The form itself does not change; what varies is the degree to which the subject is perfected by the form. Yet, in his later works, Aquinas affirms that there are some qualities that can "increase in themselves."[3] But how can it be that noth-

---

2. Important studies on the topic include Annaliese Maier, *Das Problem der Intensiven grösse in der Scholastik* (Rome: Verlage Heinrich Keller, 1939), and Jean-Luc Solère, "Plus ou moins: le vocabulaire de la latitude des formes," in J. Hamesse and C. Steel (eds.), *L'Elaboration du vocabulaire philosophique au Moyen Age* (Turnhout: Brepols, 2000), 437–88. On the significance of these views in the history of science, see, for instance, Edith Sylla's "Medieval Concepts of the Latitude of Forms. The Oxford Calculators," *Archives d'histoire doctrinale et littéraire du Moyen Âge* 40 (1974): 223–83, and *The Oxford Calculators and the Mathematics of Motion, 1320–1350: Physics and Measurement by Latitudes* (New York: Garland Publishing, 1991).

3. Jean-Luc Solère nicely summarizes the ambiguity of Aquinas's theory when he writes in his article, "The Question of Intensive Magnitudes according to some Jesuits in the Sixteenth and Seventeenth Centuries," *The Monist* 84, no. 4 (2001): 582–616, at 586: "However, Thomas's view is not devoid of ambiguity. Although he ascribes variation to participation only, he maintains that one must speak of intensification, or qualitative augmentation, with respect to the

ing can be added or subtracted from a form, and yet some forms can increase and decrease in their own perfection? In this chapter, I will argue that the key to understanding Aquinas's thought is to grasp a division that he acknowledges between different types of accidental forms, as well as a distinction between different manners in which a form might increase or decrease. There have been just as few studies on Aquinas's general views on qualitative increase and decrease.[4] The present study goes beyond the existing literature by examining in more depth the question of whether and how Aquinas thought forms could vary in themselves.

An investigation of this topic in Aquinas's thought is a fitting tribute to Fr. Wippel. Of course, Aquinas's metaphysics is one of Fr. Wippel's central interests. While he has not discussed in print Aquinas's views on the intension and remission of accidental forms, early in his career he published an influential study of Godfrey of Fontaines's views on this topic.[5] It is with gratitude to Fr. Wippel for his research and teaching that I offer this study.

This chapter is divided into two main parts. In the first section, I examine Aquinas's "participation" account of how qualities increase and decrease in their intensity and his commitment to the view that nothing can be added or subtracted to the intrinsic content of a form. In the second section, I consider his later views on how forms can increase in themselves. I show how Aquinas was able to maintain that forms increase in themselves while maintaining that nothing can be added to or subtracted from the form itself.

---

essence ('*secundum essentiam*' or '*essentialiter*') of qualities. He even on occasion speaks of latitude (in virtue)."

4. The studies devoted exclusively to Aquinas's views on this topic include: Jean-Luc Solère, "Thomas d'Aquin et les variations qualitatives," in C. Erismann and A. Schniewind (eds.), *Compléments de Substance: Études sur les Propriétés Accidentelles offertes à Alain de Libera* (Paris: Vrin, 2008), 147–65, and Gloria Frost, "Aquinas on the Intension and Remission of Accidental Forms," *Oxford Studies in Medieval Philosophy* 7 (2019): 116–46. Solère also discusses Aquinas's position at length in his article, "Les variations qualitatives dans les théories post-thomistes," *Revue Thomiste* (2012): 157–204; there is also some discussion of Aquinas's views on qualitative intensification in Barry Brown, *Accidental Esse* (New York: University Press of America, 1985), 168–84.

5. John F. Wippel, "Godfrey of Fontaines on Intension and Remission of Accidental Forms," *Franciscan Studies* 39, no. 1 (1979): 316–55.

AQUINAS'S PARTICIPATION SOLUTION AND THE INVARIABILITY OF FORMS

In order to understand Aquinas's approach to the intensification and weakening of qualities, it is necessary first to review a few important points about his thinking about accidental qualities more generally. In Aquinas's view, every way in which a substance exists is due to the inherence of a form. He writes: "Every existence is from some inhering form, just as existing as white is from whiteness, and existing as a substance is from a substantial form. It is unintelligible that a wall be white without [the form of] whiteness inhering."[6] Every quality that a substance has is through an accidental form inhering in it. As the quotation explains, a wall has the quality of being white in virtue of the form of whiteness inhering in it. Aquinas explains elsewhere that forms are not themselves subjects *that exist*, but rather they are that *by which* substances exist in determinate ways. He writes: "In this way whiteness is said to exist not because it subsists in itself, but because something has existence-as-white by it (*habet esse album ea*)."[7] The form of whiteness is not itself a substance that exists. Rather, whiteness is that through which a substance exists as white.

Aquinas claims that numerically distinct substances have numerically distinct forms.[8] For instance, a white wall and a white ball each has its own numerically distinct form of whiteness. The sameness between the forms of numerically distinct substances is sameness of species, rather than numerical sameness.[9] Numerically distinct forms are of the same species if, when considered in abstraction from their subjects, their account (*ratio*) is the same.[10] An analogy can help to illustrate the respect in

---

6. *In Sent.* I, d. 17, q. 1, a. 1 (Mandonnet-Moos 1.393): "Constat enim quod omne esse a forma aliqua inhaerente est, sicut esse album ab albedine, et esse substantiale a forma substantiali ... Non potest intelligi quod paries sit albus sine albedine inhaerente." See ibid. (1.395): "nullum esse potest recipi in creatura, nisi per aliquam formam."

7. *Quod.* IX.2.2 (Leon. 25/1.94:56–58): "Sicut albedo dicitur esse, non quia ipsa in se subsistat, set quia ea aliquid habet esse album."

8. *De ente*, c. 3 (Leon. 43.375:80–83): "[I]n Sorte non inuenitur communitas aliqua, sed quicquid est in eo est indiuiduatum."

9. *De prin. nat.* (Leon. 43.47:63–67): "Eorum igitur que sunt idem numero, forma et materia sunt idem numero, ut Tullii et Ciceronis; eorum autem que sunt idem in specie, diversa numero, etiam materia est forma non est eadem numero, sed specie, sicut Sortis et Platonis." See also *In Sent.* II, d. 17, q. 1, a. 1.

10. On the difference between a form considered in abstraction and considered as it exists in an individual, see *De ente*, c. 2. For a helpful discussion of Aquinas's views on sameness and

which forms of the same species differ and the respect in which they are the same. Consider a computer monitor that is displaying a passage from Aquinas's *Summa theologiae* and a book that is open to that same passage. In this example, there are two numerically distinct texts and there are various differences regarding how the text is displayed (e.g., font, size, brightness) which arise from the two distinct media that have received the text. Yet we recognize the texts as the same because the account (*ratio*), which is the text *itself* (i.e., leaving aside all of the features which arise from the medium), is *identical* in both instances. In a similar way, there is a sameness of account (*ratio*) in numerically distinct forms that belong to the same substantial or accidental species. For example, while there may be various differences in two concrete white objects, such as a dingy white wall and a freshly bleached white sheet, Aquinas thinks that everything intrinsic to the whiteness of each is the same. The sameness of the form itself is what secures the sameness of species between numerically distinct forms of the same type. With this background in place about Aquinas's views on accidental forms, we can now turn to his account of how qualities increase and decrease in their intensity.

Aquinas discusses the intension and remission of forms in major works over the course of his career, and the core of his solution remains the same over time.[11] It may be helpful to begin with Aquinas's critique of one prominent medieval theory about how qualities increase and decrease in intensity, the "addition to form" theory, as his critique of this theory highlights an important constraint that he tried to meet in his own theory.[12] The "addition to form" theory maintained that the accidental forms that admit of intensification and remission are quantitatively divisible into separable parts.

According to this theory, substances can be informed by some parts of the form while not being informed by others. In a change of intensification, the relevant form gains a part that it previously lacked. For instance, when an object becomes more intensely white, a form-part is added to its

---

difference that obtains between distinct forms of the same species see Jeffrey Brower, "Aquinas on the Problem of Universals," *Philosophy and Phenomenological Research* 92 (2016): 715–35.

11. Aquinas's major discussions of the intension and remission of forms occur in the following texts that treat of questions surrounding the increase of habits and virtues: *In Sent.* I, d. 17, q. 2, aa. 1–5; *Quod.* IX.6.un.; *ST* I-II, q. 52, aa. 1–3, and q. 66, aa. 1–2; *ST* II-II, q. 24, aa. 4–10; *De virt. in com.* 11; and *De virt. card.* 3.

12. On Aquinas's critique of the other medieval theories on the intension and remission of forms, see my "Aquinas on the Intension and Remission of Accidental Forms," 119–24.

form of whiteness. Likewise, when a quality becomes less intense, a part of its form is lost. Thus, changes of qualitative increase or decrease involve a change in the number of form parts that actualize a substance. What is especially significant about this theory is that it implies that the form changes *in itself*. The form itself varies with respect to the number of its parts. Furthermore, numerically distinct forms of the same species differ in themselves from one another. For instance, the form of whiteness in a freshly bleached white sheet would have more parts of the form of whiteness than the form of whiteness in a dingy white wall.

Aquinas's critique of the "addition to form" theory reveals his own commitment to the unity and indivisibility of forms. Aquinas worries that if a form were to gain or lose something from itself, this would entail a change in its species. Aquinas claims, for instance, that adding to or subtracting from a substance's form of paleness will not give rise to a more or less intense paleness; rather it will give rise to black or white, which is an altogether different species of color.[13] In his *Disputed Questions on the Virtues* he writes: "It is necessary to understand the specific principle of something as indivisible. For differences of this kind of principle vary the species. If this principle were added to or subtracted from, the species would necessarily be varied. Accordingly, the Philosopher says in Metaphysics VIII that the species of things are like numbers in so far as an added or subtracted unit varies the species."[14] Aquinas sees forms as indivisible units from which nothing can be gained or lost.[15] The essence of courage, for instance, is a basic unit, which cannot be divided into separable parts. Any addition or subtraction from the form

13. *ST* I-II, q. 52, a. 2 (Leon. 6.334): "Si autem ex parte ipsius formae, iam dictum est quod talis additio vel subtractio speciem variaret; sicut variatur species coloris, quando de pallido fit album."

14. *De virt. card.* 3 (Marietti 618): "Oportet enim principium specificum accipi in aliquo indivisibili. Differentia enim huiusmodi principii speciem variat, et ideo, si hoc principio esset additio vel subtractio, ex necessitate species variaretur. Unde et philosophus dicit in VIII Metaph., quod species rerum sunt sicut numeri, in quibus unitas addita vel subtracta variat speciem." See also *SCG* III, c. 97, and IV, c. 14. In the latter text Aquinas attributes the view that "forms are like numbers" to Plato as well. On Aquinas's claim that forms are like numbers, see Rudi te Velde, *Participation and Substantiality in Thomas Aquinas*, Studien und Texte zur Geistesgeschichte des Mittelalters 46 (Leiden: Brill, 1995), 227–30.

15. *SCG* IV, c. 41 (Marietti 484): "[N]atura dicitur quod quid rei, continens ea quae ad speciei pertinent integritatem ... Est autem impossibile quod alicui speciei in sua integritate iam constitutae aliquid extraneum uniatur in unitatem naturae, nisi species solvatur. Cum enim species sint sicut numeri, in quibus quaelibet unitas addita vel subtracta variat speciem, si quid ad speciem iam perfectam addatur, necesse est iam aliam speciem esse."

itself would make it something other than courage. Just as the number two "becomes" the number three when a unit is added to it, so too would one form cease to be and another replace it if something were added or subtracted to the nature of a quality itself.

In his own theory, Aquinas aims to uphold the unity and indivisibility of forms themselves. Rather than locate the metaphysical flux that underlies the change in qualitative intensity in a variability within the subject's form, Aquinas instead locates it in the subject's relationship to the form.[16] On Aquinas's view, one and the same invariable form can perfect its subject to varying degrees.[17] According to Aquinas, forms themselves do not confer a determinate intensive degree of perfection on their subjects. For example, the form of heat does not determine the extent to which a pot of water exists as hot.

This is an important difference between Aquinas's view and the "addition to form" theory. In the latter theory, it is the form itself and, more precisely, the number of its parts that determines the intensive degree of the subject's perfection. For example, a form of heat with more parts makes a subject exist as hotter. On Aquinas's view, however, the form determines only the species or nature of the subject's quality.[18] The individuating conditions of the quality, such as its precise degree of intensive perfection, arise from how the form is received in the subject.[19] For example, the water on the stove does not merely exist as hot. It exists with a determinate degree of heat, for example, 150 degrees. Yet the form of

---

16. Elsewhere, I have explained and analyzed Aquinas's "participation" solution to the intension and remission of forms in more depth and detail. See my "Aquinas on the Intension and Remission of Accidental Forms." For the purposes of this chapter, I repeat just the most important and relevant elements of the theory.

17. It should be noted that Aquinas does not think that every form can be intensified or remitted. He discusses two reasons for why a particular form cannot be subject to variation in intensity in *De virt. in com.* 11 (Marietti 524): "Sed hoc non contingit in omnibus formis, propter duo. Primo quidem ex ipsa ratione formae; eo scilicet quod id quod perficit rationem formae, est aliquid indivisibile, puta numerus. Nam unitas addita constituit speciem: unde binarius aut trinarius non dicitur secundum magis et minus ... Alio modo ex comparatione formae ad subiectum; quia inhaeret ei modo indivisibili. Et propter hoc forma substantialis non recipit intensionem vel remissionem, quia dat esse substantiale, quod est uno modo: ubi enim est aliud esse substantiale, est alia res." See also *ST* I-II, q. 52, a. 1, and *De virt. card.* 3.

18. Aquinas identifies "form" and "species" in *ST* I, q. 5, a. 5 (Leon. 4.63): "Ipsa autem forma significatur per *speciem*: quia per formam unumquodque in specie constituitur."

19. *Quod.* VII.4.3 (Leon. 25/1.23): "[I]n albedine et qualibet alia qualitate corporali est duo considerare: scilicet ipsam naturam albedinis, per quam speciem sortitur; et individuationem eius, secundum quod est haec albedo sensibilis ab alia albedine sensibili distincta."

itself does not determine the degree to which a subject exists through it. Rather, the receiving subject limits the extent to which the form perfects it. Aquinas writes in his *Summa contra Gentiles*: "Every act that inheres in another is limited by the one in which it exists. This is because whatever exists in another exists in it according to the mode of the receiver. Therefore, an act that exists in nothing is in no way limited."[20]

At the end of this passage, Aquinas states that if a form were not received in a subject, it would not be limited in its intensive perfection. Each form is such that it could confer a quality with unlimited intensive perfection. The limitation of a quality to a determinate degree of perfection arises solely through the receiving subject. Aquinas writes elsewhere: "The fullness of form is contracted by matter. Hence the infinity that belongs to a form not determined by matter has the nature of perfection."[21] The subject that functions as matter for the form limits the degree of perfection that the form confers. Different subjects limit the same species of form in different ways because substances vary in their capacity for receiving certain forms. For example, a metal substance has a greater capacity for receiving the form of coldness than a wool substance. Because of their differing prior qualities, different types of subjects are able to receive further qualities with a greater or lesser degree of perfection.

So how does it happen that the same subject's quality increases in its degree of intensity? Aquinas thinks that a subject that is already actualized by a form might have further potential for being more perfectly actualized by that same form. For example, water that is already hot may not be as hot as it is fully able to be. Even while being hot, it has a potential to be hotter. This potential is not a potential to acquire the form of heat, because it already has that form. Rather it is a potential to exist more perfectly through the form. Aquinas states that an agent capable of heating can actualize this potential. Aquinas writes: "But that which is less hot or less white is not in potency to a form since it already has a form in act, but it is in potency to a more perfect mode of participation; and this it

---

20. *SCG* I, c. 43 (Leon. 13.124): "Omnis actus alteri inhaerens terminationem recipit ex eo in quo est: quia quod est in altero, est in eo per modum recipientis. Actus igitur in nullo existens nullo terminatur."

21. *ST* I, q. 7, a. 1 (Leon. 4.72): "[S]ed magis per eam [i.e., materiam] eius [i.e., formae] amplitudo contrahitur: unde infinitum secundum quod se tenet ex parte formae non determinatae per materiam, habet rationem perfecti." On Aquinas's notion of infinity see John Tomarchio, "Aquinas's Concept of Infinity," *Journal of the History of Philosophy* 40 (2002): 163–87.

receives through the agent's action."[22] On Aquinas's model, changes of intensification involve the same elements as other changes, namely an agent cause capable of producing the change and a patient with the potential to undergo the change. The only difference is that the potential involved in a change of intensification is not the potential to acquire a new form (or new form part). Rather, it is a potential for existing more perfectly through an already inherent form. An agent with the power to actualize the form in a substance that lacks it, can likewise cause a perfect participation in the form in a patient that already has the form.

While Aquinas's core solution to the problem of intension remains constant throughout his career, the terminology in which he expresses it develops. In his earliest extended treatment of intensification in his *Commentary on the Sentences* question on whether charity increases by addition, Aquinas expresses the variable relationship between a subject and its inherent accidental forms in terms of the Aristotelian notions of potency and act. According to him, a subject's quality increases in virtue of the subject being more perfectly actualized by its form. He writes: "The increase of it is from it being educed from imperfect toward perfect infused act."[23] In intensification, the subject does not gain or lose any forms, nor does the subject's form gain or lose any parts. Rather, an already inherent form actualizes the subject's potentiality to a greater degree.

In later works, Aquinas appeals to the Platonic notion of "participation" to express the variable relationship which a subject has to its inherent forms. According to later texts, the intensity of a subject's quality increases in virtue of the subject "participating more" in the relevant form. Aquinas writes in *De virt. in com.* 11: "For a quality to be increased is

---

22. *ST* I-II, q. 52, a. 2, ad 3 (Leon. 6.334): "Sed id quod est minus calidum aut album, non est in potentia ad formam, cum iam actu formam habeat: sed est in potentia ad perfectum participationis modum. Et hoc consequitur per actionem agentis." See also *In Sent.* I, d. 17, q. 2, a. 2 (Mandonnet-Moos 1.415–16): "Qualitates autem primae et simplices intenduntur ex causis suis, scilicet ex agente et recipiente. Agens enim intendit reducere patiens de potentia in actum suae similitudinis, quantumcumque potest. Sicut autem non calidum est potentia caloris; ita minus calidum est potentia respectu magis calidi. Unde sicut per potentiam calidi efficitur de non calido calidu ... ita etiam efficitur magis calidum per actionem calidi ... et hoc contingit, secundum quod potentia subjecta actui, quae quidem, quantum in se est, ad multa se habet, magis ac magis terminatur ab actu illo; vel quia augetur virtus agentis, sicut ex conjunctione plurium luminarium intenditur illuminatio; vel ex parte ipsius materiae, secundum quod efficitur susceptibilior illius actus, sicut aer quanto plus attenuatur, fit susceptibilior luminis."

23. See *In Sent.* I, d. 17, q. 2, a. 2, co. (Mandonnet-Moos 1.416): "[A]ugmentum ejus est per hoc quod de imperfecto ad perfectum actus infusus educitur." This text refers to "infused" act because charity was conceived of as a form infused by God into the creature.

nothing other than for the subject to participate more in the quality; for a quality has no existence except for in a subject."[24] He repeats this idea again in the *Summa theologiae* when he writes: "The increase of habits and other forms of this kind does not happen through an addition of form to form, rather it happens through the subject participating more or less perfectly in one and the same form."[25] In his later *De virt. in com.* 11, Aquinas identifies his earlier seemingly more Aristotelian "degrees of actualization" solution with the "Neo-Platonic participation" solution.[26] He writes: "form is act; thus, for a subject to receive more of a form is nothing other than for it to be reduced more to the act of that form."[27]

For our purposes, that which is most noteworthy about Aquinas's "participation" and "degrees of actualization" account of how qualities increase in their intensity is that it involves no variation in the form itself. What varies is how the subject receives or is actualized by the form. The form itself does not gain or lose anything. The fact that the form is not of itself determined to a particular degree of perfection makes it possible for the form to remain invariable while the existence that the subject has through the form varies.

---

24. *De virt. in com.* 11 (Marietti 523–24): "Nihil enim est aliud qualitatem aliquam augeri, quam subiectum magis participare qualitatem; non enim est aliquod esse qualitatis nisi quod habet in subiecto."

25. *ST* I-II, q. 52, a. 2 (Leon. 6.334): "Et ideo huiusmodi augmentum habituum et aliarum formarum, non fit per additionem formae ad formam; sed fit per hoc quod subiectum magis vel minus perfecte participat unam et eandem formam." See also *ST* I-II, q. 52, a. 2, ad 2 (Leon. 6.334): "[Q]uod causa augens habitum, facit quidem semper aliquid in subiecto, non autem novam formam. Sed facit quod subiectum perfectius participet formam praeexistentem ..."

26. Between his earliest discussions of intension in the *Sentences* and his later treatments of the topic in the *Summa theologiae* and *Disputed Questions on the Virtues*, Aquinas read the ancient philosopher Simplicius's commentary on Aristotle's *Categories*. This text greatly influenced how he framed the questions associated with qualitative increase. Simplicius's *Commentary on the Categories* was written in Greek around 538 and translated into Latin by William Moerbeke in 1266. Aquinas appears to be the first Scholastic author to reference this work. See Michael Chase, "The Medieval Posterity of Simplicius' Commentary on the *Categories*: Thomas Aquinas and Al-Farabi," in L. A. Newton (ed.), *Medieval Commentaries on Aristotle's Categories* (Leiden: Brill, 2008), 9–10. For the relevant passage in Simplicius see his *Commentaire sur les Catégories d'Aristôte. Traduction de Guillaume de Moerbeke*, ed. A. Pattin, 2 vols. (Louvain: Publications universitaires de Louvain, 1971/1975); 2:392.80–89. On Simplicius's influence on medieval discussions see Maier, *Das Problem der intensiven Grösse in der Scholastik*, 10.

27. *De virt. in com.* 11 (Marietti 524): "[F]orma actus est; unde subiectum magis percipere formam, nihil aliud est quam ipsum reduci magis in actum illius formae."

AQUINAS ON HOW SOME FORMS INCREASE IN THEMSELVES

We have just seen that Aquinas's account of how qualities increase and decrease in their intensity was tailored around his commitment to the view that nothing can be added to or subtracted from a form. In his view, forms are in themselves not susceptible to gain or loss. What varies in qualitative increase is the extent to which forms perfect their subject, or to use his later terminology, the extent to which the subject participates in the form. Given Aquinas's denial that anything can be added to or subtracted from a form, it may come as a surprise to see that in his very latest discussions of the intension and remission of forms, he admits that some forms can increase in perfection *in themselves*. He explicitly contrasts this type of increase in perfection with the type of increase that comes from the subject participating more perfectly in the form. For a form to increase in perfection in itself is for it to be more perfect when it is considered in abstraction from its subject. How can it be that a form can become more or less perfect in itself if nothing can be added to or subtracted from a form? Did Aquinas falter in his commitment to the unity and indivisibility of forms themselves?

The key to understanding Aquinas's thinking on this matter is to grasp a distinction that he recognized between different types of forms. In Aquinas's view, not all forms have their species in the same way. This is to say that there are different criteria according to which different forms are designated as forms of a certain kind. In order for a form to be such that it can increase in perfection in itself, that is, such that it can become a more perfect form of its type, it must receive its species in a particular way. Aquinas explains these points in the following passage:

> It must be observed that [the principle] according to which anything is sorted into its species must be fixed and stationary, as if indivisible, so that whatever attains it is contained under the species, and whatever recedes from it, by either more or less, pertains to another species either more or less perfect ... If, therefore, some form, or any thing (*res*) whatsoever, should be sorted into the account (*rationem*) of its species according to itself or something belonging to it, it is necessary that considered in itself it would have a determinate nature (*ratio*) that could neither be exceeded by more or fallen short of by less. To this kind belong heat and whiteness and other such qualities that are

not named in relation to another, and much more substance, which is a *per se* being. Those things that receive their species from another to which they are ordered are able to be diversified in themselves according to more or less and nevertheless, they are of the same species on account of the unity of that to which they are ordered, from which they receive their species.[28]

Aquinas begins in this passage by explaining that the criterion or measure according to which a form has its species must be fixed and invariable. In order for it to be possible to sort forms into different species, there must be a determinate standard for whether the form is or is not of a particular species. Aquinas notes that there are two different types of standards for determining the species of a form. First, some forms are of a certain species based on the form's intrinsic account (*ratio*). These forms belong to certain species based on what they are in themselves. Examples of such forms are simple sensible qualities, such as whiteness and heat. A form is whiteness or heat through itself. Forms that are sorted into their species in this way cannot be more or less perfect in themselves, that is, more or less perfect forms of the species, because being a certain fixed and invariable way in themselves is what makes the form of a particular species.[29] Because what the form is in itself is the standard for including it in the species, there is no room for any variation in such forms. Each of these forms within the same species is exactly the same in itself because being a certain, determinate way in themselves is that through which they belong to their species.

As the passage quoted above explains, there is another way in which

---

28. *ST* I-II, q. 52, a. 1 (Leon. 6.331): "[C]onsiderandum est quod illud secundum quod sortitur aliquid speciem, oportet esse fixum et stans, et quasi indivisibile, quaecumque enim ad illud attingunt, sub specie continentur; quaecumque autem recedunt ab illo, vel in plus vel in minus, pertinent ad aliam speciem, vel perfectiorem vel imperfectiorem ... Si igitur aliqua forma, vel quaecumque res, secundum seipsam vel secundum aliquid sui, sortiatur rationem speciei; necesse est quod, secundum se considerata, habeat determinatam rationem, quae neque in plus excedere, neque in minus deficere possit. Et huiusmodi sunt calor et albedo, et aliae huiusmodi qualitates quae non dicuntur in ordine ad aliud, et multo magis substantia, quae est per se ens. Illa vero quae recipiunt speciem ex aliquo ad quod ordinantur, possunt secundum seipsa diversificari in plus vel in minus, et nihilominus sunt eadem specie, propter unitatem eius ad quod ordinantur, ex quo recipiunt speciem."

29. See also *De virt. card.* 3 (Marietti 618): "Quaedam vero formae sunt quae sortiuntur speciem per aliquid suae essentiae, sicut omnes formae absolutae, sive sint substantiales sive accidentales; et in talibus impossibile est quod in eadem specie secundum hunc modum una forma maior alia inveniatur, non enim est una albedo secundum se considerata, magis albedo quam alia. Quaedam vero formae sunt quae sortiuntur speciem ex aliquo extrinseco ad quod ordinantur, sicut motus sortitur speciem ex termino."

other forms have their species. Some forms are classified as forms of a given species not because of what they are in themselves, that is, in their own intrinsic account (*ratio*), but rather because they order their subject to something. Health is an example of such a form.[30] On the medieval view, which Aquinas adopted, health was understood as a certain proportion of humors that preserves the nature of the animal. A certain proportion was designated as a form of health not because of what it is in itself, that is the particular proportion that it is, but rather because of its order to preserving the animal. Aquinas reasons that it must be through an order to something outside of itself that a particular form is of the species of health, as no one proportion of humors constitutes health in all animals. For instance, if a lion had the amount of blood that is healthy for a fish, it would be dead. Thus, one cannot consider a proportion in itself and know if it has the species of health. One must also consider the subject in which the proportion inheres and how this proportion relates to the subject's preservation. Thus, a form only has the species of health when taken together with an order to the well-being of its subject.[31]

What is significant about this manner in which forms receive their species, that is, through order to something outside of the form, is that it offers an invariable standard that can be either met or not met, and yet, it can be met in more or less perfect ways. Different forms can order their subject more or less perfectly to the same invariable term. For example, different proportions of wetness and heat can both be considered in the species of health insofar as they both preserve an animal's nature, and yet one proportion might preserve the animal's nature more perfectly than the other. Because the standard for species membership is order to something else, and not what is intrinsic to the form itself, it is possible for forms that differ within themselves to be of the same species. Furthermore, they can be more or less perfect than one another depending on how well they order the subject to the term.[32]

Aquinas does not think, however, that *every* form that has its species through an order to an external term can increase or decrease in itself.

---

30. See, for instance, *ST* I-II, q. 52, a. 1.
31. See ibid. and *De virt. card.* 3.
32. It should be noted that the term to which the form orders must be outside of the form, however, it need not be outside of the subject of the form. The animal's state of well-being, for example, is extrinsic to the proportion of humors that preserves it, but it is not extrinsic to the animal that is its subject.

Virtues are another type of form that have their species through an order to an external term. A quality is a virtue insofar as it orders an agent to the mean of right reason. Aquinas, however, explicitly denies that virtues can increase or decrease in themselves.[33] In addition to being a form that has its species through an order to an external term, for the form to be able to vary in itself it must satisfy one of these two further conditions: the form must either (1) be an order among other forms or integral parts in a subject, or (2) be a form that is a science or habit that can regard differing numbers of particulars falling under its general object.[34] Let us examine the nature of these two types of forms and how they can increase in themselves.

First, let us examine forms that are orders among forms or parts of a subject. Health, as we have seen, is an example of such a form. A proportion among the four bodily humors (i.e., blood, phlegm, yellow bile, and black bile) has the species of health when it is ordered rightly to the preservation of an animal's body. In the following passage, Aquinas explains how it is that forms that are orders or proportions can increase and decrease in themselves. He writes:

> When there is some form which in its *ratio* implies a certain proportion of many things ordered to one, such a form also admits of more or less in itself (*secundum propriam rationem*). This is evident concerning health and beauty, both of which imply a proportion fitting to the nature of the subject which is said to be beautiful or healthy. Since a proportion of this kind is able to be more or less fitting, beauty and health considered in themselves are said to be more and less.[35]

33. See, e.g., *ST* I-II, q. 66, a. 1.

34. Aquinas references the distinction between simple qualities and forms that are orders or proportions between things in *ST* I-II, q. 49, a. 4. Aquinas's discussion of whether pleasures can increase in themselves also makes clear that some connection with multiplicity is necessary for a form to vary in itself; see *In Ethic.* X.3 (Leon. 47/2.559–60:74–88): "Si vero dicant delectationem recipere magis et minus ex parte ipsarum delectationum, considerandum est ne forte eorum ratio non referatur ad omnes delectationes, sed assignent causam quod quaedam delectationes sunt simplices et immixtae, puta delectatio quae sequitur contemplationem veri, quaedam autem delectationes sunt mixtae, puta quae sequuntur contemperantiam aliquorum sensibilium, sicut quae sequuntur harmoniam sonorum, aut commixtionem saporum seu colorum. Manifestum est enim, quod delectatio simplex secundum se non recipiet magis et minus, sed sola mixta, inquantum scilicet contemperantia sensibilium quae delectationem causat potest esse magis vel minus conveniens naturae eius qui delectatur."

35. *In Ethic.* X.3 (Leon. 47/2.559.46–55): "Quando autem est aliqua forma quae in sui ratione importat quandam proportionem multorum ordinatorum ad unum, talis forma etiam secundum propriam rationem recipit magis et minus, sicut patet de sanitate et pulchritudine,

Aquinas on How Accidental Forms Vary in Themselves

Aquinas realizes that with regard to one and the same animal, different levels of humors, such as a greater degree of yellow bile or a lesser degree of phlegm, can preserve the animal's physical well-being over time.[36] Aquinas thinks that when an animal's proportion of humors changes, the animal's form of health has varied in itself. For example, when an animal body loses some blood, the animal's proportion-form that is its health varies in itself. If this change better preserves the animal's life, then the form of health has increased in itself. But if the change in the proportion is worse for the preservation of the animal's life, the form of health has then decreased in itself.

It is important to note that the way in which Aquinas thinks an order or proportion form increases in itself is entirely different from how the "addition to form" theory claims that forms increase. When an animal's health increases, the forms that inhere in the animal do not gain or lose any form parts, nor does one health form replace another health form. Rather, what varies is the proportion that obtains among parts or forms within the subject. If a form is order among other forms, the proportion among those forms changes in virtue of the subject participating in one or more of those forms to a greater or lesser degree. He writes in the *Summa theologiae*: "If a subject is changed to have a more perfect commensuration, this happens on account of transmutation of simple qualities, which are not increased except in intensity through the subject's participation."[37] Aquinas uses his participation theory to account for how a form that is a proportion among forms can vary without the subject gaining or losing a form or form-parts.

It is worth noting that Aquinas maintains that forms that are orders or proportions among other forms or integral parts, such as health, can both be participated in more perfectly by their subject and can also

---

quorum utrumque importat proportionem convenientem naturae eius quod dicitur pulchrum vel sanum, et quia huiusmodi proportio potest esse vel magis vel minus conveniens, inde est quod ipsa pulchritudo vel sanitas in se considerata dicitur secundum magis et minus."

36. One especially clear statement of this is found in *In Ethic.* VIII.1 (Leon. 47/2.380:55–62): "[C]onsonantia enim sive contemperantia alicuius rei non consistit in indivisibili, sed habet latitudinem quandam, sicut patet de contemperantia humorum in corpore humano, salvatur enim natura humana et cum maiori vel cum minori caliditate, et similiter contemperantia humanae vitae salvatur secundum diversas maneries affectionum."

37. *ST* I-II, q. 52, a. 2 (Leon. 6.334): "Quod autem ad perfectiorem commensurationem perducatur, hoc contingit secundum transmutationem simplicium qualitatum; quae non augentur nisi secundum intensionem, ex parte subiecti participantis."

increase in themselves. For example, a subject can both (1) be more perfectly healthy and (2) have a greater health in itself. [38] It may seem that Aquinas has here posited a distinction without a difference. It would seem that having a greater form of health would entail that a subject is also more perfectly healthy. Thus, once Aquinas posits that a form can vary in itself it seems that there is no longer a need to appeal to degrees of participation to explain differences in qualitative intensity. Aquinas, however, believes that in our ordinary experience we observe that there are two distinct ways in which a quality, such as health, can be more or less perfect. He writes: "Similarly, health can be unequal either because the grade of commensuration in one is closer to the fitting and perfect equality than the other's grade of commensuration; or because concerning the same grade of commensuration, one has it more firmly and perfectly than the other."[39]

According to Aquinas, it is possible that one and the same grade of commensuration or proportion can be possessed by a subject more or less perfectly. Consider, for example, a hospital patient who is receiving IV fluids and ice packs as part of treatment for heat exhaustion. His proportion of humors might now have the same degree of proportion as the doctor who is treating him, yet the patient will possess this grade of commensuration less perfectly. If the treatment is not continued, the proportion will be easily lost. Thus, as Aquinas sees it, different subjects can have the very same proportion of humors more or less perfectly. The degree to which the subject participates in the form that is the order or proportion explains how "firmly" the subject has the quality. Thus, he appeals to degrees of participation in the proportion to explain the metaphysics behind possessing a quality more or less perfectly; and he appeals to variation in the proportion itself to explain differences in qualities themselves.

In addition to forms that have their species by being ordered to something else, Aquinas recognizes that there is another type of form that can

---

38. Ibid. (6.330): "Inquantum igitur attenditur perfectio formae secundum ipsam formam, sic dicitur ipsa esse parva vel magna; puta magna vel parva sanitas vel scientia. Inquantum vero attenditur perfectio formae secundum participationem subiecti, dicitur magis et minus; puta magis vel minus album vel sanum. Non autem ista distinctio procedit secundum hoc, quod forma habeat esse praeter materiam aut subiectum: sed quia alia est consideratio eius secundum rationem speciei suae, et alia secundum quod participatur in subiecto."

39. *De virt. card.* 3 (Marietti 619): "Similiter potest esse sanitas inaequaliter, vel quia gradus commensurationis in uno est propinquior debitae et perfectae aequalitati quam in alio, vel quia circa eumdem gradum commensurationis unus firmius se habet quam alius, et melius."

increase in itself, namely sciences and other habits that can potentially regard a number of different particulars that fall under its general object. A habit or science is a form that allows an agent to reason either practically or speculatively about a certain generic object. The science of geometry, for example, allows an agent to reason about geometrical conclusions, while the habit of music allows an agent to play music. These forms can increase in themselves by relating to more particulars that fall under the general object of the habit or science. A person's science of geometry, for example, increases in itself when the person learns a new conclusion.[40] A person's musical habit increases in itself when she learns to play a new instrument or song. The way the form increases is by extending to more particulars, but it retains its same species because it has the same order to the general object that it regards (e.g., music, geometrical figures). Incidentally, Aquinas denies that virtues can increase in this way because the virtuous person, as a condition of possessing virtue, must be able to act according to the mean with regard to every particular that the virtue regards.[41] The temperate person, for instance, must be able to eat with moderation no matter what particular foods he is presented with. Thus, a form of temperance cannot increase by extending to a new type of food. All forms of temperance by nature extend to every particular pleasurable object.

To summarize Aquinas's views on forms that can increase in themselves, he thinks that there are two types of forms that admit of such an increase. The first type is forms that are orders or proportions among other forms or integral parts, such as health and beauty, which have their species in virtue of an order to something else. Such forms increase in themselves when the proportion among the forms varies in such a way that they order their subject more perfectly to that through which they have their species. As we have seen, proportions among forms vary in virtue of the subject participating more or less perfectly in the forms involved in the order or proportion. The second type of form that can increase in itself, as we have just seen, is habits and sciences. Such forms increase in themselves when their subject relates to more particulars through them. With regard to both types of forms that can increase in

40. See, e.g., *De virt. in com.* 11, ad 10 (Marietti 525): "Unde scientia potest augeri ... secundum numerum obiectorum." Aquinas sometimes speaks of sciences and habits as having a greater "quantity of power" (*quantitas virtualis*) insofar as it relates to more objects. See *In Sent.* I, d. 17, q. 2, a. 1, ad 2, and *ST* II-II, q. 24, a. 4, ad 1.
41. *ST* I-II, q. 66, a. 1.

themselves, it is worth emphasizing that increase happens without any addition to or subtraction from the form itself. Forms that are orders or proportions that regard other forms or parts are indivisible. Nothing is added to or subtracted from them when they vary. Rather, they vary in themselves through the subject participating more or less perfectly in the forms they regard. In the case of sciences and habits, it is likewise the case that nothing is added to or subtracted from the form itself when it increases in its own perfection. The form remains a simple unity. It becomes more perfect in itself by extending to more particulars.

CONCLUSION

In addition to being an important topic in its own right, Aquinas's views on the increase of qualities also highlight some of his more general commitments about accidental forms. First, his writings on this topic reveal that he was committed to a class of accidental forms that are orders or proportions among forms or integral parts. Second, as we have seen, Aquinas thought that not all forms have their species based on what they are in themselves. Some forms have their species in virtue of an order to something else. Aquinas capitalizes on these two commitments to show how some forms can increase in themselves in a manner other than by addition of a part to the form. Forms that are orders or proportions among forms can vary in terms of order or proportion without any forms or form-parts being added to the subject. Such forms vary through their subjects participating more or less perfectly in the forms that the orders or proportions regard. Furthermore, order or proportion forms can vary in themselves and still remain of the same species so long as they retain their order to that from which they receive their species. Thus, even while acknowledging that some forms can increase in themselves, Aquinas was able to remain steadfast to his commitments that the principle of species must be fixed and invariable and that forms are not susceptible to addition or subtraction.[42]

---

42. I am grateful to Therese Scarpelli Cory and Gregory T. Doolan for their helpful comments on an earlier draft of this chapter.

Part 4 ∽ First Causal Principles
From Finite Being to Uncreated Being

Francis Feingold

8 ☙ Can Angels Know Being without Judgment?

Hallmarks of Aquinas's metaphysical thought include the real distinction of essence from existence, the analogy of being, and the close study of angelic nature that helped earn him the title "Angelic Doctor."[1] Yet there is an apparent tension between the first two hallmarks and the third.

As many recent Thomists have emphasized (John F. Wippel prominent among them), it follows from the first two claims that neither "existence" (*esse*)[2] nor "being as being" (*ens inquantum ens*) can be originally known by the act of the mind that conceptualizes essences, usually called "simple apprehension" in the Scholastic tradition, as neither "existence" nor "being as being" signify a univocal essence. Rather, Aquinas holds that they are both originally grasped by the act of the mind by which we "compose and divide" conceptualized essences, usually called

---

1. For the origin of the title "Angelic Doctor," see Pierre Mandonnet, "Les titres doctoreaux de saint Thomas d'Aquin," *Revue Thomiste* 17 (1909): 597–608, at 607–8, where he says that Aquinas approached his angelology "non pas comme une oeuvre d'art, curieuse et rare, mais comme un anneau puissant qui relie les grands éléments de l'objet de sa pensée philosophique et théologique, et aussi comme une idée maîtresse qui éclaire et unifie ses conceptions de penseur intellectualiste." See Arthur-G. Albert, "Pourquoi 'Docteur Angélique,'" *Revue Dominicaine* 39 (1933): 129–34, at 132; Julien Péghaire, "L'intellection du singulier matériel chez les anges et chez l'homme," *Revue Dominicaine* 39 (1933): 135–44, at 135; and Francis Cardinal George, "Saint Thomas: Timeless and Timely," in *Thomas Aquinas: Teacher of Humanity*, ed. John Hittinger and Daniel Wagner (Newcastle upon Tyne: Cambridge Scholars Publishing, 2015), 6.

2. Following Étienne Gilson's recommendation in "Propos sur l'être et sa notion," in *San Tommaso e il pensiero moderno*, Studi tomistici 3, ed. Antonio Piolanti (Rome: Città Nuova Editrice, 1974), 7–17, at 10, I will use the term "existence" rather than "being" to translate *esse* throughout this chapter, even though "existence" is etymologically derived instead from *existentia*, in order to reserve the term "being" for *ens*.

"judgment": "existence" by "composition" in a positive existential judgment, "being as being" by "division" in the negative metaphysical judgment of *separatio*.

Nonetheless, Aquinas also holds that angels neither compose nor divide. Does this mean that, in Aquinas's view, angels cannot perceive real existence or enjoy metaphysical knowledge? Surely not. Does it mean then that Aquinas admits that existence and being are directly conceptualizable, univocal essences after all? This seems equally unpalatable. Are contemporary Thomists wrong then to attribute such high stakes to the thesis that existence and being are originally known by judgment? Not exactly.

Rather, I propose that, while contemporary Thomists are right to hold that the thesis carries these high stakes in humans, this fact is due as much to the subjective peculiarities of human knowing as it is to the objective character of existence and being. The angel's radically different mode of knowing, however, allows him to judge existence compositionlessly without reducing it to an essence; likewise, it allows him to grasp the analogical richness of being without *separatio*.

To make good on this proposal, I will proceed as follows. First, I will present Aquinas's claims that existence and being as being are known by composing and dividing, respectively, along with the import that contemporary Thomists attach to these claims. Second, I will present Aquinas's absolute denial of angelic composing and dividing. Third, I will seek to account for angelic compositionless knowledge of existence by appealing, on the one hand, to the active character of the angel's knowledge as a participation in God's creative knowing, and on the other hand to our own reliance on our senses as the reason for the ontological complexity of our human judgments. Finally, I will seek to account for angelic divisionless knowledge of "being as being" by appealing to the angel's ability to distinctly discern the whole intelligible content of his concept without needing to form new, more abstract concepts in the process. As side benefits, I also hope to shed more light on angels' preeminent role in Aquinas's cosmology; on how God can know genuinely free creaturely acts without passivity; and on the idiosyncrasies of our own human way of knowing being.

AQUINAS'S CLAIM THAT WE MUST COMPOSE AND DIVIDE TO GRASP "BEING AS REAL" AND "BEING AS BEING"

Wippel opens *The Metaphysical Thought of Thomas Aquinas* with the role of the mind's "second act" in knowing being:

> One of the more notable developments in recent decades in our understanding of Aquinas's metaphysical thought has been a growing appreciation of the distinctive way in which he accounts for our discovery of being *as real* or as existing and, consequent upon this, for our knowledge of being *as being*. . . . Thomas's point is this: if it is through the intellect's first operation that we discover quiddities or understand what things are, it is only through its second operation that we discover their existence (*esse*). . . . Equally important for our appreciation of Thomas's understanding of metaphysics is . . . [that] he singles out a special kind of judgment, a negative one which he refers to as *separatio*, which he closely connects with metaphysics and presumably with our discovery of being as being.[3]

Our knowledge of being, and with it the possibility of metaphysics, depends on the mind's second act: the act of "composing or dividing," which Wippel, following common usage, identifies with "judgment."[4] (For reasons that will become clear in the next section, this identification is only appropriate in human knowledge; in this section, however, I will use the terms "judgment" and "composition and division" interchangeably, following the usage of the authors discussed here.) We depend on judgment in two ways: for discovering the *existence* of things, and, subsequently, for discovering being *as being*. Let us begin with the claim that judgment alone lets us discover existence.

A key text for this first claim is Aquinas's *In De Trin.*, q. 5, a. 3.[5]

---

3. John F. Wippel, *The Metaphysical Thought of Thomas Aquinas: From Finite Being to Uncreated Being* (Washington, DC: The Catholic University of America Press, 2000), 3–4 (emphasis added); see 23–25 (on knowing being as *real*) and 44–49 (on knowing being as *being*). For the same twofold role of judgment, see also Wippel's "Metaphysics and *Separatio* in Thomas Aquinas," in *Metaphysical Themes in Thomas Aquinas* (Washington, DC: The Catholic University of America Press, 1984), 69–104, at 69–70, and his "Maritain and Aquinas on Our Discovery of Being," *Studia Gilsoniana* 3 (2014): 415–43, at 416–18 and 431–34.

4. Wippel, *Metaphysical Thought*, 3–4.

5. For the importance of this text, see Étienne Gilson, *Being and Some Philosophers*, 2nd ed. (Toronto: Pontifical Institute of Mediaeval Studies, 1952), 203n23; Jacques Maritain, *Existence and the Existent*, trans. Lewis Galantiere and Gerald Phelan (New York: Pantheon Books, 1948), 28n14; Joseph Owens, *An Elementary Christian Metaphysics* (Milwaukee, WI: Bruce Publishing, 1963), 49n12, "Quiddity and Real Distinction in Aquinas," *Mediaeval Studies* 27,

Aquinas here first distinguishes the mind's two operations: simple apprehension (*intelligentia indiuisibilium*), by which we know the quiddities of things (*quid est*), and "composing and dividing," by which we form positive or negative propositions (*enuntiationem*).[6] He then ties these two acts to the two fundamental principles of the object's being, essence and existence:

> And these two operations correspond to two [principles] (*duobus*) that are in things. *The first operation regards* (*respicit*) *the very nature of the thing*, according to which the thing known possesses a certain rank (*gradum*) among beings. . . . *The second operation regards the very existence* (*esse*) *of the thing*: which in composite things results from the union (*congregatione*) of the thing's principles, or else which, as in simple substances, accompanies the thing's simple nature itself.[7]

Judgment ("the second operation") alone grasps a thing's real existence initially and directly. Existence lies beyond simple apprehension's scope; Gilson argues that the verb "is," even in its substantivized grammatical forms, is meaningful only in reference to its use in judgment.[8] More-

---

no. 1 (1965): 1–22, at 3n7, *An Interpretation of Existence* (Houston, TX: Center for Thomistic Studies, 1985), 29n9, "Judgment and Truth in Aquinas," *Mediaeval Studies* 32, no. 1 (1970): 138–58, at 150n22, and "Aquinas on Knowing Existence," *The Review of Metaphysics* 29, no. 4 (1976): 670–90, at 675n9; John F. X. Knasas, "The Intellectual Phenomenology of '*De ente et essentia*,' Chapter 4," *The Review of Metaphysics* 68, no. 1 (2014): 107–53, at 113n13; and Bernard Muller-Thym, "The Common Sense, Perfection of the Order of Pure Sensibility," *The Thomist* 2, no. 3 (1940): 315–43, at 336–39.

6. Aquinas relies for this distinction between the two first acts of the mind on Aristotle, *De anima* III.6.430a26–28, where they are called "τῶν ἀδιαιρέτων νόησις" and "σύνθεσις νοημάτων ὥσπερ ἓν ὄντων," respectively.

7. Aquinas, *In De Trin.*, q. 5, a. 3 (Leon. 50.147a:96–105): "Et hee quidem due operationes duobus que sunt in rebus respondent. Prima quidem operatio respicit ipsam naturam rei, secundum quam res intellecta aliquem gradum in entibus obtinet, siue sit res completa, ut totum aliquod, siue res incompleta, ut pars uel accidens. Secunda uero operatio respicit ipsum esse rei; quod quidem resultat ex congregatione principiorum rei in compositis, uel ipsam simplicem naturam rei concomitatur, ut in substantiis simplicibus." All translations from Aquinas are my own.

8. See, e.g., Gilson, *Being and Some Philosophers*, 190–201. Obviously *esse* is a concept that can be used as the subject of further predication. The point is that it is a derivative concept, formed by reflecting on one's own act of judgment, rather than a concept abstracted directly from experience. See, e.g., Gilson, *Being and Some Philosophers*, "Appendix" (216–33); Maritain, *Existence*, 33–34, and "Reflections," 221; Owens, *An Interpretation of Existence*, 46–51, *An Elementary Christian Metaphysics*, 57–58, "The Content of Existence," 28–29, "Maritain's Three Concepts of Existence," 296–99, "Judgment and Truth," 152–55, and "Aquinas on Knowing Existence," 672 and 687; and Wilhelmsen, "Existence and Esse," *The New Scholasticism* 50, no. 1 (1976): 20–45, at 30–31.

over, Aquinas seems at least to hint here that the reason for judgment's exclusive claim on existence is the ontological composition that always accompanies existence: a composite object, it would seem, can only be grasped by a composing act.

Two other famous texts bear out the claim. In *In Sent.* I, d. 19, q. 5, a. 1, ad 7, we again find the statement that "the first operation [of the mind] regards (*respicit*) the thing's quiddity; the second regards its existence." What is new here is that Aquinas makes this statement the reason for his (frequent[9]) assertion that only judgment is, properly speaking, true or false: for truth is primarily based in existence rather than essence.[10] This text also clearly implies that all judgments concern existence, not only existential judgments ("Socrates exists") but also attributive ones ("men are mortal"), since truth and falsity, which are based in existence, pertain to all judgments.[11] And in *In Sent.* I, d. 38, q. 1, a. 3, after again asserting that the intellect's first two operations correspond to (*respondent*) and grasp (*apprehendit, comprehendit*) the thing's quiddity and existence, respectively, Aquinas both strengthens and qualifies the reason hinted at in *In De Trin.*, q. 5, a. 3, for the correlation between judgment and *esse*. Here he states that existence has to be known by a "composing" act because (a) existence lies in (*consistit in*) the object's composition (matter-form or subject-accident), and (b) our knowledge of this composite existence is derived from the composite object.[12] The implied

---

9. For Aquinas's claim that truth and falsity properly belong to the "intellect composing and dividing," see also, e.g., *ST* I, q. 16, a. 2, and q. 17, a. 3; *De ver.*, q. 1, aa. 3 and 11 (see also a. 9, though it uses the term *iudicium* instead of *compositio et divisio*); *SCG* III, c. 108, n. 2836; *In De an.* III.5 (Leon. 45/1.224a–26a:1–90); *In Peri herm.* I.3 (Leon. 1*/1.14b–17b:31–197); and *In Meta.* VI.4, nn. 1232–38 and IX.11, n. 1896. For the claim's origins, see, e.g., Aristotle, *Metaphysics* VI.4.1027b25–29 and *De anima* III.6.430a26–b6.

10. Aquinas, *In Sent.* I, d. 19, q. 5, a. 1, ad 7 (Mandonnet 1:489): "Prima operatio respicit quidditatem rei; secunda respicit esse ipsius. Et quia ratio veritatis fundatur in esse, et non in quidditate, ut dictum est, ideo veritas et falsitas proprie invenitur in secunda operatione." As the article's corpus makes clear, *quidditas* and *esse* here, just like in *In De Trin.*, q. 5, a. 3, refer to a duality in the thing, not merely in the mind: "Cum autem *in re* sit quidditas ejus et suum esse, veritas fundatur in esse rei magis quam in quidditate" (Mandonnet 1:486; emphasis added). Both Wippel and Owens cite this text in all their treatments of *esse* as the proper object of judgment.

11. For this claim that all attributive judgments imply an underlying existential judgment, and that this is why truth and falsity properly speaking are found in every judgment and only in judgment, see, e.g.: Gilson, *Being and Some Philosophers*, 199–201 and 203; Maritain, *Existence*, 12; Owens, "Aquinas on Knowing Existence," 681; and Wippel, *Metaphysical Thought*, 27, and "Maritain and Aquinas," 421. In Aquinas, see *In Peri herm.* I.5 (Leon. 1*/1.31b:395–402).

12. Aquinas, *In Sent.* I, d. 38, q. 1, a. 3, co. (Mandonnet 1:903): "Cum in re duo sint,

premise seems to be that a composite object must cause a composite act of knowing.

What is at stake in this claim that we know real existence only in the composing act of judgment? Above all, several Thomists see this claim as inextricably tied to the irreducibility of existence to essence. Owens, for example (following Aquinas's *In Sent.* I, d. 38, q. 1, a. 3), says that it is "because there are the two factors, quiddity and existence, in the thing itself" that "there are the two corresponding activities in the intellect";[13] and he insists that "the importance of this consideration" (namely that "existence is originally apprehended through judgment") "is obviously fundamental. If existence is approached as though it were originally known through a concept ... it would be placed on the same level as the essential aspects of the thing."[14] We find Gilson drawing the same connection between judgment's unique role and the real distinction:

> Because it lies beyond essence, existence lies beyond abstract representation, but not beyond the scope of intellectual knowledge; for judgment itself is the most perfect form of intellectual knowledge, and existence is its proper object. The most serious mistake made by the various metaphysics of essence is their failure to realize ... that ... there is, in the object of every concept, something that escapes and transcends its essence.... What [the object] contains over and above its formal definition is its act of existing, and, because

---

quidditas rei, et esse ejus, his duobus respondet duplex operatio intellectus. Una quae dicitur a philosophis formatio, qua apprehendit quidditates rerum, quae etiam a Philosopho, in III *De anima*, dicitur indivisibilium intelligentia. Alia autem comprehendit esse rei, componendo affirmationem, quia etiam esse rei ex materia et forma compositae, *a qua cognitionem accipit, consistit in* quadam compositione formae ad materiam, vel accidentis ad subjectum" (emphasis added). See also ad 2 (Mandonnet 1:904): "Intellectus noster, *cujus cognitio a rebus oritur,* quae *esse compositum* habent, non apprehendit illud esse nisi componendo et dividendo" (emphasis added). The phrase *consistit in* is puzzling. Owens (who, like Wippel, cites this passage too in all his treatments of the subject) takes it to mean that a material thing's *esse* simply *is* the synthesis of its matter and form ("Aquinas on Knowing Existence," 674 and 681–83); Wippel instead takes it, I think rightly, to mean that the *esse* is merely "constituted by" that synthesis (*Metaphysical Thought*, 29–31). A final text from which Owens and Wippel draw support is *ST* II-II, q. 83, a. 1, arg. 3, where Aquinas again assigns essence (*quid est*) to the mind's first act (*indivisibilium intelligentia*) and being (*esse vel non esse*) to the second (*compositio et divisio*). Aquinas's reply leaves this premise unchallenged.

13. Owens, "Judgment and Truth," 150. See ibid.: "The reason why the activity that grasps the thing's existence has to do so by composing an affirmative assertion is that the existence of a thing composed of matter and form *consists in* the composition of form and matter or of accident and subject." Owens's concern here is to counter Rahner's "transcendental Thomist" view that the intellect's activity structures the object rather than being structured by it; but in so doing he seems to claim that composite objects require a composing cognition.

14. Owens, *Interpretation*, 29.

such acts transcend both essence and representation, they can be reached only by means of judgment. The proper function of judgment is to say existence, and this is why judgment is a type of cognition distinct from, and superior to, pure and simple abstract conceptualization.[15]

That is, the irreducible distinction between simple apprehension and judgment results from the irreducible distinction between their proper objects: essence and existence. The "duality of our intellect's operations" follows directly from the "metaphysical composition" of finite being; and in Gilson's view only God can know this composition without this duality.[16]

Maritain too thinks that judgment's unique role in grasping existence is rooted in the fundamental fact that "existence is not an essence" but rather "is shut off from the whole order of essence."[17] In his view, "notionalism"—that is, the reduction of the world to a "universe of essences," of which he thinks even Aristotle is guilty—can be avoided only by "really *thinking*" the existential "judicative act," which, instead of applying "an attribute to a subject," affirms "the subject itself." To genuinely affirm this judgment just "is . . . to grasp intuitively, or *to see*, the being, the existence, the extra-mental *esse* of that subject," which Maritain calls the "intuition of being."[18]

Now, Maritain's theory of an "intuition of being" was controversial; Gilson rejected it,[19] followed by Wippel[20] and Owens,[21] for two reasons. First (paradoxically), Gilson thought it too essentialist. In his view "intuition" or "seeing" by definition is aimed at existing beings, which it "sees" as existing. Hence, since existence is not itself an existing being (except in God's case), it follows that, short of the Beatific Vision, there is no intellectual intuition of existence; to say otherwise confuses existence with an existing, conceptualizable thing. Second, he held that we

---

15. Gilson, *Being and Some Philosophers*, 202. See also 204, where he calls "the abstract essence of being" a "metaphysical monster."

16. Ibid., 229–30.

17. Maritain, *Existence*, 22–23; see also 16–18.

18. Jacques Maritain, "Reflections on Wounded Nature," in Maritain, *Untrammeled Approaches*, ed. and trans. Bernard Doering (Notre Dame, IN: University of Notre Dame Press, 1997), 207–42, at 216–19. This essay was originally published as "Réflexions sur la nature blessée et sur l'intuition de l'être," *Revue Thomiste* 68, no. 1 (1968): 5–40.

19. See Gilson, "Propos sur l'être et sa notion," esp. 10–11 and 16.

20. See Wippel, "Maritain and Aquinas," 428–29 and esp. 441–43, and *Metaphysical Thought*, 3n1 and 40n55.

21. See Owens, "Aquinas on Knowing Existence," 687–88 (though his endorsement of Gilson's critique is more reserved than Wippel's).

have no intellectual intuition at all, since we perceive beings as existing only *in* our sensory perceptions, via the "return to the phantasm," not on the purely intelligible level as an "intellectual intuition" would require.[22]

I think Gilson's critique misses the mark, though, in both respects. First, Maritain would simply reject the critique's stipulation that, definitionally, the object of "intuition" is a conceptualizable *subject* of existence. To "intuit being" for him is not to affirm the reality *of* existence as an existent in its own right (which would indeed be impossible, as Gilson insists), nor is it a further conceptualizing act beyond the original existential judgment.[23] Rather, it is simply grasping the reality of *things*, by which those things are placed "outside of nothingness."[24] That is, it is simply judgment's *apprehensio* of things' *esse*, which we saw Aquinas affirm in *In Sent.* I, d. 38, q. 1, a. 3, taken in its full import. Second, Maritain clearly does not think that an "intuition" of being must be unmediated by the senses, as Gilson and Wippel seem to assume;[25] on the contrary, in a passage that Wippel himself quotes, Maritain asserts that "the intellect reaches the *actus essendi* (in judging) . . . *by the mediation of sensorial perception.*"[26] Indeed, Gilson himself uses "intuition" in Maritain's looser way when he asserts that "our direct knowledge" of beings "includes an *intuitive experience* of their very acts of existing."[27] Rightly understood, then, Maritain's "intuition of being" seems a helpful way to highlight the gulf between existence and essence.

The stakes of the claim that judgment or "intuition" alone grasps

---

22. For Gilson's claim that there is simply no "intellectual intuition" at all, see also his *Elements of Christian Philosophy* (New York: Doubleday, 1960), 130.

23. Maritain clearly stipulates that such conceptualization *follows* on the intuition as the fruit of self-reflection, rather than preceding that intuition by providing it with its object ("existence"); see "Reflections," 220.

24. Maritain, "Reflections," 225; see also his "No Knowledge without Intuitivity," in *Untrammeled Approaches*, 310–49, at 310–11.

25. The passage they both cite (Gilson, "Propos sur l'être et sa notion," 15; Wippel, "Maritain and Aquinas," 437) is "Reflections," 222, where Maritain states that the concept of *esse* gained by reflecting upon the intuition of being "was not drawn from phantasms by the abstractive operation, like all the other objects of concepts." But Maritain's point here is simply that the immediate source of this concept is judgment rather than abstraction from phantasms—not that we can somehow intuit the existence of things around us without using our senses.

26. Maritain, *Existence*, 27n13; see Wippel, "Maritain and Aquinas," 426. Nor is this merely an early view from which Maritain later withdraws: see his "Reflections," see 223–25, where he makes clear that the "intuition of being" simply causes what was already "implicitly and blindly contained" in the intellect's grasp of the sensory act to become "unveiled explicitly."

27. Gilson, *Being and Some Philosophers*, 207 (emphasis added).

Can Angels Know Being without Judgment? 235

existence, then, seem high indeed: it appears that the real distinction between essence and existence stands or falls with it. One might, however, wonder whether the stakes are really this high. Wippel, notably, criticizes Maritain for claiming that the "existence" grasped by judgment is the object's *actus essendi*.[28] Rather, he argues that the existential judgment at first grasps *only* the object's "facticity"; after all, everyone makes existential judgments, but only Thomist metaphysicians have demonstrated the real distinction between essence and the *actus essendi*, and hence can grasp the latter as such.[29] This is why Wippel insists one cannot, *pace* Aquinas's famous *intellectus essentiae* argument, infer that essence is really distinct from existence just because simple apprehension cannot grasp existence.[30] One can indeed infer from this that the *fact* of existence lies outside the "essence" grasped by simple apprehension, but not that either this "facticity" or the "essence" from which it is excluded are two distinct realities: for they might simply be two aspects or consequences of one single actuality-principle,[31] as Suárez claims.[32] And indeed, even Gilson and Owens, despite attaching such importance to the claim that only judgment grasps existence, likewise deny that one can infer the real essence/*actus essendi* distinction simply from that claim.[33] Hence, although Wippel too thinks it is vital for avoiding "essentialism"

28. Wippel spares Gilson from this criticism, however, even though Gilson makes this claim as well in the passage just quoted in note 15 above; see also *Being and Some Philosophers*, 207 and 228).

29. Wippel, *Metaphysical Thought*, 31–33, and "Maritain and Aquinas," 416–17, 428, 428n37, 430. Wippel attributes the formulation of the facticity/*actus essendi* distinction to Cornelio Fabro, citing his "The Intensive Hermeneutics of Thomistic Philosophy: The Notion of Participation," *The Review of Metaphysics* 27, no. 3 (1974): 449–91, at 470 and 470n68, and "Elementi per una dottrina tomistica della partecipazione," in *Esegesi tomistica* (Rome: Libreria ed. della Pontificia Università Lateranense, 1969), 421–48, at 435.

30. Aquinas makes the *intellectus essentiae* argument—namely, that existence really differs from essence because one can fully understand a thing's essence without knowing whether it actually exists—in several early texts: *De ente*, c. 4; *In Sent.* I, d. 8, exp. prim. and q. 4, a. 2; II, d. 1, q. 1, a. 1; II, d. 3, q. 1, a. 1; *De ver.*, q. 10, a. 12. These passages are catalogued by Wippel, "Essence and Existence in Other Writings," in *Metaphysical Themes*, 133–61, at 134n2, in turn relying on Leo Sweeney, "Existence/Essence in Thomas Aquinas's Early Writings," *Proceedings of the American Catholic Philosophical Association* 37 (1963): 97–131, at 105.

31. See Wippel, "Essence and Existence in the *De Ente*, Ch. 4," in *Metaphysical Themes*, 107–32, at 113, and *Metaphysical Thought*, 141, 407, 410, 588.

32. See Suárez, *Disputationes metaphysicae*, 31.6.15 (ed. Vivès, 26:246b–47a); see also Owens, *An Elementary Christian Metaphysics*, 71n5.

33. See Gilson, *Elements of Christian Philosophy*, 128 and 130–31; Owens, "Quiddity and Real Distinction," 8–14, and "Aquinas' Distinction at *De ente et essentia* 4.119–123," *Mediaeval Studies* 48, no. 1 (1986): 264–87, at 277–81.

not to reduce the *actus essendi* to essence, it seems that in his view the mere fact that judgment alone grasps "facticity" says little about the *actus essendi*'s irreducibility.[34]

Nonetheless, further reflection shows that existence's irreducibility is indeed tightly linked to judgment's privileged role. To begin, it seems reasonable to understand "facticity" not as naming something real in its own right over and above the *actus essendi*, but rather as naming the *actus essendi* itself precisely insofar as it is understood imperfectly and prephilosophically (i.e., without awareness of its real distinction from, and actualization of, essence).[35] Aquinas himself seems to imply that judgment attains the *actus essendi* itself (as Maritain held) when he says, in all three of the passages quoted above, that the distinction between simple apprehension and judgment corresponds to essence and existence taken as *duobus in rebus* (or *in re*), two principles in things—not merely in the mind.

But if "facticity" indeed signifies the *actus essendi* as imperfectly understood, then it remains vitally important that it can be accessed only by judgment, not simple apprehension (at least by us humans). For even if our judgment's privileged access to existence does not of itself demonstrate the real distinction, it is still a necessary condition for the real distinction. After all, real distinction presupposes at least the possibility of

---

34. See Wippel, *Metaphysical Thought*, 32.

35. Owens and Wilhelmsen endorse this view; see Owens, "Aquinas on Knowing Existence," 689, and "Aquinas on Being and Thing," in *Thomistic Papers III*, ed. Leonard Kennedy (Houston, TX: Center for Thomistic Studies, 1987), 3–34, at 32n28; Frederick Wilhelmsen, "Existence and Esse," esp. 42–43, and "The Concept of Existence and the Structure of Judgment: A Thomistic Paradox," *The Thomist* 41, no. 3 (1977): 317–49, at 318, 320–21, 340. On this issue they are opposing Fabro, who presents facticity as the "result" of *esse*; see "The Intensive Hermeneutics of Thomistic Philosophy," 470. Wippel seems to side with Owens and Wilhelmsen insofar as he insists that "facticity" signifies "actuality" in *Metaphysical Thought*, 33–35, and denies endorsing Fabro's framing of "facticity" as "result" at 31n29. At 33n33, however, Wippel insists that *esse* is "prior in the order of nature" to facticity; this seems similar to Fabro's "result" relation between *esse* and facticity, and incompatible with their real identity. But if "facticity" were really the "result" of the *actus essendi* rather than identical thereto, then, as it is certainly not an additional metaphysical principle in its own right, "facticity" would have to be *relational* rather than absolute: that is, merely the object's *presence* in and ability to *interact* with our world. "Facticity" in this relational sense is what Maritain terms "Dasein"; and he thinks it is originally known by abstraction, not existential judgment (Maritain, "Reflections," 221–31), which seems quite reasonable, since relations are quidditative predicates. (Owens seems to miss this relational, and therefore quidditative, nature of Maritain's "Dasein," in his "Maritain's Three Concepts of Existence," *New Scholasticism* 49, no. 3 [1975]: 295–309, at 300–303.) But then Aquinas cannot have meant "facticity" in this relational sense when he assigned "existence" exclusively to judgment. And so it seems reasonable to take the "existence" originally grasped in existential judgment to be instead really identical to the *actus essendi*, even if imperfectly known.

conceptual distinction; and the conceptual distinction between essence and existence is possible for us precisely because our concepts, which give us access only to essences, do not directly grasp existence. If our concepts did directly grasp existence, then there would be no grounds for even the *intellectus essentiae* argument's conceptual distinction between essence and existence, let alone a real distinction. Rather, existence (whether as act or as fact) would perforce be something quidditative in its own right, as in Giles of Rome's "two things" (*duae res*) view of the distinction,[36] and *contra* Kant's famous insight that existence is not a "real predicate" (i.e., has no conceptual content).[37] And if existence were indeed held to be something quidditative in its own right, then one would rightly observe that it adds nothing to the original essence, and either follow Suárez in discarding this hypostatized existence as useless,[38]

---

36. For Giles of Rome's description essence and existence as *duae res*, see, e.g., *Theorems on Existence and Essence (Theoremata de esse et essentia)*, trans. Michael Murray (Milwaukee, WI: Marquette University Press, 1953), theor. 19 (94–99). Giles, of course, denies that existence is a kind of quiddity, and therefore insists that nothing is added to our knowledge of, e.g., "rose" when we know that a rose exists; see theor. 12 (61–62). (This was both the point of Aquinas's *intellectus essentiae* argument and of Kant's famous point about the hundred thalers; for the latter, see note 37 below.) The question, however, is whether Giles's understanding of the real distinction is consistent with this denial. For discussion, see Gilson, *Being and Some Philosophers*, 99–100; Owens, "Quiddity and Real Distinction," 20, "Aquinas' Distinction," 284–85, *An Elementary Christian Metaphysics*, 104–5 and 105n11, and "Aquinas on Being and Thing," 6; Wilhelmsen, *The Paradoxical Structure of Existence*, 53.

37. For Kant's famous insistence that "being," in the sense of actual existence, "is not a real predicate," see his *Critique of Pure Reason*, trans. Paul Guyer and Allen Wood (Cambridge: Cambridge University Press, 1998), Ak. A598–99/B626–27 (567). Gilson and Owens place Kant's insight at the forefront of their discussions of knowing existence: see Gilson, *Being and Some Philosophers*, 3–4 (see also 124–32, where Gilson commends Kant for refusing either to reduce existence to essence or to deny existence outright, but faults him for choosing to "bracket" it instead), and Owens, *An Interpretation of Existence*, 2–5, *An Elementary Christian Metaphysics*, 43–45, and "Aquinas on Knowing Existence," 671.

38. For Suárez's understanding of the "real distinction" thesis in Giles's terms of *duae res*, see his *Disputationes metaphysicae*, 31.1.3, 31.3.7, 31.6.1 (ed. Vivès, 26:225a, 26:235a, 26:241b); see also 31.4.5 (ed. Vivès, 26:236b) for Suárez's insistence on identifying what "existence" is (*quid existentia sit*). For Suárez's view that existence so conceived (as a *res* over and above essence) could add nothing to the essence, see esp. 31.6.1 ("nihil addit rei"; ed. Vivès, 26:242a); see also 31.5.10 (ed. Vivès, 26:240b) and 31.12.6 (ed. Vivès, 26:285a), where he says that an existence that is separable from essence "nihil esse, cum nullum habeat effectum neque utilitatem." (Suárez of course does not reject existence as such—only existence taken as really distinct from essence.) For discussion of the link between Suárez's conceptualized understanding of existence and his rejection of the real distinction, see Gilson, *Being and Some Philosophers*, 100–107 and 223; Owens, "Aquinas on Being and Thing," 13–17, and *An Elementary Christian Metaphysics*, 104–5 and 105n11–12; and Wilhelmsen, *The Paradoxical Structure of Existence*, 54.

or follow Hegel in simply identifying it with "nothing."[39] As Gilson puts it, the upshot of such essentialism is "reducing to nothingness the very act in virtue of which being actually is."[40]

This, I take it, is the chief significance of denying that simple apprehension grasps existence: it makes nonessentialist metaphysics possible. Moreover, this claim in turn implies also that only judgment grasps being as real—that is, the prephilosophical notion of "being" (*ens*). This is because "being" (*ens*) is simply short for "that which is" and hence includes a reference to existence. Therefore, if "being" were known purely by abstraction, either existence would be too (reducing it to a kind of essence) or else "being" would have to abstract not only from all essential differences but also from "existence" too, leaving it empty indeed.[41]

What then of the other claim—that only judgment knows being as being? This second claim is based primarily on a single, though thorough, text: again, *In De Trin.*, q. 5, a. 3. Previously (5.1) Aquinas had divided speculative science into natural philosophy, mathematics, and metaphysics, and he had identified the subject of metaphysics with natures that do not depend on matter for either their being or their intelligibility (including both spiritual substances and metaphysical notions such as being, substance and accident, act and potency, etc.). In 5.3 he now correlates these three sciences to three degrees of "abstraction" from matter. The first two kinds of abstraction, corresponding to natural philosophy and mathematics, both pertain to simple apprehension because, in both cases, the forms (physical essences and mathematical quantities, respectively) still depend for their *existence* on their union with the matter from which they are being abstracted. Hence the "abstractions" in question consist simply in isolated *consideration* of the relevant form; they do not assign any *ontological* isolation to that form. The third, metaphysical

---

39. See Hegel, *The Science of Logic*, trans. George di Giovanni (Cambridge: Cambridge University Press, 2010), GW 21:69 (59), culminating in the famous line that "pure being and pure nothing are therefore the same." For the view that Hegel's view of being results from conceptualizing existence, see Frederick Wilhelmsen, *The Paradoxical Structure of Existence*, 3rd ed. (New Brunswick, NJ: Transaction Publishers, 2015), 71–75, and "Existence and Esse," 29; Owens, "The Content of Existence," in *Logic and Ontology*, ed. Milton Munitz, 21–35 (New York: New York University Press, 1973), esp. 22 and 34, *An Elementary Christian Metaphysics*, 61n7, and "Aquinas' Distinction," 280; and Gilson, *Being and Some Philosophers*, 209.

40. Gilson, *Being and Some Philosophers*, 207.

41. See Wippel, *Metaphysical Thought*, 48, and "Metaphysics and *Separatio*," 81; Maritain, *Existence*, 31; Owens, "Metaphysical Separation in Aquinas," *Mediaeval Studies* 34, no. 1 (1972): 287–306, at 302–4; and Wilhelmsen, "The Concept of Existence," 337.

Can Angels Know Being without Judgment? 239

type of abstraction, however, goes further: it *asserts* that the forms it has abstracted can indeed *exist* in isolation from matter.

Hence, metaphysical abstraction is not merely an isolating "consideration," an instance of simple apprehension: it is an isolating judgment, asserting that its object is really (not merely conceptually) separable from matter. Aquinas therefore says, in his final revision to the text,[42] that this third "abstraction" is only improperly so called, because properly speaking one "abstracts" X from Y only if X and Y are really united (*simul secundum rem*). Since metaphysical notions signify realities that are *not* necessarily really united to matter, the corresponding third "abstraction" is better named "separation" (*separatio*). It is only by this negative judgment of "separation" that thought reaches the level of metaphysics.[43] And the reason that metaphysics depends on this "separation" is simple: to understand "being as being," the subject of metaphysics,[44] one must

---

42. As Armand Maurer notes in *St. Thomas Aquinas: The Division and Methods of the Sciences*, 3rd ed. (Toronto: The Pontifical Institute of Mediaeval Studies, 1963), xxv, "in the first redaction St. Thomas makes no mention of the distinction between apprehension and judgment: the distinction that later becomes the keystone of his solution"; and though the second redaction does mention judgment, it is only the third redaction that gives judgment its foundational role in metaphysics. For a discussion of Aquinas's autograph of this article and the careful development of Aquinas's thought revealed therein, see especially Louis-Bertrand Geiger, "Abstraction et séparation d'après S. Thomas: In De Trinitate, q. 5, a. 3," *Revue des sciences philosophiques et théologiques* 31 (1947): 3–40, at 15–20; see also Wippel, *Metaphysical Thought*, 49n82, and "Metaphysics and *Separatio*," 80.

43. Aquinas, *In De Trin.*, q. 5, a. 3. The main parallel text on the "degrees of abstraction" is *ST* I, q. 85, a. 1, ad 1–2. Although Aquinas does not here use the term *separatio*, and speaks only of three kinds of *abstractio*, the central point remains the same: the third, metaphysical type of abstraction, unlike the first two types, pertains to judgment (*modum compositionis et divisionis*) rather than simple apprehension (*modum simplicis et absolutae considerationis*). For discussion of *ST* I, q. 85, a. 1, see Maurer, *The Division and Methods of the Sciences*, xxiv; Wippel, *Metaphysical Thought*, 50–51, and "Metaphysics and *Separatio*," 81–82. Aquinas also lists the three degrees of abstraction in *In Meta.*, prol.; he does not make reference to judgment there, but does insist that metaphysics abstracts from matter *secundum esse*, and not just *secundum rationem* as mathematics does. In addition, see *ST* I, q. 88, a. 2, co. and ad 2, where he insists that immaterial things cannot be known simply by abstraction, but only *per viam remotionis*, which seems to imply the use of judgments of separation. Maritain discusses the three degrees of abstraction at length, though without singling out judgment's role, in his *The Degrees of Knowledge*, 4th ed., trans. Gerald Phelan (New York: Charles Scribner's Sons, 1959), 35–46, 136–38, 209–18. He does, however, emphasize negative judgment's role in the third degree of abstraction in *Existence*, 28n14.

44. The famous claim that the subject of metaphysics is *ens inquantum ens* originates from Aristotle's *Metaphysics*, esp. IV.1–3 and VI.1. Aquinas frequently repeats this claim. See, e.g., his commentary on those texts at *In Meta.* IV.1, n. 529–33; IV.4, nn. 571 and 584–87; IV.5, n. 593; VI.1, nn. 1144–52 and 1170. See also III.4, n. 384; III.6, n. 398; VII.1, n. 1245; XI.3, nn. 2194 and 2204; XI.4, nn. 2206–09; XI.7, nn. 2248, 2259, 2266; XII.1, n. 2421. See also the prologue,

transcend the limitation of understanding "being" only "as material."[45]

But what exactly is at stake in claiming that this "separation" must consist in negative judgment, rather than the ordinary abstraction of simple apprehension? Arguably, it is the analogical richness of the notion of "being." In *In De Trin.*, q. 5, a. 3, Aquinas seems to be thinking primarily of the analogy within the category of "substance" that unites corruptible bodies, incorruptible bodies, and immaterial substances (sometimes called "analogy of genus").[46] In Aquinas's view, we need *separatio* to grasp immaterial substances not only because they lie outside our experience, and thus can be known only by nominal definitions, but also because they do not share any natural (i.e., metaphysical or real, as opposed to logical) genus with anything in our experience. This means that we cannot form our nominal definitions of them by the normal recourse to a remote genus; instead we are forced to arrive at them by negation—that is, a judgment of *separatio*.[47]

---

although there Aquinas instead uses the term *ens commune* to refer to the subject of metaphysics. In his Aristotle commentaries, see also *In De an.* I.1 (Leon. 45/1.4a:1–10), *In Phys.* I.1, n. 4 and III.6, n. 2, and *In Ethic.* VI.5 (Leon. 47/2.350a:97–106). In his theological works, see esp. *In De Trin.*, q. 5, a. 4, as well as *ST* I-II, q. 66, a. 5, ad 4, and *In Sent.* III, d. 27, q. 2, a. 4, ad 2 (though in these latter two again he uses the term *ens commune* instead).

45. For the link between *separatio* and attaining "being as being," see especially *In De Trin.*, q. 5, a. 4 (Leon. 50.154a–b:157–62 and 182–98), where Aquinas says that the metaphysical science "que habet subiectum *ens in quantum est ens* . . . est de his que sunt *separata* a materia et motu *secundum esse*" (emphasis added). Although Aquinas does not mention the judgment of *separatio* here, he had just stated in q. 5, a. 3 that this judgment is needed to grasp objects which are independent of matter *secundum esse*. Wippel attributes great significance to *separatio*'s role in metaphysics; see his "Metaphysics and *Separatio*," 74–80, and *Metaphysical Thought*, 44–47. In this he is following Geiger; see his *La participation dans la philosophie de S. Thomas d'Aquin* (Paris: Vrin, 1942), 315–21, and "Abstraction et séparation," 12–23.

46. For the sense in which there can be analogy—albeit metaphysical rather than logical—even within the Aristotelian category of substance, see esp. *In Sent.* I, d. 19, q. 5, a. 2, ad 1 (the second of the three meanings of analogy distinguished there), as well as *In Sent.* II, d. 3, q. 1, a. 1, ad 2, *De ver.*, q. 18, a. 5, ad 6, and *In De Trin.*, q. 6, a. 3 (which, though without using the word "analogy," emphasizes that we can only know incorruptible and immaterial substances by *negations*—presumably judgments of "separation"). These texts (excepting *De ver.*) rely on Aristotle's claim at *Metaphysics* X.10.1058b26–1059a15 that corruptible and incorruptible substances do not share a genus. For discussion of this doctrine of "metaphysical analogy" within the category of substance, and its link to the metaphysical judgment of *separatio*, see Gregory T. Doolan, "Substance as a Metaphysical Genus," in *The Science of Being as Being: Metaphysical Investigations*, ed. Gregory T. Doolan (Washington, DC: the Catholic University of America Press, 2012), 99–128, esp. 101 and 115–18; Doolan, "The Metaphysician's vs. the Logician's Categories," *Quaestiones Disputatae* 4, no. 2 (2014): 133–55, at 149 and 151–54; and Armand Maurer, "St. Thomas and the Analogy of Genus," *The New Scholasticism* 29, no. 2: 127–44, esp. 142–44.

47. See esp. *In De Trin.*, q. 6, a. 3. See also *ST* I, q. 88, a. 2; *Q. de an.* 16; *SCG* III, c. 41; *In Meta.* II.1, n. 285; and *De ver.*, q. 18, a. 5, co. and ad 6.

However, the trans-categorial analogy of being seems to be at stake as well, and with it the whole Aristotelian response to Parmenides's dilemma, even if Aquinas does not emphasize this point here. For if "being" were known by ordinary abstraction, then, such abstraction consists simply in nonconsideration of extraneous content, there would be nothing left to "being" at all: it would simply be the monolithic block envisioned by Parmenides, and rightly identified by Hegel with "nothing."[48] By assigning knowledge of "being as being" instead to judgment, Aquinas is rejecting this pursuit of a single, isolatable, generic "core" of being underlying the ten categories,[49] and instead insisting that "being" cannot be identified with *any* of the ways in which it manifests itself: substance or accident, material or immaterial, matter or form.[50]

The point, then, is that whenever one considers "being as being," what one directly conceptualizes is always some given kind of being (substance *or* accident, material *or* immaterial), while simultaneously correcting that conceptualization by *denying* that "being as being" is restricted to that particular kind of being.[51] One might also add that the same is true of the abstract concept "existence" (*esse*): it cannot be rightly understood without a corrective negative judgment (*separatio*) asserting that, despite its grammatical noun form, "existence" is not a nature![52] Without *separatio*, our key metaphysical concepts would be distorted

---

48. See note 39 above. For discussion of Hegel's notion of "being" in the context of metaphysical abstraction, see Maritain, *The Degrees of Knowledge*, 216, and Wilhelmsen, "The Concept of Existence," 329, 331, 348.

49. For a small sample of the texts where Aquinas claims that "being" is analogical across the ten categories, see *In Phys.* I.3, I.6, and III.5, n. 15; *In Meta.* I.9, nn. 138–39, IV.1, nn. 534–43, IV.3, n. 568, V.9, nn. 889–90, XI.3, n. 2197; *De principiis naturae* 6; and *De ver.*, q. 1, a. 1. See *ST* I, q. 13, a. 5; *De ver.*, q. 2, a. 11; *SCG* I, c. 34; *De pot.*, q. 7, a. 7; and *In Sent.* I, prol. q. 1, a. 2, ad 2; d. 19, q. 5, a. 1, ad 1; and I, d. 35, q. 1, a. 4, which discuss trans-categorial analogy in the context of God-creatures analogy.

50. See esp. Wippel, *Metaphysical Thought*, 48–49, "Metaphysics and *Separatio*," 80–81, and "Maritain and Aquinas," 433–34, along with Geiger, "Abstraction et séparation," 27–28. See also Klubertanz, *Introduction to the Philosophy of Being*, 2nd ed. (New York: Appleton-Century-Crofts, 1963), 56; Schmidt, "L'emploi de la séparation en métaphysique," *Revue philosophique de Louvain* 58 (1960): 373–93, at 389; Maritain, *The Degrees of Knowledge*, 212–14; and Wilhelmsen, "Existence and Esse," 35–36, and "The Concept of Existence," 337 and 349.

51. Obviously *ens inquantum ens*, like *esse*, is a concept which can be simply apprehended and used as the subject of further predication. Again, the point is that, like *esse*, it is a *derivative* or *reflexive* concept, formed by reflecting on an insight originally attained in judgment (see above, note 8)—here, the negative judgment of *separatio*.

52. See Wilhelmsen, "Existence and Esse," 30–31 and 34; "The Concept of Existence," 322, 339, 343.

into signifying univocal essences. Metaphysics thus not only ends but also begins with the *via negativa*.

AQUINAS'S CLAIM THAT ANGELS DO NOT COMPOSE OR DIVIDE

It would seem, then, that judgment is indispensable for knowing both existence and being as such. Existence cannot be known by simple apprehension under pain of turning it into one more essence; being-as-being cannot be known by simple apprehension without removing both its reference to existence and its intrinsically analogical nature. Yet, on the other hand, it seems that Aquinas *must* hold that both existence and being-as-being are in fact known at least to angels by simple apprehension, since he denies that they engage in acts of "composition and division" at all, at least on the natural plane. Let us turn then to the texts where Aquinas excludes composition and division from angelic knowledge.

Although Aquinas argues for this claim in at least two other passages (notably both from relatively late works),[53] his fullest treatment is in *ST* I, q. 58, a. 4, an article dedicated to this purpose:

53. See *ST* I, q. 85, a. 5, and *De malo*, q. 16, a. 6, ad s.c. 1. See also *In De an.* III.5 (Leon. 45/1.227b:242–46), which makes the same claim but without argument, and *In De div. nom.* 7.2, n. 711, where he denies that angelic knowledge involves our judgment's composition on the basis of angelic immateriality. This claim that angels know only by simple apprehension is not only absent from Aquinas's earlier works; he actually seems to deny it at *De ver.*, q. 15, a. 1, ad 5 (Leon. 22.481b:479–86): "Eadem potentia in nobis est quae [1] cognoscit simplices rerum quiditates et quae [2] format propositiones et quae [3] ratiocinatur, quorum [3] ultimum proprium est rationis in quantum est ratio; alia duo possunt esse etiam intellectus in quantum est intellectus. Unde [2] *secundum invenitur in angelis cum per plures species cognoscant*, sed in Deo est solum [1] primum." (emphasis added) Harm Goris takes this to be an early affirmation of angelic composition and division which Aquinas later simply abandons; see "Angelic Knowledge in Aquinas and Bonaventure," in *A Companion to Angels in Medieval Philosophy*, ed. Tobias Hoffmann, (Leiden: Brill, 2012), 149–85, at 171n66. Even in this early text, though, the curt reason given (namely that angels know through multiple species) seems to imply only a limited use of angelic composition and division: merely comparing things which fall under different angelic species, not knowing the existence or accidents of a given subject known under a single angelic species. This limitation is necessary, I think, to reconcile this passage with other passages in the *De ver.* affirming angels' changeless knowledge of changing things (see below, note 72), and also with, e.g., the earlier *In Sent.* II, d. 7, q. 2, a. 1, ad 4, where Aquinas insists that *one* species allows the angel to know both a thing and whatever belongs to that thing (*ea quae in re sunt*). One might also take Aquinas here to be taking "composition" in the different, very loose sense of "using multiple species to know something wholly and perfectly," to quote John of St. Thomas, *Cursus theologicus*, 42.4, n. 43 (Paris: Desclée, 1946), 4:679b; Benoît Garceau also seems to take this approach in *Judicium. Vocabulaire, sources, doctrine de saint Thomas d'Aquin* (Paris: Vrin, 1968), 133 and 139–40.

Can Angels Know Being without Judgment?   243

The conclusion is compared to the principle in the intellect's reasoning (*intellectu ratiocinante*) just as the predicate is compared to the subject in the intellect's composing and dividing (*intellectu componente et dividente*). Now if the intellect were to see the truth of the conclusion immediately in the principle itself, it would never understand by discursive reasoning (*discurrendo vel ratiocinando*). So likewise, if the intellect, in its apprehension of the subject's quiddity, were immediately aware (*haberet notitiam*) of everything which can be attributed to or removed from the subject, it would never understand by composing and dividing, but only by understanding the thing's essence (*quod quid est*).

Therefore it is clear that it is for the same reason that our intellect understands by discursive reasoning, and by composing and dividing: namely, because it cannot instantly inspect whatever is virtually (*virtute*) contained in something newly apprehended in its first apprehension thereof. This is due to the weakness of the intellectual light in us, as has been said [I, q. 58, a. 3]. Hence, since there is a perfect intellectual light in the angel ... it follows that the angel, just as it does not understand by reasoning (*ratiocinando*), so neither does it understand by composing or dividing.

Nonetheless, the angel understands the composition and division of propositions (*enuntiationum*), just as it understands the reasoning of syllogisms: for it understands composite things simply, and changeable things changelessly (*mobilia immobiliter*), and material things immaterially.[54]

---

54. *ST* I, q. 58, a. 4 (Leon. 5.85a–b): "Sicut in intellectu ratiocinante comparatur conclusio ad principium, ita in intellectu componente et dividente comparatur praedicatum ad subiectum. Si enim intellectus statim in ipso principio videret conclusionis veritatem, nunquam intelligeret discurrendo vel ratiocinando. Similiter si intellectus statim in apprehensione quidditatis subiecti haberet notitiam de omnibus quae possunt attribui subiecto vel removeri ab eo, nunquam intelligeret componendo et dividendo, sed solum intelligendo *quod quid est*. Sic igitur patet quod ex eodem provenit quod intellectus noster intelligit discurrendo, et componendo et dividendo: ex hoc scilicet, quod non statim in prima apprehensione alicuius primi apprehensi, potest inspicere quidquid in eo virtute continetur. Quod contingit ex debilitate luminis intellectualis in nobis, sicut dictum est. Unde cum in angelo sit lumen intellectuale perfectum ...; relinquitur quod angelus, sicut non intelligit ratiocinando, ita non intelligit componendo et dividendo. Nihilominus tamen compositionem et divisionem enuntiationum intelligit, sicut et ratiocinationem syllogismorum: intelligit enim composita simpliciter, et mobilia immobiliter, et materialia immaterialiter." For contemporary discussions of angelic composition-free knowing in Aquinas, see, e.g., Serge-Thomas Bonino, *Angels and Demons: A Catholic Introduction*, trans. Michael Miller (Washington, DC: The Catholic University of America Press, 2016), 150–51; Goris, "Angelic Knowledge," 171–73; Tiziana Suarez-Nani, *Connaissance et langage des anges selon Thomas d'Aquin et Gilles de Rome* (Paris: Vrin, 2002), 65–68; James Collins, *The Thomistic Philosophy of the Angels* (Washington, DC: The Catholic University of America Press, 1947), 180–84; and Anton Pegis, "In Umbra Intelligentiae," *The New Scholasticism* 14, no. 2 (1940): 146–80, at 168. Of these, only Bonino and Goris explicitly apply Aquinas's claim to judgments with existential import. For more extensive treatments, see Cajetan, *In* ST I, q. 58, aa. 4–5 (Leon. 5.85–88), and John of St. Thomas, *Cursus theologicus*, 42.4, nn. 42–50.

Aquinas here certainly seems to exclude composition and division categorically from the angelic mind. He can do so because of his view (expressed in the final sentence) that there is no intrinsic contradiction in a simple cognitive act with a composite object.[55] Our own human need for further composing and dividing is therefore due not to the complexity of judgment's *object*, but rather to the imperfection of our *mode of knowing* ("the weakness of the intellectual light in us"), which makes our initial grasp of the object incomplete.[56] By contrast, an angel, thanks to his "perfect intellectual light," can see immediately, by a simple act, everything that is virtually contained in his intellectual starting-points: both (1) the full implications of an axiom, which obviates further reasoning,[57] and (2) "everything which can be attributed to or removed from the subject" whose quiddity he grasps, which obviates further composing and dividing.[58]

55. This claim is a fixture of Aquinas's discussions of God's knowledge, where he frequently insists that the divine intellect, despite its lack of composition and division, possesses par excellence both truth and knowledge of *enuntiabilia* (roughly meaning "states of affairs" precisely insofar as they can be expressed in propositions; see esp. *In Sent.* I, d. 41, q. 1, a. 5). See *In Sent.* I, d. 19, q. 5, a. 1, and d. 38, q. 1, a. 3, co. and ad 2; *De ver.*, q. 2, a. 7; *SCG* I, c. 58, n. 493, and c. 59, n. 495; *ST* I, q. 14, a. 14; a. 15, ad 3; q. 16, a. 5, ad 1; and *In Peri herm.* I.3 (Leon. 1*/1.17a–b:193–97).

56. For this claim that composition and division presupposes that the object has already been grasped imperfectly, see also Aquinas's treatments of God's simple knowledge in, e.g., *SCG* I, c. 58, n. 487, and *ST* I, q. 14, a. 14.

57. Aquinas makes this relatively straightforward claim throughout his career. For his early treatments of angelic nondiscursivity, see, e.g., *In Sent.* II, d. 3, q. 1, aa. 2 and 6; d. 7, q. 1, a. 2; d. 9, q. 1, aa. 3–4; *De ver.*, q. 8, a. 15 (see also q. 2, a. 1, ad 4; q. 8, a. 4, ad 14; and q. 24, a. 10); *In De div. nom.* 4.7 (though Jean-Pierre Torrell notes that this work may have been written during the later Rome period; see *Saint Thomas Aquinas*, vol. 1, *The Person and His Work*, rev. ed., trans. Robert Royal [Washington, DC: The Catholic University of America Press, 2005], 127); and *SCG* III, c. 49, n. 2265, and III, c. 108, n. 2836. Later treatments include *ST* I, q. 58, a. 3 (see also q. 64, a. 2), and II-II, q. 180, a. 6, ad 2; *De spir. creat.* 2, ad 12; and *De malo*, q. 16, aa. 4 and 6. For Dionysius's influence on Aquinas's theory of angelic nondiscursivity, see *De div. nom.* 7.2.868B. For discussions of angelic nondiscursivity in Aquinas, see Cajetan, *In ST* I, q. 58, a. 3; John of St. Thomas, *Cursus theologicus*, 42.4, nn. 2–41; Bonino, *Angels and Demons*, 149–50; and Harm Goris, "Angelic Knowledge," 169–71. Suarez-Nani, Collins, and Pegis treat angelic nondiscursivity together with angelic nonpropositionality; see above, note 54.

58. Aquinas thus identifies a single root for discursive and propositional knowing (namely, the inability to grasp a whole essence at a glance), which seems to imply that excluding the latter from angels presents no more difficulty than excluding the former. Suarez-Nani therefore treats this twofold exclusion as a single claim (*Connaissance*, 65). Conversely, Bonino (rightly, I think) takes the "no-composition" claim to be more fundamental than the "no-discursivity" claim; see *Angels and Demons*, 150. Although Goris does not rank the two claims, he (again rightly, I believe) claims that the root of the "no-judgment" thesis is actually different from that of the "no-discursivity thesis," despite Aquinas's apparent contrary view in both *ST* I, q. 58, a. 4, and *De malo*, q. 16, a. 6, ad s.c. 1; see "Angelic Knowledge," 173.

Can Angels Know Being without Judgment? 245

Notably, however, this argument does not obviate judging. Aquinas does not use the term *iudicare* in this article, but he attributes it freely to angels in the very next article (I, q. 58, a. 5), as well as in the parallel *De malo*, q. 16, a. 6, even as he reiterates in both texts that they do not compose and divide. Elsewhere Aquinas states that God too judges (*iudicat*) without composition and division.[59] The clear implication is that Aquinas himself, unlike the contemporary Thomists discussed in the previous section, sharply distinguishes "judgment" (*iudicium*) from "composition and division" (the "second act of the mind"). "Judgment" implies composition only in the *object known*; it signifies any cognitive act, whether simple or complex, whose object is a composite state of affairs (an *enuntiabile*), including even the act of sense perception.[60] "Composition and division," by contrast, implies composition in the *intellect itself*; it signifies only complex intellectual acts, which grasp states of affairs by adding to (or subtracting from) a subject already imperfectly known by a prior simple act.[61] The argument of *ST* I, q. 58, a. 4, is meant to exclude only "composition and division" (hereafter C/D), not "judgment."[62]

---

59. See esp. *ST* I, q. 16, a. 5, ad 1 (Leon. 5.212b): "Licet in intellectu divino non sit *compositio et divisio*, tamen secundum suam simplicem intelligentiam *iudicat* de omnibus, et cognoscit omnia complexa" (emphasis added). See also *In Sent.* I, d. 38, q. 1, a. 3 (one of the *loci classici* examined earlier for the claim that existence is known by "composition and division"), where Aquinas, though without using the term *iudicium*, claims that God knows *affirmations and negations* without "composition and division."

60. Aquinas frequently refers to the activity of the senses as a *iudicium* without ascribing "composition" to them. See esp. *Quod.* VIII.2.1 (Leon. 25/1.56b:69–73), where Aquinas describes the proper operation of the senses in general as "iudicium de propriis obiectis." See also *In De an.* II.28 for the *iudicium* of the senses in general; *In De an.* II.13, II.30, III.2, and III.5–6 for the *iudicium* of the external senses; *ST* I, q. 78, a. 4, ad 2, and *In De sensu* 16 and 18 for the *iudicium* of the external senses contrasted with that of the common sense; *In De an.* II.27 and *In De sensu* 18 for the *iudicium* of the common sense; *In Ethic.* II.11 and *ST* I-II, q. 45, a. 4, for the *iudicium* of the estimative sense; and *In De an.* III.6, where Aquinas indicates that the *iudicium* of the estimative sense, like the intellect's and unlike the external senses', really is a kind of "composing." I thank Therese Cory for drawing my attention to these texts and their significance. For discussion of the "sense judgment" in Aquinas, see Owens, "Judgment and Truth," esp. 138–47.

61. See, e.g., *SCG* I, c. 58, n. 490, and c. 59, n. 495; *ST* I, q. 14, a. 14, and q. 58, a. 4, co. and ad 3; and *De ver.*, q. 2, a. 7. For discussion, see Cajetan, *In ST* I, q. 58, a. 5, n. 4 (Leon. 5.88b), and John of St. Thomas, *Cursus theologicus*, 42.4, n. 50 (Desclée 4.681b).

62. Francis A. Cunningham and Benoît Garceau have emphasized the difference between "judgment" and "composition and division" in Aquinas's usage. See Cunningham, "Judgment in St. Thomas," *The Modern Schoolman* 31, no. 3 (1954): 185–212, and "The Second Operation and the Assent vs. the Judgment in St. Thomas," *The New Scholasticism* 31, no. 1 (1957): 1–33; and Garceau, *Judicium*, esp. 7–14, 30–35, and 101–51. Moreover, Cunningham leans on the fact that Aquinas attributes judgment but not C/D to the angels, as well as to God and to the senses;

Now, this argument certainly seems successful in obviating C/D in angelic knowledge of *essential* properties, which are indeed virtually contained in the essence. (1) It is not at all clear, however, that the essence also virtually contains what belongs merely *contingently* to particular subjects that instantiate the essence—least of all their existence! And so it is not clear that the argument successfully obviates acts of "composing" the fully-grasped essence with these contingent predicates. (2) Nor does Aquinas explain here how to reconcile his denial of angelic C/D with his other claim, which we examined above, that only C/D, not simple apprehension, grasps existence—even though the real distinction itself seemed to be at stake in that claim! He does elsewhere explain why God can know created essence and existence by a single act, namely because he knows them by being the single exemplar of both,[63] but this explanation hardly seems applicable to angels.

One strategy to resolve both problems is to adopt a deflationary reading of *ST* I, q. 58, a. 4, as in fact excluding only C/D about necessary essential properties—not about contingent accidents or existence, which after all are not specifically named in the article. This strategy, however, fails. Even in the article itself Aquinas explicitly speaks of knowing "everything which can be attributed to or removed from the *subject*"—not just what pertains to the subject's *essence*. And two parallel passages definitively eliminate the deflationary strategy. In *ST* I, q. 85, a. 5, Aquinas says that the things that angels know without C/D include not only properties (*proprietates*) but also accidents (*accidentia*) and relations (*habitudines*) "surrounding" the essence (*circumstantes rei essentiam*). And more importantly, in *De malo*, q. 16, a. 6, ad s.c. 1, Aquinas insists that "the angel, by simple apprehension of the subject, knows *existence and*

---

see "*Judgment* in St. Thomas," 185, 191n16, and 205, and "The Second Operation," 5, 26, and 27. Garceau too brings up angelic C/D-less judgment at *Judicium*, 133 and 139–40. Cunningham, however, does not link "judgment" to grasping existence, and, oddly, actually excludes genuine "judgment" from the act of "composing and dividing" ("*Judgment* in St. Thomas," 207; "The Second Operation," 30–31). Garceau's more nuanced approach grants, versus Cunningham, that in Aquinas's view the "judgment" by which intellectual beings grasp truth is indeed a kind of C/D (*Iudicium*, 151). However, Garceau thinks that even angels have this kind of judicative C/D; what they lack, in his view, is a different, non-judicative kind of C/D that consists strictly in adding to an initially imperfectly grasped concept (*Iudicium*, 139–40). As we will see, Aquinas actually denies that angels have *either* kind of C/D. I therefore propose instead that (1) *all* C/D is judgmental, but (2) angelic judgments need not be acts of C/D, for reasons to be discussed below.

63. Aquinas, *In Sent*. I, d. 38, q. 1, a. 3, co. and ad 2. For discussion, see Wippel, *Metaphysical Thought*, 29–30.

nonexistence" (*Angelus per simplicem apprehensionem subiecti cognoscit esse vel non esse*). This seems unequivocal: angels can grasp (judge) existence by simple apprehension.

Perhaps even more strikingly, Aquinas states in *ST* I, q. 58, a. 5, and the parallel *De malo*, q. 16, a. 6, co. and ad s.c. 1, that fallen angels can not only judge existence but even judge it falsely without C/D,[64] precisely because they, unlike us, can grasp *esse* by simple apprehension.[65] This is even more striking because the reason that angels are supposed to be able to prescind from C/D is that their initial grasp of each thing's essence is already complete. But if it was already odd to say that a thing's essence virtually contains the thing's contingent substantial and accidental existence, it is surely much odder to say that the essence virtually contains existence that does not actually belong to the thing! Rather, false judgment seems to require wrongly adding something to or subtracting something from the initially grasped essence. Indeed Aquinas uses the term "break out" (*prorumpunt*), which might seem to suggest that something new has been added to the original simple apprehension; and this in turn would certainly imply C/D. Nonetheless, Aquinas clearly denies that this *falsum opinium* or *iudicium* is an act of C/D, and so he must think that it is instead somehow already contained in a flaw in the fallen angel's initial grasp of the essence, traceable to his corrupt will.[66]

---

64. *ST* I, q. 58, a. 5 (Leon. 5.87a–b): "Angelus non intelligit componendo et dividendo, sed intelligendo *quod quid est*.... Sic igitur per se non potest esse falsitas aut error aut deceptio; sed per accidens contingit.... Daemones vero, per voluntatem perversam subducentes intellectum a divina sapientia, *absolute interdum de rebus iudicant* secundum naturalem conditionem. Et ... decipi possunt quantum ad ea quae supernaturalia sunt," (emphasis added). *De malo*, q. 16, a. 6 (Leon. 23.310b:281–85 and 288–89): "In malis angelis propter inordinatam et superbam uoluntatem potest esse respectu huiusmodi cognoscibilium etiam *defectus false opinionis*, in quantum exhibent presumptuose suum intellectum ad iudicandum de his que eos excedunt ... in quantum scilicet *absolute in falsum iudicium prorumpunt*" (emphasis added). Aquinas holds here that, although all angels are inerrant with respect to the natural objects of their knowledge, their natural knowledge does not extend to supernatural matters, and so fallen angels may make false judgments about those supernatural matters. Before their fall, however (up to and including the moment of their sin), Aquinas elsewhere holds that angels could not have an actual false belief. Instead their sin was due to "nonconsideration" of something that they should have been considering at the moment of choice. See *SCG* III, c. 110, n. 2851; *De malo*, q. 16, a. 2, ad 4–5 and 7 (see also q. 16, a. 6, ad s.c. 3, for a similar contrast between mere "not knowing" and actual false opinion).

65. The claim we just saw in *De malo*, q. 16, a. 6, ad s.c. 1, that angels know *esse* by simple apprehension is made precisely to counter the objection (s.c. 1) that simple apprehension (*simplex intelligentia*) cannot be false.

66. Specifically, I would interpret Aquinas's claim at *ST* I, q. 58, a. 5, that the demons "by

For present purposes, it suffices to note Aquinas's intransigent commitment to denying angelic C/D even in the false-judgment case, where C/D would seem to be required most of all.

Still further evidence (albeit less direct) that Aquinas thinks that angels know contingent existence without C/D is his view that they begin to know changing events without undergoing any mental change. C/D knowledge of changing things requires mental change, as Aquinas insists in discussing God's changeless knowledge:

> God's knowledge would be changeable if he knew states of affairs (*enuntiabilia*) in the way proper to states of affairs (*per modum enuntiabilium*), that is, by composing and dividing, as is the case with our own intellect. This is why our knowledge is changeable, either between truth and falsity—for example if we retained the same opinion of a thing even after it had changed—or between different beliefs, for example if we first believe that someone is sitting and then believe they are not sitting.[67]

In other words, if one knows contingent existence by C/D, one will then need a new act of C/D for every new contingent reality that one grasps, since the negation "X is not" is clearly opposed to the affirmation "X is." But even in the early *Quodlibet* VII, q. 1, a. 3, ad 2,[68] Aquinas claims that angels' awareness of changeable things—somewhat like God's, and unlike ours—is changeless: "When something begins to be present, the angel begins to know (*de novo cognoscit*) it without any change (*innovatione*) in the angel himself, but rather in the knowable thing."[69] It follows

---

perverse will cause their intellect to fall away from God's wisdom" to mean that the demons' pride corrupts their simple notion of "wisdom" in two ways: (1) in general, by removing its analogical openness to a supernatural wisdom beyond their comprehension; (2) in particular, by removing from it the note of humility. They would therefore falsely believe in general that they could understand the workings of God's wisdom, and in particular that God's wisdom was incompatible with, e.g., taking on creaturely form in the incarnation; and this false judgment would be due solely to a flaw in their original grasp of the simple notion, not to any subsequent act of addition or subtraction.

67. *ST* I, q. 14, a. 15, ad 3 (Leon. 5.195b): "*Esset* autem ex hoc scientia Dei variabilis, si enuntiabilia cognosceret per modum enuntiabilium, *componendo et dividendo*, sicut accidit in intellectu nostro. Unde cognitio nostra variatur, vel secundum veritatem et falsitatem, puta si, mutata re, eandem opinionem de re illa retineamus: vel secundum diversas opiniones, ut si primo opinemur aliquem sedere, et postea opinemur eum non sedere" (emphasis added). Indeed, as Aquinas states more explicitly in *De ver.*, q. 2, a. 13, ad 7, this lack of C/D is a necessary condition of God's eternal presence to all times.

68. According to sources gathered by Torrell, *Quodlibet* VII is generally dated between 1255 and 1257; see *Saint Thomas Aquinas*, 1:211.

69. *Quod.* VII.1.3, ad 2 (Leon. 25/1.15a:194–99): "Quando aliquid incipit esse presens,

Can Angels Know Being without Judgment?   249

that angelic knowledge of changing realities, like God's, must be C/D-free.

In *De ver.*, q. 8, a. 9, ad 3, Aquinas both reiterates and provides a reason for this remarkable claim that nothing changes in an angel when it begins to know something new:

> Since knowledge takes place (*sit*) through the knower's becoming similar (*assimilari*) to the known thing, one gains new knowledge of something in the same way that one becomes newly similar to something. This happens in two ways: first, by one's own movement; second, by something else's movement toward a form one already possesses. Likewise, someone newly begins to know something in one way by newly receiving the form of the thing known, as happens in us; in another way, by the fact that the known thing newly attains the form that is in the knower. And it is in the latter way that the angels newly know present things that previously had been future. For example, if something was not yet a man, the angelic intellect will not yet have become similar to it by the form of man that the angel possesses; but when it begins to be a man, the angelic intellect begins to be similar to it according to that same form, without any change on its side.[70]

The reason, then, why angels can know changing things changelessly is that the act of knowing X requires *only* intentional likeness to X. Achieving this likeness requires humans, who know contingent things by receiving new sensible species from them, to change. But, as Aquinas had insisted in the article's corpus, angels cannot receive forms from physical objects, because they lack the intermediary senses needed for a spiritual intellect to be affected by matter. Instead, angels are created by God already fully-stocked with all their intelligible species.[71]

---

angelus de nouo cognoscit illud, non facta aliqua innouatione in ipso angelo, set in re cognoscibili, in qua est aliquid quod prius non fuit, quod simul ea cognita cognoscitur" (emphasis added). See also ad 1.

70. *De ver.*, q. 8, a. 9, ad 3 (Leon. 22/2.251a:217–36): "Cum enim cognitio sit per assimilationem cognoscentis ad cognitum, hoc modo contingit novam cognitionem de aliquo accipere, quomodo contingit de novo aliquid alicui assimilari; quod quidem contingit dupliciter: uno modo per motum suum, alio modo per motum alterius ad formam quam ipse iam habet; et similiter aliquis incipit aliquid de novo cognoscere uno modo per hoc quod cognoscens de novo accipit formam cogniti, sicut in nobis accidit, alio modo per hoc quod cognitum de novo pervenit ad formam quae est in cognoscente. Et hoc modo angeli de novo cognoscunt praesentia quae prius fuerunt futura, ut puta si aliquid nondum erat homo, ei non assimilabatur intellectus angelicus per formam hominis quam habet apud se, sed cum incipit esse homo, secundum eandem formam incipit intellectus angelicus sibi assimilari *sine aliqua mutatione facta circa ipsum*" (emphasis added). For discussion of this passage, see Goris, "Angelic Knowledge," 181. Torrell dates *De ver.* to 1256–59; see *Saint Thomas Aquinas*, 1:62.

71. For this argument in Aquinas, besides *De ver.*, q. 8, a. 9, see also *In Sent.* II, d. 3, q. 3,

Hence, an angel who has already activated one of these intelligible species in simple apprehension need do nothing except wait for an object to match that species. Once it does, that object somehow simply *becomes present* in the angel's ongoing act of simple apprehension—that is, of interiorly "speaking" the concept—without altering that act or requiring a new one (C/D or otherwise). The act remains unaltered because its ontological term is not a proposition (which must be changed to "keep up with" changing events) but rather simply a concept.

Now, how this is supposed to work is quite mysterious, and will be discussed in more detail below. But for our present purposes, Aquinas's point is clear: knowledge of changing things can be changeless *if* it consists in simple apprehension, rather than C/D. Given that Aquinas claims that angels have changeless knowledge of changing events in a number of passages across his career, both early and late (mostly in the context of denying that angels see future events),[72] it clearly follows that, in Aquinas's view, angels cannot grasp contingent existence by C/D.

A final, related reason for thinking that this is Aquinas's view lies in his more general claim that *every* angelic act (not just angelic knowledge of changing events) is in itself changeless and therefore timeless (*supra tempus*),[73] which in turn implies that angelic acts must take place in a kind of "discrete" time that, unlike our "continuous" time, is composed of actual, discrete instants, each of which is occupied by one

---

a. 1, ad 2; *ST* I, q. 55, a. 2, ad 2, and q. 84, a. 6; *De ver.*, q. 19, a. 1; and *SCG* II, c. 96 (esp. n. 1812). For discussion of this argument, see Péghaire, "L'intellection du singulier matériel," 137–44. For other arguments for the doctrine of angelic concreated intelligible species, see also Aquinas's *In De caus.* 10 and *In De div. nom.* 7.2, nn. 710–12.

72. Even as early as *In Sent.* II, d. 7, q. 2, a. 1, ad 4 (Mandonnet 2:188), Aquinas claims that demons do not "gain knowledge from things" (*cognitionem a rebus non accipiat*); they "learn" (*scientia acuitur*) only in the sense that new things become present to them, without any corresponding new mental furniture. Moreover, they know whatever is in a thing simply through the thing's single species (*per speciem enim rei quam habet innatam cognoscit rem, et ea que in re sunt*). See also II, d. 11, q. 2, a. 4. For similar claims in *De ver.*, see q. 8, a. 11, ad 9 (Leon. 22/2.257a:300–306), a. 12, ad 1 and ad 7–8, and a. 15, ad 4 and ad 7. Later texts where Aquinas repeats the claim that angels know change without mentally changing include *ST* I, q. 57, a. 3, ad 3–4, and q. 64, a. 1, ad 5; *Q. de an.* 20, ad 4; and *De malo*, q. 16, a. 7, ad 6, 9, 13. For discussion of this claim, see esp. John of St. Thomas, *Cursus theologicus* 42.2, esp. nn. 1, 8, 25–32 (though, as we shall see, he waters down Aquinas's claim significantly). See also Cajetan, *In ST* I, q. 57, a. 2, n. 18, and q. 58, a. 5, n. 3; Bonino, *Angels and Demons*, 146n42; and Collins, *The Thomistic Philosophy of Angels*, 230–31.

73. See *De ver.*, q. 8, a. 14, arg. 12 and ad 12; *SCG* II, c. 96, n. 1820; *De sub. sep.* 20 ad fin.; and *Quod.* V.4, all of which rely on *Liber de causis* 6 (see also Aquinas's commentary at *In De caus.* 7).

Can Angels Know Being without Judgment? 251

angelic act.[74] Now, the changeless and therefore timeless nature of angelic acts certainly does not *ipso facto* exclude angelic C/D: changeless acts of C/D seem no more problematic than changeless acts of simple apprehension. But if changeless acts of C/D were angels' only access to continuous physical change, it is hard to see how angels could stay abreast of that change: for, unless their series of C/Ds about a temporally finite physical change were infinite, they would perforce be limited to static "snapshots" of that change with intervening gaps, which seems odd. (Human C/Ds avoid this problem by their connection to sensory knowledge, which is physical and therefore continuous.)[75] Whereas, because simple apprehension of X does not vary depending on whether X is Y or not-Y (unlike the proposition "X is now Y," which is replaced by the subsequent proposition "X is now not-Y"), a single changeless, timeless simple apprehension of X would be able to cognize the whole range of continuous change that X undergoes. Hence, if Aquinas is committed both to angelic "discrete time" and to angels' gapless knowledge of physical history, he must hold that they access that history (i.e., physical contingent existence) by simple apprehension, not by C/D.

We have, then, abundant evidence that Aquinas's exclusion of C/D from angelic knowledge in *ST* I, q. 58, a. 4, is meant to be categorical: both direct evidence (notably Aquinas's explicit statements at *ST* I, q. 58, a. 5, and *De malo*, q. 16, a. 6, co. and ad s.c. 1, in the context of angelic error)

---

74. According to Aquinas, the angels' *tempus discretum* is complementary to their *aevum*: while their undivided *aevum* measures their incorruptible existence, their divided *tempus discretum* measures their sequential actions. See esp. *In Sent.* I, d. 37, q. 4, aa. 1 and 3; *Quod.* II.3 and XI.4. See also *ST* I, q. 10, a. 6; *In Sent.* I, d. 8, q. 3, a. 3, co. and ad 4; d. 19, q. 2, a. 1; II, d. 2, q. 1, a. 1, ad 4; II, d. 3, q. 2, a. 1, ad 5; *ST* I, q. 53, a. 3, co., ad 1 and ad 3; q. 63, a. 6, ad 4; I-II, q. 113, a. 7, ad 5; and *De ver.*, q. 8, a. 14, ad 12. For discussion of angelic discrete time in Aquinas and his contemporaries, see esp. Pasquale Porro, *Forme e modelli di durata nel pensiero medievale. L' 'aevum', il tempo discreto, la categoria 'quando'* (Leuven: Leuven University Press, 1996), 267–384, and "Angelic Measures: *Aevum* and Discrete Time," in *The Medieval Concept of Time: The Scholastic Debate and its Reception in Early Modern Philosophy*, ed. Pasquale Porro (Leiden: Brill, 2001), 131–59.

75. See again *De ver.*, q. 8, a. 14, ad 12; *SCG* II, c. 96, n. 1820; and *De sub. sep.* 20 (see also *In Sent.* I, d. 8, q. 3, a. 3, ad 4; d. 38, q. 1, a. 3, ad 3; and IV, d. 17, q. 1, a. 5, qc. 2, ad 3), where Aquinas argues that, whereas human existential judgments "take time" *per accidens* owing to their connection to our continuous sensory activity, angelic judgments take no time at all. It is unclear whether Aquinas thinks that our intellect's connection to our senses means that our intellectual judgments are updated continuously, or only in "snapshots"; but at least our *sensory* judgment updates continuously, which still seems to give us a significant advantage over a hypothetical angel who knew change only through judgment.

and the indirect evidence of Aquinas's ascription to angels of changeless knowledge of changing events, which is incompatible with knowledge by C/D. Significant questions remain, however, about how this C/D-less knowledge is supposed to work. (1) First, with regard to grasping being as real: given that creaturely existence is neither an essence nor contained in any essence, how can grasping an essence already contain a grasp of existence, rather than needing to be composed with such a grasp? What does this C/D-less judgment of existence consist in precisely, if it is not an act of "composing"? (2) Second, with regard to grasping being as being: how can angels do so without *separatio* and yet still retain being's analogous character? To answer these questions, we must first explore the peculiar nature of the intelligible species by which angels know.

EXPLAINING ANGELIC COMPOSITION-LESS EXISTENTIAL JUDGMENT

The central distinctive feature of angelic intelligible species, as Aquinas understands them, is their origin: they are received directly from God, not from creatures. Angels cannot simply do without received intelligible species altogether because their own essence (unlike God's) is not itself a perfect likeness of other things, and so it would give them only general, not proper, knowledge of those things.[76] But as we saw, Aquinas denies that they receive these intelligible species from material creatures because angels lack sense organs and thus cannot be causally affected by anything material.[77] He furthermore denies that they receive intelligible species from any creatures, including from other angels, because it befits pure intellects to have their creaturely potency fully actualized by nature, given the intermediate place they occupy between humans' *tabula rasa* and God's sheer actuality. Hence, the angels' intelligible species must have been received directly from God at their creation.[78] Thus

---

76. See *ST* I, q. 55, a. 1; q. 84, a. 2; q. 87, a. 1; I-II, q. 50, a. 6; q. 51, a. 1, ad 2; *SCG* II, c. 98, nn. 1829–35; *De ver.*, q. 8, a. 8; *In Sent.* II, d. 3, q. 3, a. 1; III, d. 14, q. 1, a. 1, qc. 2, ad 1.

77. See the first five texts cited in note 71.

78. See *ST* I, q. 55, a. 2; *SCG* II, c. 98, n. 1839; *In Sent.* II, d. 3, q. 3, a. 1; and *In De caus.* 10 (Saffrey 68–69). For discussion of Aquinas's theory of angelic concreated species, see John of St. Thomas, *Cursus theologicus*, 41.3, nn. 1–58, and 41.4, nn. 35–36; Cajetan, *In ST* I, q. 55, aa. 1–2; Therese Cory, "Embodied Vs. Non-Embodied Modes of Knowing in Aquinas," *Faith and Philosophy* 35, no. 4 (2018): 417–46, at 422–27; Suarez-Nani, *Connaissance et langage des anges*, 24–32; Bonino, *Angels and Demons*, 134–39; Goris, "Angelic Knowledge," 155–59; and Collins, *The Thomistic Philosophy of Angels*, 165–67 and 171–80.

Can Angels Know Being without Judgment? 253

Aquinas, following Augustine,[79] strikingly claims that God's creative ideas "flowed out" (*effluxerunt*) from him in not one but two ways: not only "to subsist in their own proper natures" with real existence in the act of creation, but also, independently, "into the angelic intellect," to exist there with intentional existence.[80]

Aquinas relies most heavily on angels' cognitive participation in God's own creative ideas when he seeks to account for angels' knowledge of individuals, especially material individuals; accordingly, let us explore this account of angelic singular knowledge first, as it will give us key clues for our own question about existential knowledge. To begin with, knowing *spiritual* individuals as individuals poses no difficulty for Aquinas. It is perhaps a common misconception that in Aquinas's view intellection can only grasp universals, not singulars, and that this is why intellection must be immaterial. His real view is subtler: intellection in itself is perfectly compatible with singularity on the part of both the object and the mental likeness by which it is understood, and is incompatible only with material singularity on the part of the mental likeness,[81] inasmuch as a material mental likeness (i.e., a phantasm) would prevent grasping the singular object in its universal dimension (e.g., as a "substance"). In the case of one angel knowing another, the knower's mental likeness is a singular likeness of a singular object in its singularity; yet because it is a spiritual likeness, it yields properly intellectual knowledge of what the known angel is, rather than merely a peculiar kind of

---

79. Augustine, *De Genesi ad litteram* II.8, esp.: "Quae infra [Angelos] sunt, ita creantur, ut prius fiant in cognitione rationalis creaturae, ac deinde in genere suo" (Patrologia Latina 34:269). Other sources on which Aquinas relies for the broader claim that angels know by innate species include the famous line in *Liber de causis* 10 stating that each angel is *plena formis*, (in turn relying on Proclus's phrase πλήρωμα εἰδῶν in *The Elements of Theology*, 2nd ed., ed. E. R. Dodds (Oxford: Clarendon Press, 1963), 177 (156), and Dionysius's claim in *De divinis nominibus*, in *Corpus Dionysiacum*, vol. 1: *De divinis nominibus*, ed. Beate Regina Suchla, Patristische Texte und Studien 33 (Berlin: Walter de Gruyter, 1990), 4.1.693C (144), that angels "τοὺς τῶν ὄντων οἰκείως ἐλλάμπονται λόγους."

80. *ST* I, q. 56, a. 2 (Leon. 5.65a): "Ea quae in Verbo Dei ab aeterno praeextiterunt, dupliciter ab eo effluxerunt: uno modo, in intellectum angelicum; alio modo, ut subsisterent in propriis naturis." Aquinas reiterates this "double flowing" thesis in many texts: *De ver.*, q. 8, aa. 8 and 10, and q. 10, a. 4; *ST* I, q. 55, a. 2, ad 1; *In Sent.* II, d. 3, q. 3, a. 1, ad 2; *Q. de an.* 18; and all the passages cited below (note 89) on angelic knowledge of singulars.

81. See, e.g., *ST* I, q. 86, a. 1, ad 3 (Leon. 5.347b): "Singulare non repugnat intelligibilitati inquantum est singulare, sed inquantum est materiale." See also *ST* I, q. 56, a. 1, ad 2; *SCG* II, c. 75, n. 1553; and *De unit. int.* 5 (Leon. 43.312b). For discussion, Therese Cory, *Aquinas on Human Self-Knowledge* (Cambridge: Cambridge University Press, 2013), 12.; Péghaire, "L'intellection du singulier," 143; Goris, "Angelic Knowledge," 156; and Bonino, *Angels and Demons*, 141.

sensation.[82] Nor is this simply due to Aquinas's theory that there can be only one instance of any species of angel,[83] and that therefore to know an angel's species universally just is to know who that angel is as an individual. Rather, Aquinas also thinks that we humans (even though we all share a species) can know our own individual spiritual minds directly, without need for phantasms,[84] and that after death we will be able to know other individual separated (spiritual) souls despite lacking phantasms.[85]

Knowing material individuals as individuals, however, requires having what Aquinas calls a "proper likeness" (*propria similitudo* or *propria ratio*) not only of their common form but of their individuating matter. Human intelligible species, derived from abstraction, lack this "proper likeness" of matter altogether; they are proper likenesses only of common form. Instead, our "proper likeness" of individuating matter resides in our sensory knowledge, which is why we need to "return to the phantasm" in order to know material singulars rather than relying on our intellects alone.[86] A reason Aquinas frequently gives for this human deficiency is that our intelligible species are caused in us by extra-mental objects' forms, not by their matter, since only form is active; but form, as such, is not individual, and so the likeness it imprints on our intellects will also not be individual, unless it is re-individualized by being received in a physical sense organ.[87]

---

82. For Aquinas's account of how one angel knows another, see *SCG* II, c. 98; *De ver.*, q. 8, a. 7, esp. ad 3 (*prima series*); and *ST* I, q. 56, a. 2.

83. See *ST* I, q. 50, a. 4; *In Sent.* II, d. 3, q. 1, a. 4 (see also d. 32, q. 2, a. 3, and IV, d. 12, q. 1, a. 1, qc. 3, ad 3); *SCG* II, c. 93; *De spir. creat.* 8; *Q. de an.* 3; and *De ente*, c. 5.

84. See esp. *ST* I, q. 87, a. 1, and *De ver.*, q. 10, a. 8; for discussion, see Cory, *Aquinas on Human Self-Knowledge*, esp. chaps. 3–4.

85. See *ST* I, q. 89, a. 2, and *Quod.* III, q. 9, a. 1.

86. For discussion of Aquinas on human knowledge of singulars and an extensive collection of the relevant texts, see esp. Klubertanz, "St. Thomas and the Knowledge of the Singular," *The New Scholasticism* 26, no. 2 (1952): 135–66. See also Camille Bérubé, *La connaissance de l'individuel au Moyen Âge* (Montreal: Presses de l'Université de Montréal, 1964), 42–64, and Goris, "A Reinterpretation of Aquinas' Correspondence Definition of Truth," in *Intellect et imagination dans la Philosophie Médiévale. Actes du XIe Congrès International de Philosophie Médiévale de la Société Internationale pour l'étude de la Philosophie Médiévale* (S.I.E.P.M.), Porto, du 26 au 31 août 2002, Rencontres de philosophie médiévale 11 (Turnhout: Brepols, 2006), 3:1431–43, at 1433–38.

87. For this argument, see esp. *De ver.*, q. 8, a. 11. See also *De ver.*, q. 2, aa. 5 and 6, and q. 19, a. 2; *In Sent.* IV, d. 50, q. 1, a. 3; and *SCG* I, q. 65, n. 537. For discussion of this argument, see Robert Pasnau, "Aquinas and the Content Fallacy," *The Modern Schoolman* 75, no. 4 (1998): 293–314, at 308–12, and Therese Cory, "Rethinking Abstractionism: Aquinas's Intellectual Light

Can Angels Know Being without Judgment? 255

Angels obviously cannot know material individuals this way, as they lack phantasms; so they must somehow know them through their intelligible species instead. Fortunately, Aquinas thinks that spiritual intelligible species may be proper likenesses not only of common forms and of spiritual singulars but even of individuating matter. Such a species would grant knowledge of a material singular in both its universal and singular dimensions. But what could it mean for a spiritual intelligible species to be a "proper likeness" of matter, and how might the angels have acquired a species of this remarkable sort?

Here Aquinas's theory of concreated species provides the key. According to Aquinas, God can know singulars because the "intelligible species" through which he knows all things (his own essence) is also their cause: not only of physical creatures' forms but also of their matter. Hence, unlike the practical ideas in the minds of human craftsmen who only cause form (which in itself is universal), God's creative ideas contain knowledge of individual matter as well as of universal form and, thus, are "proper likenesses" of material individuals in their individuality.[88] And this is why the angels' intelligible species are also "proper likenesses" of material individuals: because, rather than being derived passively, like ours, from the universal action of material creatures' forms, they are instead copies of God's active, causal knowledge of material creatures in their individuality.[89]

---

and Some Arabic Sources," *Journal of the History of Philosophy* 53, no. 4 (2015): 607–46, at 624–25. Pace Bérubé (*La connaissance de l'individuel*, 49–51), this extended argument seems necessary to me to explain *why* abstraction cannot produce a proper likeness of matter, even though Aquinas omits this extended argument in other treatments (e.g., *De ver.*, q. 10, a. 5; *ST* I, q. 85, a. 1; and *In De an.* II.12).

88. For Aquinas's thematic treatments of God's proper knowledge of singulars, see *De ver.*, q. 2, aa. 5 and 7; *ST* I, q. 14, a. 11; *SCG* I, cc. 54 and 65, nn. 537 and 540; *In Sent.* I, d. 36, q. 1, a. 1; and *Comp. theol.* I.133. See *De ver.*, q. 3, a. 5; *Quod.* VIII.1.2; and *ST* I, q. 15, a. 3, ad 4, for discussions specifically of divine *ideas* of singulars. *De ver.*, q. 2, a. 5 (Leon. 22/1.63a:280–313) also arguably identifies the divine ideas (*similitudo rei quae est in intellectu divino*), rather than simply the divine essence, as the proper likeness of singulars). Aquinas also examines God's knowledge of material singulars in comparison to spiritual creatures' knowledge thereof at *De ver.*, q. 8, a. 11, and q. 19, a. 2; *ST* I, q. 57, a. 2, and q. 89, a. 4; *Q. de an.* 20; and *In Sent.* II, d. 3, q. 3, a. 3. For discussion, see, e.g., Gregory Doolan, *Aquinas on the Divine Ideas as Exemplar Causes* (Washington, DC: The Catholic University of America Press, 2008), 164–66.

89. For Aquinas's thematic treatments of angelic knowledge of singulars through participation in God's *rationes factivae*, see *ST* I, q. 57, a. 2; *De ver.*, q. 8, a. 11; *SCG* II, c. 100, n. 1856; *Quod.* VII.1.3; and *In Sent.* II, d. 3, q. 3, a. 3. In other contexts, see *De ver.*, q. 2, aa. 5 and 6; q. 10, a. 5; q. 19, a. 2; *In Sent.* IV, d. 50, q. 1, a. 3; and *Q. de an.* 20, co. and ad 8. For discussion, see Cajetan, *In ST* I, q. 57, a. 2, nn. 9–14 (Leon. 5.72a–73b); John of St. Thomas, *Cursus theologicus*,

If angelic knowledge's divine origin explains how angels can know material individuals without bodily senses, does it perhaps also explain how they can know real existence and "being as being" without separate acts of judgment? That this is indeed the key is suggested by the fact that Aquinas, in *In Sent.* I, d. 38, q. 1, a. 3, had attributed our need to know existence by an act of "composing" to the fact that we derive this knowledge from the composite existent.[90] If angels instead derive their knowledge of existence from God, they escape this reason for needing to "compose." Besides, this strategy has some inherent plausibility. God, after all, knows the existence of things as well as their universal and individual "content" (*ratio*). If angelic knowledge is simply a (limited) copy of God's knowledge, should this copy not include things' existence as well as their content?

One easy way to run this argument would be as follows: (1) God's creative ideas are likenesses of each creature's *esse*;[91] (2) angelic intelligible species are copies of God's creative ideas;[92] therefore, (3) angelic intelligible species are likenesses of creatures' *esse*. This appeal to God's ideas is problematic, however, in both premises. Against the first, Doolan argues convincingly that, in Aquinas's view, it is God's essence (*ipsum esse*), not his ideas, that exemplifies creaturely *esse*;[93] and indeed Aquinas says that

---

41.4, nn. 2–8, 31–41, 50, and 42.2, nn. 26–32; Bonino, *Angels and Demons*, 144–45; Péghaire, "L'intellection du singulier matériel," 141–43; Suarez-Nani, *Connaissance et langage des anges*, 52–54; Collins, *The Thomistic Philosophy of Angels*, 221–28; and esp. Cory's eloquent treatment at "Embodied Vs. Non-Embodied Modes of Knowing," 427–35 and 439–42.

90. See note 12.

91. For this claim, see Gilson, *Being and Some Philosophers*, 212: "The *esse* of each being is included in its divine idea." Gilson's argument is that (1) what God knows in an idea is a particular way of imitating him, and (2) things imitate God in different ways thanks to their unique *esse* (relying on *De ver.*, q. 2, a. 5, and q. 3, a. 2). This claim finds some support in *De ver.*, q. 2, a. 3, ad 20, and *In Sent.* I, d. 38, q. 1, a. 3, ad 1.

92. Aquinas seems to say that angelic intelligible species are imperfect copies specifically of the divine ideas at *De ver.*, q. 8, a. 8, ad 1, and a. 11; *De malo*, q. 16, a. 7, ad 8; *In Sent.* II, d. 3, q. 3, a. 2, ad 1, and a. 3, ad 3; and *De spir. creat.* 5, ad 7.

93. Doolan, *Aquinas on the Divine Ideas*, 213–28, relying chiefly on *De pot.*, q. 3, a. 4, ad 9, and *In Sent.* III, d. 27, q. 2, a. 4, ad 1 (see also I, d. 19, q. 5, a. 2, ad 5), and on the discussions in Montagnes, *The Doctrine of the Analogy of Being*, 38; Fabro, *Participation et causalité selon s. Thomas d'Aquin* (Louvain: Publications Universitaires, 1961), 435 and 518–19; and Geiger, *La participation*, 232–33. The rationale for aligning the "twofold exemplarity" of God's ideas and essence with creaturely essence and *esse*, respectively, is that God's multiple "ideas" correspond to the multiple ways God can be imitated—that is, to the varied measures and limits on creatures' participation in God's essential perfection, which are precisely creaturely essences. Creaturely *esse* and the ensuing transcendental perfections, by contrast, are not distinguishing and limiting measures on creatures' participation in God, but rather constitute that participation

Can Angels Know Being without Judgment? 257

God knows the existence of states of affairs (*enuntiabilia*) precisely by this essential exemplification.[94] Against the second, although Aquinas does frequently simply call the angelic intelligible species copies of God's ideas (*rationes ideales*), there are a number of texts where he clarifies that the proper analogy is between angelic intelligible species and God's essence. Just as the single divine essence is "multiplied" into many ideas by virtue of the multiplicity of cognitive objects of which it is the "proper likeness" (*propria ratio*), so each angelic species is "multiplied" (into the equivalent of "ideas") inasmuch as it is the "proper likeness" of all the individuals and kinds that fall under it.[95] However, angelic intelligible species are highly imperfect copies of the divine essence, for they do not capture its identity to *esse:* no angel has an innate intelligible species of *ipsum esse subsistens*.[96] Hence, though God can know creaturely *esse* through his essence's exemplification thereof, an angelic intelligible species is too poor a copy of the divine essence to serve the same function.

A more promising strategy is to appeal to causality rather than exemplification. Even though angelic intelligible species do not represent God's exemplification of *esse*, they do (unlike human intelligible species) represent essences precisely as flowing out into reality from God's causal power, as we saw above. To draw out this fact's implications, let

---

itself; and so they are not exemplified by the multiplicity of divine ideas but rather by the single divine essence.

94. For Aquinas's discussions of God's exemplification-based knowledge of creaturely *esse*, see two of his treatments of whether God knows *enuntiabilia*: *In Sent.* I, d. 38, q. 1, a. 3 (one of our original texts for assigning knowledge of existence to judgment), and *ST* I, q. 14, a. 14, ad 2. For discussion of God's exemplification of creaturely *esse*, see Doolan, *Aquinas on the Divine Ideas*, 218–19 and 222–23.

95. See esp. *ST* I, q. 57, a. 2 (Leon. 5.71a), where Aquinas calls the angelic intelligible species "quaedam repraesentationes multiplicatae illius *unicae et simplicis essentiae*," and *De ver.*, q. 8, a. 10, ad 3 (Leon. 22/2.253b:124–31), where Aquinas says: "Non est inconveniens si una *forma* intellectus angelici sit ratio propria plurium secundum diversas eius *habitudines* ad res, sicut et divina *essentia* est propria ratio plurium secundum diversas *habitudines* eius ad res; ex quibus *habitudinibus* consurgit pluralitas *idearum*" (emphasis added). This second text is especially noteworthy insofar as it explicitly aligns God's "ideas" not with the angelic species itself, but with the species's relations (*habitudines*) to individual things. See also *In Sent.* II, d. 3, q. 3, a. 3, ad 3, which is noteworthy because, even though in the corpus Aquinas had aligned the angelic species to God's *rationes ideales*, here he aligns the angelic species with God's essence, and aligns God's ideas (*ideae*) instead with the angelic species's relations to individuals; *ST* I, q. 55, a. 3, ad 3; and *SCG* II, c. 100, n. 1856. For discussion, see John of St. Thomas, *Cursus theologicus*, 41.4, n. 37 (ed. Desclée, 4:612a–b).

96. See the texts where Aquinas denies that angels have a natural vision of God's essence, esp. *ST* I, q. 12, a. 4, and *SCG* III, c. 49, n. 2269. See also *ST* I, q. 56, a. 3; *De ver.*, q. 8, a. 3; and *In Sent.* II, d. 23, q. 2, a. 1.

us first consider how humans arrive at their existential judgments about extra-mental things.

In Aquinas's view, human intelligible species, in the process of abstraction, lose not only their singularity but also their causal relation to the world: though derived from real things, they do not include this derivation in their content.[97] For our intellect to regain this causal connection to extra-mental reality, we have to "return to the phantasm," for three reasons. First, because without this "return" we cannot think intellectually at all—even about already abstracted universals.[98] Second, because in order to make existential judgments about individual things we first have to be able to think about those individual things; and as we saw, without this "return" we cannot think about individual things.[99] The singularity lost in abstraction must be restored by connecting the universal species to the singular phantasm in the imagination and cogitative sense.[100] Finally, third, we arguably need this "return" in order to restore the connection to real existence, which was also lost in abstraction.[101] Aquinas does not speak in this context of a *reditio* or *reflexio*, or even a *conversio*, to the phantasm,[102] but in *ST* I, q. 86, a. 3, he does describe the intellect's grasp of contingent existence as "indirect" and sense-mediated

---

97. See esp. *ST* I, q. 86, a. 3, which surprisingly is Aquinas's only dedicated treatment of our intellect's indirect, sense-mediated grasp of contingent existence. See also Aquinas's frequent claim that *intellectus abstrahit ab hic et nunc*, in, e.g., *ST* I, q. 16, a. 7, ad 2; q. 46, a. 2; q. 86, arg. 1 and ad 1 (Aquinas's reply here seems to accept the principle as formulated in the objection); *De ver.*, q. 2, a. 6, ad 1; *SCG* II, c. 96, n. 1820, and III, c. 84, n. 2588; *In Peri herm.* I.2 (Leon. 1/1:10a:40–41); and *De malo*, q. 16, a. 7, ad 5.

98. See *ST* I, q. 84, a. 7, and q. 89, a. 1; *In Sent.* III, d. 31, q. 2, a. 4, and II, d. 20, q. 2, a. 2, ad 3; *SCG* II, c. 73, n. 1523; c. 80, n. 1618; c. 81, n. 1625; and *De ver.*, q. 19, a. 1 (see also q. 10, a. 2, ad 7). For the Aristotelian source of this claim, see *De anima* III.7.431a15–17; see Aquinas's commentary at *In De an.* III.6 (Leon. 45/1.231a–b:104–34). For a vivid explanation of the human need to exercise all intellectual activity conjointly with the imagination, see Cory, "Embodied Vs. Non-Embodied Modes of Knowing," 435–39.

99. Goris argues that, properly speaking, the term "*return [reditio]* to the phantasm" applies only to the intellect's knowledge of the singular; the intellect's basic and constant use of phantasms simply for *universal* knowledge, by contrast, is just its innate orientation, the "turn [*conversio*] to the phantasm." "Angelic Knowledge," 172–73; see "Reinterpretation," 1437.

100. For Aquinas's discussions of how the human intellect joins itself to the phantasm to achieve its indirect cognition of singulars, see the array of texts quoted in Klubertanz, "St. Thomas and the Knowledge of the Singular," 141–54.

101. For this language of "restoring" the connection to existence, see esp. Maritain, *Existence*, 11–12 and 16–17, and Gilson, *Being and Some Philosophers*, 203–4.

102. For texts where Aquinas specifically uses *reflexio* to describe the intellect's use of phantasms to know the singular, see Klubertanz, "St. Thomas and the Knowledge of the Singular," 146–48.

Can Angels Know Being without Judgment? 259

in just the same way as the intellect's grasp of singulars, which seems to imply that, if the latter grasp involves a "return (*reflexio*) to the phantasm," then so does the former.[103]

Thus, to intellectually grasp a singular's real existence, we must connect the known universal-in-the-singular back to our senses' original passive reception of the external object's influence. But this original passive reception is the object of the "common sense," the power by which we, like other animals, perceive that our external senses are engaged.[104] Hence, though Aquinas does not state this in so many words, it seems that human existential judgment requires the universal-in-the-singular to be "re-connected" back either to the common sense itself (if the external sensation is ongoing) or to memory's retention of the common sense's activity (if the external sensation happened in the past). Thus, a twofold "return to the phantasm" seems to be required: a first one to the phantasm in the imagination and cogitative in order to both make actual conceptualization possible and also to recover singularity, and then a second one to the phantasm in the common sense or memory in order to recover existence.

Our need to go through this complex process is, I take it, the reason why human existential judgment—at least about extra-mental things — has to be a different kind of act from simple apprehension, even when they are temporally simultaneous:[105] namely, because it requires "com-

---

103. *ST* I, q. 86, a. 3 (Leon. 5.351b): "Dictum autem est supra [a. 1] quod per se et *directe* intellectus est universalium; sensus autem singularium, quorum etiam *indirecte* quodammodo est intellectus, ut supra dictum est [a. 1]. Sic igitur contingentia, prout sunt contingentia, cognscuntur *directe* quidem sensu, *indirecte* autem ab intellectu" (emphasis added). Notably, Klubertanz himself thinks that there is no real difference between the language of *indirecte* and that of *reflexio* in the context of intellectual knowledge of singulars ("St. Thomas and the Knowledge of the Singular," 148).

104. For Aquinas's view that, though the external senses can distinguish between or "judge" their proper objects, it is by the common sense alone that we "perceive that we perceive," see *ST* I, q. 78, a. 4, ad 2, and *In De an.* II.13 (Leon. 45/1.120a:104–5), II.26 (Leon. 45/1.178a:8–14), and II.27 (Leon. 45/1.182a:1–8). See Aristotle, *De somno*, 2.455a13–22; for discussion, see Muller-Thym, "The Common Sense," 339–41. Does it follow that Aquinas thinks the common sense is the basis for intellectual existential judgment? Though Aquinas does not say so explicitly, it seems plausible, especially since Aquinas does give a central role to "perceiving that we perceive" and "knowing that we know" in our existential judgments about *ourselves* at *De ver.*, q. 10, a. 8, relying on Aristotle's *Nicomachean Ethics* IX.9.1170a33. See esp. Robert Schmidt, "The Evidence Grounding Judgments of Existence," in *An Etienne Gilson Tribute*, ed. C. J. O'Neil, 228–44 (Milwaukee, WI: Marquette University Press, 1959), at 237–39, endorsed and developed by Wippel in *Metaphysical Thought*, 35–40, esp. 36n47.

105. For the simultaneity of the existential judgment with our first simple apprehension

posing" the terms of two separate acts, exercised by two separate powers. One, which provides the judgment's subject, is the term of the intellect's act of simple apprehension: the abstracted intelligible species, taken as already reunited to the singular phantasm to yield an intellectually grasped singular (e.g., "this man"). The other, which provides the judgment's predicate, is the term of the common sense's act of "perceiving that one perceives"—that is, of perceiving the external senses' passivity (ongoing or remembered) to external causal stimulus. Only by putting the terms of these two acts together—that is, by composing them—can one grasp that, for example, "this man is." Without this act of "composing" or "reconnecting" the grasped intelligibility ("this man") with the original experience of sensory passivity, one would have no way to determine whether the intelligible content under consideration was real or merely possible.

A key issue to note here is that this "composition" is not only logical but also ontological. By "logical" composition I mean simply the normal sense of "composition" in logic, namely linking subject to predicate; by "ontological" composition I mean joining the terms of two ontologically distinct acts. Now, in human attributive judgment (at least in the simple case of essential predication), the two types of composition are closely correlated: the logical composition of conceptualized subject to conceptualized predicate occurs precisely by ontologically composing the two corresponding concepts, each of which is the term of a distinct act of simple apprehension. The logical composition requires the ontological composition because our initial imperfect grasp of the subject did not include the predicate. In human existential judgment, however, the logical composition is the intellect's affirmation of the singular subject's union to its nondirectly-conceptualizable act of existing, while the ontological composition consists in the twofold "return to the phantasm" described above, which involves joining the terms of acts which differ not only in number but also in kind. Here too the logical composition requires the ontological composition, but for a slightly different reason: because our concept of the subject had lost, through abstraction, not the existential

---

of the object, see, e.g., Cory, *Aquinas on Human Self-Knowledge*, 81–82; Wippel, *Metaphysical Thought*, 40, and "Maritain and Aquinas," 427; Owens, "Aquinas on Knowing Existence," 679, and "Judgment and Truth," 149; Gilson, *Being and Some Philosophers*, 209; and Maritain, *Existence*, 23. As Wippel notes, however, Aquinas himself does not seem to take a position on this problem.

predicate itself (which was never in the phantasm to begin with), but rather the phantasm's causal link to existence. The object's causal action on us is our sole window onto the object's own inner existence.[106]

Now, Aquinas to my knowledge does not explicitly make this distinction between "logical" and "ontological" composition, and he certainly never describes the "turn to the phantasms" as a "composition" of any sort. Nonetheless, I think the relation between these two types of composition is crucial for understanding why Aquinas uses the term "composition" in the way he does. Specifically, I would suggest that, when Aquinas affirms angelic "judgment" but denies angelic "composition and division," we should understand "judgment" to refer to the act of grasping logical composition (subject and predicate), and understand "composition and division" to refer to the kind of judgment that requires ontological composition, and which therefore is an act of compos*ing* two ontologically separate terms rather than simply an act of perceiving their already-given compos*ition*.[107]

Understanding "composition and division" in this way is, I think, the best way to explain why Aquinas uses the term "composition" for human rational judgments (both existential and attributive) but not for human intellectual knowledge of singulars, sense judgments, or angelic judgments. Human intellectual knowledge of singulars does require ontological composition (the "turn to the phantasms"); but it does not itself have the structure of a logical composition, that is, a judgment (there is no predicate[108]), so it is not C/D in Aquinas's sense. Conversely, external

---

106. Norris Clarke stresses this principle that action reveals being, as a corollary of the principle that action follows upon being. See, e.g., his "Action as the Self-Revelation of Being: A Central Theme in the Thought of St. Thomas Aquinas," in *History of Philosophy in the Making: A Symposium of Essays to Honor Professor James D. Collins on His 65th Birthday*, ed. Linus Thro (Washington, DC: University Press of America, 1982), 63–80.

107. In this regard I concur, up to a point, with Cunningham's view that the difference between judgment and C/D is the difference between the logical and the ontological. Cunningham takes this point much too far, however, by insisting that judgment properly speaking is a purely "logical entity," as opposed to a "real entity" ("The Second Operation," 4; see also 6–7 and 23). In my view, the act of angelic judgment is no less a "real entity" than the act of human C/D; what is "logical" is just the distinction between the terms that the angel's judgment unites.

108. That is, there is no predicate in the intellect's grasp of "this dog," though this composite perception is certainly ordered to the judgment "this *is* a dog." Klubertanz seems to have confused the composite perception of the singular with the "composition" of judgment, which I think is why he strikingly claims that "the intellectual knowledge of the material singular is, in the first instance at least, a judgment" ("St. Thomas and the Knowledge of the Singular," 165). I concur with Cory's critique of this claim and her suggestion that, instead, existential

sense judgments, by which, for example, an animal perceives that this object is white rather than black, are called "judgments" because they are indeed particular logical compositions;[109] but they do not require ontological composition of two different acts, so they are not "compositions" in Aquinas's sense either. (Notably, though, Aquinas is willing to say that the judgment of the internal estimative sense, e.g. "this red object is tasty," is at least analogous to intellectual C/D.[110] This makes perfect sense since it does require ontologically composing external sense data, e.g., "this red object," with a feature perceptible only to the internal sense, e.g. "tasty.")

Similarly, angels' judgments do involve logical compositions, since they thereby grasp the union of subject and predicate. But, if the angel's intelligible species of the subject itself somehow contained a causal connection to existence—the causal connection that, in humans, is supplied instead by the common sense, whose act must be "composed" with the intellect's—then the angel's existential judgment would not need the ontological composition of synthesizing the terms of two ontologically separate acts; and so angelic judgment, like the external sense judgment, would not be C/D.

But how is it possible for the angelic intelligible species to contain a causal connection to existence? Aquinas does not say explicitly. As we saw above, however, Aquinas thinks that the reason why angels can know singulars directly through their infused intelligible species, without needing to join those species to any particular sensory phantasm, is that those species are copies of God's active causal knowledge of things, that is, of God's creative art: the infused species therefore represent natures precisely as God knows and causes them, in both their shared form and their individuating matter.[111] I would simply suggest that, in addi-

---

judgment is simultaneous with intellectual perception of the singular but distinct from it and dependent on it (*Aquinas on Human Self-Knowledge*, 83n57; see also 188n45).

109. See note 60 above.

110. See *In De an.* III.6 (Leon. 45/1.230b:45–61), where Aquinas says that, though the "simplex apprehensio et *iudicium* sensus assimilatur *speculationi* intellectus," and though "*formare affirmationem et negationem* est proprium intellectus," nonetheless "sensus facit aliquid *simile* huic [scil. formare affirmationem et negationem] quando apprehendit aliquid ut delectabile uel triste" (emphasis added). See *ST* I, q. 78, a. 4, where Aquinas explicitly describes the cogitative power's act as a "comparison" (*collatio*).

111. See all the texts on angelic participation in God's *rationes factivae* cited above in note 89, e.g. *Quod.* VII.1.3 (Leon. 25/1.14:110–15): "Sicut autem ille rationes ydeales *effluunt* in res producendas in *esse* suo naturali, in quo particulariter unumquodque subsistit in forma et

Can Angels Know Being without Judgment? 263

tion, Aquinas thinks that these infused species, as active blueprints, represent natures precisely as to-be-caused by God: that is, that they represent not only what God makes (form and matter), but the making itself, the nature's flowing-forth into reality from its divine cause. If this is right, then the angel's infused species do contain a causal connection to real existence, just as our external senses do, but in reverse: the angelic connection is active rather than passive. Thanks to this active causal connection, the angel can do in one act, without any ontological composition, what we must do by "composing" the acts of three powers: the intellect's universal representation, the imagination's singular representation, and the common sense's perception of causality.[112] Thus, the angel's simple apprehension of a nature—that is, the angel's inner act of activating or "uttering" one of the intelligible species with which his intellect is endowed[113]—just is an act of affirming that nature's real existence in actual individuals. The angel's inner word is never a mere concept but always a judgment, an echo of the original divine "Let there *be* . . . !"[114]

---

materia, ita *procedunt* in mentes angelicas ut sint in eis principium *cognoscendi* res secundum suum *totum esse* in quo subsistunt" (emphasis added), and *In Sent.* IV, d. 50, q. 1, a. 3 (Parma 7/2:1250a–b): "Sed in illa cognitione quae est per formas quae sunt rerum *causae*, vel earum *impressiones*, pervenitur usque ad singularia, quamvis hujusmodi formae sint omnino immateriales, eo quod causa rei prima est quae rebus *esse influit: esse* autem communiter materiam et formam respicit. Unde hujusmodi formae ducunt directe in cognitionem utriusque, scilicet materiae et formae; et propter hoc per talem cognitionem cognoscuntur res et in universali et in singulari" (emphasis added).

112. Goris similarly grounds the difference between human propositional knowing and angelic nonpropositional knowing in the fact that our intellects, unlike angels', naturally depend on the senses, though he does not appeal to the causal nature of angelic species; see "Angelic Knowledge," 172–73.

113. It is important to remember that, in Aquinas's view, simple apprehension is no less of an *act* than judgment; it is distinct from, and presupposes, the intellect's prior reception of form (either through abstraction, in the human case, or through divine infusion, in the angelic case). For this point with respect to all acts of knowing in general, see esp. *De ver.*, q. 8, a. 6 (see also *In Sent.* II, d. 11, q. 2, a. 1), where Aquinas compares occurrent knowing to actual "shining" (*lucere*) and the mere intentional possession of form (which itself is distinguished from the prior "reception") to merely "having light" (*habet lucem*). For clear statements that simple apprehension in particular is an act (the *formatio* of a concept) rather than a mere reception of form, see also *De spir. creat.* 9, ad 6; *Quod.* VIII.2.1; and *In Sent.* I, d. 19, q. 5, a. 1, ad 7 (one of our main texts for assigning grasping *esse* to the act of C/D, discussed above at note 10). From this it follows that, when Aquinas identifies the act of judgment with simple apprehension in angels, he is equating it with an action, not a passion.

114. If this account of why angelic existential judgment is C/D-free is right, it may also imply that humans too exercise a non-C/D existential judgment in one unique case: namely, knowing "I exist" in prephilosophical self-awareness. The reason is that, arguably, Aquinas would deny that our grasp of our own mind's existence is originally derived from the

What exactly does it mean, though, to say that the angel grasps existence by grasping the nature precisely as causally flowing-forth from God's power? Does it mean that God's particular creative actions toward all the relevant individual things are already inscribed in the angel's intelligible species from the very beginning? That is, does the angel know contingent events by a kind of Leibnizian "preestablished harmony," entirely independently of the actual events? Péghaire thinks so.[115] This interpretation, however, implies that angels should naturally know the future no less than the past, and Aquinas vigorously denies this.[116]

To avoid this difficulty, one might instead adopt John of St. Thomas's view. By this view, the angel's intelligible species still contains God's particular creative actions, but instead of containing the whole history of God's relevant creative actions inscribed in it from the start, it is being constantly updated to reflect God's current creative actions. John of St. Thomas's rationale is that, because the angel's intelligible species represent created natures precisely as flowing out from God's power, and because those natures flow out from God sequentially rather than all-at-once, the angelic species should represent the current status of that sequential outpouring.[117]

However, although this view neatly avoids implying that angels have

senses at all (though of course, like all our thinking, it presupposes some sensory activity). Rather, instead of perceiving our external senses' causal *passivity* via the common sense, in self-awareness the intellect perceives its own causal *activity* as agent of its thinking about other things. See esp. *De ver.*, q. 10, a. 8; *SCG* III, c. 46; *In De an.* III.3; and *ST* I, q. 87, a. 1, which Cory carefully examines at *Aquinas on Human Self-Knowledge*, 49–57. Since the causal connection to reality here is embedded in our own intellect-as-acting, and since our intellect-as-acting itself is immediately present to us in self-awareness (see note 81 above), there is no need to "compose" this self-awareness with the term of any other act to achieve the (prephilosophical) judgment that "I exist." Hence, if "ontological composition" is indeed necessary for an act of judgment to count as an act of "composing," then judging "I exist" does not "compose" anything with the merely apprehended "I": rather, to think "I" just is to affirm "I exist."

115. Péghaire, "L'intellection du singulier matériel," 143. Goris, unlike Péghaire, does not use the term "harmonie préétablie," but he too does say that angelic intelligible species contain "everything that is accidental and proper" to the individual things known thereby, including "their own unique histories" ("Angelic Knowledge," 160). Suarez-Nani, though without explicitly saying that the angelic intelligible species contains individual "history," seems to imply it when she says that its *a priori* character releases angels from "toute dépendance à l'égard des objets de connaissance" (*Connaissance et langage*, 54).

116. For Aquinas's denial that angels can by nature directly see future events, see *De malo*, q. 16, a. 7; *ST* I, q. 57, a. 3, and II-II, q. 95, a. 1; *De ver.*, q. 8, a. 12; *In Sent.* II, d. 3, q. 3, a. 3, ad 4, and d. 7, q. 2, a. 2; *Quod.* VII.1.3, ad 1; and *SCG* III, c. 154, n. 3268. For the same claim applied to any non-divine intellect, see also *ST* I, q. 86, a. 4, and *In Sent.* I, d. 38, q. 1, a. 5.

117. John of St. Thomas, *Cursus theologicus*, 42.2, nn. 25–61 (Desclée 4:644a–655b).

Can Angels Know Being without Judgment? 265

natural knowledge of the future, it instead runs afoul of two other claims we have seen Aquinas make. First, by introducing change into the angel's intelligible species, it contradicts Aquinas's claim that angelic knowledge of changing events is itself entirely changeless.[118] Second, the change introduced into the angel's intelligible species would have to be continuous, which contradicts Aquinas's claim that all angelic change is discrete and therefore measured by their own "discrete time."[119]

I therefore would caution against taking my proposal (namely, that angels grasp existence by way of active causality) too strongly. Specifically, I would deny that angels grasp existence by way of having God's particular creative actions, or the determination of which particular things he creates, inscribed in their intelligible species at all. Rather, in my view, that species is a determinate likeness of just three things: (1) shared form, (2) individuating matter, and (3) God's act of "making" just as such—not his act of making this particular individual. Items (1) and (2), which we saw Aquinas explicitly affirm, together allow the angel's intelligible species to be a proper likeness of all individuals whatsoever that actually possess the corresponding shared form at a given time. Item (3), which I contend is at least implicit in Aquinas's view, allows the angel's act of conceptually grasping these individuals to also be an act of existential affirmation, in that it allows the angel to grasp them precisely as brought into reality by God. But *which* individuals' existence the angel thereby affirms to be made by God is determined, not *a priori* by the content of the angel's intelligible species (*pace* John of St. Thomas), but rather

---

118. See the texts cited in notes 69, 70, and 72 above. John of St. Thomas (*Cursus theologicus*, 42.2, nn. 26, 29, 56, and 60 [Desclée 4:644a, 645b, 653b, and 654b–55b]) insists that his theory still somewhat preserves the unchangeability of the angel's knowledge, inasmuch as the changes that he posits in the angel's intelligible species are all directed by the species's original blueprint (*ex vi primae infusionis*), like a rock which, by virtue of the heaviness it acquired at its original generation, falls down anew whenever it is removed from the center yet still retains the same original heaviness. (A better example might be a streaming video: the stream changes constantly, but the regulating program remains unchanged.) Nonetheless, internally directed change is still change, and even John of St. Thomas admits that he is proposing a "variatio … intrinseca" (*Cursus theologicus*, 42.2, n. 56 [Desclée 4:653b]), which Aquinas categorically excludes from the angelic intelligible species. What is at stake here, as we will see, is a question highly relevant to divine foreknowledge: can the medium by which one knows contingent events be entirely changeless without somehow pre-containing all the determinate complexity of those contingent events? John of St. Thomas, like any good Bañezian, thinks it cannot, which is why he requires the angelic intelligible species to constantly receive new determinations; Aquinas, I would submit, thinks it can.

119. See the texts cited above at notes 73–74.

simply by the occurrent existence of the individuals themselves, as Aquinas clearly stipulates in all his discussions of the topic.

The key here is to keep in mind that, when Aquinas says that the angelic species, just like the divine essence, is a "proper likeness" of individuating matter,[120] he does not mean that it is a proper likeness of certain parcels of individuating matter *as opposed to* other parcels. That would make the angelic species (or the divine essence) into a kind of complex, interiorly determined spreadsheet filled out with a particular determinate set of individuals. Rather, in his discussions of angelic knowledge of singulars, Aquinas frequently insists that the angelic intelligible species, like the divine essence, is simple, multiplied only extrinsically in its "relations" (*respectus*) to individual things.[121] To explain how a simple thing can be a "proper likeness" of many, Aquinas distinguishes two senses of "proper likeness" (*propria ratio*): a merely "adequate" sense, and an "excelling" (*excellens*) or "superexceeding" (*superexcedens*) sense.

"Adequate" proper likeness, which is all that human knowledge is capable of thanks to its passive origin, is always one-to-one (genus to genus, species to species, individual to individual). Angels, however, enjoy an "excelling" proper likeness, just as God does; and this likeness can be one-to-many, because the "excelling" form contains "uniformly" (*uniformiter*) and universally what the represented things contain "dividedly" (*divisim*).[122] And although the texts where Aquinas develops this distinction are concerned primarily with how more universal angelic ideas can be proper likenesses of specific kinds, Aquinas also explicitly appeals

---

120. See the texts cited above in notes 88–89 for, respectively, divine and angelic knowledge of singulars.

121. For the intrinsic simplicity of the intelligible species by which the angel knows individuals, see *Q. de an.* 20; *SCG* II, c. 100, n. 1854; and *ST* I, q. 57, a. 2. For the species's multiplication only by way of extrinsic relation rather than by intrinsic determination, see *Quod.* VII.1.3, co. (Leon. 25/1.14a:142–48): "per unam formam possunt cognoscere omnia indiuidua eiusdem speciei, ita quod illa species efficitur propria similitudo uniuscuiusque particularium secundum *diuersos respectus* eius ad particularia, sicut *essencia diuina* efficitur propria similitudo singulorum secundum *diuersos respectus*" (emphasis added) and ad 5. See also *De ver.*, q. 19, a. 2, ad 1, and *In Sent.* II, d. 3, q. 3, a. 3, ad 3.

122. See Aquinas's comparison of the angel's intelligible species to the divine essence in *ST* I, q. 55, a. 3, ad 3, and esp. *De ver.*, q. 8, a. 10, ad 3 (Leon. 22.253a–b:113–31): "id quod <est> unum, non potest esse propria ratio plurium si sit eis *adaequatum*; sed si sit *superexcedens*, potest esse plurium propria ratio quia continet in se *uniformiter* propria utriusque quae in eis *divisim* inveniuntur" (emphasis added). See also *SCG* II, c. 98, n. 1837; *In Sent.* II, d. 3, q. 3, a. 2, ad 3; *De sub. sep.* 16; and *In De caus.* 10.

Can Angels Know Being without Judgment? 267

to this distinction to explain angelic knowledge of individuals.[123] Thus, though an angel's intelligible species is indeed a proper likeness of individuating matter, it (like God's essence) is a proper likeness of *any* individuating matter, not just of the particular parcels of matter that have actually been created. Hence the reason why an angel is aware of only the actually existent individuals, to the exclusion of merely possible ones, is not some *a priori* determination intrinsic to the angel's intelligible species (*pace* Péghaire and John of St. Thomas), but rather simply the fact that only the actual individuals are actually similar to that intelligible species.

In my view, then, the active causal connection provided by the angel's copies of God's creative knowledge has a sharply delimited role: it simply (1) allows the angel to *affirm* as existent (made by God) whatever is actually present to the angel by way of likeness. The active causal connection does not additionally (2) determine *which* things are present to the angel; that is determined only by which things actually exist. (In this respect the angels' active causal connection is radically different from our passive causal connection through the senses, which is the basis for both our ability to *affirm* existence and our awareness of *which* individual things' existence to affirm, and which is the basis for the latter too precisely because our "proper likenesses" of those individuals are passively acquired rather than innate.) An angel's knowledge of contingent events is therefore really dependent on those events themselves, rather than on divinely-sourced information—even though those events do not add any new determination to the angel's mind, or actualize any potency in him. Aquinas can hold this because he rejects John of St. Thomas's assumption that the mental likeness by which one knows contingent events must itself be intrinsically determined to those particular events. If this is right, then the implications may extend well beyond angelology (and the topic of the present chapter) by providing a new way to approach the classic problem of how God himself can have changeless, nonreceptive,

---

123. See esp. *De ver.*, q. 8, a. 11, ad 6 (Leon. 22/2.257a:287–91), where Aquinas, responding to an objection against angelic knowledge of singulars, argues that "una species potest esse propria ratio diversorum in quantum est *superexcedens*, ut ex supra dictis patet [a. 10, ad 3]; per unum autem medium *adaequatum* non possunt diversa distincte cognosci" (emphasis added). See also *ST* I, q. 57, a. 2, ad 3, where Aquinas similarly responds to an objection against angelic knowledge of singulars by referring back to q. 55, a. 3, ad 3 (the parallel to *De ver.*, q. 8, a. 10, ad 3), where he had distinguished between "excelling" and merely "adequate" likenesses.

purely actual knowledge of creatures' free actions without actively controlling them.

For present purposes, however, what we have established is that Aquinas does have available to him a coherent solution to the problem of how angels can grasp existence without C/D, even though he does not explicitly spell it out. The solution lies in appealing to the active-causal status of the angel's innate intelligible species, which they enjoy as copies of the divine art. This active-causal connection to existence replaces our passive-causal connection to existence via our external senses: the angels' grip on reality, rather than deriving like ours from objects' causal actions on them, derives instead from God's causal action on created objects.

This does not mean that angels have *a priori* knowledge of which individual objects and events God causes, which I take to be incompatible with various aspects of Aquinas's view; rather, the sole role of the active-causal connection is to let the angels grasp essences as proceeding into some real existence, so that they can enjoy the "intuition of being" rather than being trapped in a world of pure possible essences. This limited role suffices, however, to make every angelic act of conceptualization also an act of affirmation: of affirming the real existence of any extant individual of which the angel's concept is currently a proper likeness. But because, ontologically speaking, this affirmative judgment involves only one act (internally "speaking" the concept) and one term (the concept itself), this judgment cannot involve ontological composition; and so this judgment does not constitute C/D, since C/D is the kind of judgment that does involve ontologically "composing" two distinct terms of two distinct acts. Positing C/D-less grasp of existence in this way presents no danger of essentialism, *pace* Gilson and his followers, since the theory in no way involves reducing existence itself to a directly conceptualizable pseudo-essence (or essential property) in its own right. Rather, angels simply (a) conceptualize essences and (b) affirm their existence, just as we do; the difference is that, in the angels, one and the same act performs both the conceptualizing and the judicative roles.

Now, I believe the strategy I have just proposed for explaining angelic composition-less existential judgments is a novel one.[124] Indeed, I

---

124. John of St. Thomas perhaps comes closest in his explanation of angelic knowledge of contingent events at *Cursus theologicus*, 42.2, nn. 25–32 and 54 (Desclée 4:644a–47a and

am not aware that even the problem itself has been directly formulated—perhaps because the Scholastic commentators were insufficiently interested in the connection between judgment and existence, whereas modern Thomists have been insufficiently interested in angelology. But if the strategy succeeds, then it follows that Gilson, Maritain, and Owens are not quite right in holding that what prevents us humans from grasping existence by simple apprehension is simply existence's irreducibility to essence. If it were, then angelic simple apprehension would be equally inadequate to the task.

What existence's irreducibility does entail is merely that simple apprehension cannot grasp existence directly in an isolated concept *of its own*, which holds true for angels too. But existence's irreducibility by itself does not preclude grasping existence in a simple apprehension *of the existent nature*; that is, it does not entail an act of composing that simply apprehended nature with existence. Rather, humans' need to "compose" is due to existence's irreducibility together with another factor: the abstracted intelligible species's loss of the senses' causal connection to reality. Thus, arguably one of the greatest benefits of this study of angelic knowledge is actually the light it sheds on our own human way of knowing.

EXPLAINING ANGELIC DIVISION-LESS KNOWLEDGE OF BEING AS BEING

Thus far, we have examined how angels can affirm being *as real* without an act of "composing." We have yet to show how angels can grasp being *as being* without an act of either "composing" or "dividing" (*separatio*). Let us briefly recall the two main reasons why humans do need such an act for this purpose. First, humans require an at least implicit act of positive "composing" to grasp not only existence but also the prephilosophical notion of "being" (*ens*), since "being" means "that which is."[125] Second, humans require an act of negative "dividing" (*separatio*) to advance

---

652b–53a), as his explanation, like mine, leans heavily on angels knowing natures as proceeding from God's causality. But even he does not appeal to this quality of angelic knowledge to explain angelic composition-less knowledge (which he discusses at 42.4, nn. 42–53 [Desclée 4:679a–682b]), nor does he contrast the angelic intelligible species' active grip on reality with our senses' passive grip.

125. See note 41 above.

to the metaphysical notion of "being as being" without losing its analogical richness.

Now, it should already be clear that the first reason does not apply to angels. If indeed angels can affirm X's real existence without composition, they should have no trouble knowing X as an instance of "that which is" (i.e., as prephilosophical "being") without composition either. As for the second reason, at least part of it does not apply to angels either. After all, angelic intellects are built for knowing immaterial realities; they hardly need corrective *separatio* to conceptualize them adequately!

Two problems do remain, however. First, although angelic intellects are indeed built for knowing immaterial creatures, it seems they would still need corrective *separatio* in order to conceptualize God, given that God's essence cannot be naturally grasped by any creature.[126] Second, without corrective *separatio*, it is unclear how the angelic notion of "being" could retain its analogical richness, either across the ten categories or across the three grades of substance (corruptible bodies, incorruptible bodies, and immaterial substances).[127]

Both remaining problems can, however, be resolved by simply denying that angels have distinct intelligible species either for "God" or for "being." Instead, I would contend, Aquinas's angels have intelligible species (adequate or supereminent) only of actual created natures; and these species suffice for discerning therein both the known creature's First Cause and the creature's analogical commonality to other categories of being, with no need to form (as we must) a new nominal definition for "First Cause" or "being as being." To show that this is in fact Aquinas's view, let us consider first the problem of angelic knowledge of God, to which Aquinas gives considerable attention; this will then give us the tools to understand the problem of angelic knowledge of "being as being," to which, to my knowledge, Aquinas gives no attention at all.

When Aquinas discusses how angels naturally know God, his answer is invariably that they do so primarily by knowing their own similarity to God as their first cause.[128] Just as angels need not move discursively

---

126. This claim that God's essence cannot be naturally grasped by creatures is ubiquitous in Aquinas. See, for example, *In Sent.* II, d. 4, q. 1, a. 1; d. 23, q. 2, a. 1; IV, d. 49, q. 2, a. 6; *De ver.*, q. 8, a. 3; *SCG* III, cc. 49, 52; *ST* I, q. 12, a. 4; q. 64, a. 1, ad 2; q. 94, a. 1, co. and ad 3; I-II, q. 5, a. 5.

127. For these two kinds of analogy, see notes 49 and 46, respectively.

128. See esp. *ST* I, q. 56, a. 3 (Leon. 5.67b): "Quia enim imago Dei est in ipsa natura angeli

from grasping principles to grasping conclusions,[129] and just as they need not have a separate intelligible species for each individual of a kind,[130] but rather know the conclusions in the principle and the individuals in the innate species, so too with cause and effect: they can see the cause in the effect and vice versa, by a single act through a single intelligible species.[131] Aquinas compares this angelic ability to know ordinary causes in their effects, in a single act, to seeing a man in a "mirror" (*speculum*): just as there is no need to see the mirrored image first in its own right before seeing the man, so there is no need to grasp the effect in its own right before grasping the cause of which it is the likeness.[132] Aquinas also sometimes uses this "mirror" analogy to describe angelic knowledge of the divine cause, by contrast to our discursive method;[133] but elsewhere he says that angelic knowledge of God is even more immediate than this, because the angel can see God's image directly stamped on his own angelic essence (the "effect"), with no need to peer into anything outside himself (like seeing a man directly by his likeness in our sight, rather than indirectly by his likeness in a mirror).[134]

The point, for our purposes, is this: the angel's only natural "idea" (species) of God is his own angelic essence. Unlike us in our postlapsarian state,[135] the angel need not form a separate idea of God, any more than he need form separate ideas of individual human beings: rather, he sees both in one of his connatural "ideas." Hence, the angel can do his

---

impressa per suam essentiam, angelus Deum cognoscit, inquantum est similitudo Dei." See also *ST* I, q. 12, a. 4, ad 1; *De ver.*, q. 8, a. 3, co. and ad 17–18; *SCG* III, c. 49, nn. 2265 and 2271; and *In Sent.* II, d. 4, q. 1, a. 1; d. 23, q. 2, a. 1; and IV, d. 49, q. 2, a. 6, ad 1. In these texts Aquinas frequently quotes *Liber de causis* 8.

129. *De ver.*, q. 8, a. 15; *ST* I, q. 58, a. 3; *SCG* III, c. 49, n. 2265; and *De malo*, q. 16, a. 6, co. and ad s.c. 1. See also *ST* I, q. 79, a. 8, and q. 85, a. 5, and *De ver.*, q. 15, a. 1.

130. Besides the previously cited texts (notes 121–123) on angelic knowledge of many singulars through a single species, see also Aquinas's texts on angels' ability to *simul plura intelligere*: *De ver.*, q. 8, a. 14; *ST* I, q. 58, a. 2; *In Sent.* II, d. 3, q. 3, a. 4; and *SCG* II, c. 101, n. 1859.

131. *De ver.*, q. 8, a. 15, ad 6–7; *ST* I, q. 58, a. 3, ad 2; and *SCG* III, c. 49, n. 2265.

132. See *De ver.*, q. 8, a. 15, and *ST* I, q. 58, a. 3, ad 1; see also *ST* I, q. 93, a. 1, ad 3 (in the context of human prelapsarian knowledge of God rather than angelic knowledge of causes).

133. See *SCG* III, c. 49, n. 2265.

134. *ST* I, q. 56, a. 1; *De ver.*, q. 8, a. 3, ad 17; and *In Sent.* II, d. 4, q. 1, a. 1, and d. 23, q. 2, a. 1; cf. *SCG* III, c. 49, n. 2265, where Aquinas says that angels know God both by the "mirror" way in other creatures, and by the more immediate way in their own essence.

135. For Aquinas's claim that prelapsarian Adam knew God nondiscursively like the angels, though by a kind of spiritual light rather than by self-knowledge, see *In Sent.* II, d. 23, q. 2, a. 1; *De ver.*, q. 18, a. 1, ad 1; and *ST* I, q. 94, a. 1, co. and ad 3.

version of "metaphysics"—namely, consider the divine substance whose essence is its *esse*, and which therefore lies above angelic natural understanding—without needing to arrive at a suitable concept of "God" by an act of denying its essence-existence composition, simply because he needs no distinct concept of "God" at all.

If knowledge of God is the angelic equivalent to human metaphysical knowledge of positively immaterial being, knowledge of *esse* is their equivalent to human metaphysical knowledge of neutrally immaterial being.[136] Does *separatio* at least need to play a role for angels here? The only text I am aware of where Aquinas discusses angels' knowledge of *esse* as such, in the abstract, is *ST* I, q. 12, a. 4, ad 3. Aquinas here draws a comparison between angelic knowledge of abstract *esse* and human knowledge of abstract form. Even though it is natural (*connaturale*) for human intellects to know (*cognoscere*) abstracted common natures in the concrete material things from which we abstracted them,[137] we can still also consider (*considerare*) those same abstracted natures by themselves, in the abstract. So too, even though it is natural (*connaturale*) for angels to know (*cognoscere*) existence in a concrete nature, they can still also set apart (*secernere*) existence from that nature, inasmuch as they know (*cognoscere*) *that* the thing is not identical to its existence.[138]

What is the import of that key term *secernere*? At first it might seem like a straightforward synonym for *separare*, which would imply that angels do in fact have to perform a separate act of "dividing" in order to grasp a thing's *esse* as such. It seems more likely, however, that *secernere* here—while indeed doing the work that *separatio* does in us—is instead meant to describe simply grasping the distinct contents of a cognitive act in their distinction, within the original cognitive act (rather than making a new cognitive act of distinguishing what was previously blurred together, followed by another new cognitive act of considering one of the newly distinguished items). This reading would certainly harmonize better with what Aquinas says elsewhere about the nondiscursiveness of angelic knowledge. It also, however, fits better with the

---

136. For (human) metaphysics as concerned with both positively immaterial being (separate substances) and neutrally or negatively immaterial being (*ens commune*), see esp. Wippel, *Metaphysical Thought*, 8–9 and 52–53, and *Metaphysical Themes*, 30–31 and 72–73.

137. See the texts cited above in note 98, where Aquinas insists that all human intellectual thought requires returning to the phantasm.

138. *ST* I, q. 12, a. 4, ad 3 (Leon. 4.121b).

fact that Aquinas reserves the discursive terms *considerare* and *resolvere*[139] solely to the human side of the analogy,[140] while instead using the immediacy-connoting term *cognoscere* (which he uses throughout for knowing concrete form-in-matter and *esse*-in-essence) to describe how angels know the essence-*esse* distinction. If this reading is right, then the angel can know *esse* as such without needing to consider it in isolation, in a pseudo-concept produced by *separatio*.

Finally, if this account of angels' knowledge of God and *esse* is correct, it seems easy enough to apply it to their knowledge of *ens inquantum ens*, despite Aquinas's silence on the subject. There is no danger that their lack of *separatio* would reduce their conception of "being" to trans-categorial univocity, simply because they need no such conception in the first place. Rather, they need only their innate intelligible species; and a single one of these species lets them discern the secondary, derived character of the known thing's various modes of accidental being, just as they can discern its *esse* and its similitude to the First Cause.

CONCLUSION

The primary purpose of this investigation was to resolve a conundrum posed by the apparent tension between two of Aquinas's claims: that "being as real" and "being as being" are known by acts of composition and division, respectively, and that angels neither "compose" nor "divide," although they do still "judge" as an aspect of their single simple cognitive act. To explain angels' knowledge of "being as real" without composition, I argued that Aquinas's theory that angelic intelligible species are derived from God's creative knowledge allows angels to have an active causal connection to existence that inversely parallels our own passive, sense-mediated causal connection to existence. The crucial difference between the angelic version and our sense-mediated version is that, where our sense-mediated connection to existence requires ontological

---

139. See, e.g., Jan Aertsen's discussion of *resolutio* as metaphysical discursive *ratiocinatio* in his *Medieval Philosophy and the Transcendentals: The Case of Thomas Aquinas* (Leiden: Brill, 1996), 130–36, relying primarily on *In De Trin.*, q. 6, a. 1.

140. While Aquinas does apply the term *resolutio* to both human and angelic abstract cognitions at the very end of *ST* I, q. 12, a. 4, ad 3, he there qualifies it with a *quaedam* ("resolutionis cuiusdam"). This suggests that he does not mean the term *resolutio* to apply to the angelic version in its technical, discursiveness-denoting meaning.

"composing" between intellectual and sensory activity, the angels' active causal connection is already pre-contained in their innate intelligible species, thus eliminating the need for ontological (though not logical) "composing." Finally, to explain angels' knowledge of "being as being" without division (*separatio*), I argued that angels do not need to form an isolated concept of "being" at all, but rather simply grasp "being" in their innate species of created natures. Hence, since we humans need *separatio* for metaphysics only because our (abstracted) concept of being would be univocal and empty without it, the fact that angels simply have no such concept eliminates their need for metaphysical *separatio*.

The payoffs of this investigation, however, go beyond simply resolving the conundrum. In the first place, it sheds further light on the pride of place that Aquinas assigns to the angels in his cosmology. Specifically, it highlights how angels, as Aquinas understands them, are quasi-divine not only in their nature and in their causal power over the material world but also in their way of knowing individual existents: actively rather than passively, thanks to a kind of participation in God's own creative knowledge. Moreover, the more obvious preeminence in the line of efficient causality that Aquinas attributes to angels in, for example, *ST* I, q. 110, presupposes their preeminence in knowing individual existents, as without the latter they could not exercise their providential role; and, in Aquinas's view, both of these preeminences are required for the unity and order of the cosmos.[141]

A second payoff is that, because there are significant parallels between angelic knowledge and God's knowledge, this investigation also arguably helps us understand the latter. Specifically, I would argue that Aquinas's model of how angels know changing events by an active causal connection, without changing or receiving anything from the object of their knowledge, yet still *because* they happen (as evinced by their lack of future-knowledge), sheds important light on how God, too, without changing or receiving anything from creatures, can know changing events simply because they happen, rather than because he had "already" decreed them to happen thus. If so, this has important implications for the problem of how to reconcile the pure actuality and nonpassivity of God's knowledge with creatures' free will.

141. For this emphasis on the importance of the angelic mode of knowing individuals for understanding angelic *praesidentia* over the cosmos, see Suarez-Nani, *Connaissance et langage*, 54 (referring to *ST* I, q. 61, a. 4).

Finally, highlighting the contrast between angelic and human knowledge helps us to better understand our own human way of knowing. In particular, it shows that, although recent Thomists are right to insist that we grasp being by acts of composing and dividing, the reason we do so is not solely the objective character of *esse* and of *ens inquantum ens*, as they claim, but also and equally our human-specific way of knowing, which is in fact rather idiosyncratic in the intellectual realm. Thus, our need to grasp *esse* by positive "composition" is due not only to *esse*'s non-essential character, but also to the fact that our causal connection to the world requires a complex intellect-sense-hybrid process. Likewise, our need to grasp *ens inquantum ens* by negative "separation" is due not only to being's analogous character, but also to the fact that, in order to know being and its transcendental properties distinctly, we need to form separate pseudo-concepts for them, rather than simply discerning them in an original rich and simple concept as angels do.[142] In short, investigating angelic consciousness is a fruitful way to discern which parts of our own human experience are due to its objects and which are due, instead, to the peculiarities of our own nature.[143]

---

142. Here I would echo Domenic D'Ettore's recent suggestion in his *Analogy After Aquinas: Logical Problems, Thomistic Answers* (Washington, DC: The Catholic University of America Press, 2019), 191, that, regarding our understanding of Thomistic analogical predication, "the way forward ... involves exploring the formation and development of concepts, beginning with the initial abstraction of concepts from phantasms and proceeding through the development of concepts by the possible intellect."

143. See Tobias Hoffmann's introduction to *A Companion to Angels in Medieval Philosophy*, 2–3; in the same volume, Bernd Roling, "Angelic Language and Communication," 223–60, at 223–25; and Dominik Perler, "Thought Experiments: The Methodological Function of Angels in Late Medieval Epistemology," in *Angels in Medieval Philosophical Inquiry: Their Function and Significance* (Aldershot: Ashgate, 2008), 143–54. I would like to thank Therese Cory and Gregory T. Doolan for inviting me to contribute to this volume, and for their invaluable suggestions and comments; this chapter is much the better for them.

Gaven Kerr

9 ⁂ Aquinas's Metaphysical Way to God

Anybody who has even a casual acquaintance with Aquinas's thought knows that he endeavored to offer philosophical demonstrations for God's existence. The five ways are the arguments on which both Thomists and non-Thomists often focus. It seems to me that these ways are so popular for three reasons: they do not seem to require any in-depth knowledge of Thomistic metaphysics beforehand, they are all intuitively familiar, and they appear at the beginning of Thomas's most famous work, the *Summa theologiae*. But these reasons for popularity can translate into seeming weaknesses. Unless one is familiar with the metaphysical background out of which the ways emerge, Thomas may appear to be making use of an outdated physics, to be adopting a premodern notion of causality, to be falling into obvious logical fallacies, to be presupposing the impossibility of an infinite regress.[1] Even among Thomists, there are divisions on how to read the various ways to God, with some arguing that they are not actually demonstrative proofs as opposed to a way of deepening an already established faith, others holding that they are demonstrative proofs but drawn from philosophy of nature or physics, and others holding that they are demonstrative metaphysical proofs.[2]

---

1. For a presentation of the five ways that is problematic (in my estimation) precisely because it fails to engage with the metaphysics that Aquinas utilizes to buttress the ways, see Anthony Kenny, *The Five Ways* (London: Routledge & Kegan Paul, 1969). One can also consult the myriad presentations of the ways by non-Thomists in generic philosophy of religion textbooks for further engagements that present the ways in isolation from their wider metaphysical background.

2. See Fergus Kerr, *After Aquinas: Versions of Thomism* (Oxford: Blackwell, 2002), chap. 4, for an interpretation that leans heavily toward the view that the ways deepen an already

Beyond the five ways we can look to other proofs of God's existence that Thomas offers. To my mind the most compelling is that of *De ente*, c. 4.[3] One of the reasons for the attractiveness of the *De ente* proof is that unlike the more famous five ways, the *De ente* spells out the metaphysical commitments of the proof explicitly beforehand. Given the clear-cut metaphysical procedure of the *De ente* proof, some Thomists have argued that it stands as the backdrop to *any* Thomistic proof of God's existence.

For instance, Joseph Owens and John Knasas have argued that the proof of God that reasons from the participated *esse* of a thing to its unparticipated source is Aquinas's characteristic way of demonstrating God's existence and accordingly it is to be found as the backdrop to the various other proofs in Aquinas's works, especially the five ways. In particular, Knasas has recently held that any proof of God offered by Aquinas must be a metaphysical proof, and as such it pertains to the being of things under consideration in the proof itself. So, for example, in the proof from motion, while Thomas is considering motion, his consideration thereof is with a view to its sharing in the common character of being: *sub ratione entis*. And with that Knasas makes the connection with *esse* such that the motion that anything has its own *esse* for which we are seeking an account in the proof itself. Hence, the proof from motion is not seeking to explain the motion of a thing, but the *esse* of the motion; Knasas offers similar considerations for the other *viae*.[4]

---

established faith; see Wippel, *Metaphysical Thought*, 51–52, for details of those who hold that divine being is established prior to metaphysics (and thereby presupposed for metaphysics) in which case the proofs of God are drawn from philosophy of nature; note also the recent volume devoted to the five ways, Robert Arp, *Revisiting Aquinas' Proofs for the Existence of God* (Leiden / Boston: Brill / Rodopi, 2016) in which several, though not all, contributors take the ways to be arguments from philosophy of nature; see the relevant papers by Joseph Owens in *St. Thomas Aquinas on the Existence of God: The Collected Papers of Joseph Owens*, ed. John R. Catan (Albany: State University of New York Press, 1980), and John Knasas, *Thomistic Existentialism and Cosmological Reasoning* (Washington, DC: The Catholic University of America Press, 2019), who argue that the five ways are robust metaphysical demonstrations of God's existence. Wippel's own thinking in *The Metaphysical Thought of Thomas Aquinas* (Washington, DC: The Catholic University of America Press, 2000) is that each of the five ways begins with some physical reality, but in reasoning from those physical realities to God, Aquinas quickly moves to the level of metaphysical consideration.

3. For my engagement with this proof, see *Aquinas's Way to God: The Proof in "De Ente et Essentia"* (Oxford: Oxford University Press, 2015).

4. See, e.g., John Knasas, "Thomistic Existentialism and the Proofs *Ex Motu* at *Summa Contra Gentiles*, I, C. 13," *The Thomist* 59, no. 4 (1995): 591–615, note in particular §4, and more recently his treatment of the five ways in both *Summa contra Gentiles* and *Summa theologiae* in *Thomistic Existentialism and Cosmological Reasoning*, chaps. 8–9.

I am sympathetic to these existentialist readings of Aquinas's thought, and I do think that his proofs for God presuppose his metaphysics of *esse*. However, I think it is a little too strong to hold that what is really at stake in the various proofs is the reality of *esse*. Certainly, there are some proofs that deal with *esse* and seek a cause thereof, for example, *De ente*, c. 4; *In Sent*. I, d. 3; *De pot.*, q. 3, a. 5; and (arguably) the Fourth Way.[5] Nevertheless, there are other proofs that do not appear to be dealing with *esse* in any way, for example, the proof from motion, so that while the primary cause arrived at in those proofs may be shown to be a cause of *esse*, the conclusion is not immediate that the primary cause is such.

Yet I believe there is something to be said about adopting a unified approach to Aquinas's proofs for God's existence. In this respect, the view that I propose in this chapter is that what is up for grabs in the various demonstrations of God's existence is some sort of causal actuality derivatively possessed, and that this actuality is only accounted for by arriving at some cause that is *per se* in respect of that actuality. This is a move from participated to unparticipated being, or from what is *per aliud* to what is *per se*. Accordingly, creatures only exist insofar as they participate in some actuality, fundamentally the act of existence, which actuality is derived from God; the proof from *esse* falls within this argument schema, but does not exhaust it. Thus, the mode of reasoning I take to be common in Aquinas's proofs of God's existence involves the following: the identification of some actuality possessed not *per se* but *per aliud*, thereby motivating the inference to what is *per se* in order to account for such actuality. This is what I call Aquinas's way to God.

In what follows, I shall begin by exploring Aquinas's thought on the divisions of the sciences and how God's existence is established in metaphysics and only in metaphysics. Having done that, I will argue that Aquinas's various demonstrations of God all proceed by way of consideration of some derived actuality to an affirmation of the existence of a *per se* source thereof.

---

5. For a reading of the Fourth Way in which the actuality of *esse* plays a pivotal role, see my article, "A Reconsideration of Aquinas's Fourth Way," in Gaven Kerr, *Collected Articles on the Existence of God* (Neunkirchen-Seelscheid: Editiones Scholasticae, 2023), chap. 10.

GOD'S EXISTENCE AND THE DIVISIONS OF THE SCIENCES

Aquinas has a clear vision of how the sciences are hierarchically ordered, particularly regarding how philosophy relates to theology. Nowhere is this more apparent than in his *In De Trin.*, qq. 5–6. Herein, Aquinas argues that sciences are divided based on their formal objects, and that the formal objects of the sciences are distinguished based on the intellectual operations used to consider those objects.[6]

Accordingly, our intellects can engage with things either to consider their truth or to put such truth to some practical use; correspondingly there are speculative and practical sciences.[7] Remaining with the speculative sciences, we find that they in turn are divided based on the formal object that the intellect considers. Following Aristotle, Thomas reasons that objects are knowable according to the degree to which they are universal and necessary, and the degree to which an object is such is the degree to which it is dependent (or not) on matter. Hence those things that are dependent on matter to a high degree are least knowable, whereas those things dependent on matter to very little or no degree are most knowable.[8] With these comments in mind, Aquinas proceeds to divide the speculative sciences.

Some things open for scientific investigation depend on matter both for their being and for their being understood. Hence, they can neither exist nor be understood without matter. Such objects are studied by the natural sciences.[9] Other things are open for investigation that depend on matter for their being but not for their being understood. Hence, they cannot be without matter, but they can be understood without matter; such are the objects of mathematical investigation.[10] Finally, there are

---

6. Aquinas, *In De Trin.*, and Maurer's translation of qq. 5–6, *The Division and Methods of the Sciences* (Toronto: Pontifical Institute of Mediaeval Studies, 1986). For general discussion see Wippel, *Metaphysical Thought*, 3–10. For in-depth treatment of the intellectual operation (*separatio*) by which the subject matter of metaphysics is distinguished, see Wippel, *Metaphysical Themes in Thomas Aquinas* (Washington, DC: The Catholic University of America Press, 1984), chap. 4.

7. *In De Trin.*, q. 5, a. 1 (Leon. 50.137:92–96).

8. Ibid. (Leon. 50.138:123–31). For the Aristotelian patrimony of Thomas's reasoning here, see Aristotle, *Posterior Analytics* I.6.74b5–75a37, in *The Complete Works of Aristotle*, ed. Jonathan Barnes (Princeton, NJ: Princeton University Press, 1984), and Aquinas, *In Post. an.* I.13.

9. *In De Trin.*, q. 5, a. 1 (Leon. 50.138:141–49).

10. Ibid. (149–54).

things that can be investigated that depend on matter neither for their being nor for their being understood. Hence, they do not need to be material in order to be and matter does not enter into their intelligible content; such are the objects of theology.

At this point Aquinas makes a subdivision between: (i) objects that are immaterial in the sense that they can never be found to be in matter, for example, God and angels (Wippel calls these positively immaterial) and (ii) objects that are immaterial in the sense that they need not be found in matter even though sometimes they are found that way, for example, substance, quality, being, potency, act, etc. (Wippel calls these neutrally immaterial.) Revealed theology deals with (i) as its subject matter, whereas the theology of the philosophers, that is, metaphysics or first philosophy, deals with (ii) as its subject matter, and with (i) as the principles of its subject matter.[11]

Aquinas has accordingly distinguished the subject matter of metaphysics as first philosophy insofar as it studies certain realities (substance, quality, being, potency, act) that are equally applicable to both material and immaterial beings. Given that these realities can be found among both material and immaterial beings, a study of such will not be limited to a single domain of being but will embrace a study of being as being.

Revealed theology deals with substances that are themselves immaterial. Later in the same work Aquinas makes an important observation, already noted by Aristotle, to the effect that owing to the supreme intelligibility of divine things, our intellect relates to them as the eye of an owl to the sun. We cannot think about such things using natural reason unless we are led to do so by means of their effects.[12] Consequently, in dealing with being *qua* being, metaphysics deals with objects that are positively immaterial insofar as they are causes of being, but not in themselves; whereas owing to divine revelation, revealed theology can consider divine things as they are in themselves.[13]

---

11. Ibid. (154–67). Note in particular the division of what is positively immaterial from what is neutrally immaterial: "Quedam uero speculabilia sunt que non dependent a materia secundum esse, quia sine materia esse possunt, siue numquam sint in materia, sicut Deus et angelus, siue in quibusdam sint in materia et in quibusdam non, ut substantia, qualitas, ens, potentia, actus, unum et multa, et huiusmodi."

12. Ibid. (149–54). See Aristotle, *Metaphysics* II.1.993b10–11, for the comparison of the eye of the owl looking at the sun.

13. Ibid. (175–82): "Sic ergo theologia siue scientia diuina est duplex: una in qua considerantur

Turning to the commentary on the *Metaphysics*, Aquinas offers a similar position to the one he advanced in the commentary on the *De Trinitate*. In the prologue to the *Metaphysics* commentary, Thomas argues that there needs to be a single science that is regulative for the rest and bears the title of wisdom. Such a science studies that which is maximally intelligible. In agreement with what he holds in the commentary on the *De Trinitate*, Aquinas reasons that what are maximally intelligible are the highest beings that are both free from matter and motion as well as the cause of being for all else. Accordingly, he concludes that it belongs to a single science to consider common being (*ens commune*) and its causes. But in considering the causes of *ens commune*, such a science does not treat them as its subject matter; for the cause of the subject matter of any science is not considered at the outset of the science, but as its goal. Hence, consideration of God as the cause of being in metaphysics is not considered or taken for granted from the outset but is arrived at as the goal of metaphysics.[14]

The subject matter of metaphysics then is *ens commune*; this is the being common to both material and immaterial things, and it comprises such parts as substance, quality, potency, act, etc., parts that we have already seen Thomas attribute as belonging to the subject matter of metaphysics in the commentary on the *De Trinitate*.[15] Thomas denies that God and angels, that is, substances that are separated from matter, are dealt with in metaphysics as its direct subject matter; rather they are

---

res diuine non tamquam subiectum scientie, set tamquam principia subiecti, et talis est theologia quam philosophi prosequntur, que alio nomine metaphisica dicitur; alia uero que ipsas res diuinas considerat propter se ipsas ut subiectum scientie, et hec est theologia que in sacra Scriptura traditur."

14. Aquinas, *In Meta.*, proem. (Marietti 2): "Unde oportet quod ad eamdem scientiam pertineat considerare substantias separatas, et ens commune, quod est genus, cuius sunt praedictae substantiae communes et universales causae. Ex quo apparet, quod quamvis ista scientia praedicta tria consideret, non tamen considerat quodlibet eorum ut subiectum, sed ipsum solum ens commune. Hoc enim est subiectum in scientia, cuius causas et passiones quaerimus, non autem ipsae causae alicuius generis quaesiti. Nam cognitio causarum alicuius generis, est finis ad quem consideratio scientiae pertingit. Quamvis autem subiectum huius scientiae sit ens commune, dicitur tamen tota de his quae sunt separata a materia secundum esse et rationem. Quia secundum esse et rationem separari dicuntur, non solum illa quae nunquam in materia esse possunt, sicut Deus et intellectuales substantiae, sed etiam illa quae possunt sine materia esse, sicut ens commune."

15. For further details see Wippel, *Metaphysical Thought*, 20–21, and my article "The Meaning of *Ens Commune* in the Thought of Thomas Aquinas," *Yearbook of the Irish Philosophical Society* (2008): 32–60.

considered directly in revealed theology.[16] The philosopher can obtain a knowledge of these beings by considering them as causes of the common being that he considers in metaphysics. Hence the end of metaphysics is characterized by a consideration of the cause of being, in which case metaphysics affirms the existence of God as its goal, not as its starting point. Metaphysics, therefore, does not begin with God, but ends with him.[17] There is no commitment then to the existence or otherwise of immaterial beings at the outset of metaphysics to establish its subject matter, though of course one may arrive at the affirmation of the existence of such within metaphysics.

By contrast, some commentators have argued that there needs to be some awareness of the existence of immaterial beings (God, angels, and even the human soul) in order to undertake metaphysics as a science distinct from physics.[18] On this view, for metaphysics to be a science dis-

---

16. A caveat is due here on angels. While Thomas has affirmed that they enter into consideration in metaphysics only as the principles of its subject matter, that is, *ens commune*, they nevertheless fall under and are included within *ens commune*, since they are substances composed of potency and act. Nevertheless, when it comes to the subject matter of metaphysics as a science, such things are not open to direct consideration by us, even though they fall under the subject matter of metaphysics; for discussion, see Gregory Doolan, "Aquinas on Separate Substances as the Subject Matter of Metaphysics," *Documenti e studi sulla tradizione filosofica medievale* 22 (2011): 347–82. Part I of this article is devoted to the divisions of the sciences and the place of the angels therein. Part II deals with whether the angels are included in the subject matter of metaphysics given that they are principles of *ens commune*; Doolan argues that qua divine/immaterial, angels are principles of *ens commune*, but qua substances they fall under *ens commune*. Part III deals with how angels can be principles of *ens commune* while falling under it; Doolan argues that while angels cannot be direct causes of *esse*, for such is reserved for God alone, angels can be preserving secondary causes of *esse* and thus principles of *ens commune*.

17. *SCG* III, c. 25 (Marietti 68): "Ipsaque prima philosophia tota ordinatur ad Dei cognitionem sicut ad ultimum finem, unde et scientia divina nominatur."

18. For details and discussion, see Wippel, *Metaphysical Thought*, 50–62; Lawrence Dewan, *Form and Being: Studies in Thomistic Metaphysics* (Washington, DC: The Catholic University of America Press, 2006), chap. 4; Benedict Ashley, *The Way toward Wisdom: An Interdisciplinary and Intercultural Introduction to Metaphysics* (Notre Dame, IN: University of Notre Dame Press, 2006), chap. 4; Ralph McInerny, "The Prime Mover and the Order of Learning," in *Being and Predication: Thomistic Interpretations* (Washington, DC: The Catholic University of America Press, 1986), 49–57; Leo Elders, "St. Thomas Aquinas' Commentary on the *Metaphysics* of Aristotle," and "La connaissance de l'être et l'entrée en métaphysique," in *Autour de Saint Thomas d'Aquinas: recueil d'études sur sa pensée philosophique et théologique* (Paris: FAC-éditions, 1987), 123–47 and 207–27; and Daniel De Haan, "Is Philosophy of Nature Irrelevant?," *Proceedings of the American Catholic Philosophical Association* 93 (2019): 327–48. De Haan's position is interesting here, because while in agreement with Ashley, McInerny, et al., that there must be some knowledge of substantially immaterial being in order to secure the subject matter of metaphysics, this is discovered within the dialectic of doing metaphysics itself, rather than formally established from the outset.

tinct from physics, there is required some proof of immaterial being prior to the investigation of *ens commune*. Accordingly, God's existence can be proved in a science prior to metaphysics, notably, physics or what has come to be called philosophy of nature. By contrast, the reading I have been offering here stresses that the subject matter of metaphysics is not immaterial being *per se*, that is, the positively immaterial, but the neutrally immaterial. One can know such being and thereby secure the subject matter of metaphysics without knowing the existence of positively immaterial beings, in which case we need not have a proof of God before entering metaphysics.

Nevertheless, even granting that metaphysics does not begin with the existence of God, this does not in itself entail that a science prior to metaphysics cannot offer demonstrative proof of God's existence. Accordingly, let us proceed to consider whether a proof of God's existence can be offered *only* in metaphysics; for if the latter is the case, then any way to God must be a metaphysical way.[19]

Physics is the study of mobile being; it is not the study of being *qua* being, or the being common to all beings.[20] Systematically speaking, physics presupposes a background metaphysics by which change, space, time, causality, etc. are understood, but this is presupposed only because the proper subject matter of physics is some domain of being itself. Given that the subject matter of physics is mobile being, any proof of God advocated therein will begin with a consideration of the being of mobile beings. But unless a more metaphysical viewpoint is taken, there is no guarantee that a cause for mobile being is a cause of being *tout court*. Indeed, in his commentary on the *De Trinitate* Thomas argues for this by claiming that divine beings are studied by the philosophers only insofar (*nisi prout*) as they are the principles of all things. Hence, they are taken for consideration in the science that studies all things and has as its subject matter being *qua* being, not the science that takes mobile being as its subject matter.[21]

---

19. In what follows I shall leave consideration of the argument from motion until the next section.
20. Aquinas, *In Phys.* I.1.
21. Aquinas, *In De Trin.*, q. 5, a. 4 (Leon. 50.154:157–63): "Unde et huiusmodi res divinae non tractantur a philosophis, nisi prout sunt rerum omnium principia. Et ideo pertractantur in illa doctrina, in qua ponuntur ea quae sunt communia omnibus entibus, quae habet subiectum ens in quantum est ens; et haec scientia apud eos scientia divina dicitur."

Furthermore, when we look at what Thomas has to say on the demonstrability of God in general, we can obtain further clarification that God's existence can only be established in metaphysics. In both the *Summa contra Gentiles* and the *Summa theologiae*, Thomas considers the objection that insofar as we have no knowledge of the essence of God sufficient for a middle term of demonstration, we can have no demonstration of God's existence.[22] Aquinas's solution to this problem is well known, and it is to distinguish between a *propter quid* demonstration, whose middle term tells us something about the essence of the subject, and a *quia* demonstration, whose middle term is drawn from some effect and leads to an affirmation of some cause for that effect.[23] Accordingly, we can offer a *quia* demonstration for God's existence given that we have some effects that can lead us to God.

What these clarifications establish is that created effects point us toward God as their cause. But it cannot be created effects considered in just any way, for a physical or a mathematical consideration of creatures will not reveal God as their cause. Rather, per the *De Trinitate*, God is considered as cause of all things in the science that considers the very being of things. Hence, our consideration of created effects must be in terms of their being; otherwise we fail to consider God as cause of such being. Hence, it is in metaphysics that God's existence is established, for only metaphysics considers creatures in terms of their being.

Let us add to this the fact that in dealing with the metaphysics of creation Aquinas offers us further reason to hold that we need to consider creatures metaphysically in order to arrive at God as a universal cause

---

22. *SCG* I, q. 12, and *ST* I, q. 2, a. 2.
23. *ST* I, q. 2, a. 2. For the division of demonstrations *quia* and *propter quid*, see *In Post. an.* I.23–25, noting in particular 23 (Leon. 1*/2.85:37–53): "Scire 'quia' est quando fit syllogismus non quidem per media, id est per mediata, set per inmediata, set non fit per causam, set fit per conuertentia, id est per effectus conuertibiles et inmediatos; et tamen talis demonstratio fit per notius, alias non faceret scire: non enim peruenimus ad cognitionem ignoti nisi per aliquid magis notum. Nichil enim prohibet duorum eque praedicantium, id est conuertibilium, quorum unus sit causa et aliud effectus, notius esse aliquando non causam, sed magis effectum; nam effectus aliquando est notior causa quo ad nos et secundum sensum, licet causa sit semper notior simpliciter et secundum naturam. Et ita per effectum notiorem causa potest fieri demonstratio non faciens scire 'propter quid', sed tantum 'quia.'" For discussion, see Rudi te Velde, *Aquinas on God: The 'Divine Science' of the "Summa Theologiae"* (Aldershot: Ashgate, 2006), 42–47, and David B. Twetten, "To Which 'God' Must a Proof of God's Existence Conclude For Aquinas?," in *Laudemos Viros Gloriosos: Essays in Honour of Armand Maurer, CSB*, ed. R. E. Houser (Notre Dame, IN: University of Notre Dame Press, 2007), 146–84.

of all beings. Thomas offers two short histories of philosophical reflection on the meaning of creation, one in *De pot.*, q. 3, a. 5, and the other in *ST* I, q. 44, a. 2. In both, he argues that it was not until philosophers began considering being in its universality, that is, being as not restricted to this or that or to such and such a being, that philosophers were able to come upon a cause of such being and therefore a creator.[24] These histories make it clear that creatures are beings because of their *esse*. It is only in isolating that metaphysical principle by which a creature is something rather than nothing that one can in turn rise to a consideration of the cause of such a principle and thus a creator.

What this tells us is that to reason from the being of things to God, we must consider creatures in terms of their very being. Attempting to arrive at an affirmation of God's existence in the philosophy of nature will involve reasoning from *ens mobile* to some primary cause thereof. But a primary cause of *ens mobile* will not be a primary cause of the being of things. Hence, it is only in metaphysics that divine beings, God in particular, are studied as the cause of all things. Whatever primary cause is established in physics or philosophy of nature, it will not be the primary cause of all, and so it will not be God.[25]

There is, then, something about the being of things that can lead us to consider God as the cause of such being. Whatever feature of a creature's being we take to springboard us into a proof of God's existence,

---

24. Aquinas, *De pot.*, q. 3, a. 5 (Marietti 49): "Posteriores vero philosophi, ut Plato, Aristoteles et eorum sequaces, pervenerunt ad considerationem ipsius esse universalis; et ideo ipsi soli posuerunt aliquam universalem causam rerum, a qua omnia alia in esse prodirent, ut patet per Augustinum. Cui quidem sententiae etiam Catholica fides consentit"; *ST* I, q. 44, a. 2 (Leon. 4.301): "Et ulterius aliqui erexerunt se ad considerandum ens inquantum est ens, et consideraverunt causam rerum, non solum secundum quod sunt haec vel talia, sed secundum quod sunt entia. Hoc igitur quod est causa rerum inquantum sunt entia, oportet esse causam rerum, non solum secundum quod sunt talia per formas accidentales, nec secundum quod sunt haec per formas substantiales, sed etiam secundum omne illud quod pertinet ad esse illorum quocumque modo." For discussion see Gaven Kerr, *Aquinas and the Metaphysics of Creation* (Oxford: Oxford University Press, 2019), chap. 1; Fernand Van Steenberghen, *Le problème de l'existence de Dieu dans les Écrits de s. Thomas d'Aquin* (Louvain: Éditions de l'institut supérieur de philosophie, 1980), 138; John F. Wippel, "Aquinas on Creation and the Preambles of Faith," *The Thomist* 78, no. 11 (2014): 1–36.

25. Both Owens and Knasas have pointed out that the proof from motion in Aristotle's *Physics* VIII needs to be augmented by the proof from *Metaphysics* XII; otherwise we are left with nothing more than a world soul that moves the outermost sphere. See Joseph Owens, "Aquinas and the Proof from the 'Physics,'" *Mediaeval Studies* 1 (1996): 119–50, and Knasas, *Thomistic Existentialism and Cosmological Reasoning*, 176–77.

such a feature must pertain to the being of *anything* other than God. But whatever is other than God is *per aliud*. Accordingly, I submit that what launches any proof for God's existence in Aquinas's thought is a consideration of the *per aliud* character of the beings that are under consideration in the context of the proof itself, from which consideration Aquinas moves to the affirmation of what is *per se*. In the following section I will explore how this argument structure is to be found in Aquinas's various demonstrations of God's existence.

AQUINAS'S WAY TO GOD

I have stated above that Aquinas reasons from the caused and thereby *per aliud* character of a thing's being to an uncaused *per se* source thereof; in other contexts, Aquinas speaks of what is *per participationem* as depending on what is *per se*. Nevertheless, the inference structure is from what is in a derived and participated sense through another to that which is in itself.[26] This is what in fact binds creatures to God precisely as creatures: the participated and derived status of their being as dependent on God, whose being participates in nothing but is *per se*.[27] With that in mind,

---

26. There are many instances in which Aquinas affirms this move. See *ST* I, q. 61, a. 1 (Leon. 5.393): "Solus enim Deus est suum esse; in omnibus autem aliis differt essentia rei et esse eius ... Et ex hoc manifestum est quod solus Deus est ens per suam essentiam; omnia vero alia sunt entia per participationem. Omne autem quod est per participationem, causatur ab eo quod est per essentiam"; *SCG* II, c. 15 (Marietti 27): "Item: quod per essentiam dicitur, est causa omnium quae per participationem dicuntur: sicut ignis est causa omnium ignitorum in quantum huiusmodi. Deus autem est ens per essentiam suam, quia est ipsum esse. Omne autem aliud ens est per participationem: quia ens quod sit suum esse, non potest esse nisi unum ... Deus igitur est causa essendi omnibus aliis"; *In Meta*. II.2, n. 296 (Marietti 85): "Omnia composita et participantia, reducantur in ea, quae sunt per essentiam, sicut in causas"; and *De ente*, c. 4 (Leon. 43.377:137–39): "Omne quod est per aliud reducitur ad id quod est per se sicut ad causam primam." For a detailed study see Denis Bonnette, *Aquinas' Proofs for God's Existence. St. Thomas Aquinas on 'The Per Accidens Necessarily Implies the Per Se'* (The Hague: Martinus Nijhoff, 1972); he holds (62–63) that this principle is what establishes the existence of a primary cause and not the impossibility of an infinite regress of *per se* ordered series, a view also held by Joseph Bobik in *Aquinas on Being and Essence: A Translation and Interpretation* (Notre Dame, IN: University of Notre Dame Press, 1965), 175, and John Knasas in *Thomistic Existentialism*, 60–63, and "The Analytical Thomist and the Paradoxical Aquinas: Some Reflections on Kerr's *Aquinas's Way to God*," *Annals of Philosophy* 67, no. 4 (2019): 84–85. Concerning the application of this principle in the proof in the *De ente*, I have argued in agreement with Wippel that it depends on the impossibility of an infinite regress, see *Aquinas's Way to God*, chap. 5, and for Wippel, see *Metaphysical Thought*, 408–9.

27. For details of Aquinas's participation metaphysics see Cornelio Fabro, *La nozione metafisica di partecipazione secondo s. Tommaso d'Aquino* (Turin: Società Editrice Internazionale,

the way to God will involve two components: (i) the designation of what is *per aliud* as properly *per aliud* and (ii) some justification for arriving at a *per se* source for the *per aliud*. In this section I will begin by considering (i) and (ii) in turn. Having done that, I will proceed to consider how (i) and (ii) are disclosed in the different proofs offered by Thomas throughout his career.

The *per aliud* utilized in a demonstration of God's existence will ultimately have to express some sort of dependence for actuality. This is because whatever is *per aliud* is dependent precisely for some actuality that it has not of itself, but through another. Hence, there is in every demonstration of God's existence an appeal to some derived actuality pertaining to the very being of the thing; this actuality in turn points to the existence of something that is *per se*. The metaphysics of *esse* stands as an important backdrop here, since every dependency for actuality subsequent to existential dependency itself reveals existential dependency; this is because in every dependent relationship there is something in potency that is actualized in some respect. But *esse* is the act of all acts, the perfection of all perfections.[28] So, unless a thing is pure act, it is subject to essence/*esse* composition, in which case no matter what the dependency, it will reveal some element of potency and thus dependency for *esse*. Nevertheless, *pace* Owens and Knasas, this is not to say that existential actuality is itself what is under consideration in each of Aquinas's demonstrations of God's existence, but only that it provides a metaphysical backdrop for understanding such dependency.

Given that what is *per aliud* is such because it is dependent on another for actuality, Aquinas justifies the reduction to the *per se* through consideration of *per se* ordered series. A *per se* ordered series is a causal series in which the members of the series do not possess the causality of the series essentially. For example, in the hand moving the stick to move the stone, the hand-stick-stone do not have the power of motion of the series of themselves; they require a cause for the motion that they have, and such

---

1950), *Participation et causalité selon s. Thomas d'Aquin* (Louvain / Paris: Publications Universitaires de Louvain / Béatrice-Nauwelaerts, 1961); Louis-Bertrand Geiger, *La participation dans la philosophie de s. Thomas d'Aquin* (Paris: Librairie Philosophique J. Vrin, 1953); Rudi te Velde, *Participation and Substantiality in Thomas Aquinas* (Leiden: E. J. Brill, 1995); Wippel, *Metaphysical Thought*, chap. 4; and Gregory T. Doolan, "Aquinas on *esse subsistens* and the Third Mode of Participation," *The Thomist* 82, no. 4 (2018): 611–42.

28. *De pot.*, q. 7, a. 2, ad 9.

a cause is the mind or mental agent. Accordingly, the hand-stick-stone themselves are immobile without some cause of motion that does have the causality of motion *per se* and not from something else.

On the other hand, *per accidens* series are causal series in which the causality of the series *is* possessed essentially by the members of the series. For example, in the series of fathers producing sons, Peter can beget James and James can beget John. Peter, James, and John all have the causality of the series in virtue of what they are, that is, biologically functioning males. Given the latter, it follows that as earlier members of the series pass away, later members can continue. This is because the later members are not causally dependent on the earlier members in the way that the hand-stick-stone are dependent on the mind or mental agent. In *per accidens* series, a member of the series is only causally dependent on its immediately preceding member. And having been caused in the series, a member of a *per accidens* series possesses the causality of the series of itself. Hence Peter can beget James and pass away without hindering James's ability to produce John.

By contrast, the mind or mental agent cannot induce motion to the hand-stick-stone, drop out of the series, and hope that the series continues. Consider Dr. Smith going to the golf course. As he sets up his swing, he suffers some irreparable brain damage by which his causal input ceases. It follows that his swing will not follow through to move the ball unless some other source of motion intervenes that continues the motion that Dr. Smith imparted to his hands and club. In short, when you remove the originating cause from the *per se* series, you remove the causality of the series (or as the Second Way states, remove the cause and you remove the effect). This is because members of the *per se* series are dependent on another for their causality, such that if there were no cause for their causality, there would be no causality and thus no causal series in question.

Given that members of *per se* series have the causality of the series not of themselves but through another, they are *per aliud*; hence without a primary cause through which such members have their causality, there would be no causal series in question. But the primary cause of such a series cannot itself be *per aliud* in respect of the causality in the series; for then it would not be the primary cause. Rather, the primary cause in a *per se* series must be something that does have the causality of the series *per se* and in turn can originate that causality in others. So, the metaphysics of a *per se* series justifies the inference from what is *per aliud* to what is *per se*.[29]

Aquinas applies the same reasoning then *mutatis mutandis* to created things in arriving at the affirmation of God's existence. In every such demonstration, Thomas seeks to arrive at some *per se* source of being for all that is. It is a *per se* source given the metaphysics of *per se* causal series we have just considered. It is the source of all that is because, as we have seen, the *per aliud* character of things reveals their dependency for actuality and ultimately for *esse*; hence the *per se* to which the *per aliud* are ultimately reducible will be that from which all actuality is drawn, without which there is nothing. Thus, there is a move from the participated or *per aliud* character of the causal feature in question to the affirmation of some unparticipated *per se* source.

At this point, then, it will be well to look at Aquinas's various proofs for God's existence to see this argument schema emerge; in particular, the argument from motion may be the most challenging for my contention that Aquinas's way to God is a *metaphysical* way. In what follows, I shall outline several categories of argumentation by which the various proofs of God can be streamlined with differences not so much pertaining to the kind of proof offered, but more to the phraseology involved. This is not to say that the arguments in each category are identical to

29. For further consideration of the metaphysics of causal series see Gaven Kerr, "Essentially Ordered Series Reconsidered," *American Catholic Philosophical Quarterly* 86, no. 4 (2012): 155–74, and "Essentially Ordered Series Reconsidered Once Again," *American Catholic Philosophical Quarterly* 91, no. 2 (2017): 541–55; Caleb Cohoe, "There Must be a First: Why Thomas Aquinas Rejects Infinite, Essentially Ordered, Causal Series," *British Journal for the History of Philosophy* 21, no. 5 (2013): 838–56; and Wippel, *Metaphysical Thought*, 460–62. Note also the references to Bonnette, Bobik, and Knasas in note oo above, who argue that the reduction of the *per aliud* to the *per se* is established independently of considerations of *per se* ordered series. For my part, other than its fittingness within a general Thomistic metaphysical picture, I cannot see any justification for the principle that what is *per aliud* is reducible to what is *per se* unless we establish that in every *per se* ordered series, what is *per aliud* in the series would be lacking the causality of the series without a *per se* source. Knasas has asked, in "The Analytical Thomist and the Paradoxical Aquinas," 84–85, how one can entertain the possibility of an infinite regress in light of the priority of *esse*. I would suggest that, in this context, the priority of *esse* rests on the knowledge of some *per se* source of *esse*. Hence the priority of *esse* rests on the conclusion that a *per se* source exists, in which case the priority of *esse* itself cannot justify the principle that what is *per aliud* is reducible to what is *per se*, since the latter principle itself is used to establish the existence of a *per se* source and thus the priority of *esse*. Therefore, we need a proof of the principle that what is *per aliud* is reducible to what is *per se*, and this proof is the denial of an infinite regress in *per se* ordered series.

each other, since there are differences in the way that Aquinas on different occasions justifies various premises; yet in affirming the latter, we should not overlook the remarkable commonalities found among Aquinas's proofs, both in argumentative structure and even down to the wording of the premises.[30]

As I see it, there are four general categories under which Aquinas's proofs of God can be considered; they are: (i) arguments from motion, (ii) arguments from causality, (iii) arguments from modality, and (iv) arguments from actuality/*esse* itself. Arguments from motion are very familiar in Aquinas's work and they begin by observing that things are moved. Invoking the Aristotelian principle that whatever is moved is moved by another, the argument proceeds to set up a series of moved movers, and through denial of an infinite regress of such movers the argument concludes to a prime mover not moved by another.

Arguments from causality focus on the causal efficacy that a thing has. These arguments reason that such causal efficacy is not possessed by the thing essentially and so a cause is required for such causality. By denial of an infinite regress of causes the argument arrives at a primary cause without which there would be no such causal efficacy. As I see it, argumentation from causality is not restricted to efficient causality, but pertains also to final causality; in his ways from the order/providence/finality of creatures, Thomas reasons that the activity of creatures for some goal or purpose would be lacking were there not some primary final cause causing that activity.[31]

Arguments from modality are familiar from the Third Way and the proof in *SCG* I, c. 15. In these arguments Thomas reasons that the

---

30. For a chronological list of the proofs that Aquinas offers, see Jules A. Baisnée, "St. Thomas Aquinas's Proofs for the Existence of God Presented in their Chronological Order," in *Philosophical Studies in Honor of the Very Reverend Ignatius Smith*, ed. John K. Ryan (Westminster, MD: Newman Press, 1952), 29–64. I would slightly amend Baisnée's list here by excluding some of the arguments; this is because he includes arguments for God's unity, eternity, etc., which appear to me to presuppose a proof of God already offered rather than offering a stand-alone proof.

31. In this respect, my categorization differs from Baisnée's insofar as he lists the arguments from the order of the world as independent from arguments from causality. I have defended reading the Fifth Way as a causal proof in "Design Arguments and Aquinas's Fifth Way," *The Thomist* 82, no. 3 (2019): 447–71; also, I have argued that all efficient causality presupposes some primary final cause in "Essentially Ordered Series Reconsidered Once Again." See also Edward Feser, "Between Aristotle and William Paley: Aquinas's Fifth Way," *Nova et Vetera* 11, no. 3 (2013): 707–49.

existence of whatever is possible to be and not to be points to the existence of some necessary being; and given such a necessary being, its necessity is either from another or absolute. If from another, there must be a cause of such necessity, whence Thomas denies an infinite regress of causes and thereby arrives at some absolutely necessary being that is primary and cause of all else.

Arguments from actuality/*esse* consider actuality or *esse* itself, observe its *per aliud* character and through the denial of an infinite regress arrive at something that is actual/*esse per se*. I include in this group arguments based on the degrees of being, because in all such arguments Thomas isolates some metaphysical feature(s) possessed by a thing in terms of its actuality. Accordingly, such things are limited in being because they are limited in actuality and thereby depend on what is not so limited, that is, on what is *per se*.[32] Arguments in this group most clearly exhibit Aquinas's way to God.

These summaries in no way articulate the subtle and delicate moves that Thomas makes in the various arguments that fall under them; indeed, in some individual instances of his argumentation Thomas can be accused of making a serious mistake, for example, the so-called shift fallacy in the Third Way, that he does not make when the same argument reappears elsewhere, for example, *SCG* I, c. 5. I present these argument forms here because I believe that they categorize all the various arguments for God's existence that Thomas offers.

Given the foregoing categorization, I think they all manifest what I have called Aquinas's way to God. This is because in each argument form Aquinas takes some derived or dependent feature that a thing has nonessentially and thus *per aliud* and thence reasons to some primary *per se* source on which all such depend. Furthermore, I think argument forms (ii)–(iv) can be considered metaphysical arguments. This is because the consideration of causality, modality, and actuality all pertain to the consideration of a thing's being, as opposed to its being in motion. Hence, such forms of argument are not physical arguments drawn from the philosophy of nature, but metaphysical arguments.[33] However, the

---

32. For my interpretation of the Fourth Way in this regard see "A Reconsideration of Aquinas's Fourth Way." Given this categorization, we can include herein many of the standalone arguments that Baisnée outlines, thereby revealing this form of argumentation to be the one most frequently offered by Aquinas.

33. With regard to the argument from causality, while it is the case that the philosopher of

argument from motion can be taken as a challenge to what I take to be Aquinas's *metaphysical* way to God, and this is the case because on some readings of the argument, it is one made within the philosophy of nature.

Recent work engaging with the argument from motion has made the case that it is a metaphysical argument concerned with act and potency.[34] This work follows that of Owens who argued that the actuality at stake in the *prima via* and in the argument from motion more generally is that of metaphysical act. If we look initially at the *prima via*, we see there that while Thomas adverts to motion as manifest, he quickly moves to the consideration of motion in terms of act and potency. From there he proceeds to justify the principle that whatever is moved is moved by another. His reasoning is that if something is moved, it stands in potency in some respect, and in being moved its potency is actualized. Now, while this notion of actualized potency is in accord with the general account of motion given in *Physics* II, Thomas gives no indication in the *prima via* that he restricts it to physical motion. Thus, we can take Thomas to be reasoning in the *prima via* on the basis of the actualization of any potency, in which case what is at stake is not some physical motion dealt with in the science that deals with *ens mobile*, but the actualization of potency as such, dealt with in the science that deals with *ens commune*.

With the latter in mind, then, the moved movers in the *prima via* are beings that are in act and so can move others, but they are not pure actuality, since they have been moved/actualized. Hence, when Thomas reasons to a primary mover, he reasons to something that is in potency in no respect; for if it were, it would be a moved mover and not the prime mover.

Not only is this reading of the *prima via* in accord with what I have termed Aquinas's way to God, it is also eminently metaphysical insofar as

---

nature does consider the causes of things, Thomas is explicit that he does not consider them *qua* causes, that is, in terms of their causality; rather, the philosopher of nature considers causes as causes of this and that, but not in terms of the causal actuality that they have. See Aquinas, *In Phys.* II.5, n. 176.

34. See David Twetten, "Clearing a Way for Aquinas: How the Proof from Motion Concludes to God," *Proceedings of the American Catholic Philosophical Quarterly* 70 (1996): 259–78; Wippel, *Metaphysical Thought*, 446–47; Knasas, *Thomistic Existentialism*, 176–77; and Gaven Kerr, "A Deeper Look at Aquinas's First Way," in *Collected Articles on the Existence of God*, chap. 7. For a more general consideration of the argument from motion heavily influenced by both Aristotle and Aquinas and indeed presenting it as a metaphysical argument, see Edward Feser, *Five Proofs for the Existence of God* (San Francisco, CA: Ignatius Press, 2017), chap. 1.

its concern is with the actualization of potency *per se*, and not just as the latter is manifest in some physical motion. Understood in these terms, the argument from motion does not threaten the contention here that Aquinas's way to God is a metaphysical way.

Nevertheless, the *Summa contra Gentiles* does raise a thorny problem. Therein Thomas offers us his most in-depth treatment of the argument from motion (and indeed of any argument for God's existence); and while the metaphysical reasoning pertaining to act and potency is not absent from that treatment, it is to be found in the company of the more physical reasoning found in *Physics* VII and VIII. One might argue that the *Summa contra Gentiles* offers a clear counterexample to what I am arguing regarding the argument from motion.

I have argued elsewhere that the disproportionate length devoted to the argument from motion in the *Summa contra Gentiles* discloses Thomas's discomfort with the argument.[35] In *SCG* I, c. 13, Thomas offers five proofs for God's existence, the first two are from motion and they run to 2,281 (Latin) words, whereas the remaining three arguments run to 268 words. By comparison, the five ways run to 773 words in total. Accordingly, the space devoted to just the first two arguments from motion in the *Summa contra Gentiles* is almost nine times the space devoted to the remaining three ways, and almost three times the space given over to the five ways in the *Summa theologiae*. An account of why this is the case will take us too far off target here, but a plausible reason is that, given the context of writing, Thomas adopts a more explicitly Aristotelian and thereby physical approach in the *Summa contra Gentiles*, an approach that, while not denying the metaphysical stature of the argument from motion, focuses on the more physical argumentation to convince other, non-Catholic, Aristotelians.

Furthermore, it should be noted that in the *Summa contra Gentiles*, Thomas himself holds that even when we establish a prime mover on the basis of the physical argumentation, we need to appeal to metaphysical reasoning to show that this is a wholly separate unmoved mover.[36] In this

---

35. See "The *Summa Contra Gentiles* and Aquinas's Way to God," in *Collected Articles on the Existence of God*, chap. 6.
36. *SCG* I, c. 13 (Marietti 4): "Sed quia Deus non est pars alicuius moventis seipsum, ulterius Aristoteles, in sua metaphysica, investigat ex hoc motore qui est pars moventis seipsum, alium motorem separatum omnino, qui est Deus. Cum enim omne movens seipsum moveatur per appetitum, oportet quod motor qui est pars moventis seipsum, moveat propter appetitum

regard, Twetten notes that Thomas's various redactions of c. 13 reveal that the proof from motion leads to nothing more than a world soul, and so the argumentation requires augmentation from metaphysics.[37]

Finally, despite the emphasis on the physical argumentation in the *Summa contra Gentiles*, the metaphysical defense of each stage of the argument is not missing; and indeed, it is only these metaphysical defenses that are preserved in the later *prima via*. Hence, in incorporating such metaphysical reasoning within physical reasoning, the *SCG* proof does not limit itself to physical motion, and so can be taken to envisage the more streamlined argumentation offered later in the *prima via*.

Based on these considerations, I do not think the argument from motion in the *Summa contra Gentiles* offers a clear counterexample to the thesis that I have been advocating in this chapter, viz., that there is a metaphysical way to God in Aquinas's thought, a way that is schematic for all his various arguments and so can unify the different argument forms. As we have seen, this way to God is metaphysical and so in accord with what Aquinas holds independently about the demonstrability of God, it isolates some derived actuality in the thing, and it proceeds to reason to some *per se* source.

CONCLUSION

In this concluding note, I want to engage briefly with the issue of what exactly Thomas establishes in his way to God. I bring this up here because while it is not the focus of this chapter, it is somewhat relevant. On my reading, we can demonstrate that God exists because we can demonstrate that a primary cause exists without which there is nothing. As we have seen, we arrive at this conclusion by appeal to the *per aliud* character of creatures and their dependence on a *per se* source. The acknowledgment that this is God minimally involves the commitment to the view that whatever else God is, he is the primary cause from which all things come to be. In establishing that this exists, we establish that God exists.

Accordingly, Aquinas's way to God does not establish that some

---

alicuius appetibilis. Quod est eo superius in movendo: nam appetens est quodammodo movens motum; appetibile autem est movens omnino non motum. Oportet igitur esse primum motorem separatum omnino immobilem, qui Deus est."

37. Twetten, "Clearing a Way," 269.

instance of divinity exists, and then proceeds to carve out that instance of divinity as the only such instance with all the various divine attributes subsequently affirmed thereof. Rather, given that God on this account is the *per se* source of all that is, it would be absurd to hold that God's existence so established is only an instance of divinity; for what is *per se* is not subject to any kind of distinction, as otherwise there would be some degree to which it is not *per se*. That being the case, there is no distinction between essence and supposit in God; whereas such cannot be affirmed even of the angels, given that they are *per aliud* and thus are subject to the distinction of essence and supposit.[38] Hence, God is not simply an instance of divinity; he is divinity itself.

Consequently, if we have genuinely established the existence of what is *per se*, then we have established the existence of an utterly unique primary cause of all that is, which is God. This is not to say that there are no further things we can affirm about God, but that we do so on the basis of his being *per se*. Hence, we do not add proof upon proof on top of the demonstration of God's existence, but rather we deepen the furrow carved out already by that demonstration. Should there be some revelation of God to creatures that reveals something that cannot be directly established about God by natural reason, so much the better for our understanding of God not only as the primary cause of all that is, but also as the proper object of the assent of faith. Accordingly, the understanding of Aquinas's proofs of God offered in this chapter stands in contrast to a view that would hold that we only establish some instance of divinity, and that we gradually specify what that entails by additional proofs and ultimately by assent through faith to what God has revealed.[39]

---

38. It is true that Aquinas's general reasoning for this position turns on considerations of matter and form such that what is composed of matter and form is subject to distinction of supposit and essence; hence, the angels could be seen to be subsisting supposita in themselves. However, see the important discussion in *Quaestiones Quodlibetales* II.2.2, wherein Thomas argues that precisely insofar as even the angels are *per aliud* (or *per accidens*) they are subject to distinction of supposit and essence; for discussion see Wippel, *Metaphysical Thought*, 243–53, and my discussion of the same in *Aquinas and the Metaphysics of Creation*, chap. 5, §1.2.

39. See John O'Callaghan, "Can we Demonstrate that 'God Exists,'" *Nova et Vetera* 14, no. 2 (2016): 619–44. A full consideration of O'Callaghan's position would take me too far away from my primary concern in this paper, which is teasing out a unified way to God in Aquinas's thought. Nevertheless, the primary thrust of such a response would be to argue as I have above, that if we establish the existence of what is genuinely *per se*, then it is subject to no distinction in its being, and so no distinction of supposit and essence; this is something that can be said of no other being, in which case we have an utterly unique primary cause of all that is, not simply some instance of divinity.

Aquinas's proofs of God's existence cause both fascination and frustration in the nonspecialist reader. The arguments rely on a metaphysical backdrop that is often presupposed and only occasionally developed in the proof itself. Not only that, the proliferation of what are ostensibly different ways to God can often cause consternation in the reader who may wish for a unified approach to such a worthy topic. Msgr. Wippel has done the community of Thomistic scholars and the wider community of interested readers a great service in his systematic presentation of various metaphysical themes from the thought of Aquinas. Part of the appeal of Wippel's work is that he draws together Thomas's various disparate treatments of some metaphysical issue to present it as his (Thomas's) unified metaphysical view.

In this chapter I have sought to do something similar by discerning a common argumentative structure that I believe is to be found in Aquinas's various arguments for God's existence. While Wippel himself does not appear to endorse the view that there is a unifying theme to Aquinas's arguments for God's existence, and indeed in his consideration of the five ways he rejects a unified reading of them, I think it is nevertheless defensible to read Aquinas's proofs of God's existence in a more schematic fashion as moving from participated being to unparticipated being, a schema that can be applied to the various arguments that Thomas endorses. If this is correct, then what I have argued here falls within the spirit of Wippel's work in its endeavour to unearth just how profound and systematic a thinker St. Thomas actually was.

Brian Carl

10 ❧ The Kataphatic and Apophatic Propriety of '*Qui Est*'

INTRODUCTION

St. Thomas Aquinas famously characterizes 'he who is' (*qui est*) as the most proper name of God, tying the propriety of this name to his identification of God as *ipsum esse per se subsistens*.[1] The centrality of '*qui est*' and '*ipsum esse*' as divine names has consequently been commonly recognized by Thomas's interpreters, although this centrality has been understood in different ways, in accordance with varying emphases upon and interpretations of the positive and negative elements within Thomas's account of our knowing and naming God in this life.

On the more kataphatic extreme, it was a common thesis among Thomists from the late seventeenth to the early twentieth century that *ipsum esse subsistens* is the "formal constituent of the divine essence in our understanding" or the "metaphysical essence of God," playing a role in our knowledge of the divine essence in this life comparable to a difference or definition in our knowledge of a created essence, as the notion that distinguishes God from all creatures and serves as the root (*radix*) from which all the divine attributes can be derived, just as in the case of a creaturely essence properties are derived from a definition.[2] For these

---

1. Thomas mentions or discusses the propriety of '*qui est*' in *In Sent.* I, d. 8, q. 1, aa. 1 and 3; *SCG* I, c. 22; *Contra errores Graecorum* 1; *In De div. nom.* 5; *De pot.*, q. 7, a. 5; *ST* I, q. 13, a. 11. See also *Lectura Romana*, d. 2, q. 3, a. 3, ad 3. All translations are my own.
2. For some discussion of the history of the notion of a formal constituent of the divine nature among Thomists, see Brian T. Carl, "The Formal Constituent of the Divine Nature in Peter Ledesma, John of St. Thomas, and Vincent Contenson," *The Thomist* 82 (2018): 59–88.

Thomists, the divine self-revelation of God's name to Moses in Exodus 3:14 is taken to support their way of understanding the centrality of *esse* in human knowledge of God in this life.

In contrast, many interpreters over the last century have attributed a strict apophaticism to Thomas,[3] and the supreme propriety of the name '*qui est*' or the centrality of *ipsum esse* can be understood in apophatic terms.[4] Aiding this interpretation, we find in Thomas's earliest treatment of the propriety of '*esse*' and '*qui est*' as divine names that the knowledge of God as *qui est* is characterized as a penultimate step in the progress of the *via remotionis*, which terminates in the intellect's remaining "in a shadow of ignorance" in which it can be joined to God "in the darkness in which God is said to dwell." In this penultimate step, it is known only that God is, but we have left behind all other more determinate names, leaving the intellect "in a certain confusion."[5]

The more fundamental question regarding whether human beings *in statu viae* can attain any positive knowledge concerning the divine essence has long occupied the attention of Thomas's interpreters.[6] This

---

3. See, e.g., Antonin-Gilbert Sertillanges, *Les grandes thèses de la philosophie thomiste* (Paris: Bloud and Gay, 1928), 67–80; Anton Pegis, "Penitus Manet Ignotum," *Mediaeval Studies* 27 (1965): 212–26; Herbert McCabe, "The Logic of Mysticism," in *God Still Matters*, ed. Brian Davies, OP (London: Continuum, 2002), 13–28; David Burrell, *Aquinas: God and Action*, 3rd ed. (Eugene, OR: Wipf and Stock, 2016); J. B. M. Wissink, "Aquinas: The Theologian of Negative Theology," *Jaarboek Thomas Instituut te Utrecht* (1993): 15–83; Herwi M. Rikhof, "Thomas at Utrecht," in *Contemplating Aquinas: On the Varieties of Interpretation*, ed. Fergus Kerr, OP (Notre Dame, IN: University of Notre Dame Press, 2003), 105–36.

4. For an influential treatment, see Burrell, *Aquinas: God and Action*, 47–61. I would suggest that there are sometimes echoes of the Thomist position (held in the seventeenth through twentieth centuries) concerning the "metaphysical essence" of God found even among interpreters who attribute a strict apophaticism to Thomas, by the claim that everything further said about God can be derived from the claim that in God essence and *esse* are identical. See, e.g., David Burrell, *Knowing the Unknowable God*, 49 and 59–61, in which Burrell points to the identity of essence and *esse* in God as the conclusion about God from which "are derived the consequent formal features, as well as every essential attribute" (59).

5. *In Sent.* I, d. 8, q. 1, a. 1, ad 4. Joseph Owens devotes a study to the exposition of this text. See Joseph Owens, "Aquinas—'Darkness of Ignorance' in the Most Refined Notion of God," *The Southwestern Journal of Philosophy* 5, no. 2 (1974): 93–110.

6. John F. Wippel, "Quidditative Knowledge of God," in *Metaphysical Themes in Thomas Aquinas* (Washington, DC: The Catholic University of America Press, 1984), 215–41. For some treatment of the history of this dispute from Thomas to Sylvester of Ferrara, see Igor Agostini, "The Knowledge of God's *Quid Sit* in Dominican Theology: From Saint Thomas to Ferrariensis," *American Catholic Philosophical Quarterly* 93, no. 2 (2019): 191–210. There was early occasion for dispute about Thomas's position on this question due to the presence in the 1277 Parisian condemnation of the proposition "Quod de Deo non potest cognosci nisi quia ipse est, sive ipsum esse," which was likely directed against Thomas's view. For discussion, see John F.

debate centers upon what sort of knowledge about the divine nature is expressed through positive divine names like 'goodness' and 'wisdom,' names that Thomas says are predicated properly of God. The characterization of *'qui est'* as the most proper divine name is made by way of comparison to these other names. The present study will examine Thomas's treatments of *'qui est'* in light of this debate.[7] Wippel has made an important contribution to this debate by calling attention to certain developments in Thomas's thinking over the course of his career. This study will suggest that some of the developments in Thomas's treatments of the propriety of *'qui est'* can be understood in light of Wippel's claims.[8]

As I will show, Thomas's explanation of the supreme propriety of *'qui est,'* particularly in his most mature treatment in *ST* I, q. 13, a. 11, balances the positive and negative elements in his understanding of our knowing and naming God, particularly in its use of the distinction between *res significata* and *modus significandi*. This study will proceed in four parts. In the first, I will provide a brief overview of the debate among Thomas's interpreters concerning the possibility of positive knowledge concerning the divine essence *in statu viae*. The second part will introduce Thomas's discussion and defense of the supreme propriety of *'qui est'* as a divine name in *ST*, articulating a number of interpretive questions concerning the argumentative structure of this text and the meaning of its conclusion. In the third part, I will examine a parallel treatment of the question of the supreme propriety of *qui est* from Thomas's early *Sentences* commentary, as I will argue that this text furnishes several interpretive keys for answering the questions raised concerning *ST* I, q. 13, a. 11. The fourth part will analyze the *ST* text, concluding that its "threefold" argument establishes the uniquely supreme propriety of *qui est* insofar as this name is least improper, for apophatic reasons, among the positive names said properly of God. In the conclusion, I will suggest that Wippel's thesis about development in Thomas's views about our positive knowledge concerning God *in statu viae* help to explain the parallel developments in his treatment of the propriety of *qui est*.

Wippel, "Thomas Aquinas and the Condemnation of 1277," *The Modern Schoolman* 72, no. 1 (1995): 266–67.

7. The connection between these themes is suggested by *De pot.*, q. 7, a. 5, which addresses directly the question of whether positive divine names signify the divine essence and concludes with a discussion of the supreme propriety of *'qui est.'*

8. Wippel, "Quidditative Knowledge of God."

THOMAS AQUINAS AND POSITIVE KNOWLEDGE ABOUT GOD *IN STATU VIAE*

We find in Thomas's writings many statements that seem strictly apophatic. Thomas asserts that the highest knowledge we attain of God is to know that he exceeds our understanding, and he insists that despite any progress we make in our understanding, what God is remains entirely unknown to us.[9] Throughout his career, he tells us that we are limited to understanding *that* God is without ever grasping *what* he is.[10] Many interpreters of St. Thomas over the last century have emphasized these apophatic elements in his philosophical theology to the exclusion of any claim that we attain some positive knowledge about God's essence *in statu viae*.[11]

Maritain and Wippel, by contrast, stand out as prominent advocates for the view that Thomas allows for a positive (albeit imperfect) knowledge of the divine essence through knowing divine attributes like goodness and wisdom. Wippel documents that although Thomas denies throughout his career that human beings can attain knowledge in this life of what God is in himself, in his mature writings Thomas also contends that positive divine names like goodness and wisdom signify the divine essence and are predicated essentially of God. On Wippel's view, when Thomas says that we cannot know what God is, he is denying that we can in this life attain any definitional or comprehensive knowledge of the divine essence.[12] Wippel maintains that this is a matter regarding which there is some development over the course of Thomas's career, such that Thomas's mature assertions about our positive knowledge regarding the divine essence serve to soften the claims, particularly pronounced in earlier texts, that God's essence remains entirely unknown to us.[13]

How do those who interpret Thomas in more strictly apophatic terms interpret these assertions about positive, proper divine names said

---

9. *In De Trin.*, q. 1, a. 2, ad 1; *De ver.*, q. 2, a. 1, ad 9; *De pot.*, q. 7, a. 5, ad 14.

10. *In Sent.* I, d. 8, q. 1, a. 1, and d. 34, q. 3, a. 1; *In De Trin.*, q. 1, a. 2, ad 1; *De ver.*, q. 2, a. 1, obj. 9 and ad 9; *SCG* III, c. 41; and *ST* I, q. 2, a. 1.

11. See note 3 above.

12. For support for this interpretation, see *De pot.*, q. 7, a. 5, ad 6 (Marietti 199–200): "Deus non potest nominari nomine substantiam ipsius definiente vel comprehendente vel adaequante: sic enim de Deo ignoramus quid est."

13. See Wippel, "Quidditative Knowledge of God," 228.

essentially of God? To take one influential source,[14] Burrell contends that all of the perfection terms that Thomas holds can be properly predicated of God are terms that are of themselves "inherently analogous in structure."[15] For example, Burrell explains that we are able to predicate the term 'living' of God precisely because we recognize that we can use this term "to express many ways of being alive, without thereby exhausting the range of this term." On Burrell's view, this is what allows us to assert that God is living, without making any claim that we understand what we mean by this.[16] We find a similar approach in Davies, for example in his use of Geach's claim that 'good' is a logically attributive adjective, a term whose meaning is always a function of the subject of which it is predicated: we can affirm that God is good (and is his goodness) without suggesting that we understand what it is for God to be good.[17]

For Burrell, the centrality of the identification of God's essence with *esse* is also an expression of Thomas's apophaticism. Unlike the inherently analogous perfection terms that we can grasp in their range of meanings, in no case can we conceptualize what *esse* is. For this reason, to identify God as *esse* is only to assert that "God *is* what it is for God-language to obtain."[18] We do not in fact possess "a God-language," but only "some very general remarks about its syntax."[19] Consequently, Thomas's identification of God as *ipsum esse* in no way contradicts the apophatic assertion that we are entirely ignorant of God's essence. On Burrell's account, it is precisely the inherently analogous character of perfection terms and the nonconceptual character of *esse* that permit the "proper" predication of these terms of God, as terms that can be predicated while we can still profess ignorance about what it means to say that

---

14. Herwi Rikhof, "Thomas at Utrecht," 108: "In particular, Burrell's analysis of the opening of the *Summa theologiae* has influenced profoundly the way Thomas is read at Utrecht."

15. Burrell, *Aquinas: God and Action*, 76. See Rikhof, "Thomas at Utrecht," 126–27. Although I will not explore this point in this chapter, I would suggest that if terms like 'wise' and 'just' are in fact univocal in the creaturely applications that are the *a quo nomen imponitur* from which these divine names are taken, then this reliance upon the inherently analogous character of all perfection terms is a potential weakness in Burrell's and Rikhof's account, along with that of Davies.

16. Rikhof, "Thomas at Utrecht," 72–73.

17. See Brian Davies, *Thomas Aquinas's "Summa Theologiae": A Guide and Commentary* (Oxford: Oxford University Press, 2014), 53.

18. Burrell, *Aquinas: God and Action*, 55.

19. Ibid.

God is living or that God is *esse*. For Burrell, then, the propriety of both perfection terms like goodness and wisdom and that of *esse* thus reflects Thomas's apophaticism.

At an opposite extreme from Burrell's apophatic reading of *ipsum esse*, there is the position of Thomists from the late seventeenth into the early twentieth century who characterize *ipsum esse subsistens* as the formal constituent of the divine essence in our understanding. For these Thomists, *ipsum esse subsistens* formally constitutes the divine essence insofar as this notion both distinguishes God from all creatures and serves as the root (*radix*) from which all of the divine attributes can be derived, just as in the case of a creaturely essence the properties are derived from the definition or difference.[20] In this way, *ipsum esse subsistens* is understood to radically unify (i.e., unify in their *radix*) our knowledge of the divine essence, just as a difference or definition radically unifies knowledge of a created essence. These Thomists thus understand the centrality of *esse* in human knowledge of God by an explicit analogy with the sort of perfect quidditative knowledge expressed by a definition from which properties can be demonstrated. On this interpretation of Thomas's philosophical theology, the sort of reasoning presented in the second argument of *ST* I, q. 4, a. 2—which argues that *ipsum esse subsistens* must possess every perfection—is the avenue through which one concludes that every pure perfection belongs properly to God.[21] On this interpretation, it is what the notion of *ipsum esse* positively contains or implies that makes it the supremely proper name of God.

It will become apparent from what follows that Thomas's reasons for the supreme propriety of *qui est* are quite different from those who characterize *ipsum esse* as the formal constituent of the divine essence. It is not my purpose in this chapter to enter at length into the dispute concerning the positive signification of the divine attributes, but I will

20. For an account of some of the history of this notion of a "formal constituent of the divine essence in our understanding" among Aquinas's commentators, see Brian Carl, "The Formal Constituent of the Divine Nature in Peter Ledesma, John of St. Thomas, and Vincent Contenson," *The Thomist* 82 (2018): 59–88.

21. A similar emphasis upon the centrality of universal perfection (as the avenue through which Thomas proceeds to argue for the attribution of perfections to God) is found in Norman Kretzmann, *The Metaphysics of Theism: Aquinas's Natural Theology in "Summa Contra Gentiles" I* (Oxford: Clarendon Press, 1997). Burrell, by contrast, passes over *ST* I, q. 4, a. 2, without remark in his discussion of q. 4 and in his chapter devoted to *esse* as a divine name. See Burrell, *Aquinas: God and Action*, 29–30 and 47–61.

suggest that some of the points of development and clarification in Thomas's mature treatment of *qui est* could lend support to Wippel's claim about the development in Thomas's thinking, concerning that more fundamental question.

QUESTIONS CONCERNING THE SUPREME PROPRIETY OF 'QUI EST'

The question about the supremely proper name of God is not original to Thomas,[22] as it is a question directly inspired by the contents of Damascene's *De fide orthodoxa* 1.9.[23] In addition to identifying *qui est* as the supremely proper name of God, Thomas also refers to this scriptural name as first (*principalius*) among the divine names, quoting Damascene.[24] Three central candidates for the status of *maxime proprium nomen Dei* in *ST* I, q. 13, a. 11—'*qui est*,' '*Deus*,' and '*bonus*'—are all discussed in Burgundio's Latin translation of the *De fide orthodoxa*. The Burgundio translation of *De fide orthodoxa* 1.9 includes a remark indicating that Dionysius offers 'good' as the first divine name, with an assertion of the equal priority of this name with the name '*qui est*.' The Kotter critical edition of the Greek text identifies this remark about Dionysius as an addition in a minority of Greek manuscripts.[25] Thomas thus derives the question about the most proper divine name (and the broad outlines of his answer to this question) ultimately from Damascene, but more precisely from the Latin Damascene.

Thomas introduces *ST* I, q. 13, a. 11, with the claim that the name '*qui est*' "is for a threefold reason the supremely proper name of God." Three questions should be raised here. First, I have used here the definite article, *the* supremely proper name of God. But it will be worth considering,

---

22. Thomas is indebted to earlier *Sentences* commentaries and likely to the *Summa fratris Alexandri*, lib. 1, par. 2, inq. 2, tr. 1, q. 1, cap. 2, a. 2 (Quaracchi 522–23), for the explicit formulation of this question, ultimately inspired by the text of Damascene. See Armand Maurer, "St. Thomas on the Sacred Name 'Tetragrammaton,'" *Mediaeval Studies* 34 (1972): 275, reprinted in *Being and Knowing*, 59.

23. For Damascene, I cite the book and chapter division found in the Buytaert critical edition of the Latin translation by Burgundio.

24. *De fide orthodoxa* 1.9 (Buytaert 48–49): "Igitur videtur quidem omnibus principalius eorum quae in Deo dicuntur nominibus esse 'qui est,' quemadmodum 'ipse oraculo loquens Moysi in monte,' ait: 'Dic filiis Israel: Qui est misit me.'"

25. See *Expositio Fidei*, in *Die Schriften des Johannes von Damaskos*, vol. 2, ed. Kotter (Berlin: Walter de Gruyter, 1969), 31.

as the argumentation of a. 11 unfolds, whether or when St. Thomas's argumentation establishes that *qui est* holds a singular status among divine names. Supremacy or "maximality" does not necessarily imply that something stands alone at the top.[26] Although I will continue to use a definite article, speaking of *the most proper* or *the supremely proper* divine name, this question should be borne in mind: at what point does Thomas's argumentation actually establish the uniquely supreme propriety of '*qui est*'?

Second, as Cajetan points out in his commentary, it is unclear on its face whether the three arguments in the body of a. 11 stand as three independent arguments for the same conclusion or as arguments for the propriety of '*qui est*' in three different respects.[27] As I will explain below, St. Thomas's "threefold reason" is in fact a single argument in three stages, with each stage establishing one of three complementary respects in which '*qui est*' is supremely proper.

Third, complicating matters further, it is unclear in what sense the term 'proper' is to be understood when it is said that '*qui est*' is the most proper divine name. Within q. 13, Thomas has already employed *nomen proprium* in more than one sense, sometimes as the opposite of a common (or appellative) name,[28] sometimes as the opposite of a metaphorical name.[29] Recognizing that Thomas's purpose in a. 11 is to defend a traditional claim made by Damascene that stands in apparent tension with Dionysius, who offers "good" as the first divine name, we might refrain from insisting that Thomas means anything particularly precise by *nomen proprium* in this context.

We could simply take *proprium* in a broad, nontechnical sense as "appropriate" or "fitting,"[30] a suggestion for which one could claim at

---

26. See *In De div. nom.* 11.1 and 11.4 for Thomas's use, in commenting on Dionysius, of *superus* and *maxime* to speak about a multiplicity of creatures that are supreme or maximal in their participation of certain perfections. My thanks to Gyula Klima for pointing me towards these texts.

27. Cajetan, *Commentarius* 1.13.11 (Leon. 4.163).

28. *ST* I, q. 13, a. 9, ad 2 (Leon. 4.159): "Hoc nomen Deus est nomen appellativum, et non proprium, quia significat naturam divinam ut in habente; licet ipse Deus, secundum rem, non sit nec universalis nec particularis." In this sense, 'God' is not a proper name at all.

29. *ST* I, q. 13, a. 3, esp. ad 1 and ad 3.

30. Armand Maurer, for example, renders *maxime proprium* in the space of one paragraph as "most appropriate," "most suitable," and "most fitting." See Armand Maurer, "St. Thomas on the Sacred Name 'Tetragrammaton,'" *Mediaeval Studies* 34 (1972): 275, reprinted in *Being and Knowing*, 59. See R. E. Houser, "Introducing the Principles of Avicennian Metaphysics into

least some textual support.[31] But when we say that it is more or less appropriate, fitting, or proper to refer to someone or something in a given way, this is often as a matter of social convention and of showing due respect. In many cases, however, in this sense of propriety it is inappropriate to address or refer to someone by his proper or personal name. Concern for this sort of propriety is not entirely foreign to the matters discussed in a. 11, as St. Thomas is aware that the tetragrammaton, to which he refers in a. 11, ad 1, is not pronounced by Jews—and by calling it the tetragrammaton, he also refrains from pronouncing it—but he tells us that the tetragrammaton is a most proper name, "imposed to signify the incommunicable (and, as if one should so speak, singular) substance of God." St. Thomas thus does not seem to use the term *proprium* in the sense of what is socially proper and respectful. As I think terms like "fitting" and "appropriate" call to mind the sense of what is conventionally proper, I will generally avoid them. It remains to be clarified, then, what St. Thomas means in calling the divine name '*qui est*' supremely proper.

AQUINAS'S EARLY TREATMENT OF THE PROPRIETY OF '*QUI EST*'

Before examining the argumentation in *ST* I, q. 13, a. 11, and looking for answers to these questions, it will be helpful to consider the arguments in Thomas's earliest treatment of the propriety of '*qui est*,' found in two articles of his *Sentences* commentary (*In Sent.* I, d. 8, q. 1, aa. 1 and 3). The former article asks whether *esse* is said properly of God, but the body of the article is devoted to arguing for the supreme propriety of '*qui est*'; the latter article (a famous text for Thomas's treatment of the transcendentals) asks whether '*qui est*' is first among the divine names, and it focuses on the priority of '*qui est*' in comparison to the names 'one,' 'true,' and 'good.'

Sacra Doctrina: Thomas Aquinas, *Scriptum super Sententiarum*, Bk. 1, d. 8," *American Catholic Philosophical Quarterly* 88, no. 2 (2014): 207.

31. See *De pot.*, q. 7, a. 5, in which Thomas refers to *qui est* as the name that supremely befits or belongs to God (Marietti 199): "Et propter hoc, nomen qui est, maxime Deo competit, quia non determinat aliquam formam Deo, sed significat esse indeterminate." Instead of saying that '*qui est*' is "most proper," Thomas says here that it "supremely befits" God. Thomas's brief argument is interesting, as it combines elements from the first and second stages of argumentation in *ST* I, q. 13, a. 11. See also *In Sent.* I, d. 8, q. 1, a. 1, ad 3, treated below, in which St. Thomas concludes that God is "more worthily" (*dignius*) named by '*qui est*.'

In *In Sent.* I, d. 8, q. 1, a. 1, Thomas advances four independent arguments in defense of the claim that '*qui est*' is the "maxime proprium nomen Dei." In the first, he appeals to the divine eternity, which knows neither past nor future and so is perfect in its *esse* in comparison to the *esse* of temporal creatures who lack what was and what will be; for this reason, it is proper to God, in comparison to others, *to be*.[32] The notion of perfection employed here is taken ultimately from Aristotle, that what is perfect lacks nothing or "has nothing of itself outside of it"; although he does not mention Boethius, Thomas also clearly has in mind the Boethian definition of eternity.[33]

The second argument of a. 1 appeals to Damascene's claim that *qui est* signifies *esse* indeterminately and not what something is; and "since in the present life we know only that [God] is and not what He is, except by negation," it follows that God will most properly be named '*qui est*.'[34] This argument is clearly apophatic in character: it is more proper to name God by a name that does not signify quiddity, because we do not in this life know the divine quiddity.

In his third argument, Thomas appeals to Dionysius, "who says that, among all other participations in divine goodness, such as life and understanding and others of this sort, *esse* is the first and as it were the principle of the others, containing (*praehabens*) in itself all the aforementioned [participations] according to a certain united mode."[35] That the containment of all other participated perfections in *esse* implies the priority of *esse* as a divine name would appear, among the arguments advanced here by Thomas, to be the most compatible with the position of the later Thomists who identify *ipsum esse* as the formal constituent of

---

32. *In Sent.* I, d. 8, q. 1, a. 1 (Mandonnet 1.195): "Prima sumitur ex littera ex verbis Hieronymi secundum perfectionem divini esse. Illud enim est perfectum cujus nihil est extra ipsum. Esse autem nostrum habet aliquid sui extra se: deest enim aliquid quod jam de ipso praeteriit, et quod futurum est. Sed in divino esse nihil praeteriit nec futurum est: et ideo totum esse suum habet perfectum, et propter hoc sibi proprie respect aliorum convenit esse."

33. Ibid. This characterization of perfection comes from *Physics* III.6.207a8–9.

34. *In Sent.* I, d. 8, q. 1, a. 1 (Mandonnet 1.195): "Secunda ratio sumitur ex verbis Damasceni, qui dicit quod qui est significat esse indeterminate et non quid est: et quia in statu viae hoc tantum de ipso cognoscimus, quia est, et non quid est, nisi per negationem, et non possumus nominare nisi secundum quod cognoscimus, ideo propriissime nominatur a nobis qui est."

35. Ibid.: "Tertia ratio sumitur ex verbis Dionysii, qui dicit, quod esse inter omnes alias divinae bonitatis participationes, sicut vivere et intelligere et hujusmodi, primum est, et quasi principium aliorum, praehabens in se omnia praedicta, secundum quemdam modum unita; et ita etiam Deus est principium divinum, et omnia sunt unum in ipso."

the divine essence insofar as it implies all of the other divine attributes.

Finally, in a fourth argument Thomas appeals to Avicenna for the claim that '*qui est*' and '*ens*' are both imposed from the act of being (*actus essendi*). Whereas anything whose quiddity is not identical with its own *esse* will be properly named from its quiddity but not from its *esse*, God is properly named by a name taken from *esse*, because his *esse* is his quiddity. For this reason, a name taken from *esse* "will be His proper name, just as the proper name of man is taken from his quiddity."[36]

It is only in the second argument—the one that is explicitly apophatic in character—that Thomas concludes that '*qui est*' is "most properly" God's name; in every other argument it is concluded somewhat more weakly that '*esse*' or '*qui est*' are "proper" or "a proper name," answering the question posed in the article of whether *esse* is said properly of God at all. The apparent difference in the force of the conclusions of these arguments raises the question of whether these other arguments in fact establish that '*qui est*' holds a unique status as *the* supremely proper name of God. I will suggest below that the same question needs to be posed concerning the various stages of argumentation in *ST* I, q. 13, a. 11; as this later text reproduces and refines some of the argumentation from *In Sent.* I, d. 8, q. 1, a. 1, I will leave aside answering this question concerning the arguments in the earlier text. Although I will also argue below that the *ST* text represents some important points of development and clarification in comparison to the *In Sent.* text, the *ST* text is difficult to interpret clearly without an awareness of some other details from the earlier presentation, particularly from the replies to objections. I will call attention to these details in my treatment of *ST* I, q. 13, a. 11.

Little needs to be said here about the treatment of '*qui est*' in *In Sent.* I, d. 8, q. 1, a. 3, which argues for the conceptual (*secundum rationem*) priority of being in comparison to 'good,' 'one,' and 'true.' As these four names "precede the other divine names absolutely according to the order of understanding, because of their universality," the conceptual priority

---

36. Ibid.: "Quarta ratio potest sumi ex verbis Avicennae in hunc modum, quod, cum in omni quod est sit considerare quidditatem suam, per quam subsistit in natura determinata, et esse suum, per quod dicitur de eo quod est in actu, hoc nomen res imponitur rei a quidditate sua, secundum Avicennam, hoc nomen quid est vel ens imponitur ab ipso actu essendi. Cum autem ita sit quod in quaelibet re creata essentia sua differat a suo esse, res illa proprie denominatur a quidditate sua, et non ab actu essendi, sicut homo ab humanitate. In Deo autem ipsum esse suum est sua quidditas: et ideo nomen quod sumitur ab esse proprie nominat ipsum, et est proprium nomen ejus: sicut proprium nomen hominis quod sumitur a quidditate sua."

of *'qui est'* makes it the first among the divine names, absolutely considered. Thomas does not indicate in this text why the greater universality of these names makes them prior as divine names, but we will find Thomas advancing a reason for the priority of these names (and of *'qui est'* among them) in *ST* I, q. 13, a. 11.[37]

THE PROPRIETY OF *'QUI EST'* IN *ST* I, Q. 13, A. 11

We can now turn to the contents of St. Thomas's "threefold argument" in *ST* I, q. 13, a. 11. I will briefly summarize the three stages of this article's argumentation and compare the structure of this article to its parallels in *In Sent.* I, d. 8, q. 1, aa. 1 and 3. The first argument (or the first stage of St. Thomas's threefold argument) establishes the propriety of *'qui est'* "on account of its signification." 'He who is' does not signify any form or nature, but existence itself (*ipsum esse*), because to say that something "is" is to signify the being or existence of that thing. But in God alone essence and *esse* are identical, "and so it is manifest that among other names this [name] most properly names God, for each thing is denominated from its form."[38] As with its parallel in the fourth argument of *In Sent.* I, d. 8, q. 1, a. 1, this argument appeals both to the identity of essence and *esse* within God and to a general principle that things are properly named from their quiddities.

The second stage of St. Thomas's argumentation appeals to the maximal universality of *'qui est'* (as compared to a name like 'wise,' which can be predicated of some things but not others) and to its conceptual priority among other maximally common names, such as 'one' and 'good.'

---

37. In his later *In De div. nom.*, Thomas finds in Dionysius the connection between the priority of certain positive divine names and their greater universality among creatures, identifying this as the fundamental rationale for the order of cc. 5–8 of *On the Divine Names*. See *In De div. nom.* 4.1, n. 263 (Marietti 87): "Si autem ipsae res in se considerentur: primum et communius, quod in eis invenitur, est esse; secundo, vivere; tertio, cognoscere; quarto iustum esse vel virtuosum. Et secundum hunc ordinem, de divinis nominibus prosequitur: primo quidem post bonum, de ente in 50 capitulo; secundo, de vita in 60; tertio, de sapientia in 70; quarto, de virtute et iustitia in 80." See Albertus Magnus, *Super Dionysii Mysticam Theologiam* 2 (Cologne 37/2.465) for a characterization of affirmative theology as proceeding according to the order of the "first and noblest" of perfections.

38. *ST* I, q. 13, a. 11 (Leon. 4.162): "Primo quidem, propter sui significationem. Non enim significat formam aliquam, sed ipsum esse. Unde, cum esse Dei sit ipsa eius essentia, et hoc nulli alii conveniat, ut supra ostensum est, manifestum est quod inter alia nomina hoc maxime proprie nominat Deum, unumquodque enim denominatur a sua forma."

The Kataphatic and Apophatic Propriety of 'Qui Est' 309

These transcendental terms are convertible with 'being' and signify a perfection really identical with being, but they add something conceptually distinct (*secundum rationem*) to 'being.' Both the names that are less universal than *esse* and the names that are convertible with it thus "in a certain way inform and determine [*esse*]." Because our intellect cannot in this life grasp the divine essence as it is in itself, "whatever mode the intellect may determine about what it understands of God, it falls short of the mode in which God exists in Himself." It follows that the less determinate a name, the more properly it is said of God. '*Qui est*' is therefore maximally proper insofar as it is most indeterminate.[39]

As with its parallel in the apophatic second argument of *In Sent.* I, d. 8, q. 1, a. 1, Thomas here points to the fact that we cannot in this life understand what God is in order to conclude that a less determinate divine name will be more proper. The argumentation of *In Sent.* I, d. 8, q. 1, a. 3, concerning the conceptual priority of *qui est* in relation to other transcendental terms is folded into this second argument by regarding conceptual addition to *ens* as a sort of informing and determining of *esse*. Finally, the third stage of argumentation in *ST* I, q. 13, a. 11, parallels the first argument of *In Sent.* I, d. 8, q. 1, a. 1, but it differs somewhat in its formulation by appealing to the fact that '*qui est*' consignifies present time, which befits divine eternity, which "knows neither past nor future, as Augustine says."[40] The parallel in a. 1 had made no mention of the notion of consignification.

The parallels to the arguments in the earlier *In Sent.* (a. 1) thus appear in reverse order in *ST* I, q. 13, a. 11. This later text also lacks any parallel

---

39. Ibid.: "Secundo, propter eius universalitatem. Omnia enim alia nomina vel sunt minus communia; vel, si convertantur cum ipso, tamen addunt aliqua supra ipsum secundum rationem; unde quodammodo informant et determinant ipsum. Intellectus autem noster non potest ipsam Dei essentiam cognoscere in statu viae, secundum quod in se est, sed quemcumque modum determinet circa id quod de Deo intelligit, deficit a modo quo Deus in se est. Et ideo, quanto aliqua nomina sunt minus determinata, et magis communia et absoluta, tanto magis proprie dicuntur de Deo a nobis. Unde et Damascenus dicit quod principalius omnibus quae de Deo dicuntur nominibus, est qui est, totum enim in seipso comprehendens, habet ipsum esse velut quoddam pelagus substantiae infinitum et indeterminatum. Quolibet enim alio nomine determinatur aliquis modus substantiae rei, sed hoc nomen qui est nullum modum essendi determinat, sed se habet indeterminate ad omnes; et ideo nominat ipsum pelagus substantiae infinitum."

40. Ibid.: "Tertio vero, ex eius consignificatione. Significat enim esse in praesenti, et hoc maxime proprie de Deo dicitur, cuius esse non novit praeteritum vel futurum, ut dicit Augustinus in V de Trin."

to the earlier text's third argument, which had appealed to the Dionysian notion that *esse* "pre-contains" all other perfections. Whereas the four arguments of *In Sent.* I, d. 8, q. 1, a. 1, also seem to stand independently of one another, I have indicated that the three arguments in *ST* I, q. 13, a. 11, constitute one ordered argument in three stages, a claim I will now defend.

The three stages of argumentation in a. 11 appeal, in turn, to "signification," "universality," and "consignification" as three respects in which '*qui est*' is supremely proper as a name of God. Signification and consignification are evidently related to one another, but how is "universality" related to them?[41] Offering a critical clue, St. Thomas claims in the reply to the first objection that the name '*qui est*' "is a more proper name of God … with respect to that from which it is imposed, namely from *esse*, and with regard to the mode of signifying and of consignifying, as was said."[42] That *esse* is the *a quo nomen imponitur* of the name '*qui est*' is part of the first stage of argumentation; and that '*qui est*' is most proper with respect to the consignification of the name is explicitly claimed in the third stage. This suggests, then, that the argument concerned with the maximal universality of '*qui est*'—and with its conceptual priority among names convertible with it—is somehow tied up with its propriety "with respect to the mode of signifying." But how so?

Here the reply to the third objection in *In Sent.* I, d. 8, q. 1, a. 1, suggests a solution. In the reply to the third objection, Thomas acknowledges that because created *esse* imperfectly represents the divine *esse*, so too the name '*qui est*' "imperfectly signifies [God], because it signifies by a

---

41. For Thomas's commentary on Aristotle's assertion that verbs consignify time, see *In De interp.* 1.5: verbs signify time because they signify *per modum actionis* and insofar as they are measured in time.

42. *ST* I, q. 13, a. 11, ad 1 (Leon. 4.162): "Ad primum ergo dicendum quod hoc nomen qui est est magis proprium nomen Dei quam hoc nomen Deus, quantum ad id a quo imponitur, scilicet ab esse, et quantum ad modum significandi et consignificandi, ut dictum est." For a treatment of Thomas's use of the *res/modus* distinction in the context of divine naming, see Gregory Rocca, "The Distinction between *Res Significata* and *Modus Significandi* in Aquinas's Theological Epistemology," *The Thomist* 55 (1991): 173–97. The crucial claim is that one can distinguish between a name's *res significata* (the very form/perfection signified by a name) and its *modus significandi* (the manner in which a given word signifies that *res*), such that two names that differ in *modus significandi* can nevertheless share the same *res significata*, as for example 'wise' (as a concrete term) and 'wisdom' (as an abstract term) signify the same form/perfection, but in different ways. One of Thomas's crucial claims concerning positive divine names (as in *ST* I, q. 13, a. 3) is that such names are affirmed of God only with respect to *res significata*, never with respect to *modus significandi*.

mode of a certain concretion and composition."[43] The concrete *modus significandi* of '*qui est*' does not befit the divine simplicity, and in this manner '*qui est*' imperfectly signifies God.[44] But other names, St. Thomas explains, signify God even more imperfectly than '*qui est*,' because when we predicate any other name of God, we also include the predication of *esse*, as when for example we declare God "to be wise." There is therefore a *duplex imperfectio* about the predication of a name such as 'wise': "one [imperfection] is on the part of the concrete *esse*, as in the name '*qui est*'; and there is added to this another [imperfection] by the proper notion (*ratio*) of wisdom."[45] The name '*qui est*' is imperfect with respect to its concrete mode of signifying *esse*, but the predication of any other divine name includes this same imperfection. It is for this reason that '*qui est*' is no more imperfect than any other name with respect to the shortcoming of its *modus significandi*.

The reply to the fourth objection, which expands upon the apophatic argument in the body (and so also parallels the second stage of argumentation in *ST* I, q. 13, a. 11), clarifies that other divine names say that God "is" according to some other determinate notion (*ratio*), while '*qui est*' expresses *esse* that is absolute and not determined by anything added.[46]

43. *In Sent.* I, d. 8, q. 1, a. 1, ad 3 (Mandonnet 196): "Ad tertium dicendum quod cum esse creaturae imperfecte repraesentet divinum esse, et hoc nomen qui est imperfecte significat ipsum, quia significat per modum cujusdam concretionis et compositionis; sed adhuc imperfectius significatur per alia nomina: cum enim dico, Deum esse sapientem, tunc, cum in hoc dicto includatur esse, significatur ibi duplex imperfectio: una est ex parte ipsius esse concreti, sicut in hoc nomine qui est; et superadditur alia ex propria ratione sapientiae. Ipsa enim sapientia creata deficit a ratione divinae sapientiae: et propter hoc major imperfectio est in aliis nominibus quam in hoc nomine qui est; et ideo hoc est dignius et magis Deo proprium."

44. It is important to note that the abstract *modus significandi* of the term *esse* similarly does not befit the divine simplicity or perfection—every name falls short with respect to *modus significandi*. See *De pot.*, q. 1, a. 1 (Marietti 9): "Sed et sciendum, quod intellectus noster Deum exprimere nititur sicut aliquid perfectissimum. Et quia in ipsum devenire non potest nisi ex effectuum similitudine; neque in creaturis invenit aliquid summe perfectum quod omnino imperfectione careat: ideo ex diversis perfectionibus in creaturis repertis, ipsum nititur designare, quamvis cuilibet illarum perfectionum aliquid desit; ita tamen quod quidquid alicui istarum perfectionum imperfectionis adiungitur, totum a Deo amoveatur. Verbi gratia esse significat aliquid completum et simplex et non subsistens; substantia autem aliquid subsistens significat sed alii subiectum. Ponimus ergo in Deo substantiam et esse, sed substantiam ratione subsistentiae non ratione substandi; esse vero ratione simplicitatis et complementi, non ratione inhaerentiae, qua alteri inhaeret."

45. *In Sent.* I, d. 8, q. 1, a. 1, ad 3, cited in note 43 above.

46. *In Sent.* I, d. 8, q. 1, a. 1, ad 4 (Mandonnet 196): "Ad quartum dicendum, quod alia omnia nomina dicunt esse secundum aliam rationem determinatam; sicut sapiens dicit aliquid esse; sed hoc nomen qui est dicit esse absolutum et non determinatum per aliquid additum."

The imperfection added by other names that are less universal or more determinate in conceptual content would thus seem to have to do with the signification of these names. This text thus also explains why even the conceptual addition made to '*qui est*' by a name convertible with it, such as 'good' or 'true,' is nevertheless more deficient as a divine name: in addition to the concrete *modus significandi* of '*qui est*' that must be denied as one affirms the name, one must also deny the further imperfection involved in whatever conceptual addition is made to '*qui est*.'

I would therefore suggest that the second stage of argumentation in *ST* I, q. 13, a. 11, is concerned in part with the propriety of '*qui est*' with respect to the mode of signifying: '*qui est*' is no more imperfect with respect to *modus significandi* than any other divine name because it is most universal, least determinate, and contained in the predication of all other divine names. The supreme propriety of '*qui est*' is in this way tied to Thomas's use of the *res/modus* distinction, so prominent throughout *ST* I, q. 13: whenever anything is affirmed properly of God, it is affirmed only with respect to *res significata*, while everything pertaining to the *modus significandi* of a term must be denied when it enters into divine predication.[47] But as we have seen, a divine name with a more determinate *res significata* less properly names God, for apophatic reasons.

There is a further respect in which we find in *ST* I, q. 13, a. 11, connected stages of argumentation rather than three independent arguments. I posed above the question of whether and when the argumentation in a. 11 successfully establishes the unique supremacy of '*qui est*.' Consider the third argument as expressed in a. 11 on its own: this argument clearly does not establish on its own the unique supremacy of '*qui est*,' because its argumentation would render any verb in the present tense or any predication in the present tense proper according to the consignification of the verb. Both "God loves" and "God is wise"—and even a metaphorical predication like "God is angry"—would be most proper with respect to consignification.

I would suggest that the first stage of the argumentation (like its parallel in the fourth argument of *In Sent.* I, d. 8, q. 1, a. 1) also falls short on its own, insofar as it rests upon the claims that a thing is denominated from its quiddity or form and that in God alone are essence and *esse* identical. Thomas also holds that in God alone essence and goodness are

---

47. The *res/modus* distinction is employed by Thomas in aa. 1, 3, 6, 11, and 12 of *ST* I, q. 13.

identical, that substance and wisdom are identical, that essence and *intelligere* are identical, and so forth. If God can be properly denominated from any name which is uniquely identical with His essence, then there is nothing about the first stage of *ST* I, q. 13, a. 11, that establishes the unique supremacy of '*qui est*.'

It is in the second stage, then, that '*qui est*' is shown to be more proper than other divine names properly signifying the divine quiddity, including those that are convertible with '*qui est*.' With respect to *modus significandi*, the name '*qui est*' is no more improper than any other name; but again, insofar as a divine name signifies according to a more determinate *ratio* added to *esse*, it will less properly name God. Finally, however, this second stage still leaves some other possible names standing, which need to be excluded as less proper by the third stage of argumentation, such as '*qui erat*' and '*qui erit*.'

At this point, we can consider what St. Thomas means in calling '*qui est*' the supremely proper name of God. As noted above, earlier in *ST* I, q. 13, St. Thomas has used *nomen proprium* as an opposite of both metaphorical names and of common (appellative) names, as 'Socrates' is a proper name in comparison to 'man' as a common name. Given that '*qui est*' is said to signify God by signifying his essence or nature—and that part of the reasoning in support of the supreme propriety of '*qui est*' appeals to its maximal universality—it is clear that St. Thomas does not mean to oppose '*qui est*' as a personal name to common or appellative names.[48] St. Thomas is arguably concerned with propriety in this sense, however, when he speaks of the tetragrammaton as having been imposed to signify the incommunicable and as it were singular substance of God.[49]

As for the opposition between proper and metaphorical names, *ST* I, q. 13, a. 3's defense of the claim that some names are said *proprie* of God appeals to the *res/modus* distinction. Given the role of the *res/modus* distinction in the argumentative structure of *ST* I, q. 13, a. 11, this suggests that there should be some continuity between the use of *proprie* in aa. 3 and 11. In a. 3, Thomas asserts that positive divine names properly belong to God with respect to their *res significata*, and indeed belong to Him more properly than they do to creatures; but with respect to their *modi*

---

48. By contrast, Denys Turner attributes to Thomas the view that '*qui est*' is a proper name comparable to 'Peter' or 'Mary.' See Denys Turner, *Faith, Reason, and the Existence of God* (Cambridge: Cambridge University Press, 2004), 43–44, esp. n37.

49. *ST* I, q. 13, a. 11, ad 1.

significandi, such names are not properly said of God. But this still leaves the question: what does proper mean in this case?

I would once again point to *In Sent.* I, d. 8, q. 1, a. 1, for clarification, this time in the reply to the first objection. The objection had urged that *esse* cannot be properly said of God, because *esse* does not belong to God alone. Thomas replies to this objection by explaining the propriety of naming as a function of whether the perfection signified belongs properly to that which is named—it is in this way that a proper name is opposed to a metaphorical name—but he then distinguishes between two senses in which a perfection is proper to something:

> When something is said to belong properly to something, this can be understood in two ways: either that by [this] propriety there is excluded everything extraneous to the nature of the subject, as when "to be risible" is said to be proper to man, since [risibility] belongs to nothing apart from the nature of man. In this way, *esse* is not called proper to God, since it also belongs to creatures. Or, insofar as there is excluded everything extraneous to the nature of the predicate, as when it is said, "this is properly gold," because it does not have an admixture of another metal; and in this way, *esse* is called proper to God, since the divine *esse* does not have an admixture of any privation or potentiality, as the *esse* of a creature [does].[50]

Again, naming is proper because it signifies a perfection that belongs properly to something; but a perfection belongs properly to something either because it belongs to it alone, or because it alone belongs to it. *Esse* is not proper to God in the former way, but it is proper to God in the latter way, because everything in God is the divine *esse*. As a name's propriety is a function of whether the perfection it signifies belongs properly in one of these senses, '*qui est*' is proper to God according to the latter sense of propriety.

This meaning of propriety fits very well with the first stage of argumentation in ST I, q. 13, a. 11, which is concerned with the *res significata* of '*qui est*' and depends upon the claim that in God alone essence and *esse* are identical. *Esse* is proper to God, because God is—as Thomas elsewhere puts it, borrowing language from the *Liber de causis*—*esse tantum*.[51] But then, as the *Liber de causis* suggests, God is also *bonitas pura*,

---

50. *In Sent.* I, d. 8, q. 1, a. 1, ad 1.

51. Richard Taylor points out that the *Liber de causis* is the source for Thomas's use of the expression *esse tantum*. See Richard Taylor, "Aquinas, the *Plotiniana Arabica*, and the Metaphysics of Being and Actuality," *Journal of the History of Ideas* 59, no. 2 (1998): 217.

just as he is also wisdom alone, and so forth.[52] This meaning of propriety is in this way consistent with the claim advanced above, that Thomas's first stage of argumentation does not establish the unique or supreme propriety of *'qui est.'*

As for the second and third stages of the argument, in these stages St. Thomas is concerned with the greater propriety of *'qui est'* not only with respect to *res significata*, but with respect to the mode of signifying and consignification. The composition implied by the *modus significandi* of any name (whether concrete or abstract) does not belong to God at all, and so with respect to its *modus significandi* no name is properly said of God; but *'qui est'* is less deficient, because it avoids the *duplex imperfectio* involved with any name that determines *esse*. And as neither past nor future belong to God, verbs consignifying past and future time are less proper than those in the present tense.

The argumentation for the propriety of *'qui est'* in *ST* I, q. 13, a. 11, thus begins with an emphasis on its positive signification. In this respect, the first stage of a. 11 presupposes the earlier conclusions of q. 13 concerning the possibility of signifying God positively. These include the conclusion of a. 2, that some positive names do signify the divine essence or substance, as well as the conclusion of a. 3, that these same positive names are predicated properly of God in the sense just explained. All of the argumentation employed in these articles concerning other positive divine names applies just as well to *esse*: *esse* is a perfection in creatures that imperfectly represents the divine essence, and so we attribute *esse* to God, and do so properly insofar as God is his *esse*.

CONCLUDING REMARKS

As indicated above, according to Wippel the view that some names signify the divine substance or essence represents a development in St. Thomas's thinking with respect to which his strict apophatic assertions seem to be softened. It is this doctrine that certain positive divine names signify the divine essence, I would suggest, that allows Thomas to reorder and unify the disparate arguments of *In Sent.* I, d. 8, q. 1, a. 1, and to begin *ST* I, q. 13, a. 11, with the positive signification of *'qui est'* as a name

---

52. For Thomas's commentary on this passage from the *Liber de causis*, see *Super Librum de causis expositio* 9 (Saffrey 64).

said properly of God insofar as it signifies the divine essence: it signifies a perfection that belongs properly to God insofar as God is *esse tantum*. But because other positive names such as 'goodness' and 'wisdom' also signify the divine essence—because these other names also signify perfections that belong properly to God—the first stage of argumentation does not establish the unique supreme propriety of '*qui est*.'

For this reason, it is with respect to the apophatic concerns at issue in the second stage of Thomas's argumentation that '*qui est*' is established as uniquely proper to the exclusion of these other names. If we emphasize only the positive signification of these divine names, as in the first stage of argumentation in *ST* I, q. 13, a. 11, then there would be reason to say that all of these names are equally proper to God. There is a thus careful balance between kataphatic and apophatic elements in St. Thomas's mature articulation of the propriety of '*qui est*.' '*Qui est*' is uniquely most proper, for apophatic reasons, among the wider set of kataphatic names that signify the divine essence.

Michael J. Rubin

11 ∞ Aquinas on 'Beauty' as a Divine Name

INTRODUCTION

In an article from 2004, Jorgen Vijgen points out that some scholars regard "the establishment of a Thomistic aesthetics"—that is, a complete account of beauty according to the mind of St. Thomas Aquinas—as resting "upon a projection of elements of modern philosophy backward into the past." Vijgen then gives this view the following rebuttal: "As John F. Wippel has convincingly shown in regard to Aquinas's metaphysics, it is legitimate to place the various elements of Aquinas's philosophical thought into a harmonious synthesis as long as one uses a sound argumentation during the 'moment of proof,' as Wippel calls it. Therefore, a sort of *Summa aesthetica* remains possible."[1] Vijgen's observations are right on the mark: if scholars imitate the careful textual analysis and solid reasoning for which Wippel is justly celebrated, they can undoubtedly recover and reconstruct Aquinas's aesthetics, and consequently determine how he would answer any number of questions about beauty.[2]

One such question that Thomists have debated for over a century is whether 'beautiful' (*pulchrum*) is a transcendental,[3] that is, a word expressing a distinct attribute of every being insofar as it is a being.[4] Since

---

1. "A Note on the Transcendental Status of Beauty," *Sapientia* 59 (2004): 83.
2. All translations are my own.
3. For a brief history of this debate, see Michael J. Rubin, "The Meaning of 'Beauty' and Its Transcendental Status in the Metaphysics of Thomas Aquinas" (PhD diss., The Catholic University of America, 2016), 88–91.
4. *De ver.*, q. 1, a. 1 (Leon. 22/1.4–5). Some scholars prefer to define the transcendentals as simply the attributes of being, and not as the words that express those attributes. For instance,

Thomas makes clear that every being is beautiful insofar as it exists,[5] what is at issue here is not whether 'beautiful' expresses an attribute of being but rather whether it expresses a *distinct* attribute of being, because while the transcendentals are identical according to the reality that they signify (namely being), they express that reality with different meanings.[6] In saying that the transcendentals are distinct in meaning, Thomas is not claiming that there is no overlap at all among their meanings because, as he makes clear, the meaning of each transcendental presupposes and includes the meanings of all the ones preceding it in their order.[7] Nevertheless, each transcendental has a unique *ratio* or meaning that it adds to the meanings of being and all prior transcendentals. Hence, no transcendental is a mere synonym for any of the others, whether taken singly or in combination.

In two authoritative studies on the transcendentals, Jan Aertsen argues that 'beautiful' does not express a distinct attribute of being because its meaning is simply 'the true taken as good,' and is therefore not a distinct transcendental in its own right but rather a mere synonym for the combination of two transcendentals, namely 'true' and 'good.'[8] Hence, scholars who write after Aertsen (and who acknowledge that 'beautiful' must have a distinct meaning to be a transcendental[9]) have

---

see W. Norris Clarke, "The Transcendental Properties of Being," in his *The One and the Many: A Contemporary Thomistic Metaphysics* (Notre Dame, IN: University of Notre Dame Press, 2001), 290–302. Thomas, however, consistently speaks of the transcendentals as the names (*nomines*) or words that express universal attributes of being, rather than the attributes themselves; for instance, in *De ver.*, q. 21, a. 3 (Leon. 22/3.598:59–63), he refers to them as "these transcending names" (*istorum nominum transcendentium*). See also *In Sent.* I, d. 8, q. 1, a. 3 (Mandonnet 1.199), and *De ver.*, q. 21, a. 1 (Leon. 22/3.593:144–52). Thomas's reason for speaking this way seems to be that, as we mention in the above paragraph, the transcendentals are identical according to the reality they signify (i.e., being) but distinct according to the meanings through which they signify that reality. Thus, the transcendentals are not properties of being that are distinct in reality from each other, but rather distinct ways of describing the same rich reality: being.

5. Thomas states that beauty is identical in reality with goodness and therefore with being. See *ST* I, q. 5, a. 4, ad 1 (Leon. 4.61), and I-II, q. 27, a. 1, ad 3 (Leon. 6.192).

6. *In Sent.* I, d. 8, q. 1, a. 3 (Mandonnet 1.199).

7. *De ver.*, q. 21, a. 3 (Leon. 22/3:598.40–63).

8. Jan Aertsen, *Medieval Philosophy and the Transcendentals: The Case of Thomas Aquinas* (Leiden: E. J. Brill, 1996), chap. 8. See also his *Medieval Philosophy as Transcendental Thought: From Philip the Chancellor (ca. 1225) to Francisco Suárez*, Studien und Texte zur Geistesgeschichte des Mittelalters 107 (Leiden: Brill, 2012), 161–76.

9. Some scholars argue that 'beautiful' can be a transcendental even though it does not have a distinct meaning, but this view contradicts Thomas's writings. For example, see Michael

focused on whether he is correct about the meaning of 'beautiful.'[10]

What has so far escaped notice in this debate is an alternate, less direct way of settling whether 'beautiful' is a distinct transcendental for Thomas: to see whether he considers 'Beauty' (*pulchritudo*) to be a distinct divine name, that is, a term expressing an attribute of God.[11] While Thomas rarely discusses transcendental beauty, he often addresses the divine beauty; hence, Thomas's writings provide far more material for determining whether 'Beauty' is a distinct divine name than whether 'beautiful' is a distinct transcendental. Moreover, Thomas holds that, since we only know God from what He creates, the divine names are all derived from terms expressing attributes of creatures and therefore have distinct meanings only because the creaturely terms from which they are derived have distinct meanings.[12] Hence, if the divine name 'Beauty'

Waddell, "Truth Beloved: Thomas Aquinas and the Relational Transcendentals" (PhD diss., University of Notre Dame, 2000), 41, and D. C. Schindler, "The Transcendentals," in *Hans Urs von Balthasar and the Dramatic Structure of Truth: A Philosophical Investigation* (New York: Fordham University Press, 2004).

10. For instance, Kevin O'Reilly, *Aesthetic Perception: A Thomistic Perspective* (Dublin: Four Courts Press, 2007), 103–11; Louis-Marie de Blignieres, *Le mystère de l'être: L'approche thomiste de Guérard des Lauriers* (Paris: J. Vrin, 2007), 123; Christopher Sevier, *Aquinas on Beauty* (Lanham, MD: Lexington Books, 2015), 126–27; and Rubin, "The Meaning of 'Beauty.'"

11. Henceforth, I will be using the concrete term 'beautiful' (*pulchrum*) to refer to the transcendental and 'Beauty' (*pulchritudo*) to refer to the divine name, for the following reasons. First, as Aertsen notes, for Thomas it is not the abstract term *esse* or "to be" that can be predicated of every being but rather the concrete term *ens* or "that which is" because no created being is the very act of being but every being is something that *has* the act of being. Aertsen, *The Transcendentals*, 187–88. Likewise, then, the transcendentals that follow 'being' (*ens*) are not the abstract terms truth (*veritas*), goodness (*bonitas*), and beauty (*pulchritudo*) but rather the concrete terms true (*verum*), good (*bonum*), and beautiful (*pulchrum*), because no created being is truth, goodness, and beauty themselves but every being is true, good, and beautiful. It is thus no surprise to find that Thomas consistently uses the concrete terms *verum*, *bonum*, and *pulchrum* when discussing the transcendentals. By contrast, it is fitting to call God truth, goodness, and beauty because, unlike creatures, God *is* the very act of being itself and is therefore likewise truth, goodness, and beauty themselves. Hence, in order to highlight this difference between created and uncreated beauty, I will refer to the divine name exclusively as 'Beauty,' although of course 'beautiful' can also be predicated of God, as Thomas makes clear in his *Divine Names* commentary (see below).

12. *ST* I, q. 13, a. 4 (Leon. 4.144–45); see *SCG* I, c. 35 (Marietti 2.46). It is important to note that the divine names and the terms from which they are derived have meanings that are neither entirely the same nor entirely different, but rather related by analogy. On the complicated relationship between the divine names and the creaturely names from which they are derived, see Gregory P. Rocca, *Speaking the Incomprehensible God* (Washington, DC: The Catholic University of America Press, 2004), chaps. 10–11; John F. Wippel, *The Metaphysical Thought of Thomas Aquinas* (Washington, DC: The Catholic University of America Press, 2000), 543–72;

derives its meaning from the transcendental 'beautiful,'[13] the former cannot be distinct in meaning unless the latter is as well; in this case, one could prove that Thomas considers 'beautiful" to be a distinct transcendental by showing that he considers 'Beauty' to be a distinct divine name.[14] The present study will attempt such a demonstration.

The success of this proof has two requirements, the first of which is to show that Thomas in fact derives the divine name 'Beauty' from the transcendental 'beautiful.' This is not a foregone conclusion because, as Brian Carl has shown,[15] when the transcendentals 'true' and 'good' are applied to God, their meanings as divine names are derived not only from their meanings as transcendentals but also from their specific meanings as perfections of the human soul.[16] For example, 'good' as a transcendental signifies the desirableness of being insofar as it exists, but has a special meaning when applied to human beings as signifying the quality by

---

and Fran O'Rourke, *Pseudo-Dionysius and the Metaphysics of Aquinas* (Notre Dame, IN: University of Notre Dame Press, 2005), chap. 2.

13. One might think not only that the divine name of 'Beauty' derives its meaning from the transcendental 'beautiful,' but even that divine beauty is an instance of transcendental beauty, because the latter extends to every being and God is a being. In fact, however, for Thomas God is not merely "a being" but subsisting being itself (*ipsum esse subsistens*), and, therefore, does not fall under "being in general" (*ens commune*) but rather stands outside of it as the cause in which it participates. Hence, transcendental beauty does not contain the divine beauty, but instead is merely the limited participation of creatures in that beauty. The same holds for truth, goodness, and the other transcendentals. On this point, see Aertsen, *The Transcendentals*, 387–95, and Wippel, *Metaphysical Thought*, 18–19 and 593–94.

14. Here I am not claiming that, if one shows 'Beauty' to be a distinct divine name, doing so would by itself be sufficient to prove that 'beautiful' is a transcendental. As will be seen below, Thomas derives some of the divine names from terms that, although they express pure perfections, are still not transcendentals for him because they do not express attributes of every being; for example, life and wisdom can be attributed to God because they do not imply any imperfection, but it does not follow that "living" and "wise" are transcendentals because as, obviously, not every being is alive or wise. Hence, for Thomas it is not the case that whatever constitutes a divine name is automatically a transcendental. To attribute this view to him would be to confuse his transcendental theory with that of Duns Scotus, for whom the pure perfections also count as transcendentals (even if they are not attributes of every being) "for the simple reason that they can be predicated of God and hence transcend the finite categories." Allan Bernard Wolter, "The Transcendentals and Their Function in the Metaphysics of Duns Scotus" (PhD diss., The Catholic University of America, 1946), 11.

15. "The Transcendentals and the Divine Names in Thomas Aquinas," *American Catholic Philosophical Quarterly* 92, no. 2 (2018): 233–42.

16. This is especially clear in the case of truth. Thomas argues that God is truth itself because truth consists either in the mind's conformity to being (i.e., logical truth) or in being's conformity to the mind (i.e., transcendental truth), and God perfectly possesses both because his being and intellect are one and the same. *ST* I, q. 16 a. 4 (Leon. 4.212); see *SCG* I, cc. 60–62 (Marietti 2.71–73).

which they are good, that is, moral goodness, which consists in choosing the good through rational and virtuous activity.[17] Moral goodness can and must be attributed to God because it is what Thomists have come to call a "pure perfection," that is, a perfection that does not imply any imperfection; hence, when we say that God is goodness itself, we do not mean simply that he is desirable insofar as he exists, but also that he perfectly possesses the goodness of reason and virtue.[18]

Now, in addition to its transcendental meaning, 'beautiful' actually has two specific meanings: it refers either to bodily (i.e., sensible) beauty, which consists in having proportioned members and the brightness of an appropriate color, or to spiritual (i.e., intelligible) beauty, which consists in a person's actions being proportioned according to the light of reason.[19] The first meaning of 'beautiful' includes matter in its definition and, therefore, can be said of God only metaphorically as all such notions imply imperfection.[20] Hence, the divine name 'Beauty' cannot be derived from 'sensible beauty' because Thomas makes clear that 'Beauty' is not said of God metaphorically, but is rather said of him properly and even essentially.[21] Like 'moral goodness,' however, spiritual beauty contains no such limitation in its meaning and is therefore a pure perfection that can be properly applied to God. Thus, Thomas could derive the divine name of 'Beauty' from spiritual beauty if he wished, in which case proving that 'Beauty' is a distinct divine name for him would not tell us whether 'beautiful' is a distinct transcendental.

The question thus arises of how to determine whether Thomas's texts on the divine name of 'Beauty' are deriving it from the transcendental 'beautiful' rather than 'spiritual beauty.' One obvious sign would be if they explicitly refer to the beauty of every being, but an equally effective proof would be if they use examples of sensible beauty while explaining

---

17. *In Sent.* II, d. 27, q. 1, a. 2, ad 2 (Mandonnet 2.699).
18. *De pot.*, q. 9, a. 7, ad 5 (Marietti 2.243); see q. 7, a. 4, ad 2 (Marietti 2.196), and *De ver.*, q. 23, a. 7 (Leon. 22/3.670).
19. *ST* II-II, q. 145, a. 2 (Leon. 10.147); see *In I Corinthios* 11.2 (Marietti 1.346) and *Contra impugnantes*, q. 2, a. 6, ad 22 (Leon. 41.121:1342–52). As will become clear, these different senses of the term "beautiful" are neither univocal nor equivocal but rather analogical, i.e., their meanings are neither entirely the same nor entirely different, just as is the case for "being" and the other transcendentals.
20. *ST* I, q. 13, a. 3, obj. 1 and ad 1 (Leon. 4.144–45).
21. Thomas states that God is the very essence of beauty in *Comp. theol.* II.9 (Leon. 42.204:393–97); see *In Sent.* IV, d. 18, q. 1, a. 2, ad 2 (Mandonnet 4.938).

the meaning of 'beauty.' As we saw, Thomas cannot derive the divine name 'Beauty' from sensible beauty because it cannot be said properly of God; thus, if Thomas mentions bodily beauty in his texts on divine beauty, he must be using it as an example of transcendental beauty, which is the only kind of beauty that both contains bodily beauty as a "genus"[22] and can be properly attributed to God.[23] Hence, if Thomas mentions sensible beauty in his texts on divine beauty, we will know that he is deriving divine beauty from the transcendental 'beautiful,' from which it follows that if he considers the former to be a distinct divine name, he must also consider the latter to be a distinct transcendental.

The second requirement for this proof's success is of course to show that 'Beauty' is a distinct divine name for Thomas. Aside from explicit statements by Thomas on the matter, the only way to establish this point is to see whether he uses distinct arguments for applying this name to God. For instance, if Thomas proves that God is beauty itself simply by arguing that he is truth and goodness itself, or if his arguments for the divine beauty are identical to his proofs of the divine truth and goodness, this would be strong evidence that the divine name 'Beauty' is a mere synonym for "both true and good" and therefore does not have its own unique meaning. On the other hand, if Thomas's arguments for the divine beauty do not appeal to God's truth or goodness and differ significantly from the arguments for these other attributes, that would be strong evidence that divine beauty has a distinct meaning. Determining whether 'Beauty' is a distinct divine name for Thomas thus requires examining his arguments for applying this name to God, of which there

---

22. Of course, transcendental beauty is not a genus strictly speaking as it is identical with being, and being is not a genus because there is nothing outside of it that can be added to it as a specific difference; e.g., see *ST* I, q. 3, a. 5 (Leon. 4.43–44). Nevertheless, being (and thus transcendental beauty) can be called a genus in a broad sense insofar as it is common to many. See *In Meta.* X.8, n. 2092 (Marietti 493), and Aertsen, *The Transcendentals*, 85–86.

23. Someone might object that there could be a type of beauty besides transcendental beauty that both contains bodily beauty and is attributable to God—perhaps qualitative beauty, as opposed to substantial beauty. There is one main problem with this view, however. Thomas makes clear that, when the term 'beauty' is used without any qualifications (such as spiritual or bodily), it is identical in reality with 'goodness' and 'being' and therefore refers to transcendental beauty (see the texts cited in note 5 above). Hence, 'beauty' could only refer to qualitative beauty if Thomas explicitly added the restriction "qualitative." Yet nowhere in his corpus does Thomas even mention the existence of a type of beauty called qualitative beauty. Hence, even if hypothetically there is some genus of beauty that contains bodily beauty and could also be attributed to God, Thomas does not seem to be even slightly concerned with it, and certainly does not derive the divine name 'Beauty' from it.

are two kinds. The first kind consists of arguments simply for predicating 'Beauty' of the divine essence and thus of all the divine Persons, whereas the second consists of arguments for applying that name in a special way to the Son—a use of the divine names that Thomas and other medieval theologians call "appropriation."

With all of the foregoing in mind, the present chapter will proceed in the following way. The first section will give a chronological survey of Aquinas's arguments for the beauty of God's essence, and the second will do the same with his arguments for appropriating 'Beauty' to the Son. As we will see, these texts provide abundant evidence not only that 'Beauty' is a distinct divine name for Thomas but also that 'beautiful' is a distinct transcendental.

AQUINAS'S ARGUMENTS FOR ATTRIBUTING BEAUTY TO THE DIVINE ESSENCE

Although Thomas's most extended treatment of the divine beauty is in his commentary on Dionysius, his corpus has multiple passages on this topic. All of these texts contain strong indications that 'Beauty' is a distinct divine name and 'beautiful' is a distinct transcendental, of which perhaps the most compelling piece of evidence is the appearance at several stages in Thomas's career of what seems to be a unique argument for God's existence from the different grades of beauty in the world.

In Sent. I, d. 3, q. 1, prooemium

One of Thomas's earliest texts on the divine beauty appears at the start of Book I in his *Sentences* commentary (1252–56).[24] Here Thomas categorizes Peter Lombard's four arguments for God's existence according to the three ways of reasoning to God described by Dionysius: while there is one argument from causality and one from negation, there are two from eminence, which are distinguished in the following way.[25] The first argument proceeds from "eminence in existence (*esse*)" and begins with the premise that "good and better are said through comparison to a best";

---

24. I will be following the dating of Thomas's texts given by Jean-Pierre Torrell in *Saint Thomas Aquinas: The Person and His Work*, rev. ed., trans. Robert Royal (Washington, DC: The Catholic University of America Press, 2005), 332.

25. For the influence of Dionysius's *triplex via* on Thomas's thought, see O'Rourke, *Pseudo-Dionysius*, 31–41, and Rocca, *Speaking the Incomprehensible God*, 49–55.

thus, because a body is good but a created spirit is better, and because the latter still does not have goodness from itself, "there must be something best from which goodness is in each."[26] The second argument is based on "eminence in knowledge," which begins as follows: "Wherever there is to be found a more and less beautiful (*speciosum*),[27] there is to be found some principle of beauty, through nearness to which one thing is called more beautiful than another. But we find that bodies are beautiful with a sensible beauty (*specie*), whereas spirits are more beautiful with an intelligible beauty." From these premises, Thomas concludes that "there must be something from which both are beautiful, to which created spirits more closely approach."[28]

For several reasons, this text provides striking evidence that 'Beauty' is a distinct divine name and 'beautiful' is a distinct transcendental for Thomas. First, the parallels between this argument and Thomas's arguments for God's existence from the natures of truth and goodness in his *Summa contra Gentiles*[29] strongly suggest that, like 'true' and 'good,' 'beautiful' has its own unique meaning. Moreover, Thomas confirms that

---

26. *In Sent.* I, d. 3, q. 1, proem. (Mandonnet 1.89): "Tertia ergo sumitur ratio per viam eminentiae in esse, et est talis. Bonum et melius dicuntur per comparationem ad optimum. Sed in substantiis invenimus corpus bonum et spiritum creatum melius, in quo tamen bonitas non est a seipso. Ergo oportet esse aliquod optimum a quo sit bonitas in utroque."

27. I am translating *speciosus* as beautiful and *species* as beauty in this text for two reasons. First, in the vast majority of texts where *speciosus* or *species* appears alongside *pulchrum* or *pulchritudo*, the terms are treated as synonyms; e.g., see *In Psalmos* 26.3 (Parma 14.238), *Super Iob* 42 (Leon. 26.230:172–91), and *In Matthaeum* 3.1 (Marietti 41), as well as *In Sent.* I, d. 31, q. 2, a. 1, and *ST* I, q. 39, a. 8. Second, in the few texts where they are not treated as synonyms, such as *Super Isaiam* 53 (Leon. 28.214:35–52) and *In Psalmos* 44.4 (Marietti 14.322), Thomas uses *species* or *speciosus* to distinguish a certain type of beauty from other types that are denoted either by *pulchrum* or other close synonyms, such as *decor*. Thomas thus evidently sees *speciosus* and *species* as close synonyms for *pulchrum* and *pulchritudo* that have slightly different connotations.

28. *In Sent.* I, d. 3, q. 1, proem. (Mandonnet 1.89): "Quarta sumitur per eminentiam in cognitione, et est talis. In quibuscumque est invenire magis et minus speciosum, est invenire aliquod speciositatis principium, per cujus propinquitatem aliud alio dicitur speciosius. Sed invenimus corpora esse speciosa sensibili specie, spiritus autem speciosiores specie intelligibili. Ergo oportet esse aliquid a quo utraque speciosa sint, cui spiritus creati magis appropinquant."

29. In *SCG* I, c. 13, Thomas argues for the existence of something supremely true (and thus supremely being) on the basis that one of two false things can be falser than the other, which is only possible if there is something supremely true to which the less false thing is nearer. In c. 38 (Marietti 2.48), Thomas argues that whatever is good by participation receives its goodness from something prior, which cannot proceed to infinity because goodness has the nature of an end and the infinite (*infinis*) is opposed to the end (*finis*); hence, there must be something that is good not by participation but by its own essence, which is God.

he considers this "argument from beauty" to be a distinct proof of God's existence with his statement that it follows a distinct way of reasoning to God, namely "through eminence in knowledge."

As for why this is an argument specifically from eminence in knowledge, Thomas does not say, but it does not seem to be the argument's form that gives it this character for him, as it is identical in structure to the other proof from eminence in this text: both argue from diverse grades of perfection to the existence of a maximum and would therefore fall under the kind of proof described by the Fourth Way in Thomas's *Summa theologiae*.[30] Hence, what makes the second argument a proof from eminence in *knowledge* seems to be simply that it argues from the beauty of creatures rather than their goodness. Thomas confirms this impression in later texts when he says that, whereas the good relates to the appetite because it is that which all desire, the beautiful relates to the cognitive power because it pleases when seen or known.[31] Likewise, that Thomas describes the proof from goodness in this passage as an argument from eminence in *existence* fits with Thomas's position that the appetite (to which the good relates) regards things as existing in reality whereas the intellect relates to them as existing in the mind.[32] Thomas is thus apparently distinguishing the two arguments from eminence in this text on the basis that one argues from the goodness of creatures and the other argues from their beauty, which strongly implies that 'beautiful' has a unique meaning of its own.

Finally, because the argument from beauty in this text mentions both sensible and intelligible beauty, the notion of beauty from which he is proving and deriving the divine name 'Beauty' here must be transcendental beauty because, as noted above, it is the only "genus" that contains both kinds of beauty. Hence, if Thomas considers 'Beauty' to be a distinct divine name in this text, he must likewise consider 'beautiful' to be a distinct transcendental.

---

30. *ST* I, q. 2, a. 3 (Leon. 4.32). As is well known, there has been extensive controversy over how to interpret this argument and even whether it is sound. On these points, see Wippel, *Metaphysical Thought*, 469–79.

31. *ST* I, q. 5, a. 4, ad 1 (Leon. 4.61); I-II, q. 27, a. 1, ad 3 (Leon. 6.192); and *In De div. nom.* 4.5 (Marietti 115).

32. See, e.g., *De ver.*, q. 1, a. 2 (Leon. 22/1:9.62–71).

Super Iob 40

We find more evidence that 'Beauty' has a distinct meaning in a much later text from the commentary on Job (1263–65),[33] in which Thomas expounds God's rebuke of Job for questioning him. At one point the Lord tells Job to "clothe yourself with beauty (*decorem*)"[34] which Thomas interprets to mean "if you are as powerful in your effects as God, attribute to yourself His beauty." Thomas then explains why God uses the word "clothe" (*circumda*): "For God does not have a clothed beauty (*decorem*) as if added on top of His Essence, but His very essence is beauty, by which is understood the very brightness or truth, and purity or simplicity, and perfection of His Essence." Thus, according to Thomas, God tells Job to "clothe" himself with beauty in order to highlight the impossibility of attributing the divine beauty to oneself, because whereas God's beauty is his essence, "man cannot have beauty except as clothed, as if participating in it from God as added above his essence."[35]

While the last text gave a proof of God's existence from the nature of beauty, here we find a different kind of argument for attributing beauty to God: an argument from other divine attributes. In saying that God's beauty consists in "the very brightness or truth, and purity or simplicity, and perfection of His Essence," Thomas mirrors the three requirements for beauty that he lists in *ST* I, q. 39, a. 8 (which was written soon after this text)[36]: integrity or perfection, harmony or due proportion, and brightness.[37] Thus Thomas is evidently arguing that God is beautiful according to his essence on the grounds that beauty consists in attributes that he has already been shown to possess. This text therefore parallels the passages where Thomas argues that God is truth and goodness

---

33. Torrell, *Saint Thomas Aquinas*, 431.

34. Like *speciosus* and *species*, *decorus* and *decor* are usually synonyms for *pulchrum* and *pulchritudo*—see, e.g., in *In Sent.* IV, d. 16, q. 2, a. 2, ad 1 (Mandonnet 4.789), and *ST* II-II, q. 145, a. 2 (Leon. 10.147)—and are distinguished from them only when Thomas wishes to denote several types of beauty, e.g., in *Super Isaiam* 53 (Leon. 28.214:35–52).

35. *Super Iob* 40 (Leon. 26.213–14:74–84): "... dicit circumda tibi decorem, quasi dicat: si tam potens es in effectibus sicut Deus, attribuas tibi eius decorem, unde signanter dicit circumda tibi: Deus enim non habet circumdatum decorem quasi superadditum eius essentiae sed ipsa essentia eius est I, per quem intelligitur ipsa claritas sive veritas, et puritas sive simplicitas, et perfectio essentiae eius; sed homo non potest habere decorem nisi circumdatum, quasi participando ipsum a Deo ut superadditum suae essentiae."

36. Torrell dates it to between 1265 and 1267; see *Saint Thomas Aquinas*, 426.

37. See page 340–44 below.

themselves because the conditions for truth and goodness have already been shown to be perfectly fulfilled in him.[38]

In a significant departure from the list in the *Summa*, however, Thomas does not attribute "harmony or due proportion" to God, but rather "purity or simplicity." Thomas seems to be saying that God fulfills this condition for beauty not by actually possessing harmony, but by having something more excellent, namely purity or simplicity. Such a position is reasonable, because God's simplicity means that He has no parts among which there could be a harmony[39]; moreover, as harmony unites divided things into a composite,[40] both harmony and simplicity seem to be types of unity, or undividedness,[41] with simplicity being the nobler kind.

By contrast, Thomas makes it clear that brightness and perfection are truly found in God, which implies that some conditions for beauty are more essential to it than others. Thomas confirms this impression in another passage where he states that, when considered "according to beauty," God "is called Light,"[42] which indicates that the divine beauty consists primarily in brightness. This text therefore suggests that brightness is beauty's nature or essential condition (just as perfection is the nature of the good),[43] whereas harmony and wholeness are conditions for beauty only because they are conditions for brightness—a conclusion supported by many other texts.[44] Hence, Thomas seems to hold that the meaning of 'beautiful' is no mere aggregate of the three conditions for beauty—as one might expect if it were a composite notion like "the true

---

38. For instance, in arguing that God is good according to his essence, Thomas proceeds from the premises that goodness consists in perfection and that God possesses every kind of perfection by his essence. See *ST* I, q. 6, a. 3 (Leon. 4.68), and *SCG* I, c. 38 (Marietti 2.48). For similar arguments that God is truth itself, see note 16 above.

39. On God's simplicity, see *ST* I, q. 3, a. 7 (Leon. 4.46–47). That harmony can only be found in things with parts is made clear by Thomas in several places: *De pot.*, q. 10, a. 3 (Marietti 2.263); *In Sent.* I, d. 20, q. 1, a. 3, sol. 1 (Mandonnet 1.509); *In Phys.* I.10.4 (Leon. 2.34); *In Politic.* II.5.2 (Leon. 48A.135:31–38); *SCG* II, c. 64.3 (Marietti 2.200); and *In De an.* I.9 (Leon. 45/1.45:100–102).

40. *In De an.* I.9 (Leon. 45/1.44:60–64); see *SCG* I, c. 64.4 (Marietti 2.200).

41. *ST* I, q. 13, a. 1 (Leon. 4.107).

42. *In Sent.* I, d. 8, q. 5, a. 3 (Mandonnet 1.236). "Secundo quantum ad pulcritudinem, et sic Deus dicitur lux."

43. *SCG* I, c. 37 (Marietti 2.47); see *ST* I, q. 5, a. 5 (Leon. 4.63).

44. For instance, see *ST* II-II, q. 145, a. 2 (Leon. 10.147), *In I Corinthios* 11.2 (Marietti 1.346), and *ST* II-II, q. 142, a. 4 (Leon. 10.136–37). For the rest of the extensive evidence that brightness is the nature or essential condition of beauty, see Rubin, "The Meaning of 'Beauty,'" 298–321.

taken as good"—but rather a single notion with one essential characteristic to which its other aspects are ordered.

Some might object, however, that *Super Iob* 40 actually provides evidence that 'beautiful' does *not* have a distinct meaning. In speaking of God's "brightness or truth," Thomas seems to identify truth with one of beauty's requirements, as he also seems to do elsewhere.[45] For example, in *In Sent*. I, d. 3, q. 2, one of Thomas's reasons for appropriating 'Beauty' to the Son is that beauty consists in splendor and "truth has the meaning (*rationem*) of splendor."[46] Moreover, as noted above, perfection is the nature of the good, so one could argue that in listing perfection as a requirement for beauty, Thomas is including 'good' in the meaning of 'beautiful.' Finally, because both harmony and simplicity seem to be types of unity, the last requirement for beauty could be seen as identical in meaning with 'unity.' Hence, one could argue that in *Super Iob* 40 Thomas is presenting the meaning of 'beautiful' as the combination not merely of 'true' and 'good,' but of 'true,' 'good,' and 'one.'[47]

There are, however, several problems with arguing this way. First, even if Thomas were identifying beauty's conditions with unity, truth, and goodness in this passage, it would not prove that the meaning of 'beautiful' is the mere sum of these attributes, but simply indicate that the meaning of 'beautiful' presupposes those of 'one,' 'true,' and 'good'; as mentioned earlier, this would still be the case if 'beautiful' comes after them in the order of transcendentals, as every transcendental includes the meanings of the ones that precede it and adds its own meaning to them.[48] Moreover, Thomas mentions neither unity nor goodness in *Super Iob* 40; as for truth, Thomas is not identifying it with brightness by using the phrase "brightness or truth" as he also speaks of God's "purity or simplicity"—terms that are obviously distinct in meaning.[49] Thomas's

---

45. *Comp. theol.* 1.106 (Leon. 42.121:14–17); *In II Corinthios* 3.3 (Marietti 1.463).

46. *Comp. theol.* 1.106: "Pulchritudo consistit in duobus, scilicet in splendore et partium proportione. Veritas autem habet splendoris rationem et aequalitas tenet locum proportionis."

47. Several scholars argue for identifying beauty's requirements with unity, truth, and goodness in this way: Richard Hunter, "Analogy and Beauty: Thomistic Reflections on the Transcendentals" (PhD diss., Bryn Mawr College, 1978), 123–24; Juan Roig Gironella, "Metafísica de la belleza," *Pensamiento* 7 (1951): 40; Jordan Aumann, "Beauty and the Esthetics Response," *Angelicum* 54 (1977): 501.

48. For this reason, it is significant that Thomas says 'beautiful' adds to the meaning of 'good' in *ST* I-II, q. 27, a .1, ad 3 (Leon. 6.192). See *In De div. nom.* 4.5, no. 356 (Marietti 115).

49. Whereas God's "simplicity" signifies his utter lack of composition, his "purity" signifies his utter lack of contamination by baser things: *In Sent*. I, d. 17, q. 2, a. 4, ad 3, and d. 44, q.

writings also provide a number of signs that brightness and truth have different meanings for him,[50] of which the most important is that brightness expresses a relation to the act of vision or apprehension,[51] while truth seems to express a relation to judgment.[52] Hence, *Super Iob* 40 is not saying that brightness and truth are synonymous, but rather that, like purity and simplicity, their meanings are very close to each other, which makes sense given that both relate to the cognitive power.

Most importantly, in *Super Iob* 40 Thomas does not say that God's beauty is his truth, but rather that it is his *brightness* or truth. In other words, that God is truth provides only indirect support for the conclusion that God is beauty, that is, by showing that God fulfills one of beauty's three conditions. The same point can be made about the text we cited from the *Sentences* commentary: truth is only a reason for appropriating 'Beauty' to the Son because it has the nature of splendor, which is one of beauty's requirements. Thomas thus apparently holds that, to prove God is beautiful, one cannot argue simply from his being true and good, but rather from beauty's own requirements—just as one would expect if 'beautiful' has its own meaning instead of being a mere synonym for "both true and good." Hence, far from showing that 'beautiful' does not have a distinct meaning, this text actually provides evidence that it does.

In De divinis nominibus 4.5

As is well known, the longest treatment of beauty in Thomas's corpus can be found in lessons 5–8 in the fourth chapter of his commentary (1266–68) on the *Divine Names* of Dionysius.[53] What has eluded attention, however, is that the fifth lesson seems to contain an argument from beauty for God's existence that is similar in structure to the proof we saw in his *Sentences* commentary, thus indicating that Thomas has a unique

---

1, a. 3, ad 3 (Mandonnet 1.424 and 1.1023); *ST* II-II, q. 7, a. 2 (Leon. 8.65).

50. For instance, brightness evidently presupposes perfection (e.g., *In Sent.* IV, d. 25, q. 2, a. 2, ad 4 [Mandonnet 7/2.910]) but truth does not (e.g., *ST* I, q. 16, a. 4 [Leon. 4.211]); moreover, the contrary of truth (i.e., falsehood) can be found only in the mind and not in reality (e.g., *De ver.*, q. 1, a. 10 [Leon. 22/1.31–32:79–138]), but the contrary of brightness (i.e., darkness) can be found in reality as well as in the mind (e.g., *ST* I, q. 93, a. 8, ad 3 [Leon. 5.411]). For a full discussion of this evidence, see Rubin, "The Meaning of 'Beauty,'" 347–56.

51. For instance, see *ST* II-II, q. 132, a. 1 (Leon. 10.78).

52. See *De ver.*, q. 1, a. 10 (Leon. 22/1.30–33). Moreover, truth relates to knowledge, which is completed in an act of judgment, as Thomas emphasizes, e.g., in *ST* I, q. 16, a. 2 (Leon. 4.208), and *De ver.*, q. 1, a. 3 (Leon. 22/1.10–11).

53. Torrell, *Saint Thomas Aquinas*, 434.

"argument from beauty" not only at the beginning of his career but even near the end of it. Due to the length of this lesson, we will not discuss it as thoroughly as we have the other texts, but rather briefly outline it and then focus on the passages containing the proof.

Lesson 5 presents a detailed exposition of Dionysius's treatment of the divine beauty, which according to Thomas has the following structure. After asserting that theologians praise God as both 'beautiful' and 'Beauty,' Dionysius claims that these names are attributed to God and creatures in different ways: in creatures 'beautiful' and 'Beauty' are distinguished as that which participates in beauty and the share of beauty that it possesses, but in God these are identical.[54] Dionysius then explains more specifically how each of these names is attributed to God: he is called 'Beauty' insofar as he gives beauty to all things, which he does by being the cause of harmony and brightness in them[55]; and he is called 'beautiful' both according to excess and as a cause. According to excess, God is both "the most beautiful" (*pulcherrimum*) and "above beautiful" (*superpulcher*), that is, God exceeds in beauty not only by having the most beauty but even by going beyond the genus of beautiful things, as he possesses all the beauty of creatures but in a more excellent way.[56] Meanwhile, God is called 'beautiful' as a cause because his beauty is not only the cause of everything in creatures, including their substantial forms, but is also their cause in every way: efficient, final, and exemplary.[57] Dionysius then spends the rest of his treatment of the divine beauty discussing each of its effects in creatures, which Thomas expounds in lessons 6–8 of his commentary.[58]

Before completing lesson 5, however, Thomas first tells us of a "certain corollary" that Dionysius infers from what he has just said about the divine beauty's causality: "And he says that, because the beautiful is the cause of all things in all ways, it follows from this that the good and the beautiful are the same, for all things desire the beautiful and the good as the cause in all ways."[59] This "corollary" suggests an intriguing

---

54. *In De div. nom.* 4.5, nn. 336–37 (Marietti 113).
55. Ibid., nn. 339–40.
56. Ibid., nn. 342–47 (Marietti 114).
57. Ibid., nn. 349–55 (Marietti 114–15).
58. Marietti 117–30. For a more thorough discussion of the lessons on beauty in Aquinas's commentary, see Brendan Sammon, *The God Who is Beauty: Beauty as a Divine Name in Thomas Aquinas and Dionysius the Areopagite* (Eugene, OR: Pickwick Publications, 2013), chap. 11.
59. *In De div. nom.* 4.5, n. 355 (Marietti 115): "Deinde ... infert quoddam corollarium ex

interpretation of lesson 5. According to Thomas, Dionysius infers that the good and the beautiful are the same because each is the First Cause of all things in every way; thus, Thomas seems to think that Dionysius is not simply assuming that the divine good is also the supreme beauty, but is rather proving that a supreme beauty exists, that it is the First Cause, and that it must therefore be identical with the good. Hence, Thomas may think that Dionysius's text contains an argument for the existence of the divine beauty.

We seem to find that argument in the section of lesson 5 on how God is called 'Beauty.' As noted above, Thomas claims here that for Dionysius God is called 'Beauty' insofar as he gives beauty to creatures by causing harmony and brightness in them, which he does in the following ways. God causes brightness by giving every creature "a share in His luminous ray, which is the font of all light"[60]; as for harmony, Thomas begins by noting that there is "a twofold harmony in creatures." The first is the order of creatures to God, which he causes by calling all things to himself as their ultimate end, and the second is the order of creatures to each other, which Dionysius mentions when he speaks of God "gathering all things into all things." In Thomas's view, one should interpret this statement "according to the opinion of the Platonists" that "higher things are in lower things according to participation," while "lower things are in higher things through a certain eminence (*excellentia*)." In other words, because lower beings possess some share or likeness of the perfection of higher beings, whereas higher beings possess all the perfection of lower beings but in a more excellent mode, each exists in the other in some way, and thus "all things are in all things."[61]

Thomas now draws a striking conclusion: "And from this [fact] that all things are found in all things with a certain order, it follows that all

---

dictis; et dicit quod, quia tot modis pulchrum est causa omnium, inde est quod bonum et pulchrum sunt idem, quia omnia desiderant pulchrum et bonum, sicut causam omnibus modis ..."

60. Ibid., n. 340 (Marietti 113): "Quomodo autem Deus sit causa claritatis, ostendit subdens, quod Deus immittit omnibus creaturis, cum quodam fulgore, traditionem sui radii luminosi, qui est fons omnis luminis ..."

61. Ibid. "Secunda autem consonantia est in rebus, secundum ordinationem earum ad invicem; et hoc tangit cum subdit, quod congregat omnia in omnibus, ad idem. Et potest hoc intelligi, secundum sententiam Platonicorum, quod superiora sunt in inferioribus, secundum participationem; inferiora vero sunt in superioribus, per excellentiam quamdam et sic omnia sunt in omnibus ..."

things are ordered to the same ultimate [thing]."[62] Here Thomas confirms that he sees some kind of argument in Dionysius's text, which appears to be an argument for God's existence with the following structure. All things become beautiful by acquiring harmony, which includes their harmony with all other beings. Beings acquire harmony with each other through an order in which all things are in all things: higher beings are in lower beings according to participation and lower beings are in higher beings through eminence. But this order is possible only if all beings are ordered to a single ultimate in which they commonly participate. Hence, there must be some ultimate beauty to which all beings are ordered as an end and which thereby causes all the harmony we find among creatures.

While this interpretation is an attractive and plausible one, it is not absolutely clear that this is an argument for God's existence. Thomas does seem to be taking the existence of God for granted throughout his commentary on this lesson, so it may be that the argument presented here is only intended to establish that God is beauty itself. Alternatively, because the argument ends by concluding that all things are ordered to the *same* ultimate reality, one could interpret the argument as being a proof solely for the unicity of the divine beauty, that is, that there can only be *one* divine beauty to which all are ordered.

Nevertheless, even if the argument from harmony presented here is only a proof of God's beauty or unicity rather than his existence, it still provides a number of strong indications that Thomas considers 'Beauty' to be a distinct divine name and 'beautiful' a distinct transcendental. First, as this proof does not appear explicitly in Dionysius's text, there is good reason to think it is Thomas's own thought, especially because he gives similar arguments elsewhere. Moreover, like the argument in the *Sentences* commentary, this proof from harmony argues to a truth about the divine beauty from the diverse grades of being, though it does so from the order among them rather than from their distinction. Thus, Thomas seems to hold that there is a distinctive type of argument for truths about the divine beauty, that is, a proof from diverse grades of being. Second, this argument in the *Divine Names* commentary is founded even more specifically on the meaning of 'beauty' than is the argument in the *Sentences* commentary: whereas the latter has the same

62. Ibid. "Et ex hoc quod omnia in omnibus inveniuntur ordine quodam, sequitur quod omnia ad idem ultimum ordinentur."

structure as other proofs from diverse grades of being (such as the proof from goodness that precedes it), the former explicitly appeals to one of beauty's conditions, namely harmony.[63] Thomas is thus giving an entirely unique argument from beauty here, which implies that the meaning of 'beauty' is similarly unique.

Finally, as this proof argues from the harmony of all beings with each other, it is clearly founded on the beauty of every being, that is, transcendental beauty, as Thomas confirms in the previous paragraph by specifically mentioning not only spiritual but also bodily beauty.[64] This argument therefore confirms that the divine name 'Beauty' is derived from transcendental rather than spiritual beauty, as is also made clear by other statements in lesson 5.[65]

In Symbolum Apostolorum 1

Still more evidence that 'Beauty' as a divine name has a distinct meaning for Thomas can be found at the end of his career in his *collatio* (or collection) of sermons on the Apostles' Creed, which most likely comes from 1273 and thus within two years of his death.[66] In explaining the words "maker of heaven and earth," Thomas dispenses with "subtle reasons" and instead uses a "rough example" to show that all things are created by God: if anyone feels heat upon entering a house, and then feels more and

---

63. It is worth mentioning that, although Thomas does not give an argument for the divine beauty from the brightness of creatures in this text, he does seem to provide the materials for one. Thomas's description of God's "luminous ray" as the "fount of all light" indicates that he sees God's brightness as a maximum whose existence is implied by the different kinds and degrees of brightness in creatures. This impression is strengthened by Thomas's statement in the previous paragraph that a thing is beautiful insofar as it has "the brightness of its genus, whether spiritual or bodily" (ibid., n. 339 [Marietti 113]) and by his statements elsewhere that intelligible brightness is greater than sensible brightness (*In Sent.* II, d. 13, q. 1, a. 2 [Mandonnet 2.330], and *In I Corinthios* 3.2 [Marietti 1.263]). One could therefore arrange these statements of Thomas into an "argument from brightness" with the same structure as the proof in the *Sentences* commentary: bodies have sensible brightness, and spirits are even brighter with an intelligible splendor; but brighter and less bright are said in comparison to a maximum, and hence there must be some maximum of brightness from which all receive brightness and to which spirits more closely approach. If Thomas accepts this argument as sound (which is plausible, as he uses similar reasoning elsewhere), then it at least seems possible for Thomas to give an "argument from beauty" for God's existence that explicitly appeals to *both* of the conditions for beauty that are mentioned by Dionysius.

64. *In De div. nom.* 4.5, n. 339 (Marietti 113).

65. For instance, Thomas states at the end of the lesson that everything is good or beautiful according to its form; ibid., n. 355 (Marietti 115); see n. 349 (Marietti 114).

66. The dating is not certain but Torrell seems to accept it. *Saint Thomas Aquinas*, 358.

more heat as he goes further inside, he will know right away that there is a fire inside the house that is causing the different levels of heat.[67] A similar line of reasoning occurs to "one considering the things of this world": "For he finds all things to be disposed according to diverse levels of beauty and nobility; and the more closely they approach God, the more beautiful and better he finds them to be. Whence heavenly bodies are more beautiful and more noble than lower bodies, and invisible things than visible things." Hence, "it must be believed that all these things are from one God, who gives His existence to singular things, and nobility."[68]

Here we find Thomas giving an argument with striking similarities to the ones we saw in the *Sentences* and *Divine Names* commentaries. Like its predecessors, this proof argues from diverse levels of beauty in creatures to a cause of that beauty, though with the difference that here he also mentions nobility.[69] Moreover, like those earlier proofs, this argument is clearly based on transcendental beauty as it explicitly mentions both sensible and intelligible beauty, and therefore shows that Thomas is once again deriving the divine name 'Beauty' from the transcendental 'beautiful.'

As with the argument in the Dionysius commentary, it is not clear that Thomas regards the argument given here as a proof of God's existence. On the one hand, the proposition that Thomas says he intends to prove is simply that all things are created and made by one God; on the other hand, the "rough example" seems to be a case of someone reasoning to the existence of a fire in the house, and therefore suggests that Thomas intends this argument to lead one to knowledge of the divine beauty's existence, not just God's causality. In any case, the similarities of this argument to its predecessors shows that whenever Thomas wishes

---

67. *In Symbolum apostolorum* 1, n. 878 (Marietti 2.196).

68. Ibid. "Sic quoque contingit consideranti res huius mundi. Nam ipse invenit res omnes secundum diversos gradus pulchritudinis et nobilitatis esse dispositas; et quanto magis appropinquant Deo, tanto pulchriora et meliora invenit. Unde corpora caelestia pulchriora et nobiliora sunt quam corpora inferiora, et invisibilia visibilibus. Et ideo credendum est quod omnia haec sunt ab uno Deo, qui dat suum esse singulis rebus, et nobilitatem."

69. One might think Thomas is identifying beauty with nobility here; as Thomas explains elsewhere, however, the very word "nobility" (*nobilitas*) signifies brightness of rank (*claritas generis*), that is, having a notable (*notabilis*) or conspicuous place in one's society. Hence, while the meanings of nobility and beauty are closely related because they both involve brightness (*claritas*), they are undoubtedly distinct. *In I Corinthios* 1.4 (Marietti 1.245).

to reason from the beauty of creatures to some truth about the divine beauty, he has a preferred way of doing so: by reasoning from the diverse grades of beauty in creatures. This text therefore heavily implies that Thomas's arguments from beauty for truths about God are genuinely distinct from other ways of reasoning to God, and consequently that the divine name 'Beauty' and the transcendental 'beautiful' have meanings that are likewise distinct.

In Psalmos 26

The last text we will examine on the beauty of the divine essence comes from Thomas's commentary on the Psalms, written in the very last year of his life.[70] In one passage, Thomas explains the multiple translations of Psalm 26:4. Where Thomas's version reads "One thing I have asked of the Lord ... that I may see the delight of the Lord (*voluptatem Domini*)," others have "the beauty of the Lord (*pulchritudinem Domini*)" and even "the will of the Lord (*voluntatem Domini*)." According to Thomas, these different translations correspond to the three things in God that man desires to see, namely beauty, delightful things, and the disposition of things by divine providence. Thomas then explains why beauty is found in God: "The highest beauty is in God Himself, for beauty consists in well-formedness (*formositate*); but God is the very form informing all."[71]

What makes this text fascinating is Thomas's surprising decision to attribute beauty to God on the basis of "well-formedness" (*formositas*), which he actually distinguishes from beauty in his commentaries on the *Sentences* and the *Ethics*: according to these texts, because one of beauty's requirements is greatness of size (*magnitudo*), small men can be "well-formed" (*formosi*) but not beautiful (*pulchri*).[72] Thus, whereas in these earlier texts Thomas understands *formositas* as being well-formed in the sense of having a pleasing sensible form or shape, here he is evidently interpreting it more widely as possessing one's substantial form or nature to an excelling degree, which would include having not only the right size but all the perfections necessary for beauty. This interpretation harmonizes with Thomas's assertion that beauty has the nature of

---

70. Torrell, *Saint Thomas Aquinas*, 420–21.
71. *In Psalmos* 26 (Parma 14.238). "Summa pulchritudo est in ipso Deo, quia pulchritudo in formositate consistit: Deus autem est ipsa forma informans omnia ..."
72. *In Sent.* I, d. 31, q. 2, a. 1, cited in note 81 below. See *In Ethic.* 4.8.4 (Leon. 47/2.226–27:50–57).

a formal cause,[73] as well as with the texts where Thomas indicates that spiritual beauty consists in the form of a thing being possessed and manifested as perfectly as possible.[74]

In any case, this text provides compelling evidence that Thomas considers 'Beauty' a distinct divine name and 'beautiful' a distinct transcendental. Not only does Thomas argue solely from the meaning of 'beauty' here rather than from those of truth or goodness, but he brings up a new aspect of this meaning that he has never mentioned before, that is, well-formedness, thus implying that he is still discovering more facets of beauty's nature even at the end of his career. This text thus confirms that beauty has a rich meaning for Thomas, one with a number of aspects that are nonetheless interrelated: pleasing when seen, relating to knowledge, requiring three conditions, etc. Finally, because the original meaning of well-formedness obviously refers to sensible beauty, Thomas's use of it here shows that he is once again deriving the divine name of 'Beauty' from transcendental beauty rather than spiritual beauty.

AQUINAS'S ARGUMENTS FOR APPROPRIATING 'BEAUTY' TO THE SON

While we already have substantial evidence that 'Beauty' is a distinct divine name and transcendental for Thomas, one finds even more compelling support for this thesis in his texts on appropriating 'Beauty' to the Son. As Thomas explains in several places, although the divine attributes are identical with God's essence and are thus common to the whole Trinity, one of these common attributes can still have a greater likeness to the proper attributes of one Person than to those of the others; hence, this common attribute can be especially associated with that Person for the sake of clarifying what is unique to him,[75] which is thus called "appropriation" because something common to the whole Trinity is being drawn *ad proprium* or "toward what is proper" to a single Person.[76] For

---

73. *ST* I, q. 5, a. 4, ad 1 (Leon. 4.61).

74. For instance, *In Sent.* III, d. 23, q. 3, a. 1, ad 1, s.c. 2 (Mandonnet 3.741), and *In I Corinthios* 11.2 (Marietti 1.346).

75. *ST* I, q. 39, a. 7 (Leon. 4.407); see *In Sent.* I, d. 31, q. 1, a. 2 (Mandonnet 1.720–22). For a helpful article on Trinitarian appropriation, see Norman Kretzmann, "Trinity and Transcendentals," in *Trinity, Incarnation, and Atonement*, ed. R. Feenstra and C. Plantinga (Notre Dame, IN: University of Notre Dame Press, 1989), 79–109.

76. *De ver.*, q. 7, a. 3 (Leon. 22/1.203:32–53).

example, Thomas appropriates the divine name 'Power' to the Father because power has the nature of a beginning (*principium*) and he is the origin of the other two Persons.[77]

Hence, in order to argue for appropriating 'Beauty' to the Son, Thomas has to show that the meaning of 'Beauty' has a special likeness to His proper attributes. These arguments are therefore especially helpful for determining whether 'Beauty' is a distinct divine name because they give us a clear understanding of what Thomas thinks about the meaning of 'Beauty.' As we will see, these arguments show not only that 'Beauty' is distinct from 'Truth' and 'Goodness' as divine names, but even that it has a special place in Thomas's theology of the Trinity.

In Sent. I, d. 31, q. 2, a. 1, co. and ad 4

In this early text, Thomas is defending St. Hilary's triad of Trinitarian appropriations, in which "eternity" is appropriated to the Father, "species" to the Son, and "use" to the Holy Spirit.[78] Thomas interprets *species* as 'Beauty' (*pulchritudo*)[79]—in accordance with a tradition that goes back to Augustine[80]—and argues that 'Beauty' should be appropriated to the Son because of his likeness to the conditions for beauty. Thomas begins by presenting these conditions:

> For the meaning of beauty (*rationem pulchritudinis*), however, two things come together, according to Dionysius ... namely harmony and brightness. For he says that God is the cause of all beauty insofar as He is the cause of harmony and brightness, just as we call human beings beautiful who have proportioned members and a brilliant color. To these two the Philosopher adds a third ... where he says that there is no beauty except in a large body; for which reason small men can be called well-proportioned and shapely but not beautiful.[81]

---

77. Ibid.
78. Because Thomas's explanations for "eternity" and "use" have more significance for our inquiry in the parallel text from the *Summa theologiae*, we will postpone examining these appropriations until our discussion of the later passage.
79. *In Sent.* I, d. 31, q. 2, a. 1, co. (Mandonnet 1.723): "et species, idest pulchritudo."
80. As Aertsen notes (*The Transcendentals*, 339), Thomas himself mentions this fact in *De 108 articulis* 57 (Leon. 42.288): "Hylarius dicit 'species est in imagine'; Augustinus autem speciem interpretatur pulcritudinem."
81. Mandonnet 1.724: "Ad rationem autem pulchritudinis duo concurrunt, secundum Dionysium ... scilicet consonantia et claritas. Dicit enim, quod Deus est causa omnis pulchritudinis, inquantum est causa consonantiae et claritatis, sicut dicimus homines pulchros qui habent membra proportionata et splendentem colorem. His duobus addit tertium Philosophus ... ubi

Thomas then claims that "according to these three, beauty conforms to the properties of the Son." Insofar as he is "the perfect image of the Father," the Son has "perfect harmony" because he is "equal and similar without inequality or unlikeness." Likewise, insofar as he is the "true Son," he has "the perfect nature of the Father," and thus has the greatness (*magnitudinem*) which consists in the perfection of the divine nature. Finally, insofar as he is the "perfect word of the Father," the Son "has the brightness which shines over all and in which all things shimmer."[82]

At this point, the article has already provided several indications that 'Beauty' is a distinct divine name and 'beautiful' a distinct transcendental. First, in justifying the appropriation of 'Beauty' to the Son, Thomas does not argue from an identity of beauty with truth or goodness, but rather from the three conditions contained in beauty's own meaning (*rationem*). Second, it is clear that he is deriving the divine name of 'Beauty' from transcendental beauty in this text, as his examples of the conditions for beauty are all instances of bodily or sensible beauty, which can be applied only metaphorically to God. Hence, if Thomas regards 'Beauty' as having a distinct meaning when writing this text, he must think the same is true of the transcendental 'beautiful.'

As instructive as the body of the article is, the reply to the fourth objection has even more significance for our inquiry. The objection begins by noting that, according to Dionysius, "the beautiful and the good follow each other"; therefore, because "goodness is appropriated not to the Son but to the Holy Spirit," neither should "species or beauty."[83] In his reply, Thomas says the following: "Beauty does not have the meaning (*rationem*) of the desirable except insofar as it takes on the meaning of good: for in this way even the true is desirable: but according to its own

---

dicit, quod pulchritudo non est nisi in magno corpore; unde parvi homines possunt dici commensurati et formosi, sed non pulchri."

82. Ibid. "Et secundum haec tria, pulchritudo convenit cum propriis filii: inquantum enim Filius est imago perfecta patris, sic est ibi consonantia perfecta; est enim aequalis et similis sine inaequalitate et dissimilitudine.... Inquantum vero est Filius verus, habet perfectam naturam Patris: et ita etiam habet magnitudinem quae consistit in perfectione divinae naturae.... Sed inquantum est verbum perfectum Patris, habet claritatem quae irradiat super omnia et in quo omnia resplendent." Thomas presents another argument from Augustine that is based entirely on proportion. As Thomas does not mention this argument in the later passage in *ST* I, q. 39, a. 8, we will not discuss it here.

83. Mandonnet 1.723: "Item, secundum Dionysium ... pulchrum et bonum se consequuntur. Unde videtur quod omnia pulchrum et bonum appetunt.... Sed bonitas non appropriatur Filio, sed Spiritui sancto. Ergo nec species vel pulchritudo."

meaning (*propriam rationem*) it has brightness and those things that were said, which have a likeness to the properties of the Son."[84]

Thomas apparently grants the objection's point that 'Goodness' is appropriated to the Spirit, but denies that 'Beauty' should be appropriated to him as well on the grounds that 'Beauty' does not have the meaning of the desirable "according to its own meaning"; rather, like 'true,' it has the meaning of desirability only insofar as it "takes on" the meaning of the good, that is, when the intellect considers it as a particular good.[85] By contrast, the things that do belong to the proper meaning of 'Beauty,' such as brightness, have a definite likeness to the Son, for which reason 'Beauty' must be appropriated to him rather than to the Spirit.

For several reasons, this short reply to an objection proves more effectively than does any other text that Thomas regards both the divine name 'Beauty' and the transcendental 'beautiful' as distinct in meaning from 'true' and 'good.' First, this reply confirms that 'beauty' is distinct in meaning both from 'good' (whose meaning beauty must take on to become desirable) and from 'true' (which becomes desirable in the same way); indeed, Thomas goes so far as to state that 'beauty' has its "own meaning" (*propriam rationem*). Second, in saying that desirability does not belong to the proper meaning of 'beauty,' this text distinguishes 'beauty' not only from 'truth' and 'goodness' taken separately but even from their combination, that is, "the true taken as good." After all, if 'beauty' were synonymous with "the true taken as good," then desirability *would* belong to the meaning of beauty because, as Thomas says in this very reply, truth becomes desirable when it takes on the meaning of good.[86] Third, as noted above, Thomas has already made clear in the corpus of the article that he is deriving the divine name of 'Beauty' from transcendental beauty; hence, what Thomas says in the reply about

---

84. Mandonnet 1.725: "Pulchritudo non habet rationem appetibilis nisi inquantum induit rationem boni: sic enim et verum appetibile est: sed secundum rationem propriam habet claritatem et ea quae dicta sunt, quae cum propriis Filii similitudinem habent."

85. For instance, see *ST* I, q. 80, a. 1, ad 1 (Leon. 10.424), and *ST* I, q. 16, a. 4, ad 1 (Leon. 4.211). This text therefore might seem to contradict Thomas's assertion in *ST* I-II, q. 27, a. 1, ad 3 (Leon. 6.192), that 'beautiful' includes and adds to 'good' in its meaning. For why this contradiction is only apparent, see note 108 below.

86. What makes this text even more significant is that Thomas composes it only a few years after writing a *reportatio* or copy of a passage where his teacher Albert explicitly states that beauty is the true accepted as good (Aertsen, *The Transcendentals*, 358). As Thomas was thus obviously familiar with this view of Albert's, his statement that beauty does *not* include the good in its meaning seems to be a quiet but conscious rejection of his teacher's opinion.

'beauty' being distinct from 'truth' and 'goodness' applies not only to the divine name 'Beauty' but also the transcendental 'beautiful.'

Finally, this text reveals that Thomas has a strong theological motivation for holding that 'Beauty' is distinct in meaning from 'Truth' and 'Goodness': if it were not, Thomas could not defend the appropriation of 'Beauty' to the Son by St. Hilary and St. Augustine. As we saw, the objection argues that 'Beauty' should be appropriated to the Spirit just as 'Goodness' is because the beautiful and the good follow each other; hence, when Thomas begins his reply by denying that 'Beauty' has desirability in its meaning, he does so in order to explain why 'Beauty' does not have a likeness to the Spirit and thus should not be appropriated to him. Thomas evidently holds that, if 'Beauty' *did* have desirability in its meaning, it would be appropriated to the Spirit, which naturally follows from Thomas's view that, because the Spirit proceeds as love from the Father and the Son, any divine name that relates to love or desire is appropriated to him.[87]

It thus seems that at least part of Thomas's reason for holding that 'beauty' is distinct from 'truth' and 'goodness,' whether taken separately or in combination, is that he cannot otherwise defend the theological tradition he has inherited of appropriating the divine name of 'Beauty' to the Son rather than to the Spirit. As we will see presently, Thomas continues to defend this appropriation in his most mature work, where he gives nearly identical arguments for it, so we have good reason to think that he never abandoned the view that both the divine name 'Beauty' and the transcendental 'beautiful' are distinct from truth and goodness.

ST I, q. 39, a. 8

In this article from his most famous work, Thomas aims to prove the fittingness not merely of St. Hilary's Trinitarian appropriations, but of all the appropriations Thomas has inherited from scripture and his theological predecessors. He begins by noting that, because our intellect learns of God from creatures, it must consider him in the way that it considers creatures, which follows a certain order: first, we consider a creature absolutely or insofar as it is a certain being; second, insofar as it is one; third, according to its power of acting and causing; and finally, in relation

---

87. See *In Sent.* I, d. 31, q. 1, a. 2 (Mandonnet 1.721), and *ST* I, q. 39, a. 8 (Leon. 4.409).

to its effects.[88] Thomas then spends the rest of the article showing that the different triads of appropriated attributes correspond to these four ways of considering God and therefore do not contradict each other.

It is the first consideration of God, "by which God is considered absolutely according to His Being," that yields the triad of appropriations given by St. Hilary: eternity, species, and use. 'Eternity' is appropriated to the Father because it signifies "existence without a beginning" (*esse non principiatum*) and thus has a likeness to the Father, who as the first Person of the Trinity is "a beginning not from a beginning" (*principium non de principio*).[89]

Just as he does in the *Sentences* commentary, Thomas interprets *species* as 'Beauty'[90] and argues that it should be appropriated to the Son because of his likeness to the requirements for beauty, though his presentation of these requirements is slightly different here: "First indeed, integrity or perfection, for those things that are diminished are for this very reason ugly. And due proportion or harmony. And again brightness, for which reason those things that have a shining color are said to be beautiful (*pulchra*)."[91] While Thomas may seem to have replaced "greatness" (*magnitudo*) with integrity or perfection in this text,[92] he then states that integrity has a likeness to the second Person insofar as he is the Son and thus possesses truly and perfectly the nature of the Father, which is the same reason Thomas gave for the Son's likeness to greatness. Thus "integrity or perfection" is clearly just a more precise description of the same condition for beauty as "greatness," which Thomas confirms elsewhere.[93] Likewise, the rest of Thomas's account here is simply a more developed version of what he says in the *Sentences* commentary: "due proportion or harmony" befits the Son "insofar as He is the expressed image of the Father," because "we see that any image is said to be beautiful if it perfectly represents a thing, however ugly"; and brightness

---

88. *ST* I, q. 39, a. 8 (Leon. 4.408).
89. Ibid.
90. Leon. 4.409: "Species autem, sive pulchritudo, habet similitudinem cum propriis filii."
91. Ibid. "Nam ad pulchritudinem tria requiruntur. Primo quidem, integritas sive perfectio, quae enim diminuta sunt, hoc ipso turpia sunt. Et debita proportio sive consonantia. Et iterum claritas, unde quae habent colorem nitidum, pulchra esse dicuntur."
92. Aertsen interprets the text this way in *The Transcendentals*, 339.
93. In *ST* I, q. 42, a. 1, ad 1 (Leon. 4.435–36), Thomas notes that, when applied to spiritual things, greatness means perfection. See *In Sent.* I, d. 19, q. 3, a. 1 (Mandonnet 1.473).

conforms to the Son insofar as he is the Word, "which is a certain light, and the splendor of the intellect."[94]

Thomas now finishes his defense of St. Hilary's triad by explaining why "use" should be appropriated to the Holy Spirit. He notes that "use" has a likeness to the properties of the Holy Spirit only if we take the term "in a broad sense" that can include enjoying (*frui*). As Thomas notes elsewhere, the strict meaning of "using" (*uti*) is to order something to another object as a means to an end, and is thus contrasted with "enjoying" (*frui*), which means to delight in something as an end in itself; however, in a sense we still "use" an end by enjoying it because we are ordering it to a further good, namely our own delight.[95] Hence, as Thomas observes here, the broader meaning of "use" is simply to take something into the power of the will, in which case "to enjoy" means "to use with joy." According to this broader meaning, the use by which the Father and the Son enjoy each other has a likeness to the Spirit insofar as he is love, and the use by which we enjoy God has a likeness to the Spirit insofar as he is gift.[96] Having thus completed his account of Hilary's appropriations, Thomas devotes the rest of the main body of the article to explaining how the three other triads of appropriations correspond to the three other ways of considering God: we appropriate "unity, equality, and union" to the Trinity insofar as God is one, "power, wisdom, and goodness" insofar as he has a power of acting, and "from Whom, by Whom, and in Whom" insofar as he is related to his effects.[97]

This text is interesting because it gives 'Beauty' a special place among the appropriated attributes, and even a preeminence over the true and the good. Being an appropriated attribute already gives 'Beauty' a high degree of significance in Thomas's theology, as he confirms in an earlier text;[98] in this passage, however, 'Beauty' stands out as the central mem-

---

94. *ST* I, q. 39, a. 8 (Leon. 4.409). "Quantum igitur ad primum, similitudinem habet cum proprio filii, inquantum est filius habens in se vere et perfecte naturam patris.... Quantum vero ad secundum, convenit cum proprio filii, inquantum est imago expressa patris. Unde videmus quod aliqua imago dicitur esse pulchra, si perfecte repraesentat rem, quamvis turpem.... Quantum vero ad tertium, convenit cum proprio filii, inquantum est verbum, quod quidem lux est, et splendor intellectus, ut Damascenus dicit."

95. *ST* I-II, q. 16, a. 3, co., and ad 2 (Leon. 6.115–16).

96. *ST* I, q. 39, a. 8 (Leon. 4.408).

97. Ibid. (Leon. 4.408–9).

98. In *In Sent.* III, d. 1, q. 2, a. 2 (Mandonnet 3.34), Thomas argues that it was more fitting for the Son to become incarnate than for the Father or Holy Spirit because the incarnation has a greater conformity not only to the Son's proper attributes but also to his appropriated

ber in the first triad of appropriations, that is, those said of God "absolutely" or according to his being (*esse*).[99] By contrast, goodness belongs only to the third triad of appropriations, namely those said of God according to his power of acting, and truth does not even belong to a triad but is considered only in the reply to the objections.[100] Thus, this text indicates that 'Beauty' is not only important for Thomas's theology of the Trinity, but even uniquely so.

In fact, this article even suggests that the triad to which 'Beauty' belongs is a description of the Trinity's own inner life. In saying that this triad is attributed to God "according to His Being (*esse*)," Thomas implies that, while the other triads describe the Persons according to some mere aspect of God, such as his unity, power of acting, or relations to his effects, St. Hilary's triad in some sense describes the "being" or essence of the Persons and their relations to each other. This impression is strengthened by Thomas's interpretation of "use" as "enjoyment" because to enjoy something simply means to take pleasure in it,[101] and as is well known, Thomas defines "beautiful" as that which pleases merely by being seen or apprehended.[102] Hence it seems natural to interpret the beauty of the Son as the reason for the enjoyment that is the Holy Spirit, especially given Thomas's insistence that the Spirit proceeds from the Father *through* the Son.[103] Finally, because Thomas says that "eternity" conforms to the Father insofar as he is "the beginning without a beginning," this appropriation seems to signify that the Father is the ultimate "beginning" or origin of the beauty that is the Son. Hence, one could argue that for Thomas, St. Hilary's triad describes the inner life of the Trinity as the

---

attributes, including beauty. Thus, due to its status as an appropriated attribute, beauty is one of the reasons that it befits the Son to become incarnate, and is therefore important for understanding the very course of salvation history.

99. It also seems significant that Thomas connects beauty's three conditions with all three personal names of the Son: integrity or perfection with "Son," harmony or due proportion with "image," and brightness with "Word."

100. There is one text where Thomas presents a triad containing truth, i.e., the appropriation of unity, truth, and goodness to the Father, Son, and Holy Spirit; however, as Aertsen acknowledges, Thomas mentions this triad only in an objection and thus "never presents the Trinitarian appropriation of the transcendentals unmistakably in his own voice." *De ver.*, q. 1, a. 1, s.c. 5 and ad s.c. 5 (Leon. 22/1.4:83–94 and 22/1.7–8:290–313). Aertsen, *The Transcendentals*, 411–14.

101. *ST* I-II, q. 11, a. 1, ad 3 (Leon. 6.90).

102. *ST* I, q. 5, a. 4, ad 1 (Leon. 4.61): "Pulchra enim dicuntur quae visa placent." *ST* I-II, q. 27, a. 1, ad 3 (Leon. 6.192): "Pulchrum autem dicatur id cuius ipsa apprehensio placet."

103. *ST* I, q. 36, a. 3 (Leon. 4.382).

begetting, beholding, and enjoyment of beauty: the Father is the origin who eternally generates beauty, the Son is the image in whom the beauty is seen, and the Spirit is the enjoyment of that beauty.[104] If such is indeed Thomas's view, it is hard to believe that 'Beauty' has so much significance for him without having a distinct meaning.

CONCLUSION

Our survey of Thomas's texts on the divine beauty has revealed abundant evidence that 'Beauty' is a distinct divine name for him, which we will now summarize:

1. Whenever Thomas argues for attributing beauty to God or appropriating it to the Son, he consistently uses one or more of the aspects that he ascribes to the meaning of beauty (the three conditions, the different types and degrees of beauty, "well-formedness," etc.), thus indicating that he thinks that beauty has a unique *ratio* to which he must appeal; moreover, some of these aspects (such as brightness) seem to be more essential to beauty than others, which implies that beauty is no mere composite notion like "the true taken as good" but in fact has a single meaning to which its various aspects are ordered.

2. Additionally, Thomas never argues for applying the name 'Beauty' to God simply on the basis of his truth or goodness. Thomas does mention truth while attributing beauty to God in *Super Iob* 40 and while appropriating it to the Son in *In Sent.* I, d. 3, q. 2, but he does so only in order to argue either that the divine essence or that the Son possesses one of beauty's requirements, namely brightness; as for goodness, Thomas never even mentions it, but instead alludes to the essential condition of the good, that is, perfection, which he does only because it is also a condition for beauty. Hence, Thomas evidently thinks that God's truth and goodness are not sufficient to prove that he is beauty unless one can use them to show that he also fulfills beauty's unique requirements.

---

104. Thomas seems to confirm that the life of the Trinity is essentially an experience of beauty in the late text *In Matthaeum* 3.2 (written 1269–70). In explaining the Father's words that he is "well pleased" in the Son, Thomas states that the Father delights in the Son "just as the artist is pleased in his beautiful artifact, and just as if a man sees his beautiful image in the mirror." Marietti 46: "*In quo mihi complacui.* In quocumque enim relucet bonum alicuius, in illo aliquid complacet sibimet, sicut artifex sibi complacet in pulchro artificio suo, et sicut si homo videat suam pulchram imaginem in speculo." Torrell, *Saint Thomas Aquinas*, 339.

3. At the very beginning of his career, Thomas presents an argument for God's existence from the diverse grades of beauty in his *Sentences* commentary, and we find very similar arguments near the end of his career in his *Divine Names* commentary and his *collatio* on the Apostles' creed. Thomas therefore seems to have an "argument from beauty" for God's existence (or for his unicity and causality) that is truly distinct from other ways of reasoning to God, which strongly implies that he considers beauty a distinct attribute of God and of being.

4. In an early text on appropriating 'Beauty' to the Son, Thomas explicitly distinguishes 'beauty' from 'truth' and 'goodness' and implicitly distinguishes it from 'the true taken as good'; moreover, he makes clear that, if 'beauty' were simply "the true taken as good," it would have to be appropriated to the Holy Spirit, whereas Thomas holds throughout his career that 'Beauty' must be appropriated to the Son. Thus, Thomas has a powerful theological motivation for holding that 'Beauty' is a distinct divine name: his respect for St. Hilary's appropriation of 'Beauty' to the Son.

5. Finally, 'Beauty' has a surprising degree of significance in Thomas's theology as an appropriated attribute because it belongs to the triad of appropriations that is said of God according to his being (*esse*). It therefore seems that for Thomas the very inner life of the Trinity can be described as the begetting, beholding, and enjoyment of beauty.

The only reasonable conclusion to be drawn from such evidence is that Thomas does consider 'Beauty' to be a distinct divine name, and even one of some importance.

Furthermore, the texts we have examined show not only that 'Beauty' is a distinct divine name but also that 'beautiful' is a distinct transcendental. In his passages on the divine beauty, Thomas never mentions spiritual beauty without sensible beauty, but frequently does the reverse. Thus, because bodily beauty cannot be attributed to God, these texts are clearly deriving the divine name of 'Beauty' from the only 'genus' that contains both bodily and spiritual beauty, that is, transcendental beauty, from which it follows that 'Beauty' is not a distinct divine name unless 'beautiful' is also a distinct transcendental. As Thomas evidently considers 'Beauty' to be a distinct divine name, he must likewise consider 'beautiful' to be a distinct transcendental.

This conclusion naturally raises certain questions about Thomas's treatment of beauty. First, if Thomas considered 'Beauty' to be a distinct divine name, and even an important one, why does he give such passing attention to beauty, particularly in his *Summa theologiae*? Thomas does not devote a separate *quaestio* or inquiry to beauty, as he does with the other divine attributes, but instead discusses it only in the articles on goodness, and often in a mere reply to an objection. Moreover, if Thomas considered 'beautiful' to be a distinct transcendental, why does he never mention it in his texts on the transcendentals, particularly the most extensive one in *De veritate*, q. 1, a. 1?[105]

Two reasons can be given as an explanation of these facts. First, although beauty is clearly important to Thomas, it is not as foundational a notion for his philosophy and theology as the other transcendentals. For one thing, unlike truth and goodness, beauty is not the object of a distinct power of the human soul,[106] and thus does not need to be discussed in order to understand the soul's structure and activity. Moreover, as mentioned earlier, in Thomas's order of the transcendentals the meanings of the later terms include and add to the meanings of earlier terms; consequently, earlier terms are necessary for understanding later terms, but not vice versa.[107] Now Thomas makes clear that 'beautiful' comes at the end of the order of transcendentals; he says that its meaning includes and adds to the meaning of 'good,'[108] which is the last transcendental that

---

105. *De ver.*, q. 1, a. 1 (Leon. 22/1.4–5:95–161).

106. Many (such as Aertsen) regard this fact as sufficient proof that beauty cannot be a distinct transcendental. But such an argument assumes that the only way for a transcendental to express a unique relation to the human soul is by expressing a relation to a distinct power of the human soul. As Kovach and others have suggested, there remains the possibility of expressing a relation to both powers of the human soul simultaneously, which could happen through relating to one power directly and the other indirectly. I have argued in my doctoral dissertation that beauty expresses just such a relation, as I mention below in note 111.

107. *De ver.*, q. 21, a. 3, cited in note 7 above.

108. *ST* I-II, q. 27, a. 1, ad 3 (Leon. 6.192). This view of Thomas might seem to contradict his earlier statement in *In Sent.* I, d. 31, q. 2, a. 1, ad 4, that 'beauty' does not have the meaning of the desirable unless it takes on the meaning of 'good,' just as 'true' does (see note 85). In fact, however, the contradiction is only apparent. While 'beautiful' does include the meaning of 'good,' it also adds to the meaning of good its own unique meaning (just as every transcendental does to the one preceding it); moreover, this unique *ratio* that is added to 'good' by 'beautiful' cannot itself contain 'good' or it will not be distinct from what it is added to. Hence, when Thomas says that 'beautiful' does not have the meaning of the desirable or the good, he is referring to the "proper meaning" (*propriam rationem*) of the beautiful, i.e., the unique *ratio* that 'beautiful' adds to 'good,' whereas when he says that 'beautiful' includes and adds to the meaning of 'good,' he is referring to what one might call the complete meaning of 'beautiful,' i.e., the meaning that is the result of combining 'good' and the proper meaning that 'beautiful' adds to it.

he lists. Hence Thomas does not need to devote as much explicit attention to beauty because it is not needed to explain any of the other transcendentals. In fact, quite the opposite is true: precisely because 'beautiful' is the last transcendental and thus includes all the others, one cannot fully understand beauty without fully understanding *all* the transcendentals. Hence, in devoting more attention to the earlier transcendentals, Thomas is doing exactly what needs to be done in order to lay the groundwork for a complete account of beauty. As Eric Gill famously said, "look after goodness and truth, and beauty will look after herself."

Second, Thomas does not seem to have ever pinned down the meaning of beauty to his complete satisfaction. In one of his latest texts on beauty, Thomas writes that 'beautiful' adds to the good "a certain relation" (*quendam ordinem*) to the cognitive power,[109] thus indicating that he has not fully determined the nature of this relation. Moreover, the word *quendam* does not appear in the earlier but parallel text in the *Divine Names* commentary,[110] which suggests that Thomas has become more uncertain about the meaning of 'beautiful' since then. Finally, as we saw, Thomas seems to be discovering new aspects of beauty even at the end of his career, such as "well-formedness." Hence, Thomas may have decided not to devote as much attention to beauty because he was not as confident about its precise meaning as he was about those of goodness and truth. If so, then fully determining the elusive *ratio* of beauty[111] is a task that Thomas has left for his followers.[112]

---

109. *ST* I-II, q. 27, a. 1, ad 3 (Leon. 6.192). "Et sic patet quod pulchrum addit supra bonum, quendam ordinem ad vim cognoscitivam ..."

110. *In De div. nom.* 4.5, n. 356 (Marietti 115).

111. For one account of the meaning of 'beautiful,' see Rubin, "The Meaning of 'Beauty,'" chaps. 3–6. There I argue that 'beautiful' expresses being's ability to be possessed and enjoyed by the will through the mere apprehension of it by the intellect, which is a relation *to* the will but *through* the intellect, and thus distinct from the meanings of 'true' and 'good.'

112. I am grateful to Brian Carl, Thérèse Cory, and Gregory Doolan for their help with this chapter.

Jason A. Mitchell

12 ∞ Aquinas on Divine Application

In the late sixteenth and early seventeenth centuries, Dominican and Jesuit scholars were sharply divided on the theme of how God influences the creature's operation, especially the rational creature's free operation. Domingo Báñez, OP, proposed that God physically pre-moves the creature from potency to act,[1] while Luis de Molina, SJ, developed a theory of divine concurrence in which God acts with the creature and not on the creature.[2] Although each theory has had its supporters through the centuries, neither theory has been able to establish itself definitively as representing either the authentic doctrine of Thomas Aquinas or as adequately resolving the problem of divine causality and human freedom.[3] At least three problems should be acknowledged in this debate:

1. R. J. Matava, *Divine Causality and Human Free Choice: Domingo Báñez, Physical Premotion and the Controversy "de Auxiliis" Revisited* (Leiden: Brill, 2016), 9: "Physical premotion was advanced by Báñez as an account of what *Deus operatur in omni operante* (ST I.105.5) means: God operates in all creaturely agents – including free creaturely agents – by moving them to act."

2. Ibid., 109: "Molina conceives of God's causation not as taking place *on* the human agent (*pace* Báñez), but rather *with* the human agent on the human agent's action and effect. Since the human agent is endowed with causal powers of its own, it needs no divinely added perfection to move from rest to operation. Rather, the human agent is already poised to act. It only needs God's general concurrence for its own autonomous self-determination to obtain."

3. Brian J. Shanley, "Divine Causation and Human Freedom in Aquinas," *American Catholic Philosophical Quarterly* 77 (1998): 110: "Quite apart from the troubling implications of *praemotio* for human freedom and its lack of textual warrant, other interpreters of Aquinas argue that the doctrine is not only unnecessary but also at odds with Aquinas's basic attempt to uphold the reality of secondary causation. For if every exercise of secondary causation requires a specific divine push or premotion that is passively receive by the created power, then the secondary cause is not really an active agent." Réginald Garrigou-Lagrange, *The Trinity and God the Creator* (Jackson, MI: Ex Fontibus Company, 2015), 452–53: "Molina, however, found

the metaphysical question about interplay between divine and creaturely causation; the anthropological question about the relationship between human freedom and divine providence; and the theological question about the role of divine grace as an effect of divine predestination. This chapter will focus primarily on the first metaphysical problem.[4] It is my contention that the theories of Báñez and Molina each suffer the consequences of the late Scholastic move toward essentialism,[5] which tends to gives priority to essence over being (*esse*) and dissociates being and operation.

In this chapter, I want to propose divine application as a third alternative, an alternative I believe more closely aligns with Aquinas's thought. Instead of saying with Báñez that God physically and predeterminately pre-moves the creature from potency to act or with Molina that God generally concourses with the creature by sustaining the creature in existence while the creature specifies its acts,[6] we will see that Aquinas proposes that God moves the creature by applying the creature's operative potencies to their operations.[7]

---

himself at variance with this teaching of St. Thomas. He said: '[...] I cannot see or understand that movement and that application in second causes by which God moves these causes to act.' For Molina the influx of God's general power is simultaneous, it does not flow into the second cause and apply it to action but flows directly into the effect of the second cause, 'not unlike two men rowing a boat.' Suárez maintained the same view."

4. I will deal indirectly with the second problem in this paper. I dealt extensively with the third problem in my recent dissertation: Jason A. Mitchell, *Aquinas's Theology of Grace: Metaphysics and the New Perspective* (Charlotte, N.C.: Spirit of Wisdom Press, 2024).

5. The move toward essentialism can be seen especially in Francisco Suárez. See his *Disputationes Metaphysicae* 31.4.6: "Ergo huiusmodi esse quo res formaliter constituitur actu extra causas est existentia." See also 31.13.18: "Unde cum existentia nihil aliud sit quam essentia in actu constituta, sicut essentia actualis per seipsam vel per sua intrinseca principia est formaliter limitata, ita etiam existentia creata limitationem habet ex ipsa essentia, non ut est potentia in qua recipitur, sed quia in re nihil aliud est quam ipsamet actualis essentia."

6. Kirk R. MacGregor, *Luis de Molina: The Life and Theology of the Founder of Middle Knowledge* (Grand Rapids, MI: Zondervan, 2015), 160: "[Molina] denied that secondary agents must be moved by God to use their causal power. Further, Molina argued that, intrinsically, God's general concurrence is neither efficacious nor inefficacious. Rather, it is intrinsically neutral and is extrinsically made efficacious or inefficacious by the pertinent secondary agents." Matava, *Divine Causality and Human Free Choice*, 111: "For Molina, it is from the secondary cause that actions get their particular species. The function of the secondary cause, for Molina, is to particularize God's nonspecific causal influx (general concurrence)." Molina and Suárez do not see existence as the intrinsic source of perfection but as what constitutes an essence outside of its cause.

7. Aquinas, *ST* I, q. 105, a. 5 (Leon. 4:476): "Deus movet non solum res ad operandum, quasi applicando formas et virtutes rerum ad operationem ... sed etiam dat formam creaturis agentibus, et eas tenet in esse."

John F. Wippel first dealt with divine application in an article that contrasted Thomas Aquinas and Henry of Ghent on the problem of divine knowledge, divine power, and human freedom.[8] Wippel dealt with it again in an article on creatures as causes of *esse*.[9] In his *The Metaphysical Thought of Thomas Aquinas*, Wippel deals with divine application in the context of his presentation of Aquinas's First Way.[10] This is important because one of the examples employed by Aquinas in the First Way is that of a staff (*baculus*) that is moved by a hand. Aquinas's example, which posits that the series of moved movers needs to arrive to a First Immobile Mover, does not specify how the human will moves the hand or how God, as First Mover, applies and moves the human will to its operations. Divine application, then, is not a fringe metaphysical topic, but one essential to the proofs of God's existence and, therefore, central to metaphysics.

In this chapter, I want to explore Aquinas's understanding of how God applies the created operative powers of irrational and rational creatures to their respective operations and the role of the notion of participation in this understanding. I propose that it is Aquinas's metaphysics of *actus essendi* and participation that leads him to a theory of divine application.[11]

To approach Aquinas's theory on divine application we need to understand both the intrinsic relationship between the act of being (*actus essendi*), essence, operative powers, operative habits, and operation in a creature, and the extrinsic relationship between the threefold divine causality and created beings. In the first part of this chapter, I will establish the basic tenets of what we can call Aquinas's metaphysics of operation. In the second part, dedicated to divine causality, I strive to avoid the bifurcation of efficient causality and exemplar causality into two separate corresponding lines of participation.[12] Aquinas's texts can be interpreted

---

8. John F. Wippel, "Divine Knowledge, Divine Power and Human Freedom in Thomas Aquinas and Henry of Ghent," in *Metaphysical Themes in Thomas Aquinas* (Washington, DC: The Catholic University of America Press, 1984), 243–70, esp. 258–63. Throughout Wippel refers favorably to Fabro's work.

9. John F. Wippel, "Thomas Aquinas on Creatures as Causes of *Esse*," in *Metaphysical Themes in Thomas Aquinas II* (Washington, DC: The Catholic University of America Press, 2007), 172–93.

10. Wippel, *Metaphysical Thought*, 451–52.

11. Some interpreters of Aquinas see operation as something added to the existing essence instead of as a mediated expansion of the perfection of the act of being, which itself remains *fixum et quietum* in a being (*ens*).

12. Alain Contat, "*Esse, essentia, ordo*. Verso una metafisica della partecipazione operativa,"

in such a way that both causalities are kept together in a single line of participation, which can even incorporate the notion of final causality. By keeping all three extrinsic causalities together in one line of participation between creature and Creator, we can better account for the real composition of created *ens*, its order of the creature to its ultimate end, and how the creature attains its end through its operation.[13] The third and final part attends especially to Aquinas's texts on application. This overview will bring to light how Aquinas contextualizes divine application and how divine application presupposes the creation and conservation of the creature's operative powers. We will see that Aquinas does not speak about predetermining or pre-moving the human will, but about inclining the human will and applying it to the creature's operation in accord with the creature's rational nature.

METAPHYSICS OF OPERATION

Aquinas holds that the subject of metaphysics is being insofar as it is being (*ens inquantum est ens*) or common being (*ens commune*). Being (*ens*), as studied in metaphysics, is "that which finitely participates in being" (*esse*).[14] Wippel has pointed out that, according to Aquinas, this participation of being (*ens*) in being (*esse*) is threefold: participation in *esse commune*, participation in *actus essendi*, and participation in *Esse subsistens*.[15] I have argued elsewhere, with Daniel De Haan and Gregory Doolan, that the three participations can be linked to Aquinas's three modes of participation. Formally, participation in *esse* refers to the participation

---

Espíritu 61 (2012): 17–18. The bifurcation of efficient causality and exemplar causality associates exemplar causality with the essence and leads some Scholastics to separate participation into "participation by composition" and "participation by similitude." This leads to a dualistic view of *ens* as a composition of two acts: (1) essence (formal act and perfection) which relates to God according to exemplar causality and is like God by similitude and (2) existence (existential act and perfection) which relates to God according to efficient causality. Operation, in this view, tends to be seen as a third act or perfection added to these two acts.

13. A single line of participation between God and the creature rather than two lines of participation better integrates efficient, exemplar, and final causality. When we say that the creature has being by participation, this means that its being depends on God, imitates God, and is ordered to God. The interpretation that employs two lines of participation associates being with efficient causality and essence with exemplar causality and tends to leave final causality out of the picture. Suárez, for example, tends to deny that final causality is a real cause.

14. Aquinas, *In De caus.* (Saffrey 47): "ens autem dicitur id quod finite participat esse."

15. Wippel, *Metaphysical Thought*, 110–31.

of a finite substance in its act of being (*actus essendi*) according to the second mode of participation. Foundationally, it refers to the participation of a created substance in a likeness of *Esse subsistens* according to the third mode of participation. Notionally, it refers to the participation of an individual substance in *esse commune* according to the first mode of participation.[16]

The Thomistic interpretation developed in large part by Cornelio Fabro and Étienne Gilson[17] understands the act of being (*actus essendi*) as the "actuality of all acts" and "the perfection of all perfections."[18] The act of being, according to this interpretation, is the actuating act and the ultimate, intrinsic source of all the perfection of a finite being. The role of the essence (as *potentia essendi*) is not to add another perfection to the act of being, but rather to limit, determine, measure, and specify the act of being. In the Fabrian view, the order (*ordo*) of the creature to its end is not reduced completely to the essence, but rather is seen as consequent upon the specification of the essence and rooted intrinsically in the act of being, which seeks to communicate itself to the highest possible degree.[19] This interpretation, then, opposes the Scholastic view that created *ens* is a mixture of two perfections, with the essence conferring formal perfection to the substance apart from existence, and existence adding a separate existential perfection to this formal perfection.

It is important to grasp how the two interpretations oppose each other, as this will ultimately affect the interpretation of Aquinas's thought on divine motion and divine application. The classical or Baroque Thomist

---

16. Jason A. Mitchell, "Aquinas on *esse commune* and the First Mode of Participation," *The Thomist* 82 (2018): 566. See Daniel D. De Haan, "Aquinas on *actus essendi* and the Second Mode of Participation," *The Thomist* 82 (2018): 573–609; Gregory T. Doolan, "Aquinas on *esse subsistens* and the Third Mode of Participation," *The Thomist* 82 (2018): 611–42.

17. Alain Contat outlines the three main interpretations of Aquinas's metaphysics that have emerged. While the classical approach (Cajetan, D. Báñez, R. Garrigou-Lagrange, L.-B. Geiger, T. Tyn) is often characterized by a dualism of formal and existential perfection, and the transcendental approach (K. Rahner, J. B. Lotz) is marked by the role of knowledge in the relation between finite being and infinite being, the approach of Fabro and Gilson, which is sometimes labeled "intensive Thomism," intrinsically roots the creature's perfection in the act of being (*actus essendi*) which, in turn, causally participates in divine being. See, e.g., Alain Contat, "La constitution de l'étant dans le thomisme contemporain: Tomas Tyn, Johann Baptist Lotz, Cornelio Fabro," in *Actus essendi. Saint Thomas d'Aquin et ses interprètes*, ed. Matthieu Raffray (Paris: Parole et Silence, 2019), 369–433.

18. See Thomas Aquinas, *De pot.*, q. 7, a. 2, ad 9.

19. See Alain Contat, "*Esse, essentia, ordo*. Verso una metafisica della partecipazione operativa," *Espíritu* 61 (2012): 29.

view tends to see being (*ens*) as a subsistent essence to which existence is added.[20] The Fabrian or Gilsonian view sees being (*ens*) as a participated act of being measured and specified by its correlative essence.

According to the late Scholastic view, being (*ens*) is like a dualistic mixture of two perfections, one formal and the other existential. Accidental perfections and operation tend to be seen as a third perfection that is added to the existing essence. This is seen in the interpretation of *esse accidentale*. Rather than root "accidental *esse*" in the substance's sole *actus essendi*, these interpreters posit an additional "*esse*" conferred by the accidental form that is distinct from and not truly connected to the creature's *actus essendi*.[21] For example, Báñez's metaphysics dissociates the *esse* of an accident from the *esse* of substance. The reason he gives is that the *esse* of an accident is dependent on a subject while the *esse* of a substance is an independent act. The *esse* of an accident is "existence in another" or "in-existence." Báñez also gives a theological reason: "The third argument is from the actuality of accidents in the supernatural order. Such accidents must, by proportion, be actuated by *esse* in the supernatural order. There is only one actual substance in the supernatural order, however: namely, the divine substance. Hence, supernatural accidents found in natural substances do not exist by the *esse* of the natural substances they modify; hence, substantial and accidental *esse* must be really distinct."[22]

In the Baroque Scholastic view, a created *ens*, then, is viewed as a composite mixture of three perfections. Formal perfection is conferred by the essence and this makes the being (*ens*) what it is. Existential perfection is conferred to the essence by *esse* which places a finite essence outside of nothingness and its cause. Accidental perfections are conferred by accidental forms or operation, which are added to the existing subsistent essence. In the end, this view dissociates operation from being and posits it as an additional perfection without rooting it in the

---

20. See Alain Contat, "Le figure della differenza ontologica nel tomismo del Novecento (seconda parte)," *Alpha Omega* 11 (2008): 232.

21. See Wippel, *Metaphysical Thought*, 254: "At least as far back as Capreolus in the early fifteenth century, leading commentators may be found who hold that Thomas assigns an existence or *esse* to accidents which is distinct from that of their substantial subject. This reading continues to have its defenders down to the present day, and includes many twentieth-century interpreters of Aquinas."

22. Benjamin S. Llamzon, "Suppositi and Accidental *Esse*: A Study in Banez," *The New Scholasticism* 39 (1965): 180.

creature's act of being. This conception of created being leads Báñez to set up a parallel between the cause of being and the cause of action and posit divine pre-motion as that which moves the creature, which is in potency, from non-act to act, from non-operation to operation. Seemingly absent in Báñez's metaphysics is the recognition that the creature is already in act in some way and has the capacity and participated power to act. A more nuanced view of the operative powers of the creature is warranted.

In the Fabrian and Gilsonian view, *actus essendi* is *fixum et quietum* in a created *ens*[23] and is the intrinsic source of *all* perfection. The created essence does not confer a distinct perfection, but rather specifies the perfection of being and orders it to its ultimate end. The Fabrian distinction between "being as act" (*esse ut actus*) and "being in act" (*esse in actu*) allows the metaphysician to distinguish the essence from the act of being at the level of principles and to contemplate various levels of potency and actuality in the finite *ens*. Substantial *esse*, then, can refer either to the *actus essendi* that the substance has by participation or to the being-in-act (*esse in actu*) of the substance. In this interpretation, accidents do not confer their own *actus essendi* to the substance. Accidental *esse* is the being-in-act (*esse in actu*) of the accident, which inheres in the substance and thus depends intrinsically on the *actus essendi* of the substance. This line of interpretation also sees *actus essendi* rather than the essence as *virtus essendi*, that is, the actuating capacity of *esse* itself.

Aquinas's explicit text on the threefold perfection of a thing does not divide it, as do some Scholastics, into formal (*esse essentiae*), existential (*esse existentiae*), and operative (*esse accidentis*). Rather, Aquinas distinguishes: (1) the perfection of its constitution in being (*esse*); (2) its accidental perfections which are necessary for its perfect operation; and (3) the perfection of attaining its end.[24] According to the Fabrian and Gilsonian interpretation, the entire perfection of a thing belongs to its being.[25] Thus, the constitution in *esse* does not refer to an admixture of two perfections, but to a limitation and specification of the perfection of being by the essence. Accidental perfections are added to the substance, but depend on the substance's one act of being. The attainment of the end

---

23. *SCG* I.20 (Leon. 13.54): "Esse autem est aliquid fixum et quietum in ente."
24. *ST* I, q. 6, a. 3.
25. *ST* I, q. 4, a. 2.

through operation refers back intrinsically to the actuating power (*virtus*) of the act of being, mediated by the essence, operative powers, and operative habits.

In the human being, the operative powers of intellect and will flow from the essence of the human soul,[26] which measures and specifies the rational creature's act of being. Operative habits (such as the acquired virtues) have the operative powers as their subject. Good habits dispose the creature to operate for the good. In Aquinas's metaphysics of operation, the good (*bonum*) plays a fundamental role. On the one hand, the finite creature is constituted in its first perfection through the act of creation and is said to be good in a relative way (*bonum secundum quid*); on the other hand, the finite creature is ordered to its ultimate end and perfection (*bonum simpliciter*), which is attained through its proper operation.

The usage of the analogical notions of act and potency enable us to understand how Aquinas relates the various principles and powers. Compared to the act of being, the created essence is the potency of being (*potentia essendi*). The essence itself is an actuated act and specifying principle.[27] The operative powers are specified by the essence and actuated by the creature's act of being. They are actuated acts, and yet are ordered to and are in potency to second acts. For example, the human being has eighteen operative powers of the soul ordered to various objects and operations.[28] The operative habits, which are accidental qualities, reside in the powers and dispose the operative powers to operation, or second act. The soul as such is not an act ordered to an ulterior act, but is the ultimate term of generation.[29] Hence, that it be in potency to another act, does not belong to it according to its essence, insofar as it is a form, but according to its power. And so the soul itself, as the subject of its powers, is called the first act, ordered to a second act through its powers.[30]

---

26. *In Sent.* II, d. 3, q. 7, a. 2, ad 2.
27. *ST* I, q. 77, a. 1.
28. The eighteen powers are the three vegetative powers (nutritive, augmentative, and generative), the five exterior sensitive powers (touch, smell, hearing, sight, and taste), the four interior sensitive powers (common sense, imagination, cogitative power, memory), the two sensitive appetitive powers (concupiscible and irascible), the locomotive power, the possible intellect, the active intellect, and the rational appetite.
29. *ST* I, q. 77, a. 1 (Leon. 4.237): "Non enim, inquantum est forma, est actus ordinatus ad ulteriorem actum, sed est ultimus terminus generationis."
30. Ibid. "Unde quod sit in potentia adhuc ad alium actum, hoc non competit ei secundum

Because Aquinas holds that the creature's operative powers—which are rooted in the creature's act of being and specified, determined, and measured by the creature's essence—are active powers yet still in potency to operation, it will be necessary to posit a First Mover who reduces the operative powers to act by applying them to the creature's operation. Let us consider divine causality in general before looking at the causality of divine application in particular.

DIVINE CAUSALITY

Metaphysics seeks not only to know the intrinsic principles of *ens inquantum ens* and what belongs to it, that is, the transcendentals, but also the extrinsic causes. Aquinas defines a "cause" as "that from which the being of something follows."[31] Cause adds to "principle" the notion of an influx or influence on the being of the effect (*causatum*).[32] I have argued elsewhere that Aquinas's metaphysical causality elevates and transforms Aristotelian physical-metaphysical causality in several ways.[33] At the level of intrinsic causality, Aquinas posits that the actuating act of a created substance is no longer the accidental or substantial form (in act), but rather its participated *actus essendi*. With respect to the act of being, the essence or form is a potency principle that limits and specifies the act of being. And this real composition of act of being and essence instills a teleology within the created substance, ordering and directing it from within to its end, which is attained through its proper operation.

At the level of extrinsic causality, Aquinas first sees that the ultimate efficient cause is not just a moving cause (as in Aristotle), but rather is that which produces *ex nihilo* both the creature's *actus essendi* and its specifying essence. Second, God knows not just himself, but also knows all other things through himself, and, as the ultimate exemplar cause, intellectually measures what is produced. Third, the ultimate final cause is not indifferent to its creatures, but rather providentially orders each creature to himself as to its ultimate end. Divine governance is the execution

---

suam essentiam, inquantum est forma; sed secundum suam potentiam. Et sic ipsa anima, secundum quod subest suae potentiae, dicitur *actus primus*, ordinatus ad actum secundum."

31. *De princ. nat.* 3.

32. *In Meta.* V.1, n. 751.

33. Jason Mitchell, "From Aristotle's Four Causes to Aquinas' Ultimate Causes of Being: Modern Interpretations," *Alpha Omega* 16 (2013): 409.

of this providential plan (*executio providentiae*).³⁴ In this execution, the divine cause moves his creatures, in accord with their rational or irrational natures, to their ultimate end. To understand this divine motion in creatures and the divine application of operative powers to operation, we need to consider divine causality and its integration with the notion of participation.

Aquinas's treatment of creation in *ST* I, qq. 44–119, is divided according to a threefold consideration of the procession of creatures from God: *efficient causality* concerns the production of creatures (qq. 44–46); exemplar causality concerns the distinction of creatures (qq. 47–102); and final causality concerns the conservation and governance of creatures (qq. 103–19).³⁵ It is interesting to note that while Suárez considers concurrence and application under the notion of efficient causality, Aquinas considers divine motion and application in the section on final causality.³⁶

With regard to efficient causality, Aquinas holds that God is the efficient cause of created *ens* insofar as he gives it participated *esse*: "All others [apart] from God are not their own being (*esse*), but rather participate being (*esse*). Therefore, it is necessary that all that are diversified according to diverse participation of being, so as to be more or less perfect, are caused by the one First Being."³⁷ In creating, God simultaneously gives *esse* and produces that which receives *esse*.³⁸ The properly metaphysical consideration of being is not as *this* being (*hoc ens*) or as *such* a being

---

34. *In Sent.* I, d. 39, q. 2, a. 1, ad 1. See also *ST* I, q. 23, a. 2 (Leon. 4.273): "Sed executio providentiae, quae gubernatio dicitur, passive quidem est in gubernatis; active autem est in gubernante."

35. Rudi te Velde, *Aquinas on God* (Aldershot: Ashgate, 2006), 125–26: "The aspect of *production* is unmistakably associated with the efficient cause (*causa efficiens*); the *distinction* refers to the extrinsic formal cause (*causa exemplaris*), and the couple *preservation/government* is related to the final cause (*causa finalis*)."

36. Francisco Suárez, *On Creation, Conservation, & Concurrence. Metaphysical Disputations 20–22*, trans. A. J. Freddoso (South Bend, IN: St. Augustine's Press, 2002); see esp. 169–208 on his theory of application. Suárez tends to see the creature's action as only needing a sustaining efficient cause, while Aquinas sees the creature's operation as needing an efficient moving cause and a final cause. According to Suárez's view, the creature is in charge of the direction of its operation and specifies its act. According to Aquinas's view, the creature is inclined to its ultimate end and operates to attain that end.

37. *ST* I, q. 44, a. 1 (Leon. 4.455): "Relinquitur ergo quod omnia alia a Deo non sint suum esse, sed participant esse. Necesse est igitur omnia quae diversificantur secundum diversam participationem essendi, ut sint perfectius vel minus perfecte, causari ab uno primo ente, quod perfectissime est."

38. *De pot.*, q. 3, a. 1, ad 17.

(*tale ens*), but rather the consideration of being as being (*ens in quantum est ens*), and the consideration of the cause of things, not as these or as such, but insofar as they are beings. "Therefore whatever is the cause of things insofar as they are beings, must be the cause of things, not only according as they are *such* by accidental forms, nor according as they are *these* by substantial forms, but also according to all that belongs to their being at all in any way."[39]

With regard to exemplar causality, I recall first that every created being has being (*actus essendi*) according to the measure of its essence. The essence itself is predetermined by the divine idea, which is nothing other than the divine essence known by God as imitable and participable. Divine efficient causality always involves exemplar causality.[40] Just as God's being and essence are really identical, so also God's essence and his divine ideas are identical *secundum rem*. Louis-Bertrand Geiger's interpretation of Aquinas tends to divide efficient causality and exemplar causality into two different lines or systems of participation.[41] Fabro's interpretation, on the other hand, rejects this bifurcation of participation, and argues for one line of participation between the creature (effect) and God (cause).[42] This one line of participation can be considered according to the three extrinsic causalities. With regard to the aspect of exemplar causality, Gregory Doolan has articulated the notion of participation as follows:

---

39. *ST* I, q. 44, a. 2 (Leon. 4.458): "Hoc igitur quod est causa rerum inquantum sunt entia, oportet esse causam rerum, non solum secundum quod sunt talia per formas accidentales, nec secundum quod sunt haec per formas substantiales, sed etiam secundum omne illud quod pertinet ad esse illorum quocumque modo."

40. Alain Contat, "*Esse, essentia, ordo*. Verso una metafisica della partecipazione operativa," 17. See Aquinas, *In Sent.* II, d. 3, q. 3, a. 1.

41. Louis-Bertrand Geiger, *La participation dans la philosophie de S. Thomas d'Aquin* (Paris: Vrin, 1942).

42. Cornelio Fabro, "The Intensive Hermeneutics of Thomistic Philosophy: The Notion of Participation," in *Selected Works of Cornelio Fabro* (Chillum: IVE Press, 2016), 83: "To assert, as has been done (Geiger), that Thomas holds as distinct participation by similitude (*secundum similitudinem*) and participation by composition (*secundum compositionem*), is to break the Thomistic synthesis at its center, which is the assimilation and mutual subordination of the couplets of act-potency and *participatum-participans* in the emergence of the new concept of *esse*." Alain Contat, "*Esse, essentia, ordo*: Verso una metafisica della partecipazione operativa," 19 (author's translation): "It is true, therefore, that created being (*ens*) proceeds from the Creator according to two causal lines, efficient and exemplar; but there is only one relation of participation of finite *ens* to Infinite Being, and it is the participation that, resulting from the composition of *esse* – the created act of being – with its *essentia* – correlative potency of being, founds a relation of likeness between this *ens* and the Being from which it proceeds."

Although the created essence does not participate in its exemplar idea, the finite [*ens*] of which it is a principle does participate in a likeness of the exemplar that is the divine nature. Through such participation, the created essence receives and limits *esse*. This limitation, however, is dependent upon the ontologically prior formation of the divine idea that determines the created essence's limited mode of being. Thus, while the divine nature is imitable in itself, a finite being actually imitates it only because God knows his nature as imitable and wills it actually to be imitated.[43]

Doolan also argues that the mode of being of the essence is determined by the divine idea; its actuality is determined by the participation of the finite being (*ens*) in a likeness of the divine nature. For Aquinas, divine exemplarism is twofold.[44] Doolan writes: "As the exemplar cause of created essence, the divine ideas are the causes of a principle of potency that requires a principle of act; as the exemplar cause of the act of being, the divine nature is the cause of an act that requires a principle of limitation."[45]

To the causalities of efficient production and exemplar determination, we must add that of final ordination. God the Creator freely communicates his goodness to creatures, which, in turn, intend to acquire their perfection, which is a likeness of divine perfection and goodness.[46] This sequence has been articulated by Alain Contat as follows:

> The *exitus a principio* of the created substance carries with itself the ontological demand of the *reditus in finem*: the gift of being to *ens* is fulfilled in the return of the one who receives the gift to the giver by means of the fecundity of the gift, which "pushes" the created supposit to its perfection. Thus, if the creature refers to God according to a nexus of procession, as an *ens per participationem* to Being *per essentiam*, then the same creature will be ordered to God as a good *per participationem* to Goodness *per essentiam* according to a nexus of finality. The *ens per participationem* refers to God as the first efficient [cause] insofar as its act of being is composite with its essence, and to God as

---

43. Gregory T. Doolan, *Aquinas on the Divine Ideas as Exemplar Causes* (Washington, DC: The Catholic University of America Press, 2008), 242.

44. Gregory T. Doolan, "Fabro's Double Participation and Aquinas's Double Exemplarism," in *Studia Fabriana. Cornelio Fabro. Essential Thinker. Philosopher of Being and of Freedom*, ed. Nathaniel Dreyer (Chillum: IVE Press, 2017), 67–88.

45. Doolan, *Aquinas on the Divine Ideas as Exemplar Causes*, 243.

46. *ST* I, q. 44, a. 4 (Leon. 4.461): "Sed primo agenti, qui est agens tantum, non convenit agere propter acquisitionem alicuius finis; sed intendit solum communicare suam perfectionem, quae est eius bonitas. Et unaquaeque creatura intendit consequi suam perfectionem, quae est similitudo perfectionis et bonitatis divinae."

first exemplar [cause] insofar as the same *esse* is measured by the concreated essence; now, the same *ens per participationem* refers to God as ultimate end insofar as its particularized goodness—because it is participated—is ordered *per se* to the goodness *per essentiam* of the Subsistent Being. This third causal line founds a new aspect of participation, which is manifested as a dynamic assimilation of the creature to the Creator.[47]

The relation of causal participation between creature and Creator, under the aspect of efficient causality, stresses the composite creature's ontological dependence on the simple Creator. The relation of participation, under the aspect of exemplar causality, underscores the creature's imitation of the divine nature according to the intellectual measure of the divine exemplars. The relation of participation, under the aspect of final causality, emphasizes the creature's order to the divine goodness, attained through operation. The *ordo* of the creature is consequent upon the essence, but ultimately rooted in the creature's *esse*.

DIVINE APPLICATION

In the first section, I argued that, according to Aquinas, the creature's operation is intrinsically rooted in its act of being. The creature's essence, operative powers, and operative habits mediate between the act of being and operation in various ways. I presented this in opposition to the Scholastic view that tends to hold that accidents and operations have being (*esse*) apart from the creature's act of being. In the second section, I argued that God produces, measures, and orders the created being (*ens*). The creature depends on God, imitates God, and is drawn toward God through its ordered operation. I opposed this to the Scholastic view that posits two causal lines, one for the essence and one for existence, and emphasizes almost exclusively how the creature depends on God.

With the framework of intrinsic and extrinsic causality in place, we now turn to Aquinas's theory that God moves rational and irrational creatures by applying their operative powers to their operation. Key to Aquinas's view is that the creature not only has participated being (*esse*) from God, but also has a participated power and capacity to operate. Aquinas holds that the created substance is for the sake of its operation,[48]

---

47. Alain Contat, "*Esse, essentia, ordo*: Verso una metafisica della partecipazione operativa," 21 (author's translation).

48. *SCG* I, c. 45 (Leon. 13.136): "omnis substantia est propter suam operationem."

through which it attains its end. In the creature, there are natural operative powers that are really distinct from and flow, so to speak, from the substantial essence.[49] These created operative powers need to be applied to action according to the principle that "all that is moved is moved by another" (*omne quod movetur ab alio movetur*).[50] Let us now review chronologically Aquinas's principal texts on divine application. We will see that development of Aquinas's doctrine is fairly consistent and leads to a nuanced view of how the spiritual creature's will is moved.

Scriptum super libros Sententiarum (1256–59)

Bernard Lonergan posits that application does not appear in Aquinas's early works because Aquinas "had not solved the speculative problems incident to the conception of the causal certitude of providence."[51] Lonergan writes: "In the commentary on the *Sentences* and the *De veritate* God operates the operation of creatures because he is creator and conserver; in later works other grounds are more prominently asserted, namely, application, instrumentality, finality. In parallel fashion earlier works state that the creatures cannot operate without God, while later works state that they cannot operate without divine motion."[52] Now, despite the fact that the term "application" does not appear, there is at least one text in the *Scriptum* where Aquinas does speak about God's power acting as an intermediary that joins the creature's power to its effect. Aquinas writes: "In fact, the power of a creature cannot achieve its effect except by the power of the Creator, from whom is all power, preservation of power, and order to effect. For this reason, as is said in the same place of the *Book of Causes*, the causality of the secondary cause is rooted (*firmatur*) in the causality of the primary cause."[53]

Here Aquinas appeals to the *Liber de causis*, which greatly influences

---

49. *De spir. creat.* 11.
50. Contat, "*Esse, essentia, ordo*," 62.
51. Bernard Lonergan, *Grace and Freedom: Operative Grace in the Thought of St. Thomas Aquinas* (Toronto: University of Toronto Press, 2000), 82.
52. Ibid., 92–93.
53. *In Sent.* II, d. 1, q. 1, a. 4 (Parma 6.589): "non enim virtus alicujus creaturae posset in suum effectum, nisi per virtutem creatoris, a quo est omnis virtus, et virtutis conservatio, et ordo ad effectum; quia, ut in libro de causis dicitur, causalitas causae secundae firmatur per causalitatem causae primae." Steven E. Baldner and William E. Carroll, trans., *Aquinas on Creation: Writings on the "Sentences of Peter Lombard"* (Toronto: Pontifical Institute of Medieval Studies, 1997), 85–86.

his thought on divine application and asserts that "the operation, by which the second cause causes an effect, is caused by the First Cause." In his exposition of the book, written much later, Aquinas writes that "the First Cause aids the second cause, making it act."[54] The second cause has both its substance and its power to act (*potentiam sive virtutem operandi*) from the First Cause.[55] The second cause is able to act on its effect only by the power of the First Cause: "The effect, then, proceeds from the second cause only through the power of the First Cause. The power of the First Cause thus enables the effect to be affected by the power of the second cause. Therefore, it is affected first by the power of the First Cause."[56] Even though Aquinas's exposition of the *Liber de Causis* was written much later, the ideas contained in the *Liber de Causis* already inform Aquinas's views in the *Scriptum*.

Summa contra Gentiles (1259–65)

In *SCG* III, Aquinas deals with the order of creatures to God as to their end, establishes that God is the end of all things, and posits that "to become like God (*assimilari ad Deum*) is the ultimate end of all things."[57] Each created thing imitates divine goodness according to its mode and tends toward the divine similitude through its operation.[58] After establishing that God is the end of all things and that God governs the universe through divine providence, Aquinas takes up the problem of divine motion in III, c. 67, and provides six arguments to prove that God is the cause of operating in all operating agents. The first three arguments establish that the creature's operative powers depend on God. The fourth argument holds that God also applies the powers to operation. The fifth argument introduces the distinction between God's principal causality and the creature's instrumental causality. The sixth addresses God as final cause of the creature's operation.

---

54. *In De caus.* 1 (Saffrey 7): "sed operatio qua causa secunda causat effectum, causatur a causa prima, nam *causa prima adiuvat causam secundam* faciens eam operari."

55. Ibid.: "causa enim secunda, cum sit effectus causae primae, *substantiam* suam habet a causa prima; sed a quo habet aliquid substantiam, ab eo habet *potentiam* sive virtutem operandi; ergo causa secunda habet potentiam sive virtutem operandi a causa prima."

56. Ibid. (Saffrey 7–8): "Causa secunda non agit in causatum suum nisi virtute causae primae; ergo et causatum non procedit a causa secunda nisi per virtutem causae primae; sic igitur virtus causae primae dat effectui ut attingatur a virtute causae secundae; prius ergo attingitur a virtute causae primae."

57. *SCG* III, c. 20.

58. *SCG* III, c. 21.

The first argument focuses on the fact that all operating agents are caused by God and, insofar as they themselves cause being, they are said to operate by the power of God. Aquinas writes: "Now, every *operans* is in some way a cause of being (*causa essendi*), either according to substantial *esse* or accidental *esse*. But, nothing is the cause of being unless and insofar as it acts by the power of God. Therefore, every *operans* operates through the power (*virtutem*) of God."[59] Implicit in this argument is the notion of participated causality. Operating agents are causes of being, not in an absolute sense of producing being *ex nihilo*, but insofar as they influence the substantial *esse* of a finite *ens* (as a cause of generation and corruption) and the accidental *esse* of finite beings (as a cause of accidental changes).[60] Aquinas's second argument complements the first and focuses on the operative power of the created agent, which has been given to it by God. He argues: "Every operation that results from a certain power (*virtutem*) is attributed as a cause to that thing which has given that power ... Now every power in any agent is from God, as from a first principle of all perfection. Therefore, since every operation stems from a power, the cause of every operation must be God."[61] The third argument holds that the operative power given to the created agent is conserved by God. If the divine influence were to cease, all operation would cease.[62]

The fourth argument touches on the theme that is at the heart of this chapter. The first three arguments have dealt with created causes influencing the being of their effects by the power of God, with God as the cause of the operative powers of created agents and as the conserver of

---

59. SCG III, c. 67 (Leon. 14.190): "Omne enim operans est aliquo modo causa essendi, vel secundum esse substantiale, vel accidentale. Nihil autem est causa essendi nisi inquantum agit in virtute Dei, ut ostensum est. Omne igitur operans operatur per virtutem Dei."

60. Wippel, *Metaphysical Themes in Thomas Aquinas II*, 193: "Whenever a new substance is efficiently caused by a natural or created agent, that agent's causation applies both to the act of being itself (*esse*) of the new substance and to a particular determination of *esse* as realized in that substance. Causation of the particular determination (this or that kind of form) is owing to the created efficient cause insofar as it operates by its own inherent power as a principal cause. Causation of the act of being itself (*esse*) is assigned to it as an instrumental cause acting with the power of God, and to God himself as the principal cause of the same."

61. SCG III, c. 67 (Leon. 14.190): "Omnis operatio quae consequitur aliquam virtutem, attribuitur sicut causae illi rei quae dedit illam virtutem: sicut motus gravium et levium naturalis consequitur formam ipsorum, secundum quam sunt gravia et levia, et ideo causa motus ipsorum dicitur esse generans, qui dedit formam. Omnis autem virtus cuiuscumque agentis est a Deo, sicut a primo principio omnis perfectionis. Ergo, cum omnis operatio consequatur aliquam virtutem, oportet quod cuiuslibet operationis causa sit Deus."

62. Ibid.: "Unde, cessante influentia divina, omnis operatio cessaret. Omnis igitur rei operatio in ipsum reducitur sicut in causam."

their operative powers. Now, Aquinas argues that God not only causes and conserves operative powers but also applies them to operation. That which applies an active power to action is said to be the cause of that action. Every application of power (*virtus*) to operation is principally and primarily by God.[63] The reason is that operative powers are applied to their proper operations by some movement of body or soul and God is the first principle of both types of movement because God is the entirely immobile First Mover.[64] In saying that God applies the creature's operative power to operation, Aquinas does not deny that the creature is the cause of its action. In the *Summa theologiae*, a later work, Aquinas addresses how the will applies the soul's powers to operation. Aquinas highlights in particular how God moves the will of the intellectual creature: "Similarly, every movement of a will whereby powers are applied to operation is reduced to God, as to a first object of appetite and to a first *volens*. Therefore, every operation should be attributed to God, as to a first and principal agent."[65] As well, in *ST* I, q. 105, a. 4, Aquinas clearly establishes the two ways that God moves the will: as the sufficient object of the will and as the one who efficiently inclines the will to its ultimate end.

Aquinas's fifth argument concentrates on how all created agents act through God's power. Aquinas here introduces the distinction between principal agent and instrumental agent. All subsequent agent causes act through the power of the First Cause. God is the First Cause, and so all lower agent causes act through his power. But the cause of an action is the one by whose power the action is done rather than the one who acts: the principal agent, for instance, rather than the instrument. Therefore, God is more especially the cause of every action than are secondary agent causes.[66]

---

63. Ibid.: "Quicquid applicat virtutem activam ad agendum, dicitur esse causa illius actionis [...]. Sed omnis applicatio virtutis ad operationem est principaliter et primo a Deo."

64. Ibid.: "Applicantur enim virtutes operativae ad proprias operationes per aliquem motum vel corporis, vel animae. Primum autem principium utriusque motus est Deus. Est enim primum movens omnino immobile."

65. Ibid.: "Similiter etiam omnis motus voluntatis quo applicantur aliquae virtutes ad operandum, reducitur in Deum sicut in primum appetibile et in primum volentem. Omnis igitur operatio debet attribui Deo sicut primo et principali agenti."

66. Ibid.: "In omnibus causis agentibus ordinatis semper oportet quod causae sequentes agant in virtute causae primae: sicut in rebus naturalibus corpora inferiora agunt in virtute corporum caelestium; et in rebus voluntariis omnes artifices inferiores operantur secundum imperium supremi architectoris. In ordine autem causarum agentium Deus est prima causa,

The sixth argument holds that all created agents are ordered, through their operation, to God as to their end. Every agent is ordered through its operation to an ultimate end, for either the operation itself is the end, or the work (*operatum*), which is the effect of the operation, is the end. Now, to order things to their end is the prerogative of God. And so, it is necessary to say that every agent acts by the divine power. Therefore, he is the one who is the cause of the action of all things.[67]

Chapter 70 also takes up the problem of application. In the agent, Aquinas distinguishes between the thing itself that acts and the power by which it acts. The power of the lower agent depends on the power of the superior agent, insofar as the superior agent gives the power to the lower agent whereby it may act; or preserves it; or even applies it to action. The natural thing does not produce its proper effect except by divine power. At the same time: "The same effect is not attributed to a natural cause and to divine power in such a way that it is partly done by God, and partly by the natural agent; rather it is wholly done by both, according to a different mode, just as the same effect is wholly attributed to the instrument and also wholly to the principal agent."[68]

In summary, Aquinas holds that God is the cause of the actions of all things insofar as he creates and conserves the being (*esse*) and operative powers of the creature. Both the being and operative powers can be seen according to the notion of participation. The creature exercises a participated causality, having been given both being and power by God. Second, God is the cause insofar as he directs the creature to its ultimate end through its operation. Third, God is the cause of all operation insofar as he applies the created operative powers of the creature to their operation. This application can be likened to the relationship between a principal cause and an instrumental cause.

---

ut in primo ostensum est. Ergo omnes causae inferiores agentes agunt in virtute ipsius. Causa autem actionis magis est illud cuius virtute agitur quam etiam illud quod agit: sicut principale agens magis quam instrumentum. Deus igitur principalius est causa cuiuslibet actionis quam etiam secundae causae agentes."

67. Ibid.: "Omne operans per suam operationem ordinatur ad finem ultimum: oportet enim quod vel operatio ipsa sit finis; vel operatum, quod est operationis effectus. Ordinare autem res in finem est ipsius Dei, sicut supra ostensum est. Oportet igitur dicere quod omne agens virtute divina agat. Ipse est igitur qui est causa actionis omnium rerum."

68. SCG III, c. 70 (Leon. 14.207): "Patet etiam quod non sic idem effectus causae naturali et divinae virtuti attribuitur quasi partim a Deo, et partim a naturali agente fiat, sed totus ab utroque secundum alium modum: sicut idem effectus totus attribuitur instrumento, et principali agenti etiam totus."

Quaestiones disputatae De potentia (1265–66)

Aquinas deals with application in *De pot.*, q. 3, a. 7. He asks: "Whether God works in the operations of nature?" After discarding different theories, Aquinas argues that God is the cause of the creature's action in four ways.[69] First, God is the cause that gives the effect the power to operate (*virtutem operandi*). Thus, God is the cause of a creature's action by causing or constituting in being the creature's natural power.[70] Second, the conserver of a power is said to cause the effect's action: thus, God is the cause of a creature's action by conserving in being the creature's natural power.[71]

The third way that a thing is said to cause another's action is by moving it to act: thus, God is the cause of a creature's action by moving and applying (*movens et applicans*) the creature's natural power to what is to be done. This argument proceeds as follows: nothing moves or acts of itself unless it be a nonmoved mover (*movens non motum*), therefore the action of a moved mover is caused by the first immobile mover not only insofar as the First Mover causes and conserves the active power, but also insofar as it applies the power to action (*applicatio virtutis ad actionem*). Aquinas gives the example of how a man is the cause of incision by applying the form of the "sharpness" of a knife to the operation of cutting by moving it. The second cause is compared to the first cause as an instrument to a principal agent: the axe is the cause of the craftsman's work not by its own form, but by the power of the craftsman who moves it so that it participates in his power.[72]

The fourth way that a thing is said to cause another's action is insofar

---

69. Wippel, *Metaphysical Thought*, 451–52: "As Thomas points out in q. 3, a. 7 of his *De pot.*, God may be said to cause the actions performed by created agents in four different ways: (1) by giving to a created agent the power by means of which it acts; (2) by continuously sustaining (conserving) this created power in being; (3) by moving or applying the created operative power to its activity; (4) by serving as principal cause of that of which the created agent is an instrumental cause. With respect to point 4 it should be noted that at times Thomas uses the language of first cause and second cause rather than that of principal cause and instrumental cause to express this relationship between God and other agents."

70. Wippel, *Metaphysical Themes in Thomas Aquinas II*, 185: "First, this may happen because [the cause] grants to that other things its very power of acting. In this way God does indeed produce the actions of created nature, since he gives to natural things the powers by means of which they act."

71. *De pot.*, q. 3, a. 7.

72. Ibid.

as the instrumental cause participates in something of the power of the principal cause through the cause's motion: thus, God is the cause of a creature's action insofar as the power of the secondary cause participates in his power.[73] This fourth argument opens up the possibility of seeing the operative power of the creature as a participated power: a created power that participates in the power of its cause. While the first way of causing the creature's action focuses on the production and consequent dependence of the creature's power on God, this fourth way invokes the notion of participation, which means that the creature truly has received the power to act.

Aquinas's *De potentia* has followed a similar outline to that of the *Summa contra Gentiles*. Aquinas first establishes that God creates and conserves the operative powers of the creature. He then argues that these same powers, because they are not immobile movers, must be reduced to act by a first unmoved and immobile mover. As active powers that flow from the creature's essence and being, they are not completely in potency in themselves, but are in potency to their operation.

Compendium theologiae (1265-73)

Comp. theol. I.130 contains a very concise presentation of divine motion. The text adds that the creature's movement and divine motion are simultaneous:

> Second causes do not act except through the power of the first cause; thus instruments operate under the direction of art. Consequently, all the agents through which God carries out the order of his government can act only through the power of God himself. The action of any of them is caused by God, just as the movement of a mobile is caused by the motion of the mover. And *movens* and *motum* must be simultaneous. Hence God must be interiorly present to any agent as acting therein whenever he moves the agent to act.[74]

---

73. Wippel, *Metaphysical Themes in Thomas Aquinas II*, 192-93: "According to this mode, God causes the action of every natural agent or cause in the way in which a principal cause causes the action performed by an instrumental cause. Consequently, Thomas holds (in according with the physical worldview of his time) that no purely natural cause can exercise causality with respect to a species of lower things except insofar as it acts through the power of, as an instrument of, a heavenly body. And no purely natural agent can exercise causality with respect to *esse* except insofar as it acts with the power of God."

74. *Comp. theol.* I.130 (Leon. 42.130): "Quia uero cause secundę non agunt nisi per uirtutem prime cause, sicut instrumenta agunt per directionem artis, necesse est quod omnia alia agentia per que Deus ordinem sue gubernationis adimplet, uirtute ipsius Dei agant. Agere igitur cuiuslibet ipsorum a Deo causatur, sicut motus mobilis a motione mouentis; movens autem

Aquinas's view on the simultaneity of divine motion (as *movens*) and the creature's motion (as *motum*) mitigates somewhat against the Scholastic tendency to label divine motion as pre-motion, even though "pre-" is said to refer to the causal priority and not temporal priority of divine motion.

Summa theologiae (I: 1265–68; I-II: 1271)

Aquinas's treatment of divine application in *ST* I, q. 105, a. 5, does not follow *De potentia*'s fourfold outline of creator of natural power, conserver of natural power, applier of natural power, and source of participated power, but rather a threefold outline of end, agent, and form, to which he adds the creation and conservation of the forms of created agents.[75] Application is considered under the third rubric of form. Matter, Aquinas states, is not a principle of action, but rather is the subject that receives the effect of action. The order of the three principles of action is the following: the first principle of action is the *end* which moves the agent; the second is the *agent*; the third is the *form* of that which the agent applies to action (although the agent also acts through its own form).[76] God, Aquinas argues, works in every worker (*operans*) according to these three principles of action and insofar as he gives and preserves created agents and their operative powers.

First, God is the cause of every operation as an end: every operation is for the sake of some good, and nothing is good except insofar as it participates in a likeness of the supreme good, which is God. Hence, God himself is the cause of every operation as its end.[77] Second, God is the

---

et motum oportet esse simul: oportet igitur quod Deus cuilibet agenti assit interius quasi in ipso agens, dum ipsum ad agendum mouet."

75. Wippel, *Metaphysical Thought*, 452: "In the *Summa theologiae* I, q. 105, a. 5, Thomas makes the same point in slightly different fashion. God works in the activities performed by created agents: (1) by serving as the final cause of such agents; (2) by acting as an efficient cause of their operations inasmuch as second causes act by reason of the first cause which moves them to act; (3) by giving to created agents the forms which are their principles of operation and by keeping these in being. As I have indicated elsewhere, we might combine into one the third and fourth ways mentioned in the text from the *De potentia*, as Thomas himself seems to do, and view this as equivalent to the second way of the text from ST I, q. 105."

76. *ST* I, q. 105, a. 5 (Leon. 4.475–76): "Ad cuius evidentiam, considerandum est quod, cum sint causarum quatuor genera, materia quidem non est principium actionis, sed se habet ut subiectum recipiens actionis effectum. Finis vero et agens et forma se habent ut actionis principium, sed ordine quodam. Nam primo quidem, principium actionis est finis, qui movet agentem; secundo vero, agens; tertio autem, forma eius quod ab agente applicatur ad agendum (quamvis et ipsum agens per formam suam agat)."

77. Ibid. (Leon. 4.476): "Primo quidem, secundum rationem finis. Cum enim omnis

cause of every operation as an agent: the second agent always acts in virtue of the first agent; all agents act in virtue of God himself, and therefore he is the cause of action in every agent.[78] Third, God is the cause of every operation insofar as he applies the forms and powers of secondary agents to operation.[79] Aquinas adds that not only does God apply the powers to operation, but he is the cause of every operation insofar as he gives created agents their form, which is the principle of action,[80] and insofar as he conserves the forms and powers of created agents.[81]

In various places in the *Summa theologiae*, Aquinas takes up the question of what moves the will. In *ST* I, q. 105, a. 4, Aquinas argues that God moves the will sufficiently and efficaciously to its object, the universal good: *sufficiently* insofar as he is the universal good and alone fills the will; *efficaciously* insofar as he causes the power of willing and interiorly inclines the will to the universal good.[82] This does not exclude that the will is moved in other ways. In fact, in I-II, q. 9, Aquinas posits that the will is moved in four ways. Aquinas first argues that the will is moved by the human intellect insofar as it presents a good object to it and, second, that it is moved by the sensitive appetite.[83] Third, the will, through its volition of the end, moves itself to will the means to the end.[84] Lastly, the will is moved in the exercise of its act by God alone as an exterior principle.[85] In I-II, qq. 15–16, Aquinas states that, in the case of the rational creature, the will moves the soul's powers to their acts, and applies them to operation.[86]

---

operatio sit propter aliquod bonum verum vel apparens; nihil autem est vel apparet bonum, nisi secundum quod participat aliquam similitudinem summi boni, quod est Deus; sequitur quod ipse Deus sit cuiuslibet operationis causa ut finis."

78. Ibid.: "Similiter etiam considerandum est quod, si sint multa agentia ordinata, semper secundum agens agit in virtute primi, nam primum agens movet secundum ad agendum. Et secundum hoc, omnia agunt in virtute ipsius Dei; et ita ipse est causa actionum omnium agentium."

79. Ibid.: "Tertio, considerandum est quod Deus movet non solum res ad operandum, quasi applicando formas et virtutes rerum ad operationem, sicut etiam artifex applicat securim ad scindendum, qui tamen interdum formam securi non tribuit."

80. Ibid.: "Unde non solum est causa actionum inquantum dat formam quae est principium actionis."

81. Ibid.: "sed etiam dat formam creaturis agentibus, et eas tenet in esse."

82. *ST* I, q. 105, a. 4.

83. *ST* I-II, q. 9, aa. 1–2.

84. *ST* I-II, q. 9, a. 3.

85. *ST* I-II, q. 9, aa. 1–6.

86. *ST* I-II, q. 16, a. 1 (Leon. 6.114): "voluntas est quae movet potentias animae ad suos actus; et hoc est applicare eas ad operationem."

In saying, on the one hand, that the will moves itself and applies the soul's powers to its operation and, on the other, that God applies the creature's operative powers to operation, Aquinas is not contradicting himself. Wippel references this problem in connection to *ST*, I, q. 83, a. 1, where Aquinas replies to the objection that because God moves the will, the human being is not free. Wippel summarizes Aquinas's reply as follows:

> In replying Thomas notes that the will is a cause of its own motion, since by means of free will man moves himself to act. Still, adds Thomas, the presence of freedom does not require that a free agent be the first cause of its own motion. Thus, for something to be regarded as the cause of something else, it need not be a first cause; it can be a second cause. So too, God, as first cause, moves both natural agents and voluntary agents. Just as his moving natural causes does not destroy the fact that they are causes, neither does his moving voluntary agents militate against the fact that they are still voluntary causes. Rather, he moves each in accord with its nature.[87]

CONCLUSION

In the introduction I posited that the deficiencies in Molina's theory of general concurrence and Báñez's theory of physical pre-motion can be overcome by better grasp of Aquinas's metaphysics of *actus essendi* and participation and a more attentive reading of Aquinas's thought on divine application. According to the intensive interpretation of Aquinas's metaphysical thought articulated by Cornelio Fabro and Alain Contat, operative activity is the ultimate actuality which "emanates" from the intensive and emergent act of being (*actus essendi*) and not something completely extraneous to the act of being that is extrinsically added to the creature. Operation brings the created supposit to its fulfillment and ultimate perfection.

Insofar as the creature's operative powers are in potency, however, they ultimately need to be reduced to act and applied to operation by the First Unmoved Mover. As Contat writes, divine application can be seen as God liberating the creature's dynamic participated power:

> On the metaphysical level, the potentiality of the created essence reverberates in its operative powers, which cannot act or operate without an actuating mo-

---

87. Wippel, *Metaphysical Themes in Thomas Aquinas*, 263.

tion, by virtue of the principle ... *quidquid movetur ab alio movetur*. For this reason, in the transcendental order, the "application" of the created operative power to its operation—namely, the passage from first act to second act—requires an intervention of the First Cause, which takes away the potentiality of the created agent and "frees," so to speak, its dynamic power.[88]

For Aquinas the ordering of a creature to its ultimate end and perfection is rooted in its *actus essendi*. The intensive act of being emerges in *operari* mediated by the essence and its operative powers. A natural inclination or order is consequent upon the created essence but ultimately rooted intrinsically in the creature's act of being, which seeks to unite itself to its principle and seeks to communicate itself as far as possible. Aquinas's metaphysics of *actus essendi* argues for various levels of act and correlative potency, founded on the two fundamental principles in a finite creature.[89] Ultimately, every causal reduction from potency to act requires the causal influence of the First Mover, who is said, in this case, to apply the creature's operative power to its action.

According to the notion of efficient causality, God simultaneously gives *esse* and produces that which receives *esse*. According to the notion of exemplar causality, God, through knowing his being as imitable and participable, intellectually measures the production of the creature. According to the notion of final causality, God orders the irrational creature to participate, according to its nature, in divine goodness. The operation of the irrational creature is marked by determination and there is no difficulty posed by Aquinas's thesis that God applies the operative powers of the irrational creature to their operations. The operation of the free rational creature is not marked by determination. Aquinas affirms that, on the one hand, the rational appetite of the creature applies itself to its operation, and, on the other, that God applies the operative power of the will to operation not only sufficiently as the ultimate and universal good that fills the will, but also effectively insofar as God inclines the creature's will to himself. The inclination of the rational creature's will by God to himself is not the same as the determination of the irrational creature's appetite by God to one thing and, in this way, the free choice of the rational creature is not compromised.[90]

88. Contat, "*Esse, essentia, ordo*," 62.
89. Ibid., 58.
90. Wippel, *Metaphysical Themes in Thomas Aquinas*, 263: "This seems to be Thomas's final philosophical thought on this point. God moves every created agent to act in accord with

Throughout this chapter, I have shown that, in the case of the free operation of the rational creature, Aquinas speaks of inclination and application, and not of physical pre-motion, predetermination, or concurrence. It is my hope that my reading of Aquinas's work in the light of the exegesis of scholars such as Fabro, Gilson, Contat, Wippel, Shanley, and Doolan, contributes to a more authentic understanding of the role of divine causality in created operation.

---

its nature. He moves freely acting agents to act in accord with their nature, which is to say, freely. Neither the certitude of divine science nor the causal character of the divine will detracts from man's freedom. In fact, remarks Aquinas, it would be more repugnant to the divine motion if the created will were thereby moved to act necessarily rather than to act freely. Only the latter kind of divine motion is in accord with the nature of the created will."

Appendix

Vita Sapientis: A Biographical Interview with John F. Wippel

The following biography, composed by Miriam Pritschet, is drawn from an interview with John F. Wippel conducted by Nick Kahm on September 4, 2020.

Celebrated as one of the most distinguished Thomists of our day, Msgr. John F. Wippel began his life quietly in rural Ohio. There, tucked away along an anonymous gravel road, three Wippel farms stretched through the countryside—those of his father, two uncles, and their families. These farms, first established by Wippel's grandfather, carved out the backdrop of an Ohio childhood. Born in 1933 to life on the farmstead, Wippel entered into a steady rhythm of work, play, and prayer. The ebb and flow of these early years with his family, with boyhood joys and challenges, would serve to foster within him a discipline that would prove invaluable in his later work and scholarship.

In reflecting on his childhood, Wippel recounted that there was never a dull moment on the family farm, with plenty to keep a growing boy busy: tractors needed driving, drifts of snow needed shoveling, old machinery needed fixing—and the young Wippel was put to work wherever he could be of use. With these daily efforts as part of his childhood, he was no more a stranger to the strain of physical labor than he was to the intellectual agility needed for such efforts, cultivating in him ingenuity, creativity, and problem-solving. These many tasks were made lighter, however, by the company of his brother, Patrick, and of his beloved collie Rover—a faithful companion to the Wippel boys in all their adventures. Under the guidance of their father Joseph, Wippel and his brother became well versed in the many skills required by the demands of farm life.

Whereas his brother took after their father with a passion for mechanics, Wippel himself shared more fully in their father's love of baseball. From the time he was old enough to throw a ball, Wippel was an enthusiast of the game. Thus, as a teenager, he could be found joining other boys and young men from the neighboring farms, scattered across a stretch of some twenty miles of countryside. His dedication to the sport would continue into adolescence, and the hours devoted to it did not go to waste, as Wippel would eventually play in two different semi-professional leagues in the positions of pitcher and outfielder. He came to see baseball as a "philosopher's game"—as demanding mentally as it was physically. Physics and geometry colored the field for him, with consideration of the speed of a pitch, of a runner's pace between bases, and of the dimensions unique to a given outfield. Complementing this less conventional education from the baseball diamond was Wippel's grade school education. He and his brother Patrick attended the best school in the county: a two-room schoolhouse called Sacred Heart that was staffed by two Sisters of the Divine Providence who had come to Ohio from France prior to World War I. Each sister instructed four grades. Wippel recounted that each day their father would drive them six miles to and from Sacred Heart—a distance that threatened to disrupt their schooling when World War II rationing made gasoline hard to come by, along with salt, sugar, and rubber.

Life changed during the war for Wippel and his family. Whereas his mother was of Irish and English descent, his father's side of the family was German, and Wippel's father grew up exclusively speaking German to his own father but English to others. But with the First World War, he had dropped the language completely because speaking German, at that time, was considered unpatriotic. Wippel recounted that many of the families nearby nevertheless continued to speak it—much to the annoyance of their non-German neighbors. At the time, the area relied upon a party-line telephone, and there were a dozen or so families who shared the same phone line with the Wippels. Complaints were lodged against the German-speaking folk by neighbors who worried that, by virtue of the shared line, the use of the language would somehow "spoil" their own phones. So, given this political climate, Wippel did not grow up speaking German at home with his family. Nevertheless, he learned to understand it when he heard German spoken, and he recalled the concern his father had hearing Hitler's addresses broadcast over the shortwave radio. Wippel's father saw no choice but for the United States to enter the war, even though their neighbors were mostly isolationists.

Throughout the upheaval brought by World War II, the Wippel boys' parents remained deeply committed to their children's education and were determined that it should not lead to absences from the Sacred Heart school. They enlisted the help of a handful of neighbors who worked in town to take turns giving Wippel and his brother rides to school. Each morning, the boys would walk the mile from their farm to the main road, where the neighbors would stop to pick them up. They would then be dropped off downtown to walk the final half mile from the riverfront to their school. After school, they would stay there until the appointed neighbor was finished with his day's work and could assist with the reverse commute, often getting the boys home late in the evening.

The Sisters who ran the Sacred Heart school took a deep interest in their students' learning, and the Sister who taught Wippel's final four grades would send him home with a new book every night. These early, formative years nurtured a great love of reading in him, and he gradually made his way through all of the volumes in the school's library. Wippel noted that he discovered a passion for history during this time. He was especially captivated by the Civil War, a topic of special interest to him even to this day. The Sisters' successful efforts to instill a love of learning in the children was paired with their equal determination to ingrain in them a mastery of grammar—a foundation that would greatly facilitate Wippel's later Latin learning.

Discerning a call to the priesthood while still in grade school, Wippel began his formation with the Diocese of Steubenville at the recently founded minor seminary. At the time, the seminary was being built from the ground up, and Wippel was a member of one of their initial cohorts. He and his brother were both called upon to use the skills acquired through their country upbringing to further develop the growing seminary, driving tractors and putting in long hours at the large horse farm that was attached to it. Wippel's semesters of study there were balanced with summers of work as varied as his farmhouse chores had been: from the construction job that had him painting guardrails and mowing alongside highways; to his time at a factory cutting, bending, and hand-shaping the steel tops for Jeeps; to his work at the steel mill across the river, from which he would trek home at night coated in a dark dust of charcoal. This blend of work experiences complemented Wippel's time in the classroom with growth in new competencies and with friendships with people from all walks of life. He especially enjoyed his time in the local railroad yard as a brakeman—throwing switches to shoot cars first down one line and then down another. There, Wippel worked late into the night using the light of electric lanterns to signal from one end of the train to the other when to speed up, to slow down, and to stop. It was demanding work, as an inattentive mistake could result in a literal train wreck. Yet Wippel noted that he found the task engaging and that he savored the challenge and the sharpness of intellect that it fostered.

This quickness of mind and willingness to tackle difficult undertakings transferred well to Wippel's studies, which led him to The Catholic University of America in 1953. He arrived there thanks to his admission to the Theodore B. Basselin Scholars Program, which even today brings together bright seminarians from across the country for academic and priestly formation—a program that begins with an undergraduate major in philosophy. Although the seeds of Wippel's love of philosophy were already planted during his sophomore year of seminary back in Ohio, it was during his time at CUA as a Basselin Scholar that they truly came into full bloom. Wippel's first encounter with the philosophical thought of Thomas Aquinas paralleled this broader discovery of philosophy as a whole, and his fascination with one grew alongside the other. At the time of Wippel's attendance, the approach of the philosophy faculty at CUA was predominately Thomistic, and he was captivated by the courses he took there on Aquinas's thought. He avidly read the works of the leading Thomists of the day, such as Jacques Maritain and Étienne Gilson.

In this manner, Wippel completed his undergraduate studies and his first year of graduate work at Catholic University with great academic enthusiasm, earning first his Bachelor and then his Master of Arts degrees as a Basselin Scholar there in 1955 and 1956 respectively. He went on to earn his Licentiate in Sacred Theology from the same institution in 1960, becoming an instructor at CUA that same year. The following year, Wippel took a two-year leave of absence from his work there to study for his doctorate at l'Université Catholique de Louvain in Belgium, where he would remain until 1963. At Louvain, he took classes from the prominent

Thomistic philosopher Fernand Van Steenberghen, a figure who would prove deeply influential for Wippel in his scholarly ventures. It was Van Steenberghen who introduced Wippel to Godfrey of Fontaines—the subject of his dissertation. Wippel had initially planned to write about Aquinas on analogy but had been "beaten to the punch" by the recent publication of a dissertation on that topic by Bernard Montagnes, O.P.. Van Steenberghen and Wippel determined that another dissertation on the theme would therefore be redundant, and thus began Wippel's work on Godfrey, who was a younger contemporary of Aquinas and a fellow Scholastic philosopher.

Wippel recalled that he found Godfrey's Latin a "tougher nut to crack" than the straightforward writing of Aquinas, but his time at Sacred Heart and at the Steubenville seminary had well equipped him for the challenge, and he read through the whole of Godfrey's philosophical and theological corpus. He amassed a collection of index cards summarizing all of the philosophical content he could glean from this reading, organizing it into an alphabetical collection of Godfrey's thoughts that he kept until his dying day. Having completed this momentous task, Wippel brought his collection of cards to Van Steenberghen, under whose direction he was to write his dissertation. This direction was rather minimal in character, however; the two met for all of one day, poring over the index cards and working up an outline. After this meeting, Wippel simply went home and completed the entire dissertation, bringing it back to present to Van Steenberghen only once he had completed the entire project.

Wippel defended the resulting dissertation, entitled "Fundamental Metaphysical Themes in the *Quaestiones Quodlibetales* of Godfrey of Fontaines," in 1963, passing "avec la plus grande distinction"—a great honor, comparable to the American distinction of *summa cum laude*. Following this successful defense, Wippel returned to CUA to continue his work as an instructor. He was awarded his PhD in philosophy from Louvain in 1965 upon the appearance of his first publication, at which point he was promoted at CUA to the position of assistant professor. He then served in this position a mere two years before rising to the rank of associate professor in 1967. Subsequently, Wippel spent the spring of 1969 as a visiting associate professor at the University of California, San Diego. He thoroughly enjoyed his semester there—a time that showcased his ability to inspire his classes, with even student protestors at that university taking interest in his stories of the riots in medieval Paris by university students. After this eventful time in San Diego, Wippel returned to CUA to resume his research and teaching there, reaching the rank of ordinary (or full) professor in 1972, which he enjoyed until his retirement in December 2021, when he was made a professor emeritus.

Wippel's work throughout his career was marked not only by a deep dedication to his students, but also by his abundant and rigorous scholarship. In addition to his seminal works—*The Metaphysical Thought of Godfrey of Fontaines: A Study in Late Thirteenth-Century Philosophy* (1981), *Metaphysical Themes in Thomas Aquinas* (1984), *The Metaphysical Thought of Thomas Aquinas: From Finite Being to Uncreated Being* (2000), *Metaphysical Themes in Thomas Aquinas II* (2007), and *Metaphysical Themes in Thomas Aquinas III* (2021)—Wippel was the editor or co-editor of numerous other volumes. And, of course, there are his extensive journal publications of over a hundred articles spanning his entire academic career.

Of all the aforementioned works, Wippel noted that he was most proud of *The Metaphysical Thought of Thomas Aquinas* and *The Metaphysical Thought of Godfrey of Fontaines*. The latter book emerged from his work for his postdoctoral degree in philosophy from l'Université Catholique de Louvain, which he was awarded in 1981. This prestigious degree, the "Maître-Agrégé de l'Ecole Saint Thomas d'Aquin," requires the authoring of a book as well as the production of fifty theses ranging over the whole of philosophy, culminating in the successful defense of both. This degree would not be the last received by Wippel: in 2005 he was awarded a doctorate of letters, *honoris causa*, by the Pontifical Institute of Mediaeval Studies in Toronto. He noted that he felt especially honored by this conferral considering his criticism of Gilson, who had been the Institute's founding director. In addition to this honor, Wippel was twice awarded a fellowship from the National Endowment for the Humanities (their Younger Humanist Fellowship in 1970–71 and their Fellowship for Independent Study and Research in 1984–85), as well as, in 2001, the chair of Theodore Basselin Professor of Philosophy in the School of Philosophy at CUA.

In addition to Wippel's celebrated research achievements, there is also his extensive service to the academic community, in particular at CUA. After having first served as the assistant academic vice president for graduate studies in 1989, Wippel served as the academic vice president from 1989–96, and finally as the University's provost from 1996–97. Although he had not sought these positions, when asked to serve in them Wippel accepted willingly, agreeing at first to fill the need for a three-year commitment that wound up being stretched into eight. In the end, he was happy to return to his faculty position and to research after those years in administration, but Wippel noted that he found aspects of his various administrative positions to be both enriching and enjoyable. In particular, he discovered that speaking with the deans and meeting with people from all areas across CUA allowed him to grow in knowledge of his beloved university that an academic position limited to a single field had not afforded.

Wippel's academic service was thus not limited to his own School of Philosophy at CUA. Among his other accomplishments there, he co-founded the program on Medieval and Byzantine Studies at Catholic University, serving as its director for a time. Beyond Wippel's contributions to CUA, he served as vice president and then president of the American Catholic Philosophical Association; likewise, he served as vice president and, subsequently, president of the Society for Medieval and Renaissance Philosophy, of which he was a founding member; and for ten years he served on the board of directors for the *Journal of the History of Philosophy*. Throughout the entirety of his academic career of teaching, scholarship, and administrative services, Wippel also served faithfully as a priest. Although a priest of the Diocese of Steubenville, given his work at CUA and his residence in the Washington, D.C., area, Wippel helped out chiefly at parishes in northern Virginia and Maryland, most recently at a German-speaking parish in Maryland.

Wippel's love of learning and research did not diminish with his retirement, as he continued to wrestle with philosophical quandaries and Thomistic investigations that for him never ran dry. In his last months, he noted one problem that he found to be particularly perplexing: Aquinas's treatment of the unity of substantial form in the body of Christ in the tomb prior to the resurrection. Wippel expressed the hope of meeting St. Thomas in the next life to ask the Angelic Doctor about this topic. Be that as it may, in his final months, Wippel's focus was on his project of editing works of Siger of Brabant, a figure whom Dante, in his *Divine Comedy*, had placed in paradise in conversation with St. Thomas.

Wippel was still working on this project when he passed away on September 11, 2023, at the age of ninety. With his death, we can only imagine that, through God's grace, he has now joined Siger and St. Thomas in their conversation in the next life, enriching it in the same way that, in this one, he enriched the conversations of generations of students and scholars alike.

Select Bibliography

Aertsen, Jan. "Method and Metaphysics: The *via resolutionis* in Thomas Aquinas." *New Scholasticism* 63 (1989): 405–18.

——. *Medieval Philosophy and the Transcendentals: The Case of Thomas Aquinas.* Leiden: Brill, 1996.

——. "What is First and Most Fundamental? The Beginnings of Transcendental Philosophy." In *Was ist Philosophie im Mittelalter?*, edited by J. A. Aertsen and A. Speer, 177–92. Berlin: De Gruyter, 1998.

——. *Medieval Philosophy as Transcendental Thought: From Philip the Chancellor (ca. 1225) to Francisco Suárez.* Studien und Texte zur Geistesgeschichte des Mittelalters 107. Leiden: Brill, 2012.

Agostini, Igor. "The Knowledge of God's *Quid Sit* in Dominican Theology: From Saint Thomas to Ferrariensis." *American Catholic Philosophical Quarterly* 93, no. 2 (2019): 191–210.

Albert, Arthur G. "Pourquoi 'Docteur Angélique.'" *Revue Dominicaine* 39 (1933): 129–34.

Albertus Magnus. *Liber Posteriorum Analyticorum.* Edited by A. Borgnet. Paris: Vivès, 1890.

——. *Super Dionysii Mysticam Theologiam.* Vol. 37/2 in *Alberti Magni Opera Omnia.* Berlin: Aschendorff, 1978.

Alexander of Hales. *Summa fratris Alexandri.* 5 vols. Quaracchi: Collegium S. Bonaventurae, 1924, 1928, 1930, 1948, 1979.

Amerini, Fabrizio. *Tommaso d'Aquino e l'intenzionalitá.* Pisa: Edizioni ETS, 2013.

Aristotle. *The Complete Works of Aristotle.* Edited by Jonathan Barnes. 2 vols. Princeton, NJ: Princeton University Press, 1984.

——. *Metaphysica, Lib. I–X, XII–XIV, Translatio Anonyma sive 'Media.'* Vol. XXV/2 in *Aristoteles Latinus.* Leiden: Brill, 1976.

——. *Metaphysica, Lib. I–XIV, Recensio et Translatio Guillelmi de Moerbeke.* Vol. XXV/3.2 in *Aristoteles Latinus.* Leiden: Brill, 1995.

Aquinas, Thomas. *Commentaria in octo libros Physicorum Aristotelis* (= *In Phys.*). Vol. 2 in *Sancti Thomae de Aquino Opera Omnia.* Rome: Commissio Leonina, 1884.

——. *Commentum in quatuor libros Sententiarum* (= *In Sent.*). Vol. 6 in *Sancti Thomae Aquinatis Opera Omnia.* Parma: Fiaccadori, 1856. [See Mandonnet/Moos edition below under *Scriptum*.]

———. *Compendium theologiae seu Brevis compilatio theologiae ad fratrem Raynaldum* (= *Comp. theol.*). Vol. 42 in *Sancti Thomae de Aquino Opera Omnia*. Rome: Editori di San Tommaso, 1979.

———. *Contra errores Graecorum ad Urbanum papam* (= *Contra errores Graegorum*). Vol. 40A in *Sancti Thomae de Aquino Opera Omnia*. Rome: Sancta Sabina, 1967.

———. *Contra impugnantes*. Vol. 41A in *Sancti Thomae de Aquino Opera Omnia*. Rome: Sancta Sabina, 1970.

———. *De ente et essentia* (= *De ente*). Vol. 43 in *Sancti Thomae de Aquino Opera Omnia*. Rome: Editori di San Tommaso, 1976.

———. *De principiis naturae ad fratrem Sylvestrum* (= *De princ. nat.*). Vol. 43 in *Sancti Thomae de Aquino Opera Omnia*. Rome: Editori di San Tommaso, 1976.

———. *De substantiis separatis* (= *De sub. sep.*). Vol. 40D in *Sancti Thomae de Aquino Opera Omnia*. Rome: Sancta Sabina, 1968.

———. *Expositio libri Peryermeneias* (= *In Peri herm.*). 2nd ed. Vol. 1*/1 in *Sancti Thomae de Aquino Opera Omnia*. Rome / Paris: Commissio Leonina / J. Vrin, 1989.

———. *Expositio super Iob ad litteram* (= *Super Iob*). Vol. 26 in *Sancti Thomae de Aquino Opera Omnia*. Rome: Commissio Leonina, 1965.

———. *Expositio super Isaiam ad litteram* (= *Super Isaiam*). Vol. 28 in *Sancti Thomae de Aquino Opera Omnia*. Rome: Editori di San Tommaso, 1974.

———. *In duodecim libros Metaphysicorum Aristotelis expositio* (= *In Meta.*). Edited by M.-R. Cathala and R. M. Spiazzi. Rome: Marietti, 1964.

———. *In librum Beati Dionysii De divinis nominibus expositio* (= *In De div. nom.*). Edited by C. Pera, P. Caramello, and C. Mazzantini. Rome: Marietti, 1950.

———. *In librum primum Aristotelis De generatione et corruptione expositio* (= *In De gen.*). Vol. 3 in *Sancti Thomae de Aquino Opera Omnia*. Rome: S. C. de Propaganda Fide, 1886.

———. *In Symbolum Apostolorum, scilicet "Credo in Deum"* (= *Symbolum Apostolorum*). In *Opuscula theologica*, vol. 2, edited by R. M. Spiazzi. Rome: Marietti, 1953.

———. *In psalmos Davidis expositio* (= *In Psalmos*). Vol. 14 of *Opera omnia*. Parma: Typis Petri Fiaccadori, 1863.

———. *Lectura romana in primum Sententiarum Petri Lombardi* (= *Lectura Romana*). Edited by L. E. Boyle and J. F. Boyle. Toronto: Pontifical Institute of Mediaeval Studies, 2006.

———. *Liber de veritate catholicae Fidei contra errores infidelium seu Summa contra Gentiles* (= *SCG*). Edited by C. Pera and P. Caramello. Vols. 2–3. Rome: Marietti, 1961.

———. *Quaestio disputata de spiritualibus creaturis* (= *De spir. creat.*). Edited by J. Cos, OP. Vol. 24/2 in *Sancti Thomae de Aquino Opera Omnia*. Rome / Paris: Commissio Leonina / Éditions Du Cerf, 2002.

———. *Quaestio disputata de virtutibus cardinalibus* (= *De virt. card.*). Edited by P. A. Odetto. In *Quaestiones disputatae*, 8th rev. ed., vol. 2. Rome: Marietti, 1949.

———. *Quaestio disputata de virtutibus in communi* (= *De virt. in com.*). Edited by P. A. Odetto. In *Quaestiones disputatae*, 8th rev. ed., vol. 2. Rome: Marietti, 1949.

———. *Quaestiones disputatae de anima* (= *Q. de an.*). Edited by B. C. Bazán. Vols. 24/1–2 in *Sancti Thomae de Aquino Opera Omnia*. Rome: Commissio Leonina, 1996.

———. *Quaestiones disputatae de malo* (= *De malo*). Vol. 23 in *Sancti Thomae de Aquino Opera Omnia*. Rome: Commissio Leonina, 1982.

———. *Quaestiones disputatae de potentia* (= *De pot.*). 2 vols. Edited by P. M. Pession. In *Quaestiones disputatae*, 8th rev. ed., vol. 2. Rome: Marietti, 1949.

———. *Quaestiones disputatae de veritate* (= *De ver.*). Vols. 22/1–3 in *Sancti Thomae de Aquino Opera Omnia*. Rome: Commissio Leonina, 1970.

———. *Quaestio disputatio de caritate* (= *De car.* / also *De virtutibus*, q. 2). Edited by P. A. Odetto. In *Quaestiones disputatae*, 8th rev. ed., vol. 2. Rome: Marietti, 1949.

———. *Quaestiones de quolibet* (= *Quod.*). Vols. 25/1–2 in *Sancti Thomae de Aquino Opera Omnia*. Rome / Paris: Commissio Leonina / Éditions Du Cerf, 1996.

———. *Scriptum super libros Sententiarum magistri Petri Lombardi episcopi Parisiensis* (= *In Sent.*). Vols. 1–2, edited by P. Mandonnet. Vols. 3–4, edited by Maria Fabianus Moos. Paris: Lethielleux, 1929, 1933. [See Parma edition above under *Commentum*.]

———. *Sentencia libri De anima* (= *In De an.*). Vol. 45/1 in *Sancti Thomae de Aquino Opera Omnia*. Rome: Commissio Leonina, 1984.

———. *Sentencia libri De sensu et sensato cuius secundus tractatus est De memoria et reminiscencia* (= *In De sensu*). Vol. 45/2 in *Sancti Thomae de Aquino Opera Omnia*. Rome: Commissio Leonina, 1984.

———. *Sententia libri Ethicorum* (= *In Ethic.*). Vol. 47/1–2 in *Sancti Thomae de Aquino Opera Omnia*. Rome: Sancta Sabina, 1969.

———. *Sententia libri Politicorum* (= *In Politic.*). Vol. 48 in *Sancti Thomae de Aquino Opera Omnia*. Rome: Sancta Sabina, 1971.

———. *Summa contra Gentiles* (= *SCG*) Vols. 13–15 in *Sancti Thomae de Aquino Opera Omnia*. Rome: Typis Riccardi Garroni, 1918, 1926, 1930. [See Marietti edition above under *Liber de veritate*.]

———. *Summae theologiae* (= *ST*). Vols. 4–12 in *Sancti Thomae de Aquino Opera Omnia*. Rome: Commissio Leonina, 1888, 1889, 1891, 1892, 1895, 1898, 1899, 1903, 1906.

———. *Super Boetium De Trinitate* (= *In De Trin.*). Vol. 50 in *Sancti Thomae de Aquino Opera Omnia*. Rome / Paris: Commissio Leonina / Éditions Du Cerf, 1992.

———. *Super Evangelium S. Matthaei lectura* (= *In Matthaeum*). Edited by R. Cai. Turin: Marietti, 1951.

———. *Super librum De Causis expositio* (= *In De caus.*). Edited by H. D. Saffrey. Fribourg: Société philosophique, 1954.

———. *Super primam Epistolam ad Corinthios lectura* (= *In I Corinthios*) and *Super secundam Epistolam ad Corinthios lectura* (= *In II Corinthios*). Vol. 1 of *Super*

Epistolas S. Pauli lectura, 8th ed., edited by P. Raphael Cai. Turin: Marietti, 1953.

Arp, Robert, ed. *Revisiting Aquinas' Proofs for the Existence of God*. Leiden: Brill, 2016.

Ashley, Benedict. *The Way toward Wisdom: An Interdisciplinary and Intercultural Introduction to Metaphysics*. Notre Dame, IN: University of Notre Dame Press, 2006.

Ashworth, E. J. "Signification and Modes of Signifying in Thirteenth-Century Logic: A Preface to Aquinas on Analogy." *Medieval Philosophy and Theology* (1991): 39–67.

——. "Analogy and Equivocation in Thirteenth-Century Logic: Aquinas in Context." *Mediaeval Studies* 54 (1992): 94–135.

Augustine. *De Genesi ad litteram*. In *Patrologia Latina* 34. Paris: Migne, 1850.

Aumann, Jordan. "Beauty and the Esthetic Response." *Angelicum* 54 (1977): 501.

Bailer-Jones, Daniela M. "Models, Metaphors and Analogies." In *The Blackwell Guide to the Philosophy of Science*, 108–27. Oxford: Blackwell, 2002.

Baisnée, Jules A. "St. Thomas Aquinas's Proofs for the Existence of God Presented in Their Chronological Order." In *Philosophical Studies in Honor of the Very Reverend Ignatius Smith*, edited by John K. Ryan, 29–64. Westminster, MD: Newman Press, 1952.

Baumgaertner, William. "Metaphysics and the Second Analytics." *New Scholasticism* 29 (1955): 423–26.

Bérubé, Camille. *La connaissance de l'individuel au Moyen Âge*. Montreal: Presses de l'Université de Montréal, 1964.

Blanchette, Oliva. *Philosophy of Being: A Reconstructive Essay in Metaphysics*. Washington, DC: The Catholic University of America Press, 2003.

Bobik, Joseph. "Dimensions in the Individuation of Bodily Substances." *Philosophical Studies (Maynooth)* 4 (1954): 60–79.

——. "Some Remarks on Father Owens' St. Thomas and the Future of Metaphysics.'" *The New Scholasticism* 33 (1959): 68–85.

——. "Some Disputable Points Apropos of St. Thomas and Metaphysics." *The New Scholasticism* 37 (1963): 411–30.

——. "Some Remarks on Fr. Owens' 'St. Thomas and Elucidation.'" *The New Scholasticism* 37 (1963): 59–63.

——. *Aquinas on Being and Essence: A Translation and Interpretation*. Notre Dame, IN: University of Notre Dame Press, 1965.

Bonino, Serge-Thomas. *Angels and Demons: A Catholic Introduction*. Translated by Michael Miller. Washington, DC: The Catholic University of America Press, 2016.

Bonnette, Denis. *Aquinas' Proofs for God's Existence. St Thomas Aquinas on: "The Per Accidens necessarily implies the Per Se."* The Hague: Martinus Nijhoff, 1972.

Brock, Stephen. "On Whether Aquinas's *Ipsum Esse* is 'Platonism.'" *The Review of Metaphysics* 60 (2006): 269–303.

——. "Harmonizing Plato and Aristotle on *esse*: Thomas Aquinas and the *De hebdomadibus*." *Nova et Vetera* 5 (2007): 478–88.

——. "How Many Acts of Being Can a Substance Have? An Aristotelian Approach to Aquinas's Real Distinction." *International Philosophical Quarterly* 54, no. 3 (2014): 317–31.

———. *The Philosophy of Saint Thomas Aquinas*. Eugene, OR: Cascade Books, 2015.
Brower, Jeffrey. *Aquinas's Ontology of the Material World: Change, Hylomorphism, and Material Objects*. Oxford: Oxford University Press, 2014.
———. "Aquinas on the Problem of Universals." *Philosophy and Phenomenological Research* 92 (2016): 715–35.
Brower, Jeffrey E., and Susan Brower-Toland. "Aquinas on Mental Representation: Concepts and Intentionality." *The Philosophical Review* 117, no. 2 (2008): 193–243.
Brown, Barry. *Accidental Esse*. New York: University Press of America, 1985.
Burrell, David. *Aquinas: God and Action*. 3rd ed. Eugene, OR: Wipf and Stock, 2016.
Cardinal George, Francis. "Saint Thomas: Timeless and Timely." In *Thomas Aquinas: Teacher of Humanity*, edited by John Hittinger and Daniel Wagner. Newcastle upon Tyne: Cambridge Scholars Publishing, 2015.
Carl, Brian. "The Formal Constituent of the Divine Nature in Peter Ledesma, John of St. Thomas, and Vincent Contenson." *The Thomist* 82 (2018): 59–88.
———. "The Transcendentals and the Divine Names in Thomas Aquinas." *American Catholic Philosophical Quarterly* 92, no. 2 (2018): 233–42.
Carlo, William. *The Ultimate Reducibility of Essence to Existence in Existential Metaphysics*. The Hague: Martinus Nijhoff, 1966.
Chase, Michael. "The Medieval Posterity of Simplicius' Commentary on the *Categories*: Thomas Aquinas and Al-Farabi." In *Medieval Commentaries on Aristotle's Categories*, ed. L. A. Newton. Leiden: Brill, 2008.
———. "*Quod est primum in compositione, est ultimum in resolutione*. Notes on Analysis and Synthesis in Late Antiquity." *Anuario Filosófico* 48 (2015): 103–39.
Chossat, M. "Dieu. Sa nature selon les scolastiques." In *Dictionnaire de théologie catholique*, vol. 4. Paris: Letouzey et Ané, 1910.
Clarke, W. Norris. "Limitation of Act by Potency: Aristotelianism or Neoplatonism." *The New Scholasticism* 26, no. 2 (1952): 167–94.
———. "What Cannot Be Said in St. Thomas' Essence-Existence Doctrine." *The New Scholasticism* 48, no. 1 (1974): 19–39.
———. "The Role of Essence within St. Thomas' Essence-Existence Doctrine: Positive or Negative Principle? A Dispute within Thomism." In *Tommaso d'Aquino nel suo settimo centenario: Atti del Congresso Internazionale*, vol. 6: *L'Essere*, 109–15. Naples: Edizioni Domenicane Italiane, 1977.
———. "Action as the Self-Revelation of Being: A Central Theme in the Thought of St. Thomas Aquinas." In *History of Philosophy in the Making: A Symposium of Essays to Honor Professor James D. Collins on His 65th Birthday*, ed. Linus Thro, 63–80. Washington, DC: University Press of America, 1982.
———. *The One and the Many: A Contemporary Thomistic Metaphysics*. Notre Dame, IN: University of Notre Dame Press, 2001.
Cohoe, Caleb. "There Must Be a First: Why Thomas Aquinas Rejects Infinite, Essentially Ordered, Causal Series." *British Journal for the History of Philosophy* 21, no. 5 (2013): 838–85.
Collins, James. *The Thomistic Philosophy of the Angels*. Washington, DC: The Catholic University of America Press, 1947.

Contat, Alain. "Le figure della differenza ontologica nel tomismo del Novecento (seconda parte)." *Alpha Omega* 11 (2008): 213–50.

———. "*Esse, essentia, ordo*. Verso una metafisica della partecipazione operativa." *Espíritu* 61 (2012): 9–71.

———. "La constitution de l'étant dans le thomisme contemporain: Tomas Tyn, Johann Baptist Lotz, Fabro, Cornelio." In *Actus essendi. Saint Thomas d'Aquin et ses interprètes*, ed. Matthieu Raffray, 369–433. Paris: Parole et Silence, 2019.

Cory, Therese. *Aquinas on Human Self-Knowledge*. Cambridge: Cambridge University Press, 2014.

———. "Rethinking Abstractionism: Aquinas's Intellectual Light and Some Arabic Sources." *Journal of the History of Philosophy* 53, no. 4 (2015): 607–46.

Coughlin, Glen. "The Role of Natural Philosophy in the Beginning of Metaphysics." *The Thomist* 84, no. 3 (2020): 395–434.

Cross, Richard. "Angelic Time and Motion: Bonaventure to Duns Scotus," in *A Companion to Angels in Medieval Philosophy*, ed. Tobias Hoffman, 117–48. Leiden: Brill, 2012.

Cunningham, Francis. "Judgment in St. Thomas." *The Modern Schoolman* 31, no. 3 (1954): 185–212.

———. "The Second Operation and the Assent vs. the Judgment in St. Thomas." *The New Scholasticism* 31, no. 1 (1957): 1–33.

———. *Essence and Existence in Thomism: A Mental vs. the "Real Distinction?"* Lanham, MD: University Press of America, 1988.

Damascene, John. *De fide orthodoxa: Versions of Burgundio and Cerbanus*. Edited by E. M. Buytaert. St. Bonaventure, NY: Franciscan Institute, 1955.

———. *Expositio Fidei*. In *Die Schriften des Johannes von Damaskos*, vol. 2, edited by Bonifatius Kotter. Berlin: Walter de Gruyter, 1969.

D'Ettore, Domenic. *Analogy After Aquinas: Logical Problems, Thomistic Answers*. Washington, DC: The Catholic University of America Press, 2019.

———. "*Una ratio* versus *Diversae rationes*: Three Interpretations." *Nova et Vetera* 17, no. 1 (2019): 39–55.

Davies, Brian. *The Thought of Thomas Aquinas*. Oxford: Clarendon Press, 1992.

———. *Thomas Aquinas's "Summa Theologiae": A Guide and Commentary*. Oxford: Oxford University Press, 2014.

de Blignieres, Louis-Marie. *Le mystère de l'être: L'approche thomiste de Guérard des Lauriers*. Paris: J. Vrin, 2007.

De Haan, Daniel. "Aquinas on *actus essendi* and the Second Mode of Participation." *The Thomist* 82 (2018): 573–609.

———. "Is Philosophy of Nature Irrelevant?" *Proceedings of the American Catholic Philosophical Association* 93 (2019): 327–48.

Deferrari, Roy. *A Lexicon of St. Thomas Aquinas Based on the "Summa Theologica" and Selected Passages of His Other Works*. Washington, DC: The Catholic University of America Press, 1948.

del Prado, Norbertus. "La vérité fondamentale de la philosophie chrétienne selon saint Thomas." *Revue thomiste* 18, nos. 2–3 (1910): 209–27.

———. *De veritate fundamentali philosophiae Christianae*. Fribourg: Société Saint Paul, 1911.

Del Punta, F., S. Donati, and C. Luna. "Egidio Romano." In *Dizionario biografico degli Italiani* 42:319–41. Rome: Istituto della Enciclopedia italiana, 1993.

Dewan, Lawrence. *The Doctrine of Being of John Capreolus: A Contribution to the History of the Notion of "esse."* PhD diss., University of Toronto, 1967.

———. "Being *per se*, Being *per accidens*, and St. Thomas's Metaphysics." *Science et Esprit* 30 (1978): 169–84.

———. "St. Thomas, Metaphysics, and Formal Causality." *Laval théologique et philosophique* 36 (1980): 285–316.

———. "Saint Thomas, Joseph Owens, and the Real Distinction between Being and Essence." *The Modern Schoolman* 61, no. 3 (1984): 145–56.

———. "St. Thomas, Metaphysical Procedure, and the Formal Cause." *The New Scholasticism* 63 (1989): 173–82.

———. "Thomas Aquinas, Creation, and Two Historians." *Laval théologique et philosophique* 50, no. 2 (1994): 363–87.

———. "The Individual as a Mode of Being according to Thomas Aquinas." *The Thomist* 63 (1999): 403–24.

———. "Etienne Gilson and the *Actus Essendi*." *Maritain Studies* 15 (1999): 1–27.

———. "Discussion on Anthony Kenny's *Aquinas on Being.*" *Nova et Vetera* 3, no. 2 (2005): 335–400.

———. *Form and Being: Studies in Thomistic Metaphysics*. Washington, DC: The Catholic University of America Press, 2006.

———. "St. Thomas, Physics, and the Principle of Metaphysics." In *Form and Being: Studies in Thomistic Metaphysics*. Studies in Philosophy and the History of Philosophy 45. Washington, DC: The Catholic University of America Press, 2006.

———. *St. Thomas and Form as Something Divine in Things*. Aquinas Lecture 71. Milwaukee, WI: Marquette University Press, 2007.

———. "Maritain and Aquinas on Our Discovery of Being." *Studia Gilsoniana* 3 (2014): 415–43.

Dolan, Edmund. "Resolution and Composition in Speculative and Practical Discourse." *Laval Théologique et Philosophique* 6 (1950): 9–62.

Donati, Silvia. "Studi per una cronologia delle opere di Egidio Romano." *Documenti e studi sulla tradizione filosofica medievale* 1 (1990): 1–111; 2 (1991): 1–74.

Doolan, Gregory T. *Aquinas on the Divine Ideas as Exemplar Causes*. Washington, DC: The Catholic University of America Press, 2008.

———. "Aquinas on Separate Substances as the Subject Matter of Metaphysics." *Documenti E Studi Sulla Tradizione Filosofica Medievale* 22 (2011): 347–82.

———. "Aquinas on *Substance* as a Metaphysical Genus." In *The Science of Being as Being: Metaphysical Investigations*, edited by Gregory T. Doolan. Washington, DC: The Catholic University of America Press, 2012.

———. "Aquinas on the Demonstrability of Angels." In *A Companion to Angels in Medieval Philosophy*, edited by Tobias Hoffmann, 13–44. Leiden: Brill, 2012.

———. "The Metaphysician's vs. the Logician's Categories." *Quaestiones Disputatae* 4, no. 2 (2014): 133–55.

———. "Fabro's Double Participation and Aquinas's Double Exemplarism." In *Studia Fabriana. Cornelio Fabro. Essential Thinker. Philosopher of Being and of Freedom*, edited by Nathaniel Dreyer, 67–88. Chillum: IVE Press, 2017.

———. "Aquinas on *esse subsistens* and the Third Mode of Participation." *The Thomist* 82 (2018): 611–42.

———. "Aquinas's Methodology for Deriving the Categories: Convergences with Albert's *Sufficientia Praedicamentorum*." *Documenti e studi sulla tradizione filosofica medievale* 30 (2019): 654–89.

Druart, T.-A. "*Shay*' or *Res* as Concomitant of 'Being' in Avicenna." *Documenti e studi sulla tradizione filosofica medievale* 12 (2001): 125–42.

Dulles, Avery R., James M. Demske, and Robert J. O'Connell. *Introductory Metaphysics: A Course Combining Matter Treated in Ontology, Cosmology, and Natural Theology*. New York: Sheed and Ward, 1955.

Dumont, Stephen. "Duns Scotus's Parisian Question on the Formal Distinction." *Vivarium* 43, no. 1 (2005): 7–62.

Elders, Leo J. "St. Thomas Aquinas' Commentary on the *Metaphysics* of Aristotle." *Divus Thomas* 86, no. 4 (1983): 307–26.

———. *Autour de Saint Thomas d'Aquinas: recueil d'études sur sa pensée philosophique et théologique*. Paris: FAC-éditions, 1987.

———. "La connaissance de l'être et l'entrée en métaphysique." In *Autour de Saint Thomas d'Aquinas: recueil d'études sur sa pensée philosophique et théologique*. Paris: FAC-éditions, 1987.

———. *The Metaphysics of Being of St. Thomas Aquinas in a Historical Perspective*. Leiden: Brill, 1993.

Fabro, Cornelio. "Circa la divisione dell'essere in atto e potenza." *Divus Thomas* 42 (1939): 529–62.

———. "Un itinéraire de saint Thomas." *Revue de Philosophie* 39 (1939): 285–310.

———. "Neotomismo e Neosuarezismo: una battaglia di principi." *Divus Thomas* 44 (1941): 167–215.

———. *La Nozione Metafisica di Partecipazione secondo s. Tommaso d'Aquino*. Turin: Società Editrice Internazionale, 1950.

———. "Sviluppo, significato e valore della 'IV via.'" *Doctor Communis* 7 (1954): 71–109.

———. "Per la semantica originaria dell' *esse* tomistico." *Euntes Docete* 9 (1956): 437–66.

———. *Participation et causalité selon s. Thomas d'Aquin*. Louvain: Publications Universitaires de Louvain, 1961.

———. "The Problem of Being and the Destiny of Man." *International Philosophical Quarterly* 1 (1961): 407–36.

———. "Il fondamento metafisico della 'IV via.'" *Doctor Communis* 18 (1965): 49–70.

———. "Existence." In *The New Catholic Encyclopedia*, 5:721–24. Washington, DC: The Catholic University of America Press, 1966.

———. "L' 'esse' tomistico e la ripresa della metafisica." *Angelicum* 3 (1967): 281–314.

———. "The Intensive Hermeneutics of Thomistic Philosophy. The Notion of Participation." *The Review of Metaphysics* 27, no. 3 (1974): 449–91.

———. *La preghiera nel pensiero moderno*. Rome: Edizioni di storia e letteratura, 1983.

Feser, Edward. "Between Aristotle and William Paley: Aquinas's Fifth Way." *Nova et Vetera* 11, no. 3 (2013): 707–49.
———. *Five Proofs for the Existence of God*. San Francisco, CA: Ignatius Press, 2017.
Fine, Gail. *On Ideas: Aristotle's Criticism of Plato's Theory of Forms*. Oxford: Oxford University Press, 1993.
Fontana, Elvio. "Notes pour la fondation métaphysique de l'être." *Revue Thomiste* 111 (2011), Hors-série: 113–39.
Forest, Aimé. *La structure métaphysique du concret selon Saint Thomas d'Aquin*. 2nd ed. Paris: Vrin, 1956.
Fox, Rory. *Time and Eternity in Mid-Thirteenth-Century Thought*. Oxford: Oxford University Press, 2006.
Frost, Gloria. "Aquinas on the Intension and Remission of Accidental Forms." *Oxford Studies in Medieval Philosophy* 7 (2019): 116–46.
———. *Aquinas on Efficient Causation and Causal Powers*. Cambridge: Cambridge University Press, 2022.
Galluzzo, Gabriele. "Aquinas on Common Nature and Universals." *Recherches de Théologie et Philosophie Médiévales* 70 (2004): 131–71.
———. "Two Senses of 'Common'. Avicenna's Doctrine of Essence and Aquinas's View on Individuation." In *The Arabic, Hebrew and Latin Reception of Avicenna's Metaphysics*, ed. Amos Bertolacci and Dag Hasse, 309–37. Berlin: De Gruyter, 2011.
Garceau, Benoît. *Judicium. Vocabulaire, sources, doctrine de saint Thomas d'Aquin*. Paris: Vrin, 1968.
Gardeil, A. "'Destruction des destructions' du R. P. Chossat." *Revue thomiste* 18 (1910): 361–91.
Garrigou-Lagrange, Réginald. *The Trinity and God the Creator*. Jackson, Miss.: Ex Fontibus Company, 2015.
Geach, Peter. "Form and Existence." *Proceedings of the Aristotelian Society* 55 (1954–55): 251–72.
Geiger, Louis-Bertrand. "Abstraction et séparation d'après S. Thomas: In De Trinitate, q. 5, a. 3." *Revue des sciences philosophiques et théologiques* 31 (1947): 3–40.
———. *La participation dans la philosophie de s. Thomas d'Aquin*. Paris: Librairie Philosophique J. Vrin, 1953.
Giles of Rome. *Aegidii Romani Theoremata de esse et essentia*. Edited by E. Hocedez. Louvain: Museum Lessianum, 1930.
———. *Apologia*. Vol. III/1 in *Aegidi Romani Opera Omnia*. Edited by R. Wielockx. Florence: Leo S. Olschki, 1985.
———. *Reportatio lecturae super libros I–IV Sententiarum: Reportatio Monacensis. Excerpta Godefridi de Fontibus*. Vol III/2 in *Aegidii Romani Opera Omnia*. Edited by C. Luna. Florence: SISMEL, 2003.
Gilson, Étienne. *The Spirit of Mediaeval Philosophy*. Translated by Alfred Howard Campbell Downes. New York: C. Scribner's Sons, 1936.
———. *Being and Some Philosophers*. 2nd ed. Toronto: Pontifical Institute of Mediaeval Studies, 1952.
———. *Elements of Christian Philosophy*. Garden City, NY: Doubleday, 1960.

———. *L'esprit de la philosophie médiévale (Gifford lectures, Université d'Aberdeen).* 2nd rev. ed. Paris: Vrin, 1969.

———. *Introduction à la philosophie chrétienne.* 2nd ed. Paris: Vrin, 2007.

Gironella, Juan Roig. "Metafísica de la belleza." *Pensamiento* 7 (1951): 29–55.

Goris, Harm. "A Reinterpretation of Aquinas' Correspondence Definition of Truth." In *Intellect et imagination dans la Philosophie Médiévale. Actes du XIe Congrès International de Philosophie Médiévale de la Société Internationale pour l'étude de la Philosophie Médiévale (S.I.E.P.M.), Porto, du 26 au 31 août 2002*, edited by Maria Cândida da Costa Reis Monteiro Pacheco and José Francisco Meirinhos, 3:1431–43. Rencontres de philosophie médiévale. Turnhout: Brepols, 2006.

———. "Angelic Knowledge in Aquinas and Bonaventure." In *A Companion to Angels in Medieval Philosophy*, edited by Tobias Hoffmann, 149–85. Leiden: Brill, 2012.

Grabmann, M. "Doctrina S. Thomae de distinctione reali inter essentiam et esse ex documentis ineditis saeculi XIII illustratur." In *Acta hebdomadae Thomisticae Romae celebratae 19–25 Novembris 1923 in laudem S. Thomae Aquinatis*, 131–90. Rome: Apud sedem Academiae S. Thomae Aquinatis, 1924.

Gredt, Joseph. *Elementa Philosophiae Aristotelico Thomisticae*, vol. 2. Freiburg: Herder, 1937.

Hesse, Mary B. *Models and Analogies in Science.* Notre Dame, IN: University of Notre Dame Press, 1966.

Hocedez, E. "Gilles de Rome et Henri de Gand sur la distinction réelle (1276–1287)." *Gregorianum* 8 (1927): 358–84.

———. "Le premier quodlibet d'Henri de Gand (1276)." *Gregorianum* 9 (1928): 92–117.

———. "Gilles de Rome et Saint Thomas." In *Mélanges Mandonnet. Études d'histoire littéraire et doctrinale du Moyen-Âge*, 1:385–409. Paris: Vrin, 1930.

Hochschild, Joshua. "Form, Essence, Soul: Distinguishing Principles of Thomistic Metaphysics." In *Distinctions of Being: Philosophical Approaches to Reality*, edited by Nikolaj Zunic, 21–35. Washington, DC: American Maritain Association, 2013.

———. "Proportionality vs. Divine Naming: Did Aquinas Change His Mind about Analogy?" *The Thomist* 77 (2013): 531–58.

Houser, R. E. "The Real Distinction and the Principles of Metaphysics." In *Laudemus viros gloriosos: Essays in Honor of Armand Maurer, CSB*, edited by R. E. Houser, 75–108. Notre Dame, IN: University of Notre Dame Press, 2007.

———. "Introducing the Principles of Avicennian Metaphysics into *Sacra Doctrina*: Thomas Aquinas, *Scriptum super Sententiarum*, Bk. 1, d. 8." *American Catholic Philosophical Quarterly* 88, no. 2 (2014): 207.

Hunter, Richard. "Analogy and Beauty: Thomistic Reflections on the Transcendentals." PhD diss., Bryn Mawr College, 1978.

Imbach, R. "Averroistische Stellungnahmen zur Diskussion über das Verhältnis von Esse und Essentia." In *Studi sul XIV secolo in memoria di Anneliese Maier*, edited by A. Maieru and A. P. Bagliani, 299–319. Rome: Storia e letteratura, 1981.

John, Helen. *The Thomist Spectrum.* New York: Fordham University Press, 1966.

Kenny, Anthony. *The Five Ways*. London: Routledge & Kegan Paul, 1969.
Kerr, Fergus. *After Aquinas: Versions of Thomism*. Oxford: Blackwell, 2002.
Kerr, Gaven. "The Meaning of *Ens Commune* in the Thought of Thomas Aquinas." *Yearbook of the Irish Philosophical Society* (2008): 32–60.
———. "Essentially Ordered Series Reconsidered." *American Catholic Philosophical Quarterly* 86, no. 4 (2012): 155–74.
———. *Aquinas's Way to God: The Proof in "De Ente et Essentia."* Oxford: Oxford University Press, 2015.
———. "The Relevance of Aquinas's Uncaused Cause Argument Today." In *Revisiting Aquinas' Proofs for the Existence of God*, edited by Robert Arp, 71–86. Leiden / Boston: Brill / Rodopi, 2016.
———. "Essentially Ordered Series Reconsidered Once Again." *American Catholic Philosophical Quarterly* 91, no. 2 (2017): 541–55.
———. *Aquinas and the Metaphysics of Creation*. Oxford: Oxford University Press, 2019.
———. "Design Arguments and Aquinas's Fifth Way." *The Thomist* 82, no. 3 (2019): 447–71.
———. "A Reconsideration of Aquinas's Fourth Way." *American Catholic Philosophical Quarterly* 95, no. 4 (2021): 595–615. Reprinted in his *Collected Articles on the Existence of God*. Neunkirchen-Seelscheid: Editiones Scholasticae, 2023.
———. "A Deeper Look at Aquinas's First Way." *Nova et Vetera* (English Edition) 20, no. 2 (2022): 461–84. Reprinted in his *Collected Articles on the Existence of God*. Neunkirchen-Seelscheid: Editiones Scholasticae, 2023.
———. "The *Summa Contra Gentiles* and Aquinas's Way to God." *Nova et Vetera* (English Edition) 20, no. 4 (2022): 1273–88. Reprinted in his *Collected Articles on the Existence of God*. Neunkirchen-Seelscheid: Editiones Scholasticae, 2023.
King, Peter. "Rethinking Representation in the Middle Ages." In *Representation and Objects of Thought in Medieval Philosophy*, edited by H. Lagerlund, 84–85. Aldershot: Ashgate, 2005.
Klima, Gyula. "Ontological Alternatives vs. Alternative Semantics in Medieval Philosophy." *S: European Journal for Semiotic Studies* 3, no. 4 (1991): 587–618.
———. "The Semantic Principles Underlying Saint Thomas Aquinas's Metaphysics of Being." *Medieval Philosophy and Theology* 5 (1996): 125–27.
———. "The Demonic Temptations of Medieval Nominalism: Mental Representation and 'Demon Skepticism.'" *Proceedings of the Society for Medieval Logic and Metaphysics* 4 (2004): 37–44.
———. "Tradition and Innovation in Medieval Theories of Mental Representation." *Proceedings of the Society for Medieval Logic and Metaphysics* 4 (2004): 4–11.
———. "Intentional Transfer in Averroes, Indifference of Nature in Avicenna, and the Representationalism of Aquinas." *Proceedings of the Society for Medieval Logic and Metaphysics* 5 (2005): 33–37.
———. "The Anti-Skepticism of John Buridan and Thomas Aquinas: Putting Skeptics in Their Place vs. Stopping Them in Their Tracks." In *Rethinking the History of Skepticism*, edited by Henrik Lagerlund, 145–70. Leiden: Brill, 2010.
———. "Being." In *Encyclopedia of Medieval Philosophy: Philosophy Between 500 and 1500*, edited by Henrik Lagerlund, 150–59. Dordrecht: Springer, 2011.

———. "Thought-Transplants, Demons, and Modalities." In *The Language of Thought in Late Medieval Philosophy: Essays in Honor of Claude Panaccio*, edited by Jenny Pelletier and Magali Roques, 369–81. Dordrecht: Springer, 2017.

Klubertanz, George. "St. Thomas and the Knowledge of the Singular." *The New Scholasticism* 26, no. 2 (1952): 135–66.

———. *St. Thomas Aquinas on Analogy: A Textual Analysis and Systematic Synthesis*. Chicago: Loyola University Press, 1960.

———. *Introduction to the Philosophy of Being*. 2nd ed. New York: Appleton-Century-Crofts, 1963.

Knasas, John. "Thomistic Existentialism and the Proofs *Ex Motu* at *Summa Contra Gentiles*, I, C. 13." *The Thomist* 59, no. 4 (1995): 591–615.

———. *Being and Some Twentieth-Century Thomists*. New York: Fordham University Press, 2003.

———. "The Intellectual Phenomenology of '*De ente et essentia*,' Chapter 4." *The Review of Metaphysics* 68, no. 1 (2014): 107–53.

———. "The Analytical Thomist and the Paradoxical Aquinas: Some Reflections on Kerr's *Aquinas's Way to God*." *Annals of Philosophy* 67, no. 4 (2019): 84–85.

———. *Thomistic Existentialism and Cosmological Reasoning*. Washington, DC: The Catholic University of America Press, 2019.

König-Pralong, C. *Avènement de l'aristotélisme en terre chrétienne*. Paris: Vrin, 2005.

———. *Être, essence et contingence. Henri de Gand, Gilles de Rome, Godefroid de Fontaines*. Paris: Les Belles Lettres, 2006.

Kretzmann, Norman. "Trinity and Transcendentals." In *Trinity, Incarnation, and Atonement*, edited by R. Feenstra and C. Plantinga, 79–109. Notre Dame, IN: University of Notre Dame Press, 1989.

———. *The Metaphysics of Theism: Aquinas's Natural Theology in "Summa Contra Gentiles" I*. Oxford: Clarendon Press, 1997.

———. *The Metaphysics of Creation: Aquinas's Natural Theology in "Summa Contra Gentiles" II*. Oxford: Clarendon Press, 1999.

LaZella, A. T. "As Light Belongs to Air: Thomas Aquinas and Meister Eckhart on the Existential Rootlessness of Creatures." *American Catholic Philosophical Quarterly* 87 (2013): 567–91.

Leftow, Brian. "Aquinas on Attributes." *Medieval Philosophy and Theology* 11, no. 1 (2003): 1–41.

LeNotre, Gaston G. "Determinate and Indeterminate Dimensions: Does Thomas Aquinas Change His Mind on Individuation?" *American Catholic Philosophical Quarterly* 94 (2020): 503–46.

Leo XIII, Pope. *Aeterni Patris*. Encyclical Letter. August 4, 1879. Available at www.vatican.va.

Llamzon, Benjamin S. "Suppositral and Accidental *Esse*: A Study in Banez." *The New Scholasticism* 39 (1965): 170–88.

Lonergan, Bernard. *Grace and Freedom: Operative Grace in the Thought of St. Thomas Aquinas*. Toronto: University of Toronto Press, 2000.

Long, Steven. *Analogia Entis: On the Analogy of Being, Metaphysics, and the Act of Faith*. Notre Dame, IN: University of Notre Dame Press, 2011.

Longeway, John. "Aegidius Romanus and Albertus Magnus vs. Thomas Aquinas on the Highest Sort of Demonstration (*demonstratio potissima*)." *Documenti e studi sulla tradizione filosofica medieval* 13 (2002): 373–434.

———. *Demonstration and Scientific Knowledge in William of Ockham: A Translation of "Summa Logicae" III-II: "De Syllogismo Demonstrativo," and selections from the Prologue to the "Ordinatio."* Notre Dame, IN: University of Notre Dame Press, 2007.

Luna, C. "Nouveaux textes d'Henri de Gand, de Gilles de Rome et de Godefroid de Fontaines: les questions du ms. Bologne, Collegio di Spagna 133. Contribution à l'étude des questions disputées." *Archives d'histoire doctrinale et littéraire du moyen âge* 65 (1998): 151–272.

MacDonald, Scott. "The *Esse/Essentia* Argument in Aquinas's *De ente et essentia*." *Journal of the History of Philosophy* 22, no. 2 (1984): 157–72.

MacGregor, Kirk R. *Luis de Molina: The Life and Theology of the Founder of Middle Knowledge*. Grand Rapids, MI: Zondervan, 2015.

Maier, Annaliese. *Das Problem der Intensiven grösse in der Scholastik*. Rome: Verlage Heinrich Keller, 1939.

Mandonnet, Pierre. "Les titres doctoreaux de saint Thomas d'Aquin." *Revue Thomiste* 17 (1909): 597–608.

———. "Les premières disputes sur la distinction réelle entre l'essence et l'existence." *Revue thomiste* 18 (1910): 741–65.

Manser, Gallus. *Das Wesen des Thomismus*. 3rd ed. Fribourg: Paulusverlag, 1949.

Maritain, Jacques. *A Preface to Metaphysics: Seven Lectures on Being*. New York: Sheed and Ward, 1945.

———. *Existence and the Existent*. Translated by Lewis Galantiere and Gerald Phelan. New York: Pantheon Books, 1948.

———. *The Degrees of Knowledge*. 4th ed. Translated by Gerald Phelan. New York: Charles Scribner's Sons, 1959.

———. "Reflections on Wounded Nature." In *Untrammeled Approaches*, edited and translated by Bernard Doering, 207–42. Notre Dame, IN: University of Notre Dame Press, 1997.

Matava, R. J. *Divine Causality and Human Free Choice: Domingo Báñez, Physical Premotion and the Controversy "de Auxiliis" Revisited*. Leiden: Brill, 2016.

Maurer, Armand. "St. Thomas and the Analogy of Genus." *The New Scholasticism* 29, no. 2 (1955): 127–44.

———. "St. Thomas on the Sacred Name 'Tetragrammaton.'" *Mediaeval Studies* 34 (1972): 275–86.

———. "Dialectic in the *De ente et essentia* of St. Thomas Aquinas." In *Roma, magistra mundi. Itineraria culturae medievalis: Mélanges offerts au Père L.E. Boyle à l'occasion de son 75e anniversaire*, 573–83. Textes et études du moyen âge 10. Louvain-la-Neuve: Fédération des Instituts d'Etudes Médiévales, 1998.

McCabe, Herbert. "The Logic of Mysticism." In *God Still Matters*, edited by Brian Davies, OP. London: Continuum, 2002.

McInerny, Ralph. *The Logic of Analogy: An Interpretation of Aquinas*. The Hague: Martinus Nijhoff, 1961.

———. *Being and Predication: Thomistic Interpretations*. Washington, DC: The Catholic University of America Press, 1986.
———. *Praeambula Fidei: Thomism and the God of the Philosophers*. Washington, DC: The Catholic University of America Press, 2006.
———. *Aquinas and Analogy*. Washington, DC: The Catholic University of America Press, 2012.
Meehan, F.-X. "Efficient Causality in Aristotle and St. Thomas." PhD diss., The Catholic University of America, 1940.
Meliadò, Mario. "Axiomatic Thought: Boethius' *De hebdomadibus* and the *Liber de causis* in Late-Medieval Albertism." *Bulletin de philosophie médiévale* 55 (2013): 71–131.
Mercier, S. *Gilles de Rome. Théorèmes sur L'être et L'essence*. Paris: Les Belles Lettres, 2011.
Mitchell, Jason A. *Being and Participation: The Method and Structure of Metaphysical Reflection according to Cornelio Fabro*. Rome: Ateneo Pontificio Regina Apostolorum, 2012.
———. "From Aristotle's Four Causes to Aquinas' Ultimate Causes of Being: Modern Interpretations." *Alpha Omega* 16 (2013): 399–414.
———. "Aquinas on *esse commune* and the First Mode of Participation." *The Thomist* 82 (2018): 543–72.
———. "Knowledge of *ens* as *primum cognitum* and the Discovery of *ens qua ens* according to Cornelio Fabro and Jan Aertsen." In *The Discovery of Being & Thomas Aquinas: Philosophical and Theological Perspectives*, edited by Christopher M. Cullen and Franklin T. Harkins, 106–24. Washington, DC: The Catholic University of America Press, 2019.
———. *Aquinas's Theology of Grace: Metaphysics and the New Perspective*. PhD diss., Ateneo Pontificio Regina Apostolorum, 2023.
Mondin, Battista. *The Principle of Analogy in Protestant and Catholic Theology*. 2nd rev. ed. The Hague: Martinus Nijhoff, 1968.
Montagnes, Bernard. *The Doctrine of the Analogy of Being According to Thomas Aquinas*. Translated by E. Macierowski. Milwaukee, WI: Marquette University Press, 2004.
Morris, Michael. *An Introduction to the Philosophy of Language*. Cambridge: Cambridge University Press, 2006.
Muller-Thym, Bernard. "The Common Sense, Perfection of the Order of Pure Sensibility." *The Thomist* 2, no. 3 (1940): 315–43.
O'Reilly, Kevin. *Aesthetic Perception: A Thomistic Perspective*. Dublin: Four Courts Press, 2007.
O'Rourke, Fran. *Pseudo-Dionysius and the Metaphysics of Aquinas*. Notre Dame, IN: University of Notre Dame Press, 2005.
Oeing-Hanhoff, L. "Die Methoden der Metaphysik im Mittelalter." In *Die Metaphysik im Mittelalter, Ihr Ursprung und ihre Bedeutung*, edited by Paul Wilpert and Willehad P. Eckert, 71–91. Berlin: De Gruyter, 1963.
———. "Analyse/Synthese." *Historisches Wörterbuch der Philosophie* 1 (1971): 232–48.

Owens, Joseph. "Common Nature: A Point of Comparison Between Thomistic and Scotistic Metaphysics." *Mediaeval Studies* 19 (1957): 1–14.

———. *St. Thomas and the Future of Metaphysics*. Milwaukee, WI: Marquette University Press, 1957.

———. "The Accidental and Essential Character of Being in the Doctrine of St. Thomas Aquinas." *Mediaeval Studies* 20 (1958): 1–40.

———. "Thomistic Common Nature and Platonic Idea." *Mediaeval Studies* 21 (1959): 211–23.

———. "Aristotle on Categories." *The Review of Metaphysics* 14 (1960): 73–90.

———. "St. Thomas and Elucidation." *The New Scholasticism* 35 (1961): 59–63.

———. *An Elementary Christian Metaphysics*. Milwaukee, WI: Bruce, 1963.

———. "Existential Act, Divine Being, and the Subject of Metaphysics." *The New Scholasticism* 37 (1963): 359–63.

———. "The 'Analytics' and Thomistic Metaphysical Procedure." *Mediaeval Studies* 20 (1964): 83–108.

———. "Quiddity and Real Distinction in Aquinas." *Mediaeval Studies* 27, no. 1 (1965): 1–22.

———. "Judgment and Truth in Aquinas." *Mediaeval Studies* 32, no. 1 (1970): 138–58.

———. "Metaphysical Separation in Aquinas." *Mediaeval Studies* 34, no. 1 (1972): 287–306.

———. "Aquinas—'Darkness of Ignorance' in the Most Refined Notion of God." *The Southwestern Journal of Philosophy* 5, no. 2 (1974): 93–110.

———. "Aquinas on Knowing Existence." *The Review of Metaphysics* 29, no. 4 (1976): 670–90.

———. *St. Thomas Aquinas on the Existence of God: The Collected Papers of Joseph Owens*. Edited by John R. Catan. Albany: State University of New York Press, 1980.

———. *Aquinas on Being and Thing*. Niagara Falls, NY: Niagara University Press, 1981.

———. *An Interpretation of Existence*. Houston: Center for Thomistic Studies, 1985.

———. "Aquinas' Distinction at *De ente et essentia* 4.119–123." *Mediaeval Studies* 48 (1986): 264–87.

———. "Aquinas and the Proof from the 'Physics.'" *Mediaeval Studies* 1 (1996): 119–50.

Panaccio, Claude. "Ockham and Locke on Mental Language." In *The Medieval Heritage in Early Modern Metaphysics and Modal Theory, 1400–1700*, edited by Russell Friedman and Lauge Nielsen, 37–51. Dordrecht: Springer, 2003.

Pasnau, Robert. "Aquinas and the Content Fallacy." *The Modern Schoolman* 75, no. 4 (1998): 293–314.

Paulus, J. "Les disputes d'Henri de Gand et de Gilles de Rome sur la distinction de l'essence et de l'existence." *Archives d'histoire doctrinale et littéraire du moyen âge* 13 (1940–42): 323–58.

Pawl, Timothy. *A Thomistic Account of Truthmakers for Modal Truths*. PhD diss., St. Louis University, 2008.

———. "A Thomistic Truthmaker Principle." *Acta Philosophica* 25 (2016): 45–64.

Peghaire, Julien. "L'intellection du singulier matériel chez les anges et chez l'homme." *Revue Dominicaine* 39 (1933): 135–44.
Pegis, Anton. "In Umbra Intelligentiae." *The New Scholasticism* 14, no. 2 (1940): 146–80.
———. "Penitus Manet Ignotum." *Mediaeval Studies* 27 (1965): 212–26.
Perler, Dominik. "Thought Experiments: The Methodogical Function of Angels in Late Medieval Epistemology." In his *Angels in Medieval Philosophical Inquiry: Their Function and Significance*, 143–54. Aldershot: Ashgate, 2008.
Pierson, Daniel J. "Aquinas on the Principle *Omne agens agit sibi simile*." PhD diss., The Catholic University of America, 2015.
Pinborg, Jan. "Diskussionen um die Wissenschaftstheorie an der Artistenfakultät." *Miscellanea medievalia* 10 (1976): 254–68.
Porro, Pasquale. "Ancora sulle polemiche tra Egidio Romano e Enrico di Gand: due questioni sul tempo angelico." *Medioevo* 14 (1988): 107–48.
———. *Forme e modelli di durata nel pensiero medievale. L' 'aevum', il tempo discreto, la categoria 'quando'.* Leuven: Leuven University Press, 1996.
———. "Angelic Measures: *Aevum* and Discrete Time." In *The Medieval Concept of Time: The Scholastic Debate and its Reception in Early Modern Philosophy*, edited by Pasquale Porro, 131–265. Leiden: Brill, 2001.
———. *Tommaso d'Aquino. L'ente e l'essenza.* Milan: Bompiani, 2002.
———. *Thomas Aquinas: A Historical and Philosophical Profile.* Translated by Joseph G. Trabbic and Roger W. Nutt. Washington, DC: The Catholic University of America Press, 2015.
Proclus. *The Elements of Theology.* 2nd ed. Edited by E. R. Dodds. Oxford: Clarendon Press, 1963.
Pseudo-Dionysius. *Corpus Dionysiacum*, vol. 1: *De divinis nominibus.* Edited by Beate Regina Suchla. Patristiche Texte und Studien 33. Berlin: Walter de Gruyter, 1990.
Quine, Willard Van Orman. "Natural Kinds." In his *Ontological Relativity and Other Essays.* New York: Columbia University Press, 1969.
———. "Use and its Place in Meaning." *Erkenntnis* 13 (1978): 1–8.
———. "Indeterminacy of Translation Again." *Journal of Philosophy* 84 (1987): 5–10.
Régis, L.-M. "Analyse et synthèse dans l'oeuvre de saint Thomas." *Studia Medievalia* (1948): 303–30.
Reichmann, James B. "Logic and the Method of Metaphysics." *The Thomist* 29 (1965): 341–95.
Renard, Henri. "What Is St. Thomas' Approach to Metaphysics?" *The New Scholasticism* 30, no. 1 (1956): 64–83.
Rikhof, Herwi M. "Thomas at Utrecht." In *Contemplating Aquinas: On the Varieties of Interpretation*, edited by Fergus Kerr, OP, 105–36. Notre Dame, IN: University of Notre Dame Press, 2003.
Robert, J. D. "Le principe: 'Actus non limitatur nisi per potentiam subjectivam realiter distinctam.'" *Revue philosophique de Louvain* 47 (1949): 44–70.
Rocca, Gregory. "The Distinction between *Res Significata* and *Modus Significandi* in Aquinas's Theological Epistemology." *The Thomist* 55 (1991): 173–97.
———. *Speaking the Incomprehensible God.* Washington, DC: The Catholic University of America Press, 2004.

Roland-Gosselin, Marie-Dominique. "La distinction réelle entre l'essence et l'être." In *Le « De ente et essentia » de saint Thomas d'Aquin. Texte établi d'après les manuscrits parisiens. Introduction, notes et études historiques par M.-D. Roland-Gosselin*, 135–205. Paris: Vrin, 1948.

Rosemann, Philipp W. *Omne Agens Agit Sibi Simile: A "Repetition" of Scholastic Metaphysics*. Louvain Philosophical Studies 12. Leuven: Leuven University Press, 1996.

Rousseau, Edward. *The Distinction between Essence and Supposit in the Angel according to St. Thomas Aquinas*. PhD diss., Fordham University, 1954.

Rubin, Michael J. "The Meaning of 'Beauty' and Its Transcendental Status in the Metaphysics of Thomas Aquinas." PhD diss., The Catholic University of America, 2016.

Russell, Bertrand. *Philosophy of Logical Atomism* (1918). In his *Logic and Knowledge*, edited by R. C. Marsh. London: Allen & Unwin, 1956.

Sadler, Gregory B., ed. and trans. *Reason Fulfilled by Revelation: The 1930s Christian Philosophy Debates in France*. Washington, DC: The Catholic University of America Press, 2011.

Schindler, D. C. *Hans Urs von Balthasar and the Dramatic Structure of Truth: A Philosophical Investigation*. New York: Fordham University Press, 2004.

Schmidt, Robert. "The Evidence Grounding Judgments of Existence." In *An Etienne Gilson Tribute*, edited by C. J. O'Neil, 228–44. Milwaukee, WI: Marquette University Press, 1959.

———. "L'emploi de la séparation en métaphysique." *Revue philosophique de Louvain* 58 (1960): 373–93.

Sertillanges, Antonin-Gilbert. *Les grandes thèses de la philosophie thomiste*. Paris: Bloud and Gay, 1928.

Sevier, Christopher. *Aquinas on Beauty*. Lanham, MD: Lexington Books, 2015.

Shanley, Brian J. "Divine Causation and Human Freedom in Aquinas." *American Catholic Philosophical Quarterly* 77 (1998): 99–122.

Solère, Jean-Luc. "Plus ou moins: le vocabulaire de la latitude des formes." In *L'Elaboration du vocabulaire philosophique au Moyen Age*, edited by J. Hamesse and C. Steel, 437–88. Turnhout: Brepols, 2000.

———. "The Question of Intensive Magnitudes according to Some Jesuits in the Sixteenth and Seventeenth Centuries." *The Monist* 84, no. 4 (2001): 582–616.

———. "Thomas d'Aquin et les variations qualitatives." In *Compléments de Substance: Études sur les Propriétés Accidentelles offertes à Alain de Libera*, edited by C. Erismann and A. Schniewind, 147–65. Paris: Vrin, 2008.

———. "Les variations qualitatives dans les théories post-thomistes." *Revue Thomiste* (2012): 157–204.

Suarez-Nani, Tiziana. *Tempo ed essere nell'autunno del Medioevo: Il 'De tempore' di Nicola di Strasburgo e il dibattito sulla nature ed il senso del tempo agli inizi del XIV secolo*. Amsterdam: B. R. Grüner, 1989.

———. *Connaissance et langage des anges selon Thomas d'Aquin et Gilles de Rome*. Paris: Vrin, 2002.

Suárez, Francisco. *On Creation, Conservation, & Concurrence: Metaphysical Disputations 20–22*. Translated by A. J. Freddoso. South Bend, IN: St. Augustine's Press, 2002.

Svoboda, David. "Aquinas on Real Relation." *Acta Universitatis Carolinae Theologica* 6 (2016): 147–72.
Sweeney, Eileen. "Three Notions of *Resolutio* and the Structure of Reasoning in Aquinas." *The Thomist* 58 (1994): 197–243.
Sylla, Edith. "Medieval Concepts of the Latitude of Forms: The Oxford Calculators." *Archives d'histoire doctrinale et littéraire du Moyen Âge* 40 (1974): 223–83.
———. *The Oxford Calculators and the Mathematics of Motion, 1320–1350: Physics and Measurement by Latitudes.* New York: Garland Publishing, 1991.
Taylor, Richard. "St. Thomas and the *Liber de causis* on the Hylomorphic Composition of Separate Substances." *Mediaeval Studies* 41 (1979): 506–13.
———. "Aquinas, the *Plotiniana Arabica*, and the Metaphysics of Being and Actuality." *Journal of the History of Ideas* 59, no. 2 (1998): 217–39.
te Velde, Rudi. *Participation and Substantiality in Thomas Aquinas.* Leiden: Brill, 1995.
———. "Metaphysics, Dialectics and the *Modus Logicus* According to Thomas Aquinas." *Recherches de Théologie et Philosophie médiévales* 63 (1996): 15–35.
———. *Aquinas on God: The 'Divine Science' of the "Summa Theologiae."* Aldershot: Ashgate, 2006.
———. "The Knowledge of Being: Thomistic Metaphysics in the Contemporary Debate." In *The Discovery of Being & Thomas Aquinas*, edited by Christopher M. Cullen and Franklin T. Harkins, 46–50. Washington, DC: The Catholic University of America Press, 2019.
Thomas of Sutton?. *De principio individuationis* and *De quatuor oppositis.* In Thomas Aquinas, *Opuscula philosophica*, edited by R. Spiazzi, OP. Turin: Marietti, 1954.
Tomarchio, John. "Aquinas's Division of Being According to Modes of Existing." *The Review of Metaphysics* 54, no. 3 (2001): 585–613.
Torrell, Jean-Pierre. *Saint Thomas Aquinas: The Person and His Work.* Rev. ed. Translated by Robert Royal. Washington, DC: The Catholic University of America Press, 2005.
———. *Initiation à saint Thomas d'Aquin: Sa personne et son œuvre*, Nouvelle édition profondément remaniée, vol. 1. Paris: Éditions du Cerf, 2015.
Turner, Denys. *Faith, Reason, and the Existence of God.* Cambridge: Cambridge University Press, 2004.
Twetten, David B. "Clearing a Way for Aquinas: How the Proof from Motion Concludes to God." *Proceedings of the American Catholic Philosophical Quarterly* 70 (1996): 259–78.
———. "Really Distinguishing Essence from *Esse*." In *Wisdom's Apprentice: Thomistic Essays in Honor of Lawrence Dewan, O.P.*, edited by Peter Kwasniewski. Washington, DC: The Catholic University of America Press, 2007.
———. "To Which 'God' Must a Proof of God's Existence Conclude For Aquinas?" In *Laudemos Viros Gloriosos: Essays in Honour of Armand Maurer, CSB*, edited by R. E. Houser, 146–84. Notre Dame, IN: University of Notre Dame Press, 2007.
———. "Aristotelian Cosmology and Causality in Classical Arabic Philosophy and its Greek Background." In *Ideas in Motion in Baghdad and Beyond: Philosoph-*

ical and Theological Exchanges between Christians and Muslims in the Third/Ninth and Fourth/Tenth Centuries, edited by Damien Janos. Leiden: Brill, 2015.
———. "How Save Aquinas' 'Intellectus essentiae' Argument for the Real Distinction between Essence and esse?" Annals of Philosophy 67 (2019): 129–43.
Tyn, Tomas. Metafisica della sostanza: Partecipazione e "analogia entis." Verona: Fede & Cultura, 2009.
Urráburu, Johannes. Institutiones philosophicae quas Romae in Pontificia Universitate Gregoriana, vol. 2: Ontologia. Vallisoleti: Cuesta, 1891.
Van Steenberghen, Fernand. Maître Siger de Brabant. Louvain: Publications Universitaires, 1977.
———. Le problème de l'existence de Dieu dans les Écrits de s. Thomas d'Aquin. Louvain: Éditions de l'institut supérieur de philosophie, 1980.
Vargas, Rosa. Thomas Aquinas on the Apprehension of Being: The Role of Judgment in Light of 13th C. Semantics. PhD diss., Marquette University, 2013.
Vijgen, Jorgen. "A Note on the Transcendental Status of Beauty." Sapientia 59 (2004): 83.
Waddell, Michael. "Truth Beloved: Thomas Aquinas and the Relational Transcendentals." PhD diss., University of Notre Dame, 2000.
West, Jason. "Aquinas on the Real Distinction between a Supposit and its Nature." In Wisdom's Apprentice: Thomistic Essays in Honor of Lawrence Dewan, O.P., edited by Peter Kwasniewski, 85–106. Washington, DC: The Catholic University of America Press, 2007.
White, Roger M. Talking About God: The Concept of Analogy and the Problem of Religious Language. Burlington, Vt.: Ashgate, 2010.
White, Thomas Joseph. "How Barth Got Aquinas Wrong: A Reply to Archie J. Spencer on Causality and Christocentrism." Nova et Vetera (English Edition) 7 (2009): 241–70.
Wielockx, Robert. Aegidi Romani Opera Omnia III.1. Apologia. Florence: Leo S. Olschki, 1985.
Wilhelmsen, Frederick. "Existence and Esse." The New Scholasticism 50, no. 1 (1976): 20–45.
———. "The Concept of Existence and the Structure of Judgment: A Thomistic Paradox." The Thomist 41, no. 3 (1977): 317–49.
———. "A Note: The Absolute Consideration of Nature in Quaestiones Quodlibetales, VIII." The New Scholasticism 57 (1983): 352–61.
———. The Paradoxical Structure of Existence. 3rd ed. New Brunswick, NJ: Transaction Publishers, 2015.
Winandy, Jacques. "Le Quodlibet ii, art. 4 de saint Thomas et la notion de suppôt." Ephemerides theologicae Lovanienses 2 (1934): 5–29.
Wippel, John F. "The Title First Philosophy According to Thomas Aquinas and His Different Justifications for the Same." The Review of Metaphysics 27 (1974): 585–600.
———. "Metaphysics and Separatio According to Thomas Aquinas." The Review of Metaphysics 31 (1978): 431–70.
———. "Godfrey of Fontaines on Intension and Remission of Accidental Forms." Franciscan Studies 39, no. 1 (1979): 316–55.

———. "Essence and Existence." In *The Cambridge History of Later Medieval Philosophy*, edited by N. Kretzmann, A. Kenny, and J. Pinborg, 385–410. New York: Cambridge University Press, 1982.

———. *Metaphysical Themes in Thomas Aquinas*. Washington, DC: The Catholic University of America Press, 1984.

———. "Quidditative Knowledge of God." In his *Metaphysical Themes in Thomas Aquinas*, 215–42. Washington, DC: The Catholic University of America Press, 1984.

———. "Thomas Aquinas on What Philosophers Can Know About God." *American Catholic Philosophical Quarterly* 66, no. 3 (1992): 279–97.

———. "Thomas Aquinas and the Condemnation of 1277." *The Modern Schoolman* 72, no. 1 (1995): 266–67.

———. *The Metaphysical Thought of Thomas Aquinas: From Finite Being to Uncreated Being*. Washington, DC: The Catholic University of America Press, 2000.

———. *Metaphysical Themes in Thomas Aquinas II*. Rev. ed. Washington, DC: The Catholic University of America Press, 2007.

———. "Thomas Aquinas and the Axiom that Unreceived Act Is Unlimited." In Wippel, *Metaphysical Themes in Thomas Aquinas II*, 123–51. Washington, DC: The Catholic University of America Press, 2007.

———. "Thomas Aquinas and the Axiom 'What is Received is Received According to the Mode of the Receiver.'" In *Metaphysical Themes in Thomas Aquinas II*, 113–22. Washington, DC: The Catholic University of America Press, 2007.

———. "Thomas Aquinas on Creatures as Causes of *Esse*." In *Metaphysical Themes in Thomas Aquinas II*, 172–93. Washington, DC: The Catholic University of America Press, 2007.

———. "Thomas Aquinas on Our Knowledge of God and the Axiom that Every Agent Produces Something Like Itself." In *Metaphysical Themes in Thomas Aquinas II*, 157–71. Washington, DC: The Catholic University of America Press, 2007.

———. "Aquinas on Creation and the Preambles of Faith." *The Thomist* 78, no. 1 (2014): 1–36.

———. "Cornelio Fabro on the Distinction and Composition of Essence and *Esse* in the Metaphysics of Thomas Aquinas." *The Review of Metaphysics* 68, no. 3 (2015): 573–92.

Wisnovsky, R. "Notes on Avicenna's Concept of Thingness (Šay'iyya)." *Arabic Sciences and Philosophy* 10 (2000): 181–221.

Wissink, J. B. M. "Aquinas: The Theologian of Negative Theology." *Jaarboek Thomas Instituut te Utrecht* (1993): 15–83.

Wolter, Allan B. "The Transcendentals and Their Function in the Metaphysics of Duns Scotus." PhD diss., The Catholic University of America, 1946.

Wreen, Michael. "Existence as a Perfection." *History of Philosophy & Logical Analysis* 20 (2017): 161–72.

———. "Existence as a Property." *Acta Analytica* 32 (2017): 297–312.

Contributor Biographies

STEPHEN L. BROCK is a priest of the Prelature of Opus Dei and Ordinary Professor of Medieval Philosophy at the Pontifical University of the Holy Cross in Rome. He has written on Thomas Aquinas's action theory, ethics, and metaphysics. Among his publications are *The Philosophy of Saint Thomas Aquinas: A Sketch* (2015), *The Light that Binds: A Study in Thomas Aquinas's Metaphysics of Natural Law* (2020), and *Action & Conduct: Thomas Aquinas and the Theory of Action* (2021).

BRIAN CARL is Associate Professor of Philosophy and Director of the Center for Thomistic Studies at the University of St. Thomas in Houston, Texas. He specializes in medieval philosophy, metaphysics, and the philosophy of religion. He has published articles in journals including *American Catholic Philosophical Quarterly*, *Nova et Vetera*, *Scientia et Fides*, and *The Thomist*.

THERESE SCARPELLI CORY is the John and Jean Oesterle Associate Professor of Thomistic Studies at the University of Notre Dame, and Director of the Maritain Center and History of Philosophy Forum. Her work focuses on medieval theories of cognition and the human person, especially in Thomas Aquinas, Albert the Great, and their Greco-Arabic sources. She is the author of *Aquinas on Human Self-Knowledge* (2014) and numerous articles on topics such as self-knowledge, consciousness, abstraction, imagination, the soul, attention, and selfhood, in medieval thinkers.

GREGORY T. DOOLAN is Associate Professor in the School of Philosophy at the Catholic University of America. He specializes in medieval philosophy, metaphysics, and the thought of Thomas Aquinas. Doolan is author of *Aquinas on the Divine Ideas as Exemplar Causes* (2008) and editor of the volume *The Science of Being as Being: Metaphysical*

Investigations (2011). His articles have appeared in such journals as *International Philosophical Quarterly*, *Documenti e studi sulla tradizione filosofica medievale*, and *The Thomist*.

FRANCIS FEINGOLD is Associate Professor of Philosophy at Kenrick-Glennon Seminary in St. Louis, Missouri. His research interests center on Aquinas's metaphysics (especially God's relation to the world, the nature of action, and the notion of the good) and ethics (chiefly the common good, friendship-love, and natural law); they also include medieval philosophy more generally, as well as figures such as Pascal and Dietrich von Hildebrand. His publications include articles on Aquinas's theory of love (individual, political, and divine) and of natural law, on von Hildebrand's value theory, and on Pascal's theory of faith.

GLORIA FROST is Professor of Philosophy at the University of St. Thomas in Minnesota. She specializes in medieval philosophy and is the author of *Aquinas on Efficient Causation and Causal Powers* (2022). Her articles have appeared in journals such as *Ergo*, *Journal of the History of Philosophy*, *British Journal for the History of Philosophy*, and *Oxford Studies in Medieval Philosophy*.

MARK D. GOSSIAUX is Professor of Philosophy at Loyola University New Orleans. His research focuses on the history of medieval philosophy, with a particular interest in the metaphysical thought of thinkers in the late thirteenth century. He has published articles in such journals as *Vivarium*, *Recherches de Théologie et Philosophie Médiévales*, *Augustiniana*, and *American Catholic Philosophical Quarterly*.

NICK KAHM wrote his dissertation under Msgr. Wippel at The Catholic University of America and turned it into a book: *Thomas Aquinas on Emotion's Participation in Reason* (2019). He has also published in the *British Journal for the History of Philosophy*, *History of Philosophy Quarterly*, and *American Catholic Philosophical Quarterly*. After teaching philosophy at St. Michael's College in Vermont for five years, he left academia and is currently the founder and CEO of the Kahm Clinic and the Kahm Center for Eating Disorders.

GAVEN KERR is a lecturer in philosophy at St Patrick's Pontifical University Maynooth, Ireland. His philosophical interests are wide ranging, including the thought of Aquinas and Kant, as well as metaphysics and epistemology more generally. Kerr is the author of two monographs on Aquinas's thought: *Aquinas's Way to God: The Proof in "De Ente et Essentia"* (2015), *Aquinas and the Metaphysics of Creation* (2019), as well as a collection of articles entitled *Collected Articles on the Existence of God* (2022). He has also published in such journals as the *American Catholic Philosophical Quarterly*, *International Philosophical Quarterly*, and *The Thomist*. Kerr is also a Third Order Dominican and a martial artist.

JASON A. MITCHELL taught philosophical theology at *Regina Apostolorum* Pontifical Athenaeum from 2007 to 2015 and metaphysics at Gannon University from 2015 to 2022. His doctorate in philosophy is entitled *Being and Participation: The Method and Structure of Metaphysical Reflection according to Cornelio Fabro* (2012). His doctorate in sacred theology is entitled *Aquinas's Theology of Grace: Metaphysics and the New Perspective* (2023).

MIRIAM PRITSCHET is a PhD candidate in the School of Philosophy at the Catholic University of America. Her research interests focus upon metaphysics and the thought of St. Thomas Aquinas, particularly in regard to questions surrounding the fulfillment of man, and his relation to divine knowledge, causation, and will.

FR. PHILIP-NERI REESE, OP, is a Dominican friar of the Province of St. Joseph, Professor of Philosophy at the Pontifical University of St. Thomas in Rome, and the principal investigator for the Angelicum Thomistic Institute's Project on Philosophy and the Thomistic Tradition. His main areas of research are metaphysics and anything adjacent thereto (the history of metaphysics, the methodology of metaphysics, etc.), with a special emphasis on the metaphysical thought of St. Thomas Aquinas and its subsequent reception and interpretation. His publications include articles on metaphysics, philosophical anthropology, ethics, and (Scholastic) economics.

MICHAEL J. RUBIN earned his master's and doctoral degrees in philosophy at The Catholic University of America, where Msgr. Wippel directed his dissertation on whether beauty is a distinct transcendental for Aquinas. Since then, his research on beauty and the transcendentals in Aquinas's thought has won multiple awards, including First Place at the 2017 Veritas et Amor Contest hosted in Aquino, Italy, and the Karen Chan Young Scholar Award at the 2020 Meeting of the American Catholic Philosophical Association. Rubin has taught at The Catholic University of America, the University of Mary Washington, and Thomas Aquinas College, and he currently teaches philosophy at Christendom College in Front Royal, Virginia.

DAVID TWETTEN, Professor of Philosophy at Marquette University, has his licentiate from PIMS and PhD from the University of Toronto in Philosophy and Medieval Studies. He works in classical and contemporary philosophy in the areas of metaphysics, semantics, natural philosophy and philosophical theology, with a special focus on Averroes, Albert the Great, and Aquinas.

Index of Terms

Abstraction, 9–10, 11n22, 14–15, 17, 20, 128n70, 161, 170, 173, 217, 234n25, 236n35, 238–41, 254, 255n87, 258, 260, 263n113, 275n142

Accident (accidental, accidentally), xiv, xvi, xvii, xx, 8, 15–17, 21–23, 26, 27n61, 33–35, 37n85, 40, 52, 57, 72, 78–79, 82–84, 98, 101n13, 102n14, 106, 112n33, 118, 121, 123n56, 124, 136–37, 139, 145n50, 153n71, 154, 157–60, 170, 184–85, 194, 198, 205–6, 207–24, 231, 232n12, n13, 238, 241, 242n53, 246, 264n115, 273, 353–56, 358, 360, 363

Act (*actus*), xvi–xvii, 7, 13n28, 56, 58, 60, 67, 70, 76, 84–90, 98, 102, 104, 123–24, 135n20, 177–206, 214, 215n23, 216, 238, 252, 267–68, 270, 280–81, 282n16, 292–93, 348–49, 351n12, 354–56, 358n42, 359, 371; act of being / existence (*actus essendi*) (see also Being, *esse*), xx, 4n4, 60, 68, 70, 76, 79, 84–87, 94, 96, 98, 99n8, 100, 104–5, 107–13, 123–26, 128n70, 178, 185–86, 188n55, 190, 193–94, 197, 199, 201, 203–4, 232, 234–38, 260, 278, 287, 307, 319n11, 350, 352, 354–56, 358–60, 363n60, 370–71

Actuality (*actualitas*), xviii, 5, 24, 28, 152, 186, 192–93, 198, 203–4, 206, 235, 274, 278, 287, 289–92, 294, 359; degrees of actualization, 216

Aesthetics, 317

Agent cause, (see causality)

Agency, (see causality)

Angel, xvii–xviii, 7, 24n53, 88–92, 101n13, 125, 144, 160, 171, 183, 184n44, 188–89, 195, 203n135, 227–75, 280–82, 295

Apophatic, xix, 297–316

Application: divine, xx, 348–72

Apprehension: simple, xviii, 8, 227, 230, 233, 235–36, 238–40, 242, 246–47, 250–51, 259–60, 263, 269

Beauty, xix–xx, 220, 223, 317–47; appropriation of 'Beauty' to the Son; 323, 329, 336–45; argument for God from diverse grades of beauty; 323–25, 329–35, 345; bodily or sensible beauty, 321–22, 325, 333–34, 336, 338, 345; divine beauty, xix, 317–47; spiritual or intelligible beauty; 321, 325, 333–34, 336, 345; transcendental beauty, 317–47

Being (*ens*), xiii–xiv, 3–41, 42–63, 74, 76n17, 77n21, 78, 80–91, 112n33, 124–25, 132, 227–43, 252, 256, 268–75, 280–86, 292, 309, 319, 350–54, 356–60, 363; being by participation, 51–54, 58–61, 63, 99, 128, 202n132, 278, 296, 351–53, 360; *ens inquantum ens*, 34, 55, 227, 239n44, 241n51, 275, 285, 317–18, 321, 324n29, 331–32, 340, 351; *per accidens* being, 55; *per se* being, 55, 218, 283, 294–95

Being (*esse*), xvi–xix, 3–41, 51n24, 55–61, 67–95, 96–129, 154n75, 177–206, 210, 227–75, 277–78, 282n16, 285, 286n26, 287, 289, 291, 297–98, 301–2, 305–16, 319n11, 320n13, 323, 341, 343, 345, 349–60, 363, 365–67, 368n75, 371

Body, xvii, 5, 19, 21–23, 30–33, 37, 39, 75, 89–92, 97n3, 116, 123, 135, 144, 154, 158, 160–61, 159n94, 160–62, 165, 171, 183, 193, 194n91, 197, 199, 201–2, 220–21, 240, 270, 324, 333n63, 334, 337, 364, 367n73, 379

Causality: agent, xvi, 73, 89, 130, 131n3, 132, 151n63, 152–53, 155, 158–61, 162n101, 163, 167, 169n119, 170–73, 182, 189, 190n70, 191–93, 195–96, 200, 214–15, 220, 223, 264n114, 288, 348n1, n2, 349n6, n7, 359n46, 362–72; analogous, 152n66, 153n71, 163–67, 171; caused by another, 51, 53–54, 59–62, 76; cause of being (*esse*), 71, 113, 178, 181,

405

Index of Terms

Causality: cause of being (*esse*) (*cont.*) 182n32, 183, 185–86, 189–92, 199, 278, 281–83, 286n26, 354, 363; efficient, 50n22, 54, 57, 61–63, 112, 115, 123n56, 131n3, 186, 191–93, 196, 200, 290, 350–51, 356–58, 360, 363n60, 368n75, 371; equivocal, 132n9, 135n20, 150, 151n63, 153n71, 157n87, 161, 164, 166; exemplar, 155n77, 246, 256n93, 330, 350, 351n12, 356–60, 371; final, 290, 351, 356, 357, 368n75, 371; first, xiii, 6n6, 46, 58n47, 73–76, 96–97, 113, 122–23, 126, 153, 186, 192, 270, 273, 331, 362, 364, 366–67, 368n75, 370, 371; formal, 47, 123n56, 182, 186, 189, 190–91, 193, 200, 202, 336, 357n35; univocal, 132–33, 150, 151n63, 153n71, 155, 163, 167

Change, 62, 120, 124, 161, 187n51, 195n97, 200–201, 242n53, 243, 248–51, 265, 267, 283; accidental, 207–24, 363; substantial, 198

Composition, xvi–xviii, 44, 48n18, 58, 60, 70, 72–73, 76–78, 86–87, 98, 100n10, 110n27, 228–29, 231, 232nn12–13, 233, 239n43, 242–45, 252, 260–62, 264n114, 268, 269n124, 270, 272–73, 275, 287, 311, 315, 328n49, 351, 356, 358n42

Composing and dividing (C/D), xviii, 8, 227–28, 230, 231n9, 242–52, 275

Create, creator, creation (act of), xvii, xx, 77, 86n42, 88, 92–93, 97–98, 124, 132, 153n71, 167, 187, 192, 196, 228, 253, 255–56, 262, 264–65, 267, 273–74, 285, 319, 351, 358n42, 359–61, 368

Created, creature, creation (created world), xiv, xvi, xviii–xix, xx, 19, 22n49, 24, 27n60, 45, 49–54, 61–63, 67–68, 71–74, 76–79, 82, 85–94, 97n3, 99n8, 106, 110nn27–28, 112n34, 113, 114n40, 123–25, 127–29, 130–31, 135–36, 153n71, 154, 159n93, n96, 167, 170–71, 177–206, 210n6, 215n23, 228, 241n49, 246, 248n66, 249, 250n71, 252–53, 255–57, 264, 267–68, 270, 271n134, 274, 278, 284–86, 289–90, 294–95, 297, 301n15, 302, 304, 306, 307n36, 308n37, 310, 311nn43–44, 313–15, 319, 320n13, 324–25, 330–35, 340, 348–72

Demonstration, xiv, 26n57, 28n65, 34–35, 44–49, 52, 54, 59, 61–63, 98, 99n8, 127, 277n2, 278, 284, 286–87, 289, 295

Divine Names, xix–xx, 297–300, 301n15, 302n21, 303–16, 317–47

Ens (see Being, *ens*); *ens commune*, xiii–xiv, 3–41, 54–56, 58–61, 63, 124, 132, 191, 240n44, 272n136, 281–83, 292, 320, 351

Entity (see also Being, *ens*), 5, 29, 56, 58, 60, 97n5, 112n33, 177–79, 181–83, 186n50, 191, 194, 196–98, 204–6, 261n107

Esse (see Being, *esse*; see also *actus essendi*); *esse subsistens*, 61, 257, 297–98, 302, 320,

Essence, xiv–xx, 3, 15, 21n47, 22, 28n64, 39n90, 48, 50, 52, 56, 58, 60, 67–95, 96–129, 136, 147n55, 155, 157, 159–60, 166n111, 178, 182–90, 193, 196n102, 198, 203, 205–6, 208n3, 212, 227–28, 230–38, 242–43, 244n58, 246–47, 252, 255–57, 260, 266–73, 284, 286n26, 287–88, 290, 295, 321, 327–28, 344, 349–61, 367, 370–71; divine, xvii, xix, 71, 73, 78, 101n13, 205, 255n88, 257, 266, 297, 299–300, 302, 307, 309, 315–16, 323, 335, 343–44, 358; formal constituent of divine, 297, 302

Enuntiabilia, 244n55, 257

Eternity, xix, 93, 290n30, 306, 309, 337, 341, 343

Existence, (see Being, *esse*; see also *actus essendi*), xii, xiv–xvi, xviii–xix, 3–41, 67–95, 97–98, 101, 102n15, 109n27, 111, 122–26, 128n70, 145, 186, 188n55, 193n87, 199n115, 210, 216, 227–75, 276–96, 308, 323–26, 329, 331–34, 341, 345, 349–53, 360; active causal connection to, 263, 267–68; as distinct from essence, xiv–xvi, xviii, 67–95, 96–129, 178, 182, 227–75, 352–53, 360; as distinct from facticity, 235–36; as real, 229, 252, 269, 273; grasped by existential judgement (see also composing), 10, 17, 20, 228, 231, 235, 236n35, 251–69; passive causal connection to, 267–68

Form (see also causality), xvi–xvii, 10n20, 15–16, 17n34, 23n50, 27n62, 38n90, 47–48, 49n18, 57, 59–60, 74, 83, 84n37, 88–93, 97n5, 98n5, 106, 107n21, 108, 110n28, 111nn31–32, 113n38, 116, 122–24, 129, 131n4, 135, 137–38, 143–45, 146n52, 148–50, 155–56, 158–59, 161–62, 163n106, 164, 166–70, 172–73, 178–206, 207–24, 232, 238–39, 241, 248–49, 253n79, 254–55, 257n95, 262, 263n111; n113, 265–66, 272–73, 279, 285n24, 295n38, 297n2, 298n4, 302, 306,

308, 310n42, 312, 330, 333n65, 335–36, 349n5; n7, 351–59, 363nn60–61, 366, 368–69, 379
Fourth Way, 125, 278, 291n32, 325

Generation (generate, generative), 126, 130, 132, 135n17; n20, 149n59, 152, 155, 158, 159n92, 160n98, 161, 166, 171, 182, 184, 195, 198, 265n118, 344, 355, 363
God, xvii–xx, 7, 21, 24n52, 38n89, 39n90, 40n94, 49, 50n22, 51, 55n31, 61–62, 67, 71–78, 82, 86–94, 97, 99n8, 101, 103–4, 110, 111n32, 114n40, 115, 122–29, 130–33, 135–36, 146n52, 147, 151n63, 153n71, 159n93, 167, 169, 171, 181–82, 186–92, 196–200, 204, 206, 208, 215n23, 228, 233, 241n49, 244nn55–56, 245–46, 248–49, 252–53, 255–57, 262–74, 276–96, 297–316, 319–45, 348–51, 356–72; proof of, 101, 122–26, 277, 283, 285–86, 290n30, 325–26, 332, 334; proper name, xix, 297, 302–3, 304n28, 305, 307, 310, 313–14
Goodness (good), 74, 190, 321, 323–25, 326, 333; as a divine name, 299–308, 312, 316, 319n11, 320–22, 324–33, 336–46; as a transcendental, 318–33, 342–47

Habit, 34n80, 76n17, 132n9, 153n70, 211n11, 216, 220, 223–24; operative, 350, 355, 360
Health, xvii, 219–23

Identity (see sameness), 72, 75, 107n21, 111n32, 127, 134, 189, 236n35, 257, 298n4, 308, 338
Intelligible species: human, 254, 257–58, 260, 269; concreated (angelic, innate), 249–52, 255–57, 262–75
Intuition of being, 233–34, 268

Judgement (judge), xii–xiv, xvii–xviii, 4, 8–15, 17–20, 39–40, 109n27, 110n27, 128, 227–75; as distinct from "composing and dividing," xviii, 228, 244–75; In sense, 228, 234, 245, 249, 251–52, 254, 256, 258–263, 267–69, 273–75; possibility of error without "composing and dividing," 247–48, 251

Kataphatic, xix, 297, 316
Knowledge, angelic natural, 227–75

Life, 183–84, 200, 297–98, 300, 306, 309, 320n14, 343, 344n104, 345
Likeness, xvi, 61n55, 130–74, 252–54, 331, 336–42, 352, 358n42, 359, 368; and agency, xvi, 73, 130–33, 150–68, 171–74, 270–71; and intellect, 15n31, 114, 131–32, 156, 249, 253–57, 265–68, 271

Material (materiality), xii–xiv, 4–5, 7, 10–15, 18, 23–24, 28–30, 35, 37n84, 41, 47, 71, 88, 90n60, 106, 149n59, 156, 158n90, 193, 202n132, 232n12, 240–41, 243, 252–56, 261n108, 272, 274, 281
Matter, xvi, 4, 6–8, 10n20, 11n22, 13–19, 22n49, 27n62, 28n65, 32n73, 38n90, 48n18, 57, 62, 74, 78, 83, 88–90, 98n5, 104, 105–6, 108, 123, 125, 154, 160, 170, 180–202, 203n135, 205n143, 214, 232nn12–13, 238–39, 240n45, 241, 249, 254–55, 262–63, 265–67, 273, 279–81, 295n38, 321, 368
Metaphysics, xiii–xiv, 3–10, 13n28, 14, 18, 20n47, 25–27, 30–41, 43–45, 49, 54–56, 63, 67, 68n3, 80–81, 83, 96, 97n4, 110, 118, 120, 122, 124–27, 132–33, 165, 170, 173, 177–79, 182, 185, 188, 196, 209, 222, 229, 232, 238–39, 240n45, 242, 272, 274, 276–85, 286n27, 287, 289, 294 317, 350–51, 352n17, 353–56, 370–71; subject matter of, 3–6, 13n28, 13–14, 39, 49, 54–55, 124, 177, 179, 279n6, 238–39, 280–83, 351
Middle term, 45–49, 53, 59, 61, 284
Mode of being, 20n47, 21, 22n49, 113, 150, 152, 155–61, 166n111, 182, 195, 315, 359
Modus significandi, 299, 310n42, 311–13, 315
Motion, 7–8, 13, 16, 18–19, 28n65, 31–32, 34n80, 38, 39n90, 124, 154, 179–80, 202, 277–78, 281, 283n19, 285n25, 287–94, 348, 352, 354, 357, 361–62, 367–68, 370, 372

Object, 6–8, 13n28, 15, 17, 31, 32n73, 35n82, 82, 84, 108n22, 110, 118–21, 156, 158, 180, 203n135, 220, 223, 230–36, 239, 244–45, 247n64, 249–50. 253–54, 257, 259, 261–62, 268, 274–75, 279–280, 295, 346, 355, 364, 369
Omne agens agit sibi simile, 73, 130–33, 152n68, 161n100, 164n107, 165, 168n116, 172–73

Index of Terms

Operation, xx, 8–11, 14–15, 17, 20–21, 27, 70, 110n27, 115, 136, 179–80, 183–84, 200n120, 229–31, 233, 234n25, 245n60, 279, 348–51, 353–57, 360–72

Order, xii–xiii, xvi–xvii, 6n6, 16, 40n94, 49n19, 74, 78, 81, 84, 99n8, 113, 123n56, 131–32, 143–44, 148, 150, 153–54, 160, 165, 167–68, 169n119, 171–72, 174, 184–89, 194–95, 203, 206, 218–24, 233, 236n35, 261n108, 274, 279, 286n26, 287, 289n29, 290, 307, 308n37, 318, 328, 331–32, 340, 342, 344, 346, 351, 352–56, 359–60, 361–62, 365, 367–68, 371

Participation, xvii–xviii, 51–63, 71–72, 75, 78, 79n24, 92–94, 97n4, 98, 99n8, 100n9, 104n17, 114n40; n43, 127–28, 128nn70–71, 129, 135n23, 149, 159, 166–67, 206, 208n3, 209–10, 213n16, 214, 215–16, 228, 253, 255n89, 256n93, 262n111, 274, 286, 304n26, 306, 320n13, 324n29, 331–32, 350–52, 354, 357–60, 365, 367, 370; causal, 57, 59, 61, 167n115, 360; degrees of, 221–22; formal, 57, 59–61; logical, 57, 59–60

Property, 23, 45–49, 52, 59, 61–62, 102, 108–9, 111n31, 115, 117, 120–21, 123n56, 145, 148, 150, 154, 171n128, 246, 268, 275, 297, 302, 318n4, 338–39, 342

Per aliud, xviii, 76, 78n23, 79n24, 278, 286–289, 291, 294–295

Per se, 21n48, 22, 52, 55, 60n51, 73, 76, 82, 83n35, 89, 90n60, 123n56, 124, 126, 152, 153n71, 172–73, 190n70, 191–92, 194–95, 198–99, 203, 205n143, 218, 247n64, 259n103, 278, 286–89, 291, 294–95, 297, 360; *per se* accident, 26, 36n84, 52; *per se nota*, xiv, 47–48, 54, 56, 58–59, 61–62, 114, 128; *per se nota* to all, 47n13, 56; *per se nota* to the wise, 47, 56, 58, 128

Perfection, intensive, 213–16

Potency, xvi–xvii, 7, 13n27, 56, 58, 61, 67, 74, 75n15, 76, 78, 84, 86–90, 91n63, 96n2, 98, 102, 110, 128n70, 152n67, 177–206, 214–15, 238, 252, 267, 280–81, 282n16, 287, 292–93, 348–49, 352, 354–56, 358n42, 359, 367, 370–71

Power, operative, 348–372

Predicate, predication, 26, 27n62, 33–35, 47–49, 52–54, 58–59, 62, 77, 82, 102, 106, 107n21, 108–9, 110n31, 111n32, 112n33, 117, 122n54, 132n11, 133, 150, 154n75, 168n117, 169n118, 170n128, 203, 230n8, 236n35, 237, 241n51, 243, 246, 260–62, 275, 308, 323; of God, 299–301, 311–12, 314–15, 319n11, 320n14

Proportion, xvii, 37n85, 132n9, 135n23, 138n33, 140, 142, 149n59, 150–53, 160, 162–65, 166n111, 168–73, 191, 194, 219–24, 321, 326–27, 328n46, 337, 338n82, 341, 343n99, 353

Propter quid, xiv, 42–63

Quality, xvii, 7, 15n30, 16, 116, 135n23, 145n46, 159, 161, 165, 207–24, 280–81, 320, 322n23, 355; degrees of perfection of, 143–44, 154, 163n104, 207–24; unity of, xvi, 134, 136–41, 143–44, 146, 149, 153, 155n77, 169n120, 172

Qualitative variation (variation in qualities), 207, 208n3, 209n4, 213n17, 216, 218

Quia, 27, 44–45, 49n19, 99n8, 284

Qui est, xix, 297–316

Reasoning, discursive, 243, 244n58, 270–71, 273

Relation, xvi, 101n13, 121, 131, 133–39, 142, 144–51, 153–54, 156, 164–65, 168, 169n120, 172, 174, 236n35, 246, 257, 266, 343, 347, 358n42, 360; causal, 49–51, 61–62, 130–74, 258, 341, 343, 360, 365, 366n69; of dependence, 16, 287

Ratio, xix, 4–5, 13–25, 27n61, 28, 39–40, 111n31, 137, 140, 142, 144, 152, 155–61, 163, 166–68, 173–74, 203n137, 205, 220, 257, 266, 267n123, 307, 309, 311, 313, 318, 328, 337–39, 344, 346n108, 347; *ratio entis*, 4–5, 49–63, 84n38, 277; Ratio-Nondependence Principle, 19–25; real *ratio*, 59–60

Resolutio, 34, 40, 44, 273nn139–140

Res significata, 299, 310n42, 312–15

Sameness, 102, 107, 111n31, 114, 119–22, 126, 133, 137–42, 145–46, 148, 151–53, 155n79, 173, 210–11

Separatio, xiii, 3–19, 21, 23–25, 30, 39–40, 228–29, 239–41, 252, 269–70, 272–75, 279n6

Series, ordered, 286n26, 287–89

Soul, 56, 58, 60, 80, 88, 97n3, 107n21, 123n56,

124–25, 156, 178, 183–85, 193, 194n91, 195, 200–201, 203, 205, 254, 282, 285n25, 294, 320, 346, 355, 364, 369–70
Subject, xvii, 15, 32, 34, 46, 47n16, 48, 56–59, 77, 101n13, 107n21, 111n32, 112n33, 117, 134n13, 139–41, 143, 150, 180, 184, 186, 187n51, 205–6, 207–8, 210, 213–17, 219–24, 230n8, 231–34, 241n51, 242n53, 243–46, 260–62, 284, 301, 314, 353, 355, 368; subject matter, xiii–xiv, 3–6, 10, 13–14, 18, 25–26, 30, 32–34, 35nn81–82, 36–37, 38n87; n89, 39–40, 49, 54–55, 124–125, 177, 179, 238–39, 279n6, 280–83, 351
Subsistence (subsist, subsistent), 21–23, 25, 38, 61, 86, 90, 94, 101n13, 105–6, 124n57, 183, 187–89, 192n86, 195, 202, 204–5, 210, 253, 257, 295n38, 297, 302, 311n44, 320n13, 352–53, 360
Substance, xiii–xiv, xvi–xvii, 3–41, 48n18, 58, 74, 76, 82, 83n35, 84, 87n46, 88–90, 98, 100n10, 101–2, 104–8, 111n31, 114, 123n56, 124, 126, 134, 136–41, 143, 149, 153–54, 161, 170–71, 174, 183, 185–86, 197, 199, 200n121, 205–6, 210–12, 214–15, 218, 230, 238, 240–41, 270, 272, 280–81, 282n16, 305, 313, 315, 352–54, 356, 359–60, 362, 363n60; immaterial, xiii–xiv, 12, 13n28, 19, 24, 28n65, 90, 240, 270; orders or grades of, 270

Substantial form, 27n62, 124, 183, 197–98, 202, 205n143, 206, 210, 330, 335, 356, 358, 379

Transcendentals, xx, 81, 111n31, 112n33, 125, 128, 146, 256n93, 275, 309, 317–47, 356
Trinity, xix, 145n46, 194n92, 336–37, 340–45; appropriations, 323, 336–43; inner life of, 343–45
Truth, 9, 45, 55, 70–71, 108, 118, 231, 243, 244n55, 246n62, 248, 279; as a Divine Name, 322, 326–29, 337–38, 340, 343–44; as a transcendental, 319n11, 320n13; n16, 324, 328–29, 336, 339–40, 345, 346–47
Unity, xvi–xvii, 111n31, 133–134, 136–174, 189n69, 202, 212, 213, 217–218, 224, 274, 290n30; as a divine name, 343; as a transcendental, 74, 81–82, 328; of the subject of metaphysics, 6, 30–39; relation to harmony and simplicity, 32–328

Use (*uti*), 342–343

Via compositionis, 44
Via resolutionis, 34, 40, 44

Will, 369, 370–371

Index of Names

Aertsen, Jan, 32n73, 33n77, 35n81, 44n7, 273n139, 318, 319n11, 320n13, 322n22, 337n80, 339n86, 341n92, 343n100, 346n106

Albert (Albertists), 42, 45–48, 107n21, 114, 132n9, 153n71, 308n37, 339n86

Aristotle, xiv, 8, 9n17, 13n28, 14, 26, 27n62, 31–36, 38, 45n10, 46, 47n14, 55n31, 56n40, 77n22, 80–83, 102n15, 104n17, 105, 108, 114–15, 118–20, 125, 128, 130, 134, 136–43, 163n104, 165, 170, 172, 178–85, 189n69, 190n73, 196n102, 200n118, 202–4, 206n148, 215–16, 231n9, 233, 239n44, 240n46, 241, 258n98, 259n104, 279–80, 285n25, 290, 292n34, 293, 306, 310n41, 356

Ashley, Benedict, 4–5, 13–15, 17n36, 18, 24, 30, 35, 36n83, 37, 43n4, 186n50, 282n18

Averroes, 76n17, 80–83, 89–90, 100n9, 130

Avicenna, 6, 80–84, 89–90, 96, 102, 103n16, 104n17, 107, 113, 115, 125, 158, 307

Báñez, Domingo, xx, 265n118, 348–49, 352n17, 353–54, 370

Boethius, 5–6, 26n59, 43, 47n13, 56–57, 100n10, 104n17, 106, 134, 136, 139, 306

Brock, Stephen, 24n53, 39n90, 57n43, 148n57, 189n63

Burrell, David, 298n4, 301–2

Cajetan, 97, 243n54, 244n57, 245n61, 250n72, 252n78, 255n89, 304, 352n17

Carl, Brian, 297n2, 302n20, 320, 347n112

Contat, Alain, 99n8, 110n30, 127n69, 128n70–71, 185, 350n12, 352n17; n19, 353n20, 358n40; n42, 359–61, 370–72

Cory, Therese, 41n95, 224n42, 245n60, 252n78, 253n81, 254n84; n87, 258n98, 260n105, 264n114, 275n143, 347

Cunningham, Francis, 98n6, 245, 246n62, 261n107

Damascene, John, 303–6, 309n39, 342n94

De Haan, Daniel, 57n44, 60n50; n53, 282n18, 351, 352n16

Dewan, Lawrence, 35n82, 36n83, 43n4, 44n6, 55n28, 97n3, 100n10, 113, 123, 154, 181n25, 182n32, 188, 201n125, 282n18

Dionysius, 143, 244n57, 253n79, 303–4, 306, 308n37, 310, 323, 329–34, 337–38

Doolan, Gregory, 22n49, 34n78, 49n18, 57n44, 61n55, 126n63, 154n74, 156n83, 167n115, 224n42, 240n46, 255n88, 256, 257n94, 275n143, 282n16, 287n27, 347n112, 351, 352n16, 358–59, 372

Fabro, Cornelio, 35n81, 68n3, 96n1, 97n4, 98–99, 100nn9–10, 103–4, 109, 110n28; n30, 113–14, 123n55, 127–29, 152n66, 185–87, 188n55, 189n62; n66, 197, 235n29, 236n35, 256n93, 350n8, 352–54, 358, 370, 372

Frost, Gloria, 131n3, 143n40, 209n4

Garceau, Benoît, 242n53, 245n62

Geiger, Louis-Bertrand, 240n45, 241n50, 256n93, 287n27, 352n17, 358

Giles of Rome, xv, 43n5, 45, 67–79, 85–88, 94–95, 237

Gilson, Étienne, 22n49, 43n2, 97–98, 100n10, 104, 105n20, 109n26, 110n28, 123n56, 185–86, 187nn51–52, 193n87, 201n126, 227, 229n5, 230, 231n11, 232–35, 237nn36–38, 238, 256n91, 258n101, 260n105, 268–69, 352–54, 372, 376, 378

Goris, Harm, 242n53, 243n54, 244nn57–58, 249n70, 252n78, 253n81, 254n86, 258n99, 263n112, 264n115

Index of Names

Hegel, Georg Wilhelm Friedrich, 11n22, 42, 238, 241
Henry of Ghent, xv, 68–69, 83n35, 85–95, 350
Hilary, St., 337, 340–43, 345

John of St. Thomas, 99n8, 242n53, 243n54, 244n57, 245n61, 250n72, 252n78, 255n89, 257n95, 264–65, 267, 268n124, 302n20

Kant, Immanuel, 120, 122, 237
Kerr, Gavin, 59n49, 60n52, 186n47, 199n115, 278n5, 285n24, 286n26, 289n29, 292n34,
Klubertanz, George, 241n50, 254n86, 258n100; n102, 259n103, 261n108

Laval School, 4–5
Liber de Causis, (Book of Causes), 43n5, 74, 166, 202, 250n73, 253n79, 271n128, 314, 315n52, 361–62
Lonergan, Bernard, 361

Maritain, Jacques, 110n27, 229n5, 231n11, 233–36, 238n41, 239n43, 241n48; n50, 258n101, 260n105, 269, 300, 376
McInerny, Ralph, 4–5, 12–14, 17n36, 18, 24–25, 28–30, 35, 36n83, 37, 112n33, 170n128, 174n130, 282n18
Mitchell, Jason, 35n81, 57n44, 60n50, 96n1, 99n8, 349n4, 352n16, 356n33
de Molina, Luis, xx, 348–49, 370

Owens, Joseph, xviii, 44n6, 68n3, 97n5, 102n15, 104, 107n21, 110–111, 112nn33–34, 113n38, 123n56, 147n55, 186n47, 187n51, 193n87, 196n102, 199n115, 229n5, 230n8, 231nn10–11, 232–33, 235, 236n35, 237nn36–38, 238n39; n41, 245n60, 260n105, 269, 277, 285n25, 287, 292, 298n5

Peghaire, Julien, 250n71, 253n81, 256n89, 264
Plotinus, 42, 188n53

Porro, Pasquale, 67n2, 68n4, 88n54, 186n50, 187, 188nn53–54, 189n66, 193n88, 251n74,
Pseudo-Dionysius the Areopagite (Dionysius), 143, 244n57, 253n79, 303–4, 306, 308n37, 310, 323, 329–332, 337–338

River Forest School, xiii, 4–5, 35n82
Rubin, Michael, 317n3, 319n10, 327n44, 329n50, 347n111

Scotus, John Duns, 98n5, 109, 113, 115, 320n14
Siger of Brabant, xv, 69, 80–85, 94–95, 196n102, 379–80
Suárez, 109n27, 113n39, 235, 237, 349nn3–5; n6, 351n13, 357

Thomas of Sutton, 193, 194n90
Twetten, David, 39n90, 96n1, 100n9, 109n25, 114n40, 284n23, 292n34, 294

Wilhelmsen, Frederick, 110n29, 230n8, 236n35, 237n36; n38, 238n39; n41, 241n48; n50; n52
Wippel, John F., xi–xx, 3–41, 43, 44n7, 49n18, 54n26, 58n45, 59n49, 60n52, 68n3–4, 73n13, 87n47, 100n10, 101, 104, 107n21, 130n1, 132n10–11, 133, 154, 168n117, 177–78, 182n33, 187n52, 188n55, 191n76; n82, 196n106, 209, 227, 229, 231nn10–11, 232n12, 233–35, 236nn34–35, 238n41, 239nn42–43, 240n45, 241n50, 246n63, 259n104, 260n105, 272n136, 277n2, 279n6, 280, 281n15, 282n18, 285n24, 286n26, 287n27, 289n29, 292n34, 295n38, 296, 298n6, 299–300, 303, 315, 317, 319n12, 320n13, 325n30, 350–51, 353n21, 363n60, 366n69, n70, 367n73, 368n75, 370, 371n90, 372, 373–80

Vijgen, Jorgen, 317